GUINNESS
WORLD RECORDS™
2002

www.guinnessworldrecords.com

introduction

Welcome to *Guinness World Records 2002*! This year we've added hundreds of amazing new records and record categories. Check out Colin Winkelmann's amazing power-assisted BMX ramp jump (page 225), Mikael Bigersson's concrete-crushing feats (page 245), NFL-star Corey Dillon's rushing record (page 202) and Madonna's largest-ever live audience (page 172)!

It's not just new records – 2002 has more interactive features than ever. Whenever you see this symbol 🖳 you'll be able to access the Bulletin Boards and hook up with Guinness World Records fans across the globe.

You can also download amazing icons and ringtones to your mobile phone! Check out this symbol 🖭 for icons and this symbol 🎵 for ringtones.

Clockwise from top:
Most Expensive Washroom
Most Rhinestones on a Body,
Tina-Marie Stoker
Youngest US No.1 solo rapper,
Lil Bow Wow

And for those of you really into the details around a particular record or subject, use the great new short-codes to go straight online and discuss with other fans on your chosen subject! You never know, you could even be online to the record breaker themselves.

We really enjoyed putting this year's edition together - we hope you'll love it too!

Clockwise from top:
Most Contortionists in a Box
Youngest NBA Player, Kobe Bryant
Sword Swallower, Brad Byers
Furthest Distance Shot with a Bow and
Arrow using the Feet, Hang Thu Thi Ngyuen
Most Tattooed Man, Tom Leppard
Guinness World Records *Primetime* host,
Mark Thompson, with Skateboard Plummet
record holder, Brian Patch
Larry and Danny Ramos Gomez
from the World's Hairiest Family
Most Jumps by a Dog, Olive Oyl
Man with Longest Fingernails,
Shridar Chillal

GUINNESS
WORLD RECORDS

how to use this book

Guinness World Records 2002 is even more action-packed than ever, with lots of new ways to find out more about our amazing records. As well as all the great new records that you have come to expect, this year's book is crammed with extra information and opportunities to interact with other Guinness World Records enthusiasts on our hot new website. Follow our symbols to find out what's been shown on TV, where we have super-fast record links and where to find fantastic icons and ringtones to download on to your phone!

SUBJECT URL

The URL shown here, is a subject URL. If you go to our website at **www.guinnessworldrecords.com** and type this address in, it will take you straight to the section of the site devoted to Unusual Skills.

ACCESS CODES

If you type in this number at the GWR website, you will go straight to the record featured in the box for even more information and related ringtones or SMS icons.

AWESOME ICONS

This year we have dreamt up hundreds of cool, record-related icons for you to download. Check them out on the web and ring 0901 6070 700. Calls will cost no more than 60p per minute.

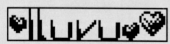

---

www.guinnessworldrecords.com/unusualskills

unusual skills

MOST FOOT-JUGGLING FLIPS OF A TABLE USA
Chester Cable (USA) flipped a table 3.03 m (9 ft 11.75 in) long, 88.9 cm (35 in) wide and 69.21 cm (27.25 in) high a total of 17 times, using his feet, on 1 Oct 1998.

MOST FOOT-JUGGLING FLIPS OF A PERSON FR
On 26 Oct 2000 Ali Bandbaz (Iran) 'juggled' his brother Massoud through 12 consecutive 360° revolutions, using only his feet. Ali lay on his back with Massoud sitting on his feet, and the pair completed each revolution in the same position.

LARGEST BUBBLE-GUM BUBBLE BLOWN WITH NOSE USA
Joyce Samuels (USA) blew a bubble-gum bubble with a diameter of 27.94 cm (11 in) on 10 Nov 2000.

LARGEST BALLOON INFLATED WITH A TANDEM NOSE BLOW USA
On 10 Nov 2000 Ryan Barker (USA) inflated an 118.11-cm (46.5-in) balloon held in his wife Marilee's mouth by blowing through her nose.

LONGEST-DISTANCE MARSHMALLOW NOSE BLOW USA
The greatest distance that a marshmallow has been shot from one person's nostril and caught in another person's mouth is 4.96 m (16 ft 3¼ in). Americans Scott Jeckel (the launcher) and Ray Perisin (the catcher) set this record on 13 Aug 1999.

FASTEST PANCAKE MARATHON
On 24 Oct 1999 Mike Cuzzacrea (USA) ('The Pancake Man') ran the 42.1-km (26.2-mile) Casino Niagara International Marathon in Buffalo, New York, USA, in 3 hr 2 min 27 sec, while flipping a pancake continuously in a frying pan. He came 46th out of 1,319 finishers.

FASTEST SANDWICH MADE USING FEET USA
On 10 Nov 2000 Rob Williams (USA) made a bologna, cheese and salad sandwich in 1 min 57 sec, using just his feet.

LOUDEST BURP UK
On 5 April 2000 Paul Hunn (UK) registered a burp of 118.1 dB – similar to being in the front row at a rock concert, and only slightly quieter than the noise made by an aeroplane on a runway.

MOST STEPS CLIMBED ON A BICYCLE
Javier Zapata (Colombia) broke his own world record by hopping up 943 steps on a bicycle, without touching the ground, on 20 May 2000. The feat took him 43 min 26 sec.

CATAPULT EARS USA
On 29 Oct 1999 Monte Pierce (USA, left) shot an American 10 cent coin a distance of 3.306 m (10 ft 10.5 in), using his ear as a catapult. This is the furthest a coin has been propelled by an ear lobe. Monte began pulling at his ears as a child to relieve earache, and now, aged 20, can pull them up over his eyes, pull them down to meet under his chin, or roll them up like earplugs. His left ear stretches to a length of 12–12.7 cm (4.75–5 in), and his right ear to a length of 11.4 cm (4.5 in). He has perfect hearing, and doctors assure him that he is not damaging his ears in any way by performing these feats.

www.guinnessworldrecords.com/catapultears
ACCESS CODE: ‹54633›

FASTEST TIME TO MEMORIZE A PACK OF CARDS
Andi Bell (UK) memorized a pack of 52 shuffled cards and repeated out loud the order in which they appeared in 34.03 seconds on 28 Aug 1998.

LONGEST TIME TENNIS BALL KEPT IN AIR WITH FEET
On 11 Nov 1999 Jacek Guzowski (Poland) kept a tennis ball up in the air, using only his feet, for 5 hr 28 min 59 sec. A counter showed that he touched the ball 35,000 times – an average of approximately 107 times per minute, or 1.8 times per second.

LARGEST SCORPION HELD IN MOUTH USA
Dean Sheldon (USA) was able to hold a 17.78-cm (7-in) scorpion in his mouth for 18 seconds on 21 Dec 2000.

MOST SCORPIONS IN MOUTH USA
Dean Sheldon (USA) put a total of 20 scorpions in his mouth, holding them there for 21 seconds, on 21 Dec 2000.

INSECT MORSEL MUNCHIES
Retired rat-catcher and part-time entertainer Ken Edwards (UK, left) ate 36 medium-sized cockroaches, in one minute on 5 March 2001, setting the record for the most cockroaches ever eaten by a human. Eating cockroaches is "like having an anaesthetic at the back of the throat" he says, as they let off a scent to ward away predators. His other bizarre stage acts include stuffing 47 rats down a pair of tights he was wearing, and inviting people to throw darts at a cork placed in his navel.
On 20 Oct 1998 Dr Norman Gary (USA) held 109 honeybees in his closed mouth for 10 seconds – but didn't eat them. Gary is Emeritus Professor at the University of California, USA, where his specialist subject is the behaviour of bees.

www.guinnessworldrecords.com/cockroacheater
ACCESS CODE: ‹54654›

66

SMS ICONS

You can download a crazy icon on to your phone every time you see this symbol. Go to the Guinness World Records website and type in the access code shown in this space. For this creepy cockroach, for example, type in /cockroacheater. Follow the instructions and he will be all yours!

CHAPTER SYMBOLS
Every chapter has its own symbols to identify it. These pages come from the chapter on Human Achievement.

HOTTEST METAL IN MOUTH
 USA
On 18 Dec 1998 Yim Byung Nam held a silver-dollar-sized piece of metal, heated to 487.8°C (910°F), in his mouth for 14 seconds. When Yim spat it out, it was hot enough to fry bacon.

LONGEST TIME IN A BOX BY THREE CONTORTIONISTS
FR
Bonnie Morgan, Daniel Smith and Leslie Tipton (all USA) fitted into a box measuring 66.04 x 68.58 x 55.88 cm (26 x 27 x 22 in) and stayed there for 2 min 40 sec on 31 Jan 2001.

LONGEST BASKETBALL SHOT MADE WITH HEAD
USA
On 10 Nov 2000 Eyal Horn (Israel) shot a basketball with his head while standing 7.62 m (25 ft) from the backboard. He also scored a record 15 consecutive lay-ups (shooting and catching the ball with the head).

MOST CHERRY STEMS KNOTTED IN ONE HOUR
On 4 Sept 1997 Al Gliniecki (USA) knotted 911 cherry stems with his tongue in one hour – an average of 15 stems per minute.

MOST SKIPS ON A UNICYCLE IN ONE MINUTE
DE
On 31 Aug 2000 Peter Rosendahl (Sweden) who resides in Germany, set the record for the most revolutions of a jump rope made on a unicycle. He managed 169 revolutions in just one minute.

GREATEST DISTANCE TO SPIT A CRICKET
USA
Danny Capps (USA) spat a dead cricket a total distance of 9.17 m (30 ft 1.2 in) on 26 June 1998.

FASTEST HUMAN BEER BOTTLE OPENER
USA
Daniel Lambert (Sweden) used his teeth to open 50 conventional crown-cap bottles on 11 March 2001. He achieved this in only one minute.

FASTEST TYRE FLIPPER
SE
On 31 Jan 2001 in Stockholm, Sweden, Jorma Paananen (Sweden) completed a 20-m (65-ft) course – 10 m (32 ft 6 in) there and back – of flipping a Michelin Radial Steel Cord X26.5R25 (XHA) tyre in a time of 1 min 6 sec. The tyre weighed 420 kg (925.9 lb).

AMAZING FEET OF ARCHERY
USA
www.guinnessworldrecords.com/archeryfeet

Hang Thu Thi Nguyen (Vietnam, left) set the record for the furthest distance shot with a bow and arrow using the feet. On 12 Aug 1999 she hit a target that was 5 m (16 ft 5 in) away. Thu Hang, whose father is a lighting technician at Ho Chi Minh City Circus, first became interested in circus skills as a child. She spends three hours a day practising her act. Although shy by nature, Thu Hang is very focused and confident on stage.

ACCESS CODE: 154461

TV ICONS
These symbols show which records have been performed and shown on TV and in which country they originated.

USA – USA, FOX

FR – France, TF1

DE – Germany, ARD

SE – Sweden, TV3

FIN – Finland, NELONEN

UK – UK, LWT

BULLETIN BOARDS
Now you have the chance to say what you think about some of the records in the book. This symbol means that there is a bulletin board on our website for the featured record. Get in there, see what everybody is talking about and have your say!

SMS ICON   SMS RINGTONE   BULLETIN BOARD   WORLD RECORDS TV

ICON MENU
If you forget what each icon means, just look along here to find out.

SMS RING TONES
Download hundreds of cool ringtones from the GWR website. Just type in the access code for the record and follow the instructions on the web.

how to use the web

Get a piece of the action when you log on to http://www.guinnessworldrecords.com. Choose from hundreds of crazy videos to watch, play games, discuss our amazing records with your mates, customize your mobile phone, and catch the latest world record news. Here's how ...

GWR NEWS
Click here for the latest Guinness World Records news, gossip and info – valiant attempts, records in progress, celebrity record breakers, hilarious failures and lots more. With daily updated record news, there's always something to come back for.

FIND YOUR CATEGORY!
This year's Guinness World Records website is more exciting than ever with lots of new and exciting ways of finding out more about all our amazing records. Search the category menu to find the subject area you're looking for ...

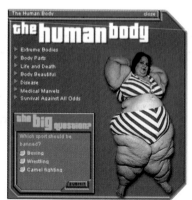

Click on different menus to find records featured in the Guinness World Records book.

What do YOU think of these records?

Have your say with the fully interactive 'The Big Question'.

GO STRAIGHT TO THE ACTION
Go straight to your favourite record for even more amazing pictures and information using the access codes in this book!

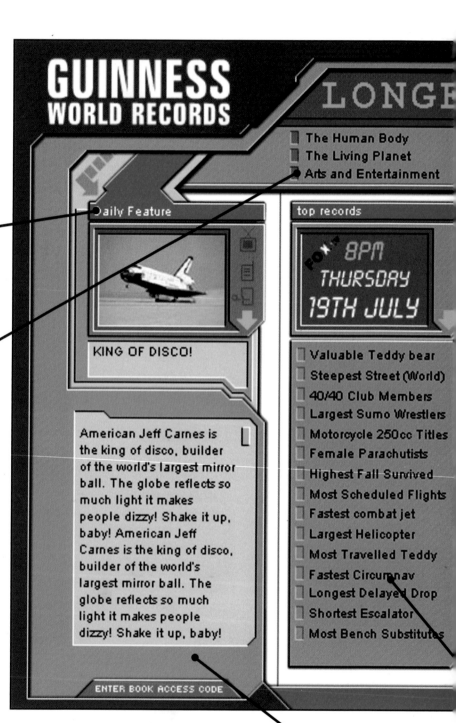

GUINNESS WORLD RECORDS

LONGE

- The Human Body
- The Living Planet
- Arts and Entertainment

Daily Feature

KING OF DISCO!

top records

FOX 8PM THURSDAY 19TH JULY

- Valuable Teddy bear
- Steepest Street (World)
- 40/40 Club Members
- Largest Sumo Wrestlers
- Motorcycle 250cc Titles
- Female Parachutists
- Highest Fall Survived
- Most Scheduled Flights
- Fastest combat jet
- Largest Helicopter
- Most Travelled Teddy
- Fastest Circumnav
- Longest Delayed Drop
- Shortest Escalator
- Most Bench Substitutes

American Jeff Carnes is the king of disco, builder of the world's largest mirror ball. The globe reflects so much light it makes people dizzy! Shake it up, baby! American Jeff Carnes is the king of disco, builder of the world's largest mirror ball. The globe reflects so much light it makes people dizzy! Shake it up, baby!

ENTER BOOK ACCESS CODE

HOT BUTTONS
Amazed at what you've just seen? Hook up with some e-buddies and say what you think! Want to see more? Check out the video! Still want more? Why not download a record-breaking ringtone or icon for your mobile phone?

FANTASTIC SHORT CUTS
Use the access codes shown in Guinness World Records 2002 to get straight to the action! Follow the directions on pages 6-7 and go directly to the record you want!

KEYWORD SEARCH
Use our keyword search to locate one of the thousands of Guinness World Records home pages.

INSTANT UPDATE
Hit the ticker tape when a world record flashes by and get the full details – instantly.

GREAT T-SHIRTS
Pick up some of the coolest, newest Guinness World Records T-shirts.

SEARCH

T HOVERCRA

SHOP GUINNESS WORLD RECORDS

ame and Money
orld Matters
Technology

Human Achievements
The Material World
Sports

favourite videos

interactive

The Video Vault
car balancing

the Video vault

MORE PICTURES

LAUNCH WINDOWS MEDIA PLAYER · 14.4KB · 56KB MODEMS
LAUNCH WINDOWS MEDIA PLAYER · ISDN, ADSL, CABLE, T1-T3 CONNECTIONS
LAUNCH REAL PLAYER · 14.4KB · 56KB MODEMS
LAUNCH REAL PLAYER · ISDN, ADSL, CABLE, T1-T3 CONNECTIONS

Windows Media Player

top five videos

Heaviest car balanced o
Coin throwing - 24 hour
Dog weaving
Fastest pantomime hors
First virtual newscaster

past favourites

Fastest system frame scaff
Most heads shaved in 4 ho
Tallest paper cup
Bow and arrow speed shoc
Tallest tomato plant
Heaviest train pulled
Longest bicycle
Largest accordion ensemt

top five game scores

nemo 22 55555
winboy 34
no doubt 56
poke y2 43
wormy 23

top 5 games

nemo 22
winboy
no doubt
poke-y2
wormy

Contact Us

Submit a Claim
Enquires

PRIVACY   CREDITS   ABOUT US   CONTACT

VIDEO VAULT
Choose from hundreds of great record film clips straight from the Guinness World Records video vault.

INTERACTIVE GAMES
Test your skill and see how you rank against all the other Guinness World Record challengers by playing our interactive games.

TOP RECORDS
Find the top records here, from the biggest, smallest, longest, highest, oldest, youngest, loudest and deepest, to the wettest, hottest, hairiest, fastest, slowest, coolest, smelliest and richest ...

WANT TO BREAK A RECORD?
Have you broken a Guinness World Record? Do you want to break a Guinness World Record? Send us your claim over the web for a fast response or contact us for information. You're only a click away, and you could be in next year's book ...

GUINNESS WORLD RECORDS

contents

Josh Tenge – see page 225

Robonaut
– see page 179

Alex Rodriguez – see page 201

Crash Bandicoot – see page 169

GUINNESS WORLD RECORDS

www.guinnessworldrecords.com/thehumanbody

the human body

extreme bodies

GREATEST HEIGHT DIFFERENCE BETWEEN A MARRIED COUPLE

When Fabien Pretou and Natalie Lucius (both France) walked down the aisle on 14 April 1990, they became the married couple with the greatest difference in height. He is 188.5 cm (6 ft 2 in) tall, while she is only 94 cm (3 ft 1 in) – a difference of 94.5 cm (3 ft 1.2 in).

GREATEST WEIGHT DIFFERENCE BETWEEN A MARRIED COUPLE

Jon Brower Minnoch weighed 635 kg (1,400 lb) when he married his 50-kg (110-lb) wife, Jeannette, (both USA) in March 1978. At 585 kg (1,289.7 lb), this is the greatest recorded difference in weight for a married couple. Jon was also the heaviest person in medical history. He suffered from obesity as a child and by 1963, when he was 22-years-old and 1.85 m (6 ft 1 in) tall, he weighed a huge 178 kg (392 lb). By Sept 1976 he weighed 442 kg (974 lb). He died in 1983, still weighing more than 362 kg (798 lb).

MOST WEIGHT GAINED BY A WOMAN

Doris James (USA) is alleged to have gained 147 kg (324 lb) in the 12 months before her death in Aug 1965. At this time she was aged 38, weighed 306 kg (675 lb) and measured 1.57 m (5 ft 2 in) in height.

MOST WEIGHT GAINED BY A MAN

Arthur Knorr (USA), who was born in 1916 and died in 1960, gained a record 133 kg (293 lb) in the last six months of his life.

HEAVIEST WOMAN USA

Rosalie Bradford (USA) is claimed to have registered a peak weight of 544 kg (1,199 lb) in Jan 1987, aged 43. After following a controlled diet, she weighed 128 kg (282 lb) in Feb 1994.

LIGHTEST PERSON

Lucia Xarate (1863–89, Mexico), an emaciated ateleiotic dwarf of 67 cm (26.8 in) who weighed 1.1 kg (2.8 lb) at birth, weighed only 2.13 kg (4.7 lb) at the age of 17. She had fattened up to 5.9 kg (13 lb) by her 20th birthday. The lightest recorded adults of normal height are those suffering from Simmond's Disease (*hypophyseal cachexia*). Losses of up to 65% of the original body weight have been recorded in females, with a 'low'

of 20 kg (44 lb) in the case of Emma Shaller (USA) who stood 1.57 m (5 ft 2 in). Edward C Hagner, alias Eddie Masher (USA), is alleged to have weighed only 22 kg (48 lb) at a height of 1.7 m (5 ft 7 in). He was also known as the 'Skeleton Dude'.

HEAVIEST TWINS AT BIRTH

The world's heaviest twins were born to JP Haskin (USA) on 20 Feb 1924. They had a combined weight of 12.6 kg (27 lb 12 oz).

CROWD PULLERS

The world's most elastic man is double-jointed Pierre Beauchemin (Canada, left), who earned the nickname 'Mr Gumby' for his amazing ability to turn his arms and legs around in extremely contorted positions. Doctors believed that Pierre would be crippled by the time he was 30, but at 34 he continues to entertain people.

Gary Turner (UK) has skin that stretches further than that of any other known human being. His favourite trick is to stretch his neck skin over his mouth to create a human turtle neck, although this does not beat his stomach trick – on 29 Oct 1999 he stretched the skin of his stomach 15.8 cm (6.25 in). Gary, who was born in 1964, has been entertaining people with this ability since school days.

www.guinnessworldrecords.com/elasticman
← ACCESS CODE: ‹53928›

HEAVIEST TWINS

Billy Leon and Benny Loyd McCrary, alias McGuire (both USA), were normal in size until the age of six. In Nov 1978, just before their 32nd birthday, Billy and Benny weighed 337 kg (743 lb) and 328 kg (723 lb) respectively, and both had waists measuring 2.13 m (84 in). They became professional tag wrestling performers. When weighed before competitions, they clocked weights of up to 349 kg (769 lb).

WASTING THOSE INCHES

Cathie Jung (USA, left) has a 38.1-cm (15-in) waist – the smallest waist on a living person. She is 1.73 m (5 ft 8 in) tall. Cathie and husband Bob worked together to develop her tiny waist as part of their enthusiasm for Victorian dress. At 38, the mother of three started wearing a 15-cm (6-in) wide training belt to reduce her waist gradually. She does not eat a special diet or exercise to maintain her waist.

The smallest waist ever of a person of normal height was 33 cm (13 in). Ethel Granger (UK) reduced to this measurement from a natural 56 cm (22 in) between 1929 and 1939, by wearing specially constructed corsets.

A measurement of 33 cm (13 in) was also claimed for French actress Mademoiselle Polaire (real name Emile Marie Bouchand) who died in 1939.

www.guinnessworldrecords.com/tinywaist
← ACCESS CODE: ‹54595›

LIGHTEST TWINS

Two sets of twins have been born with a combined weight of 860 g (30.33 oz). Roshan Maralyn (490 g or 17.28 oz) and Melanie Louise (370 g or 13.05 oz), were born to Katrina Gray (Australia) at the Royal Women's Hospital, Brisbane, Qld, Australia, on 19 Nov 1993. Wendy Morrison (Canada) gave birth to Anne (420 g or 14.81 oz) and John (440 g or 15.52 oz) at Ottawa General Hospital, Ontario, Canada, on 14 Jan 1994.

SHORTEST LIVING TWINS   USA

The shortest living twins are John and Greg Rice (USA), born on 3 Dec 1951. They are identical twins and both measure 86.3 cm (2 ft 10 in).

SHORTEST TWINS EVER

The shortest twins on record were Matyus and Béla Matina (Hungary, later USA; 1903–c.1935), who were both 76 cm (2 ft 6 in) tall.

SHORTEST LIVING MAN

Younis Edwan (Jordan) is believed to be 65 cm (2 ft 1.5 in) tall. He was born c.1971, and is the sixth sibling in a family of seven sisters and brothers.

SHORTEST MAN EVER

The shortest mature man for whose height there is independent evidence was Gul Mohammed (India). When examined at Ram Manohar Hospital, New Delhi, in 1990, he was found to be just 57 cm (1 ft 10.5 in) tall.

ACCESS CODE: ‹56075›

DADDY LONGLEGS

At the age of 17, Sam Stacey (UK, right) has the world's longest verified legs. They measured 126.36 cm (49.75 in) in Jan 2001. Sam has always been taller than average and at the age of 17, she is 2.08 m (6 ft 4 in) – about the same height as her father. At a height of 1.77 m (5 ft 10 in), Sam's mother actually looks short. Her younger brother and sister are both of average height. Although Sam has occasionally considered a career in modelling, she is studying to become a nurse.

He died at the age of 39 in 1997, after a long struggle with asthma and bronchitis.

SHORTEST LIVING WOMAN

Madge Bester (South Africa) is just 65 cm (2 ft 1.5 in) tall. Sadly, she suffers from *osteogenesis imperfecta* (characterized by brittle bones and deformities of the skeleton) and is confined to a wheelchair.

SHORTEST WOMAN EVER

The shortest-ever female was Pauline Musters (1876–1895), who measured 30 cm (1 ft) at the time of her birth in Ossendrecht, Netherlands, and 55 cm (1 ft 9.6 in) at the age of nine. A postmortem carried out after her death, from pneumonia and meningitis, at the age of 19 in New York City, New York, USA, showed her to be 61 cm (2 ft) tall, although there was evidence of elongation of the body after death.

TALLEST LIVING MAN　　UK

The tallest living man is Radhouane Charbib (Tunisia), who measures 2.35 m (7 ft 8.9 in). He is one of 11 brothers and sisters, who all measure a normal 1.7 m (5 ft 6 in).

TALLEST MAN EVER

The tallest man in medical history was Robert Wadlow (USA). When measured in June 1940, shortly before his death, he was 2.72 m (8 ft 11.1 in) tall. His greatest recorded weight was 222.71 kg (491 lb) on his 21st birthday. He weighed 199 kg (438 lb) at the time of his death. His shoe size was 37AA (47 cm or 18.5 in long) and his hands measured 32.4 cm (12.75 in) from the wrist to the tip of the middle finger. His arm span was 2.88 m (9 ft 5.75 in) and his peak daily food consumption was 8,000 calories. At the age of nine, he was able to carry his father, Harold F Wadlow, who stood 1.8 m (5 ft 11 in) and weighed 77 kg (170 lb), up the stairs of the family home.

TALLEST LIVING WOMAN　　USA

Sandy Allen (USA) is 2.31 m (7 ft 7.25 in) tall, making her the tallest living woman. A 2.95-kg (6-lb-8-oz) baby, her abnormal growth began soon after birth. She stood 1.90 m (6 ft 3 in) by the age of 10 and was 2.16 m (7 ft 1 in) by 16.

TALLEST WOMAN EVER

The tallest woman for whose height there is reliable evidence was Zeng Jinlian (China). She was 2.48 m (8 ft 1.75 in) tall when she died on 13 Feb 1982, aged 17.

LARGEST WAIST　　USA

The largest waist was that of Walter Hudson (USA), which measured 3.02 m (9 ft 11 in) at his peak weight of 545 kg (1,201 lb).

GUINNESS WORLD RECORDS™

body parts

LARGEST BELLY CIRCUMFERENCE
Gut barger contestant David White (UK), also known as 'Mad Maurice Vanderkirkoff', had a belly circumference of 137.7 cm (54.2 in) when measured on 12 March 2001.

FEWEST TOES
The two-toed syndrome exhibited by some members of the Wadomo tribe of the Zambezi Valley, Zimbabwe, and the Kalanga tribe of the eastern Kalahari Desert, Botswana, is hereditary, via a single mutated gene.

MOST FINGERS AND TOES
An inquest held on a baby boy on 16 Sept 1921 in London, UK, reported that he had 14 fingers and 15 toes. This condition, known as polydactylism, can be caused by any one of over 30 rare congenital medical syndromes (syndromes that are present at birth). The condition is relatively common, with as many as two in 1,000 births affected. These extra digits are most commonly fleshy bumps without any bones, but can be complete fingers or toes.

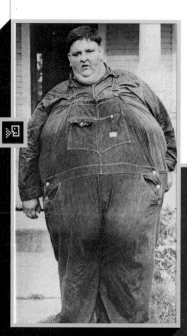

LIVING PERSON WITH MOST FINGERS
Godfrey Hill (UK) has 10 fingers and two thumbs. Born in 1928, when 12 pennies made a shilling, his extra fingers were an advantage at school where he topped the class at adding. His condition has won him attention around the world, especially in Tunisia, where he was mistaken for a descendant of Allah.

MOST DEVELOPED THIRD FOOT USA
José López (originally Mexico, now USA) has a third foot, consisting of an ankle and four toes, growing out from the ankle of his left leg.

HEAVIEST BRAIN
The heaviest brain ever recorded weighed 2.3 kg (5 lb 1.1 oz). It belonged to a 30-year-old male, and was reported by Dr T Mandybur of the Department of Pathology and Laboratory Medicine at the University of Cincinnati, Ohio, USA, in Dec 1992. An average-sized brain for an adult would weigh 1.3 to 1.4 kg (2.8 to 3 lb).

LONGEST NOSE
There are historical accounts that Thomas Wedders, who lived in the UK during the 1770s and was a member of a travelling freak circus, had a nose measuring 19 cm (7.5 in) long.

LIGHTEST BRAIN
The world's lightest normal (non-atrophied) brain weighed just 680 g (1 lb 8 oz). It belonged to Daniel Lyon (Ireland), who died in New York, USA, in 1907, aged 46. He was just over 1.5 m (5 ft) tall and weighed 66 kg (145 lb).

MOST VALUABLE TOOTH
In 1816 a tooth belonging to scientist Sir Isaac Newton (UK, 1642–1727) was sold in London for £730 ($3,633). This is approximately £25,000 ($35,700) in today's terms. It was purchased by an aristocrat who had it set in a ring.

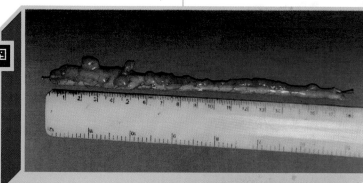

HORRENDIX APPENDIX
The appendix (above) removed from the abdomen of Mr Mahendra (India) on 11 Aug 2000 measured a record 17.5 cm (6.8 in) in length. An average appendix measures just 8–10 cm long (3–4 in). The operation was performed by Dr Teekappa at Vishwamanava Hospital, Birur, India.

On 25 Oct 1998 surgeon Kadri Al-Ban (Yemen) removed the biggest bladder stone ever recorded from one of his patients in an operation at the Al-Kadri Clinic, Ibb, Yemen. Mohammed Ali A Al-Muleiki (Yemen) had a vesical (bladder) stone that weighed a record-setting 260 g (9.15 oz), with a diameter of about 7 cm (2.75 in).

www.guinnessworldrecords.com/appendix
← ACCESS CODE: ‹53572›

LONGEST MOUSTACHE
The moustache of Kalyan Ramji Sain (India) spanned 3.39 m (133.4 in). In July 1993 the right side measured 1.72 m (67.7 in) and the left measured 1.67 m (65.7 in). The moustache had been growing since 1976.

LONGEST HAIR USA
The world's longest documented hair belongs to Ho Sateow, a tribal medicine man from Chiang Mai, Thailand. On 21 Nov 1997 his hair was unravelled and it was officially measured at 5.15 m (16 ft 11 in) long. He had not had a haircut in over 70 years. He fell sick after cutting his hair when he was aged 18 and vowed never to cut it again. The hair is washed annually with detergent and worn wound up in a fashionable beehive.

LONGEST-BEARDED MAN
The beard of Hans Langseth (Norway) measured 5.33 m (17 ft 6 in) at the time of his burial at Kensett, Iowa, USA, in 1927. He started growing his beard at the age of 30 and it took 51 years to grow to this length. It grew at an average rate of 2 mm (0.007 in) per week, and was presented to the Smithsonian Institution, Washington DC, USA, in 1967.

GET IT OFF YOUR CHEST
Robert Earl Hughes (USA, left) had a chest measurement of 3.15 m (10 ft 4 in). His parents believed that a bout of whooping cough at the age of three months caused an endocrine imbalance that accounted for his incredible weight gain. At the age of six, he weighed 92 kg (203 lb). By 10 he weighed 171 kg (378 lb) and at age 25 he reached 406 kg (896 lb). In Feb 1958, just before his death, Robert weighed 484 kg (1,067 lb). His waist was 3.1 m (10 ft 2 in), and each upper arm was 1.02 m (3 ft 4 in) in circumference.

The largest muscular chest measurement is that of Isaac Nesser (USA) at 1.88 m (6 ft 2 in).

www.guinnessworldrecords.com/bigchest
← ACCESS CODE: ‹48481›

LONGEST-BEARDED WOMAN

The beard of the 'Bearded Lady', Janice Deveree (USA), was measured at 36 cm (14 in) long in 1884.

LONGEST-BEARDED LIVING WOMAN 📺 USA

Vivian Wheeler (USA) grew a full beard in 1990. The longest strand from the follicle to the tip of hair was measured at 27.9 cm (11 in) in 2000. Wheeler, who has married four times, was shaving her face at age seven.

LONGEST MALE FINGERNAILS 📺 USA

The world's longest fingernails are those of Shridhar Chillal (India), who last cut his fingernails in 1952. On 8 July 1998 the nails on his left hand had a total length of 6.15 m (20 ft 2.25 in).

LONGEST FEMALE FINGERNAILS 📺 USA

The woman with the world's longest fingernails is Lee Redmond (USA). Her nails measure a total length of 6.63 m (21 ft 9 in). Lee has been growing her nails for 19 years. The longest nail is on her left thumb and measures 68.58 cm (27 in).

LARGEST GALL BLADDER

On 15 March 1989 at the National Naval Medical Center in Bethesda, Maryland, USA, Prof Bimal C Ghosh removed a gall bladder weighing a record-breaking 10.4 kg (23 lb) from a

www.guinnessworldrecords.com/bigfeet

BIGFOOT 📷 USA

The biggest feet of a living person (excluding cases of the disease elephantiasis) are those of Matthew McGrory (USA, right) who wears US size 28.5 (UK size 28) shoes. Unsurprisingly, he has to have all his shoes custom-made to fit. Both his big toes measure 12.7 cm (5 in) in length, and his little toes are 3.81 cm (1.5 in) long.

69-year-old woman. This is more than three times the weight of an average newborn baby. The patient made a full recovery after the operation.

LARGEST BICEP

The right bicep of Denis Sester (USA) measures 77.8 cm (30 in) when cold. He built up his amazing muscles by performing arm curls with a 68-kg (150-lb) bucket of sand. As a youngster he wrestled hogs weighing 180 kg (400 lb) on his parents' farm to get fit.

GUINNESS WORLD RECORDS

age and youth

OLDEST LIVING WOMAN

Maude Farris-Luse (neé Davis) born on 21 Jan 1887 in Morley, Michigan, USA, is the world's oldest living woman whose date of birth can be fully authenticated.

OLDEST PERSON EVER

The greatest fully authenticated age to which any human has ever lived is 122 years 164 days by Jeanne Louise Calment (France). She was born on 21 Feb 1875 and died on 4 Aug 1997.

THREE OF A KIND

Marjory Skeaping (neé Scott), Sheila Botterill (neé Scott) and David Scott (UK, above) have been verified as the oldest triplets living in the world. They were born in Edinburgh, UK, on 19 May 1920. Interestingly their uncle, aunt and their mother's first cousin also celebrate their birthdays on 19 May.

The longest-lived triplets ever recorded were Faith, Hope and Charity Cardwell (USA) who were born on 18 May 1899. Faith died first, on 2 Oct 1994, aged 95 years 137 days.

The oldest quadruplets were the Ottmans (Germany). Adolf, Anne-Marie, Emma and Elisabeth were born on 5 May 1912. All four quads lived to the age of 79.

In Nov 2000 there were 992 sets of quadruplets worldwide. Identical quads are quite rare – only about 20 sets worldwide.

www.guinnessworldrecords.com/oldtriplets

ACCESS CODE: ‹54715›

Centenarians surviving beyond their 113th year are extremely rare. It is thought that only one 115-year life can be expected in 2.1 billion lives.

OLDEST MOTHER

Rosanna Dalla Corte (Italy), born in 1931, gave birth to a baby boy on 18 July 1994 when she was 63. The baby was conceived through artificial insemination of donor eggs.

On 7 Nov 1996, 63-year-old Arceli Keh (USA) gave birth to daughter Cynthia having undergone IVF treatment.

OLDEST MOTHER TO HAVE QUADRUPLETS

The oldest mother to have quadruplets is Merryl Thelma Fudel (Australia) who gave birth to three girls and one boy on 18 April 1998, at the age of 55 years 286 days, at Sharp Memorial Hospital, San Diego, California, USA. One baby died at birth due to respiratory failure.

OLDEST MALE TWINS

The oldest twins ever documented are Eli Shadrack and John Meshak Phipps (USA), born on 14 Feb 1803 in Affington, Virginia, USA. Eli died on 23 Feb 1911 at the age of 108 years; his brother John died on 10 Dec 1916 at the age of 113. The chance of identical twins both reaching and surpassing the age of 100 is about one in 700 million.

OLDEST LIVING MALE CONJOINED TWINS

USA

Born in 1952, Ronnie and Donnie Galyon (both USA) are the oldest living conjoined male twins. For 36 years they travelled in side shows, carnivals and circuses. In 1991 they retired and now live in Ohio, USA.

OLDEST LIVING FEMALE CONJOINED TWINS

Masha and Dasha Krivoshlyapova (USSR), born on 3 Jan 1950, are a rare form of conjoined twins – *dicephales tetrabrachius dipus* (two heads, four arms and two legs). Now aged 51 years old, they reside in a Moscow old people's home.

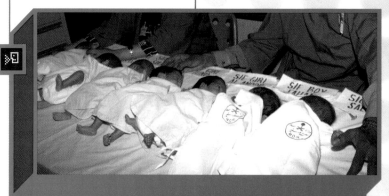

IN SEVENTH HEAVEN

The most surviving children from a single birth is seven. The septuplets (above) were born eight weeks premature on 14 Jan 1998 to 40-year-old Hasna Mohammed Humair (Saudi Arabia). There were four boys and three girls, the smallest of which weighed just under 907 g (2 lb).

Bobbie McCaughey (USA) also had septuplets on 19 Nov 1997. Named Kenneth, Nathaniel, Brandon, Joel, Kelsey, Natalie and Alexis, they weighed between 1,048 g and 1,474.3 g (2 lb 5 oz and 3 lb 4 oz) and were delivered at 31 weeks by Caesarean in the space of 16 minutes.

www.guinnessworldrecords.com/septuplets

ACCESS CODE: ‹48315›

OLDEST MALE CONJOINED TWINS EVER

Giacomo and Giovanni Battista Tocci (Italy) were born on 4 Oct 1877 and lived to be 63 years old. They were separate above the waist, but shared an abdomen, pelvis and two legs.

MOST LIVING ASCENDANTS

At her birth on 16 May 1982, Megan Sue Austin (USA) had a full set of parents, grandparents and great-grandparents, and five great-great-grandparents, making 19 direct ascendants.

GREATEST NUMBER OF DESCENDANTS

At the time of his death on 15 Oct 1992 aged 96, Samuel S Mast (USA), had 824 living descendants. The roll call comprised 11 children, 97 grandchildren, 634 great-grandchildren and 82 great-great-grandchildren.

In polygamous countries, the number of a person's descendants can become incalculable. The last Sharifian emperor of Morocco, Moulay Ismail, who died in 1727, was reputed to have fathered a total of 525 sons and 342 daughters by 1703 and had his 700th son in 1721.

MOST COINCIDENT BIRTHDAYS IN A FAMILY

Ralph Betram Williams (USA) was born on 4 July 1982. His father, grandfather and, in 1876, his great-grandfather, were also born on 4 July.

Veera Tuulia Tuijantyär Kivistö (Finland), who was born in 1997, shares her birthday of 21 March with her mother (1967), her grandfather (1940) and great-grandfather (1903).

MOST COINCIDENT BIRTHDAYS OF SIBLINGS

Catherine (1952), Carol (1953), Charles (1956), Claudia (1961) and Cecilia (1966) were born to Carolyn and Ralph Cummins (both USA) – all of them on 20 Feb. The random odds against five single siblings sharing a birthdate are one in 17,797,577,730.

Heidi (1960), Olav (1964) and Leif-Martin (1968) Henriksen (Norway), all celebrate their birthdays on leap year day (29 Feb).

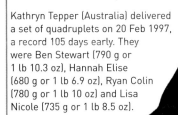

AGE BEFORE BEAUTY

At 112, Antonio Todde (right), born on 22 Jan 1889 in Tiana, Sardinia, Italy, is the oldest living man in the world. He puts his longevity down to a lifetime of hard work and a daily glass of locally produced red wine. Sardinia's exceptionally high concentration of centenarians is attributed mainly to genes. Both Antonio's parents lived well into their nineties, and his four children are all in their eighties.

The greatest age to which any man has ever lived is 120 years 237 days. Shigechiyo Izumi, of Isen on Tokunoshima, an island 1,320 km (820 miles) south-west of Japan, was born on 29 June 1865 and died on 21 Feb 1986. He worked until he was 105. He drank *sho-chu* (distilled from barley) and took up smoking at the age of 70. He attributed his long life to 'God, Buddha and the Sun'.

MOST SOUTHERLY BIRTH

Emilio Marcos Palma (Argentina) was born on 7 Jan 1978 at the Sargento Cabral Base, Antarctica. To date, he is the only infant known to have been born on the icy southern continent.

LONGEST INTERVALS BETWEEN BIRTHS

The longest interval between the birth of two children to the same mother, but in separate confinements, is 41 years. Elizabeth Ann Buttle (UK) had a daughter, Belinda, in 1956 and a son, Joseph David, on 20 Nov 1997, at the age of 60.

Jackie Iverson (Canada) gave birth normally to a boy, Christopher, on 21 Nov 1993, a girl Alexandra, on 29 Nov 1993, and was delivered (by Caesarean) of another boy and girl, Matthew and Sarah, on 30 Nov 1993. This period of nine days is the longest interval between the births of quadruplets.

MOST PREMATURE BABIES

On 20 May 1987, James Elgin Gill was born to Brenda and James Gill (both Canada). 128 days premature, he weighed only 624 g (1 lb 6 oz).

Born on 8 April 1996 in Riverside, Ohio, USA, Devin and Dorraine Johnson (both USA) are the most premature twins. They were 119 days premature.

The most premature triplets are Guy, Kathryn and Marcus Humphrey (UK), born on 28 Feb 1992 in Manchester, UK, 108 days early.

Kathryn Tepper (Australia) delivered a set of quadruplets on 20 Feb 1997, a record 105 days early. They were Ben Stewart (790 g or 1 lb 10.3 oz), Hannah Elise (680 g or 1 lb 6.9 oz), Ryan Colin (780 g or 1 lb 10 oz) and Lisa Nicole (735 g or 1 lb 8.5 oz).

MOST PROLIFIC MOTHER

The wife of Feodor Vassilyev from Shuya, Russia, gave birth to 69 children in 27 confinements. A total of 16 pairs of twins, seven sets of triplets and four sets of quadruplets were born between 1725 and 1765. Only two of the children failed to survive infancy.

GUINNESS WORLD RECORDS

CERTIFICATE

Antonio Todde
who was born on
22 January 1889
in Tiana, Sardinia, Italy
is the world's oldest living man

Keeper of the Records
GUINNESS WORLD RECORDS LTD

GUINNESS WORLD RECORDS

body beautiful

COUNTRY WITH MOST PLASTIC SURGEONS

The USA has the world's most plastic surgeons, with approximately 5,965, followed by Brazil and then Japan, according to the International Confederation for Plastic, Reconstructive and Aesthetic Surgery. This figure is equal to almost half of the world's plastic surgeons. New York City has the highest concentration, but San Francisco is the city with the most plastic surgeons per capita.

MOST PLASTIC SURGERY

Cindy Jackson (USA) has spent $99,600 (£69,104) on 28 cosmetic operations over 15 years. Born in Ohio in 1955, Jackson has had three full facelifts, two nose operations, knee, waist, abdomen and jawline surgery, thigh liposuction, breast reduction and augmentation, and semi-permanent make-up.

MOST EXPENSIVE SKIN BEAUTY TREATMENT

The 'Botaenica Dual-Mud Kit' made by a New York City luxury store is the most expensive skin beauty treatment in the world. It sold out after just four days at a price of $845 (£534) per unit. Each of the Dual-Mud systems was obtained from different geological compositions – the first from the Dead Sea and the second from the emanation of an Arctic Ocean floor volcanic vent, a very rare mud found only at this depth.

BODY TALK 📺 USA

Fashion designer Tina-Marie Stoker (USA) adorned the body of a model (left) with a record-breaking 29,540 rhinestones in Munich, Germany, on 20 Jan 2000.

Adornment of a different kind makes Luis Antonio Agüero (Cuba), a record-holder as the world's most pierced man. He sports 230 piercings on his head and body. His face alone carries over 175 rings. Agüero uses a sterilized needle to do all his own piercing, and the 230 piercings have taken him 10 years.

The world's fastest henna artist is Ash Kumar (UK). On 1 April 2001 he completed 96 traditional henna armband tattoos in one hour at Cannon High School, Middlesex, UK.

www.guinnessworldrecords.com/rhinestonebody
← ACCESS CODE: ‹54611›

LARGEST LIP JEWELLERY

The Ethiopian Mursi tribe is renowned for their practice of inserting large, circular clay plates behind the lower lips of their women as a sign of true beauty. At puberty, the lip is stretched with a clay plate, and the size is increased periodically. A girl's goal is to wear a plate at least the size of a teacup saucer (15 cm or 6 in in diameter), before she is married.

LONGEST NECK

The maximum known extension of a human neck is 40 cm (15.75 in). This was created by the successive fitting of copper coils, as practised by the women of the Padaung or Kareni tribe of Myanmar (Burma) as a sign of beauty. Only initial discomfort is reported after the coils are fitted, yet the distance from earlobe to collarbone lengthens to more than double the average. The women's necks eventually become so long and weak that they cannot support their heads without the coils.

MOST WOMEN WITH BOUND FEET

In China, 38% of women aged 80 or older have bound feet. The practice of foot binding began in the Sung dynasty (960–976 AD) as a symbol of beauty. Chinese women's feet were bound tightly with strips of cloth to stop them from growing, so that their feet would resemble three-inch golden lotus flowers. By the time a girl turned three, all but the first of her toes were broken, and because of the cloth strips, her feet would grow no larger than 10 cm (3.9 in).

MOST VALUABLE PAIR OF 'FALSIES'

A pair of flesh-coloured foam and cotton bra pads once belonging to film star Marilyn Monroe (USA), sold at auction for $5,000 (£3,450) in Bedford, New Hampshire, USA, on 15 April 2000. The 'falsies', with nipple-shaped tips, were given to the Westwood Village Mortuary, Los Angeles, by Monroe's housekeeper, but were not used when preparing

Marilyn's body for burial. They were rescued from the mortuary's bin by Allan Abbott, who kept them for 37 years, finally selling them for $2,100 (£1,500) in 1999.

MOST EXPENSIVE PERFUME

The world's most expensive perfume, launched in June 2000, is *Parfum VI*, designed by British perfumer Arthur Burnham. The 10.2-cm (4-in) bottle, made with platinum, 24-carat gold, rubies and diamonds, costs £47,500 ($71,380) and was inspired by the Phantom VI Rolls-Royce. Only 173 bottles were made and Michael Jackson and Mike Tyson were among the first to place orders.

LARGEST GLOBAL BEAUTY PAGEANT

As of Feb 2001, there were 89 entrants from 89 countries competing for the title of Miss World. India and Sweden tie for the most Miss World titles, with five each in the pageant's history.

BEAUTY PAGEANT WITH THE OLDEST CONTESTANTS

The 'Ms Senior America' pageant is only open to women aged 60 years or older. It was founded in 1971 to draw attention to the positive aspects of ageing in response to the then bleak media image of America's elderly.

HEAVIEST MS OLYMPIA CONTESTANT

Nicole Bass (USA) weighed 92.5 kg (204 lb) when she participated in the 1997 Ms Olympia contest. As

BODY OF EVIDENCE

Although she no longer appears regularly on the catwalk, Elle MacPherson ('The Body'), is said to be the world's richest supermodel, worth a massive £23 million ($38.12 million). Her business interests include her own line of lingerie, 'Elle MacPherson Intimates'. Elle has also appeared in several films, including *Sirens* (Australia/UK, 1994), *Jane Eyre* (USA, 1996) and *Batman & Robin* (USA, 1997). Most recently, she appeared in the US TV sitcom, *Friends*.

The largest international model agency is Elite Model Management. It is currently based in 22 countries around the world, with 11 offices in Europe and five in the USA. The company also has offices in Brazil, Hong Kong and China.

www.guinnessworldrecords.com/ellethebody
← ACCESS CODE: ‹52258›

well as the heaviest, she is also the tallest-ever contestant, at 1.87 m (6 ft 2 in). Nicole was the overall winner of the 1997 NPC National Bodybuilding Championships before she went into Pro Wrestling. She is now working at independent shows worldwide. She has a 127-cm (50-in) chest, 76-cm (30-in) waist, 45.7-cm (18-in) arms, 71-cm (28-in) thighs and 45.7-cm (18-in) calves.

www.guinnessworldrecords.com/hairyboys

CROWNING GLORY USA

Victor 'Larry' and Gabriel 'Danny' Ramos Gomez (below) are 98% covered by a thick coat of fur, caused by a condition called hypertrichosis. The boys are very positive about their condition and have become stars in the Mexican National Circus, thanks to its owner Mundo Carpa. As Danny says, "We have learnt that people who are different can still have dignity." Many others in their family – the De Jesus clan – also have hypertrichosis, earning them the title of 'the world's hairiest family'.

ACCESS CODE: ‹5383›

MOST TATTOOED MAN USA

Tom Leppard (UK) has approximately 99.9% of his body covered in tattoos. Tom's all-body tattoo portrays a leopard-skin design – dark feline spots, with a leopard-like yellow tattooed on the skin in between. Tom now lives as a hermit on the Isle of Skye, UK, and estimates he has spent over £4,857 ($7,000) on his amazing bodywork.

MOST TATTOOED WOMAN

The world's most tatooed woman is strip artiste Krystyne Kolorful (Canada). Tattoos cover 95% of her body and took 10 years to complete.

TALLEST HAIRSTYLE

Ladies' hairstyles literally reached their 'high point' in the mid-1770s when the French Queen Marie Antoinette's hair stood an amazing 91.44 cm (36 in) tall on her head. Ribbons, feathers and other decorations made it even taller. These elaborate hairstyles were expected to last a month – with unsavoury results, since the hair had to be mingled with lard and whiting to keep it in place.

MOST HAIR 'UPDOS' STYLED IN ONE MINUTE DE

With only one minute on the clock, hairdresser Timo Zimmermann (Germany) twisted the hair of 22 women into a chignon-style 'updo' using a chopstick-type implement, in Munich, Germany, on 2 Dec 1998.

LARGEST FITNESS CHAIN

The world's largest fitness franchise is Curves International Inc, with over 1,700 locations throughout the USA. Curves opens a new location approximately every 12 hours and was founded in 1992. *Entrepreneur Magazine* ranked Curves the No.1 Top New Franchise and No.14 Fastest Growing Franchise in Jan 1999 and Jan 2000 respectively.

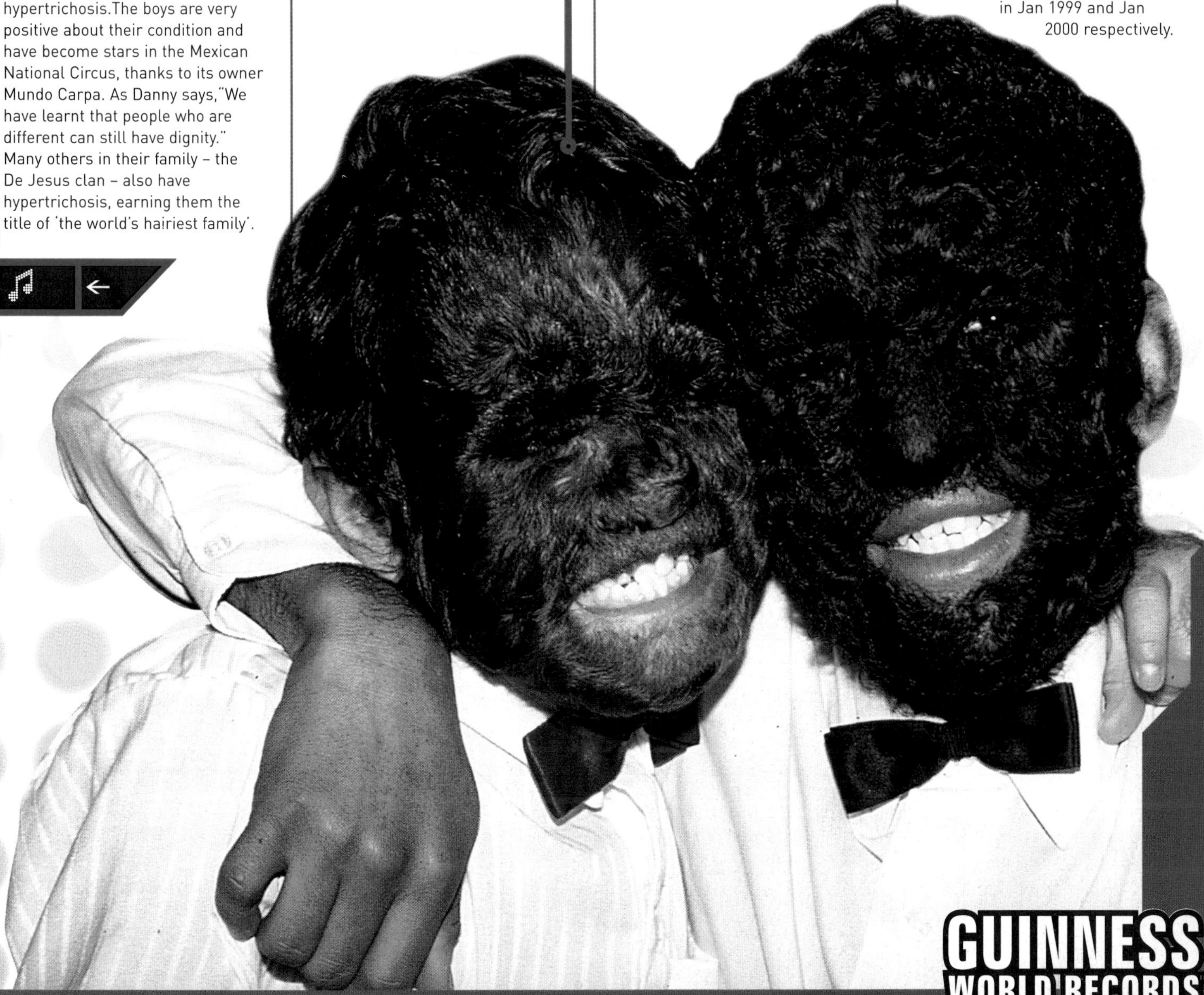

GUINNESS WORLD RECORDS™

disease

RAREST DISEASE

The world's rarest disease is smallpox. In May 1978 the WHO (World Health Organization) registered zero cases in the previous six months worldwide. The last case of smallpox, in Aug 1978, resulted in death when a medical photographer at Birmingham University, W Midlands, UK, was infected by a sample kept for research purposes. There have been no cases since.

LEADING CAUSE OF DEATH

In industrialized countries, diseases of the heart and blood vessels (cardiovascular disease) currently account for over 50% of deaths. The most common of these are heart attacks and strokes, commonly due to atheroma (degeneration of the arterial walls) obstructing the flow of blood. Of the 53.9 million deaths in 1998, 16.71 million, or 31%, were caused by cardiovascular diseases.

MOST COMMON CAUSE OF SUDDEN DEATH

Coronary heart disease is the most common cause of sudden death. Smoking, high blood pressure and high levels of cholesterol in food put an individual at high risk.

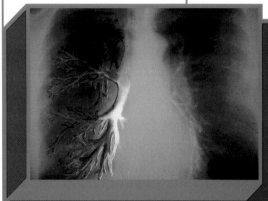

www.guinnessworldrecords.com/badcigs

← ACCESS CODE: ‹52507›

GOVERNMENT HEALTH WARNING

The world's most urgent health problems are tobacco-related. The WHO estimates that by 2020, tobacco-related illnesses including heart disease, cancer, lung disease (left) and respiratory disorders will be the world's leading killers, responsible for more deaths than AIDS, tuberculosis, road accidents and suicide put together – around seven million people per year. Populations in developing countries face the greatest risk as 85% of all smokers will come from the poorer countries. Health care costs associated with these illnesses result in a global net loss of £140 billion ($200 billion) per year.

WORST FLESH-EATING DISEASE

Dubbed the 'flesh-eating bug' by the media in May 1994, the rare and deadly necrotising fasciitis (NF), has been around since World War I. The cunning *Streptococcus A* bacteria first attacks a layer of tissue below the skin, leaving gangrene in its wake, for which there is only one cure – surgical removal of the infected area. The mortality rate for patients contracting NF is 15%. But if NF combines with streptococcal toxic shock syndrome – severe pain and fever – the death rate soars to 70%.

MOST DISEASE OUTBREAKS

According to the 1999 WHO Report on Infectious Diseases, as of 15 April 1999, the year 1998–1999 saw 45 reported outbreaks of cholera. The second was the potentially fatal meningococcal disease – infection of the spinal cord – with 29 reported outbreaks.

DEADLIEST AVIAN FLU OUTBREAK IN HUMANS

Avian flu, a strain of influenza previously only known to affect birds, was found to have infected 16 people in Hong Kong, China, in 1997. Four people died from the virus. This is the first virus to have been passed directly from birds to humans.

MOST VIRULENT DISEASE

Dengue, a viral disease carried by mosquitoes, and its more serious variant, dengue haemorrhagic fever (DHF), are probably the most widespread re-emerging diseases. In 1998 there were 1.2 million cases of dengue and DHF reported. Over 15,000 of these cases led to deaths.

MOST COMMON NON-CONTAGIOUS DISEASE

Periodontal diseases like gingivitis (inflammation of the gums) are the world's most prevalent non-contagious disease. Few people used to escape the effects of tooth decay but the 1981 level of 93% among UK schoolchildren had fallen to 55% by 1992. Sources state that up to one third of American adults suffer from it.

LONGEST SNEEZING FIT

Donna Griffiths (UK) started sneezing on 13 Jan 1981 at the age of 12, and sneezed an estimated million times in the next 365 days. She achieved her first sneeze-free day on 16 Sept 1983 – the 978th day.

MOST NOTORIOUS CARRIER

The most publicized of all typhoid carriers is Mary Mallon (real name Maria Anna Caduff), known as 'Typhoid Mary', who was born in Switzerland in 1855 and emigrated to the USA in 1868. In her job as a cook, she was the source of 53 typhoid outbreaks, including the

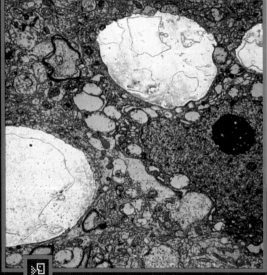

MAD, BAD AND DANGEROUS TO HAVE

The most recently discovered infectious human disease is a new type of Creutzfeld Jacob disease (CJD, left), which leads to dementia. It is probably caused by a prion (a tiny piece of protein) transmitted from cattle suffering from the disease bovine spongiform encephalitis (BSE).

In 1999, the WHO recognized the south-east Asian Nipah virus as the newest virus. A Hendra-like paramyxovirus, it is clinically similar to Japanese encephalitis (JE), although probably not transmitted by mosquitoes but through direct contact with the tissue fluids of infected animals. This disease is associated with pig farming and has caused illness and death in both humans and pigs in Malaysia. The first human case of Nipah virus occurred in Sept 1998.

1903 epidemic of 1,400 cases in Ithaca, New York, USA, and three deaths. She was placed under permanent detention at Riverside Hospital on North Brother's Island, East River, New York, USA, from 1915 until her death from broncho-pneumonia on 11 Nov 1938.

HIGHEST MORTALITY

The three diseases that are generally considered to be universally fatal are AIDS, rabies encephalitis and plague. Acquired Immune Deficiency Syndrome (AIDS) is a fatal transmittable breakdown of the immune system, caused by the human immunodeficiency virus (HIV). HIV attacks and destroys the immune system, leaving the infected individual vulnerable to infections that will cause death. AIDS is the last stage of HIV infection, during which time these diseases have taken hold.

Rabies, a viral infection of the central nervous system, is commonly caused by being bitten by a rabid animal. The majority of rabies cases occur in wild animals like racoons, bats and foxes. Early symptoms in humans include fever, headache and sickness, followed progressively by hallucinations, insomnia, anxiety, hypersalivation and hydrophobia (fear of water). Death can occur within days of the start of symptoms, but with immediate treatment, chances of survival are high.

In the world's worst pandemic, the Black Death, an estimated third of the world's population died. From 1347 to 1351, this pneumonic form of plague (bacterial infection) spread through Asia, North Africa and Europe, crossed the English Channel into England and Scotland, then went on into Norway, Sweden, Denmark, Iceland and Greenland. It killed everyone who caught it – some 75 million people worldwide.

EARLIEST AIDS CASE

In Jan 1998, Dr Tuofo Zhu (USA) from the Aaron Diamond AIDS Research Institute in New York, USA, found the oldest known specimen of HIV in a blood sample taken in 1959 in Leopoldville, Zaire (now Democratic Republic of Congo). This pinpoints the beginning of the AIDS (Acquired Immune Deficiency Syndrome)

epidemic to a decade earlier than first thought. Comparison of the specimen's genetic material to current strains, suggest that HIV first crossed from monkeys to humans around that time. The HIV virus mutates very rapidly and charting its evolutionary changes will help to predict how much the virus will change in the future.

SMALLEST PARASITE

The smallest parasitic animals comprise various unicellular, protozoan parasites, some of which are only a few micrometres long. The smallest of these is *Pneumocystis carinii*, which is only 0.5-1 mm (about 0.02 in) long. It inhabits the lungs and causes pneumonia in humans.

LONGEST-LIVING PARASITE

A lifespan of 27 years has been reliably recorded for the medicinal leech (*Hirudo medicinalis*). The length of a leech's body ranges from miniscule to about 20 cm (8 in), and longer when the animal stretches. The medicinal use of leeches dates from antiquity and reached its peak in the first half of the 19th century. Hirudin, an extract from leeches, is used as a blood anticoagulant. The leech's saliva contains substances that anaesthetize the wound and prevent the blood from clotting.

www.guinnessworldrecords.com/leprosy

ACCESS CODE: ‹48530›

UNDER YOUR SKIN

Although plague and cholera are mentioned in the Old Testament of the Bible, leprosy (below) is thought to be the world's oldest disease. Cases of leprosy were described in ancient Egypt as early as 1350 BC. The disease is described by the World Health Organization (WHO) as 'a chronic infectious disease caused by the bacterium *Mycobacterium leprae*'. It mainly affects the skin, the peripheral nerves, mucosa of the upper respiratory tract and the eyes, and it causes body mutilation.

Tuberculosis schistosomiasi, an infectious disease of the lungs, has also been seen in Egyptian mummies from the 20th dynasty (1250 to 1000 BC). Sophisticated techniques such as DNA extraction are now used to uncover the secrets of ancient illness. The first successful diagnosis was made from a Byzantine skeleton found in Turkey, which shows tuberculosis damage.

GUINNESS WORLD RECORDS

medical maruels 1

MOST ARTIFICIAL JOINTS

Diagnosed with arthritis at the age of 13, Anne Davison (UK) had 12 major joints (both shoulders, elbows, wrists, hips, knees and ankles) and three knuckles replaced by the age of 47. Her right knee was the first joint to be replaced, when she was 27 years old.

LONGEST TIME SURVIVED WITHOUT A PULSE

The longest time a human has survived without a pulse is three days. Julie Mills (UK) was at the point of death on 14 Aug 1998 owing to severe heart failure, when cardiac surgeons at the John Radcliffe Hospital, Oxford, Oxon, UK, used a special blood pump to support her for one week, during which time her heart fully recovered and the pump was removed. This was the first time a patient survived the procedure.

BIGGEST PREGNANCY

In 1971 Dr Gennaro Montanino (Italy) announced that he had removed 15 foetuses from the uterus of a 35-year-old woman who was four months pregnant. A fertility drug was responsible for this unique incidence of quindecaplets.

BABY IT'S YOU

Louise Brown (UK, left) was the world's earliest test-tube baby. Weighing 2.6 kg (5 lb 12 oz), she was delivered by Caesarean section on 25 July 1978 in Oldham General Hospital, Lancashire, UK. Louise's mother had been told for years that she could not have her own child. The miracle birth was down to the work of UK gynaecologist Patrick Steptoe and two Cambridge doctors, Robert Edwards and Barry Bavister. The trio pioneered a new technique by which an egg could be taken from a woman's ovary and fertilized in a test tube before being returned to the womb to develop normally.

www.guinnessworldrecords.com/louisebrown
← ACCESS CODE: ‹53414›

YOUNGEST PERSON TO HAVE A PACEMAKER FITTED

Stephanie Gardiner (UK) was just four hours old when she was fitted with a tiny pacemaker, which was the size of a stamp, on 11 March 1995.

MOST PACEMAKERS FITTED IN ONE PERSON

Mark D Smith Jr (USA) has used a record-breaking 18 pacemakers in his lifetime. His first pacemaker was implanted in Sept 1964, when he was just two years old and, because of complications over the years, he has had a grand total of five temporary and 13 permanent pacemakers fitted and replaced.

Pacemakers were invented in 1930, with the first implant performed on 8 Oct 1958, only five years prior to Smith's first implant.

LONGEST WORKING PACEMAKER

The longest working pacemaker is a lithium battery-powered Biotec 777 which was fitted into János Szilágyi (Hungary) on 18 Jan 1979 and was last confirmed on 7 April 2000 to be operating as normal.

LEAST BLOOD TRANSFUSED DURING A TRANSPLANT OPERATION

In June 1996 a transplant team led by surgeon Stephen Pollard (UK) at St James University Hospital, Leeds, W Yorks, UK, performed a liver transplant on 47-year-old housewife Linda Pearson (UK) without a drop of blood being transfused. This operation usually requires up to 2.3–3.4 litres (4.8–7.2 pints) of blood, but as a Jehovah's Witness, Pearson could not receive any blood that was not her own.

RECIPIENT OF MOST BLOOD

A 50-year-old haemophiliac, Warren Jyrich (USA), was given a record 2,400 units of blood, equivalent to 1,080 litres (285.3 gal), when he underwent open-heart surgery at the Michael Reese Hospital, Chicago, Illinois, USA, in Dec 1970. An average human body contains around 5 litres (10.5 pints) of blood.

OLDEST PATIENT TO UNDERGO AN OPERATION

The oldest age at which anyone has undergone an operation is 111 years 105 days. James Brett (USA) had a successful hip operation on 7 Nov 1960, but died a year later of old age.

LARGEST GALLSTONE

The largest gallstone ever to be reported in medical literature weighed 6.29 kg (13 lb 14 oz) and

ARMS TRADE

🖵 USA

At only four weeks old, Chong Lih Ying (Malaysia, left) was the youngest person to have a full limb transplanted when surgeon Dr V Pathmanathan (Malaysia) and his team of 55 transplanted her twin sister's left arm to her body in May 2000, during a 15-hour operation. Her twin sister, who was born with a severe brain abnormality, had no hope of survival before the operation. Chong was born with a deformed left arm and no hand. She was the first person in the world to undergo a transplant for a whole limb and was expected to create another medical first after not having to receive any carcinogenic drugs to prevent rejection of the limb. This was anticipated because Chong's identical twin had the same blood group and cell make-up as she did, making the operation a complete success.

www.guinnessworldrecords.com/babyarm
← ACCESS CODE: ‹54824›

ACCESS CODE: ‹56505›

www.guinnessworldrecords.com/handtransplant

HANDYMAN

The most amputations on the same arm have been endured by Clint Hallam (New Zealand, right), who has had his right hand amputated a total of three times. He first lost his hand in 1984 after an accident with a circular saw. Surgeons managed to reattach the severed limb but an infection developed and it was removed again in 1988. In Sept 1998 doctors performed a pioneering hand transplant on Hallam at a hospital in Lyons, France. However, he later requested that it be amputated once more as he was in continual pain. An operation to meet his demand successfully took place at a London hospital on 2 Feb 2001.

was removed from an 80-year-old woman at Charing Cross Hospital, London, UK, on 29 Dec 1952.

LARGEST BRAIN TUMOUR

A tumour weighing a record-breaking 570 g (1lb 5 oz) was successfully removed from the brain of four-year-old Kaushal Choudhary (India) at Curewell Hospital, Indore, India, on 25 May 2000. The child was admitted to hospital on 24 May 2000 and was allowed to leave on 30 May 2000.

LARGEST TUMOUR REMOVED INTACT USA

The largest tumour ever removed intact was a multicystic mass from an ovary weighing 137.6 kg (303 lb). The giant growth had a diameter of 1 m (3 ft 3 in) and was removed in Oct 1991 from the abdomen of a 34-year-old woman. The operation was performed by Professor Katherine O'Hanlan of Stanford University Medical Center, California, USA, and took over six hours.

MOST BENEFICIAL USA
PARASITE TO HUMANS

The medical leech *Hirudo medicinalis*, traditionally used by doctors for bloodletting, has made a comeback. In 1991 a team of Canadian surgeons led by Dr Dean Vistnes took advantage of the anticoagulants in leech saliva to drain away blood and prevent it from clotting during an operation to reattach a patient's scalp. The leeches used had been specially cultured in sterile conditions.

GUINNESS WORLD RECORDS

 SMS ICON   SMS RINGTONE   BULLETIN BOARD   GUINNESS WORLD RECORDS TV

medical maruels 2

YOUNGEST DOUBLE HEART-VALVE TRANSPLANT

The youngest-ever double heart-valve transplant patient is Cameron Miles (UK), who was born with one heart valve missing and another not functioning. He was just three weeks old when he received a donor replacement on 14 Dec 1998 and another on 23 Dec 1998, at Leeds General Infirmary, Leeds, W Yorks, UK.

YOUNGEST LIVER TRANSPLANT PATIENT

Five-day-old Baebhen Schuttke (Ireland) was given a new liver in an operation lasting seven hours at King's College Hospital, London, UK, after she collapsed with liver failure 24 hours after she was born.

YOUNGEST MULTI-ORGAN TRANSPLANT PATIENT

Sarah Marshall (Canada) was only six months old when she was given a liver, a bowel, a stomach and a pancreas at London's Children's Hospital, Western Ontario, Canada, on 7 Aug 1997. She had been born with an enlarged bladder, a small colon and an abnormal bowel.

MOST HEART STOPPAGES IN AN OPERATION

Rudolph A Cizmar (USA) died twice on the operating table on 16 Sept 1999 at Baptist Memorial Hospital in Mississippi (USA). He had to be given

electrical shocks to restore a heart rhythm twice by doctors, once at 3.20 pm for 25 minutes, and again at 5.20 pm. He made a full recovery.

LONGEST HEART STOPPAGE

The longest recorded heart stoppage is 3 hr 40 min in the case of Jean Jawbone (Canada), who at the age of 20 was revived by a team of 26, using peritoneal dialysis, on 8 Jan 1977 at the Health Sciences Center, Winnipeg, Manitoba, Canada.

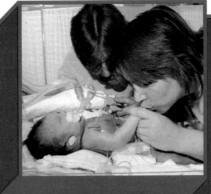

LONGEST SURVIVING KIDNEY TRANSPLANT PATIENT

The longest surviving kidney transplant patient is Johanna Rempel (Canada), who was given a kidney from her identical twin sister on 28 Dec 1960 when she was 12 years old in an operation at the Peter Bent Brigham Hospital, Boston, Massachusetts, USA. Both Johanna and her sister have continued to enjoy excellent health and both have had healthy children.

FAKING IT

The longest surviving recipient of an artificial heart (left) was William Schroeder (USA), who lived for 620 days from 25 Nov 1984 to 7 Aug 1986.
Made of plastic, aluminium and polyester, the earliest artificial hearts date back to the 1950s. The best-known is the *Jarvik-7*, named after its designer, Robert K Jarvik, an American physician. Designed to function like the natural heart, the *Jarvik-7* has two pumps (like the ventricles), each with a disk-shaped mechanism that pushes the blood from the inlet valve to the outlet valve.
The longest surviving recipient of a real heart was Dirk van Zyl (South Africa) who lived for 23 years 57 days after a heart transplant at the Groote Schuur Hospital, Cape Town, South Africa, on 10 May 1971.

www.guinnessworldrecords.com/heart
← ACCESS CODE: ‹48472›

LONGEST SURVIVOR OF A PORCINE HEART VALVE REPLACEMENT

An unnamed American lived a record 22 years, 8 months and 22 days after a porcine (pig) aortic valve replaced a defective heart valve. He died on 28 Dec 1998.

Harry Driver (UK) received a porcine aortic valve replacement on the 12 April 1978. It was still functioning on 12 May 2000, a total of 22 years and one month later.

CHANGE OF HEART

On 8 Nov 1996, one-hour-old Cheyenne Pyle (USA, left) became the youngest-ever recipient of a donor heart. The six-hour operation at Jackson Children's Hospital, Miami, Florida, USA, involved draining her blood and cooling her body to 17°C (62.6°F), the temperature at which organs cease to function. Surgeons had an hour to complete the operation to prevent damage to her other organs.
Sophie Parker (UK) is the youngest recipient of two donor hearts. In 1992, aged two, she underwent an operation at Harefield Hospital, London, UK, to give her a donor heart to complement her weak natural heart. In March 1998 her natural heart no longer functioned properly, so she had a second donor heart transplant to aid her donor heart.

www.guinnessworldrecords.com/youngestheartop
← ACCESS CODE: ‹48446›

MOST ANEURYSMS SURVIVED

An aneurysm is a ballooning-out of the wall of an artery, vein or the heart, due to weakening of the wall by disease, injury or an abnormality present at birth, and is often caused or aggravated by high blood pressure. Sheryl Evette Kessee (USA) has survived surgery for a record-breaking three aneurysms – two of which burst in the front of her head and a third that was removed intact from behind her right ear.

MOST EXTENSIVE SKULL RECONSTRUCTION
📺 USA

Ahad Israfil (USA) holds the record for having the world's most extensive cranial reconstruction, after he was nearly killed by a close-range .357 Magnum revolver wound to the head when his employer mistook him for an intruder and shot him. A local surgeon, Dr James Apesos, literally rebuilt Ahad's skull using a silicon mould and, after nearly a dozen separate operations, the reconstruction was complete.

MOST EXTENSIVE FACIAL PROSTHESIS
📺 USA

Leonard McQueeny (Australia) lost his nose and upper palate to a cancerous tumour and had them replaced with snap-on prosthetics made from silicon rubber and surgical-grade titanium.

SMALLEST SUBMARINE FOR MEDICAL USE

In 1999 German company microTEC produced a micro-submarine just 4 mm (0.157 in) in length with a diameter of 0.65 mm (0.025 in). Made with computer-guided lasers, it will be used to travel to sites of blockage or damage in blood vessels and repair them from within the body.

GREATEST NUMBER OF SEX-CHANGE OPERATIONS PERFORMED
📺 USA

Surgeon Stanley Biber (USA) has performed sex-change operations for 30 years in Trinidad, Colorado, USA. He has conducted 3,000 male to female operations and over 250

BACK TO MY ROOTS

Adrian Targett (UK), the living link to the oldest known family tree in the world, can trace his family back further than any other person. He has been shown to be a direct descendant, on his mother's side, of 'Cheddar Man', a 9,000-year-old skeleton found in a cave in Cheddar Gorge, Somerset, UK. Scientists took a DNA sample from a molar from Cheddar Man and found a near perfect match in Adrian Targett, who lives less than half a mile away.

ACCESS CODE: ‹4834›

female to male operations. The three-hour operation costs approximately $30,000 (£18,750).

LARGEST OBJECT REMOVED FROM HUMAN SKULL
USA

The largest object removed from a human skull is a 20.32-cm (8-in) survival knife with a serrated blade, which was plunged into the head of 41-year-old Michael Hill (USA) on 25 April 1998. Surgeons had to remove parts of Hill's skull to take the knife from his head successfully.

OLDEST SURGICAL PROCEDURE
USA

Trepanation – the process of removing bone from the cranial vault – is the oldest surgical procedure practised by mankind. The oldest evidence of trepanation was found at a 7,000-year-old burial site at Ensisheim, France, and belonged to a 50-year-old man.

MOST SUCCESSFUL ARTIFICIAL EYE

On 17 Jan 2000 it was announced that Jeremiah Teehan (USA), who lost his sight 36 years ago due to a blow to his head, can now see again thanks to an artificial eye developed by William Dobelle, an American eye specialist who worked to create this device for approximately 30 years. The device consists of a miniature camera and ultrasonic rangefinder that feeds signals via two computers into electrodes planted in Teehan's brain.

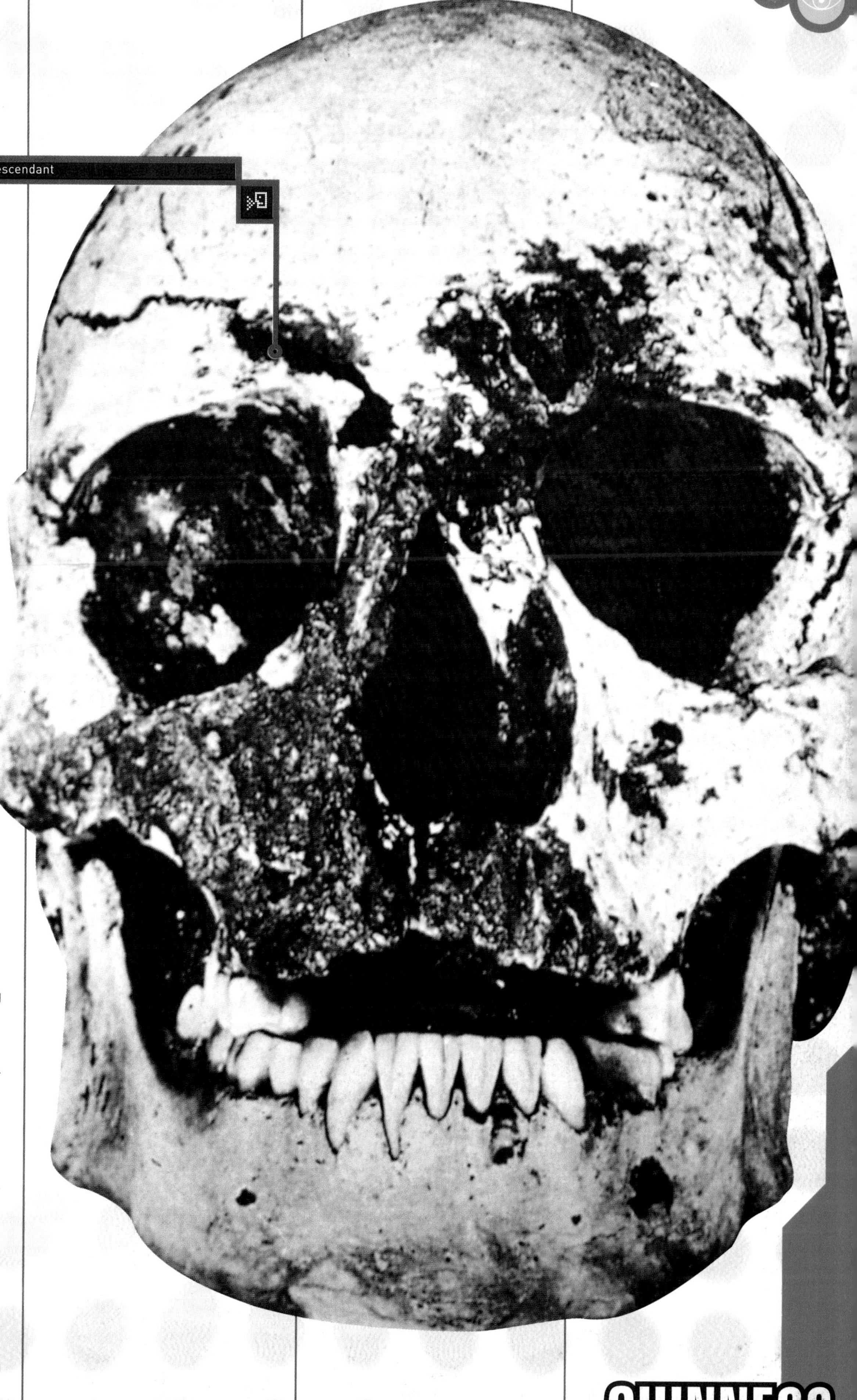

GUINNESS WORLD RECORDS

against all odds

MOST LIGHTNING STRIKES SURVIVED

In the USA, the average number of deaths from lightning is just over 100 a year. Ex-park ranger Roy C Sullivan (USA) was struck by lightning a record seven times. Sullivan's attraction for lightning began in 1942 (lost big toe nail), followed by 1969 (lost eyebrows), July 1970 (left shoulder seared), 16 April 1972 (hair set on fire), 7 Aug 1973 (new hair re-fired and legs seared), 5 June 1976 (ankle injured) and 25 June 1977 (chest and stomach burns). Sadly, despite his many escapes, he died in 1983.

THIRTEEN – LUCKY FOR SOME

Millvina Dean (UK, left) was just nine weeks old when she travelled third class on the cruiseliner *Titanic* with her parents and 18-month-old brother, Bertram. Millvina, along with her mother and brother, all managed to get into a lifeboat (No 13) and survived when the 'unsinkable' ship sank after hitting an iceberg in the infamous 1912 tragedy. Her father, Bert, was not so fortunate and was among the 1,517 passengers who perished. Of the 706 passengers who travelled in third class, down in the bowels of the ship, only 178 survived – 75 of the 462 men, 76 of the 165 women, and 27 of the 79 children. In total there were 109 children on board the ship, 57 of whom were saved.

www.guinnessworldrecords.com/titanicbaby
← ACCESS CODE: ‹52780›

LONGEST SURVIVING HEADLESS CHICKEN

On 10 Sept 1945 a Wyandotte chicken called Mike had its head chopped off but went on to survive for 18 months. Mike's owner, Lloyd Olsen (USA) fed and watered the headless chicken directly into his gullet using an eyedropper. Mike eventually choked to death in an Arizona motel. He now has a website dedicated to him: www.miketheheadlesschicken.org

GREATEST RESCUE WITHOUT LOSS OF LIFE

The greatest rescue without any loss of life was from the American vessel *Susan B Anthony*, which was carrying 2,689 people, all of whom survived when it was sunk off the coast of Normandy, France, on 7 June 1944.

LONGEST SURVIVAL ALONE ON A RAFT

The longest recorded survival alone on a raft is 133 days by Second Steward Poon Lim (Hong Kong) of the UK Merchant Navy, whose ship, the *SS Ben Lomond*, was torpedoed in the Atlantic Ocean 910 km (565 miles) west of St Paul's Rocks on 23 Nov 1942. He was picked up by a Brazilian fishing boat off Salinópolis, Brazil, on 5 April 1943, and was able to walk ashore.

LONGEST TIME ADRIFT AT SEA IN A FISHING BOAT

Fishermen Tabwai Mikaie and Arenta Tebeitabu, from the island of Nikunau in the Republic of Kiribati, survived for 177 days adrift at sea in their 4-m (13-ft) fishing boat. They were caught in a cyclone after setting out on a trip on 17 Nov 1991 and were found washed ashore in Western Samoa, 180 km (111 miles) away, on 11 May 1992. A third man on the boat died a few days before reaching Western Samoa.

LONGEST UNDERWATER SUBMERGENCE SURVIVAL

In 1986, two-year-old Michelle Funk (USA) made a full recovery after spending 66 minutes underwater, having fallen into a swollen creek.

DEEPEST UNDERWATER ESCAPE WITHOUT EQUIPMENT

The greatest depth from which an escape without any equipment has been made is 68.6 m (225 ft), by Richard A Slater (USA) from the rammed submersible *Nekton Beta* off Catalina Island, California, USA, on 28 Sept 1970.

DEEPEST UNDERWATER RESCUE

The deepest-ever underwater rescue was that of Roger R Chapman and Roger Mallinson (both UK) from the mini-sub *Pisces III*, in which they were trapped for 76 hours when it sank to 480 m (1,575 ft), 240 km (150 miles) southeast of Cork, Ireland, on 29 Aug 1973. It was hauled to the surface on 1 Sept by the cable ship *John Cabot* after work by *Pisces V*, *Pisces II* and the remote-control recovery vessel *CURV* (Controlled Underwater Recovery Vehicle).

FURTHEST VERTICAL SKI FALL USA

In April 1997, while competing in the 1997 World Extreme Skiing Championships in Valdez, Alaska, USA, 25-year-old Bridget Mead (New Zealand) fell a vertical distance of nearly 400 m (1,312.4 ft), suffering bruises and severe concussion but no broken bones. At that time, Mead was the highest-ranked female extreme skier. Her doctors credit her survival to her excellent physical condition and to the fact that she was wearing a helmet.

LONGEST LIFT FALL SURVIVED

On 25 Jan 2000, US office workers Shameka Peterson and Joe Mascora dropped 40 floors – 121 m (400 ft) – in a lift in four seconds down the Empire State Building, New York City, New York, USA, when their lift-cable failed. Stopping just four floors from the ground, both suffered only minor bruising.

HIGHEST G FORCE ENDURED VOLUNTARILY

The highest G value voluntarily endured is 82.6 G for 0.04 seconds by Eli L Beeding Jr (USA) on a water-braked rocket sled at Holloman Air Force Base, New Mexico, USA, on 16 May 1958. He was hospitalized for three days.

INVASION OF THE BODY SNATCHERS

A team of 21 firemen and one woman from the Malaysian Fire and Rescue service carried out the highest high-rise external snatch and rescue operation on 17 April 1998. The rescue was from a gondola lift which had stopped 378.25 m (1,241 ft) from the ground, on the 88th (top) floor of the Petronas Towers (left), Kuala Lumpur, Malaysia – the world's tallest office building. Owing to strong winds and the building design, the 'victims' had to be carried down from the top to the ground in five stages – from the 88th to the 82nd floor, from the 82nd to the 73rd, from the 73rd to the 60th, from the 60th to the 6th and from the 6th to the ground. The entire operation, an exercise to test the competency and ability of the fire crew, took only 20 minutes.

www.guinnessworldrecords.com/snatchrescue
← ACCESS CODE: ‹53086›

HIGHEST G FORCE ENDURED INVOLUNTARILY

Racing driver David Purley (UK) survived a deceleration from 173 km/h (108 mph) to zero over 66 cm (26 in) in a crash at Silverstone Race Track, Northants, UK, on 13 July 1977. He endured a G force of 179.8 G and suffered 29 fractures, three dislocations and six heart stoppages. He recovered and continued racing.

LONGEST SURVIVAL WITHOUT FOOD AND WATER

The longest recorded case of survival without food and water is 18 days by 18-year-old Andreas Mihavecz (Austria). He was put into a holding cell in a local government building in Höchst, Austria, on 1 April 1979, but was totally forgotten by the police. On 18 April 1979, he was discovered close to death. Mihavecz had been a passenger in a crashed car.

LONGEST POST-EARTHQUAKE SURVIVAL BY A CAT

In Dec 1999, 80 days after an earthquake struck Taiwan on 21 Sept 1999, killing an estimated 2,400 people, a cat was discovered alive after being trapped in the rubble of a collapsed building in Taichung, Taiwan. The cat, dehydrated and barely breathing, was treated immediately in a veterinary hospital and eventually made a full recovery.

LONGEST SURVIVAL WITH HEART OUTSIDE BODY 🖵 USA

Christopher Wall (USA), born on 19 Aug 1975, is the longest known survivor of the condition known as *ectopia cordis*, where the heart lies outside the body. The mortality rate is high, with most patients not living beyond 48 hours. The condition occurs in between 5.5 and 7.9 per one million live births according to the American Heart Association. Wall now works for a Philadelphia construction company.

LOWEST BODY TEMPERATURE

The lowest authenticated body temperature is 14.2°C (57.5°F) for two-year-old Karlee Kosolofski, (Canada) on 23 Feb 1994. She had accidentally been locked outside her home for six hours in a temperature of -22°C (-8°F). Despite severe frostbite, which meant the amputation of her left leg above the knee, she has made a full recovery.

LOWEST PARACHUTE ESCAPE

RAF officer Terence Spencer (UK) achieved the lowest-ever aircraft escape when he was blown out of his aircraft at a height of 9–12 m (30–40 ft) over Wismar Bay, Germany, on 19 April 1945. He managed to swim ashore but his plane crashed on land.

www.guinnessworldrecords.com/frostbite

WEATHER-ING THE STORM

On 10 May 1996 Dr Seaborn 'Beck' Weathers (USA, right) miraculously survived being left for dead on Mt Everest when he was caught in a blizzard with winds up to 145-km/h (90-mph). The snowstorm claimed the lives of eight other climbers – the most deaths on Mt Everest in a single day. Weathers lay exposed on the South Col for 16 hours, but revived and staggered to safety. He lost his right hand, some of his left hand and his nose due to the frostbite caused by the bitter -40°C (-40°F) temperatures.

GUINNESS WORLD RECORDS

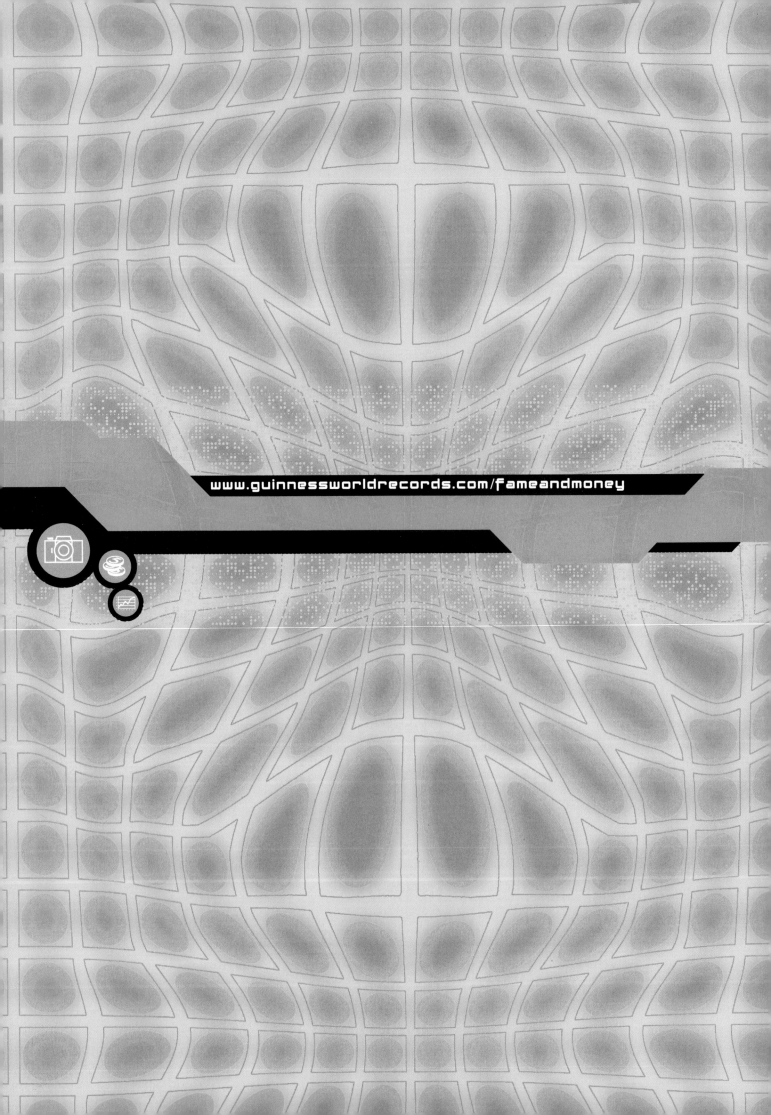

www.guinnessworldrecords.com/fameandmoney

fame and money

movie stars

HIGHEST ANNUAL EARNINGS BY A FILM ACTRESS

According to the 2001 *Forbes* Celebrity 100 list, Julia Roberts (USA) earned more in 2000 than any other actress – an estimated $18.9 million (£13.3 million).

Julia Roberts is also responsible for the highest box-office earnings generated by any actress. Since 1987 her 24 films have earned a total box-office gross of $1,532.6 million (£1,054 million). Eight of her films have taken over $100 million (£71.4 million); the highest earner, *Pretty Woman* (USA, 1990), made $463.4 million (£331 million).

MOST BEST ACTOR OSCAR NOMINATIONS FOR THE SAME FILM

At the 1935 Academy Awards, three out of the four Best Actor nominees were from the same film. Clark Gable, Charles Laughton and Franchot Tone (all USA) were all nominated for *Mutiny On The Bounty* (USA, 1935). However, it was fourth nominee Victor McLaglen (UK), who won the award for his role in *The Informer* (USA, 1935).

ACTOR WITH THE MOST OSCAR NOMINATIONS

Jack Nicholson (USA) has notched up a record 11 Oscar nominations since his 1958 film debut. Four were for Best Supporting Actor, with the remaining seven for Best Actor.

AND THE OSCAR GOES (AGAIN) TO...

Katharine Hepburn (USA, left) has been nominated for and won more Oscars than any other actor. She won the Best Actress Oscar for her roles in *Morning Glory* (USA, 1933), *Guess Who's Coming to Dinner* (USA, 1967), *The Lion in Winter* (USA, 1968) and *On Golden Pond* (USA, 1981). She has been nominated for an Oscar a record 12 times.

www.guinnessworldrecords.com/oscarwinner
← ACCESS CODE: <50660>

MOST BEST ACTOR OSCARS WON

Seven American actors have twice won the Best Actor Oscar at the Academy Awards. They are Spencer Tracy for *Captains Courageous* (USA, 1937) and *Boys Town* (USA, 1938); Fredric March for *Dr Jekyll and Mr Hyde* (USA, 1932) and *The Best Years of Our Lives* (USA, 1946); Gary Cooper for *Sergeant York* (USA, 1941) and *High Noon* (USA, 1952); Marlon Brando for *On the Waterfront* (USA, 1954) and *The Godfather* (USA, 1972); Jack Nicholson for *One Flew Over the Cuckoo's Nest* (USA, 1975) and *As Good As It Gets* (USA, 1997); Dustin Hoffman for *Kramer vs. Kramer* (USA, 1979) and *Rain Man* (USA, 1988); and Tom Hanks for *Philadelphia* (USA, 1993) and *Forrest Gump* (USA, 1994).

MOST OSCAR NOMINATIONS WITHOUT WINNING

Actors Richard Burton and Peter O'Toole (both UK) have both been nominated seven times for the Best Actor award, but neither has won.

YOUNGEST OSCAR WINNER

The youngest Oscar winner is Tatum O'Neal (USA), who was aged 10 years 148 days when she received the Best Supporting Actress award for *Paper Moon* (USA, 1973) on 2 April 1974.

YOUNGEST WINNER OF A BEST ACTRESS OSCAR

Marlee Matlin (USA) was 21 years 219 days old when she accepted the Best Actress award on 31 March 1987, for her role as a deaf-mute in *Children of a Lesser God* (USA, 1986).

YOUNGEST WINNER OF A BEST ACTOR OSCAR

Richard Dreyfuss (USA) won the Best Actor award on 13 April 1978 for his performance in *The Goodbye Girl* (USA, 1977), aged 29 years 166 days.

OLDEST WINNER OF A BEST ACTOR OSCAR

Henry Fonda (USA) won a Best Actor Oscar on 29 March 1982 for his performance in *On Golden Pond* (USA, 1981), aged 75 years 318 days.

OLDEST WINNER OF A BEST ACTRESS OSCAR

British-born actress Jessica Tandy won a Best Actress award for *Driving Miss Daisy* (USA, 1989) on 29 March 1990, at the age of 80 years 295 days.

YOUNGEST RECIPIENT OF AN OSCAR

Shirley Temple (USA) won a special Juvenile award from the Academy on 27 Feb 1935, aged six years 310 days, the year she became the youngest person to reach No.1 at the box office. She became the youngest, self-made, dollar millionairess in 1938.

OLDEST WINNER OF AN HONORARY OSCAR

Comic genius Groucho Marx (USA) was 83 years 182 days old when he received an Honorary Award on 2 April 1974. The wisecracking actor, famed for his greasepaint moustache, died on 19 Aug 1977.

OLDEST ACTOR WITH AN OSCAR NOMINATION

American actor Richard Farnsworth (1920–2000), was 79 years 270 days old when he was nominated for a Best Actor Oscar for his role in *The Straight Story* (USA, 1999) in Feb 2000.

OLDEST ACTRESS WITH AN OSCAR NOMINATION

British-born American actress Eva LeGallienne was aged 82 years 80 days when she was nominated as Best Supporting Actress for her role in *Resurrection* (USA, 1980).

ONLY ACTORS TO WIN A BEST DIRECTOR OSCAR

In 1996 Mel Gibson (Australia) became the fifth actor to receive a Best Director Oscar, which he won for his film *Braveheart* (USA, 1995). He shares the record with Kevin Costner (USA) for *Dances with Wolves* (USA, 1990); Clint Eastwood (USA) for *Unforgiven* (USA, 1992); Woody Allen (USA) for *Hannah and her Sisters* (USA, 1986); and Robert Redford (USA) for *Ordinary People* (USA, 1980).

GET SHORTY!

The shortest adult actor in a supporting role is Verne Troyer (USA, left), known for his role as 'Mini-Me' in *Austin Powers: The Spy Who Shagged Me* (USA, 1999), who is 81 cm (2 ft 8 in) tall. His other films include *Men In Black* (USA, 1997) and *Fear and Loathing in Las Vegas* (USA, 1998).
The shortest adult actor in a lead role is 83-cm (2-ft 9-in) tall Philippino paratrooper and martial-arts expert Weng Wang, who stars in spoof Bond films *For Your Height Only* (Phil, 1979) and *Agent 00* (Phil, 1981).
The shortest actor with a star on the Hollywood Walk of Fame was Billy Barty (USA) who died in 2000. The 113-cm (3-ft 9-in) veteran of 130 films founded The Little People of America Inc, an organization that provides support and information for people of short stature.

www.guinnessworldrecords.com/getshorty
← ACCESS CODE: <54327>

FORD FIESTA

Actor Harrison Ford (USA, above) has been in a record 11 movies with international box-office takings of over $100 million (£71.4 million). His top five films are *Star Wars* (USA, 1977), $798 million (£570 million); *Return of the Jedi* (USA, 1983), $572.9 million (£409.2 million); *The Empire Strikes Back* (USA, 1980), $529.3 million (£378 million); *Indiana Jones and the Last Crusade* (USA, 1989), $494.8 million (£353.4 million); and *Raiders of the Lost Ark* (USA, 1981), $383.9 million (£274.2 million).

www.guinnessworldrecords.com/harrisonford

 ACCESS CODE: ← ‹54197›

FILM STAR WITH THE MOST FANMAIL

Silent movie star Charlie Chaplin (UK) received a record 73,000 fan letters in the first three days of his return home to London in 1921.

TALLEST ACTOR

Richard Kiel (USA), best known for his role as Jaws, the assassin with steel teeth, in the Bond films *The Spy Who Loved Me* (UK, 1977) and *Moonraker* (UK, 1979) stands 2.18 m (7 ft 2 in) tall.

TALLEST ACTOR IN A LEADING ROLE

Christopher Lee (UK), the tallest film actor in a leading role, is an awesome presence on set at 1.94 m (6 ft 5 in). He has been towering over movie line-ups since his film debut in 1948. His first lead role was as Dracula in the 1958 film of the same name.

TALLEST ACTRESS IN A LEADING ROLE

Brigitte Nielsen (Denmark), Margaux Hemingway, Sigourney Weaver and Geena Davis (all USA) are neck-and-neck for the tallest actress record, all at 1.82 m (6 ft) tall.

SHORTEST LIVING ADULT ACTRESS IN A LEADING ROLE

Linda Hunt (USA), who debuted in *Popeye* (USA, 1980), stands 1.43 m (4 ft 9 in) tall. She won an Academy Award in 1984 for her role as Billy Kwan, a male Eurasian cameraman in *The Year of Living Dangerously* (Australia, 1982), becoming the only actress to win an Oscar for playing someone of the opposite sex.

SHORTEST-EVER ADULT ACTRESS IN A LEADING ROLE

ET star Tamara de Treaux (USA), who died in 1990, was only 77 cm (2 ft 7 in) tall. She shot to fame after playing the role of ET in Steven Spielberg's *ET, The Extra-Terrestrial* (USA, 1982).

www.guinnessworldrecords.com/brucewillis

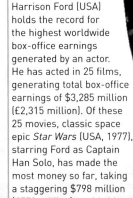

BUY HARD

Bruce Willis (USA, right) has the highest annual earnings for a film actor, earning an estimated $70 million (£46.89 million) in 2000 according to the 2001 *Forbes* Celebrity 100 list.

The highest fee earned by an actor in one film went to Jack Nicholson (USA), who was paid up to $60 million (£40 million) for playing the Joker in the hit film *Batman* (USA, 1989). His record pay cheque was a percentage of the film's worldwide box-office takings of $413.2 million (£252 million).

Harrison Ford (USA) holds the record for the highest worldwide box-office earnings generated by an actor. He has acted in 25 films, generating total box-office earnings of $3,285 million (£2,315 million). Of these 25 movies, classic space epic *Star Wars* (USA, 1977), starring Ford as Captain Han Solo, has made the most money so far, taking a staggering $798 million (£570 million) worldwide.

GUINNESS WORLD RECORDS

tv stars

HIGHEST-EVER ANNUAL EARNINGS FOR A TV ACTOR

Jerry Seinfeld (USA) earned a record-breaking $267 million (£159.5 million) for appearing in the hit comedy *Seinfeld* in 1998.

HIGHEST-PAID TV COMEDY ACTOR PER EPISODE

Kelsey Grammer (USA), who plays psychoanalyst Frasier Crane in the TV comedy series *Frasier*, will be

paid a record-breaking $1.6 million (£1.1 million) per episode for the 2002 and 2003 series.

HIGHEST-PAID TV DRAMA ACTOR PER EPISODE

In Aug 1998 Anthony Edwards (USA), who plays Dr Mark Greene in the American hospital drama *ER*, saw his salary rocket from $125,000 (£77,160) an episode to a record-breaking $400,000 (£246,913) per episode in a four-year deal totalling $35 million (£21,604,938).

HIGHEST ANNUAL EARNINGS FOR A TV CHAT-SHOW HOST

Oprah Winfrey (USA) earned a record $150 million (£100,489,047) in 2000 according to the 2001 *Forbes* Celebrity 100 list. The series *Oprah* has over 22 million viewers and is seen in 113 countries. It has won a grand total of 34 Emmy Awards.

HIGHEST ANNUAL EARNINGS FOR A TV NEWS BROADCASTER

Barbara Walters (USA) reputedly earns over $13 million (£7.84 million) a year as news correspondent and co-anchor for ABC's news magazine, *20/20*, *The Barbara Walters Specials* and *The View*. Walters was the first woman to anchor the network nightly news and she has interviewed every US president since Richard Nixon. She made journalistic history by arranging the first joint interview of President Anwar Sadat of Egypt and Prime Minister Menachem Begin of Israel in Nov 1977.

HIGHEST ANNUAL EARNINGS FOR A MAGICIAN

David Copperfield (USA) had the highest annual earnings of any magician in 2000 with $60 million (£42.8 million). The host of TV shows for both ABC and CBS, his illusions have included making the Statue of Liberty vanish and walking through the Great Wall of China.

RICHEST TV QUIZ MASTER

Chat show host Regis Philbin (USA), who is the quiz master for the US version of *Who Wants to be a Millionaire?*, earned a record $35 million (£25 million) in 2000.

LONGEST TIME PLAYING THE SAME TV ROLE

William Roache (UK) has played the character Ken Barlow without a break since the first episode of the British soap *Coronation Street* was broadcast on 9 Dec 1960.

MOST APPEARANCES BY A TV EXTRA

Vic Gallucci (UK) did his first walk-on part in *The Bill* (UK) in 1989 and has since made over 819 appearances on the show as DC Tom Baker – the most appearances ever by a TV extra. With no lines to speak, he still arrives at work early in the morning to learn his 'lurking' moves, which involve shuffling papers and wandering around the set's coffee machine. Also known as 'Trev' which stands for Totally Reliable Extra Veteran, Vic can be seen in the background shots of almost every episode.

LONGEST CAREER AS A TV CHEF

Julia Child (USA) first appeared on US TV in 1963 in a series called *The French Chef*. Pioneering the art of French cuisine on television, the series was followed by numerous others, including *Master Chef*, *Baking at Julia's* and most recently 22 episodes of *Julia and Jacques Cooking at Home* (1999) in which she teamed up with French chef Jacques Pepin.

LONGEST-SERVING ACTOR IN AN AUSTRALIAN SOAP

Three actors have appeared in the *Home and Away* TV series since it first aired in Australia on 15 Jan 1988 – Norman Coburn who plays Donald Fisher, Ray Meagher who plays Alf Stewart and Kate Ritchie who plays Sally Fletcher.

LONGEST PERFORMANCE CONTRACT IN RADIO AND TV

American entertainer Bob Hope (USA) completed the 60th year of his NBC contract on 23 Nov 1996, making this the longest performance contract ever. As well as performing on radio, TV and film, he has also entertained the US troops overseas in every war from World War II to the Gulf War.

MOST CELEBRITIES FEATURED IN A CARTOON TV SERIES

Since first appearing in 1987 as a series of 30-second spots produced by Matt Groening (USA) for the Fox network's *The Tracey Ullman Show*, *The Simpsons* has featured 240 celebrities including Dolly Parton, Buzz Aldrin and Jerry Springer (all USA) and Stephen Hawking (UK).

LONGEST CAREER AS A CARTOON VOICEOVER ARTIST

Jack Mercer (USA) first provided the voice for the cinema series *Popeye* in the film *Let You and Him Fight* in 1934. He continued to play the role for the next 45 years and 294 productions including the TV cartoons.

FIRST PERSON TO APPEAR ON A BRITISH TV ADVERT

On 22 Sept 1955, the opening night of UK Independent Television, Meg Smith (UK) beat 80 other aspiring actresses

EXCELLENT SPELLING

Aaron Spelling (USA, above) has produced over 3,842 hours of television airtime since 1956, making him the most prolific TV producer of drama. This includes 3,578 hours of TV episodes and 264 hours of TV movies. His shows have included *Mod Squad*, the original 1970s' *Charlie's Angels*, *Love Boat*, *Dynasty*, *Fantasy Island*, *Beverly Hills 90210*, *Melrose Place*, *Charmed* and *All Souls*. It would take over four months to watch all his TV shows if you watched them back-to-back for 24 hours a day.

Spelling has also erected the largest Hollywood home, dubbed 'The Manor' by his family. The building occupies an area of 5,253 m² (56,550 ft²) and has 123 rooms. The house is currently valued at $37 million (£26.4 million) and includes a gymnasium, bowling alley, swimming pool and skating rink. The previous house on the site, owned by Bing Crosby, was demolished to make way for Spelling's new house.

www.guinnessworldrecords.com/aaronspelling

ACCESS CODE: ‹51566›

MONKEY BUSINESS

The PG Tips advertising campaign, starring chimpanzees (above), began in 1956 and ran until 1994, making the chimps the most enduring commercial stars. They were first voiced by *Pink Panther* star Peter Sellers (UK) and have since starred in more than 100 adverts. The chimps put their individual fees of over £1,000 ($1,397) per commercial into a retirement fund set up by the company.

www.guinnessworldrecords.com/pgtips

ACCESS CODE:
← ‹47906›

to become Britain's first 'plug' girl – wielding a toothbrush in the 60-second advert for Gibbs SR toothpaste.

MOST STARS FROM DIFFERENT MUSIC STYLES ON ONE VIDEO

A charity recording of 'Perfect Day' by Lou Reed (USA), which was commissioned to show the diversity of music played on BBC television and radio, features a record-breaking 27 artists from 18 different musical genres. These include jazz (Courtney Pine), reggae (Burning Spear), country (Emmy Lou Harris), blues (Dr John), pop (Boyzone), rap (Fun Lovin' Criminals) and classical music (Lesley Garrett). Lou Reed himself also appears on the video.

MOST CONSECUTIVE BAFTA AWARDS

Robbie Coltrane (UK) has won a record three consecutive BAFTA (British Academy of Film and Television Arts) awards as 'Best Television Actor', for his role as forensic psychiatrist Gerry 'Fitz' Fitzgerald in Granada Television's series *Cracker*, from 1994 to 1996.

MOST TIMES MC AT THE ACADEMY AWARDS

American entertainer Bob Hope (USA) has served as Master of Ceremonies on Oscar night, alone and with others, a record-breaking 16 times and has taken part in 27 Academy Awards presentations. Hope himself received five Oscars during his acting career.

MOST DURABLE TV PRESENTER

Patrick Moore (UK) has presented the monthly *Sky at Night* without a break or a miss since 24 April 1957. By May 2001 a total of 570 shows had been broadcast. Moore has received the OBE for services to astronomy, and in 1988 he received the CBE. His guests have included first man on the Moon, Neil Armstrong (USA), and rock star Brian May (UK).

www.guinnessworldrecords.com/jenniferaniston

GIRL POWER

The highest annual earnings from female TV acting roles are paid to Jennifer Aniston (right), Lisa Kudrow and Courteney Cox Arquette (all USA), who have played the leads in NBC's *Friends* since 1994. They all earned a record-breaking $15.3 million (£10.9 million) in 2000, according to the 2001 *Forbes* Celebrity 100 list. They and their male co-stars negotiated a salary of $750,000 (£525,714) per episode in 2000 for the seventh season.

ACCESS CODE: ‹52644›

GUINNESS WORLD RECORDS

 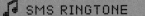

pop stars

LONGEST MUSIC VIDEO

Ghosts, Michael Jackson's (USA) 1996 part-feature film, part-music video, is 35 minutes long and was based on an original concept by cult horror writer Stephen King (USA).

MOST GRAMMY AWARDS WON IN A YEAR BY AN INDIVIDUAL

Michael Jackson took home a record eight Grammy Awards in 1984, including Best New Rhythm and

*NSYNC ARE ONE IN A MILLION

*NSYNC's (USA) 'No Strings Attached' 2000 US tour broke the record for the greatest number of tickets sold in a day when a record one million, valued at $40 million (£25,078,370), were sold on 25 March 2000, The band sold out 51 of their 52 tour dates on the first day of sales.

The most successful tour of all time is The Rolling Stones' (UK) 1989 'Steel Wheels' tour of North America, which earned an estimated $310 million (£185 million) and was attended by 3.2 million people in 30 cities.

The largest paying audience ever attracted by a solo performer was an estimated 180,000–184,000, in the Maracanã Stadium, Rio de Janeiro, Brazil, to hear a gig by ex-Beatle Sir Paul McCartney (UK) on 21 April 1990.

www.guinnessworldrecords.com/nsync

 ACCESS CODE: ‹56312›

Blues Song for hit single 'Billie Jean', as well as several awards for writing, producing and performing the legendary *Thriller* album.

FASTEST-SELLING ALBUM

The Beatles' (UK) album, *1*, sold a record 13.5 million copies around the world in its first month. Released on 13 Nov 2000, it shifted 3.6 million copies on its first day alone. Although all the tracks on the disc were more than 30 years old, it was the biggest-selling album of 2000 in the UK and was No.1 in 35 countries.

FASTEST LIVE RECORDING TO RETAIL

A limited edition of Midge Ure's (UK) 'Dear God' single, including two live B-side tracks 'All Fall Down' and 'Strange Brew', was delivered to retail just 81 hr 15 min after the songs were recorded at The Venue in Edinburgh, UK, on 21 Nov 1988.

FASTEST RAPPER USA

Rebel XD, otherwise known as Seandale Price (USA), is the world's fastest rap artist. On 24 June 1998 he rapped 683 syllables in 54.501 seconds, which works out at just over 12.5 syllables per second, beating his own previous record of 674 syllables in 54.9 seconds, or 12.2 syllables per second set in 1992.

GREATEST AGE RANGE IN A BAND

The 1997 Afro-Cuban All Stars album *A todo Cuba le Gusta* featured band members spanning four generations, ranging in age from 15 to 81. The oldest was flute player, Robert Egues, while the youngest was Julián Oviedo Sánchez (both Cuba), playing the timbales.

LARGEST SCREEN AT A ROCK CONCERT

The set for U2's (Ireland) 1997 'PopMart' tour featured the world's largest LED (light-emitting diode) screen. Measuring a gigantic 16.7 x 51.8 m (54 ft 8 in x 170 ft), the screen showed animation and pop-art masterpieces. Although U2 were originally identified with guitar-based

BACKSTREET BOYS MOVE INTO THE FAST LANE

The biggest-selling boy-band album of all time is the Backstreet Boys' (USA) *Millennium*, released in 1999, which had sales of 13 million by March 2001. The record entered the US Billboard Top 200 Album Chart at No.1 in June 1999. It sold 1,134,000 copies in its first week, shattering Garth Brooks's one-week sales world record. The Backstreet Boys earned an estimated $60 million (£43,148,714) in 1999, according to *Forbes* Celebrity 100 list (2000). The Backstreet Boys have emerged as the most successful boy-band of their generation, and their 1999 tour of the US drew 1.4 million fans.

www.guinnessworldrecords.com/backstreetboys

ACCESS CODE: ‹56422›

anthems, the 1990s saw them experimenting with samplers, dance rhythms and visual effects.

MOST SUCCESSFUL MALE COUNTRY SINGER

Garth Brooks (USA) is the most successful country artist of all time, with album sales of over 100 million since 1989. He is also the biggest-ever certified solo album artist in the USA.

Garth Brooks also holds the record for the highest-grossing country music tour with his three-year long 'Sevens' tour. Starting in March 1997, it grossed a record $105 million (£65.625 million). He played 350 shows in 100 cities, pulling crowds of around 55,000 fans at each concert.

MOST BRIT AWARDS WON BY AN INDIVIDUAL

Robbie Williams (UK) has won more BRIT (British Record Industry Trust) awards than any other artist or act. He has won a total of 12 awards, both as a solo singer and as part of Take That. Recent awards include Best British Single and Best British Video (both for 'Rock DJ') and British Male Solo Artist at the BRITS on 26 Feb 2001.

OLDEST EUROVISION SONG CONTEST WINNER

The Olsen Brothers (Jorgan and Niels), representing Denmark, won the Eurovision Song Contest aged 49 and 45 respectively. 'Fly On The Wings Of Love' won with 195 points in Stockholm, Sweden, on 13 May 2000.

LONGEST RUNNING GROUP WITH SAME LINE-UP

The Beverley Sisters (UK) made their professional debut on 13 Nov 1944, with Glenn Miller (USA) and the American Band of the AEF for the BBC's AEFP Broadcast in London. They are still regularly singing live after 57 years with the same line-up of Joy, Teddie and Babs.

MOST MUSIC VIDEOS FOR ONE SONG

There are five different videos for the 1998 song 'Timber' by UK dance act Coldcut – the original mix, the EBN remix, the LPC remix, the Clifford Gilberto remix and the Gnomadic remix. They offered the 'Timber' track to video-makers to encourage them to remix videos in the same way that dance music DJs and producers remix records.

MY BANK ACCOUNT IS THRILLING ME ...

The fastest–selling album by a female artist is Britney Spears' (USA) album, *Oops!...I Did it Again*, which sold a record 1.3 million copies in its first week of release in the US in June 2000. A further 612,500 copies were snapped up the following week. Britney Spears (right) earned $38.5 million (£25,457,225) in 2000, according to the *Forbes* Celebrity 100 list released on 2 March 2001.

The record for the highest–ever annual earnings by a female artist is held by Celine Dion, who made more money in one year than any other woman in pop. According to the *Forbes* 1999 Celebrity 100 list, the French Canadian songstress, who sings in both English and French, earned an estimated sum of $56 million (£33.5 million) in 1998.

MOST SUCCESSFUL FEMALE SOLO SINGER

The most successful female solo artist is Madonna (USA), who has sold around 120 million albums and 40 million singles. Her total sales are more than any other female music star. Madonna has had 34 American Top-10 singles and 12 Top-10 albums. In the UK she's had 48 Top-10 singles and 14 Top-10 albums.

OLDEST RAPPERS

Japanese twin sisters Kin Narita and Gin Kanie were born on 1 Aug 1892. For their 100th birthday in 1992, they recorded a 'granny rap' record that entered the Japanese pop chart. Although Gin died of a heart attack in Jan 2000, they are still household names in Japan and, in the past, appeared regularly on TV and commercials.

HIGHEST ANNUAL EARNINGS BY A BOY BAND

*NSYNC were the highest earning boy-band in 2000, with an estimated income of $42 million (£28,136,933), according to *Forbes* Celebrity 100 list.

HIGHEST ANNUAL EARNINGS BY A RAPPER

Dr Dre (USA) has made more money than any other rapper in one year. According to the 2001 *Forbes* Celebrity 100 list, Dre earned $31.5 million (£21,102,700) in 2000.

BIGGEST-SELLING FEMALE LATIN ARTIST

Cuban-born singer Gloria Estefan is the most successful female Latin artist in the world, with total global sales estimated at more than 35 million. In the USA she has amassed eight gold albums, four of which – *Primitive Love, Let It Loose, Cuts Both Ways* and *Greatest Hits* – have passed the three million sales mark.

BIGGEST-SELLING MALE LATIN ARTIST

Spanish vocalist Julio Iglesias is the world's most successful Latin music artist, with global album sales of more than 200 million. *Julio*, released in 1983, was the first foreign-language album to sell more than two million copies in the USA, and the only foreign-language record to go double platinum there.

HIGHEST-EVER ANNUAL POP EARNINGS

In 1989 Michael Jackson made the highest-ever earnings for a pop star in one year. He topped the *Forbes* list with an income of $125 million (£76,298,602).

HIGHEST-EVER ANNUAL EARNINGS BY A GIRL-BAND

The Spice Girls (UK) ranked 20th on *Forbes* list of 1998's 40 richest entertainers, with a group income of £29.6 million ($49 million).

HIGHEST ANNUAL EARNINGS BY A BAND

The Beatles, despite breaking up in 1970, were the highest-earning band in 2000, making £100.49 million ($150 million) according to the 2001 *Forbes* Celebrity 100 list.

RICHEST BAND

The Rolling Stones (all UK) are the richest band with a combined wealth of £400 million ($647 million). In 2000 lead singer Mick Jagger had an estimated fortune of £150 million ($243 million), followed by guitarist Keith Richards with £130 million ($210 million), drummer Charlie Watts with £65 million ($105 million) and guitarist Ronnie Wood with £55 million ($89 million).

GUINNESS WORLD RECORDS

super rich

RICHEST BACHELOR

Larry J Ellison (USA) is estimated to be worth $47 billion (£33 billion). He has been CEO of Oracle Corporation since he founded the company in 1977.

RICHEST PERSON

Bill Gates (USA), founder and chairman of Microsoft Corporation, is currently the richest person in the world. *Forbes* magazine estimated his wealth at $60 billion (£38 billion) in May 2000. Gates began computer programming when he was just 13. In 1986, at the age of 31, Gates became the youngest-ever dollar billionaire. For a few weeks in early 2000, Larry Ellison and Gates competed for the title of the world's richest person, but Gates soon reclaimed the title.

YOUNGEST SELF-MADE MILLIONAIRE

The youngest male ever to earn a million dollars was the child film actor Jackie Coogan (USA). Between 1923 and 1924 he earned $22,000 (£15,400) per week ($222,081 or £155,560 in today's terms) and retained about 60% of his films' profits. At 13 he was a millionaire. Unfortunately, his show-biz parents squandered his money and under

GETTING THE WANG OF THINGS

Charles B Wang (USA, left), founder and chief executive officer of Computer Associates International, earned $650,048,000 (£418,734,741) in the financial year 1999/2000 – a figure that includes his salary, bonus and stock gains. This is currently the highest annual earnings by a CEO. His total earnings over the five-year period 1996–2000 were $713,452,000 (£459,577,045). *Fortune* magazine has named Computer Associates as one of America's most admired companies and one of the best companies to work for in America. The company is a business-to-business technology and software solutions provider.

www.guinnessworldrecords.com/wang
← ACCESS CODE: ‹52160›

Californian law at the time, he had no rights to the money he made as a child. Jackie filed suit for around $4 million (£2.8 million) and in 1939, was awarded just $126,000 (£88,278). The ensuing legal case (1938) led ultimately to the Child Actor's Bill, also known as the Coogan Act, to protect the earnings of child actors.

LARGEST ANNUAL INCOME

George Soros (USA), president and chairman of Soros Fund Management LLC, a private investment management firm, earned $1.5 billion (£1 billion) in 1995 alone. Most of his earnings came from profitable investments in offshore funds such as Quantum, Quantum Emerging Growth, Quota and Quasar International.

RICHEST WORKING WOMAN

Abigail Johnson (USA), a senior vice-president of FMR Corp (Fidelity Investments), has a net worth of $7 billion (£4.4 billion), and is No.18 on the 2000 *Forbes* 400 US Rich list.

RICHEST WOMAN

Liliane Bettencourt (France), the heiress to the L'Oréal cosmetics fortune, has an estimated worth of £10.1 billion ($15.2 billion).

RICHEST INVESTOR

Warren Edward Buffett (USA), chairman of Berkshire Hathaway, is the world's richest investor, estimated to be worth $28 billion (£18.8 billion). He started playing the stock market at age 11. At 25, Buffett started his own investment company, the Buffett Partnership. In 1965 it

bought its first company, Berkshire Hathaway. Since then, the company's stock has increased by more than a stunning 300,000%.

RICHEST DESIGNER

Ralph Lauren (USA) has a personal fortune estimated at $1.7 billion (£1.03 billion). The Ralph Lauren empire is currently valued at around $3 billion (£1.8 billion). Lauren was born Ralph Lifshitz in New York City, New York, USA, in 1939.

HIGHEST-EVER ANNUAL EARNINGS BY A SUPERMODEL

According to the 1999 *Forbes* Celebrity 100 list, Claudia Schiffer (Germany) earned a record $10.5 million (£6.3 million) in 1998.

HIGHEST ANNUAL EARNINGS BY A FILM PRODUCER

Hollywood producer and director George Lucas (USA) topped the 2001 *Forbes* Celebrity 100 list, having earned a record-breaking $250 million (£175 million) in 2000

THE WRITE PAY

According to the March 2001 *Forbes* Celebrity 100 list, Stephen King (USA, left) enjoyed estimated earnings of over $44 million (£29 million) in 2000 – the highest current annual earnings by an author. King wrote his first short story at the age of seven. Since then, his horror/sci-fi books have been translated into 33 languages and published in over 35 different countries. Over 300 million copies of his novels are in circulation.

In 1999 JK Rowling (UK) earned £24 million ($40 million) – the highest annual earnings by a children's author according to the 2000 *Forbes* Celebrity 100 list. In July 2000 *Harry Potter and the Goblet of Fire* saw a first printing of 5.3 million copies with advance orders of over 1.8 million, which has made Rowling one of Britain's richest women.

after the video release of
*Star Wars: Episode 1 – The
Phantom Menace*
(USA, 1999).

RICHEST LUXURY
GOODS MAKER
Bernard Arnault (France),
who heads the luxury goods
empire LVMH (Louis Vuitton
Moët Hennessy), is worth an
estimated £8.4 billion ($12.6 billion).
LVMH owns high-profile luxury
brands such as Christian Dior,
Kenzo, Louis Vuitton, Guerlain and
Givenchy perfumes, as well as top
drinks brands, such as Dom
Perignon and Hennessy.

RICHEST JEANS TYCOON
In 1999 Robert D Haas (USA), the
great-great-grand-nephew of
the founder of jeans manufacturer
Levi Strauss Co, had amassed a
fortune of $8.2 billion (£5 billion).
As a result, he ranked 358 on
the 1999 *Forbes* 400 list.

RICHEST ROYALS
King Fahd Bin Abdulaziz Alsaud
(Saudi Arabia) is the richest monarch
in the world, with an estimated
personal wealth of £21 billion
($30 billion) in April 2001. The Saudi
dynasty is also the richest royal family.

The richest European royal house
is the Dutch House of Orange, which
has an estimated wealth of £2.6 billion
($3.69 billion). Queen Béatrix of the
Netherlands has an estimated
net worth of £2.43 billion
($3.42 billion), making her the
wealthiest queen in the world.

WEALTHIEST DOG
The largest legacy to a
dog is $15 million (£10.5
million), bequeathed by
Ella Wendel (USA) to her
poodle, Toby, in 1931.
This is equivalent to
$169 million (£118 million)
in today's terms.

www.guinnessworldrecords.com/masterp

PRODUCING THE GOODS
Master P (USA, right), chief executive
officer of No Limit Records and the
world's richest music producer, is
estimated to have a net worth of
$56.5 million (£34.1 million). Born
Percy Miller, Master P opened
his first record store in Richmond,
California, USA. He then founded
his own record label, and his first
release on No Limit Records, 'The
Ghetto's Tryin' To Kill Me', sold
100,000 copies. Although he no
longer works as a solo artist, Master
P still works with the
groups TRU and Da
504 Boyz. He has
recently set up
associated brands
such as No Limit
Films, No Limit
Sports, No Limit
Real Estate and
No Limit Clothing.
The rapper also
owns a chain of fast-
food restaurants and
petrol stations in Louisiana, USA.

GUINNESS
WORLD RECORDS™

SMS ICON   SMS RINGTONE   BULLETIN BOARD   GUINNESS WORLD RECORDS TV

big money

RICHEST HINDU TEMPLE

The Tirupati Temple in Andhra Pradesh, India, has an astonishing annual income of £35.2 million ($57.02 million). The money comes mainly from collection boxes, but the most interesting source of income is human hair. Thousands of pilgrims donate their hair as a form of sacrifice and this is auctioned annually to wigmakers and chemical and fertiliser factories.

LARGEST FAMILY FORTUNE

The Oeri, Hoffman and Sacher families of Switzerland, who jointly own Roche pharmaceuticals, have an estimated combined net worth of £8 billion ($11.5 billion).

MOST SPORTS TAX-EXILES LIVING IN ONE PLACE

Monaco has a record number of racing driver residents, including Ralf Schumacher (Germany), Pedro Diniz (Brazil), Johnny Herbert (UK), Mika Hakkinen (Sweden), David Coulthard (UK), Jacques Villeneuve (France), Alexander Wurz (Austria), Giancarlo Fisichella (Italy) and Rubens Barrichello (Brazil). A number of tennis players on the international circuit also live in the principality.

LARGEST DOWRY

In 1929 Bolivian tin millionaire Don Simon Iturbi Patío gave his daughter Elena Patío a dowry of £8 million

A GOOD TURN

On 18 Sept 1997 Ted Turner (USA, left), the founder of CNN and vice-president of Time Warner, announced that he was giving the United Nations (UN) $1 billion (£580 million) of his own money – the biggest-ever private cash donation to the UN. The money will be used to finance programmes on behalf of refugees, children, the environment and clearing landmines.

www.guinnessworldrecords.com/tedturner
← ACCESS CODE: ‹47802›

($22.48 million) – equal in 2000 to £280 million or $400 million. However, this did not make a major dent in his fortune of £125 million ($606 million) – equivalent to £5,000 million ($7,000 million) in 2000).

LARGEST CASH PRIZE WON ON RADIO

Clare Barwick (UK) won £1,000,000 ($1,600,000) – the largest cash prize ever on radio – on Chris Evans's Virgin Radio show on 17 Dec 1999. Clare correctly answered the question, "Which one of these two writers was really a woman – George Eliot or TS Eliot?" It was George, whose real name was Mary Ann Evans.

LARGEST DONATION TO A SINGLE UNIVERSITY

In Jan 2001 a record $250 million (£176 million) was given to the University of Colorado, Denver, Colorado, USA, by the chairman and co-founder of software manufacturer BEA Systems, Bill Coleman (USA).

LARGEST DONATION TO EDUCATION

In Dec 1993 philanthropist Walter H Annenberg (USA) made the biggest-ever donation to education. The publisher and diplomat split a record $365 million (£256 million) between three US universities and a US secondary school.

WEALTHIEST UNIVERSITY

In 2000 the endowment for Harvard University (USA) was $19 billion (£13 billion) – bigger than the annual operating budget of 142 of the world's countries, including Cuba, Jordan and Lithuania. Graduates include seven US presidents. Fourteen Nobel Prize winners are Harvard faculty members.

BIGGEST NON-PROFIT-MAKING RACING CLUB

In 1998 the Hong Kong Jockey Club gave over £93 million ($131.9 million) to social and educational community projects, making it the biggest non-profit-making racing club ever.

MOST EXPENSIVE CREDIT CARD

The American Express Centurion credit card, also known as the 'Black Card', has an annual fee of £700 ($1,000) and is only open to those with a minimum salary of £150,000 ($215,000). The card has no spending limits and is offered by invitation only to selected individuals.

COMPANY WITH THE MOST MILLIONAIRES

In 2001 there were 10 millionaires in the investment bank Goldman Sachs, New York City, New York, USA. They have a combined wealth of $2,200 million (£1,551 million).

LARGEST SINGLE CASH BEQUEST

On 12 Dec 1955 the Ford Foundation (USA) donated the world's biggest cash bequest of $500 million (then £178 million), to 4,157 educational and other institutions. This is the equivalent today of $4.2 billion (£2.4 billion).

LARGEST PAPER MONEY

The biggest paper money ever made was the one-guan note, which was issued between 1368 and 1399 in the Chinese Ming Dynasty. The note measured 23 x 33 cm (9 x 13 in) – bigger than an A4 sheet of paper.

LARGEST RETURN OF CASH

In May 1994 Howard Jenkins (USA) discovered that an accidental transfer had credited his bank account with an extra $88 million (£62 million). The 31-year-old employee of a roofing company withdrew $4 million (£2.8 million) for a spending spree, but his conscience got the better of him and he returned the millions in full.

LARGEST ROBBERY BY A MUGGER

A mugger made off with treasury bills and certificates of deposit worth £292 million ($435 million) after attacking a broker's messenger in London on 2 May 1990. But news of the theft spread to every major bank in the country, and none of them would accept the notes.

DEAD RICH

In the year 2000, 23 years after he died of a heart attack, the estate of Elvis Presley (USA, left) earned $35 million (£25 million), making him the richest dead celebrity. Elvis has sold more than one billion albums, generating large royalty cheques for his family. He left daughter Lisa-Marie his Graceland mansion in Memphis, Tennessee, USA, which earns $15 million (£10.5 million) annually in admission fees, while $5 million (£3.5 million) was earned by selling Presley-related articles such as T-shirts and toys. Elvis also earns through tourism with places like Heartbreak Hotel and Presley's restaurant in Memphis, as well as profits from posthumous appearances in advertisements for Lipton Iced Tea, Energizer batteries and Apple Computer.

www.guinnessworldrecords.com/elvis
← ACCESS CODE: ‹56563›

WINNER TAKES ALL

In Feb 1996 the New York State Supreme Court ruled that the actress Joan Collins (UK, above) could keep the $1.2 million (£845,000) advance for her unpublished novel *A Ruling Passion*. The publisher Random House (USA) had found her first draft unsatisfactory and sued her unsuccessfully for the return of the money – making this the world's biggest unreturned advance ever.

Joan Collins made more than 50 films before starring as the sultry Alexis in the hit 1980s' television series *Dynasty*.

www.guinnessworldrecords.com/
joancollins

ACCESS CODE:
← ‹48299›

MOST MONEY RAISED BY AN INDIVIDUAL IN A MARATHON

Retired advertising executive John Spurling (UK) raised a record-breaking £1.13 million ($1.87 million) for charity by running the London Marathon on 18 April 1999. With no previous experience, Spurling finished the race, raised the figure and divided the money between two charities – the Animal Health Trust and the Lord's Taverners, a group of ex-international cricketers and celebrities who take part in cricket matches to raise money for charity.

www.guinnessworldrecords.com/billgates

BILLION-DOLLAR BILL

Bill Gates (USA, right), founder of computer giant Microsoft, and his wife Melinda donated $6 billion (£4.2 billion) to their charity, the Bill and Melinda Gates Foundation, in Aug 1999 – the largest-ever single private donation in history. The Foundation donates funds to global healthcare programmes, education, libraries and community causes in the Pacific Northwest where Gates grew up.

In May 1999 the couple donated a record $25 million (£15.8 million) to AIDS and HIV research.

ACCESS CODE: ‹55249›

MOST MONEY RAISED IN A SINGLE TELETHON

Between 5 and 6 Sept 1999, the Jerry Lewis MDA (Muscular Dystrophy Association) telethon raised a record $53,116,417 (then £33,119,102) in pledges and contributions. About 64 million Americans in 26 million homes watched the programme, which has become a Labor Day tradition. In 1998, the programme became the first worldwide telethon, and the same year saw the launch of an Internet simulcast of the national broadcast, at www.mdausa.org.

GREATEST RANSOM

The greatest ransom ever, was a glittering hall full of gold and silver, paid in return for Atahualpa, the last emperor of the Incas, to the Spanish conquistador Francisco Pizarro. Paid from 1532 to 1533 at Cajamarca, Peru, the ransom would now be equivalent to £1 billion ($1.5 billion).

LARGEST FINE

A record fine was imposed on the US securities house Drexel Burnham Lambert in Dec 1988 for insider trading. The $650 million (£335 million) figure represented $300 million (£164 million) in direct fines, with the rest put into an account to satisfy claims of parties defrauded by Drexel's actions.

influential people

OLDEST LIVING ROYAL

Her Majesty Queen Elizabeth, The Queen Mother (UK), is the world's oldest living royal. She married Prince Albert (King George VI) on 26 April 1923, and on his coronation, became the first British-born Queen Consort since Tudor times, as well as the Last Empress of India. She celebrated her 100th birthday on 4 Aug 2000 and still enjoys a very full life. Since 1923, she has given only one interview.

YOUNGEST CURRENT QUEEN

The youngest current queen is HM Queen Rania Al-Abdullah of Jordan (b. 31 Aug 1970). She is married to the head of state, King Abdullah Bin Al-Hussein.

LONGEST REIGN

Minhti, King of Arakan, which is now part of Myanmar (Burma), is reputed to have reigned for 95 years between 1279 and 1374. However the longest well-documented reign of a monarch is that of Phiops II, an Egyptian Sixth-Dynasty pharaoh. His reign began in c. 2281 BC, when he was six years old, and lasted about 94 years.

LARGEST PRESIDENTIAL ENTOURAGE

When former US President Bill Clinton visited China in June 1998, he was accompanied by an enormous entourage of 1,200 people. The crowd consisted of 200 secret-service agents, 150 military personnel, 30 senior delegates, 375 reporters, four White House TV crews, 150 support staff and 70 senior aides and advisers.

MOST APPEARANCES ON THE COVER OF *TIME* MAGAZINE

Richard Nixon (37th President of the US) was featured on the cover of *Time* magazine a record 55 times.

LARGEST GATHERING OF WORLD LEADERS

The United Nations' Millennium Summit, held in New York City, New York, USA, from 6 to 8 Sept 2000, was the largest-ever gathering of world leaders. It brought together 144 kings, presidents, prime ministers and heads of state. There were over 1,300 official cars at the event, thousands of secret-service agents and over 2,500 journalists. On the agenda was the crisis in the Middle East, education, technology and multilateralism – the bringing together of different groups.

MOST ACCESSIBLE PRIME MINISTER

Danish premier Poul Nyrup Rasmussen, whose home telephone number is available to the public, is known to answer telephone queries from Danish citizens personally.

JUST WILLIAM

His Royal Highness Prince William of Wales (above), grandson of HM Queen Elizabeth II of the United Kingdom, has more fan clubs devoted to him than any other royal in the world. As of April 2001, there were at least 72 clubs dedicated to admiring Britain's future monarch. All fan clubs are 'unofficial' as they are not supervised by Buckingham Palace.

Prince William Arthur Philip Louis Windsor was born on 21 June 1982, the elder son of the late Diana, Princess of Wales, and HRH The Prince of Wales. He has a younger brother, Harry (b. 15 Sept 1984).

www.guinnessworldrecords.com/william
← ACCESS CODE: ‹56550›

LONGEST-SERVING FEMALE PRIME MINISTER

Sirimavo Bandaranaike was Prime Minister of Sri Lanka for a total of 17 years 208 days – from 21 July 1960 to 25 March 1965; from 29 May 1970 to 22 July 1977; and then again from 12 Nov 1994 to 10 Aug 2000.

YOUNGEST PRIME MINISTER

Swiss-born Dr Mario Frick (b. 8 May 1965) became Prime Minister of Liechtenstein at the age of 28 on 15 Dec 1993.

MOST DESCENDANTS TO BECOME PRIME MINISTER

Jawaharlal Nehru became India's Prime Minister when the country attained independence in Aug 1947. Nehru remained in power until his death in 1964. His daughter Indira Gandhi was Prime Minister from 1966 to 1977, and again from 1980 to 1984, when she was assassinated by her bodyguards. Her eldest son Rajiv Gandhi, became Prime Minister following his mother's death and won the 1984 elections by a landslide victory. He served until 1989 but was also assassinated while campaigning for the premiership in 1991.

LARGEST HUMAN RIGHTS ORGANIZATION

Amnesty International has more than 1,200,000 members in over 100 countries, offices in more than 50 countries and more than 4,200 local groups on every continent. The organization was founded in 1961 by Peter Benenson, a British lawyer, and originally began as a newspaper appeal called 'The Forgotten Prisoners'. As a result, over 1,000 people wrote in supporting the idea of an international organization to protect human rights. In 1977 Amnesty International was awarded the Nobel Prize for Peace.

POWER TO THE PEOPLE

On 28 Aug 1963 civil-rights leader Martin Luther King Jr (USA, left) led more than 250,000 demonstrators in a march down the Mall in Washington DC, USA. The march was held to promote equal civil rights for all Americans, irrespective of race or colour, and was the largest racial-equality rally ever held. From the steps of the Lincoln Memorial, King delivered his legendary "I have a dream" speech to the crowd.

Born in Atlanta, Georgia, USA, on 15 Jan 1929, Martin Luther King Jr was a Baptist minister, a civil-rights activist and winner of the Nobel Peace prize in 1964, at the time the youngest man ever to do so. He was assassinated on 4 April 1968 in Memphis, Tennessee, USA.

www.guinnessworldrecords.com/martinlutherking
← ACCESS CODE: ‹54489›

LARGEST CONSERVATION ORGANIZATION

With more than five million members, and a global network of 27 national groups and 21 programme offices, the World Wide Fund For Nature (WWF) is the world's largest conservation organization. WWF and its members are committed to preventing the degradation of the natural world and to helping people live in greater harmony with nature. Since 1985 the WWF has invested over £729 million ($1.165 billion) in 11,000 projects in 130 countries.

LARGEST FEDERATION OF ENVIRONMENTAL GROUPS

Friends of the Earth International boasts one million activists throughout the world, with member organizations in 68 countries and 13 affiliate groups – making it the world's largest federation of environmental groups. The federation aims to preserve the earth's ecological, cultural and ethnic diversity by promoting environmentally sustainable development on local, regional, national and global levels.

MOST PULITZER PRIZES

The Associated Press has received a record 45 Pulitzer Prizes. These have been awarded annually since 1917, after an endowment by newspaper publisher Joseph Pulitzer (USA) to recognize achievements in American journalism, letters, drama and music.

MOST TEMPLES CONSECRATED BY ONE PERSON

His Holiness Pramukh Swami Maharaj (India), the spiritual master of the Swaminarayan Hindu Mission, consecrated (blessed) a record 386 temples in 11 countries between 17 April 1971 and 14 May 2001.

MOST INTERNATIONAL VISITS BY A POPE

The Pope is head of the Roman Catholic church. The visit by Pope John Paul II (Poland) to Kiev, Ukraine, on 25 June 2001 was his 126th trip abroad since he became Pope on 16 Oct 1978, aged 58. He was the first non-Italian to be chosen as Pope in 456 years and the youngest in the 20th century.

LONGEST-LIVED POPE

Of the popes whose ages can be reliably confirmed, Leo XIII (Gioacchino Pecci, Italy) lived the longest. Born on 2 March 1810, he was elected Pope on 20 Feb 1878 at the age of 67. He died on 20 July 1903 at the age of 93 years 140 days.

www.guinnessworldrecords.com/georgewbush

W MONEY

George W Bush (inaugurated as the 43rd US President on 20 Jan 2001, right), has assembled the wealthiest cabinet in American history by appointing more multi-millionaires to the top rank of his government than any of his predecessors. Of the 16 full cabinet members at the heart of the Bush administration, 13 are millionaires, seven of whom own assets worth more than $10 million (£7 million). His cabinet has acquired the nickname 'tycoon's club'. Defence Secretary Donald Rumsfeld and Treasury Secretary Paul O'Neill each have declared assets of at least $61 million (£42.9 million), while Secretary of State Colin Powell has at least $18.5 million (£13 million).

GUINNESS WORLD RECORDS

big business

LARGEST SAVINGS BANK

The world's largest commercial and savings bank is Mizuho Holdings Inc (Japan). According to recently released figures, the bank generated revenues of £48,154 million ($76,851 million) and profits of £1,154 million ($1,843 million) for 2000. Mizuho Holdings Inc was created by the consolidation of the Dai-Ichi Kangyo Bank, Fuji Bank Ltd and the Industrial Bank of Japan. It is the first bank to hold over a trillion dollars in assets.

HIGHEST TECHNOLOGY COMPANY VALUATION

On 11 April 2000 Cisco Systems Inc of San Jose, California, USA, had a confirmed market capitalization of $503.4 billion (£317.7 billion). This places Cisco ahead of software giant Microsoft Corporation, whose share price suffered at the time, as a result of US judge Thomas Penfield Jackson's ruling against them over an anti-trust issue on 3 April 2000. This ruling was overturned in June 2001.

LARGEST CORPORATION

In 2000, General Motors of Detroit, Michigan, USA, generated revenues of $184,632 million (£123,306 million) In the same year the company profits were $4,452 million (£2,982 million). General Motors is the world's largest automotive corporation and vehicle manufacturer.

SUPER MARKET!

Wal-Mart Stores Inc (USA) had revenues of $191,329 million (£130,838 million) for the fiscal year ending 31 Jan 2001, the largest revenues for a retail firm. The company had profits of $6,295 million (£4,304 million) for the fiscal year ending 31 Jan 2001. As of 31 March 2000, Wal-Mart had 4,003 retail locations in 10 countries, employing 1,140,000 people. Sam Walton opened the first Wal-Mart store in 1962 in Bentonville, Arkansas, USA. A small-town merchant who had operated variety stores in Arkansas and Missouri, Walton dreamed up Wal-Mart as a discount store with a wide array of merchandise and friendly service. His son, S Robson Walton (left), is now company chairman.

www.guinnessworldrecords.com/walmart
ACCESS CODE: ‹49579›

LARGEST CHEQUE

The largest amount paid with a single cheque is £2,474,655,000 ($3,971,821,324). The record-breaking cheque was issued on 30 March 1995 as payment by Glaxo plc to Wellcome Trust Nominees Limited regarding the Trust's share in Wellcome plc. The Lloyds Bank Registrar's computer was unable to generate a cheque this big, so it was completed by an employee. The Lloyds typist was so overawed by the huge responsibility that she needed three attempts to write it correctly.

LAW FIRM WITH MOST LAWYERS

Clifford Chance LLP – created in Jan 2000 after the merger of Clifford Chance, Rogers Wells LLP and Pünder, Volhard, Weber and Axster, employs 7,400 staff, 3,580 of whom are fee-earning legal advisors and 652 are partners. The firm has 29 offices around the world and in 1999 had revenues of $1 billion (£625 million).

BIGGEST DAILY SALE OF A SINGLE STOCK

On 11 Feb 2000 over 2.1 billion Vodafone shares were traded – the biggest-ever sale of a single stock.

LONGEST TRADING SUSPENSION

In 1914 the New York Stock Exchange ceased trading for four months and two weeks from 31 July. The shutdown was due to the outbreak of World War I in Europe.

LARGEST AIRLINE CORPORATION

AMR Corporation, based in Fort Worth, Texas, USA, is the world's largest airline corporation, with a workforce of 116,054, revenues of $19.7 billion (£13.1 billion) and profits of $813 million (£544 million) in 2000. The company has a fleet of nearly 700 jetliners and its airlines serve around 170 destinations in the Americas, Europe and the Pacific Rim.

LARGEST AEROSPACE COMPANY

The world's largest aerospace company is Boeing of Seattle, Washington, USA. In 2000 the company generated revenues of $51.3 billion (£34.4 billion) with profits of $2.1 billion (£1.4 billion).

LARGEST BEVERAGE COMPANY

PepsiCo Inc, based in Purchase, New York, USA, had revenues of $20,438 million (£13,692 million) in 2000 and profits of $2,183 million (£1,462 million). Beverage brands owned by PepsiCo include Pepsi, Mountain Dew and Tropicana.

LARGEST CHEWING GUM COMPANY

The largest chewing gum company is the Wm Wrigley Jr Company based in Chicago, Illinois, USA. In 2000 it had revenues of $2,145 million (£1,436 million) and profits of $328 million (£219 million). In total, the company accounts for around 50% of all US chewing gum sales.

LARGEST FAST-FOOD CHAIN

The McDonald's Corporation (USA) is the world's largest global food service retailer. Revenues in 2000 were $14.2 billion (£9.5 billion), with profits totalling $1.9 billion (£1.2 billion) and the worldwide workforce was 364,000. McDonald's operates more than 28,000 restaurants (12,800 in the USA) in 120 countries worldwide. Non-US restaurants make up more than 60% of the company's sales and about

BABES IN TOYLAND

The world's largest toy manufacturer is Mattel Inc of El Segundo, California, USA. In 2000 the company, which employs 30,000 people, had revenues of $4,669 million (£3,127 million) and profits of a massive $430 million (£288 million). The company's best-known products include Barbie and Ken dolls (left), which are also now available in interactive games and software, Fisher-Price toys and Matchbox cars. It has also licensed Disney and *Sesame Street* items.

The world's largest toy-retail chain is Toys 'R' Us Inc of Paramus, New Jersey, USA. The first Toys 'R' Us 'toy supermarket' opened in 1957 and the company now has 1,548 stores in 25 countries worldwide. It had revenues of $11,862 million (£8,111 million) at the end of Jan 2001.

www.guinnessworldrecords.com/toptoys
ACCESS CODE: ‹57553›

50% of its profits. Brothers Dick and Mac McDonald pioneered the fast-food industry concept and later sold their business to their national franchising agent, Ray A Kroc, who created the McDonald's Corporation.

LARGEST BRA MANUFACTURER

In 2000 US clothing and food conglomerate Sara Lee controlled 33% of the US bra market. The company enjoyed total sales of $17,511 million (£11,533 million) and profits of $1,222 million (£804 million) in 2000. Sara Lee owns the Wonderbra and Playtex brands and its May 2000 takeover of UK firm Courtauld added the Berlei and Gossard brands to its portfolio.

LARGEST PR COMPANY

The largest public relations company in the world is US-based Burson-Marsteller, which enjoyed total revenues of more than $275 million (£171 million) in 1999. The company's most high-profile clients include Union Carbide, BP Chemicals and the Exxon Corporation.

LARGEST ADVERTISING BILLBOARD

In Dec 2000 an advertising billboard measuring 23.7 m (77.7 ft) high and 132 m (433 ft) long, with a surface area of 3,128.4 m² (33,661.58 ft²), was erected on the side of Fort Dunlop – the former Dunlop head office building – overlooking the M6 near Birmingham, W Midlands, UK. The construction cost was paid for by the Ford Motor Company Ltd (USA) and Ford's six-month billboard campaign, installed by Mega Profile Ltd (UK), cost £650,000 ($920,000).

LARGEST TELECOMMUNICATIONS COMPANY

The largest telecommunications company in the world is Nippon Telegraph and Telephone Corporation (NTT), based in Tokyo, Japan. In 2000 it had revenues of £69,163 million ($97,956 million) and profits of £1,991 million ($2,821 million).

www.guinnessworldrecords.com/bigmerge

TIME TO GET ONLINE

The world's largest merger was between America Online (AOL), the largest-ever internet company, and media corporation Time Warner. The $350-billion (£213-billion) deal was announced on 10 Jan 2000 by AOL CEO Steve Case (right, on left of photo) and Gerald Levin, CEO of Time Warner (on right of photo). This merger created the world's largest media company, with a major portfolio of brands including AOL, Time, CNN, Warner Bros, Netscape and Warner Music Group.

GUINNESS WORLD RECORDS™

buying and selling 1

MOST VALUABLE FOOTBALL MEDAL

The most that has ever been paid for a football medal is £124,750 ($177,280) for England goalkeeper Gordon Banks's 1966 World Cup winners medal, sold at Christie's, London, UK, on 23 March 2001.

MOST EXPENSIVE GOLF CLUB

A 200-year-old Scottish putter sold for a record £106,000 ($150,000) at Christie's in Glasgow, Scotland, UK, on 7 July 1998. It was bought by Titus Kendall (UK), a London antiques dealer, on behalf of Jaime Ortíz Patiño, a Bolivian millionaire, to display at the Valderrama Golf Club, which he owns in southern Spain.

MOST VALUABLE GOLF BALL

On 1 July 1995 Jaime Ortíz Patiño paid a record £19,995 ($31,855) in Edinburgh, Scotland, UK for a Victorian feathery ball. Golf was first played with leather balls stuffed with feathers and sticks tipped with horn.

MOST EXPENSIVE JIGSAW PUZZLE

The most expensive jigsaw puzzles in the world are the custom-made Stave Puzzles' Dollhouse Village puzzles, which cost a record £8,800 ($14,500) each in June 1999. The 2,640-piece jigsaws are hand-cut, one piece at a time, out of mahogany-backed plywood, by Steve Richardson (USA).

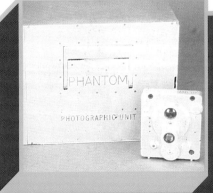

www.guinnessworldrecords.com/phantom
← ACCESS CODE: ‹43360›

PHANTOM OF THE CAMERA

The prototype Phantom Camera Unit (left), designed by British inventor and MP Noel Pemberton Billing in 1946, was sold for £146,750 ($216,826) at auction by Christie's, London, UK, on 16 Jan 2001 – making this the most valuable handheld self-contained camera in the world. The unit was designed for processing photographs on the move and includes developing tanks, paper storage and batteries. It also doubles up as an enlarger or projector.
   The Phantom never went into production as the project stopped with Billing's death in 1948. The high price paid for the camera was due to the fact that the unit is unique. It was bought by a private photographic museum.

MOST VALUABLE ANTIQUE TOY

A toy hosepipe sold for $182,545 (£128,333) at Christie's, New York City, New York, USA, on 14 Dec 1991. The work is a hand-painted tin-plate replica of the 'Charles' hose reel, a piece of fire-fighting equipment. It measures 38.1 x 58.4 cm (15 x 23 in), and was made in the 1870s by George Brown & Co, Connecticut, USA.

MOST VALUABLE DECK OF PLAYING CARDS

The highest price paid for one deck of playing cards is £99,000 ($143,352), by the Metropolitan Museum of Art, New York City, New York, USA, at Sotheby's, London, UK, on 6 Dec 1983. The cards, dating from 1470, are the oldest complete hand-painted set.

MOST VALUABLE ROBOT

A rare Masudaya Machine Man robot from the late 1950s was sold at Christie's, London, UK, in July 1999, for the record amount of £29,900

($47,203). The Machine Man is one of a set of early Japanese robots called 'The Gang Of Five'. These toys, which are about 38 cm (15 in) high, each have a lithographed tin body with graphics that resembled machine parts.

MOST VALUABLE TOY SOLDIER

A uniformed scale figure of Hitler's deputy, Rudolf Hess (Germany), was sold for £3,375 ($5,906) – the highest price ever paid for one toy soldier. The figure was among several sold by the Danish auction house Boyes in London, UK, on 23 April 1991.

MOST VALUABLE PIANO

The greatest sum ever paid for a piano was £1.45 million ($2.1 million) by singer George Michael (UK) for a Steinway Model Z upright belonging to John Lennon (UK). The piano featured on Lennon's video 'Imagine' and was sold at an auction at the Hard Rock Café, London, UK, on 17 Oct 2000.

MOST VALUABLE SINGLE MUSIC MANUSCRIPT

A record £1.4 million ($2.3 million) was paid for a manuscript of German composer Robert Schumann's Second Symphony by a private collector at Sotheby's, London, on 1 Dec 1994.

MOST VALUABLE CARTOON POSTER

A film poster for Walt Disney's film *Alice's Day at Sea*, depicting Alice astride a fish above the waves, was sold at Christie's, London, UK, in April 1994 for a record £23,100 ($34,072). The film was the start of the series of 'Alice Comedies' – 56 silent cartoons created between 1924 and 1927.

MOST VALUABLE BLACK-AND-WHITE ANIMATION CELL

In 1989 a black-and-white acetate drawing from Walt Disney's *Orphan's Benefit* (USA, 1934), depicting Donald Duck being punched by an orphan, raised £171,250 ($327,858) at Christie's, London, UK.

MOST VALUABLE FILM COSTUME

A blue-and-white gingham dress worn by Judy Garland (USA) as Dorothy in the 1939 MGM film *The Wizard of Oz* was sold at Christie's, London, UK, on 9 Dec 1999 for £199,500 ($324,188). The gingham pinafore bears a cotton wardrobe label inscribed in black ink 'Judy Garland 4228'. A New York real-estate agent bought the garment for 10 times more than the expected price.

SULTAN OF SPIN

The most expensive commercially produced yo-yos are the Cold Fusion yo-yo range (left), which cost between £90 and £150 ($150 and $250). The manufacturers, Playmaxx Inc, also produce a 24-carat, gold-plated, special-edition yo-yo, called the Gold Fusion, which sells for between £120 and £180 ($200 and $300). In 1998 Playmaxx Inc generated approximately £57.9 million ($96 million) from yo-yo retail sales and earned the 'Craze of the Year' award from the British Toy Association.
   Yo-yos date back as far as 400–500 BC in Greece, and early examples can be seen at the Metropolitan Museum of Art, New York City, New York, USA. According to the Playmaxx website, the French Emperor Napoleon Bonaparte was known to carry and use a yo-yo.

www.guinnessworldrecords.com/yoyo
← ACCESS CODE: ‹52213›

www.guinnessworldrecords.com/vangogh

PICTURE THIS

Portrait of Dr Gachet (right), by Dutch artist Vincent van Gogh (1853–90), is the world's most valuable painting. It sold in just three minutes for a record sum of $82.5 million (£49.1 million) at Christie's, New York City, New York, USA, on 15 May 1990. The artist completed this work just weeks before his suicide. The sitter, Dr Paul-Ferdinand Gachet (France), was a friend and physician to van Gogh. Shortly before his death van Gogh had a burst of creativity, producing more than one painting a day, including several versions of Dr Gachet.

MOST VALUABLE FILM SHOES

The ruby slippers worn by Judy Garland (USA) in *The Wizard of Oz* (USA, 1939), sold at Christie's, New York City, New York, USA, on 24 May 2000, for $666,000 (£450,920). The shoes were made of red silk overlaid with hand-sequinned georgette.

MOST VALUABLE JAMES BOND MEMORABILIA

The 1965 Aston Martin DB5, driven by Pierce Brosnan (UK) in *Goldeneye* (USA, 1995) sold for £157,750 ($228,264), at Christie's, London, UK, on 14 Feb 2001. The car was bought by Max Reid (UK) as a Valentine's Day present for his wife.

LARGEST SALE OF CELEBRITY CARS

On 5 June 2001 Sir Elton John (UK) auctioned 20 of his cars at Christie's, London, UK, raising £1,951,725 ($2,741,198). The top price paid was for a 1993 Jaguar XJ220, which sold for £234,750 ($329,706).

MOST EXPENSIVE SWISS ARMY KNIFE

An 18-carat gold Swiss army knife produced by Swiss jeweller Luzius Elmer has a retail price of £3,026 ($4,299). The Victorinox® Original Swiss Army™ pocketknife range, usually retails between £10 and £50 ($14 and $70).

MOST VALUABLE GUN

An 1873 .45-calibre Colt single-action army revolver, Serial No.1, was sold at Christie's, New York City, New York, USA, for a record-breaking $242,000 (£170,000) on 14 May 1987. This is equivalent to $370,000 (£285,000) in the year 2000.

MOST VALUABLE PHONECARD

In Jan 1992 the first phonecard ever issued in Japan, and therefore a rare collectors' item, was bought for a record £28,000 ($52,430).

MOST EXPENSIVE SINGLE PURCHASE OF WHISKY

On 16 Nov 2000 Norman Shelley (UK), paid £231,417 ($341,154) for 76 bottles of The Macallan malt whisky. The oldest whisky of the collection dated from 1856. The Macallan single-malt whisky has been made in Scotland since 1824.

MOST EXPENSIVE COW

The highest price paid for a live cow is $1,300,000 (£914,000) for a Friesian at auction in East Montpelier, Vermont, USA, in 1985.

MOST EXPENSIVE POST-IT® NOTE

To celebrate the 20th anniversary of the Post-It® note, artists created mini masterpieces on notes that were then auctioned online for charity. RB Kitaj's (USA) pastel-and-charcoal work sold for a record £640 ($925).

GUINNESS WORLD RECORDS™

buying and selling 2

MOST EXPENSIVE MEAL PER HEAD

In Sept 1997 three diners at Le Gavroche, London, UK, spent £13,091.20 ($20,945.92) on one meal. Only £216.20 ($345.92) went on food – cigars and spirits accounted for £845 ($1,352) and the remaining £12,030 ($19,248) was spent on six bottles of wine. The most expensive bottle, a 1985 La Romanée-Conti costing £4,950 ($7,920), was not to their liking so the generous group gave it to the restaurant staff. The diners began with a bottle of 1949 Krug champagne at £560 ($896) and followed it with clarets and burgundies – a 1985 DRC Montrachet at £1,400 ($2,240), a 1954 Château Haut Brion at £2,100 ($3,360), a 1967 Château d'Yquem at £1,070 ($1,712) and a 1961 Château Latour at £1,950 ($3,120).

MOST EXPENSIVE GLASS OF WINE

The most paid for a glass of wine is FF8600 (£982 or $1,382.80) for the first glass of 1993 Beaujolais Nouveau. The wine was released in Beaune, in the wine region of Burgundy, France. It was bought by Robert Denby in an auction at Pickwick's, a British pub in Beaune, on 18 Nov 1993.

STAMP OF APPROVAL

The most valuable single stamp in the world is the Swedish 'Treskilling Yellow', a 3-skilling stamp (left). On 8 Nov 1996 it was sold for a record Sw. Fr. 2,870,000 (£1,400,000 or $2,240,000) by David Feldman auctioneers, Geneva, Switzerland. The stamp, which should be green, was printed yellow and is the only one in existence, which makes it highly valuable to collectors. It was discovered by a schoolboy in 1885 among his grandfather's letters, and was first sold for just seven Swedish crowns – equivalent today to $1 or 70p. When sold in 1996, it became the world's most expensive item by weight.

www.guinnessworldrecords.com/stamp
ACCESS CODE: ‹43309›

MOST EXPENSIVE WINE

The most expensive commercially available wine is the Château d'Yquem Sauternes (1787), priced between £39,363 ($56,000) and £44,985 ($64,000), depending on the retailer. Château d'Yquem Sauternes is a golden-coloured dessert wine from France's Bordeaux region.

MOST EXPENSIVE FUNGUS

White truffle (*Tuber magnum pico*) is the world's most expensive edible fungus, fetching up to £2,094 ($3,000) per kilo. They can only be found in the Italian regions of Piedmont, Emilia-Romagna, Tuscany and Marches. Because they grow about a foot underground, they can only be located with the help of trained dogs.

MOST EXPENSIVE HAMBURGER

The 2001 Big Mac economic index, which compares the price of the classic McDonald's hamburger across the world, reveals that the Swiss pay the most for their burgers at $3.65 (£2.59). The price is over a dollar more than the $2.54 (£1.80) paid for a Big Mac in American McDonalds' restaurants.

MOST EXPENSIVE CAR REGISTRATION

Licence plate No.9 was sold at a Hong Kong government auction for £9 million ($13 million) on 19 March 1994 to Albert Yeung Sau-shing. In Cantonese the pronunciation of the word 'nine' is identical to the word 'dog'. This licence plate was considered lucky because 1994 was the Chinese Year of the Dog.

MOST EXPENSIVE PRIVATE JET

At $31 million ($45 million), the Gulfstream V-SP is the most expensive private jet ever made. It has a range of 6,750 nautical miles at long-range cruise speeds. The jet is powered by two Rolls-Royce BR-710 engines.

MOST EXPENSIVE MINI

The Mini Limo, an exclusive one-off commissioned by Rover Group and built by John Cooper Garages, cost £50,000 ($80,000) when it was delivered in Sept 1997. The two-door Mini boasts an £8,000 ($12,836) Alpine mini-disc sound system and seats costing £6,000 ($9,627). The car also features a custom-built dashboard and interior, leather-bound Wilton carpets, lambswool rugs, self-closing and locking systems and air-conditioning.

MOST EXPENSIVE COURSE

The Ivor Spencer International Finishing School for Young Ladies and Gentlemen, London, UK, began

DRESS TO IMPRESS

A flesh–coloured beaded gown (left) worn by Marilyn Monroe when she sang 'Happy Birthday' to President Kennedy on 19 May, 1962, is the world's most valuable dress. It was sold on 27 Oct 1999 for $1,267,000 (£885,904) at Christie's, New York City, New York, USA, to dealers Robert Schagrin and Peter Siegel. It originally cost $12,000 (£4,200).
A diamond-encrusted bikini, valued at £123,409.90 (US$194,458.97) was unveiled on 22 March 2000 at Windsor Fashion Week by Prestons of Windsor, Berkshire, UK.
In 1983 Sidney Smilove created the world's most expensive swimsuit – made from black nylon and lycra, with 19 diamonds (ranging from 0.5 to 0.003 carat) and 91 cultured pearls riveted in 14-carat gold settings. The swimsuit went on sale for $12,000 (£8,000).

www.guinnessworldrecords.com/marilyn
ACCESS CODE: ‹43411›

a one-month 'finishing' course costing £77,500 ($111,092) in 1998. Students stay at one of London's finest hotels, travel on Concorde and go to the ballet and opera. They also take lessons in etiquette, wine appreciation, and cooking.

MOST EXPENSIVE PEN

The world's most expensive pen is 'La Modernista Diamonds' made by Caran d'Ache, Geneva, Switzerland. The pricey pen was on sale in Harrods, London, UK, for £169,000 ($265,000) from Sept to Dec 1999. The rhodium-coated, solid-silver pen has an 18-carat gold nib and is pavé-set with 5,072 diamonds totalling 20 carats. At the top of the cap 96 half-cut rubies are arranged to form the Caran d'Ache company monogram.

MOST EXPENSIVE HOUSE SALE

Eric Hotung's house at 6-10 Black's Link, Hong Kong, sold for HK$778.88 million (£62,767,500 or $101,909,312) on 12 May 1997 to an anonymous buyer. Eric Hotung is an influential Hong Kong businessman, political adviser and philanthropist.

MOST EXPENSIVE HOUSE PER UNIT AREA

Two Hong Kong properties, known as Genesis and Sky High, were bought by Wong Kwan for £18,793 per m² ($2,826.54 per ft²) in Nov 1997.

MOST EXPENSIVE WEDDING CEREMONY

The wedding of Mohammed, son of Sheik Rashid Bin Saeed Al Maktoum, to Princess Salama, in Dubai in May 1981, lasted seven days and cost an estimated £22 million ($44.5 million). It was held in a purpose-built stadium for 20,000 people. This amount is equivalent to £50 million ($71 million) in the year 2000.

MOST EXPENSIVE WATCH

The Supercomplication, a Patek Phillipe watch that belonged to banker Henry Graves Jr became the most expensive timepiece ever sold when it fetched $11,002,500 (£6,820,450) on 2 Dec 1999 at a Sotheby's auction, New York City, New York, USA.

www.guinnessworldrecords.com/goldtoilet

ACCESS CODE: 56573

AWASH WITH MONEY

The world's most expensive washroom (right) was built by jeweller Lam Sai-wing for £2.4 million ($3.5 million) in his Hong Kong shop. It is made entirely out of gold and precious jewels. The toilet bowls, wash basins, toilet brushes, toilet-paper holders, mirror frames, wall-mounted chandeliers, wall tiles and doors are all made out of solid 24-carat gold. In order to use the toilet, customers must spend at least £140 ($200) in Lam's shop.

GUINNESS WORLD RECORDS

Fashion

LARGEST FASHION SHOW AUDIENCE

More than two million people watched the Victoria's Secret Fashion Show, held at Cannes, France, in May 2000, by booting up and logging on to www.victoriassecret.com. Featuring models Tyra Banks (USA), Karen Mulder (Netherlands) and Stephanie Seymour (USA), it was hosted by Elizabeth Taylor (USA) and Elton John (UK) and raised over £1.25 million ($2 million) for AIDS research.

LONGEST CATWALK

A group of 111 fashion models walked the length of a 1.111 km (0.69 miles) catwalk, built in the Seacon Square shopping centre car park, Bangkok, Thailand, between 27 and 30 May 1998. The 1.8-m-high (5-ft 9-in) catwalk was built in 16 days by 150 workmen, and was sponsored by Anglo-Dutch conglomerate Unilever. When seen from the air, it spelled out the word 'Lux', a Unilever soap brand.

MODEL FEATURED ON THE MOST MAGAZINE COVERS

Claudia Schiffer (Germany) was discovered in 1987 in a German disco at the age of 17 and has modelled ever since. She has graced the

FILLING THE GAP

Don and Doris Fisher (both USA) founded Gap Inc (left) in 1969, after Don had tried to exchange a pair of jeans and found a lack of organized clothes stores selling a sufficient range of jeans. By 2000, Gap had net sales of over £9.64 billion ($13.67 billion), and in May 2001 had 3,676 stores across the USA, Canada, UK, France, Germany and Japan, making it the world's largest fashion-retail chain. It is currently rated No.174 in the *Fortune 500* list, with a profile that has risen in recent years thanks to innovative advertising featuring songs from *West Side Story* and by Madonna (USA).

www.guinnessworldrecords.com/gap
← ACCESS CODE: ‹52438›

covers of more than 500 magazines, including *Elle*, *Harper's Bazaar*, *Vogue* and *Cosmopolitan*. Claudia has also featured on the cover of *Time* Magazine and was the first model ever to feature on the cover of *Rolling Stone* magazine's 10 Most Beautiful Women edition.

MOST EXPENSIVE BRA

The Red Hot Fantasy bra burns a scorching £10.57-million ($15-million) hole in your purse. Created by Victoria's Secret, this explosive little number is alight with over 1,300 precious stones, including 300 carats of blazing Thai rubies set among diamonds. It is home-delivered by security guards in an armoured truck.

HIGHEST HEELED SHOES COMMERCIALLY AVAILABLE

The highest heels commercially available boast a staggering combination of 27.9 cm (11 in) platforms and 40.6 cm (16 in) heels. Available in red or black leather and aptly named 'Vertigo', the shoes sell for a steep £725 ($1,092). UK firm LadyBWear who make the shoes, warn that they cannot be held responsible for any injuries clients may sustain while wearing them.

MOST VALUABLE PAIR OF JEANS

In March 1997 Levi Strauss and Co paid £15,616 ($25,000) to buy a pair of their own Levi® 501® jeans from New York vintage clothing store What Comes Around Goes Around. The jeans were found in a defunct Colorado coal mine and are believed to have been made between 1890 and 1901.

LARGEST SKATEWEAR COMPANY

Vans opened for business in 1966 in California, USA, and by the late 1970s, Vans shoes were the top footwear of choice for the Californian skater community. Today they distribute their skatewear through over 126 company-owned retail stores in the USA and in over 80 countries worldwide.

LONGEST PEARL NECKLACE

A necklace measuring 108 m (354 ft) long, weighing 8.7 kg (19 lb 2 oz) and comprising 14,400 pearls, was assembled in the Japanese town of Ago-cho Yume-kaido with the help of tourists during the town's 1995 Campaign Project.

YOUNGEST HAUTE COUTURE DESIGNER

Yves Saint Laurent (France) began his design career at the age of 17. He first worked as assistant to fashion icon Christian Dior (France), but was named head of the House of Dior when Christian died four years later.

FINANCIAL BRIEFS

When it comes to cool contemporary threads, the brand-conscious bottoms of the world choose Calvin Klein, making it the world's best-selling designer underwear. In 1998 the company sold 30 million pairs of briefs and panties, worth £256 million ($425 million). The brand has been boosted with the help of a select list of celebrities from the worlds of fashion and music, such as Kate Moss (UK), Christy Turlington (USA), Macy Gray (USA), Moby (USA) and Marky Mark (USA) all lending their street-cred to the label. Calvin Klein (USA, left) founded the company in 1968. Although it makes its ready-to-wear women's clothing its flagship, most of its income is actually generated from licensing the name to manufacturers of jeans, underwear and fragrances.

www.guinnessworldrecords.com/ralphlauren

POLO MINT

The biggest-selling designer clothing brand in the world is US-based Ralph Lauren (as modelled by Gisele, Brazil, right), with annual global wholesales of £3.2 billion ($4.5 billion) in 2000. Boasting labels such as Polo Ralph Lauren, Polo Sport and the Ralph Lauren Collection, the company has nearly 240 Polo shops and outlet stores worldwide, and also sells its designs through roughly 1,600 department stores and speciality shops.

Charles Frederick Worth (UK), who died in 1895, is the creator of the oldest designer label. He was the first designer to sign his work with a label and to show garments on live models. Worth moved from the UK to Paris, France, in 1845, where his talent for design was soon discovered by the ladies of the court of Napoleon III. His business continues today through the perfumes of the House of Worth, such as *Worth Pour Homme* and *Je Reviens*.

ACCESS CODE: ‹52317›

In 1962 he opened his own couture fashion house and in the 1970s expanded into ready-to-wear lines, household linens and fragrances.

LONGEST WEDDING DRESS TRAIN

The world's longest wedding dress train measured 204.1 m (670 ft). Made by Hege Solli (Norway) for the marriage of Hege Lorence to Rolf Rotset (both Norway) on 1 June 1996, the train needed 186 bridesmaids and pageboys to carry it.

MOST EXPENSIVE TIARA

The world's most expensive tiara, designed by Gianni Versace (Italy) in 1996, is worth £3.2 million ($5 million), and features 100-carat diamonds set in yellow gold.

LARGEST G-STRING

Unveiled at the Body Shop's UK headquarters on 15 March 2001, the world's largest G-string, a giant red and white cotton thong, was part of Comic Relief's 'Pants to Poverty' fund-raising campaign. It measured 9.2 x 4.6 m (30 x 15 ft).

LARGEST T-SHIRT

The UK's Spring Centre Trust Fund commissioned clothing firm Patz to make a giant white T-shirt measuring 29 m (95 ft 2 in) long and 23.9 m (78 ft 6 in) wide. Big enough to fill a cricket pitch, it was created to raise money for charities that support disabled children.

GUINNESS
WORLD RECORDS

www.guinnessworldrecords.com/humanachievements

human
achievements

early starters

YOUNGEST CONSULTANT
In April 2000 supermarket chain Tesco announced that it had hired seven-year-old Laurie Sleator (UK) to advise senior executives on the Pokémon craze. Laurie receives Pokémon products in return for his services.

YOUNGEST PHYSICIAN
Balamurali Ambati (USA) became the world's youngest doctor on 19 May 1995, when he graduated from the Mount Sinai School of Medicine in New York City, USA, aged 17. He also co-authored a book on AIDS with his older brother when he was 11.

YOUNGEST AUTHOR
Dorothy Straight (USA) was four years old when she wrote *How the World Began* in 1962. It was published in Aug 1964 by Pantheon Books.

YOUNGEST SINGER TO HAVE A NO.1 HIT
French singer Jordy (Lemoine) was just four-and-a-half years old when his single 'Dur Dur d'Etre Bébé' ('It's Hard To Be A Baby') reached No.1 in the French charts in Sept 1993. The song later entered the US Billboard chart.

YOUNGEST MUSICIAN TO PERFORM AT WOODSTOCK
On 23 July 1999 11-year-old Ilan Rubin (USA) became the youngest musician to perform in the 30-year history of Woodstock, kicking off the festival's three-day run in Rome, New York, USA. Ilan is a drummer in the ska-punk band F.o.N. (Freak of Nature), partly founded by his older brother, which he joined aged nine.

YOUNGEST ROCK JOURNALIST
US director/writer/producer Cameron Crowe, who was born in 1957, began a career in journalism at the age of 15, writing for such publications as *Penthouse*, *Playboy* and the *Los Angeles Times*. At 16, he joined the staff of *Rolling Stone* magazine, where he worked as a contributing editor and later as an associate editor, profiling influential musicians such as Bob Dylan, David Bowie and Eric Clapton.

YOUNGEST PERSON TO HAVE A PLATINUM ALBUM
The youngest person to record a platinum album is Billy Gilman (USA), who was 12 years 3 months old when his debut album, *One Voice*, achieved sales of one million in the USA in Aug 2000. He is also the youngest artist to have topped the country sales chart, setting this record two months earlier with the album's title song.

YOUNGEST NBA PLAYER
The youngest ever NBA player was Jermaine O'Neal (USA), who was 18 years 53 days old on the day of his professional basketball debut for the Portland Trail Blazers on 5 Dec 1996.

YOUNGEST WORLD SERIES BASEBALL PLAYER
The youngest World Series baseball player was Fred Lindstrom (USA), who was 18 years 339 days old when he played for the New York Giants (NL) on 24 Oct 1924.

YOUNGEST SOLO CIRCUMNAVIGATOR
David Griffiths Dicks (Australia) was 18 years 41 days old when he returned to Fremantle, WA, Australia, on 16 Nov 1996 after 264 days 16 hr and 49 min at sea.

YOUNGEST PERSON TO CLIMB MT EVEREST
Shambu Tamang (Nepal) is the youngest person ever to ascend Mt Everest. He reached the summit of the 8,850-m-high (29,035-ft) mountain at the age of 17 years 6 months and 15 days, on 5 May 1973.

YOUNGEST RELAY TEAM TO SWIM THE CHANNEL
The youngest six-member relay team to cross the English Channel is the Thane District AAA team from Mumbai (Bombay), India, who swam from Shakespeare Beach, Dover, Kent, UK, to Cap Gris-Nez, France, in 11 hr 23 min on 12 Aug 1996. The team members were Kaveri Thakur (13), Rahul Modi (13), Daniel Reuben (13), Rashmi Sansare (14), Gunjan Parulkar (14) and Siddesh Parab (14).

YOUNGEST PERSON TO HIKE THE APPALACHIAN TRAIL
Michael Cogswell (USA) was just six years old when he hiked the length of the Appalachian Trail with his mother and stepfather in 1980. It took the family eight-and-a-half months to finish the hike. The Appalachian Trail is the world's longest designated footpath, stretching from Katahdin, Maine, USA, to Springer Mountain, Georgia, USA – a distance of approximately 3,476 km (2,160 miles).

YOUNGEST SCHOOL GROUP TO VISIT THE NORTH POLE
On 1 April 1998 eight pupils from Robertsbridge Community College, E Sussex, UK, flew to the magnetic North Pole in Nunavut Territory, Canada, accompanied by two teachers. The students were aged between 13 and 15, and were required to complete research projects while on the expedition.

YOUNGEST PERSON TO VISIT BOTH POLES
Robert Schumann (UK) travelled to the North Pole on 6 April 1992, aged 10, and to the South Pole on 29 Dec 1993, aged 11. He arrived and left the North Pole by air, but reached the South Pole by mountain bike, having flown to within a short distance of his destination. He was accompanied by his father on both trips.

FANTASTIC GYMNASTICS
The youngest female world gymnastics champion is Aurelia Dobre (Romania, above), who won the women's overall world title aged 14 years 352 days in Rotterdam, Netherlands, on 23 Oct 1987. The overall competition involves gymnasts performing in four separate disciplines – beam, vault, floor and uneven bars – with each discipline being marked individually. Inspired by the Romanian champion gymnast Nadia Comaneci, Dobre took up gymnastics at the age of six, making her debut in junior competitions in 1983. Her first World Championship in 1987 was also her most successful competition; she won three gold medals (the team event, the all-round competition and the individual beam competition) and one bronze medal. She competed in the 1988 Olympic Games, winning silver in the team event, and repeated this achievement the following year in the World Championships. Dobre retired in 1990, aged 17, and now works as a choreographer and dance coach.

www.guinnessworldrecords.com/gymchamp

ACCESS CODE: ‹45033›

LINED UP FOR VICTORY

Siobhan Dunn (UK, above) became the world's youngest line-dance champion when she won the Junior World Line Dance Championship in Nashville, Tennessee, USA, at the boot-scootin' age of 6 years 6 months 11 days, in Jan 1998.

Two years later, the world's longest line dance involved 6,275 people (six rows of dancers, each 1.6 km (1 mile) long) in Tamworth, NSW, Australia on 20 Jan 2000, dancing for a total of 6.28 min.

www.guinnessworldrecords.com/linedancechamp

ACCESS CODE:
← ‹53295›

YOUNGEST CHEF

Justin Miller (USA) is the world's youngest chef. He became nationally famous for his cooking prowess at the age of five, and published his own cookbook, *Cooking with Justin: Recipes for Kids (And Parents)*, aged seven. Justin is currently finishing his second cookbook, *Break an Egg*, and advises the Marriot Hotel chain on its children's menus.

www.guinnessworldrecords.com/bowwow

SNOOP PUPPY PUP

Born 9 March 1987, Lil Bow Wow (USA, right) has been rapping since he was five. His single 'Bounce With Me' was the No.1 Rap single for eight weeks according to the Recording Industry Association of America, making him the youngest No.1 solo rapper on the US charts. His single 'Bow Wow (That's My Name)' was at no. 55 on the Billboard Hot 100 singles chart. He was dubbed Lil Bow Wow by multi-million-selling rap superstar Snoop Doggy Dogg.

ACCESS CODE: ‹56520›

YOUNGEST CONCRETE BLOCK BREAKER
USA

David Chu Tan (Germany), trained by his father – a martial arts master – was just 11 years old when he managed to break 24 concrete blocks with his head in 30 seconds, while doing a forward flip – one for each block. He set this record on 20 Dec 2000. David's father had been training David since he was a small child.

YOUNGEST GRADUATE

In June 1994 Michael Kearney (USA) became the world's youngest graduate when he obtained a BA in anthropology from the University of South Alabama, USA, aged 10 years, 4 months.

GUINNESS WORLD RECORDS™

golden oldies

OLDEST ACTRESS

French actress Jeanne Louise Calment (1875–1997) played herself in the film *Vincent And Me* (1990) at the amazing age of 114. The movie is about a young girl who travels through time to 19th-century France to meet the famous painter Vincent van Gogh. Calment was one of the last living people to have known Van Gogh in real life – she met him in 1888. When she died, aged 122, she was the oldest person who had concrete proof of her date of birth.

OLDEST TV PERFORMER

Myrtle Wood (b. 1900 Australia), still appears regularly on Australian television as a model on *Sale Of The Century*. She is best known for the character she played for 17 years – Granny Davis – the housewife who introduced sliced bread to Australian households in 1963.

OLDEST PROFESSIONAL PIANIST

Romanian concert pianist Cella Delavrancea (1887–1991) gave her last public recital at the age of 103 in 1990, receiving six encores.

OLDEST AUTHORS

Sisters and co-authors A Elizabeth and Sarah Louise Delany published *The Delany Sisters' Book Of Everyday Wisdom* in Oct 1994, when Sarah Louise was a spectacular 105 years

FAST AND FURIOUS

Jerry De Roye [UK, left], who was born Gerald Jones in 1927, is the world's oldest wall-of-death rider. He rides a 1927 V-Twin Indian Type 101 Scout motorbike, regularly giving 'trick'n'stunt' performances.

Prince Constantin von Lichtenstein is another death-defying pensioner. On 15 Feb 2000, at the age of 88 years 54 days, he became the oldest person to have successfully ridden the Cresta Run. This 1.2-km (0.75-mile) ice run, in St Moritz, Switzerland, is one of winter sport's legendary challenges. Riders lie head-first on small toboggans to navigate a track that drops some 157 m (515 ft), with a gradient varying from 1:2.8 to 1:8.7. As racers reach speeds of up to 145 km/h (90 mph), extreme skill is required to negotiate the terrifying corners.

www.guinnessworldrecords.com/wallofdeath
← ACCESS CODE: ‹48665›

old and A Elizabeth was 103. Following A Elizabeth's death in 1995, Sarah wrote the sequel called *On My Own At 107*, which was published in 1997 by Kodansha America.

OLDEST ADOPTEE

Born in 1940, Paula Louise Daly Winter Dolan (USA) became the oldest person in the world to be adopted on 5 Nov 1998, at the age of 58 years 5 months and 17 days. Her adopters were her aunt and uncle, John and Elizabeth Winter. Dolan had been disowned by her birth parents nearly 40 years earlier after she married a man of whom they did not approve.

OLDEST PILOT

Cole Kugel (b.1902 USA), is the oldest qualified pilot in the world at 99 years old. He was born one year before the legendary Wright Brothers took to the skies, and has been flying for the last 71 years. Cole is a member of the International Flying Farmers – where he is also the oldest member.

OLDEST WINDSURFER

Charles Ruijter (b.1915) took up windsurfing at the age of 63 in 1978, and is still windsurfing around the lakes of his native Eindhoven, Netherlands. An experienced sailor and rower, great-grandfather Charles is entirely self-taught.

OLDEST COMPETITIVE WALKER

Philip Rabinowitz (b.1904) of Hout Bay, Cape Town, South Africa, is the world's oldest active competitive walker. He regularly competes in races over 20 km (12.5 miles).

OLDEST FEMALE IN-LINE SKATER

The oldest professional female in-line skater is Donna Vano (b.1953, USA). Donna has been competing since 1991, and also takes part in skateboarding and snowboarding competitions. In-line skaters use a U-shaped ramp, from which they perform flips and other manoeuvres.

OLDEST MOTORCYCLIST

On 2 May 2000 Len Vale Onslow rode his motorcycle from his home in Birmingham, UK, to the gates of Buckingham Palace, London, UK, a distance of 194.9 km (121 miles), in order to receive a congratulatory telegram from the Queen – something that is given to every British person who reaches their 100th birthday. Len, who owns a motorbike store, has been riding motorcycles since he was seven years old.

OLDEST CIRCUMNAVIGATOR

In 1994 Fred Lasby (USA) completed a solo round-the-world flight in his single-engined Piper Comanche at the age of 82. Leaving Fort Myers, Florida, USA, on 30 June, he flew 37,366 km (23,219 miles) westwards, making 21 stops and arriving back at Fort Myers on 20 Aug.

OLDEST PERSON TO COMPLETE A MARATHON ON EACH CONTINENT

American Bill Galbrecht (b. 1928) has run a total of 56 marathons, including at least two on each of the seven continents. Most recently, he ran marathons on each of the continents between 1997, when he was 69, and 1999, when he was 71.

OLDEST SOLO TRANSATLANTIC SAILOR

Michael Richey (UK) was 80 years 25 days old when he arrived in Plymouth, Devon, UK, on 31 July 1997, having sailed single-handedly from Newport, Rhode Island, USA. An expert navigator for the British

SPRY AND NOT RETIRING

James Janssen (USA, b. 1921, left) is the world's oldest lifeguard. A retired Catholic priest, he not only guards the pool at the Davenport Outing Club, Iowa, USA, but also teaches swimming and water aerobics.

While Janssen has opted for a change of career in his retirement, other people have simply refused to retire at all. Dr Ishwar C Dalal (b. 1900, India) is the world's oldest practising physician, and has been a doctor since 1935. Leamon Ward (b. 1910, USA) has been cutting hair professionally since July 1927, and is still working four-and-a-half days per week at his one-chair barber's shop in Keystone Heights, Florida, USA, while Dr Valanjattil Kuruvilla Mani (b. 1910, India) has been practicing dentistry since 1935 and continues to do so.

www.guinnessworldrecords.com/lifeguard
← ACCESS CODE: ‹5/631›

Navy during World War II, he has made a number of solo voyages in his boat *Jester* since 1966.

OLDEST PERSON TO CLIMB MT KILIMANJARO

On 11 Feb 1999, aged 71 years 126 days, Dow Prouty (USA) became the oldest person to climb Mt Kilimanjaro, Tanzania, Africa's highest mountain at 5,895 m (19,340 ft). Mr Prouty was accompanied by his son and daughter and took six days to climb to the snowy summit.

OLDEST PERSON TO ABSEIL DOWN A BUILDING

On 25 Nov 2000 great-grandmother Dorothy 'Dos' Williams (UK, b.1916), successfully abseiled down a 30.5-m-high (100-ft) building in Flintshire, Clwyd, UK. Sponsored by the North East Wales Search and Rescue Team, Mrs Williams raised nearly £2,000 ($3,000) for cancer research.

OLDEST PERSON TO MAKE A SOLO SKYDIVE

Retired pilot Herb Tanner (USA) jumped unassisted from a single-engine plane in Cleveland, Ohio, on 19 June 1998, aged 92. He made the 1,067-m (3,500-ft) jump for the first time ever after receiving basic instruction and performing 10 practice jumps on a virtual reality simulator, with no worries about his artificial knees or hearing aid.

OLDEST TANDEM HANG-GLIDER

The oldest person to hang-glide with a tandem partner is Veronica Adams (b. 1904, Australia), who was 94 years 92 days old when she made her flight over Helensburgh, NSW, Australia, on 3 Nov 1998.

OLDEST MALE PARACHUTIST

Norwegian Bjarne Mæland (b. 1899) made his first tandem parachute jump at the age of 100 years 21 days. He jumped from a height of 3,200 m (10,499 ft).

www.guinnessworldrecords.com/cher

CHER MAGIC

The oldest female singer to top the US chart is Cher (USA, right), who was 52 years old when her single 'Believe' reached No.1 in March 1999, staying in this position for four weeks. The song came from the album *Believe*, which was released in 1998 and was the biggest-selling of Cher's long career. Cher also holds the record for having the longest gap between No.1 hits on this chart, with her previous No.1, 'Dark Lady', topping the chart in 1974.

GUINNESS WORLD RECORDS™

epic land journeys

GREATEST DISTANCE DRIVEN IN ONE YEAR

Two Opel Rekord cars, manufactured by the Delta Motor Corporation of Port Elizabeth, South Africa, covered a record distance of 573,029 km (356,063 miles) between 18 May 1988 and 18 May 1989. This is the equivalent of driving around the equator over 14 times. The cars did a daily average of 1,570 km (975 miles).

FASTEST ROUND-THE-WORLD CAR JOURNEY

Jeremy Levine, James Burke and Mark Aylett (all UK) took 19 days 10 hr 10 min (not including the time spent aboard ships) to drive a taxi around the world. Starting at Buckingham Palace, London, UK, on 16 June 2000 and arriving back on 11 Oct 2000, they covered 29,159 km (18,119 miles). They journeyed through France, Italy, Greece, Bulgaria, Turkey, Syria, Jordan, Saudi Arabia, Australia, New Zealand, USA, Spain, crossing the English Channel, Adriatic Sea, Red Sea, Indian Ocean, Tasman Sea, Pacific and Atlantic Oceans.

The first and fastest circumnavigation by car, made under the 1989 and 1991 rules and embracing more than

an equator's length of driving, is held by Neena and Mohammed Salahuddin Choudhury (both India). Their 40,075-km journey (24,901 road miles) took 69 days 19 hr 5 min from 9 Sept to 17 Nov 1989.

FASTEST ROUND-THE-WORLD CYCLE TOUR

Tal Burt (Israel) cycled 21,329 km (13,253 miles) around the world solo in 77 days 14 hr, between 1 June and 17 Aug 1992, starting and finishing in Paris, France. His average daily mileage was 277 km (172 miles).

www.guinnessworldrecords.com/solarcar
← ACCESS CODE: ‹56015›

SUN-DAY DRIVER

The longest solar-powered journey was made by the Radiance solar car (left), which travelled 7,043.5 km (4,376.62 miles) across Canada from Halifax to Vancouver in 29 days from 1 to 29 July 2000. Built by the Queen's University Solar Vehicle Team of Ontario, Canada, to an aerodynamic design, it runs on about as much energy as an average toaster, is less than 1 m (3.2 ft) high and is so flat that the driver literally has to lie down in it. The Radiance's journey cost less than CAN$5 (£2.24), compared with the estimated CAN$3,000 (£1,346.05) fuel costs for the truck that followed as a support vehicle.

Jay Aldous and Matt DeWaal (USA) cycled 22,997 km (14,290 miles) around the world from Salt Lake City, Utah, USA, in 106 days, from 2 April to 16 July 1984.

HIGHEST-ALTITUDE CYCLE RIDE

Siegfried Verheijke, Luc Belet (both Belgium) and Martin Adserballe (Denmark) rode their mountain bikes at an altitude of 7,008 m (22,992 ft) on the snowy slopes of the Muztagata peak in the Xinjiang province of China, on 11 Aug 2000. It took them 14 days to reach the required altitude, carrying their disassembled mountain bikes, which weighed between 10 and 12 kg (22 to 26 lb), on the outside of their backpacks.

LONGEST UNICYCLE JOURNEY

Hanspeter Beck (Australia) unicycled 6,237.96 km (3,876.1 miles) from Port Hedland, Western Australia, to Melbourne, Victoria, Australia, in 51 days 23 hr 25 min, from 30 June to 20 Aug 1985.

LONGEST JOURNEY BY AUTO-RICKSHAW

Between 17 Dec 1999 and 23 June 2000, Ken Twyford and Gerald Smewing (both UK) travelled from Hyderabad, India, to Lancashire, UK, using a 145-cc auto-rickshaw. These are lightweight, doorless vehicles with an average speed of 50 km/h (30 mph) widely used on the Indian subcontinent as taxis. This was a journey of 19,165 km (11,908 miles). Their route took them through India, Pakistan, Iran, Turkey, Greece, Italy, France and England.

LONGEST BICYCLE WHEELIE JOURNEY

Kurt Osburn (USA) travelled 4,569 km (2,839.6 miles) from Hollywood, California, to Orlando, Florida, USA, between 13 April and 25 June 1999. He used a standard 51-cm (20-in) BMX-style bicycle with a customized padded seat and 'fixed' wheel where the pedals pump backwards and forwards, like a unicycle. Osburn made the journey in 80-km (50-mile) stages at around 16 km/h (10 mph).

PENNY FOR THE GUY

The record for the fastest trans-American journey on a penny-farthing bicycle is held by Steve Stevens (left, USA) who cycled from San Francisco, California, to Boston, Massachusetts, from 26 May 2000 to 23 June 2000 on an 1887 Rudge penny-farthing bicycle. It took him 29 days 9 hr and 3 min and he covered a total of 5,238 km (3,255 miles). Steve, 55, averaged an astonishing 180 km (112 miles) per day on a bike with solid rubber wheels and no suspension. With its 1.37-m-tall (54-in) front wheel, Steve's 1887 Rudge Light Roadster was considerably taller than his first bicycle, which he received aged six. Steve restored his penny-farthing himself and says the trans-continental crossing had been his goal since taking up high-wheel cycling in the early 1990s.

www.guinnessworldrecords.com/pennyfarthing
← ACCESS CODE: ‹55918›

LONGEST RUN

Gary Parsons (Australia) ran 19,030.3 km (11,824.8 miles) in 274 days 8 min, beginning and ending in Brisbane, Queensland, Australia, from 25 April 1999 to 25 Jan 2000. He ran around Australia in 197 days 23 hr 49 min on 8 Nov 1999, having covered 14,399.3 km (8,947.3 miles). He then ran around Tasmania before returning to mainland Australia to complete the run. During his run he also set records for the fastest times to complete 10,000 km (6,213 miles): 135 days 9 hr 50 min; 15,000 km (9,320 miles): 205 days 23 hr 18 min; 10,000 miles (16,093 km): 221 days 1 hr 7 min.

SHORTEST TIME TO SKI DOWN MT EVEREST

Ski instructor Davo Karnicar (Slovenia) skied from the summit of Mt Everest to Base Camp in five hours on 7 Oct 2000. He did not remove his skis during the descent from 8,848 m (29,028 ft) to 5,350 m (17,550 ft). It had taken him a month to reach the summit, stopping to acclimatize to the extreme altitude.

LONGEST UNAIDED CROSSING OF ANTARCTICA

Alain Hubert and Dixie Dansercoer (both Belgium) are the first and only men to have crossed Antarctica unaided. The 3,900-km (2,423-mile) journey took 99 days between 4 Nov 1997 and 9 Feb 1998 in temperatures consistently below -10ºC (14ºF). With only skis and a parafoil, they averaged speeds of 45 km/h (28 mph) covering 1,900 km (1,180 miles) over the most favourable 20 days.

FASTEST ANTARCTIC CROSSING

Ranulph Fiennes, Oliver Shepard and Charles Burton (all UK) completed the Trans-Antarctic leg of the 1980–82 Trans-Globe Expedition in 55 days between 28 Oct 1980 and 11 Jan 1981. They used snowmobiles to make the 4,185-km (2,600-mile) journey from Sanae to Scott Base, and reached the South Pole on 15 Dec 1980. Their trip included a break of 17 days while they obtained permission to visit the Pole, and a four-day rest once they arrived there.

LONGEST DISTANCE SOLO CROSSING OF THE ANTARCTIC

Mitsuro Ohba (Japan) walked, skied and parasailed a total of 3,824 km (2,376 miles) across Antarctica in 99 days from 9 Nov 1998. Ohba began on Princess Astrid Coast on the South African side of Antarctica, and was aiming to reach Walgreen Coast on the Chilean side. He was picked up by a plane when bad weather forced him to abandon his attempt 200 km (124 miles) short of his target.

www.guinnessworldrecords.com/messner

ICE 'N' EASY DOES IT

Although there is no easy route up Mt Everest, the south face is acknowledged to be less challenging than the north, with the final ascent passing over the South Col – the major pass between the Everest and Lhotse peaks. However, on this route climbers have to pass through the Khumbu Icefall (right), where unstable, house-sized ice blocks often crash down as a result of the Khumbu glacier moving beneath them.

In May 1978 Reinhold Messner (Italy), one of history's greatest mountaineers, and Peter Habeler (Austria), reached the summit of Mt Everest without supplemental oxygen - via the deadly Khumbu Icefall.

Messner was the first person to climb the world's three highest mountains: Everest, K2 and Kanchenjunga. He has also climbed all 14 of the world's 8,000-m (26,250-ft) peaks.

GUINNESS WORLD RECORDS

air and sea heroes

FASTEST AIR SPEED

The highest aircraft speed was recorded by Captain Eldon W Joersz and Major George T Morgan Jr (both USA) in a Lockheed SR-71A 'Blackbird' on 28 July 1976. The flight took place over a 250-km (155-mile) course near Beale Air Force Base, California, USA, and averaged a speed of 3,529.56 km/h (2,193 mph) – about the same speed as a rifle bullet. In comparison, Concorde cruises at only 2,124 km/h (1,320 mph). A 'Blackbird' has flown from New York to London in 1 hr 55 min, compared with Concorde's average time of around 3 hr 50 min.

HIGHEST HORIZONTAL FLIGHT ALTITUDE

On 28 July 1976, USAF Captain Robert C Helt and USAF Major Larry A Elliot (both USA) reached an altitude of 25,929.031 m (85,073.15 ft) in horizontal flight in a Lockheed SR-71A 'Blackbird' at Beale Air Force Base, California, USA. This is approximately three times higher than the average Boeing 747 cruising at an altitude of 10,660 m (35,000 ft).

LONGEST BANZAI SKYDIVE

On 2 Sept 2000 Yasuhiro Kubo (Japan) jumped from a plane at an altitude of 3,000 m (9,842.5 ft) without a parachute and was in freefall for 50 seconds before hooking on to a parachute that had been thrown out of the plane prior to his jump.

IN AT THE DEEP END

On 13 May 2000 Audrey Mestre Ferrera (France, left) set the women's record for diving without breathing apparatus by descending to a depth of 125 m (410 ft) at Las Palmas, Canary Islands, Spain. She was underwater for a total of 2 min 30 sec.
 The record depth for a man is 152 m (498.7 ft), which was achieved by Loic Leferme (France) on 22 June 2000 in Nice, France.

www.guinnessworldrecords.com/onebreathdive
← ACCESS CODE: ‹55885›

DEEPEST UNDERGROUND BALLOON FLIGHT

On 6 May 2000 Krzysztof Rekas (Poland) used an AX-6 hot-air balloon to ascend the Staszica Chamber of Wieliczka salt mine near Krakow, Poland. Starting from an underground depth of 125 m (410.10 ft), it flew for four minutes, rising to a height of 2.13 m (6.98 ft) above the floor level of the chamber.

The altitude record for a hot-air balloon is 19,811 m (64,997 ft), set by Per Lindstrand (UK) in a Colt 600 hot-air balloon over Laredo, Texas, USA, on 6 June 1988.

LONGEST HUMAN-POWERED FLIGHT

Kanellos Kanellopoulos (Greece) kept his Daedalus 88 aircraft aloft for 3 hr 54 min 59 sec on 23 April 1988 while pedalling the 115.11 km (71.53 miles) from Heraklion to Santorini, Greece. His flight ended when a gust of wind damaged the plane's tail and caused it to crash into the sea.

FASTEST AIRCRAFT CIRCUMNAVIGATION

The fastest circumnavigational flight under the FAI (Fédération Aéronautique Internationale) rules, was 31 hr 27 min 49 sec flown by an Air France Concorde between 15 and 16 Aug 1995. Flight AF1995 flew east via Toulouse, Dubai, Bangkok, Guam, Honolulu and Acapulco from JFK airport, New York, USA.

HIGHEST PARAGLIDER

On 6 Jan 1993 Robbie Whittal (UK) paraglided using bottled oxygen and achieved an amazing height gain of 4,526 m (14,849 ft) at Brandvlei, South Africa. At this record-breaking height, ice would have started to form on his clothing and glider.

LONGEST PARAGLIDING FLIGHT

Godfrey Wennes (Australia) paraglided 335 km (208.16 miles) from Mt Borah to Ennera Station, Australia on 16 Nov 1998.

UP, UP AND AWAY

The first balloon to circumnavigate the globe non-stop was *Breitling Orbiter 3* (left), flown by Bertrand Piccard (Switzerland) and Brian Jones (UK). Taking off from Chateau d'Oex, Switzerland, on 1 March 1999, it set the circumnavigation record in 15 days 10 hr 24 min. The flight continued until 21 March, travelling a total of 40,814 km (25,361 miles) – 739 km (459 miles) longer than the Equator. The entire flight took 19 days 21 hr 47 min, thus also setting the distance and air duration records for a gas and hot-air balloon under FAI rules. The greatest distance for a solo balloon flight is 22,909 km (14,235 miles), set by Steve Fosset (USA). He took off from Mendoza, Argentina, on 7 Aug 1998 but crashed into the Pacific, 804 km (500 miles) off the coast of Australia on 16 Aug 1998.

www.guinnessworldrecords.com/circumballoon
← ACCESS CODE: ‹44059›

FASTEST ATLANTIC CROSSING

The fastest Atlantic crossing was 2 days 10 hr 34 min 47 sec between 6 and 9 Aug 1992 by the 68-m (223-ft) luxury yacht *Destriero* (*Warrior*). The gas turbine-propelled vessel maintained an average speed of 45.7 knots (84.6 km/h or 52.6 mph) despite weighing nearly 400 tonnes (881,848 lb). In comparison, the crossing of the *Mayflower* in 1620 took 66 days, and at the time of the *Titanic* (1912) the fastest crossing was still at least 4.5 days.

FASTEST CROSS-CHANNEL SWIM

Chad Hundeby of California (USA) swam across the English Channel from Shakespeare Beach, Dover to Cap Gris-Nez, France, on 27 Sept 1994 setting a world record of 7 hr 17 min. The fastest France-England time is 8 hr 5 min set by Richard Davey (UK) in 1988.

HIGHEST SPEED ON WATER

On 8 Oct 1978 Ken Warby (Australia) set the official record for the greatest speed on water with a top speed of 275.8 knots (511.11 km/h, or 317.55 mph) in his unlimited hydroplane *Spirit of Australia* on Blowering Dam Lake, NSW, Australia. However, unofficially, he had also achieved the faster estimated speed of 300 knots (555 km/h or 344.82 mph) on 20 Nov 1977.

FASTEST TRANSATLANTIC CROSSING BY ROWING BOAT

Between Oct and Nov 1997 Phil Stubbs and Rob Hamill (both New Zealand) crossed the Atlantic from Tenerife (Canary Islands, Spain) to Barbados in just 41 days in their 6.4-m (21-ft) rowing boat. Despite having to anchor for two days to ride out a 96-km/h (60-mph) storm, they beat the 1971 record by 32 days.

GREATEST DISTANCE BY PEDAL BOAT

Kenichi Horie (Japan) set a pedal-boating distance record of 7,500 km (4,460 miles), between 30 Oct 1992 and 17 Feb 1993, when he crossed the Pacific Ocean from Honolulu, Hawaii, USA, to Naha, Okinawa, Japan.

WALKING ON WATER

In 1988 Remy Bricka (France, above) 'walked' across the Atlantic Ocean on skis 4.2 m (13 ft 9 in) long. Leaving Tenerife, Canary Islands, Spain, on 2 April 1988, he covered 5,636 km (3,502 miles), arriving in Trinidad on 31 May 1988. Remy made his two-month journey on polyester floats, with no fresh water or food supplies, eating plankton on the way. He was suffering from delirium when he arrived. In April 2000 he tried to 'walk' across the Pacific Ocean, from the USA to Australia. However, he encountered problems and had to abandon his plans.

www.guinnessworldrecords.com/oceanwalk

 ACCESS CODE: ← ‹48769›

FASTEST SOLO SAILING CIRCUMNAVIGATION

Michel Desjoyeaux (France) circumnavigated the globe in 93 days 3 hr 57 min 32 sec during the 2000 Vendée Globe single-handed yacht race, starting and finishing at Les Sables d'Olonne, France. He covered a distance of 38,600 km (24,000 miles) in his yacht *PRB* from 5 Nov 2000 to 10 Feb 2001. The Vendée Globe race follows the shortest and most treacherous route around the world – navigating south and around Antarctica before heading back north.

www.guinnessworldrecords.com/ellen

VENDEE GLOBE TROTTER

Ellen MacArthur (UK, right), aged 24, broke the record for the fastest circumnavigation of the globe by a woman when she set a time of 94 days 4 hr 25 min 40 sec and finished second in the 2000 Vendée Globe single-handed yacht race, starting and finishing at Les Sables d'Olonne, France. She covered a distance of 38,600 km (24,000 miles) in her yacht *Kingfisher* from 5 Nov 2000 to 11 Feb 2001. She is also the youngest person to have completed one of the world's toughest sailing challenges.

FASTEST SOLO (UNAIDED) ROW ACROSS PACIFIC

Jim Shekhdar (UK) rowed across the Pacific Ocean in 273 days 13 hr and 12 min, starting from Ilo in Peru on 29 June 2000, and ending near Brisbane, Australia, on 30 March 2001. He made the estimated 14,650 km (9,100 mile) journey without outside support in his 10-m (33-ft) custom-built boat *Le Shark*.

DEEPEST MANNED OCEAN DESCENT

On 23 Jan 1960 Dr Jacques Piccard (Switzerland) and Lt Donald Walsh, (USA) piloted the Swiss-built US Navy bathyscaphe *Trieste* to a depth of 10,911 m (35,799 ft) in the Challenger Deep section of the Mariana Trench. Challenger Deep, situated in the Pacific Ocean, is thought to be the deepest point on Earth.

DEEPEST CAVE SCUBA DIVE

On 23 Aug 1996 Nuno Gomes (South Africa) scuba-dived to a depth of 282.6 m (927.21 ft) at the Boesmansgat Cave, South Africa. He wore seven 88-litre (19-gallon) cylinders, weighing 135 kg (298 lb) and used 54,730 litres (12,040 gallons) of mixtures of air, oxygen, nitrox and trimix.

GUINNESS WORLD RECORDS™

courage and endurance

HEAVIEST BED OF NAILS

On 24 June 2000 Lee Graber (USA) was sandwiched between two beds of nails with a weight of 752.5 kg (1,659 lb) placed on top of the upper bed. He lay between the two beds for a total of 10 seconds.

MOST LAYERED BED OF NAILS

Lee Graber, Todd Graber, Chris Smith and Doreen Graber (all USA) formed a layered four-person bed of nails at Tallmadge, Ohio, USA, on 8 Oct 2000. Lee Graber lay on a bed of nails on the ground, with Todd lying on top of a bed of nails on top of Lee followed by Chris on a bed of nails on top of Todd and finally Doreen on nails on top of Chris. The formation was held for 10 seconds after it had been created, with Lee supporting an estimated weight of 340 kg (750 lb).

LONGEST ONE-BREATH ⬛FI SWIM UNDER ICE

Wim Hof (Netherlands) swam 57.5 m (188.6 ft) under ice in a lake in Finland, on 16 March 2000. Although the water temperature was -6°C (21.2°F), he did not use any special equipment, and wore only swimming trunks and goggles. The record attempt took 1 min 1 sec to complete.

LONGEST DISTANCE CYCLED UNDERWATER

Vittorio Innocente (Italy) cycled 1,200 m (3,937 ft) underwater up and down an Olympic-sized swimming pool in 23 min 54 sec in Chiavera, Italy, on 12 April 2000. Vittorio's mountain bike was weighed down with 35 kg (77.16 lb) of lead, and the tyres were filled with water. The bike was also fitted with four spoilers and two vertical plates to provide stability.

LONGEST ⬛DE UNDERWATER EXERCISE BIKE RIDE

Without the use of any breathing equipment, Benjamin Franz (Germany) was able to clock up a distance of 558 m (1,830 ft 7 in) in 1 min 33.5 sec on a submerged Kettler 'Racer' exercise bike in a single breath on 6 Nov 2000.

LONGEST SUBMERGENCE

Michael Stevens (UK) remained underwater with no rest breaks for 212 hr 30 min from 14 to 23 Feb 1986 using scuba gear and without surface air hoses.

www.guinnessworldrecords.com/longcrawl
← ACCESS CODE: ‹48740›

FRONT CRAWL

The longest continuous voluntary crawl (with one or other knee in unbroken contact with the ground) is 50.6 km (31.44 miles), which was achieved by Peter McKinlay and John Murrie (both UK, left). They crawled around 115 laps of an athletics track, from 28 to 29 March 1992. They broke the previous record by 1.86 km (3 miles) rather than the few yards they had planned because they crawled around the outside, rather than the inside, of the track. They raised over £2,500 ($4,400) for charity. They soaked their knees in methylated spirits and trained for their record attempt for months in advance. Heavy-duty freezer gloves and miners' pads were worn to protect hands and knees, but they were still covered in bruises and blisters by the end.

LONGEST WATER-SKIING SESSION

Ralph Hildebrand and Dave Phillips (Canada) water-skied for 56 hr 35 min 3 sec around Indian Arm, Canada from 10 to 12 June 1994. They water-skied a total of 2,152.3 km (1,337.4 miles) at an average speed of 48 km/h (30 mph). While water-skiing at night, infrared binoculars and spotlights were used.

GREATEST DISTANCE RUN CARRYING A BRICK

Arulanantham Suresh Joachim (Sri Lanka) holds the record for the longest recorded distance run while carrying a 4.5-kg (10-lb) brick continuously in the same ungloved hand in an uncradled downward position. The brick was carried non-stop with no breaks for 126.67 km (78.71 miles) around a circuit of 45 m (147 ft 6 in) at the Florence St Mall Water Fountain, Hornsby, NSW, Australia, between 11 and 12 Dec 1999.

MOST COBRAS ⬛USA KISSED CONSECUTIVELY

Gordon Cates (USA) kissed 11 of the world's most venomous snakes consecutively on 25 Sept 1999. He kissed 10 monacle cobras and one 4.57-m (15-ft) King Cobra.

LARGEST NUMBER ⬛USA OF COCKROACHES IN A COFFIN

On 12 Aug 1999 'Jungle' John Lamedica (USA) was placed in a plexiglass™ coffin wearing only a pair of shorts and had 20,050 Giant Madagascan hissing cockroaches poured over him. He remained in the coffin for a minimum of 10 seconds.

BATHTUB-SITTING ⬛USA WITH MOST SNAKES

Jackie Bibby and Rosie Reynolds-McCasland (both USA) jointly hold the record for sitting in a bathtub with the most live rattlesnakes. On 24 Sept 1999 these two experienced snake handlers sat in two separate bathtubs, each with 75 Western Diamondback rattlesnakes, for a minimum of 10 seconds.

LONGEST TATTOO SESSION

Matt O'Toole (USA) holds the record for enduring the longest tattooing session of 26 hr 49 min. Matt's tattooing began at 10 am on 31 July and ended at 12:49 pm on 1 Aug 2000. The tattoos, applied by tattoo artist Scott Lunn, cover Matt's entire back, thighs, chest, calves, right ankle and right bicep, and include the Chinese symbols for 'pain' and 'suffering'.

FAITH, HOPE AND CHARITY

Terry Fox (Canada, left), who had an artificial leg, ran from St John's, Newfoundland to Thunder Bay, Ontario, Canada, in 143 days from 12 April to 2 Sept 1980, covering 5,373 km (3,339 miles). He raised the greatest recorded amount raised by a charity walk or run – CAN$24.7 million (£9.1 million). At 18, Terry had had his right leg amputated just above the knee due to bone cancer. Nonetheless, he decided to run across Canada to raise funds for cancer research. Unfortunately, Terry's cancer reappeared and he had to stop the run. He died on 28 June 1981, aged 22. His legacy, the annual Terry Fox Run, is the largest one-day cancer research fundraising event. More than 1.2 million people anually participate and, to date, it has raised CAN$270 million (£122.8 million).

www.guinnessworldrecords.com/terryfox
← ACCESS CODE: ‹47821›

LONGEST TIME SPENT BALANCING ON ONE FOOT

Arulanantham Suresh Joachim (Sri Lanka) balanced on one foot for a record 76 hr 40 min from 22 to 25 May 1997. Under the rules, the disengaged foot may not be rested on the standing foot nor may any object be used for support or balance.

LONGEST TIME SPENT MOTIONLESS

Om Prakash Singh (India) stood without moving, except for involuntary blinking, for a continuous 20 hr 10 min 6 sec from 13 to 14 Aug 1997. Singh, who was recovering from chickenpox, started his attempt on the eve of the golden jubilee of India's Independence, as a homage to unknown martyrs.

LONGEST STAY ON MT EVEREST'S SUMMIT

In May 1999 Babu Chhiri Sherpa (Nepal) remained at the summit of Mt Everest (8,848 m or 29,028 ft) for 21 hours without the use of bottled oxygen. Most climbers stay for under an hour. Chhiri, who made 10 successful ascents, climbed Everest just weeks later to become the first person to climb the mountain twice in the same season.

Babu Chhiri Sherpa also holds the record for the fastest ascent of Mt Everest. He climbed from base camp to the summit via the south face in 16 hr 56 min on 21 May 2000. Sadly, he died on Everest on 29 April 2001.

LONGEST LIFEBOAT JOURNEY

In 1916, after his ship, *Endurance*, became trapped by the ice off the shores of Antarctica, Sir Ernest Shackleton (UK) abandoned ship with his 28-strong crew and, using three lifeboats, set course to Elephant Island, 161 km (100 miles) north. Once they were there, he selected five of his best men to direct the largest lifeboat, the 6.85-m-long (22.5-ft) *James Caird*, towards a whaling station in South Georgia, 1,287 km (800 miles) away. In a journey that is still regarded as the greatest in history, Shackleton and his men reached the island after 17 days, on 19 May 1916, from where they sent a rescue ship for their stranded shipmates.

LONGEST CAR PUSH

Daniele Sangion and Giorgio Valente (both Italy) pushed a car 52.47 km (32.6 miles) in 24 hours on a 1,590-m-long (5,216-ft-6-in) track in Caorle, near Venice, Italy, between 17 and 18 Oct 1998. The car was a Fiat Uno 60 (1.1 l) weighing 840 kg (1,851.88 lb).

LONGEST LADDER CLIMB

Ten firefighters from the Bradford Shipley Fire Station, West Yorks, UK, collectively climbed a vertical height of 105 km (65.24 miles) up a standard fire-service ladder in 24 hours from 6 to 7 Oct 2000. The ladder was 10 m (32.8 ft) high; to set the record the team scaled it 10,500 times.

HIGHEST SLACKLINE WALK USA

Darrin Carter (USA) walked 30.4 m (100 ft) on a 2.54 cm (1 in) wide line, 883.9 m (2,900 ft) above the ground at Yosemite National Park, California, USA, on 19 Aug 1999. Slacklining differs from a tightrope walk in that a slackline sags significantly under body weight, whereas a tightrope does not.

LONGEST DISTANCE WALKING ON HANDS

In 1900 Johann Hurlinger (Austria) walked on his hands for 1,400 km (870 miles). In 55 daily 10-hour stints he walked from Vienna to Paris, averaging 2.54 km/h (1.58 mph).

www.guinnessworldrecords.com/iceman

THE ICEMAN COMETH 📺 USA

Wim Hof (Netherlands, right) endured standing in a tube filled with ice cubes for a record 60 min 24 sec on 20 Dec 2000. Wearing only swimming trunks, he stood on a box so that his feet did not end up in a pool of water. Hof uses meditation, yoga and breathing techniques to regulate his body temperature and keep it at a normal 37ºC (98.6ºF), even in extreme cold. Hof has been involved in various extreme outdoor activities for over 20 years, including rock climbing, canyoning, waterfall climbing and ice diving.

ACCESS CODE: ‹56038›

GUINNESS WORLD RECORDS

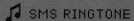

marathon efforts

LONGEST RADIO DJ MARATHON

DJ Greig Daines (UK) broadcast on Hospital Radio Chelmsford, which is based at St John's Hospital, Chelmsford, Essex, UK, for 73 hr 33 min from 6 to 9 Sept 2000. He played a total of 1,086 tracks, the first of which was Boo Radley's 'Wake Up Boo', and the last of which was 'Gold' by Spandau Ballet.

LONGEST RADIO QUIZ

Wilson Casey (USA), a DJ at WKDY-AM radio station in Spartanburg, South Carolina, USA, spent 30 hours asking 3,303 trivia questions on air from 9 to 10 Jan 1999. He used three phone lines for the event and estimated that 6,500 phone calls were fielded.

LONGEST CLAPPING SESSION

The record for continuous clapping (sustaining an average of 160 claps per minute, audible from 110 m (360 ft 11 in away) is 58 hr 9 min, by V Jeyaraman (India) from 12 to 15 Feb 1988. The record was set to raise money for the Rotary Club of Madras North's polio immunization programme, and for the Hindu Mission Hospital, Tambaram, India.

LONGEST KISS

On 5 April 1999 Karmit Tzubera and Dror Orpaz (both Israel) won a kissing contest held in Tel Aviv, Israel with a 30-hr 45-min kiss.

DRUM TILL YOU DROP!

The world's longest drumming marathon lasted for 36 hours, and was undertaken by Steven Darvill (Canada, left) from 31 Dec 2000 to 2 Jan 2001 at Angel Auto Glass, North Vancouver, British Columbia, Canada. He played 490 songs. The team record is 24 hr 15 min, by eight drummers from Cambridge High School, Ohio, USA, from 29 to 30 Dec 2000.

www.guinnessworldrecords.com/drummarathon
← ACCESS CODE: ‹54674›

LONGEST LESSON

A Hungarian language and literature lesson taught at Leõwey Klára Grammar School, Pécs, Hungary, by Szabolcs Zalay, lasted for a record-breaking 24 hours from 18 to 19 June 1999. It was attended by 34 students.

LONGEST MOVIE-WATCHING MARATHON

From 18 to 20 Feb 2000, 14 people managed to watch films for 50 hr 55 min at the Grand Entertainment Global Village cinema in Bangkok, Thailand. The marathon began with an audience of 369 and 74 of them were able to stay awake long enough to break the previous record of 37 hr 25 min.

LONGEST TAI CHI MARATHON

On 15 to 16 May 1999 Robin Nears, Keith Graham and Jo Powell (all UK) completed a tai chi marathon lasting 24 hours at St James Square, Newport, Isle of Wight, UK.

LONGEST STREET THEATRE MARATHON

From 9 to 11 July 1999, 15 members of the Thisaigal Cultural Troupe (India) performed 12 plays on a stage outside Karuna Hospital, Madurai, India, for 57 hr 30 min.

LONGEST STATIC CYCLING MARATHON

Lisa Burke (South Africa) rode an exercise bike for a record-breaking 42 hr 15 min at the Bedfordview Health and Racquet Club, Bedfordview, South Africa, from 11 to 13 Nov 2000.

GREATEST DISTANCE ON A STATIC CYCLE IN 24 HOURS

Between 19 and 20 June 1999 Steven Renata (Australia) achieved a distance of 523 km (325 miles) on an exercise bike. The record was set during the International Fitness and Healthy Lifestyle Expo at the Sydney Expo Centre, Sydney, NSW, Australia.

HAVE YOU GOT THE BOTTLE?

On 22 to 23 April 1998 Ashrita Furman (USA, left) walked a distance of 130.3 km (80.96 miles) around Victory Field track, Forest Park, New York City, USA, with a milk bottle balanced on his head. He continued for 23 hr 35 min, until he broke into a run and the milk bottle fell off. Ashrita Furman has set approximately 60 Guinness World Records – more than any other individual – and currently holds 12, as the others have been broken. A devout follower of spiritual leader Sri Chinmoy, he changed his name from Keith to Ashrita (Sanskrit for 'protected by God') in 1974. Ashrita currently manages a health food shop in Queens, New York City, and also works as the travel co-ordinator for Sri Chinmoy's international peace conferences.

www.guinnessworldrecords.com/bottlewalk
← ACCESS CODE: ‹48721›

GREATEST DISTANCE RIDDEN ON ESCALATORS

Arulanantham Suresh Joachim, who was born in Sri Lanka and now lives in Australia, travelled a total distance of 225.4 km (140 miles) up and down escalators at the Westfield Shopping Centre, Burwood, NSW, Australia, from 25 to 31 May 1998. His ride lasted for 145 hr 57 min. Joachim is currently hoping to set up a charity to help children in need around the world.

GREATEST DISTANCE TRAVELLED ON A POGO STICK

Ashrita Furman (USA) jumped a distance of 37.18 km (23.10 miles) on a pogo stick in 12 hr 27 min on 22 June 1997. The record was set on the running track at Queensborough Community College, New York, USA.

GREATEST DISTANCES TAP-DANCED

David Meenan (USA) tap-danced a record distance of 45.44 km (28.24 miles) in Red Bank, New Jersey, USA, on 31 Aug 1997. He travelled along a 0.8-km (0.5-mile) loop for seven hours, crossing railway tracks and even having a guard hold up a train for him.

MOST SKIPS IN 24 HOURS BY ONE PERSON

Ashrita Furman (USA) achieved 130,000 skips of a rope in a 24-hour period from 23 to 24 Jan 1999. The attempt began at the Sheraton Hotel in Badung, Indonesia, and moved to the nearby Hotel Chedi after six hours. Ashrita took 5-minute rest breaks per hour on a cumulative basis to preserve his strength.

GREATEST DISTANCE BY WHEELCHAIR IN 24 HOURS

Nik Nikzaban, who was born in Iran and now lives in Canada, wheeled himself a distance of 124.861 km (77.58 miles) in 24 hours between 6 and 7 April 2000. The record was set on the running track at Handsworth Secondary School, North Vancouver, British Columbia, Canada. Nik has traversed 31 countries in Europe and Asia, covering more than 60,000 km (37,282 miles) in the process.

FEEL THE BURN!

The greatest distance run on a treadmill in 24 hours is 162.19 km (100.78 miles), achieved by Rory Coleman (UK), who set the record between 17 and 18 Oct 1998. By his own admission, he is a former 'couch potato'. The women's record is 150.5 km (93.5 miles), by Patti Wixom (USA, above) at Gold's Gym, Amarillo, Texas, USA, on 28 March 1998. The idea for the record attempt came from the director of Gold's Gym, who noticed Patti's long training sessions on the treadmill and asked if she would like to try a 24-hour marathon.

www.guinnessworldrecords.com/treadmillrun

 ACCESS CODE: ← ‹51891›

GREATEST DISTANCE ON A SNOWMOBILE IN 24 HOURS

Randy Gravatt and Joe Williams (both USA) covered a distance of 2075.5 km (1,289.7 miles) in 24 hours on trails around Island Park, Idaho, USA, from 27 to 28 Jan 1998.

MOST VERTICAL FEET SKIED IN 24 HOURS

From 27 to 28 Feb 1999, Neal Weisenberg (Canada) skied 46,920 m (153,944 ft) at Kimberley Alpine Resort, British Columbia, Canada. He used a T-bar lift and made 102 runs from top to bottom – equal in distance to five times the height of Everest.

LONGEST BASKETBALL GAME

The longest game of basketball lasting a record-breaking 24 hours was played by the Suncoast Clippers at Maroochydore Eagles Basketball Stadium, Queensland, Australia, from 21 to 22 Nov 1998.

LONGEST CPR MARATHON

The world's longest cardio-pulmonary resuscitation marathon took place between 20 and 26 Sept 1998 at Merry Hill Shopping Centre, W Midlands, UK. Two teams of two – Ben Albutt and Phil Watson, and Robert Cole and Darren Fradgley – performed CPR (15 compressions alternating with two breaths) on a dummy for 144 hours. The men were all members of the West Midlands Ambulance Service.

LONGEST ARCADE MACHINE DANCE MARATHON

Mark e.t. (UK) danced on Konami's Dancing Stage arcade machine for a record eight hours without stopping at the Trocadero, London, UK, on 10 March 1999.

www.guinnessworldrecords.com/londonmarathon

RUN, BABY, RUN

The London Marathon, which has been run through the streets of London, UK, since 1981, raises more money for charity than any other single sporting event in the world. A record-breaking £24 million ($35.8 million) was raised on 16 April 2000, the last Marathon for which figures are available, and over £100 million ($149 million) has been raised altogether. Pictured right is Jerry Hoare (UK), one of 31,542 runners to complete the 2000 Marathon, and one of 445,000 who have completed it since 1981.

ACCESS CODE: ‹52445›

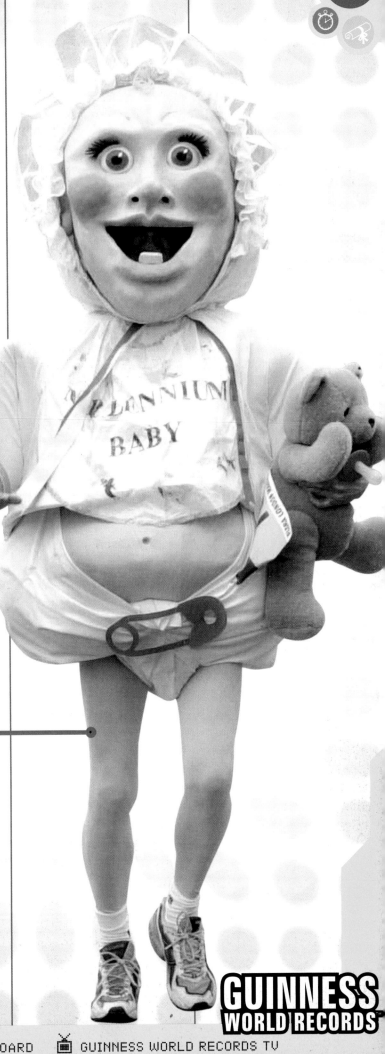

GUINNESS WORLD RECORDS

unusual skills

MOST FOOT-JUGGLING FLIPS OF A TABLE 📺 USA

Chester Cable (USA) flipped a table 3.03 m (9 ft 11.75 in) long, 88.9 cm (35 in) wide and 69.21 cm (27.25 in) high a total of 17 times, using his feet, on 16 Oct 1998.

MOST FOOT-JUGGLING FLIPS OF A PERSON 📺 FR

On 26 Oct 2000 Ali Bandbaz (Iran) 'juggled' his brother Massoud through 12 consecutive 360° revolutions, using only his feet. Ali lay on his back with Massoud sitting on his feet, and the pair completed each revolution in the same position.

LARGEST BUBBLE-GUM BUBBLE BLOWN WITH NOSE 📺 USA

Joyce Samuels (USA) blew a bubble-gum bubble with a diameter of 27.94 cm (11 in) on 10 Nov 2000.

LARGEST BALLOON INFLATED WITH A TANDEM NOSE BLOW 📺 USA

On 10 Nov 2000 Ryan Barker (USA) inflated an 118.11-cm (46.5-in) balloon held in his wife Marilee's mouth by blowing through her nose.

CATAPULT EARS 📺 USA

On 29 Oct 1999 Monte Pierce (USA, left) shot an American 10 cent coin a distance of 3.306 m (10 ft 10.5 in), using his ear as a catapult. This is the furthest a coin has been propelled by an ear lobe. Monte began pulling at his ears as a child to relieve earache, and now, aged 20, can pull them up over his eyes, pull them down to meet under his chin, or roll them up like earplugs. His left ear stretches to a length of 12–12.7 cm (4.75–5 in), and his right ear to a length of 11.4 cm (4.5 in). He has perfect hearing, and doctors assure him that he is not damaging his ears in any way by performing these feats.

www.guinnessworldrecords.com/catapultears
← ACCESS CODE: ‹54633›

LONGEST-DISTANCE MARSHMALLOW NOSE BLOW 📺 USA

The greatest distance that a marshmallow has been shot from one person's nostril and caught in another person's mouth is 4.96 m (16 ft 3½ in). Americans Scott Jeckel (the launcher) and Ray Perisin (the catcher) set this record on 13 Aug 1999.

FASTEST PANCAKE MARATHON

On 24 Oct 1999 Mike Cuzzacrea (USA) ('The Pancake Man') ran the 42.1-km (26.2-mile) Casino Niagara International Marathon in Buffalo, New York, USA, in 3 hr 2 min 27 sec, while flipping a pancake continuously in a frying pan. He came 46th out of 1,319 finishers.

FASTEST SANDWICH MADE USING FEET 📺 USA

On 10 Nov 2000 Rob Williams (USA) made a bologna, cheese and salad sandwich in 1 min 57 sec, using just his feet.

LOUDEST BURP 📺 UK

On 5 April 2000 Paul Hunn (UK) registered a burp of 118.1 dB – similar to being in the front row at a rock concert, and only slightly quieter than the noise made by an aeroplane on a runway.

MOST STEPS CLIMBED ON A BICYCLE

Javier Zapata (Colombia) broke his own world record by hopping up 943 steps on a bicycle, without touching the ground, on 20 May 2000. The feat took him 43 min 26 sec.

FASTEST TIME TO MEMORIZE A PACK OF CARDS

Andi Bell (UK) memorized a pack of 52 shuffled cards and repeated out loud the order in which they appeared in 34.03 seconds on 28 Aug 1998.

LONGEST TIME TENNIS BALL KEPT IN AIR WITH FEET

On 11 Nov 1999 Jacek Guzowski (Poland) kept a tennis ball up in the air, using only his feet, for 5 hr 28 min 59 sec. A counter showed that he touched the ball 35,000 times – an average of approximately 107 times per minute, or 1.8 times per second.

LARGEST SCORPION HELD IN MOUTH 📺 USA

Dean Sheldon (USA) was able to hold a 17.78-cm (7-in) scorpion in his mouth for 18 seconds on 21 Dec 2000.

MOST SCORPIONS IN MOUTH 📺 USA

Dean Sheldon (USA) put a total of 20 scorpions in his mouth, holding them there for 21 seconds, on 21 Dec 2000.

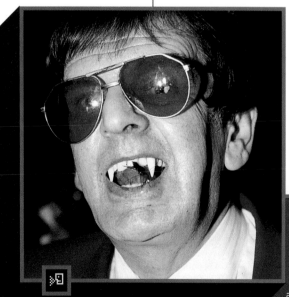

INSECT MORSEL MUNCHIES

Retired rat-catcher and part-time entertainer Ken Edwards (UK, left) ate 36 medium-sized cockroaches, in one minute on 5 March 2001, setting the record for the most cockroaches ever eaten by a human. Eating cockroaches is "like having an anaesthetic at the back of the throat" he says, as they let off a scent to ward away predators. His other bizarre stage acts include stuffing 47 rats down a pair of tights he was wearing, and inviting people to throw darts at a cork placed in his navel.
On 20 Oct 1998 Dr Norman Gary (USA) held 109 honeybees in his closed mouth for 10 seconds – but didn't eat them. Gary is Emeritus Professor at the University of California, USA, where his specialist subject is the behaviour of bees.

HOTTEST METAL IN MOUTH
📺 USA

On 18 Dec 1998 Yim Byung Nam held a silver-dollar-sized piece of metal, heated to 487.8°C (910°F), in his mouth for 14 seconds. When Yim spat it out, it was hot enough to fry bacon.

LONGEST TIME IN A BOX BY THREE CONTORTIONISTS
📺 FR

Bonnie Morgan, Daniel Smith and Leslie Tipton (all USA) fitted into a box measuring 66.04 x 68.58 x 55.88 cm (26 x 27 x 22 in) and stayed there for 2 min 40 sec on 31 Jan 2001.

LONGEST BASKETBALL SHOT MADE WITH HEAD
📺 USA

On 10 Nov 2000 Eyal Horn (Israel) shot a basketball with his head while standing 7.62 m (25 ft) from the backboard. He also scored a record 15 consecutive lay-ups (shooting and catching the ball with the head).

MOST CHERRY STEMS KNOTTED IN ONE HOUR

On 4 Sept 1997 Al Gliniecki (USA) knotted 911 cherry stems with his tongue in one hour – an average of 15 stems per minute.

MOST SKIPS ON A UNICYCLE IN ONE MINUTE
📺 DE

On 31 Aug 2000 Peter Rosendahl (Sweden) who resides in Germany, set the record for the most revolutions of a jump rope made on a unicycle. He managed 169 revolutions in just one minute.

GREATEST DISTANCE TO SPIT A CRICKET
📺 USA

Danny Capps (USA) spat a dead cricket a total distance of 9.17 m (30 ft 1.2 in) on 26 June 1998.

FASTEST HUMAN BEER BOTTLE OPENER
📺 USA

Daniel Lambert (Sweden) used his teeth to open 50 conventional crown-cap bottles on 11 March 2001. He achieved this in only one minute.

FASTEST TYRE FLIPPER
📺 SE

On 31 Jan 2001 in Stockholm, Sweden, Jorma Paananen (Sweden) completed a 20-m (65-ft) course – 10 m (32 ft 6 in) there and back – of flipping a Michelin Radial Steel Cord X26.5R25 (XHA) tyre in a time of 1 min 6 sec. The tyre weighed 420 kg (925.9 lb).

www.guinnessworldrecords.com/archeryfeet

AMAZING FEET OF ARCHERY
📺 USA

Hang Thu Thi Ngyuen (Vietnam, left) set the record for the furthest distance shot with a bow and arrow using the feet. On 12 Aug 1999 she hit a target that was 5 m (16 ft 5 in) away. Thu Hang, whose father is a lighting technician at Ho Chi Minh City Circus, first became interested in circus skills as a child. She spends three hours a day practising her act. Although shy by nature, Thu Hang is very focused and confident on stage.

ACCESS CODE: ‹54641›

GUINNESS WORLD RECORDS

speed stunts

FASTEST BACKWARDS WALK UP MT KILIMANJARO

The fastest time for a solo backwards walk up Mt Kilimanjaro, Tanzania, was 72 hr by Jurgen Gessau (South Africa), from Marangu Gate to Uhuru Peak, between 20 and 23 July 1997.

FASTEST BACKWARDS MILE

Donald Davis (USA) ran 1 mile (1.6 km) backwards in 6 min 7.1 sec on 21 Feb 1983.

FASTEST TRANS-USA BACKWARDS RUN

Arvind Pandya (India) ran backwards from Los Angeles, California, east across the USA to New York City, in 107 days, from 18 Aug to 3 Dec 1984.

FASTEST 8-KM MARCH WITH A BACKPACK

The fastest time in which anyone has run 8 km (5 miles) while carrying a 25.4-kg (56-lb) backpack is 36 min 49 sec, by Paddy Doyle (UK) at the Royal British Legion Runathon, Coventry, Warwickshire, UK, on 9 May 1999.

FASTEST POGO-STICK UP THE CN TOWER

Ashrita Furman (USA) pogo-sticked up the 1,899 steps of the CN Tower, Toronto, Canada, in 57 min 51 sec on 23 July 1999 – approximately one step every two seconds.

MOST STEP-UPS IN ONE HOUR

The most step-ups completed in one hour is 4,135, by Manjit Singh (UK, 'the Ironman of Leicester') on a 38.1-cm (15-in) bench on 4 April 1999.

MOST TRAMPOLINE SLAM-DUNKS IN 30 SECONDS

USA

Mark Odgers, Seth Botone, Shane Geraghty, Joseph Gibby and Ben Ramsey (all US) known as 'the Extreme Team' managed 15 somersaults from a trampoline, with a slam-dunk into a basketball net in 30 seconds on 21 Jan 2001.

FASTEST MIXED TEAM WHEELIE BIN RACERS

On 21 Feb 1999 Aaron Viney and Olivia Jones (Australia) completed a 110-m (361-ft) wheelie bin race in 48.53 seconds at Westfield Devils Junior Soccer Club, Launceston, Tasmania, Australia. The competitors had to sprint 10 m (33 ft) to their stationary bins before taking it in turns to be pulled over 50-m (164-ft) stretches of the course.

FASTEST TIME TO REFUEL

The record time for refuelling an aeroplane with 388.8 litres (85.5 gal) of 100-octane avgas is 3 min 42 sec, which was achieved by the Sky Harbor Air Service line crew for a 1975 Cessna 310 (N92HH) on 5 July 1992. The plane had landed at Cheyenne Airport, Wyoming, USA, during a round-the-world race. It would normally take 10 to 15 minutes to refuel an aircraft of this type.

FASTEST BRIDGE BUILDERS

On 12 Nov 1998 a team of British soldiers from 35 Engineer Regiment, based at Hameln, Germany, constructed a bridge across an 8-m (26-ft 3-in) gap using a five-bay single-storey MGB (medium girder bridge) in 8 min 19 sec.

FASTEST LUMBERJACK TRIATHLON

The fastest time to complete the three disciplines of single buck, underhand chop and tree fall, is 1 min 57 sec, by Werner Brohammer (Germany) on 31 Aug 2000.

FASTEST TIME TO LAY A MILE OF COINS

On 23 May 1998 at Ashbourne, Derbyshire, UK, eight members of the Ashbourne and District Lions Club laid out 79,200 pennies, weighing 0.25 tonnes (550 lb) in 4 hr 2 min.

FASTEST BEER BOTTLE OPENERS

 DE

On 2 April 1999 a team of three people, led by Alois Unertl of the Unertl Brewery, Mühldorf, Germany, opened 300 bottles of beer in 1 min 47 sec. Each person opened 100 bottles before passing the special opener to the next team member.

FASTEST PUMPKIN CARVER

On 16 Oct 1999 Jerry Ayers (USA) carved 914 kg (2,015 lb), of pumpkins in 7 hr 11 min. The officials weighed all pumpkins with the minimum weight being 8.1 kg (18 lb).

Stephen Clarke (USA), carved a face into a 12.47-kg (27.5-lb) pumpkin in 1 min 14.8 sec on 14 Dec 2000.

MOST BALLOON SCULPTURES IN ONE HOUR

On 10 May 1999 in one hour, John Cassidy (USA) used 371 balloons to make 367 different balloon sculptures at Gator's Restaurant, Valley Forge, Philadelphia, USA.

FASTEST HAIRCUT

On 26 Nov 1999 Trevor Mitchell (UK), cut a full head of hair in 1 min 13 sec during the BBC TV South 'Children in Need' event.

FASTEST TYPIST ON A PC

Gregory Arakelian (USA), set a PC typing speed record of 158 wpm in the Key Tronic World Invitational Type-Off, which attracted some 10,000 entrants worldwide. He recorded this speed during the three-minute semi-final on 24 Sept 1991, making only two errors.

FASTEST TIME TO MAKE A TV COMMERCIAL

A television commercial lasting 35 seconds advertising for the non-profit foundation Creative for Children, made by Thomsen AG of

TREE-MENDOUS TREE CLIMBERS

The fastest time in which anyone has climbed a 9-m (29-ft 6-in) coconut tree barefoot is 4.88 seconds, by Fuatai Solo (Fiji) at the annual Coconut Tree Climbing Competition in Sukuna Park, Fiji, on 22 Aug 1980. Climbing at this speed, Solo would be able to scale the Empire State Building, New York City, USA, in just over four minutes. He was so pleased with his win – the third in succession – that he climbed the tree again, clutching the prize money of $100 (£43) in his mouth.

The record time for fir-tree climbing is held by Guy German (USA) who climbed up a 30.5-m (100-ft) fir spar pole, and down again, in 24.82 seconds during the 1988 World Championship Timber Carnival in Albany, Oregon, USA. German also holds the record for tree topping, climbing up a spar pole of the same height and sawing off the top, which he achieved in an amazing 53.35 seconds in July 1989.

www.guinnessworldrecords.com/treeclimb

← ACCESS CODE: <48689>

KEN HE DO IT? YES, HE CAN!

Ken Moss (UK, above), who lost his sight in 1992, set the blind land speed record of 210.82 km/h (131 mph) in a single-seater prototype MG EXF car on 16 Oct 1999, at Boscombe Down, Wilts, UK. Sensors on the car gave guidance information to headphones in Ken's helmet, with bleeps in each ear telling him which way to steer.

www.guinnessworldrecords.com/
blinddriver

  ACCESS CODE: ← ‹55410›

Kiel, Germany, was created, filmed and aired in a record-breaking 1 hr 19 min on 4 Nov 1999.

FASTEST WINDOW CLEANER

Terry Burrow (UK), cleaned three standard 1,143 x 1,143-mm (45 x 45-in) office windows set in a frame with a 300-mm (11.81-in) long squeegee and 9 litres (2 gal) of water in 9.91 sec on 7 March 2001. The time taken to complete the windows was 8.91 sec, but two faults, each with a 0.5-second penalty, increased the overall time.

FASTEST RECITAL OF HAMLET'S SOLILOQUY

Sean Shannon (Canada) recited Hamlet's soliloquy 'To be or not to be' (260 words) in 23.8 sec (655 words per minute) on 30 Aug 1995.

FASTEST 10-KM PRAM PUSHING

The fastest time to complete the 10 km (6.2 miles) pram pushing race is 34 mins 26 secs by Mal Grimmett pushing his daughter Natalie, at the 1999 Olympic Dream fun run, Melbourne, Australia, on 21 Nov 1999.

www.guinnessworldrecords.com/rocketluge

ROCKET MAN 📺USA

Billy Copeland (USA, below) reached a record speed of 112.65 km/h (70 mph) on his rocket-powered street luge at Bakersfield, California, USA, on 15 May 1998.

A street luge is essentially a skateboard designed to be ridden lying down. Longer and wider than conventional boards, with bigger wheels, street luges are ridden feet-first by riders who kit up in leather motorcycle clothing and crash helmets to protect themselves from harm if they tumble off at speed. The straighter the road, the faster the luge can go. For his record attempt, Copeland used eight rockets, but he has since tested 24 rockets attached to a set of triangular wings at the back of his luge. His ambition is to become the first street-luge rider ever to reach 160 km/h (100 mph). The rockets that he uses are similar to those used by hobbyists to launch rockets over 1.6 km (1 mile) into the air.

ACCESS CODE: ‹5394›

GUINNESS WORLD RECORDS™

tests of strength

HEAVIEST HEAD BALANCE
The heaviest combined weight ever balanced on a person's head in one hour is 5,180.09 kg (11,422 lb). This record was achieved by John Evans (UK) on 23 July 2000 when, in the course of an hour, he balanced 92 people in succession on his head for at least 10 seconds each.

HEAVIEST WEIGHT LIFTED WITH A HUMAN BEARD
Using only his beard, Antanas Kontrimas (Lithuania) lifted a total weight of 59 kg (130.2 lb) – the combined weight of a girl and the harness she was in – off the ground for 10.93 seconds on 11 March 2001.

HEAVIEST VEHICLE HAIR PULL   UK
On 1 May 1999 at Bruntingthorpe Proving Ground, Leicestershire, UK, Letchemanah Ramasamy (Malaysia) pulled a Long Version Routemaster double-decker bus weighing 7,874 kg (17,362 lb) over a distance of 32.85 m (107 ft 9.5 in) using just his hair.

GREATEST WEIGHT BALANCED ON TEETH   UK
Frank Simon (USA) balanced a 61.23-kg (135-lb) motorcycle, including a helmet, on his teeth for 14 seconds on 27 April 1999, with only a tooth guard as protection.

MOST CONCRETE BLOCKS BROKEN WHILE LYING ON A BED OF NAILS   UK
On 27 April 2000 Paul Evans (UK) piled 26 concrete blocks weighing 129.72 kg (286 lb) on to his chest while lying on a bed of nails measuring 50.8 x 55.8 cm (20 x 22 in). The blocks were then smashed with a 14-lb (6.35-kg) sledgehammer. A karate teacher, Paul began training in martial arts as a Royal Marine in 1967 and first started performing on a bed of nails in 1979.

HEAVIEST TRAIN PULLED
On 1 June 1999 strongman Juraj 'Duri' Barbaric (Slovakia) single-handedly pulled a 20-freight-car train full of scrap metal weighing 1,000 tonnes (2 million lb) a distance of 4.5 m (14 ft 9 in) along a railway track at Kosice, Slovakia. On the day, he warmed up by pulling 300 tonnes (590,520 lb) for 3 m (10 ft), then 900 tonnes (1,771,580 lb) for 2.95 m (9.6 ft).

MOST CARS LIFTED
On 3 Oct 1998 Mark Anglesea (UK) lifted the rear end of a Rover Mini Metro clear off the ground 580 times in one hour – an average of almost 10 lifts a minute, in Yorkshire, UK.

HEAVIEST ONE-ARM TRUCK-PULL   FR
On 29 March 2000 William Deandreis (France) pulled a 3,128 kg (6,896 lb) truck 1.5 m (5 ft) using only a single downward arm-wrestling move.

HEAVE HO!
The record for the most tug-of-war pulls in one hour by three teams was broken by 30 members of the Holland Tug-of-War Club (UK, left) on 6 June 2000. The three teams of 10 – symbolizing the Staffordshire club's first 30 years – lifted a 425-kg (937-lb) weight (using a training rig) a total of 80 times in one hour. Each pull was over a distance of 6.86 m (22 ft 6 in). The teams took turns at the rope, and between them lifted the equivalent of a total of 34,000 kg (74,957 lb). Gantries or rigs are widely used by tug-of-war clubs for training and are trestle-like structures under which a weight is suspended by pulleys. A popular rural pastime in many parts of the world, tug-of-war was an Olympic event between 1900 and 1920.

www.guinnessworldrecords.com/tugofwar
ACCESS CODE: ‹55911›

MOST BOAT LIFTS   FI
Sami Heinonen and Juha Räsänen (both Finland) continuously lifted a boat and 10 cheerleaders with a combined weight of 653.2 kg (1,440 lb) a total of 24 times on 9 Oct 2000 (in Helsinki, Finland). The boat, a Buster XS, weighing 151 kg (332 lb), was lifted in an up-and-down motion to touch a bar 10 cm (4 in) high, ensuring the same distance was lifted every time.

HEAVIEST BOAT PULL   DE
On 19 Nov 1998 David Huxley (Australia), pulled the 1,006-tonne (20,012-lb) boat *Delphin*, with 175 cars and passengers, over 25 m (82 ft) in Rostock, Germany.

TIGHTEST FRYING PAN ROLL   USA
Craig Pumphrey (USA) rolled a 30-cm (12-in) aluminium pan with his bare hands to a circumference of 23.5 cm (9.25 in) in 30 seconds on 16 Oct 1999.

LONGEST FIRE WALK   UK
Gary Shawkey (USA) took 31 seconds to walk 50.29 m (165 ft) over burning embers of cedarwood with an average temperature of 1,800°F (982.22°C) at the Central Florida Fair in Orlando, Florida, USA, on 4 March 2000.

MOST TELEPHONE DIRECTORIES TORN
Amanda Brutus (UK) tore nine *Yellow Pages* telephone directories from top to bottom in three minutes at the Alliance & Leicester Group Property Services and Giro Services in Bootle, Liverpool, UK, on 17 Nov 2000 in aid of the BBC TV *Children in Need* charity appeal. The exact time in which she set this record was 2 min 52.46 sec. Each book contained 1,007 pages.

MOST TYRES SUPPORTED
Gary Windebank (UK), supported 96 Michelin motor tyres in a free-standing 'lift' in Feb 1984. The total weight was 653 kg (1,440 lb). The tyres used were Michelin XZX 155x13.

KEEP ON TRUCKING
The one-hour team truck-pulling record was broken by 20 Atlas Gym Power Team strongmen (left) who pulled a 15.966 tonne (31,932 lb) dump truck a distance of 5.31 km (3.3 miles) in one hour on 29 Oct 2000 in Kenosha, Wisconsin, USA. Gym owner Rhett Bobzien had the inspiration for this record while watching a strongman competition on TV. He went back to his gym and recruited 20 bodybuilders, all weighing over 90 kg (198.5 lb), and for weeks before the event Kenosha residents were treated to the sight of teachers, businessmen, factory workers and law enforcement officials pulling their cars and pickup trucks around town. On the big day 10 men would pull while 10 would rest, but importantly, the pull didn't stop for the changeover.

www.guinnessworldrecords.com/truckpull
ACCESS CODE: ‹56088›

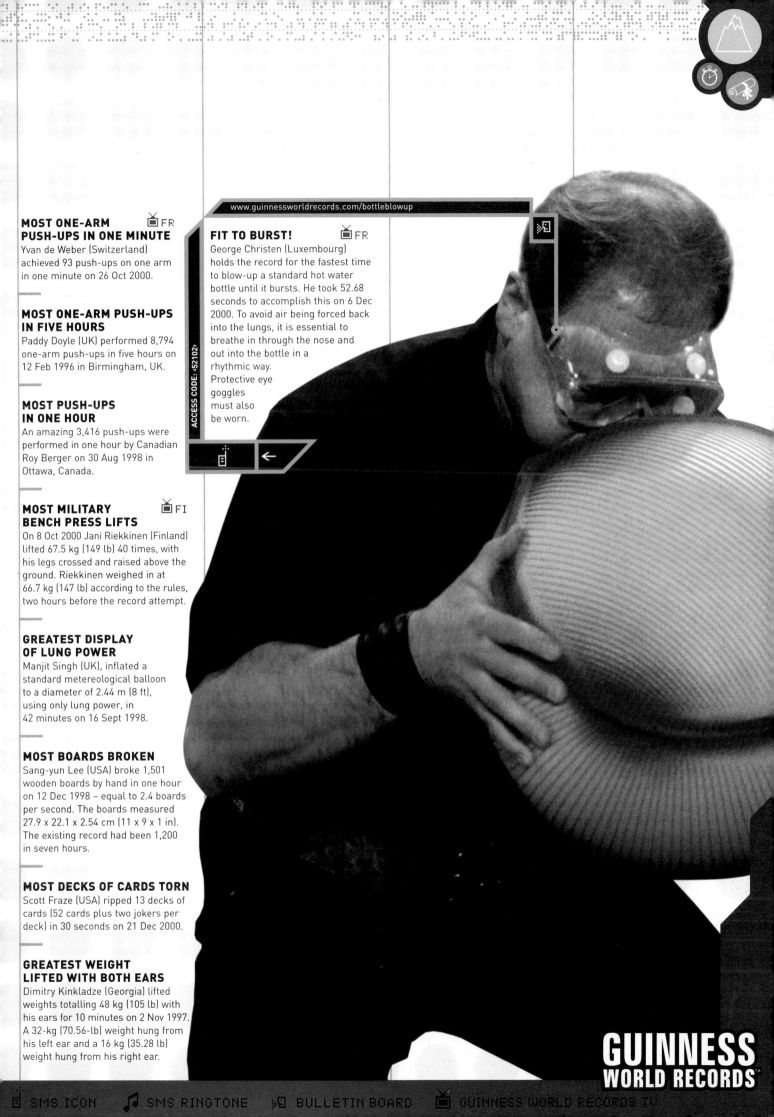

MOST ONE-ARM PUSH-UPS IN ONE MINUTE
📺 FR

Yvan de Weber (Switzerland) achieved 93 push-ups on one arm in one minute on 26 Oct 2000.

MOST ONE-ARM PUSH-UPS IN FIVE HOURS

Paddy Doyle (UK) performed 8,794 one-arm push-ups in five hours on 12 Feb 1996 in Birmingham, UK.

MOST PUSH-UPS IN ONE HOUR

An amazing 3,416 push-ups were performed in one hour by Canadian Roy Berger on 30 Aug 1998 in Ottawa, Canada.

MOST MILITARY BENCH PRESS LIFTS
📺 FI

On 8 Oct 2000 Jani Riekkinen (Finland) lifted 67.5 kg (149 lb) 40 times, with his legs crossed and raised above the ground. Riekkinen weighed in at 66.7 kg (147 lb) according to the rules, two hours before the record attempt.

GREATEST DISPLAY OF LUNG POWER

Manjit Singh (UK), inflated a standard metereological balloon to a diameter of 2.44 m (8 ft), using only lung power, in 42 minutes on 16 Sept 1998.

MOST BOARDS BROKEN

Sang-yun Lee (USA) broke 1,501 wooden boards by hand in one hour on 12 Dec 1998 – equal to 2.4 boards per second. The boards measured 27.9 x 22.1 x 2.54 cm (11 x 9 x 1 in). The existing record had been 1,200 in seven hours.

MOST DECKS OF CARDS TORN

Scott Fraze (USA) ripped 13 decks of cards (52 cards plus two jokers per deck) in 30 seconds on 21 Dec 2000.

GREATEST WEIGHT LIFTED WITH BOTH EARS

Dimitry Kinkladze (Georgia) lifted weights totalling 48 kg (105 lb) with his ears for 10 minutes on 2 Nov 1997. A 32-kg (70.56-lb) weight hung from his left ear and a 16 kg (35.28 lb) weight hung from his right ear.

www.guinnessworldrecords.com/bottleblowup

FIT TO BURST!
📺 FR

George Christen (Luxembourg) holds the record for the fastest time to blow-up a standard hot water bottle until it bursts. He took 52.68 seconds to accomplish this on 6 Dec 2000. To avoid air being forced back into the lungs, it is essential to breathe in through the nose and out into the bottle in a rhythmic way. Protective eye goggles must also be worn.

ACCESS CODE: ‹52102›

GUINNESS
WORLD RECORDS™

mass participation

MOST CHILDREN ON SPACE HOPPERS

On 23 Oct 2000, to mark the launch of the *Guinness World Records* website, 520 children bounced simultaneously down Wembley Way, London, UK, on 520 rubber space hopper toys.

LOUDEST CROWD ROAR AT AN OUTDOOR SPORTS STADIUM

On 1 Oct 2000, during an NFL game between the Denver Broncos and the New England Patriots at the 76,123-seat Mile High Stadium in Denver, Colorado, USA, a crowd roar was measured at 128.7 dB. In comparison, a car horn measures 110 dB and a rock concert generates 120 dB.

LARGEST 'YMCA' DANCE

On 1 Nov 1997, 6,907 students from Southwest Missouri State University, Springfield, Missouri, USA, danced to the song *YMCA* for five minutes while it was performed live by the famous group Village People. The record was set in the university's Plaster Stadium.

LARGEST HUG

The record for the world's largest hug was set by 899 bankers from Goldman Sachs during their IBD Global

CHICKENED OUT

An estimated 72,000 people took part in the world's largest Chicken Dance, which was staged during the Canfield Fair, Canfield, Ohio, USA, on 1 Sept 1996. The record was set as part of the Fair's 150th anniversary celebrations, and was chosen because the Fair's mascot and logo is a rooster. For 10 minutes, all rides were paused and all vendors stopped working to dance to music blaring from sound systems. The crowd was led by the rooster mascot, members of the Fair's board and a group of cheerleaders. Uniformed Springfield Township firefighters danced on top of a vintage fire truck, and many people even carried chickens as they danced.

www.guinnessworldrecords.com/chickendance
← ACCESS CODE: ‹50475›

Conference in the huge ballroom of the Hilton International, New York City, USA, on 1 Dec 2000. The slogan for the event was 'One Team, One Hug'.

LARGEST TEA PARTY

On 28 Oct 2000, 465 people gathered aboard the cruiser *The Spirit of Boston* on the Charles River, Boston, Massachusetts, USA, to break the record for the world's largest tea party. A total of 323.4 litres (71.14 gallons) of tea were consumed – or approximately 1,138 cups.

MOST PEOPLE CRAMMED ON A BUS

On 23 Oct 2000 a record-breaking 110 people crammed themselves onto a single decker bus outside Cynthia's Bar and Restaurant, London, UK. The record was set as part of the launch of the *Guinness World Records* website.

LARGEST EASTER EGG HUNT

The world's largest ever Easter egg hunt took place on 20 March 1999, during the Vision Australia Foundation's annual Easter Fair at Kooyong, Vic, Australia. A total of 150,000 solid chocolate eggs were found by the 3,000 volunteers – this is an average of 50 eggs each. The hunt was so large that army troops had to be brought in to hide the eggs within the giant field of hay.

MOST PEOPLE WALKING ON STILTS

During the Zancothon '99 parade in Santiago de Cali, Colombia, on 25 July 1999, 152 people aged six to 37 walked on stilts for 3 km (1.86 miles).

LARGEST ACCORDION ENSEMBLE

The world's largest accordion ensemble consisted of 566 musicians playing the accordion for 22 minutes. The record was set during the International Folklore Festival in Diepenheim, Netherlands, on 1 June 2000, and was organized by the Stedeker Dansers (Netherlands).

LARGEST JAPANESE DRUM ENSEMBLE

On 9 Aug 1998 a record total of 1,850 musicians gathered to play *Yamabiko* on 1,845 Japanese drums at Irie Stadium, Muroran City, Japan. The 25-minute concert was held outside as the noise of the drums would have broken the windows of an indoor venue.

LARGEST ORCHESTRA

On 15 May 2000 the world's largest orchestra, consisting of 6,452 student and professional musicians, all assembled at BC Place Stadium, Vancouver, British Columbia, Canada, to play *Ten Minutes Of Nine*,

SEEING DOUBLE?

On 12 Nov 1999 – a national holiday marking the birth of Sun Yatsen, the first president of the Republic of China – a total of 3,961 pairs of twins gathered on the square of Taipei City Hall, Taiwan, to break the record for the largest gathering of twins. The event was organized by the Mayor of Taipei, Ma Ying-Jeou, and was meant to lift people's spirits following a large earthquake two months earlier. The twins came from as far away as the UK, Germany, India and the USA, and ranged in age from one month to 88 years. National celebrities were also present, along with 37 sets of triplets and four sets of quadruplets. The participants lined up in a tree formation to symbolize the regrowth of areas damaged by the earthquake.

an arrangement from Beethoven's Ninth Symphony. The orchestra was conducted by Bramwell Tovey, the music director of the Vancouver Symphony Orchestra.

LARGEST BARBECUE
On 10 Oct 1993 a record 44,158 people attended a barbecue at Warwick Farm Racecourse, Sydney, NSW, Australia. More than 300,000 sausages, 100,000 steaks and 50,000 chicken burgers were consumed, and over 481,000 cans of beer drunk. This is equivalent to 6.7 sausages, 2.25 steaks, 1.13 chicken burgers and a whopping 10.89 cans of beer per person.

MOST PEOPLE SCUBA DIVING
On 17 April 1999, at Saipan, Northern Mariana Islands (in the western Pacific Ocean), 215 people set a record for scuba diving at the same time and at the same location.

LARGEST GAY FESTIVALS
The Lesbian Gay Bisexual Transgender Pride Parade in San Francisco, California, USA, and the Sydney Gay and Lesbian Mardi Gras in Sydney, NSW, Australia, each attract a minimum of 600,000 people annually.

MOST PARTICIPANTS IN A ONE-HOUR SWIMATHON
A record 2,533 people participated in BT Swimathon 2000, which took place at over 500 swimming pools across the UK between 6 and 7 pm on 18 March 2000.

MOST PEOPLE BUNGEE JUMPING IN 24 HOURS
On 26 Oct 2000, 505 people bungee jumped at the AJ Hackett Bungy site at Cairns, Qld, Australia – that is one bungee jump every 2.85 minutes.

www.guinnessworldrecords.com/tomatina

USA

KILLER TOMATO ATTACK!
On the last Wednesday in August, the town of Buñol, near Valencia, Spain, holds the world's largest food fight – its annual tomato festival, known as the *Tomatina*. At the 1999 event, 25,000 people spent one hour hurling approximately 120 tonnes (264,554 lb) of tomatoes at each other. The festival begins when the crowd cuts down a Serrano ham tied to the top of a greasy pole. Tomatoes are then dumped on to the streets from the backs of lorries for participants to scoop up and throw at one another. By the time the food fight is finished, the town is completely saturated with sticky tomato paste, with rivers of tomato juice running down the streets. Finally, fire trucks hose down roads and buildings, while people head down to makeshift public showers by the river. The *Tomatina* began by chance in 1944, when a lorry accidentally discharged its load of tomatoes.

ACCESS CODE: ‹49067›

GUINNESS WORLD RECORDS

teamwork

CHECKMATE

On 22 Oct 2000, 10,004 people set the record for the most people playing chess simultaneously as part of the Second Mexico City Chess Festival (above), a government initiative to bring cultural events out onto the streets for the people of the city. A team of 450 Mexican chess masters each played 20 to 25 members of the public, with 81% of the games won by the Masters, 13% won by the public and 6% drawn. The festival opened at 10 am and the last game finished at 5 pm.

A national Mexican record was also established for the largest human logo representing an enormous chessboard. The previous record (made the previous year at the same event) was for 5,046 players.

The record for the most consecutive chess games played by one person is held by Willem van Roosmalen (Netherlands), who played 719 games from 6 to 7 Nov 1998. He won 650, drew 37 and suffered only 32 defeats.

www.guinnessworldrecords.com/masschess
← ACCESS CODE: ‹55923›

LARGEST MEXICAN WAVE

The largest Mexican wave was performed on 24 June 2000 by 3,276 people. Organized by the West Sussex County Council Youth Service and the West Sussex Council for Voluntary Youth Services (both UK), the wave took seven minutes to complete and stretched for almost 5 km (3 miles).

MOST BAKED BEANS EATEN IN TWO MINUTES

On 17 Nov 2000 a team of four people living in television's *Big Brother* house in Vilvoorde, Belgium, ate a total of 335 baked beans in two minutes – an average rate of nearly 42 baked beans (spiked and eaten one at a time) – every minute.

MOST VETS INVOLVED IN AN OPERATION

In Aug 1999 over 30 vets operated on Motola, a 38-year-old cow elephant who lost her left foot after stepping on a land mine on the Thai-Burma (Myanmar) border. It took Motola three days to cover the 95.56 km (60 miles) to reach the Hang Chat Elephant Hospital in Lampang, Thailand. Enough anaesthetic to knock out 70 humans was used to put her to sleep. Vets at the Lampang Hospital said they were the worst wounds that they had ever seen at the medical centre. Motola's operation cost £64,571.70 ($105,000), and was paid for by public donation. Animal experts hoped that once Motola had recovered from her surgery they would be able to fit a prosthetic device to enable her to walk again. Elephants are cultural icons in Thai culture.

MOST RECONSTRUCTIVE SURGERY UNDERTAKEN BY A MEDICAL TEAM

Between 5 Feb and 14 April 1999, a team of volunteer doctors treated 5,139 patients in 18 countries as part of Operation Smile's 'World Journey of Hope'. The doctors repaired cleft lips and cleft palates as well as operating on facial burns, tumours and injuries. Operation Smile was founded in 1982 by Bill Magee, a plastic surgeon, and his wife Kathy, a nurse, in Norfolk, Virginia, USA.

LARGEST CIVILIAN AID CONVOY

Between 1 and 4 Dec 1992, a convoy of 105 privately owned vehicles travelled from Dover, UK, to Zagreb, Croatia, carrying donated food and other aid to refugees of the Bosnian war. The round trip was nearly 3,200 km (2,000 miles) long and was accompanied by a 3.2-km (2-mile) police escort through Slovenia.

LONGEST STRETCHER-BEARING DISTANCE

Between 27 and 30 May 1996, two teams of four men from 1 Field Ambulance, Canadian Forces Base, Calgary, Canada, carried a stretcher bearing a 63.5-kg (140-lb) 'body' a distance of 300.4 km (186.66 miles). They began in Edmonton, Alberta, and finished in Calgary, Alberta, 59 hr 19 min later.

LONGEST COAL-CARRYING DISTANCE

A team of eight men carried a 100-weight bag of coal (50.8 kg or 112 lb) over a distance of 128.7 km (80 miles) in 11 hr 28 min 33 sec on 20 May 2000. The team did 387 laps of a 333-m (1,092.52-ft) circuit of the Dewsbury Hospital car park, West Yorks, UK – just over 48 laps each.

FURTHEST 24-HOUR PRAM PUSH

Between 22 and 23 Nov 1990, a 10-man team from the Royal Marines School of Music, Deal, Kent, UK, pushed a pram containing an adult 'baby' for 24 hours over a distance of 437.3 km (271.7 miles).

FURTHEST 24-HOUR WHEELCHAIR PUSH

Between 13 and 14 Sept 1999, 88 volunteers pushed wheelchair-bound Ian Kershaw and Keith Matthews (both UK) around the track of the Copeland Athletic Stadium, Cumbria, UK, covering a distance of 348.2 km (216 miles 656 ft 2 in).

FURTHEST 24-HOUR LAWNMOWER PUSH

Between 13 and 14 Sept 1997, a team of four members of the Stowmarket and District Round Table, Suffolk, UK, pushed a standard lawnmower a distance of 162.93 km (101 miles 429 yd) in 24 hours.

LARGEST GAME OF LEAPFROG

On 8 Oct 2000, 222 people, organized by Discovery Creek Children's Museum, participated in a single game of leapfrog at Glen Echo Park, Maryland, USA.

FASTEST YOUTH WOOLSACK-RACING TEAM

A youth team from Sir William Romney School sixth form completed the World Woolsack Championship race in a time of 3 min 20.01 sec in 1997 – faster than the men's team championship record of 3 min 27.34 sec set in 1991. The event, held annually at Tetbury, Glos, UK, involves teams of four relaying up and down a steep hill while carrying a 27.21-kg (60-lb) bag of wool on their shoulders.

MOST FOUR-WAY SKYDIVING FORMATIONS IN 35 SECONDS

On 23 Sept 1999, Daniel Brodsky-Chenfeld, Jack H Jeffries, Mark Kirkby and Kirk Verners (all USA), all members of the Airspeed Arizona team, performed a record 39 skydiving formations in 35 seconds – less than one second for each formation – while falling at speeds approaching 240 km/h (150 mph) from a height of 3,050 m (10,000 ft). According to FAI (Fédération Aéronautique Internationale) rules, formations may be random but the skydivers must lose complete physical contact with each other between each formation.

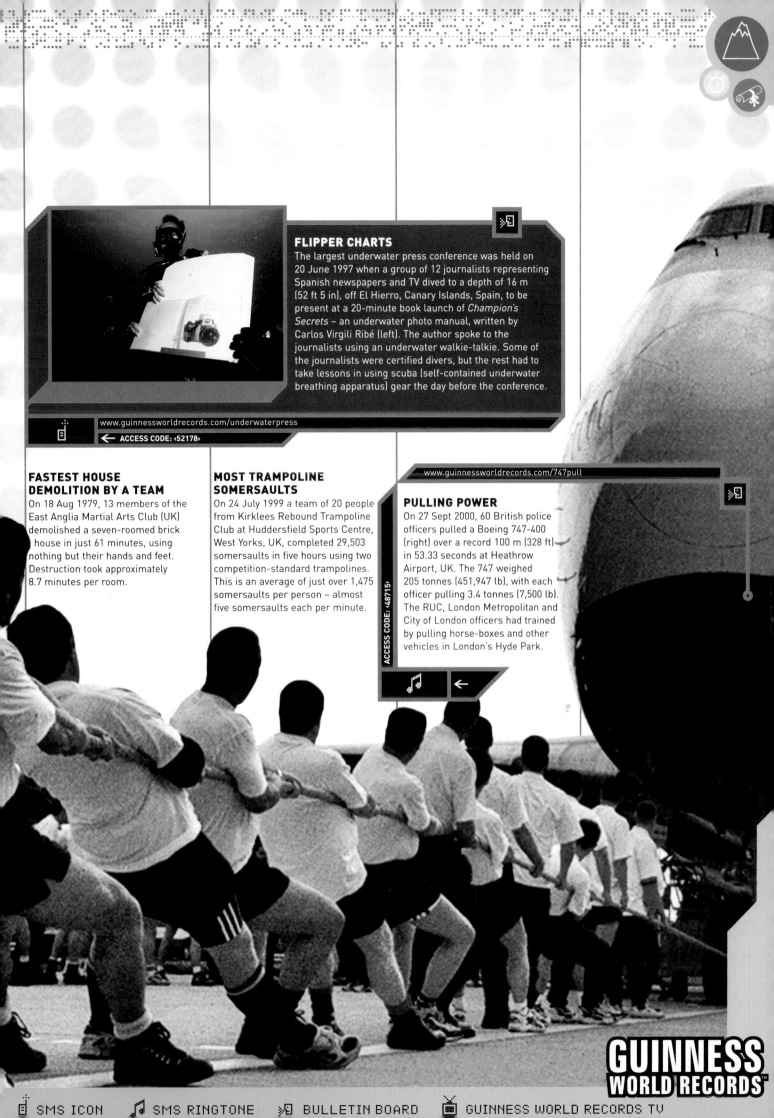

FLIPPER CHARTS

The largest underwater press conference was held on 20 June 1997 when a group of 12 journalists representing Spanish newspapers and TV dived to a depth of 16 m (52 ft 5 in), off El Hierro, Canary Islands, Spain, to be present at a 20-minute book launch of *Champion's Secrets* – an underwater photo manual, written by Carlos Virgili Ribé (left). The author spoke to the journalists using an underwater walkie-talkie. Some of the journalists were certified divers, but the rest had to take lessons in using scuba (self-contained underwater breathing apparatus) gear the day before the conference.

www.guinnessworldrecords.com/underwaterpress

← ACCESS CODE: ‹52178›

FASTEST HOUSE DEMOLITION BY A TEAM

On 18 Aug 1979, 13 members of the East Anglia Martial Arts Club (UK) demolished a seven-roomed brick house in just 61 minutes, using nothing but their hands and feet. Destruction took approximately 8.7 minutes per room.

MOST TRAMPOLINE SOMERSAULTS

On 24 July 1999 a team of 20 people from Kirklees Rebound Trampoline Club at Huddersfield Sports Centre, West Yorks, UK, completed 29,503 somersaults in five hours using two competition-standard trampolines. This is an average of just over 1,475 somersaults per person – almost five somersaults each per minute.

www.guinnessworldrecords.com/747pull

ACCESS CODE: ‹48715›

PULLING POWER

On 27 Sept 2000, 60 British police officers pulled a Boeing 747-400 (right) over a record 100 m (328 ft) in 53.33 seconds at Heathrow Airport, UK. The 747 weighed 205 tonnes (451,947 lb), with each officer pulling 3.4 tonnes (7,500 lb). The RUC, London Metropolitan and City of London officers had trained by pulling horse-boxes and other vehicles in London's Hyde Park.

GUINNESS WORLD RECORDS™

www.guinnessworldrecords.com/thelivingplanet

the living planet

the uniuerse

MOST LUMINOUS STAR

Although it cannot be seen from Earth with the naked eye, the Pistol star (identified by the Hubble telescope) is 10 million times more powerful than the Sun and, according to calculations, emits as much energy in six seconds as the Sun does in a year. Astronomers estimate that it is 25,000 light years away from Earth and more than 325 times as big as the Sun, which has a diameter of 1,391,940 km (864,910 miles). Pistol is thought to be only 1–3 million years old, in comparison with the Sun, which is five billion years old.

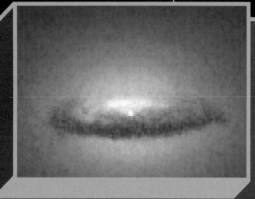

SPACE ODDITY

Normal black holes weigh several times the mass of the Sun, but supermassive black holes (left) reside in the hearts of galaxies and can be as massive as several hundred million times that of the Sun. Astronomers believe that such a terrifying force exists at the centre of the Milky Way, 30,000 light years away.

The closest black hole candidate as announced on 14 Jan 2000, is V4641 Sgr, which is only 1,600 light years from Earth. Its recent discovery was due to the dramatic changes in the intensity of X-ray radiation from V4641 Sgr as it sucks gas away from its companion star.

www.guinnessworldrecords.com/blackhole
← ACCESS CODE: ‹56351›

BRIGHTEST STAR SEEN FROM EARTH

Sirius A (Alpha Canis Majoris), or the Dog Star, is 8.64 light years away and is the brightest star visible in the night sky. A 'light year' is the distance that light travels in a year – roughly 9.5 million million km (6 million million miles). The distance between the Earth and Sirius is roughly 80 million million km (50 million million miles). Sirius has a mass 2.14 times that of the Sun, and is visually 24 times more luminous. It is also almost twice as hot, with a surface temperature of about 10,000°C (17,500°F).

NEAREST STAR

Excluding the Sun, the nearest star is the faint Proxima Centauri, (Alpha Centauri C), a red dwarf, discovered in 1915, which is 4.23 light years or 4×10^{13} km (2.49×10^{13} miles) away.

NEAREST STAR CLUSTER

The Hyades cluster in the constellation of Taurus (the bull) is the nearest star cluster to our Solar System. It contains around 300 stars, which are roughly 150 light years away and have been estimated to be 625 million years old.

BRIGHTEST SUPERNOVA OF MODERN TIMES

In 1987 a giant star in the Large Magellanic Cloud (a satellite galaxy of our own Milky Way) exploded in the brightest supernova of modern times. It was easily visible to the naked eye despite its distance from the Earth – 168,000 light years away. Supernovae occur at the end of the life of a giant star. As the star runs out of hydrogen fuel, it begins to use heavier elements as its nuclear fuel. Eventually, iron forms in the core, preventing further fusion reactions. As the star shuts down, it collapses in on itself and immediately blows itself apart as a supernova.

FASTEST PULSAR SPIN RATE

Pulsars are the rapidly spinning collapsed cores of massive stars that have blown themselves apart in a supernova. Spherical in shape and the size of a small city, a pulsar is so dense that a teaspoonful would weigh a billion tonnes. For pulsars whose spin rates have been accurately measured, the fastest-spinning is PSR B1937+214, which

was discovered by a group led by Donald C Backer (USA) in Nov 1982. It is in the minor constellation *Vulpecula* (Little Fox) 11,700 light years distant and has a pulse period of 1.5578064949 milliseconds, which is equivalent to a spin rate of 641.9282518 revolutions per second!

YOUNGEST PULSAR

A team of astronomers at Columbia University, led by Dr Eric Gotthelf (USA), discovered the youngest pulsar in 1995. The superdense stellar corpse, called PSR J1846-0258, is located on the other side of our Milky Way galaxy, some 60,000 light years away, and is only 700 years old.

CLOSEST GALAXY TO THE MILKY WAY

The closest object to Earth that is not in our galaxy is the Sagittarius Dwarf Elliptical Galaxy – a huge collection of stars and clouds made of dust and gas, which is about 82,000 light years away. The discovery by RA Ibata, G Gilmore and MJ Irwin (all UK) was announced in April 1994.

ABSOLUTELY NEBULOUS

The Orion Nebula (left) – a vast diffuse cloud of gas and dust – is the brightest nebula in the night sky. Located in the 'sword' of the constellation of Orion, the nebula is the nearest star-formation region to the Earth and is visible to the naked eye as a fuzzy patch of light. It is around 1,500 light years away.

The Boomerang Nebula, a cloud of dust and gases 5,000 light years from Earth, is where the coldest place in the universe can be found. This 'cold spot' at the outermost part of the huge wind, created by the suction of an imploding star, has a temperature of –272°C (-457.6°F). Here the gases are believed to be expanding and cooling at 595,457 km/h (370,000 mph). Colder temperatures have been achieved in laboratories on Earth.

www.guinnessworldrecords.com/orionnebula
← ACCESS CODE: ‹55562›

LARGEST GALAXY

The central galaxy of the Abell 2029 galaxy cluster, 1,070 million light years distant in the constellation of Virgo, has a major diameter of 5,600,000 light years – 80 times the diameter of our own Milky Way galaxy – and a light output equivalent to two trillion (2×10^{12}) Suns.

FARTHEST OBJECT VISIBLE TO THE NAKED EYE

The most remote heavenly body visible with the naked eye is the Andromeda Galaxy in the constellation of Andromeda, which was first noted from Germany by Simon Marius in 1611. It is a spiral galaxy similar to our Milky Way, at a distance from Earth of about 2.2 million light years, and can be seen by the naked eye as a grey smudge. Seen through binoculars or a telescope, the bright grey smudge is the combined light from more than 200,000,000,000 stars, some of which are just like our Sun.

SMALLEST CONSTELLATION

The smallest known constellation is Crux Australis (Southern Cross), which takes up an area covering just 0.16% of the sky. Until it was recognized as a constellation in 1679, it was officially part of the constellation of Centaurus. Crux Australis, which can only be seen from the southern hemisphere, is well known for the obvious difference in the colour of its stars. Three of the brightest stars are all very hot blue stars, while the other is a red giant. This striking difference can easily be seen with the naked eye.

LARGEST CONSTELLATION

Of the 88 constellations, Hydra (Sea Serpent), is the largest, covering 3.16% of the sky. It contains at least 68 stars visible to the naked eye.

MOST MASSIVE EXTRASOLAR PLANET

The discovery of the massive planet HD168443 orbiting a star 123 light years away was announced in Jan 2001. Jupiter, the largest planet in our Solar System, weighs more than all of the other planets and moons combined. HD168443 is 17 times more massive even than Jupiter.

NEAREST EXTRASOLAR PLANET

On 7 Aug 2000 a team of astronomers led by Dr William Cochran of the University of Texas McDonald Observatory (USA), announced the discovery of the nearest planet outside the Solar System. The planet – probably slightly larger than Jupiter – orbits the star Epsilon Eridani. This star, at only 10.5 light years distant, is one of the closest stars to the Sun. It is a main sequence star, which means that it is in the main phase of its lifespan.

www.guinnessworldrecords.com/helixnebula

ACCESS CODE: -56518>

GAS-TRONOMIC!

The Helix Nebula (NGC 7293, below) is the nearest planetary nebula to Earth, lying about 450 light years away in the constellation of Aquarius. It formed when a dying star cast off its outer layers as 'shells' of gas. These shells emit light as the gas is ionized by radiation from the star. They are called planetary nebulae because astronomers originally believed they were new planets, due to their often spherical shapes. The Helix Nebula covers an area around half the size of the full Moon but is not visible to the naked eye. Planetary nebulae are generally short-lived, lasting around 50,000 years before their expanding gases become too diffuse to be visible. This image was produced by the CFH12k CCD camera on the Canada-France-Hawaii telescope at Mauna Kea, Hawaii, USA, which is specially designed to image large areas of sky at a time.

GUINNESS WORLD RECORDS

the solar system

FASTEST PLANET

Mercury is the speediest planet in the Solar System, orbiting the Sun at an average of 172,248 km/h (107,030 mph), which is almost twice as fast as the Earth. The speed, coupled with the fact that Mercury is much closer to the Sun than the Earth is, means that a year on Mercury (the time it takes for Mercury to circle the Sun) lasts just 87.99 days, or roughly three months.

HOTTEST PLANET

The planet Venus has the hottest surface of any planet in the Solar System, with an average temperature of around 480° C (896° F), which makes exploration by probes on the surface rather difficult. If you were to step on to the surface of Venus you would be simultaneously crushed by the pressure, incinerated by the heat, corroded by the sulphuric acid and suffocated by the carbon dioxide.

LEAST DENSE PLANET

Saturn has no solid surface, making it the lightest planet in the Solar System. The planet is composed mostly of hydrogen and helium, the two lightest elements in the universe. It has an average density only 0.71 times that

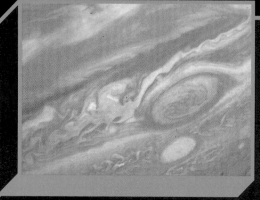

www.guinnessworldrecords.com/greatredspot
← ACCESS CODE: ‹55663›

ALL IN A SPIN

The Great Red Spot (left) on the planet Jupiter is the largest cyclone in the Solar System. It varies in size but can be up to 40,000 km (24,800 miles) long and 14,000 km (8,700 miles) wide. Three planets the size of Earth would fit along its length. This vast maelstrom has been raging for at least 300 years, ever since telescopes became powerful enough to see it from Earth, and it has probably lasted much longer. It rotates anti-clockwise at a speed of around 435 km/h (270 mph). The striking orange colour of the storm may be due to the presence of sulphur and phosphorus in the atmosphere.

of water. This means that if there was an ocean that was large enough, Saturn would float in it.

BRIGHTEST ASTEROID

The brightest asteroid is Vesta, which was discovered on 29 March 1807. Vesta is the only asteroid that is visible to the naked eye from the Earth on a clear night. This is due to the brightness of its surface, its size, – which measures 576 km (358 miles) across – and the fact that it can come as close to Earth as 177 million km (105 million miles).

LARGEST SATELLITE

The largest satellite in the Solar System is Ganymede, one of four large moons that circle the planet Jupiter. It is 2.017 times as heavy as the Earth's Moon and has a diameter of 5,267 km (3,273 miles).

SATELLITE WITH THE THICKEST ATMOSPHERE

Saturn's biggest moon Titan has the thickest atmosphere of any moon in the Solar System, exerting a surface pressure of 1.44 bar, nearly 1.5 times that of the atmospheric pressure at the Earth's surface. It consists mainly of nitrogen gas and is the most similar atmosphere to our own. Titan is the only moon in the Solar System to have a thick atmosphere – an orange smog layer obscures our view of its surface.

LARGEST CANYON IN THE SOLAR SYSTEM

The Valles Marineris on Mars is the largest canyon in the Solar System. It has an overall length of around 4,500 km (2,800 miles). At its widest,

it is 600 km (370 miles) across and is also up to 7 km (4.3 miles) deep. The immense canyon system, first discovered by NASA's *Mariner 9* spacecraft in 1971, would span the USA from coast to coast.

LARGEST SUNSPOT GROUP

On 8 April 1947 the largest sunspot group ever was found in the Sun's southern hemisphere. At its greatest length, it measured 300,000 km (187,000 miles) with a maximum width of 145,000 km (90,000 miles). It was roughly 36 times greater than the surface area of the Earth and visible to the naked eye, close to sunset.

LONGEST MEASURED COMET TAIL

The longest comet tail ever measured was 570 million km (350 million miles) long and belonged to the comet Hyakutake. This is more than three times the distance from the Earth to the Sun. The tail was discovered by Geraint Jones of Imperial College, London, UK, on 13 Sept 1999, using data gathered by

RING BOUND

The giant planet Saturn has the most massive ring system (left) of all the planets in our Solar System. The intricate system of rings around the giant has a combined mass of around 4×10^{19} kg (9×10^{19} lb) – equivalent to 30 million Mt Everests. All the other gas giants, Jupiter, Uranus and Neptune, have rings as well, but none are as extensive nor as impressive as that of Saturn. The planet's rings consist of millions of tiny, independently orbiting particles of ice and dust. It is likely that they were formed several tens of millions of years ago, when a comet smashed into a small moon shattering it into countless pieces of debris, which became the rings.

the ESA/NASA spacecraft *Ulysses* on a chance encounter with the comet on 1 May 1996.

HIGHEST CLIFFS IN THE SOLAR SYSTEM

Verona Rupes, a cliff on Miranda, a small moon that circles the planet Uranus, is roughly 20 km (12 miles) high. This is approximately 10 times higher than the walls of the Grand Canyon on Earth. The height of this cliff is particularly extraordinary given the smallness of Miranda, which has a diameter of only 472 km (265 miles). The cliff and other strange geological features on the surface may have been caused by Miranda being smashed to pieces by a comet and then reformed from the fragments.

FASTEST WINDS IN THE SOLAR SYSTEM

The planet Neptune has the fastest winds anywhere in the Solar System. Measured by NASA's *Voyager 2* probe in 1989, they gust at about 2,400 km/h (1,500 mph). This is almost five times faster than the highest wind speed recorded for a tornado on Earth.

LARGEST RECORDED IMPACT IN THE SOLAR SYSTEM

Between 16 and 22 July 1994 more than 20 fragments of comet Shoemaker-Levy 9 collided with the giant planet Jupiter. The greatest impact was made by the largest fragment, which measured 3-4 km (around 2 miles) across. It exploded with the energy of roughly 600 times all the bombs in the world going off simultaneously – equivalent to 6 million megatons of TNT. The 20 fragments ploughed into Jupiter's atmosphere at around 60 km (40 miles) per second, leaving enormous scars in Jupiter's turbulent, deep atmosphere.

COLDEST KNOWN GEOLOGICAL ACTIVITY

Active geysers on Triton, the planet Neptune's largest moon, blast freezing cold nitrogen gas several kilometres high into the atmosphere. Triton has a surface temperature of –235° C (–391° F) and is one of the coldest places in our Solar System with lakes of water that are frozen hard as steel.

LONGEST TOTAL SOLAR ECLIPSE

The longest total solar eclipse of recent date was on 20 June 1955 (7 min 8 sec), visible west of the Philippines, although it was clouded out along most of its track. The maximum possible duration of an eclipse of the Sun is 7 min 31 sec. An eclipse of 7 min 29 sec should occur in the mid-Atlantic Ocean on 16 July 2186.

LARGEST RECORDED SOLAR FLARE

On 2 April 2001 at 9:51 pm GMT, the largest solar flare ever recorded erupted from the surface of the Sun. It originated from one of the largest groups of sunspots ever recorded. The flare sent out billions of tonnes of electrified gas and radiation into the Solar System. Some of this matter collided with the Earth's upper atmosphere, causing beautiful displays of the aurora, especially in the northern hemisphere.

www.guinnessworldrecords.com/io

GREAT BALLS OF FIRE

Io, one of the four biggest moons of Jupiter, is the most volcanic body in the Solar System. In 1979, NASA's *Voyager 1* probe took the first images of volcanic eruption plumes, some reaching hundreds of kilometres into space (right, taken by NASA's *Galileo* spacecraft on 28 June 1997). Io is so active that it has 'turned inside out' at least once, with the outer layers being buried under newly erupted lava until they're so deep that they melt and re-erupt on to the surface as new lava.

ACCESS CODE: ·54814·

planet earth

LARGEST GEODE
The largest geode (a mineral-lined cave) is near Almería, Spain. It is 7.92 m (26 ft) long, 1.83m (6 ft) wide, 1.83 m (6 ft) high and is about six million years old. Most geodes are small enough to fit in the palm of a human hand.

OLDEST EARTH FRAGMENT
A tiny crystal of zircon is the oldest fragment of Earth discovered so far. Between 4.3 and 4.4 billion years old, this tiny sample is 100 million years older than any previous discovery.

LONGEST RIVER
The Nile and the Amazon are the two longest rivers in the world. Which is longer is debatable. The Nile's official length is 6,695 km (4,160 miles), but it lost a few miles after the formation of Lake Nasser behind the Aswan Dam. The Amazon has several mouths, so its end point is uncertain. If the Para estuary – its most distant mouth – is included, the river's length is approximately 6,750 km (4,195 miles).

HIGHEST ACTIVE VOLCANO
The Ojos del Salado on the border between Chile and Argentina is the world's highest active volcano at 6,887 m (22,595 ft) high.

LARGEST VOLCANO CRATER
The world's largest volcano crater is Toba, north-central Sumatra, Indonesia, covering 1,775 km^2 (685 miles^2). It is inactive and last erupted around 75,000 years ago.

LARGEST ACTIVE VOLCANO
Mauna Loa, Hawaii, USA, is 120 km (75 miles) long and 50 km (31 miles) wide, with lava flows that occupy more than 5,125 km^2 (1,980 miles^2) of the island. It has a total volume of 42,500 km^3 (16,400 miles^3), of which 84.2% is below sea level. It has averaged one eruption every 3.6 years since 1843, although none since 1984.

LARGEST OCEAN
The Pacific is the largest ocean in the world, covering more than one third of the Earth's surface at 166,241,700 km^2 (64,186,000 miles^2) with an average depth of 3,940 m (12,925 ft).

DEEPEST VALLEY
Asia's Yarlung Zangbo river valley stretching from Tibet to Bangladesh has an average depth of 5,000 m (16,405 ft) with its deepest point at 5,382 m (17,658 ft) – more than three times as deep as the Grand Canyon.

SMALLEST CONTINENT
Of all the continents (Europe, Africa, Asia, North America, South America, Australasia, Antarctica) the Australian mainland, with an area of 7,614,500 km^2 (2,939,960 miles^2), is the smallest.

MAKING WAVES
The Amazon river (above) in South America has the greatest flow of any river, discharging an amazing average of 200,000 m^3/sec (7,100,000 ft^3/sec) into the Atlantic Ocean, which increases to more than 340,000 m^3/sec (12,000,000 ft^3/sec) in full flood. The lower 1,450 km (900 miles) average 17 m (55 ft) in depth, but the river has a maximum depth of 124 m (407 ft). The Amazon is fed by over 1000 tributaries and its flow is 60 times greater than that of the Nile. The Amazon accounts for about 20% of all the fresh water that drains into the world's oceans.

www.guinnessworldrecords.com/riverflow
ACCESS CODE: ‹47578›

LARGEST CONTINENT
Asia is the largest continent in the world, covering an area of 45,036,492 km^2 (17,388,686 miles^2). Africa ranks second with a land area of 30,343,578 km^2 11,715,721 miles^2).

TALLEST MOUNTAIN
Mauna Kea ('White Mountain') on the island of Hawaii (USA) is the world's tallest mountain. Its base begins on the floor of the Pacific Ocean and rises to a peak of 10,205 m (33,480 ft). Up to 6,000 m (19,685 ft) of the

mountain is under water and 4,205 m (13,795 ft) is above sea level. In total, from base to peak, it is 1,357 m (4,452 ft) taller than Mt Everest.

HIGHEST MOUNTAIN PEAK
The eastern Himalayan peak of Mt Everest has a height of 8,848 m (29,030.8 ft) and is the highest point in the world. It was named Mt Everest after Colonel Sir George Everest (pronounced Eve-rest), formerly Surveyor-General of India.

LARGEST RIVER TO DRY UP
In 1997 and 1998, the Yellow River (Huang He), China's second-longest river, ran completely dry along its lower section for over 140 days in each year, leaving farmland parched and threatening the autumn harvest. This problem was the result of below-average rainfall, increased irrigation and the industrial demands of a growing population.

LARGEST STEAM RINGS
Sicily's active volcano Mt Etna is the highest and most active volcano in Europe. A complex physical process causes it to emit huge steam rings (similar to smoke rings) measuring about 200 m (656 ft) across, that can

SOMEWHERE UNDER THE RAINBOW
The red sandstone Rainbow Bridge, in Lake Powell National Monument, Utah, USA, is the highest natural arch in the world. It is only 82.3 m (270 ft) long, but is a massive feature rising to a height of 88.4 m (290 ft) – nearly twice the height of the Statue of Liberty. Rainbow Bridge is composed of Navajo sandstone and was formed by an ancient stream on its way to the Colorado River, which eroded away some of the weaker sedimentary rock in the area, leaving the natural bridge behind. It is considered sacred by the local Native Americans and is visted by around 300,000 people a year.

www.guinnessworldrecords.com/rainbowbridge
ACCESS CODE: ‹47585›

last up to 10 minutes or so as they drift up to a height of about 1,000 m (3,300 ft) above the volcanic vent.

FASTEST MOVING GLACIER

Measuring 54 km (34 miles) long, 4.8 km (3 miles) wide and up to 910 m (3,000 ft) high at some points, the Columbia Glacier between Anchorage and Valdez in Alaska, USA, was calculated to be flowing at an average rate of 35 m (115 ft) per day in 1999. It has almost doubled its speed over the last 20 years,

possibly because of global warming, which causes the ice to loosen and move faster.

LARGEST SUBGLACIAL LAKE

Lake Vostok in Antarctica was discovered in 1994 by analysing radar imagery of the icy continent. Buried under 4 km (2.5 miles) of the East Antarctic Ice Sheet, it is the oldest and most pristine lake on Earth, completely isolated from the rest of the world for at least 500,000 years. Covering an area of some 14,000 km² (5,400 miles²), it has a depth of at least 100 m (330 ft).

www.guinnessworldrecords.com/lambertglacier

ACCESS CODE: 475591

ICE COOL

Covering 11.4 % of the planet, glaciers are mainly found in Antartica and Greenland with about 13.5 million km² (5.2 million miles²) of Antarctica made of snow and ice. Glaciers are large, moving masses of ice formed where the rate of snowfall is greater than the rate of snow melting. As snow piles up, it is compressed into ice by the weight of more snow falling on top of it, and begins to slowly flow downhill under the force of its own weight.

Covering up to 1 million km² (386,102 miles²), the world's largest glacier is the Lambert Glacier (below) in the Australian Antarctic Territory. Lambert is up to 64 km (40 miles) wide and measures at least 700 km (440 miles) in length – longer than the state of Florida.

weather extremes

WARMEST YEAR

1998 was the warmest year since records began in 1880, with global temperatures 0.57ºC (33ºF) higher than the averages recorded between 1961 and 1990. The 1990s as a whole was also the warmest decade on record, and contained the six warmest years ever. The second warmest year was 1997.

MOST FREAKISH TEMPERATURE RISE

On 22 Jan 1943 the temperature at Spearfish, South Dakota, USA, rose from –20ºC (–4ºF) at 7.30 am to 7ºC (45ºF) at 7.32 am – a record-breaking 27ºC (49ºF) in two minutes.

GREATEST TEMPERATURE RANGES

The world's greatest temperature ranges are found around the 'cold pole' in Siberia, Russia. Temperatures in Verkhoyansk have ranged 105ºC (188ºF), from –68ºC (–90ºF) to 37ºC (98ºF). The town is in the Republic of Sakha – an area of 3.1 million km^2 (1.19 million miles^2) – and has a population of just one million, mainly because of its extreme climate.

COLDEST PLACES

The lowest outdoor temperature ever recorded is –89.2ºC (–128.6ºF), registered at the Vostok Scientific

SNOW JOKE

During a snowstorm at Fort Keogh, Montana, USA, on 28 Jan 1887, Matt Coleman discovered a snowflake that was 38 cm (15 in) wide and 20 cm (8 in) thick, which he later described as being 'larger than milk pans' in the magazine *Monthly Weather Review*. A mail courier caught in the same snowstorm witnessed the fall of these giant flakes over several miles.

www.guinnessworldrecords.com/snowflake
← ACCESS CODE: ‹53605›

Station in Antarctica on 21 July 1983. The coldest permanently inhabited place in the world is Oymyakon, a village in Yakutia, eastern Siberia, Russia, where temperatures can drop to as low as –70ºC (–94ºF). The average temperature in January, the coldest month, is –50ºC (–58ºF).

LONGEST ICE AGE

Geological evidence suggests that the Earth endured several ice ages early in its history. The longest and most severe of these occurred between 2.3 and 2.4 billion years ago and lasted around 70 million years. During this period, the entire Earth was probably covered in ice.

HIGHEST BAROMETRIC PRESSURE

Barometric pressure – the physical pressure exerted by the air on people – is measured in millibars. Pressure decreases as a person's altitude increases, as there is less of the Earth's atmosphere to weigh them

down. The highest-ever barometric pressure was 1,083.8 mb (32 in), recorded at Agata, Siberia, Russia, on 31 Dec 1968. This reading, which would normally be expected at 600 m (1,968 ft) below sea level, is made even more impressive by the fact that Agata is actually located 262 m (859 ft) above sea level.

GREATEST SNOWFALLS

Snow with a depth of 11.5 m (37 ft 7 in) was recorded at Tamarac, California, USA, in March 1911.

The most snow produced in a single snowstorm is 4.8 m (15.75 ft), which fell at Mt Shasta Ski Bowl, California, USA, between 13 and 19 Feb 1959.

HEAVIEST HAILSTONES

The heaviest hailstones on record weighed up to 1 kg (2.2 lb) each. They are reported to have killed 92 people when they struck the Gopalganj district of Bangladesh on 14 April 1986.

HIGHEST WATERSPOUT

The highest waterspout – a tornado that travels over water – was observed on 16 May 1898 off Eden, NSW, Australia. A theodolite reading taken from the shore registered its height as 1,528 m (5,013 ft), and it was about 3 m (10 ft) in diameter. Waterspouts have been known to suck up fish from the sea and drop them back down on nearby towns.

MOST RAINY DAYS

Mt Wai-`ale-`ale in Kauai, Hawaii, USA, which is 1,569 m (5,148 ft) high, has up to 350 rainy days per year – giving an average rainfall of over 10 m (32.8 ft).

MOST THUNDERY DAYS

In the 10 years between 1967 and 1976, an average of 251 days of thunder per year was recorded in Tororo, Uganda.

MOST INTENSE RAINFALL

On 26 Nov 1970, 38.1 mm (1.5 in) of rain fell on the Caribbean island of Guadeloupe in just one minute – the most rain ever recorded over that period of time.

The record for rainfall over a 24-hour period is 1.85 m (6 ft 1 in), at Cilaos on the Indian Ocean island of Réunion, between 15 and 16 March 1952.

FASTEST WIND SPEEDS

The US National Severe Storms Laboratory recorded a 512-km/h (318-mph) wind speed associated with a tornado near Bridge Creek, Oklahoma, USA, on 3 May 1999. The measurement was taken 30–60 m (100–200 ft) above the ground.

The fastest surface (ground-level) wind recorded at a high altitude is 371 km/h (231 mph), which was registered at a height of 1,916 m (6,288-ft) at the summit of Mt Washington, New Hampshire, USA, on 12 April 1934.

The low-altitude wind-speed record is 333 km/h (207 mph), recorded on 8 March 1972 at the US Air Force base at Thule, Greenland (altitude 44 m or 145 ft).

BLOWN AWAY

Tornadoes form where there is lots of warm, humid air and winds that change direction. These conditions are quite common in central USA, where there is plenty of moist air coming from the Gulf of Mexico. Between 3 and 4 April 1974, this area, which extends from central Texas (left) to Iowa and Nebraska, and is often called 'Tornado Alley', experienced a record-breaking 148 tornadoes in 24 hours.

Rather surprisingly, the record frequency of tornadoes by area is in the UK where, in an average year, one tornado is reported for every 7,397 km^2 (2,856 miles^2). The figure for the USA is one tornado for every 8,663 km^2 (3,345 miles^2). The longest distance travelled by a tornado is 471.5 km (293 miles) across Illinois and Indiana on 26 May 1917.

www.guinnessworldrecords.com/tornadoes
← ACCESS CODE: ‹47480›

TAN-FASTIC!

Children in Arizona, USA, try to beat the heat by cooling off in a livestock water trough outside their home (above). Yuma, Arizona, is one of the two sunniest places in the world, experiencing an average of 4,055 hours of sunshine (out of a possible 4,456 hours) per year. Located at an altitude of 42 m (138 ft) above sea level, the town has a population of around 71,000, and is one of Arizona's fastest-growing cities.

From Feb 1967 to March 1969 St Petersburg, Florida, USA recorded a record-breaking 768 consecutive sunny days.

www.guinnessworldrecords.com/yuma

ACCESS CODE: ‹47494›

CLOUD FORM WITH GREATEST VERTICAL RANGE

The cloud form *cumulonimbus*, which is responsible for rainstorms, snowstorms and hail, has been seen to reach a height of nearly 20,000 m (65,620 ft) in the tropics – nearly three times higher than Mt Everest.

LONGEST-LASTING SEA-LEVEL FOGS

Sea-level fogs, defined by having a visibility of less than 900 m (1,000 yd), persist for more than 120 days per year on the Grand Banks, Newfoundland, Canada.

LONGEST-LASTING RAINBOW

On 14 March 1994 a rainbow was visible over Wetherby, West Yorkshire, UK, for six hours from 9 am to 3 pm. Most rainbows last for only a matter of minutes.

www.guinnessworldrecords.com/wettest

RAINDROPS KEEP FALLING ON MY HEAD

The world's wettest place in terms of average annual rainful is Mawsynram in Meghalaya State, India (right). It experiences 11.87 m (38.94 ft) of rain per year. Most of the rain occurs during the monsoon season, between June and September.

The second rainiest place is Cherrapunji, also in Meghalaya, which has an average annual rainfall of 11.43 m (37.5 ft) per year. Amazingly, outside the monsoon season it can also suffer from serious drought.

GUINNESS WORLD RECORDS

📱 SMS ICON   🎵 SMS RINGTONE   ▶ BULLETIN BOARD   📺 GUINNESS WORLD RECORDS TV

amazing science

OLDEST EXTRACTED HUMAN DNA

In Jan 2000 scientists extracted DNA from the bone of a 60,000-year-old ancestor of modern humans. The skeleton, nicknamed 'Mungo Man', was unearthed at Lake Mungo, Australia, in 1974. This controversially challenges the theory that we are all descended from a common African ancestor.

OLDEST LIVING BACTERIA

Uncontaminated bacteria trapped in suspended animation inside salt crystals for 250 million years (older than the dinosaurs) have been revived and cultured by US scientists. Designated 'Bacillus 2-9-3', this species is 10 times older than the previous oldest revived bacteria.

HARDEST ELEMENT

Carbon (C) has many different allotropes (different configurations of atoms), but the diamond allotrope, which has an extremely strong lattice structure, has a value of 10 on Moh's relative scale of hardness (the highest value). Diamonds are formed at least 150 km (93 miles) beneath the Earth's surface, where the pressures and temperatures are great enough to force the carbon atoms to adopt this structure.

RAREST ELEMENT ON EARTH

Discovered in 1931, astatine, a member of the halogen group of elements, is the rarest element in the Earth's crust, with only around 25 g (0.9 oz) occurring naturally.

MOST DENSE MATTER

Scientists at the Brookhaven National Laboratory, Long Island, New York, USA, have created matter 20 times more dense than the nucleus of an atom. By smashing the nucleii of gold atoms together at almost the speed of light, they created subatomic particles that lasted for fractions of a second. Matter this dense may not have existed in the universe since its creation in the 'Big Bang', which occurred 12–15 billion years ago.

FINEST BALANCE

The Sartorius Microbalance Model 4108, made in Germany, can weigh miniscule objects of up to 0.5 g (0.018 oz) to an accuracy of 0.01 micrograms, or 1×10^{-8} g (3.5×10^{-10} oz) – equivalent to around 1/60 the weight of the ink on one of the full-stops on this page.

SHORTEST FLASH OF LIGHT

The shortest flash of light ever produced and measured, lasted for just 0.0000000000000045 seconds (4.5 femtoseconds). This was measured by Douwe Wiersma, Andrius Baltuska and Maxim Pshenchnikov at the University of Groningen, Netherlands, in 1998.

MOST POWERFUL X-RAY GENERATOR

The Z Machine at the Sandia National Laboratories, New Mexico, USA, can, for a few trillionths of a second, reach the temperature of the Sun's surface and give a power output (in X-rays) equal to approximately 80 times that of all the world's electrical generators combined.

LARGEST SCIENTIFIC INSTRUMENT

The Large Electron Positron (LEP) Storage Ring Collider at CERN, Geneva, Switzerland, which was created to examine the smallest particles of matter, is the world's largest scientific instrument (and arguably the largest machine). Made up of a circular tube 3.8 m (12 ft 6 in) wide and 27 km (17 miles) long, the Collider is inside a giant doughnut-shaped tunnel 100 m (328 ft) in depth. Inside, electrons and positrons are accelerated around the 'doughnut' before colliding with each other, when they produce tiny sub-atomic particles that enable physicists to study the nature of the universe. The LEP began operating in 1989 and was officially closed down at 8 am on 2 Nov 2000.

MOST POWERFUL ELECTRIC CURRENT

In April 1996 scientists at Oak Ridge National Laboratory, Tennessee, USA, sent a current of 2 million amperes per cm^2 (13 million amps per in^2) down a superconducting wire. Standard household wires carry a current of less than 1,000 amps per cm^2 (6,450 amps per in^2).

FASTEST CENTRIFUGE

Ultracentrifuges are used to separate mixtures of organic substances. The highest man-made rotary speed was achieved at Birmingham University (UK) in 1975, which registered a speed of 7,250 km/h (4,500 mph). This maximum speed is more than three times faster than Concorde flying at typical cruising speed.

MOST ACCURATE VALUE OF PI

Pi (π), one of the most important numbers in mathematics, is always equal to half the circumference of a circle, divided by its radius. Pi is also an irrational number – ie it has infinite numbers after its decimal point, which follow no repeating pattern. This lack of a pattern has inspired mathematicians to calculate pi to more and more accurate values. The most decimal places to which pi has been calculated is 206,158,430,000 by Professor Yasumasa Kanada and Dr Daisuke Takahashi (both Japan), who made the calculation by running two different computer programs in 1999.

HOTTEST FLAME

The hottest flame is produced by carbon subnitride (C_4N_2) which, at one atmosphere pressure, can generate a flame calculated to reach 4,988°C (9,010°F). The highest man-made temperature is 100,000 times hotter than this.

HIGHEST MAN-MADE TEMPERATURE

The highest man-made temperature is 510 million°C (950 million°F) – almost 30 times the temperature at the centre of the Sun – attained on 27 May 1994 at the Tokamak Fusion Test Reactor at Princeton, New Jersey, USA. The high temperatures were produced using a deuterium-tritium plasma mix.

LOWEST MAN-MADE TEMPERATURE

In 1995 Eric Cornell and Carl Wieman (both USA) cooled atoms of rubidium to a record low temperature of less than 170 billionths of a degree above absolute zero – the coldest temperature possible.

LIGHT FANTASTIC

The solid substance with the lowest density is aerogel, a silicon-based solid that is 99% air and 1,000 times less dense than glass. Aerogel (left) resembles solid smoke in appearance and weighs only three times that of air itself, yet a piece only 2.5 mm (1 in) thick will protect a human hand from the heat of a blowtorch. The lightest of these aerogels, with a density of only 0.005 g/cm^3 (5 oz/ft^3), was produced at the Lawrence Livermore Laboratory, California, USA. Aerogel is currently being flown on the Stardust planetary mission. Its unusual properties will allow tiny particles ejected from the tail of comet Wild 2 to be captured. The particles will strike the aerogel collectors at high velocities, will be slowed down by the frothy aerogel structure and trapped intact inside the substance.

www.guinnessworldrecords.com/aerogel

ACCESS CODE: ‹47186›

SMELLIEST SUBSTANCE

With a smell reminiscent of rotting cabbage, garlic, burnt toast and sewer gas, the world's smelliest substances are the gases ethyl mercaptan (C_2H_5SH) and butyl seleno-mercaptan (C_4H_9SeH). They are toxic and in large doses will cause headaches, nausea, lack of coordination and liver and kidney damage. Ethyl mercaptan is often added to odourless natural gas so that a gas leak can be detected.

ACCESS CODE: ‹5634›?

MOST BITTER SUBSTANCE

Denatonium benzoate is the world's most bitter-tasting substance. It can be detected in dilution levels as low as one part in 500 million – a

IT'S ALL IN THE GENES

www.guinnessworldrecords.com/genome

The Human Genome Project is the largest-ever biology research collaboration. It completed the final sequence of the three billion 'letters' in the genetic code for a human being in Feb 2001. Humans share 99.99% of the code; 0.01% is the tiny percentage of genes which vary among humans – accounting for all the differences between people.

dilution of one part in 100 million will leave a lingering taste. Higher levels are too bitter to be tolerated. It is used in products such as anti-freeze to deter people from swallowing them.

SWEETEST SUBSTANCE

Thaumatin (or 'Talin'), obtained from arils (appendages found on seeds) of the katemfe plant (*Thaumatococcus daniellii*) from Africa is 615,000 times sweeter than sugar. It leaves a liquorice-like aftertaste.

PIGGY BANK

The greatest number of cloned piglets born in one litter is five. Millie, Christa, Alexis, Carrel and Dotcom (above) were born on 5 March 2000 in Blacksburg, Virginia, USA. PPL Therapeutics Plc – the company that created Dolly the sheep, the first clone of an adult animal – produced the piglets as a result of nuclear transfer. This process involves transferring the nucleus of a body cell into an egg from which the nucleus and DNA have been removed. As pigs are physiologically one of the closest animals to humans, this is a potentially unlimited new source for human transplants.

www.guinnessworldrecords.com/pigclones

ACCESS CODE:
← ‹54194›

GUINNESS WORLD RECORDS™

natural disasters

MOST NATURAL DISASTERS IN ONE YEAR

Although not the most costly in terms of insurance and economic losses, the year 2000 holds the record for the most natural disasters as recorded by the world insurance industry. Extreme weather accounted for the bulk of the 850 reported catastrophes, with windstorms responsible for 73% of claims and floods for another 23%. The average number of annual natural disasters throughout the 1990s was 650.

GREATEST RECORDED IMPACT ON EARTH

A huge explosion that shook the Siberian region of Tunguska on 30 June 1908 was so powerful that it was equivalent to 10–15 megatons of high explosive, and resulted in the devastation of a 3,900-km^2 (1,500-mile^2) area. The shock wave was felt up to 1,000 km (620 miles) away. The explosion was caused when an asteroid with a diameter of 30 m (98 ft), travelling faster than the speed of sound, disintegrated at an altitude of 10 km (6.2 miles). Although no-one was killed as the area was so sparsely populated, the same explosion over a major city would have resulted in millions of deaths.

www.guinnessworldrecords.com/earthquake
ACCESS CODE: ‹52457›

COSTING THE EARTH

The earthquake that struck Kobe, Japan (left) in Jan 1995 resulted in record losses of 9,860 billion yen (£63 billion). Measuring 7.2 on the Richter scale, the quake killed more than 6,400 people and injured around 27,000. Over 106,000 buildings were damaged and hundreds of houses, particularly older wooden ones, collapsed. Japan's geographic location on the Pacific 'Rim of Fire' means that tremors are inevitable. Fortunately, Japan is relatively well prepared for this, and can draw on her large fiscal resources and modern construction techniques.

Despite these devastating statistics, asteroid collisions are – in theory – the most preventable of natural disasters, as it may now be possible to deflect their course.

MOST POWERFUL EARTHQUAKE

An earthquake that struck Chile on 22 May 1960 had a magnitude of 8.3 on the Richter scale, making it the most powerful earthquake ever recorded. In Chile, it killed more than 2,000 people, injured 3,000 and left an estimated 2 million homeless. The resultant *tsunami* (giant wave) also caused massive damage, and was responsible for around 200 deaths thousands of miles away on the US west coast, in Hawaii and Japan.

MOST PEOPLE KILLED BY AN EARTHQUAKE

It is thought that around 830,000 people died when an earthquake struck the Shanxi and Henan provinces of China on 2 Feb 1556.

MOST PEOPLE KILLED BY LANDSLIDES

On 16 Dec 1920 a series of landslides triggered by a single earthquake that hit Gansu Province, China, killed around 180,000 people.

DEADLIEST LAKE

In recent decades, toxic gases emanating from Lake Nyos in Cameroon, west Africa, have claimed an estimated 2,000 lives. On one night in Aug 1986 alone, between 1,600 and 1,800 people and countless animals were killed when a large quantity of carbon dioxide gas was naturally released from the lake. The exact source of these deadly gases is unknown, but they are thought to be either volcanic in origin or caused by the decomposition of organic material on the lakebed.

MOST PEOPLE KILLED BY A LIGHTNING STRIKE

On 8 Dec 1963 a Boeing 707 jet airliner was struck by lightning near Elkton, Maryland, USA, causing it to crash. 81 passengers were killed.

MOST DESTRUCTIVE GEOMAGNETIC STORM

The most destructive geomagnetic storm on record is the 'Great Geomagnetic Storm' of 13 March 1989, which was classified G5 (the most severe rating) on the space weather scale. The result of an abnormally strong solar wind, it caused large-scale disruption to the power grid in Canada and the USA, and even changed the orbit of a satellite.

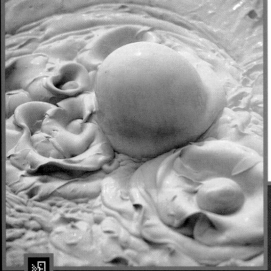

GEYSER ATTACK

Formed in 1886 when the nearby volcano Tarawera erupted, the volcanic Waimangu Valley, New Zealand, contains the world's largest hot spring. In Aug 1903 one of the geysers in this area erupted, killing four people – the greatest number of fatalities in a geyser-related accident. The power of the eruption was such that the victims, who were standing 27 m (88.6 ft) away, were blown distances of up to 800 m (2,625 ft).

There are about 700 active geysers in the world. They occur in active volcanic regions, where groundwater can circulate deep underground, and becomes superheated by molten magma. Cracks and fissures in the overlying rock allows the hot water to erupt out of the ground as a geyser when the pressure builds up.

HIGHEST TSUNAMI WASH

The highest *tsunami* (giant wave) ever reported was 524 m (1,719 ft) high and occurred along the fjord-like Lituya Bay, Alaska, USA, on 9 July 1958. Caused by a giant landslip, it moved at 160 km/h (100 mph). This wave was so high it would easily have swamped the Petronas Towers in Kuala Lumpur, Malaysia, which, at 452 m (1,483 ft), are the world's tallest office buildings.

LARGEST TIDAL BORE 📺USA

A tidal bore – caused when the Sun, Moon and Earth align to form dramatic tidal conditions – is a solitary wave that travels with great speed up a narrow river, forcing the flow upstream. The world's largest tidal bore occurred in Hangzhou Bay, China, on 18 Aug 1993. The bore was 9.14 m (30 ft) high and 321.8 km (200 miles) long, and pushed approximately 9 million litres (2 million gallons) of water per second towards the shore. It has been estimated that 100 people died as a result of the disaster.

MOST PEOPLE MADE HOMELESS BY FLOODS

During Sept 1978 monsoon rains in the Indian state of Bengal caused such extensive river flooding that, as a result, around 15 million people, out of a total population of 44 million, were made homeless. A total of 1,300 people and 26,687 cattle drowned, and 1.3 million homes were destroyed.

www.guinnessworldrecords.com/mitch

HURRICANE MITCH

Hurricane Mitch left more people homeless than any other cyclone when it struck Central America between 26 Oct and 4 Nov 1998 (below). It caused 9,745 deaths and destroyed 93,690 dwellings, leaving approximately 2.5 million people dependent on international aid efforts. It began as a tropical depression on 22 Oct 1998, and within four days had become a monster Category-Five storm on the Saffir–Simpson Hurricane scale.

The most powerful storm in the Caribbean Sea since Hurricane Gilbert in 1988, Mitch reached a maximum speed of 290 km/h (180 mph), gathering strength over the Caribbean Sea before hitting the coast of Honduras and moving slowly inland. The storm retained its Category-Five rating for 33 hours, the longest since Hurricane David sustained its fury for 36 hours in 1979.

ACCESS CODE: '49208'

GUINNESS WORLD RECORDS™

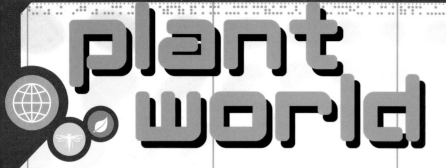

plant world

MOST DANGEROUS STINGERS

New Zealand's tree nettle (*Urtica ferox*) has killed dogs, horses and at least one human. The tree nettle can grow to 3 m (9.84 ft) in height and has fine white stinging hairs on its green leaves. These inject potent toxins into the skin; the main ones being histamine, 5-hydroxytryptamine, acetylcholine, formic acid and tryffidin. Australia's stinging trees (genus *Dendrocnide*), armed with large, hollow hairs on their leaves and twigs, are as feared as New Zealand's tree nettle. The worst, the gympie bush (*Dendrocnide moroides*), causes intense stabbing pains that can recur months later.

HIGHEST CHLOROPHYLL CONTENT

Chlorophyll is the green matter in plants that traps the energy from sunlight in order to process carbon dioxide. The chlorophyll content of the algae Kirin Chlorella M-207A7 (*Chlorella vulgaris*), measured on a dry weight basis, is 6.7% and was discovered by Dr Kouichi Nakanishi (Japan) in Jan 2000. For most plants, the chlorophyll content is between 0.6% and 1.2% on a dry weight basis. Spinach, one of the darkest green vegetables, is still only 0.9%.

TALLEST DAFFODIL

A daffodil grown in 1979 by M Lowe of Chessell, Isle of Wight, UK, reached an amazing height of 1.55 m (5 ft 1 in).

LARGEST CORK TREE

The largest cork tree is the 'Whistler Tree' in the Alentejo region of Portugal, which averages over 1.02 tonnes (2,244 lb) of raw cork per harvest – enough cork for 100,000 wine bottles. In comparison, an average cork tree produces enough cork each harvest for 4,000 wine bottles. Over 212 years old, the Whistler Tree has been producing cork every nine years since 1820, and it is anticipated that it will produce over one million corks in its lifetime.

LONGEST DISTANCE TRAVELLED BY A DRIFT SEED

The longest documented drift range for any seed or tropical fruit is for a single Mary's bean (*Merremia discoidesperma*) that travelled over 24,140 km (15,000 miles) from the Marshall Islands in the Pacific Ocean to Norway. This distance could be traced as the seed is native to only a few Pacific locations and has been researched by the world's drift seed authority, Dr Charles R Gunn (USA).

SMALLEST FRUIT

The floating duckweed (genus *Wolffia*) – the world's smallest flowering plant – produces the world's smallest fruit. As the entire plant body is less than 1 mm (0.04 in) long, the mature fruit takes up a large proportion of its parent plant. The fruit of the *Wolffia augusta* is only 0.25 mm long (0.0098 in) and weighs about 70 micrograms (0.00015 oz), making it smaller than the individual cells of many plants and animals, and smaller than an average grain of table salt.

MEDITERRANEAN MENACE

Caulerpa taxifolia (left) is the world's fastest-growing seaweed, growing at a staggering rate of 8 cm (3 in) per day. *Caulerpa taxifolia* was released from the Oceanographic Institute of Monaco into the Cote d'Azur about 16 years ago and it now covers 6,000 ha (15,000 acres) of seabed off the French coast. It has also spread as far as California. In France, the worst hit country, experts have tried using aluminium and plastic sheeting to prevent sunlight from reaching it and thereby slowing its growth rate.

The longest species of seaweed is the Pacific giant kelp (*Macrocystis pyrifera*), which grows to around 60 m (197 ft) in length. Kelp is required for a healthy marine eco-system.

www.guinnessworldrecords.com/seaweed
← ACCESS CODE: <55976>

LARGEST FLOWER

The orange-brown and white parasite *Rafflesia arnoldi* has the largest of all blooms. These attach themselves to the cissus vines of the jungle in south-east Asia. Resembling a huge poppy, they measure up to 91 cm (3 ft) across, weigh up to 11 kg (24.25 lb) with petals 1.9 cm (0.75 in) thick. There are 16 known species of *Rafflesia* (named after Sir Stamford Raffles and Dr Joseph Arnold) – the latest discovery is as recent as 1988.

GREATEST GIRTH OF A LIVING TREE

'El Arbol del Tule' in Oaxaca state, Mexico, is a 41-m-tall (135-ft) Montezuma cypress (*Taxodium mucronatum*) with a girth of 35.8 m (117 ft 6 in), measured 1.52 m (5 ft) above the ground. If 10 medium-sized cars were placed end-to-end in a circle, this would be about the same size as the girth of this tree. The largest girths are generally attributed to African baobab trees (*Adansonia digitata*).

LARGEST LEAF

The largest leaves of any plant are those belonging to the raffia palm (*Raffia farinifera* or *R. ruffia*) of the Mascarene Islands in the Indian Ocean, and the Amazonian bamboo palm (*R. taedigera*) of South America and Africa, whose leaf blades may be up to 20 m (65 ft 6 in) long, with petioles (the stalk that attaches a leaf to a plant) measuring 4 m (13 ft).

TALLEST CACTUS

The tallest cactus is the cardon (*Pachycereus pringlei*) found in the Sonoran Desert, Mexico, in April 1995. Still growing, it currently measures 19.2 m (63 ft) in height – almost the same as the length of a volleyball court.

SMELLIEST FLOWER

Also known as the 'corpse flower', the Sumatran *Amorphophallus titanum* releases an extremely foul odour, comparable to that of rotten flesh, which can be smelled from 1 km (⅔ mile) away.

TOP TOPIARY

Moirangthem Okendra Kumbi (India) has been shaping the shoots of a Sky Flower bush (*Duranta repens variegata*) in his 'Hedge to Heaven' garden since 1983. It has now grown to a height of 18.59 m (61 ft, left). Overall, with the help of a specially constructed ladder, he has cut 41 structural shapes, repeating a design of a rounded umbrella followed by two discs. Told that the Duranta plant would not grow past 6 m (20 ft), Moirangthem encouraged growth by pruning, redirecting new sprouts and fertilizing the soil. At first, the plant was displayed at local exhibitions, but when it became too large to move, it was planted in its permanent, current location. Moirangthem still climbs the tall iron railings that hold the plant up twice a day in order to tend to it.

www.guinnessworldrecords.com/topiary
← ACCESS CODE: <53209>

MOST MASSIVE TREES

The all-time most massive tree was 'Lindsey Creek' tree, a coast redwood (*Sequoia sempervirens*) in California, USA, which had a minimum trunk volume of 2,549 m³ (90,000 ft³) and a minimal total mass of 3,630 tonnes (8 million lb) – including its foliage, branches and roots – roughly equal to the weight of 800 elephants. The tree blew over in a storm in 1905.

The world's most massive living tree is 'General Sherman', the giant sequoia (*Sequoiadendron giganteum*) in the Sequoia National Park, California, USA, which stands 83.82 m (275 ft) tall, has a diameter of 11.1 m (36 ft 5 in) and a girth of 31.3 m (102 ft 8 in). The trunk has a volume of 1,487 m³ (52,508 ft³). It is estimated to contain the equivalent of 184,739 m (606,100 ft) of timber, enough to make 5 billion matches, and is thought to weigh an estimated 2,000 tonnes (4.4 million lb).

LARGEST FUNGI

A fungus growing in the Malheur National Forest in the Blue Mountains, Oregon, USA, covers 890 ha (2,200 acres) – an area equivalent to 1,220 soccer fields. The species *Armillaria ostoyae*, also known as honey mushroom, is calculated to be at least 2,400 years old.

The largest edible fungi, a giant puffball (*Calvatia gigantea*) measuring 2.64 m (8 ft 8 in) in circumference and weighing 22 kg (48 lb 8 oz), was found by Jean-Guy Richard (Canada) in 1987. A single basketball-sized puffball could produce enough spores in only a couple of generations to result in a puff ball seven times the size of the earth.

LARGEST SEED

The world's largest seed is the giant fan palm *Lodoicea maldivica*, commonly known as the double coconut or *coco de mer*, which are found wild only in the Seychelles. The single-seeded fruit can

www.guinnessworldrecords.com/talltree

ACCESS CODE: ‹47342›

BRANCHING OUT

The tallest living tree is 'Mendocino Tree', a coast redwood (*Sequoia sempervirens*, right). It is still growing at Montgomery State Reserve, California, USA. In Sept 1998 it was 112.01 m (368 ft) tall, with a diameter of 3.14 m (10.3 ft). This height is the same as the length of the average soccer pitch. The tree is about 1,000 years old.
    The oldest living tree is the 4,767-year-old bristlecone pine 'Methuselah' *Pinus longaeva* in the White Mountains, California, USA.

take 10 years to develop and weigh up to 20 kg (44 lb) – equivalent to the weight of approximately six newborn babies. They grow on the palm until they become so heavy that eventually they fall to the ground.

SMALLEST SEED

The smallest seeds are those of epiphytic (non-parasitic) orchids, at 992.25 million seeds per gram (28,129.81 million per oz). As a comparison, grass pollens have up to 170.1 billion grains per gram (6 billion grains per oz).

GUINNESS
WORLD RECORDS™

animal extremes

LARGEST MAMMAL

The world's largest mammal is the blue whale (*Balaenoptera musculus*). They have an average length of 35 m (115 ft) and can weigh up to 130 tonnes (287,000 lb). A huge specimen caught in the Southern Ocean, Antarctica, on 20 March 1947 weighed a massive 190 tonnes (420,000 lb) and measured 27.6 m (90 ft 6 in). A blue whale also has the largest offspring; the newborn calf is 6–8 m (20–26 ft) long and weighs 2–3 tonnes (4,400–6,600 lb).

LARGEST LAND MAMMAL

The largest land mammal is the male African bush elephant (*Loxodonta africana*). These huge beasts have an average shoulder-height of 3–3.7 m (9 ft 10 in– 12 ft 2 in) and an average weight of 4–7 tonnes (8,800–15,400 lb). The heaviest recorded specimen was a bull shot in Mucusso, Angola, on 7 Nov 1974, that had a projected standing height of 3.96 m (13 ft) and weighed a staggering 12.24 tonnes (26,900 lb). The tallest male African bush elephants are found in Namibia; the tallest recorded example was shot near Sesfontein, Namibia, on 4 April 1978, after allegedly killing 11 people. It

WATCH THE BIRDIE

The heaviest bird of prey is the Andean condor (*Vultur gryphus*, left), males of which average 9–12 kg (20–27 lb) and have a wingspan of 3 m (10 ft). A weight of 14.1 kg (31 lb) was claimed for a Californian condor (*Gymnogyps californianus*) now preserved in the California Academy of Sciences, Los Angeles, USA, but this species is generally smaller and rarely exceeds 10.4 kg (23 lb).

The longest feathers grown by any bird were recorded in 1972 on a Phoenix fowl or Yokohama chicken (*Gallus gallus*), whose tail covert measured 10.6 m (34 ft 9.5 in) – as long as a bus.

www.guinnessworldrecords.com/condor

← ACCESS CODE: ‹51472›

measured 4.42 m (14 ft 6 in) had a projected height of about 4.21 m (13 ft 10 in), and weighed an estimated 8 tonnes (17,600 lb).

TALLEST MAMMAL

The tallest mammal is the giraffe (*Giraffa camelopardalis*), which is only found in Africa. On average, mature giraffe males grow to a height of around 5.5 m (18 ft). George, a Kenyan Masai bull (*Giraffa camelopardalis tippelskirchi*) who arrived at Chester Zoo on 8 Jan 1959, was the tallest giraffe ever recorded. Standing 5.8 m

(19 ft) tall, his horns almost grazed the roof of the 6-m (20-ft) high giraffe house when he was nine years old. George died on 22 July 1969.

SMALLEST MAMMAL

The very tiny Kitti's hog-nosed bat (*Craseonycteris thonglongyai*) has a body no bigger than a large bumble-bee. It has a head–body length of only 2.9–3.3 cm (1.14–1.30 in), an average wingspan of 13–14.5 cm (5.1–5.7 in) and weighs just 1.7–2.0 g (0.06–0.07 oz). This tiny bat can be found in a few limestone caves on the Kwae Noi River, Thailand.

LARGEST CAMELIDAE

The dromedary or one-humped camel (*Camelus dromedarius*) is the largest even-toed hoofed mammal. Native to the Middle East, it survives as a wild animal in Australia and as a domestic animal elsewhere. It has an average head and body length of 2.3–3.5 m (7.5–11.5 ft), a shoulder height of 1.8–2.1 m (6–7 ft) (maximum 2.4 m or 7 ft 11 in) and

weighs 450–690 kg (992–1,521 lb). Incredibly, the world's tallest man (Robert Wadlow) was taller, measuring 2.72 m (8 ft).

SMALLEST HIPPOPOTAMUS

The pygmy hippopotamus (*Choeropsis liberiensis*) is the smallest species of hippo, found mainly in Liberia, west Africa. Standing at human knee-height, pygmy hippos have an average head–body length of 1.5–1.85 m (4 ft 11 in–8ft 1 in), a shoulder height of 70–100 cm (2 ft 3.5 in–3 ft 3.25 in) and a weight of 160–275 kg (353–606 lb). In comparison, the average-sized hippopotamus is about 10 times bigger and weighs a heavy duty 2,600 kg (5,733 lb).

LARGEST DEER

The world's largest deer is the Alaskan moose (*Alces alces gigas*). The largest specimen, a bull that stood 2.34 m (7 ft 8 in) and weighed an estimated 816 kg (1,800 lb), was shot in Canada in Sept 1897.

GONE TO POT!

The American or North Atlantic lobster (*Homarus americanus*, left) is the heaviest marine crustacean. On 11 Feb 1977 a specimen weighing a staggering 20.14 kg (44 lb 6 oz) and measuring 1.06 m (3 ft 6 in) from the end of the tail-fan to the tip of the largest claw, was caught off Nova Scotia, Canada, and later sold to a New York restaurant owner. The average weight of a lobster is usually 1.4 kg (3 lb).

The largest of all marine crustaceans (although not the heaviest) is the *taka-ashi-gani* or giant spider crab (*Macrocheira kaempferi*), found in the Pacific regions. A specimen with a claw-span of 3.7 m (12 ft 1 in) weighed 18.6 kg (41 lb). These spider crabs are part of a large group of slow-moving crabs that lie in wait to attack their prey.

SMALLEST DEER

The smallest true deer (family *Cervidae*) is the tiny southern pudu (*Pudu puda*), which is 33–38 cm (13–15 in) tall at the shoulder and weighs 6.3–8.2 kg (14–18 lb). An endangered species, it is found on the slopes of the Andes mountains in Chile and Argentina.

LARGEST MAMMAL EYES

The Pygmy tarsier (*Tarsius pumilus*) from South-east Asia has a head–body length of 8.5–16 cm (3.3–6.3 in) and huge forward-pointing eyes with a diameter of 1.6 cm (0.6 in). This eye-size is equivalent to eyes the size of a grapefruit in a human being. Tarsiers are also the only primates that can move their heads through 180 degrees to the left and to the right.

LARGEST WILD PIG

The largest wild pig is the extremely fierce giant forest hog (*Hylochoerus meinertzhageni*), which lives in central Africa. It has a head–body length of 1.3–2.1 m (4 ft 5 in–7 ft), a tail length of 30–45 cm (12–17.75 in), a shoulder height of 85–105 cm (2 ft 9.5 in–3 ft 8.33 in) and a weight of 130–275 kg (287–606 lb). They have sharp tusks and are highly dangerous when angry.

LARGEST OWL

The world's largest owl is the European eagle owl (*Bubo bubo*), which has an average length of 66–71 cm (26–28 in), a weight of 1.6–4 kg (3.5–8.82 lb) and a wingspan of more than 1.5 m (5 ft).

SMALLEST OWL

The world's smallest owl is the elf owl (*Micrathene whitney*) from south-western USA and Mexico, averaging 12–14 cm (4.72–5.5 in) in length and weighing less than 50 g (1.76 oz).

HEAVIEST SCORPION

The black west African species *Pandinus imperator* can weigh up to 60 g (2 oz) and is between 13–18 cm (5–7 in) in length. This is the average length of an adult human hand.

www.guinnessworldrecords.com/greatwhite

ACCESS CODE: ‹51342›

FISHY TALES

The largest predatory fish is the rare great white shark (*Carcharodon carcharias*, below). Adult specimens average 4.3–4.6 m (14–15 ft) in length, and generally weigh 520–770 kg (1,146–1,697 lb). The world's biggest fish is the rare plankton-feeding whale shark (*Rhincodon typus*), which is found in the Atlantic, Pacific and Indian Oceans. They can grow to a massive 18 m (59 ft). The whale shark also produces the largest fish egg.

GUINNESS WORLD RECORDS™

dangerous beasts

MOST SUCCESSFUL PREDATOR

African hunting dogs, also called cape hunting dogs or dog hyaenas (*Lycaon pictus*), hunt in packs and are successful in 50–70% of their hunts. This is consistently the highest figure in the mammalian world.

LARGEST LAND CARNIVORE

Adult male polar bears (*Ursus maritimus*) typically weigh 400–600 kg (880–1320 lb) and, nose-to-tail, are

2.4–2.6 m (7 ft 11 in–8 ft 6 in) in length. Excellent swimmers, they have been known to swim 100 km (approx 60 miles) to hunt seals. The polar bear has a stomach capacity of about 68 kg (150 lb) and is known to kill animals as large as walruses (500 kg or 1,100 lb) and beluga whales (600 kg or 1,320 lb) – the world's largest prey. Their digestive system is also more adapted for processing meat than plant material, making them the most carnivorous of all bear species.

Male Kodiak bears (*Ursus arctos middendorffi*), a sub-species of brown bear found on islands in the Gulf of Alaska, USA, are more robustly built than the polar bear, but are usually shorter in length.

MOST FATALITIES FROM ANIMAL ATTACKS

On 19 Feb 1945, 980 Japanese soldiers out of a group of 1,000 were killed by estuarine or saltwater crocodiles (*Crocodylus porosus*) after being forced to cross a 16-km (10-mile) mangrove swamp in order to join their infantry division. This is a survival rate of only 0.2 % – the worst-ever crocodile attack. The estuarine crocodile, found in Asia and the Pacific, is the world's largest reptile; adult males average 4.2–4.8 m (14–16 ft) long and weigh about 408–520 kg (900–1,150 lb). The largest authenticated specimens measured over 7 m (23 ft). Unauthenticated reports claim specimens up to 10 m (33 ft) in length.

Between 1764 and 1766, a wild wolf called the 'Beast of Gevauden' attacked dozens of people in the mountainous region of Lozére, France. More than 100 wolves were killed before the killer wolf was shot on 19 Jan 1766. When it was cut open, the shoulder of a young child killed the previous day was found inside its stomach.

The Champawat Tigress – said to be responsible for 436 deaths in the Champawat district, India, between 1902 and 1907 – was one of the most notorious man-eating animals in India. She was eventually shot by Colonel Jim Corbett in 1907.

ARMED AND DANGEROUS

The longest horns of any living animal belong to the wild water buffalo (*Bubalus arnee*, above) of India, Nepal, Bhutan and Thailand. The average spread is about 1 m (3 ft 3 in), but one bull shot in 1955 had horns measuring 4.24 m (13 ft 11 in) from tip to tip along the outside curve across the forehead.

The longest non-prehistoric tusks were obtained from an African elephant (*Loxodonta africana*) in Zaire (now Democratic Republic of Congo) and are kept in the New York Zoological Society, New York City, New York, USA. The right tusk measures 3.49 m (11 ft 5 in) along the outside curve, and the left 3.35 m (11 ft). Together, they weigh 133 kg (293 lb).

The Gila Lizard (*Heloderma suspectum*) is the world's most dangerous lizard, with sharp teeth and enough venom to kill two adults.

www.guinnessworldrecords.com/buffalo

 ACCESS CODE: ‹51205›

RED FOR DANGER

The tiny, brightly coloured poison dart frogs of South and Central America (*Phyllobates terribilis*, above) are the most poisonous frog species. They secrete some of the most deadly biological toxins known, including batrachotoxin, which affects the nervous system. A single drop in contact with the human body can block transmission of nerve impulses and may even stop the heart. This poison is used by native South and Central American tribes to coat arrowheads, hence the name. The 4–5-cm-long (1.6–2-in) frog produces enough toxin to kill 10 adult humans.

www.guinnessworldrecords.com/poisonfrog

← ACCESS CODE: ‹51322›

MOST FEROCIOUS FRESHWATER FISH

The piranha, especially of the genera *Serrasalmus* and *Pygocentrus*, is found in the rivers of South America. It has razor-sharp teeth and is the world's most ferocious freshwater fish. Attracted to blood and frantic splashing, piranhas can completely strip an animal as large as a horse of its flesh within minutes, leaving only the skeleton. Attacks are swift and comprehensive as they start eating their victim alive – piranhas will even often injure one another in the frenzy of an attack. On 19 Sept 1981 more than 300 people were reportedly killed and eaten when an overloaded passenger-cargo boat capsized and sank as it was docking at the Brazilian port of Obidos.

MOST ELECTRIC FISH

The electric eel (*Electrophorus electricus*), a relative of the piranha, is the world's most electric fish. Measuring up to 1.8 m (6 ft) in length, it lives in rivers in Brazil and the Guianas, and can stun its prey with an electric shock of up to 650 volts – enough to light an electric bulb or to stun a human adult.

MOST VENOMOUS FISH

The stonefish (family Synanceidae), which lives on the bottom of the Indo-Pacific Ocean, is the world's most venomous fish. *Synanceia horrida* has the largest venom glands of any known fish. Any direct contact with its spiny fins, which contain a strong, toxic poison, can prove fatal.

MOST VENOMOUS EDIBLE FISH

The puffer fish (*Tetraodon*), of the Red Sea and Indo-Pacific region, is the most poisonous edible fish, secreting a venom that is 1,250 times deadlier than cyanide. However, when cooked properly, it is a Japanese delicacy called *fugu*. The Japanese consume 10,000 tonnes (22 million lb) of *fugu* a year, resulting in an average fatality rate of 70–100 people per year.

MOST POISONOUS BIRD

The hooded pitohui (*Pitohui dichrous*) from Papua New Guinea is the only known poisonous bird in the world. Discovered in 1990, scientists do not know why its feathers and skin contain the poison homobatrachotoxin (the same one secreted by the dart frogs of South America). Like many other poisonous animals, this bird emits a foul smell and is brightly coloured.

MOST DANGEROUS BIRD

The most dangerous birds are the three species of cassowary (family Casuariidae) that live in New Guinea and north-eastern Queensland, Australia. Standing up to 2 m (6 ft 7 in) tall, they have strong claws on the three forward-pointing toes of each foot. The inner toe has a 12-cm (5-in) long spike for defensive purposes – it kicks out when cornered. They can leap into the air and kick, damaging vital organs or causing massive bleeding. Its kick is powerful enough to rip open a person's stomach or even kill.

MOST VENOMOUS MOLLUSC

The two closely related species of blue-ringed octopus, *Hapalochlaena maculosa* and *H. lunulata*, found on the coasts of Australia and south-east Asia, carry a neurotoxic venom so potent that their relatively painless bite can kill in a matter of minutes. With a radial spread of 100–200 mm (4–8 in), each individual carries enough venom to cause the paralysis (or even death) of 10 adult humans.

MOST VENOMOUS JELLYFISH

The transparent Australian sea wasp or box jellyfish (*Chironex fleckeri*) is the most venomous cnidarian and also one of the world's most venomous creatures, with enough poison to kill 60 people. Weighing an average of 6 kg (13 lb), and measuring 20–30 cm (8–12 in) across the bell, the jellyfish may have up to 60 tentacles, each one containing millions of poisonous nematocysts. At least 70 people have died from the venom in the last 100 years with death occuring in as little as four minutes.

www.guinnessworldrecords.com/venomviper

ACCESS CODE: ‹5100?›

MIND YOUR STEP!

The Gaboon viper (*Bitis gabonica*, above) from tropical Africa, produces more venom than any other snake. A single adult male is thought to have enough venom to inject lethal doses into 30 people. As they also have the longest fangs of any snake, Gaboon vipers also inject the poison more deeply – one specimen measuring 1.83 m (6 ft) had fangs 50 mm (2 in) long.

The world's longest venomous snake, the king cobra (*Ophiophagus hannah*), from India and south-east Asia, is also highly dangerous and can deliver enough venom to kill an elephant or 20 people, through fangs almost 0.5 in (12 mm) long. Averaging 3.65–4.5 m (12–15 ft), the longest known specimen measured 5.54 m (18 ft 2 in) on capture in 1937, and later grew to 5.71 m (18 ft 9 in).

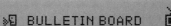

GUINNESS WORLD RECORDS

creepy crawlies

BEETLEMANIA!

The click beetle (*Athous haemorrhoidalis*, above) achieves the highest G-force of any insect without the use of its legs. The 'click' occurs when the beetle 'jack-knifes' into the air to escape predators; it bends its head and prothorax backward and then straightens up suddenly with a snapping motion, shooting up to 15 cm (6 in) high and achieving a G-force of around 400 G. One beetle measuring 1.2 cm (0.5 in) in length and weighing 40 mg (0.00014 oz) jumped to a height of 30 cm (12 in) and was calculated to have endured a peak brain deceleration of 2,300 G by the end of the movement. G-force measures the change of speed over time, and gauges how fast a person, animal or thing is accelerating from moment to moment. If sustained for longer than a few seconds, a G-force of between 4 and 6 G will cause a human being to black out. Astronauts on the space shuttle during lift-off experience a force of 3 G.

 www.guinnessworldrecords.com/clickbeetle

← ACCESS CODE: ‹51294›

LARGEST MARINE SNAIL

The largest known marine gastropod is the trumpet or baler conch (*Syrinx aruanus*) of Australia. One specimen collected off Western Australia in 1979 had a shell 77.2 cm (30.4 in) long, with a maximum girth of 101 cm (39.8 in). It weighed nearly 18 kg (40 lb) when alive.

LONGEST EARTHWORM

The longest earthworm is the *Microchaetus rappi* of South Africa. In 1967 a giant specimen was found measuring 6.7 m (22 ft) in length (when naturally extended) and 2.03 cm (0.8 in) in diameter. The average length of this species is approximately 1.8 m (6 ft) when naturally extended.

LARGEST BUTTERFLY

The largest known butterfly is the poisonous Queen Alexandra's Birdwing (*Ornithoptera alexandrae*) of Papua New Guinea. Females may have a wingspan exceeding 27.9 cm (11 in) and weigh over 25 g (0.9 oz).

SMALLEST BUTTERFLY

The smallest butterfly is the South African dwarf blue (*Brephidium barberae*). It has a wingspan of 1.4 cm (0.55 in) and weighs less than 10 mg (0.00035 oz).

LARGEST COCKROACH

The largest cockroach is *Megaloblatta longipennis* of Colombia. A specimen belonging to Akira Yokokura (Japan) is 9.7 cm (3.8 in) long and 4.45 cm (1.75 in) wide. The average cockroach measures 0.6–7.6 cm (0.24–3 in) long.

LARGEST FLEA

There are around 1,830 species of flea, of which the largest known is *Hystrichopsylla schefferi*, first found in Washington, USA, in 1913. Females of this species grow to an average length of 0.76 cm (0.3 in). As a comparison, the common flea (*Pulex irritans*) has an average length of 0.1–2.54 mm (0.04–1 in).

The champion jumper among fleas is the cat flea (*Ctenocephalides felis*), which can reach a height of 34 cm (13 in) in a single jump – 130 times its height. This requires an acceleration of over 20 times that needed to launch a space rocket.

LARGEST WASP NEST

A wasp nest found by Yoichiro Kawamura (Japan) on 18 May 1999 at Yonegaoka, Nahari Town, Japan, had a circumference of 2.45 m (8 ft) and weighed 8 kg (17.6 lb). The circumference was approximately three times the size of a basketball.

OLDEST FOSSIL ANTS

In 1998 a team of researchers from the American Museum of Natural History, New Jersey, USA, announced the dating of the oldest fossil ants ever found. The extremely rare 92-million-year-old ants, discovered in 1967, are preserved in amber. They were found in a New Jersey location where some of the most important amber-encased fossils have been located.

OLDEST INSECT

The longest-lived insects are the splendour beetles (Buprestidae). On 27 May 1983 a specimen of *Buprestis aurulenta* appeared from the staircase timber in the home of W. Euston of Prittlewell, UK, after at least 47 years as a larva.

LOUDEST INSECT

The African cicada (*Brevisana brevis*) produces a calling song with an average sound pressure level of 106.7 dB at a distance of 50 cm (19.5 in). As a comparison, the noise measured in the front row of a rock concert is 110 dB. Cicada songs play a vital role in communication.

LARGEST INDOOR SPIDER'S WEB

A spider's web 5.08 m (16 ft 6 in) long and 3.80 m (12 ft 4 in) wide, with an area of 19.35 m² (208 ft²), was discovered in the outhouse of a 17th-century cottage in Newent, Glos, UK, in Jan 1999. The web, which hung suspended like a second ceiling 1.8 m (5.9 ft) off the floor, was probably built by a succession of eight-legged inhabitants.

STRANGEST INSECT DEFENCE SYSTEM

The bombardier beetle (genus *Brachinus*) stores two relatively benign chemicals in its body. When threatened, these chemicals mix with an enzyme, causing a violent chemical reaction and the release of considerable heat (up to 100ºC or 212ºF) from the anus. This spray of irritating gas can be turned on and off an amazing 500 times a second. This system is similar to the pulse jet engine that powered the World War II German V-1 flying bomb. However the V-1 could only pulse its jet 42 times per second.

MOST EXPENSIVE INSECT

A giant 7.9-cm (3.1-in) stag beetle (*Dorcus hopei*) is reported to have been sold for JPY 10,035,000 (£57,000; $90,000) at a Tokyo store on 19 Aug 1999. A 36-year-old company president apparently bought it for his collection but refused to be identified for fear of being targeted by thieves.

FASTEST CATERPILLAR

The larvae of the mother-of-pearl moth (*Pleurotya ruralis*) can travel 38.1 cm (15 in) per second, as they curl into a ball and roll away when attacked. This is the caterpillar equivalent of 241 km/h (150 mph).

HIGHEST FLYING INSECT

The greatest height reported for migrating butterflies is 5,791 m (19,000 ft) for a flock of small tortoiseshells (*Aglais urticae*) seen over the Zemu Glacier in the eastern Himalayas. In comparison, the highest altitude recorded for a bird is 11,300 m (37,000 ft) for a Ruppell's vulture (*Gyps rueppellii*),

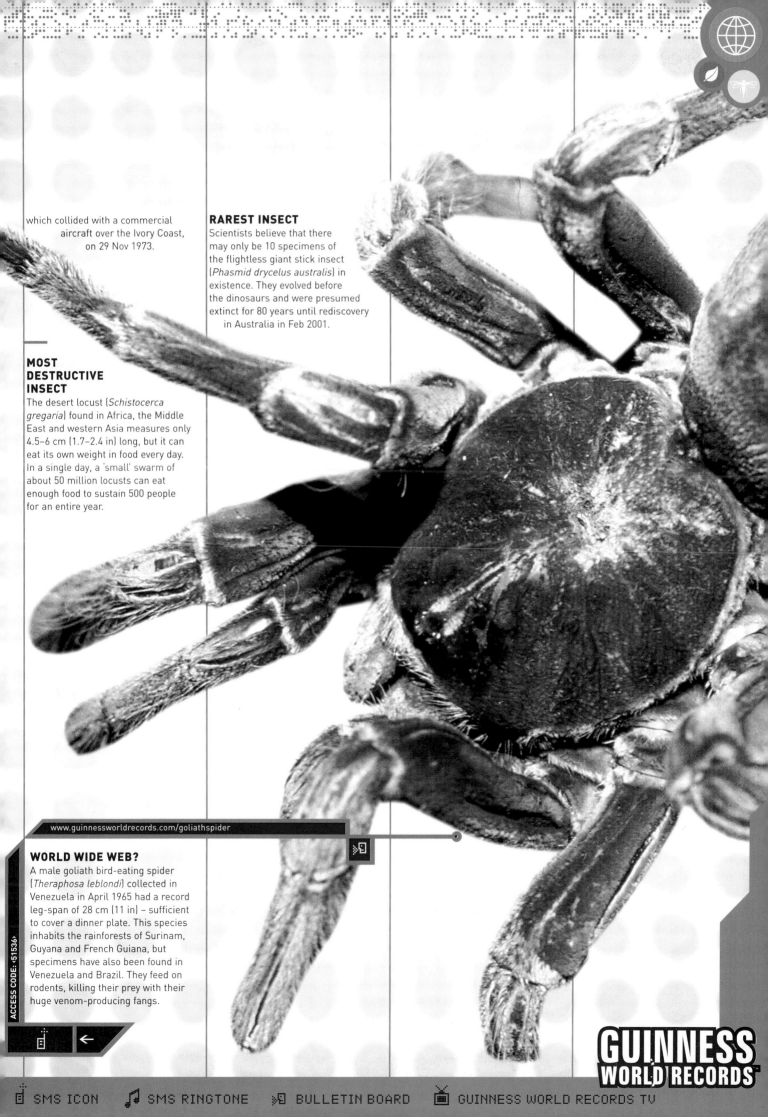

which collided with a commercial aircraft over the Ivory Coast, on 29 Nov 1973.

RAREST INSECT

Scientists believe that there may only be 10 specimens of the flightless giant stick insect (*Phasmid drycelus australis*) in existence. They evolved before the dinosaurs and were presumed extinct for 80 years until rediscovery in Australia in Feb 2001.

MOST DESTRUCTIVE INSECT

The desert locust (*Schistocerca gregaria*) found in Africa, the Middle East and western Asia measures only 4.5–6 cm (1.7–2.4 in) long, but it can eat its own weight in food every day. In a single day, a 'small' swarm of about 50 million locusts can eat enough food to sustain 500 people for an entire year.

www.guinnessworldrecords.com/goliathspider

WORLD WIDE WEB?

A male goliath bird-eating spider (*Theraphosa leblondi*) collected in Venezuela in April 1965 had a record leg-span of 28 cm (11 in) – sufficient to cover a dinner plate. This species inhabits the rainforests of Surinam, Guyana and French Guiana, but specimens have also been found in Venezuela and Brazil. They feed on rodents, killing their prey with their huge venom-producing fangs.

GUINNESS WORLD RECORDS

dinosaurs and mammoths

TALLEST DINOSAUR

The *Sauroposeidon* is thought to be the largest creature to have ever walked the Earth. Remains found in Oklahoma, USA, in 1994 indicate that it stood 18.28 m (60 ft) tall, weighed 60 tonnes (132,277 lb) and had the longest neck of any known dinosaur, with vertebrae measuring up to 1.2 m (4 ft) long. *Sauroposeidon* was giraffe-like in shape but was 30 times larger than the largest giraffe on record – as tall as a six-storey building. It lived about 110 million years ago.

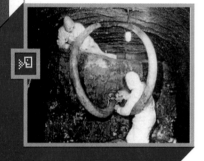

MAMMOTH TASK

The oldest intact mammoth is 'Jarkov' (above), estimated to be 23,000 years old, excavated by a group of French scientists in Oct 1999 in Siberia (Russia). It died at the age of 47 and would have stood 2.6 m (8.5 ft). Originally found by nine-year-old reindeer herder Guenadi Jarkov in 1997, the mammoth was subsequently named after his family. Much of the excavation work has been financed by the Discovery Channel and, in 2000, the entire mammoth was airlifted to a new home in its 23.34–tonne (51,456-lb) frozen cube, with its two tusks sticking out of the ice. The mammoth is now in a cave being defrosted by scientists using hairdryers. Although only a small fraction of the block has melted, mammoth bones, hair and other items have been found and sent around the world for analysis. Scientists plan to extract DNA to perform experiments.

www.guinnessworldrecords.com/mammoth

ACCESS CODE: ← ‹53392›

LARGEST CARNIVOROUS DINOSAUR

A skeleton of the largest-ever predatory dinosaur was discovered in Neuquen, Argentina in 1995. *Giganotosaurus carolinii* (giant southern reptile) was 12.5 m (41 ft) long and weighed 8 tonnes (17,637 lb). The bones suggest that it was both taller and more heavily built than *Tyrannosaurus rex*. It walked the Earth around 110 million years ago – 30 million years before the *Tyrannosaurus rex*.

SMALLEST DINOSAUR

The chicken-sized *Compsognathus* (pretty jaw), of southern Germany and south-east France, measured 60 cm (23 in) from the snout to the tip of the tail and weighed about 3 kg (6 lb 8 oz). *Compsognathus* existed during the late Jurassic period, about 145 million years ago. It was a carnivore, eating small animals such as lizards and insects. Only two specimens have been found since 1859 – an adult in Germany and a juvenile in France.

HEAVIEST DINOSAUR

Argentinosaurus, a titanosaurid from Argentina, was probably the heaviest dinosaur. Estimates made in 1994, based on its massive vertebrae, suggest it may have weighed up to 100 tonnes (220,462 lb). The heaviest UK dinosaur was the diplodocid *Cetiosaurus oxoniensis*, which lived around 170 million years ago and weighed about 45 tonnes (99,208 lb), according to estimates based on part of a femur found in Bucks, UK.

LARGEST ARMOURED DINOSAUR

Ankylosaurus, a herbivore protected with thick plates covering the skin, also had a double row of spikes running down from the back of its head to its club tail. Measuring 7.5–10.7 m (24.6–35.1 ft) long and 1.2 m (4 ft) tall, it even had plates to protect its eyes, with only its belly left unplated. With a width of up to 2.5 m (8 ft), it was also the widest known dinosaur. The last and largest of the ankylosaurids at 4 tonnes (8,618.5 lb), it lived in the late Cretaceous period, about 70–65 million years ago.

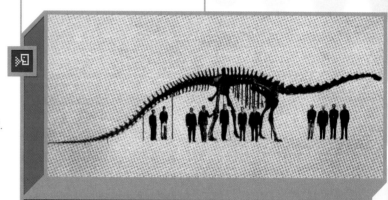

TAIL ENDING

The *Diplodocus* (double-beamed, above), a long-necked sauropod from the late Jurassic period 155–145 million years ago, had the longest tail of any dinosaur, with a length of up to 13.1 m (43 ft). The remains of a *Diplodocus carnegii* found in Wyoming, USA, in 1899 would have measured 26.6 m (87.2 ft) long when alive, with much of that length made up by a long neck and an extremely long whip-like tail. It probably weighed 5.8–18.5 tonnes (12,787–40,785 lb), with an estimate of around 12 tonnes (26,455 lb) being the most likely.

www.guinnessworldrecords.com/longtaildino
← ACCESS CODE: ‹56108›

THICKEST DINOSAUR SKULL

Pachycephalosaurus, a dome-headed herbivore that lived about 76–65 million years ago during the late Cretaceous period, had a skull measuring 65 cm (2 ft) long with a bone dome of 20 cm (7.8 in). In comparison, the thickest part of the human skull is 20 mm (0.7 in).

LONGEST PREHISTORIC SNAKE

The longest prehistoric snake was the python-like *Gigantophis garstini*, which inhabited what is now Egypt about 38 million years ago. Parts of a spinal column and a piece of jaw discovered at Fayum in the Western Desert indicate a length of about 11 m (36 ft). This is 1 m (3 ft 3 in) more than the present-day longest snake, the reticulated python (*Python reticulatus*).

LARGEST FOSSIL TRILOBITE

A fossil trilobite discovered in Canada measured over 70 cm (27.5 in) in length, more than 30 cm (11.8 in) longer than the previous largest trilobite. The discovery of this 445 million-year-old specimen was announced on 9 Oct 2000.

LARGEST PREHISTORIC FLYING BIRD

In 1979 fossil remains of the giant *Argentavis magnificens*, which lived about 6–8 million years ago in what is now Argentina, were discovered 160 km (100 miles) west of Buenos Aires. The remains indicate a wing span of over 6 m (19 ft 8 in) – possibly up to 7.6 m (25 ft) – and a weight of about 80 kg (176 lb). In comparison, the albatross (*Diomedea exulans*), which has the largest wingspan of any living species of bird, measures of 3.63 m (11 ft 11 in).

LARGEST PREHISTORIC INSECT

The largest prehistoric insect was the dragonfly *Meganeura monyi*, which lived about 280 million years ago. Fossil remains discovered at Commentry, France, indicate a wing expanse of up to 70 cm (27.5 in).

EARLIEST MAMMAL

In 1991 a partial skull of a mammal named *Adelobasileus cromptoni* (similar to a modern tree shrew) was found in 225 million-year-old rocks in New Mexico, USA.

LONGEST PREHISTORIC TUSKS

The longest prehistoric tusks were those of the straight-tusked elephant *Hesperoloxodon antiques germanicus*, which lived in what is now northern Germany about two million years ago. The average tusk-length in adult bulls was 5 m (16 ft 4.75 in).

HEAVIEST SINGLE FOSSIL TUSK

The heaviest recorded single fossil tusk weighed 150 kg (330 lb) with a maximum circumference of 89 cm (35 in), and belonged to an unknown species of mammoth. The specimen (in two pieces) is 3.58 m (11 ft 9 in) in length.

LARGEST PREHISTORIC ANTLERS

The prehistoric giant deer or Irish elk (*Megaloceros giganteus*), found in continental Europe as recently as 10,000 years ago, had the longest known antlers. One specimen, recovered from an Irish bog, had antlers measuring 4.3 m (14 ft) across, corresponding to a shoulder height of 1.83 m (6 ft) and a weight of 500 kg (1,100 lb). This compares to the largest recorded spread or 'rack' of antlers of any living species, which was 1.99 m (6 ft 6 in) from a moose (*Alces alces*) killed near the Stewart River, Yukon, Canada, in Oct 1897.

DINOSAUR WITH THE MOST TEETH

The dinosaurs with the most teeth were the duck-billed *hadrosaurs* (bulky lizards). Despite being herbivores with toothless beaks, they had up to 960 self-sharpening cheek teeth in the side of their strong jaws for chewing tough plants. *Hadrosaurs* ranged in size from 3–12 m (10–40 ft) long.

www.guinnessworldrecords.com/trex

LARGE AND EXPENSIVE

One of the largest-ever carnivores, *Tyrannosaurus rex* (above) roamed the Earth during the last part of the Cretaceous Age, between 85 and 65 million years ago. The largest and most complete *T-rex* skeleton ever is 'Sue', discovered in South Dakota, USA, on 12 Aug 1990 by fossil hunter Sue Hendrickson. The skeleton is 4 m (13 ft) tall and 12.5 m (41 ft) long and has a skull measuring 1.5 m (4.9 ft) long. She has 58 teeth in her powerful jaw, with each tooth measuring between 19 and 30 cm (7.5 and 12 in). Her estimated live weight is 6.4 tonnes (14,110 lb). The Field Museum, Chicago, USA, purchased the skeleton at a public auction in 1997 for $8,362,500 (£5,174,014) – the world's highest price for a dinosaur skeleton – and have put her on permanent display.

GUINNESS WORLD RECORDS

extraordinary animals

SLOWEST MAMMAL

The three-toed sloth of tropical South America (*Bradypus tridactylus*) has an average ground speed of 1.8–2.4 m (6–8 ft) per minute (0.1–0.16 km/h, 0.07–0.1 mph), but in the trees it can accelerate to 4.6 m (15 ft) per minute (0.27 km/h, 0.17 mph). Sloths seldom descend to the ground as they cannot walk and have to pull themselves along using their claws. Digestion for a sloth is also very slow, and it may take a month or more for food to pass from the stomach to the intestine.

LONGEST JOURNEY MADE BY A FISH

Two oyster toadfish (*Opsanus tau*), a species that inhabits the north east of the USA, travelled more than three million miles through space in the *Discovery* space shuttle mission STS-95. The fish were taken aboard to help scientists learn more about how bodies react to motion sickness.

BEST TREE-CLIMBING FISH

The climbing perch (*Anabas testudineus*), from south Asia, is remarkable for its walking and palm-tree climbing abilities. It will even walk to search for better habitat. The species has special gills that allow it to absorb atmospheric oxygen. Similarly mudskippers (of the Perciformes order like the perch) can live out of water for short periods and climb trees, holding on by their pectoral fins.

SPEEDY GONZALES

The ostrich (*Struthio camelus*, left), which is found on the plains of Africa, holds the record speed for a land bird of 72 km/h (45 mph) and has a stride that may exceed 7.01 m (23 ft). In comparison, over distances of up to 550 m (1,800 ft), the cheetah (*Acinonyx jubatus*) holds the overall animal speed record, maintaining a steady 100 km/h (60 mph) on level ground – almost the US highway speed limit. Cheetahs are found in Africa, Iran, Turkmenistan and Afghanistan. The American antelope (*Antilocapra americana*) holds the long-distance speed record for an animal, with continuous speeds of 56 km/h (35 mph) for as far as 6 km (4 miles). It is found in the USA, Canada and northern Mexico.

www.guinnessworldrecords.com/ostrich
← ACCESS CODE: ‹51481›

LONGEST RODENT HIBERNATION

Arctic ground squirrels (*Spermophilus parryi*) hold the record for the longest hibernation by a rodent. They live in northern Canada and Alaska, USA, and hibernate for nine months every year.

MOST COLD-RESISTANT ANIMAL

The Woodland frog, which lives north of the Arctic Circle, is the only animal that can survive being frozen. Glucose in the blood acts as an 'antifreeze', which protects the frogs' vital organs, while the rest of the body freezes solid. Once the weather warms up, the frogs 'come back to life'.

MOST RADIATION-RESISTANT LIFEFORM

The bacterium *Deinococcus radiodurans* can repair damage to its chromosomal DNA and thus resist 1.5 million rads of gamma radiation, which is about 3,000 times the amount that would kill a human. If the bacteria is cooled or frozen, it can take twice that amount. The bacterium survives and reproduces in environments lethal to any other organism and also resists high doses of ultraviolet radiation.

BEST ANIMAL REGENERATION

Sponges (Porifera) have the best powers of regeneration of any animal. If they lose a segment of their body, it will grow back and if a sponge is forced through a fine-meshed silk gauze, the separate fragments will re-form into a full-size sponge.

SLOWEST GROWTH RATE

The slowest animal growth rate is that of the deep-sea clam (*Tindaria callistiformis*), which inhabits the North Atlantic ocean. It takes about 100 years to grow 8 mm (0.4 in) long.

MOST FEARLESS MAMMAL

The most fearless mammal is the ratel or honey badger (*Mellivora capensis*) found in the forest and brush country of Africa, the Middle East and India. It will defend itself against animals of any size, especially if they come too close to its breeding burrow. Its tough skin is impervious to the stings of bees, the quills of porcupines and the bites of most snakes. The skin is also so loose that if a predator holds it by the scruff of the neck, the badger can turn inside its skin and bite its attacker until released.

STRONGEST ANIMAL

In proportion to their size, the strongest animals are the larger beetles of the family Scarabaeidae, which are found mainly in the tropics. In tests carried out on a rhinoceros beetle of the family Dynastinae, it was found to support 850 times its own weight on its back.

MOST DANGEROUS LOVE LIFE

The male brown antechinus (*Antechinus stuartii*), a marsupial mouse from eastern Australia, has a fatal sexual appetite. Each year the entire adult male population mates with as many females as possible. They rarely eat and spend their time fighting rival males. As a result, they all die within a matter of days, due to starvation, ulcers or infection.

MOST AERIAL LAND BIRD

A common swift (*Apus apus*) completes a non-stop flight of 500,000 km (310,000 miles) between fledging and its first landing at a potential nesting site two years, and, in some cases, up to four years later. During this time it sleeps, drinks, eats and even mates on the wing.

THE GOLDEN SHOT

The yellow-and-black banded archer fish (*Toxotes jaculator*, left) lurks near riverbanks in its native Thailand waiting for a suitable insect to alight on a water plant within its record 1.5-m (5-ft) water-spitting range. The fish shoots a pellet of water at the prey from its tubular-shaped mouth. If the fish misses, it is able to attempt again in quick fire. This semi-automatic hunting method is unique among animals and makes the archer fish the best aquatic marksman in the world.

The grotesque-looking Texas horned lizard, also known as the horned toad, or the horny toad, holds the record for the strangest defence mechanism among animals. When threatened, it can spray blood containing caustic irritants out of its eyes, warding off potential predators.

www.guinnessworldrecords.com/archerfish
← ACCESS CODE: ‹53943›

SAY 'CHEESE'!

In 1972, Koko – a gorilla born at San Francisco Zoo – was taught ASL (American Sign Language for the Deaf) by Dr Francine Patterson. By 2000, Koko (right, in a photograph that she took of herself in a mirror) had a record working vocabulary of over 1,000 signs and understood roughly 2,000 words of English. She can refer to the past and future, argue, make jokes and lie. Koko has told *Guinness World Records* that she is honoured to hold the record for the gorilla most proficient in sign language and to be in this book.

ACCESS CODE: ‹61137›

GUINNESS WORLD RECORDS

fantastic pets

OLDEST CATS

Ma, a female tabby owned by Alice St George Moore (UK) and Grandpa Rex Allen, a champion show cat owned by Jake Perry (USA) are the longest-living domestic cats ever recorded. Both felines were an amazing 34 years old when they died on 5 Nov 1957 and 1 April 1998 respectively. This is at least twice a cat's average lifespan.

HEAVIEST CATS USA

OT, short for 'Orange Thing', owned by Tom Phillips (USA) is the world's heaviest living cat, weighing in at an amazing 18.55 kg (40 lb 14 oz) on 30 Oct 1998, at the age of eight.

The heaviest domestic cat ever recorded was Himmy, a male tabby belonging to Thomas Vyse (Australia), who weighed 21.3 kg (47 lb) when he died in 1986 at the age of 10.

SMALLEST CAT

The smallest cat on record is a blue point Himalayan-Persian named Tinker Toy, who reached only 19 cm (7.5 in) when fully grown. He belongs to Katrina and Scott Forbes (USA).

HEAVIEST LIVING DOG

Kell, an English mastiff owned by Tom Scott (UK), is the heaviest living dog, weighing 130 kg (286 lb) on 18 Aug 1999. She feeds on a boxer's diet, eating lots of protein, including minced beef, eggs and goats' milk.

HEAVIEST PIG

Big Bill, a Poland-China hog owned by WJ Chappall (USA), weighed a record 1,157.5 kg (2,552 lb) before he died in 1933. He stood 1.52 m (5 ft) high at the shoulder, and was 2.74 m (9 ft) long.

OLDEST GOLDFISH

A goldfish named Tish, owned by Hilda and Gordon Hand (UK), lived for 43 years after Hilda's son Peter won him at a fairground in 1956. Tish was so old that his scales had turned from gold to silver by the time he died in 1999.

LARGEST PIGEON

A Canadian giant runt cock pigeon called Doc Yeck, owned by Leonard Yeck (Canada), weighed in at 1.8 kg (4 lb) on 6 March 1999, with a chest width of 12.7 cm (5 in). Doc Yeck is twice the size and weight of an average pigeon of the same breed.

LARGEST HAMSTER LITTER

On 28 Feb 1974, a hamster belonging to the Miller family (USA) gave birth to 26 baby hamsters. This is more than three times the average litter size, which is eight.

SHOW ME THE BUNNY!

Toby III (above), a black male English lop bred by Phil Wheeler (UK), holds the record for the longest rabbit ears – they are an astounding 75.6 cm (29.7 in) long and 18.24 cm (7.18 in) wide.

The largest rabbit ever recorded was in April 1980, when a five-month-old French lop doe weighing 12 kg (26 lb 7 oz) was exhibited at the Reus Fair in northeast Spain.

The smallest breeds – the Netherland and Polish Dwarf rabbits – are 10 times smaller than the lops, and weigh between 0.9 kg and 1.13 kg (2-2.5 lb).

www.guinnessworldrecords.com/rabbit
← ACCESS CODE: ‹51129›

CAT WITH MOST TOES

Normal cats have five toes on each forepaw and four toes on each hind paw, giving them a total of 18 toes. However, Twinkle Toes, a three-year-old owned by Gloria Boensch (USA), has a total of 25 toes – six on each of her hind paws, six on her left front paw and seven on her right.

TURTLE WITH MOST HEADS

In 1999, Lin Chi-Fa, from southern Taiwan, discovered a three-headed turtle in his garden pond. Only two of its heads were fully developed. As the turtle is regarded as a sacred animal in Chinese folklore, Lin took it to a temple to be blessed, only to notice that it walked in a zig-zag fashion as its two fully-developed heads could not agree on which direction to take.

MOST PROLIFIC CAT

A tabby cat named Dusty (USA), produced 420 kittens during her breeding life. This averages out at approximately 28 kittens a year over 15 years. She gave birth to her last litter (a single kitten) on 12 June 1952.

HIGHEST FREESTYLE JUMP BY A DOG

On 28 July 1999 during the Superdog Show at Klondike Days, Edmonton, Alberta, Canada, a Russian wolfhound named Wolf made a freestyle jump of 160 cm (5 ft 3 in). Wolf is owned and trained by Seanna O'Neill (Canada).

MOST ROMANTIC GUINEA PIG

Sooty, a three-year-old guinea pig (UK), became globally infamous when he escaped from his hutch and romanced 24 partners in a single evening. Following this impressive display of passion

LITTLE AND LARGE

The smallest living dog is a Yorkie named 'Big Boss' (left), owned by Dr Chai Khanchanakom (Thailand). Aged one year old, he measured 11.94 cm (4.7 in) tall and 12.95 cm (5.1 in) long.

The smallest dog on record was a fist-sized dwarf Yorkshire terrier owned by Arthur Marples (UK), which stood just 6.3 cm (2.5 in) tall at the shoulder, and measured 9.5 cm (3.75 in). It died in 1945, just before its second birthday.

The tallest living dog, a Great Dane called Harvey, stands a massive 1.54 m (5 ft) at the shoulder. Owned by Charles Dodman (UK), Harvey eats a huge 3.6 kg (7.9 lb) of tinned dog food a day. Great Danes usually average 75 cm (2 ft 6 in) at the shoulder.

www.guinnessworldrecords.com/dogdwarf
← ACCESS CODE: ‹51213›

in Dec 2000, Sooty became the proud father of 43 baby guinea pigs. On 14 Feb 2001 Sooty received a record 206 Valentine cards, some from as far away as New Zealand.

LONGEST DOG SWIM
On 2 Sept 1995 two Labradors called Kai and Gypsy swam the 'Maui Channel Swim' from Lanai to Maui, Hawaii, USA, with their owner, Steve Fisher (USA). They swam the 15.2-km (9.5-mile) course in 6 hr 3 min 42 sec.

DOG WITH THE LARGEST REPERTOIRE OF TRICKS
Chanda-Leah, a toy poodle owned and trained by Sharon Robinson (Canada), has a repertoire of 469 tricks, which includes playing the piano and fetching a tissue when someone sneezes.

FASTEST WEAVING DOG
A South African border collie named Jazz holds the speed record for weaving his way between 60 poles in an amazing 12.98 seconds. The record was set on 4 Dec 1999.

FARTHEST JUMP BY A FROG
Santjie, a South African sharp-nosed frog (*Ptychadena oxyrhynchus*), jumped a total of 10.3 m (33.79 ft) in three jumps at a frog Derby held at Lurula Natal Spa, Paulpietersburg, KwaZulu-Natal, South Africa, on 21 May 1977. This is about half the length of a basketball court.

BEST TALKING BIRD
A female African grey parrot (*Psittacus erythacus*) named Prudle won the 'Best talking parrot-like bird' title at the British National Cage and Aviary Bird Show for a record 12 consecutive years before retiring in 1976. Prudle came to the UK from Uganda in 1958 and boasted an amazing vocabulary of nearly 800 words.

MOST WELL-TRAVELLED CAT
In Feb 1984 a cat called Hamlet escaped from his cage on a flight from Toronto and was caught behind some panelling. He stayed there

for seven weeks, travelling just under 965,600 km (600,000 miles), approximately the same distance as going around the world 24 times.

BRAVEST ANIMALS
A St Bernard dog named Barry saved the lives of more than 40 people during his 12-year career in the Swiss Alps. His rescues included that of a boy who lay half-frozen under an avalanche in which his mother had died. Barry spread himself across the boy's body to warm him and licked the child's face until he woke up, and then carried him to the nearest dwelling.

On 19 May 1997 Murphy, an Australian Army donkey, was posthumously awarded the RSPCA Australia Purple Cross on behalf of all the donkeys that served in the 1915–16 Gallipoli campaign in World War I. Murphy carried thousands of wounded soldiers to the field hospitals.

In Dec 1999 Charlie, a three-year-old grey parrot, saved the lives of Patricia Tunnicliffe of Durham, UK, and her five children, after a fire started in their home caused by Christmas lights igniting curtains. Charlie's squawks and shouts woke up Ms Tunnicliffe, who managed to get her five children out of the house unharmed. Unfortunately, Charlie was not so lucky.

www.guinnessworldrecords.com/skydivedog

ACCESS CODE: 56167

DOGGY DIVERS TAKE PLUNGE
Katie, a Jack Russell cross (UK, above), became the first record doggy diver when she dived with her owner from 3,658 m (12,000 ft) over southern England in Oct 1987. She still holds the UK title.

However, since then, a miniature dachshund, Brutus the Skydiving Dog, excelled with a jump from a plane at an altitude of 4,572 m

(15,000 ft) above Lake Elsinore, California, USA, on 20 May 1997. Brutus currently boasts 71 skydives in his canine career.

GUINNESS WORLD RECORDS

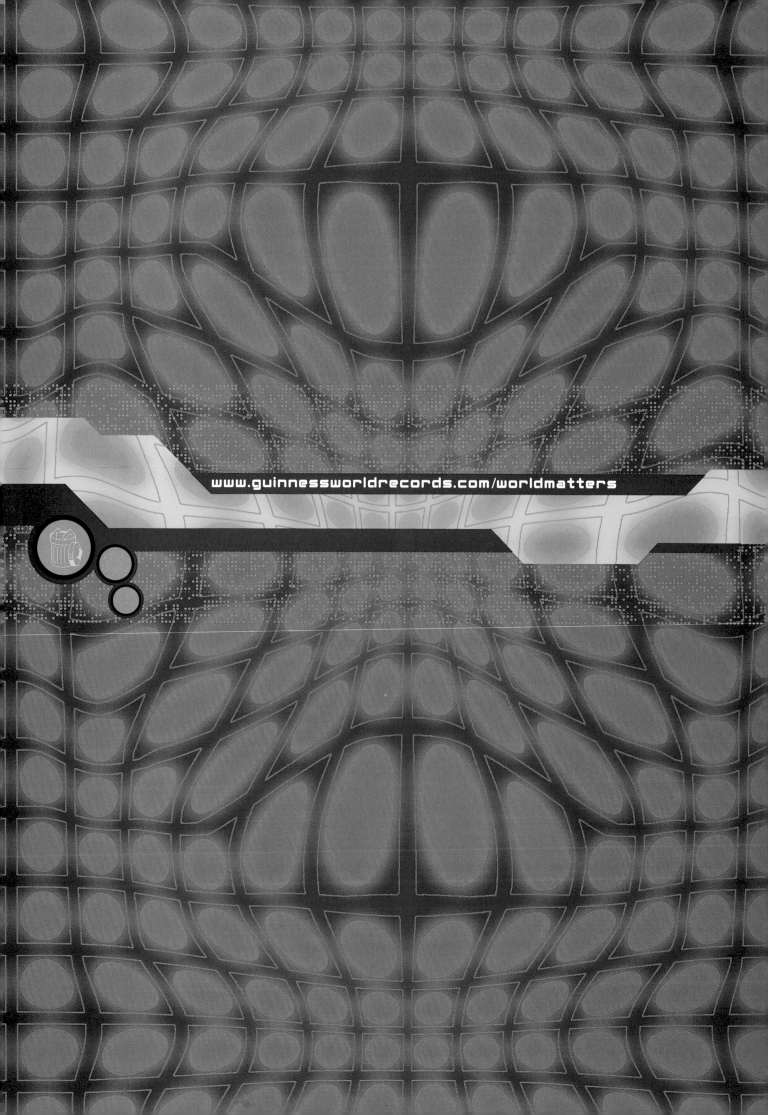

www.guinnessworldrecords.com/worldmatters

world matters

GUINNESS WORLD RECORDS

the environment

MOST POLLUTED MAJOR CITY

Mexico City is the world's most polluted city, having serious problems with sulphur dioxide, suspended particulate matter, carbon monoxide and ozone (in all of which the World Health Organization guidelines are exceeded), plus moderate to heavy lead and nitrogen dioxide pollution.

HIGHEST CARBON DIOXIDE EMISSIONS

The USA has the highest emissions of CO_2, one of the key gases responsible for the 'greenhouse effect'. In 1999 the USA emitted 5,500 million tonnes (11,000 billion lb) of CO_2.

LOWEST CARBON DIOXIDE EMISSIONS

Of the major industrialized nations in the western hemisphere, France has the lowest emissions of CO_2. In 1999 France emitted 400 million tonnes (800 billion lb) of CO_2. France's commitment to nuclear power helps cut fossil fuel-related CO_2 emissions.

LARGEST HOLE IN THE OZONE LAYER

In Sept 2000 a hole in the ozone layer was detected above Antarctica that

OIL DISASTER

Between Aug and Sept 1994, an area of the pristine Arctic tundra of the Komi Republic in Russia totalling 2,110 ha (5,213 acres) – the size of El Salvador – was contaminated with thousands of tonnes of oil flowing from damaged pipes transporting oil from an oil refining plant. Estimates of the amount of oil lost calculate that 117 million litres (31 million gal) were spilled. Known as the Usinsk accident (left), this is the worst case of land pollution ever. The cost of the accident was estimated at more than 311 billion roubles ($10 billion or £7.5 billion).

www.guinnessworldrecords.com/oildisaster

← ACCESS CODE: ‹49232›

measured about 28.3 million km² (11 million miles²), which is roughly three times the size of the USA.

LOWEST OZONE LEVELS

Between 9 and 14 Oct 1993 ozone levels reached a record low over the South Pole in Antarctica, when an average figure of 91 Dobson units (DU) was recorded. The Dobson unit measures the thickness of the ozone layer – 300 DU is considered to be adequate to shield the Earth from solar ultraviolet radiation and sustain biological systems as we know them.

Efforts are being made to reduce the global consumption of CFCs (chlorofluorocarbons) – the most prevalent ozone-depleting substance (ODS) – and it is hoped that by the year 2050 the ozone layer will have returned to safer, pre-1980 levels.

LARGEST WIND FARM

At Altamont Pass, California, USA, the Pacific Gas and Electric Company has built a wind farm that covers 140 km² (54 miles²) and has 7,300 wind turbines. Since 1981 the turbines have produced more than 6 billion kilowatt-hours of electricity – enough to give 800,000 homes power for one year.

LARGEST SOLAR ENERGY ROOF

The world's largest photovoltaic solar energy roof, which is 10,000 m² (108,000 ft²), belongs to the Nordrhein-Westfalen Mont-Cenis Academy in Herne, Germany. The one mega-watt roof has 3,185 solar cells, connected by 55 km (34 miles) of cabling, and yields over twice the annual power consumption of the building.

MOST ENERGY-EFFICIENT SUPERMARKET

J Sainsbury PLC operates a 3,251-m² (35,000-ft²) supermarket in Greenwich, London, UK, designed by architects Chetwood Associates. The supermarket's heating and electricity bill is 50% less than a normal supermarket of equivalent size. The store has a number of energy-saving features, including an on-site combined heat and power plant, wind turbines and photovoltaic cells.

LARGEST OFFSHORE OIL CONTAINMENT BOOM

An oil containment boom is a device used to contain oil spilled into the sea from pipelines, oil wells, tankers and other vessels. Usually made of rubber, they inflate quickly to float on the surface of the water and prevent an oil slick from spreading. The biggest containment boom was developed by Ro-Clean Desmi in 2000 and is called the Ro-Boom 3500. It has an overall deflated width of 3.5 m (11 ft 5 in). In tests, it contained 95% of a 95-m³ (3,355-ft³) oil slick with a thickness of 14 cm (5.5 in). It can

SAY 'NO' TO OZONE

The SULEV-rated (Super Ultra-Low Emission Vehicle) Accord EX Sedan (left), which was developed by the Japanese company Honda, has the lowest emission levels of any petrol-fuelled car. Certified by the California Air Resources Board (CARB), a SULEV engine emits only 1.04 kg (2.3 lb) of ozone-forming hydrocarbons during 161,000 km (100,000 miles) of driving, which is about the same as spilling 0.95 litres (32 fl oz) of petrol. This is an 86% reduction compared to a Low Emission Vehicle (LEV).

The rental company with the most low-emission cars is Kobe-Eco-Car (Japan), established on 30 Jan 1999. It is dedicated to the rental of environmentally friendly vehicles and has a fleet of 53, made up of electric vehicles, compressed natural gas vehicles and hybrid cars.

also contain oil travelling at speeds of up to 1.3 knots (2.4 km/h or 1.5 mph). The Ro-Boom can also contain and tow oil for long periods of time. It survived being towed for two weeks in the middle of winter and even contained oil in waves 7 m (23 ft) high.

LARGEST DEFORESTATION

Tropical forests are being cut down at a rate equivalent to 200 football pitches every minute. The greatest rate of deforestation is in Jamaica where, in the 1980s and 1990s, 7% of its forests were cut down every year. In terms of size, Brazil has cleared the greatest amount of forest each year. In most years in the 1980s and 1990s, an area the size of Belgium (30,500 km^2 or 12,000 miles^2) was cleared and burned in the Amazon Basin of Brazil to create new pastures or farming land.

MOST CONTAMINATED LAKE

Lake Karachay in the Chelyabinsk province of Russia has accumulated 120 million curies of radioactivity and absorbed nearly 100 times more strontium 90 and caesium 137 than was released at Chernobyl in 1986. If a person stood on the shore of the lake he would receive a radiation exposure rate of 600 roentgens an hour. This is 2,000 times greater radiation than that emitted during a normal chest X-ray and is strong enough to kill a person in an hour. The lake is near a Soviet nuclear facility called Mayak Chemical Combine. The plant was shut down in 1990, but radiation emitted still either evaporates and is dispersed by the wind, or is absorbed by sand particles and sediment at the bottom of the lake.

MOST ACIDIC WATER

Normally pH values range from 0 to 14, with 7 (the pH factor of water) being neutral. The lower the number, the higher the acid level of the given substance. When sampled in 1990–91, water running through the Richmond Mine at Iron Mountain, California, USA, had a pH value of -3.6. The source of the acid in the water was hot acid solutions dripping off coloured stalactites in an abandoned copper and zinc mine.

www.guinnessworldrecords.com/tankerspill

ACCESS CODE: ‹49233›

KNOCK-DOWN BLOW TO COASTAL LIFE

On 25 March 1989 the *Exxon Valdez* oil tanker collided with Bligh Reef in Prince William Sound, Alaska, USA, spilling more than 41 million litres (11 million gal) of oil and causing the worst ever coastal damage in an environmental disaster. A total of 2,400 km (1,500 miles) of coast were polluted, and the diverse and populous marine ecosystem of the sound was devastated (below). Between 3,000 and 5,000 sea otters perished, and current otter populations continue to be contaminated by the toxic hydrocarbons from the oil pollution. Sea birds suffered losses of an estimated 1,000,000, and around 20 Orca whales were killed. The company was fined £3 billion ($5 billion), on top of a clean-up bill of £2 billion ($3 billion). The captain admitted that he drank three double vodkas before setting sail with the 274.3-m (900-ft) long ship.

consumption and waste

HIGHEST GNI PER CAPITA

Of the 260 countries for which figures were available to the World Bank in 1999, Luxembourg was the country with the highest Gross National Income (the total dollar value of goods and services produced by a country in one year divided by its population) with a spending per person of 1,724,755 Luxembourg francs (£26,577, $42,960). Luxembourg is about the size of Greater London, UK, and has a population of only 429,080 (1999), 30% of which are foreign nationals. The GNI per capita for the UK is $23,590 (£14,593) and for the US is $31,910 (£19,740).

LOWEST GNI PER CAPITA

In 1999, Ethiopia had the lowest GNI per capita – 704,410 Ethiopian Birr ($100).

HIGHEST FOOD CONSUMPTION

Argentina consumes the most food per head, with each citizen consuming 183% of the 1996 FAO (United Nations Food and Agriculture Organization) recommended requirement. Portugal came second at 149%, followed by Ireland (142%), the USA, Hong Kong, Turkey, UAE and Yugoslavia (all 140%).

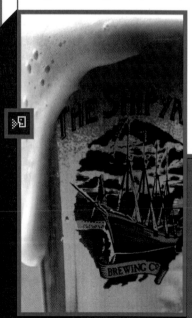

LOWEST FOOD CONSUMPTION

According to the UN's food agency the country with the lowest food consumption is Tajikistan (formerly in the USSR). Each citizen consumes only 55% of the FAO recommended minimum daily requirement. Somalia comes second with 67%.

HIGHEST PER CAPITA COFFEE CONSUMPTION

The country that consumes the most coffee per capita is Finland, where 11.3 kg (24.91 lb) of coffee per person was consumed in 1998. The total amount of coffee consumed in Finland in 1998 was 58,000 tonnes (127.8 million lb). This roughly approximates to 1,737 cups of coffee per person per year, or five cups a day. The same year the USA consumed the greatest total amount of coffee in the world – an estimated 1,148,000 tonnes (2.5 billion lb), which is 4.2 kg (9.26 lb) or 646 cups annually per person.

HIGHEST TEA CONSUMPTION

Paraguay (population 5,359,000 in 1999) is the country that consumes the most tea per person – 11.7 kg (25.79 lb) of tea each in 1998, which is roughly 14.62 cups per person per day. The UK and Ireland came joint 7th. However, India consumes the most tea overall worldwide – drinking a massive 640,000 tonnes (1.4 billion lb) in 1998, compared with Paraguay's 61,000 tonnes (1.3 billion lb). China was second to India at 466,000 tonnes (1.03 billion lb) and the UK consumed 146,000 tonnes (321.8 million lb).

A YEN FOR THE HIGH LIFE?

In 2000, for the ninth year, *The Economist* Intelligence Unit's bi-annual survey (to aid the calculation of salary packages for employees relocating overseas) revealed that Tokyo was the world's most expensive city. The survey is based on the varying costs of 90 shopping items in 126 cities. Taking New York as a median 100, Tokyo scored 164. Osaka, Japan, came second with 161, with Hong Kong third with 120. Oslo and Zurich came joint 5th as the most expensive European cities, followed by London in 7th place. New York was the most expensive US city, ranking 12th worldwide.

www.guinnessworldrecords.com/highcosttokyo

← ACCESS CODE: ‹53711›

HIGHEST CONFECTIONERY CONSUMPTION

According to a report by the sweet manufacturers Cadbury and Trebor Bassett, the UK spent more than £5 billion ($8,252,500,300) on sweets in 1997. The average UK resident ate 16 kg (35 lb) of sweets that year, ahead of the USA's 10 kg (22 lb), France's 9 kg (19 lb) and Japan's 3 kg (6.6 lb). Londoners eat the fewest sweets, spending £1.45 ($2.39) per person a week, while those living in the West Country and Wales spend the most with £2.09 ($3.44).

HIGHEST BOVINE MEAT CONSUMPTION

Argentina consumes the most bovine meat (beef and veal) per person. In 1998, each Argentinian ate 56.3 kg (124.12 lb) of bovine meat – a total of 2,033,000 tonnes (4.5 billion lb). Overall, however, in 1998 the USA consumed the most bovine meat – 12,048,000 tonnes (26.5 billion lb) – 44 kg (97 lb) per capita.

PARTY TIME

The Czech Republic is the world's leading beer consumer per capita, with each person drinking an average of 160 litres (42.6 gal) in 1998. The country as a whole consumed 1,653 million litres (436.68 million gal) during 1998. The USA consumed the greatest volume of beer in the world in the same year, drinking 24,376 million litres (6.439 million gal) – an average of 89 litres (23.5 gal) per person.

The records for the world's greatest per-capita wine consumption goes to Luxembourg with 63.3 litres (16.7 gal) per person. The smallest measurable wine consumer is Egypt, where the average yearly wine consumption is about 2 tablespoons.

www.guinnessworldrecords.com/beerdrinkers

← ACCESS CODE: ‹46083›

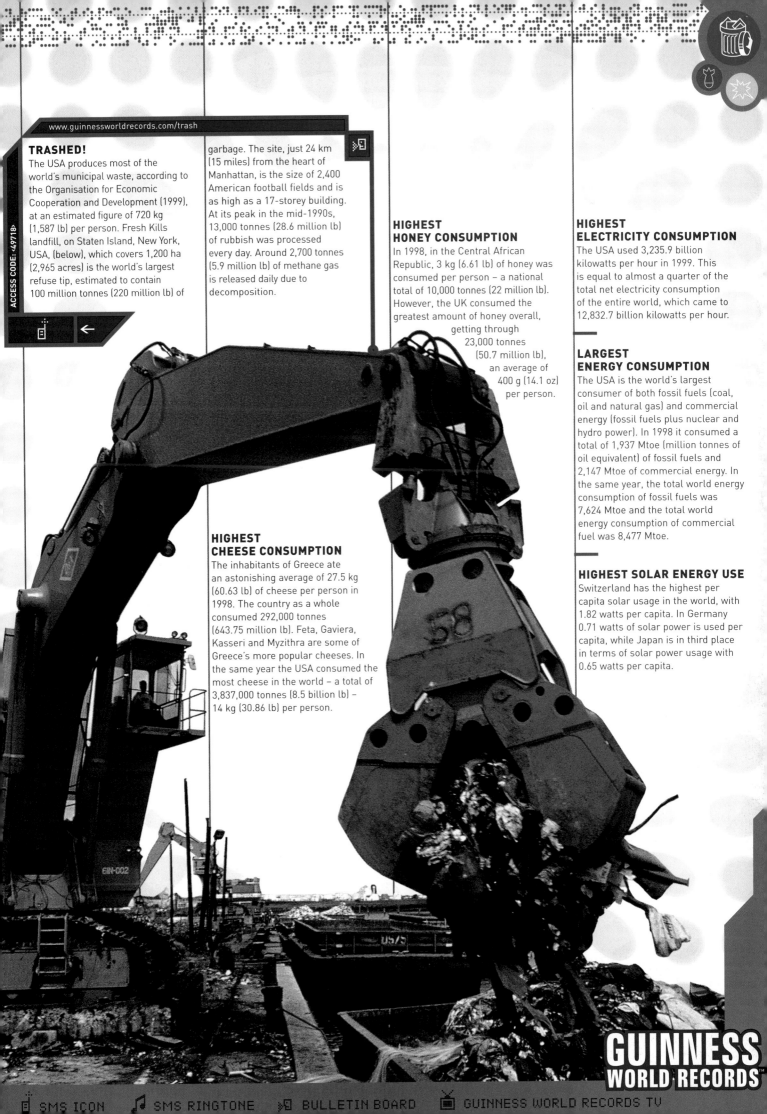

TRASHED!

The USA produces most of the world's municipal waste, according to the Organisation for Economic Cooperation and Development (1999), at an estimated figure of 720 kg (1,587 lb) per person. Fresh Kills landfill, on Staten Island, New York, USA, (below), which covers 1,200 ha (2,965 acres) is the world's largest refuse tip, estimated to contain 100 million tonnes (220 million lb) of garbage. The site, just 24 km (15 miles) from the heart of Manhattan, is the size of 2,400 American football fields and is as high as a 17-storey building. At its peak in the mid-1990s, 13,000 tonnes (28.6 million lb) of rubbish was processed every day. Around 2,700 tonnes (5.9 million lb) of methane gas is released daily due to decomposition.

HIGHEST HONEY CONSUMPTION

In 1998, in the Central African Republic, 3 kg (6.61 lb) of honey was consumed per person – a national total of 10,000 tonnes (22 million lb). However, the UK consumed the greatest amount of honey overall, getting through 23,000 tonnes (50.7 million lb), an average of 400 g (14.1 oz) per person.

HIGHEST CHEESE CONSUMPTION

The inhabitants of Greece ate an astonishing average of 27.5 kg (60.63 lb) of cheese per person in 1998. The country as a whole consumed 292,000 tonnes (643.75 million lb). Feta, Gaviera, Kasseri and Myzithra are some of Greece's more popular cheeses. In the same year the USA consumed the most cheese in the world – a total of 3,837,000 tonnes (8.5 billion lb) – 14 kg (30.86 lb) per person.

HIGHEST ELECTRICITY CONSUMPTION

The USA used 3,235.9 billion kilowatts per hour in 1999. This is equal to almost a quarter of the total net electricity consumption of the entire world, which came to 12,832.7 billion kilowatts per hour.

LARGEST ENERGY CONSUMPTION

The USA is the world's largest consumer of both fossil fuels (coal, oil and natural gas) and commercial energy (fossil fuels plus nuclear and hydro power). In 1998 it consumed a total of 1,937 Mtoe (million tonnes of oil equivalent) of fossil fuels and 2,147 Mtoe of commercial energy. In the same year, the total world energy consumption of fossil fuels was 7,624 Mtoe and the total world energy consumption of commercial fuel was 8,477 Mtoe.

HIGHEST SOLAR ENERGY USE

Switzerland has the highest per capita solar usage in the world, with 1.82 watts per capita. In Germany 0.71 watts of solar power is used per capita, while Japan is in third place in terms of solar power usage with 0.65 watts per capita.

crime and punishment

BEST POLICE DOG
The world's top police dog is Trepp, a Golden Retriever, owned by Tom Kazo (USA). Trepp, short for Intrepid, has been credited with more than 100 arrests and the recovery of narcotics worth more than $63 million (£44 million). Within his first two months on the job, Trepp had sniffed 1.52 tonnes (3,351 lb) of unlawful substances. Trepp was once set to detect 10 hidden packets of drugs at a demonstration – and found 11.

OLDEST PRISONER
Bill Wallace is the oldest prisoner on record – he spent the last 63 years of his life in Aradale Psychiatric Hospital, Ararat, Vic, Australia. He shot and killed a man in Dec 1925 and, having been found unfit to plead, was transferred to the Mental Health Department in Feb 1926. He remained there until his death on 17 July 1989, shortly before his 108th birthday.

LONGEST PRISON ESCAPE
The longest recorded escape by a recaptured prisoner was that of Leonard Fristoe, aged 77, who escaped from the Nevada State Prison, Carson City, Nevada, USA, on 15 Dec 1923. Fristoe was turned in by his son on 15 Nov 1969 at Compton, California. By then Fristoe had enjoyed nearly 46 years of freedom under the name of Claude R Willis. His crime was killing two sheriff's deputies in 1920.

ILLINOIS DEPT. OF CORRECTIONS
N 0 0 9 2 1 · 0 6 · 0 1 · 03

LONGEST STAY IN SOLITARY CONFINEMENT
Mordecai Vanunu has spent nearly 12 years in a total isolation jail cell – the longest known term of solitary confinement in modern times. Born in 1955, Vanunu was convicted of treason for giving information about Israel's nuclear programme to London's *Sunday Times* newspaper. He was held in isolation from 1986 until March 1998. Not long afterwards, the prison gate was opened, and he finally walked away a free man.

MOST COMMON METHOD OF EXECUTION
The most common method of execution is by firing squad, which is practised in 73 countries. In 45 of these countries, this is the sole method of executing criminals. Hanging is the second most common method, and is practised in 58 countries worldwide. Beheading is still practised in three countries, while electrocution is practised only in the USA.

NO GETTING AWAY WITH MURDER
The longest sentence imposed on a mass murderer was 21 consecutive life sentences and 12 death sentences. John Gacy (left), killed 33 boys and young men during a six-year killing spree from 1972 to 1978 in Illinois, USA. He was sentenced by a Chicago jury on 13 March 1980 and executed by lethal injection at Stateville Prison in Joilet, Illinois, on 10 May 1994.
The most prolific female murderer in the western world was Elizabeth Bathori, who practised vampirism on girls and young women. Throughout the 15th century, she is alleged to have killed more than 600 virgins in order to drink their blood and bathe in it – to preserve her youth. When her murderous career was discovered, she was walled up in her castle from 1610 until her death in 1614.

www.guinnessworldrecords.com/murdersentence
← ACCESS CODE: ‹55421›

MOST SECURE PRISON
The United States Penitentiary, Administrative Maximum Facility 'Supermax' Prison, set in scrubland west of Pueblo, southern Colorado, USA, is equipped with laser-beams, 1,400 remote-controlled steel doors, motion detectors, pressure pads and silent-attack dogs, and surrounded by razor wire and guard towers. With a 'level-6' security rating, inmates are often locked in their cells for 23 hours a day and for the remaining hour must wear leg-irons and handcuffs.

FOR BETTER OR FOR WORSE
One hundred and twenty inmates of Carandiru prison, Sao Paulo, Brazil, married their fiancées at the largest mass wedding ceremony in a prison on 14 June 2000 (left). Officials and evangelical pastors made Carandiru's cell block 6 into a temporary church. The brides (who traditionally show up late for weddings) and the guests had to turn up two hours before the ceremony for a body search. The grooms wore jackets and ties. The only thing that gave them away as inmates were their beige trousers, which form part of the prison uniform. The Detention House, Carandiru's formal name, houses 7,400 inmates and is best known for a massacre by police in 1992 that left 111 inmates dead.

www.guinnessworldrecords.com/prisonwedding
← ACCESS CODE: ‹54910›

MOST PROLIFIC CANNIBAL
During the 19th century Ratu Udre Udre reportedly ate between 872 and 999 people. The Fijian chief had kept a stone to record each body eaten, and these are placed along his tomb in Rakiraki, northern Viti Levu, Fiji.

LARGEST ART ROBBERY
On 14 April 1991, 20 paintings, worth around £280 million ($500 million), were stolen from the Van Gogh

Museum in Amsterdam, Netherlands. They were found in an abandoned car not far from the museum, just 35 minutes later.

LARGEST JEWEL ROBBERY
A three-man gang bearing machine-guns barged into the Carlton Hotel jewellery shop in Cannes, France, and stole gems with an estimated value of FF250 million (£31 million; $45 million) on 11 Aug 1994. This is the biggest recorded theft of jewels.

LONGEST-SERVING POLITICAL PRISONER
Kim Sung-myun served a lengthy 43 years and 10 months in prison in Seoul, South Korea, for supporting Communist North Korea. He was released at the age of 70 in Aug 1995, having never read a newspaper or watched television while in prison.

LARGEST CRIMINAL GANG
The Yamaguchi-gumi gang of the *yakuza* in Japan has 30,000 members. There are some 90,000 *yakuza* or gangsters altogether, in more than 3,000 groups. The *yakuza* go about their business openly and even advertise for recruits.

LARGEST KIDNAP RANSOM
Two Hong Kong businessmen, Walter Kwok and Victor Li, paid gangster Cheung Tze-keung a record total of £134 million ($206 million) in return for their freedom after they were kidnapped separately in 1996 and 1997 respectively. Cheung was executed in China on 5 Dec 1998.

www.guinnessworldrecords.com/oldsparky

SMS ACCESS CODE: ‹56558›

OLD SPARKY

'Old Sparky' (right), also known as the 'Texas Thunderbolt', was the first chair used for electrocutions in Texas, USA. It was built in 1923–24 by an inmate who was facing the death penalty, and was used until 1964. Before 1923, hanging was the primary means of execution in Texas.

Between Jan 1974 and April 2001, Texas executed (now by lethal injection) a record 244 criminals – more than any other US state. Virginia follows with 82 executions and Florida is third with 51.

MOST PRISONERS

According to figures released by Amnesty International in Feb 2000 the prison population in the USA topped two million. This accounts for 25% of the world's prison population, yet the USA accounts for only 5% of the world's population. The USA's per capita prison population is 565 prisoners per 100,000 people.

LEAST PRISONERS

Slovenia is the country with the least prisoners. It has under 500 prisoners in a population of just under two million. Few offenders are jailed – instead community service, probation and similar schemes are employed. The Slovene prisoners represent a mere 25 out of every 100,000 of the population.

LARGEST PRISON SYSTEM

The US state of California has the biggest prison system in the industrialized world. The single state holds more inmates in its jails and prisons than do France, Great Britain, Germany, Japan, Singapore, and the Netherlands combined. More than 626 out of every 100,000 Californians are incarcerated.

MOST ARRESTS

By 1988, Tommy Johns of Brisbane, Qld, Australia, had been arrested a total of nearly 3,000 times for being drunk and disorderly in a public place. Ironically, he died in April 1988 at the age of 66, from a brain tumour rather than a drink-related illness.

LARGEST FRAUD

Webmaster Kenneth Taves (USA) is believed to have committed the largest fraud carried out by one person, with a total of $38 million (£23,332,208) in unauthorized credit card charges. Taves got hold of credit card numbers belonging to nearly four million consumers who had bought items from merchants with accounts at Charter Pacific. The 49-year-old resubmitted up to 800,000 of the credit card numbers to his merchant service with instructions to charge each account $19.95 (£12.25) per month. Taves pleaded guilty in federal court and faces a maximum penalty of 30 years in prison.

GUINNESS WORLD RECORDS

war and weapons

BLOODIEST SIEGE

The worst siege in history was when Leningrad, USSR (now St Petersburg, Russia), was besieged by the German army for 880 days from 30 Aug 1941 until 27 Jan 1944. It was estimated that between 1.3 and 1.5 million defenders and citizens lost their lives. This number included 641,000 people who died of starvation in the city and 17,000 civilians who were killed by shelling. More than 150,000 shells and 100,000 bombs were dropped on the city.

I SPY

The smallest spy plane in existence is the palm-sized Black Widow, developed by AeroVironment of Monrovia, California, USA, for possible reconnaissance use by ground combat troops. It has a wingspan of 15.24 cm (6 in), weighs just 80 g (2.8 oz) and carries a tiny colour video camera weighing 2 g (0.07 oz). The Black Widow has a speed of 50 km/h (30 mph), a maximum range of 2 km (1.24 miles) and can stay airborne for 30 minutes. Although it has an autopilot, it will typically be controlled by a pilot navigating by live video relayed from its on-board camera. The entire ground control system and launcher fits into a briefcase-sized box. The solid wings are manufactured from lightweight expanded polystyrene foam and propulsion is provided by a battery-powered electric motor.

www.guinnessworldrecords.com/spyplane

 ACCESS CODE: ‹56237›

HIGHEST BATTLEFIELD

Since 1984 the Indian and Pakistani armies have fought each other on the Siachen Glacier, in the disputed territory of Kashmir, at a height of up to 6,700 m (22,000 ft). At this altitude, they are higher than climbers standing on the summits of the tallest mountains in Africa, North America, Australasia, Europe, and Antarctica. Reports suggest that Pakistan spends as much as £354,000 ($588,000) a month and India about £600,000 ($1 million) a month maintaining troops on the glacier.

SHORTEST WAR

The shortest war on record was between the UK and Zanzibar (now part of Tanzania) in 1896. On 25 Aug, Sultan Hamid bin Thuwaini died. Two hours later, the self-appointed Sultan Seyyid Khalid bin Bargash broke into the palace and declared himself the new ruler. The Royal Navy, under the command of Rear Admiral Harry Rawson, delivered an ultimatum. At precisely 9 o'clock on the 27th, three warships opened fire and in 45 minutes completely destroyed the palace and killed the usurper.

MOST HEAVILY ARMED TANK

The most heavily armed tanks in recent times are the Russian T-64, T-72, T-80 and T-90 tanks, which have a 12.5-cm (4.92-in) gun-missile launcher system.

LARGEST ARMY

The People's Liberation Army of China had 2.2 million service personnel as of May 2000.

LONGEST EMBASSY SIEGE

In Sept 1979 a crowd of about 500 people seized the US embassy in Tehran, Iran. Of the approximately 90 people inside the embassy, 52 remained in captivity until the end of the crisis 444 days later, making this the longest embassy siege ever. The American hostages were seized in response to the exiled Shah of Iran's admission to the USA for medical treatment. The hostage release coincided with President Reagan's inauguration day on 20 Jan 1981.

ENEMY AT THE GATE

The greatest death toll in a battle has been estimated at 1,109,000 in the Battle of Stalingrad, USSR (now Volgograd, Russia), which started in the summer of 1942 and ended with the surrender of the German Sixth Army on 31 Jan 1943.

The 142-day battle of the Somme, France (1 July–19 Nov 1916) is in the same league. There are no exact figures, but the estimate for dead and wounded is estimated to have been at least 1,220,000 men, of which 398,671 were British (57,470 on the first day) and more than 800,000 were German and French.

 www.guinnessworldrecords.com/battledeaths
← ACCESS CODE: ‹46252›

BLOODIEST WAR

The most costly war in terms of human life was World War II (1939–45), in which the total number of fatalities, including battle deaths and civilians, is estimated to have been 56.4 million – roughly equivalent to the population of the UK.

HIGHEST DEATH TOLL FROM A NON-NUCLEAR RAID

On 10 March 1945, about 83,000 people were killed in an Allied bombing raid on Tokyo, Japan. Total Japanese fatalities in World War II were 600,000 killed by conventional weapons and 220,000 by the nuclear attacks on Hiroshima and Nagasaki.

GREATEST DEATH TOLL FROM A SINGLE CHEMICAL WARFARE ATTACK

The greatest number of people killed in a single chemical weapons attack is estimated at 4,000, when President Saddam Hussein of Iraq attacked members of his country's Kurdish minority at Halabja, Iraq, in March 1988. The attack was punishment for the support the Kurds had given to Iran in the Iran–Iraq war (1980–90).

LONGEST-RANGE AIR ATTACKS

Seven B-52G bombers, which took off from Barksdale Air Force Base, Louisiana, USA, on 16 Jan 1991, flew 22,500 km (14,000 miles) to deliver cruise missiles against targets in Iraq during the Gulf War. They refuelled four times in flight, with the round-trip mission lasting 35 hours.

MOST SIBLINGS TO SERVE IN WORLD WAR II

Seven brothers from the Pritchard family (UK) served in the Armed Forces between 1939 and 1945. One, Ronald (Royal Navy), was killed in action in 1942. The six surviving sons were Idris (Royal Marines); Clifford (Parachute Regiment); Horace and David (Royal Artillery); James (Royal Army Service Corps); and Albert (Royal Pioneer Corps).

MOST EXPENSIVE PEACEKEEPING OPERATION

UNPROFOR (United Nations Protection Force) cost £2.97 billion ($4.6 billion) from 12 Jan 1992 to 31 March 1996, including all the missions in the former Yugoslavia.

CHEMICAL ABUSE

VX gas is the most deadly chemical warfare agent – a mere 10 mg (a raindrop weighs around 80 mg) on the skin will kill most people. Some nations, such as Iraq, are thought to possess such weapons and if a threat is thought to exist, the military wears protective clothing. Pictured right is a US soldier wearing nuclear-biological-chemical warfare gear during an exercise in Egypt in 1989.

GREATEST RANGE OF A GUN

The long-range gun that shelled Paris in World War I was the *Paris-Geschetz* 'Paris Gun', with a calibre of 21 cm (8.25 in), a designed range of 127.9 km (79.5 miles) and an achieved range of 122 km (76 miles).

LARGEST AIR FORCE

The largest air force, in terms of aircraft, is that of the USA, which had 4,413 combat aircraft as of Sept 1999. This total includes 179 bombers, 1,666 fighter and attack aircraft and 1,279 trainer aircraft.

MOST EXPENSIVE MILITARY AIRCRAFT

The US-made Boeing B-2 Spirit is priced at $1.3 billion (£780 million). A long-range multi-role bomber, it is capable of delivering both conventional and nuclear munitions, and has a number of stealth characteristics that enable it to penetrate an enemy's defences without being observed.

LARGEST DEFENCE CONTRACTOR

The world's largest producer of military and defence-related equipment is the Lockheed Martin Corporation (USA), which, in 1999, had global sales totalling $25.5 billion (£17.8 billion), with the US government its biggest customer.

HIGHEST RATE OF FIRE FROM A BALLISTIC WEAPON

The prototype 36-barrel gun built by Metal Storm of Brisbane, Australia, has a firing rate in excess of 1 million rounds per minute (16,666 bullets per second). Such high rates of fire are achievable because the rounds are fired electrically by computer, rather than by a 'hammer' detonator. In comparison, the fastest firing machine gun, the M134 minigun, fires at a rate of 6,000 rounds per minute.

MOST SOPHISTICATED HANDGUN

The O'Dwyer Variable Lethality Law Enforcement (VLE) prototype pistol, made by Metal Storm, has no moving parts, with projectiles fired electronically by a built-in computer processor. The gun can only be fired by someone wearing an authorized transponder ring, and is capable of firing up to three shots within 1⁄500 sec, equivalent to 60,000 rounds per minute. While it seems that only one shot has been fired, the results are far more deadly. In addition, the pistol provides audible and visual confirmation of its settings.

MOST DESTRUCTIVE NON-LETHAL WEAPON

The BLU-114/B 'graphite bomb', deployed by NATO against Serbia in May 1999, disabled 70% of its power grid with minimal 'direct' casualties. A similar device was used during the Gulf War (1990–91) to knock out 85% of Iraq's electricity generating capacity. These so-called 'soft bombs' work by exploding a cloud of hundreds of ultra-fine carbon-fibre wires over electrical installations, causing the electrical systems to short-circuit and temporarily halt supply.

HIGHEST DEFENCE SPEND

It is estimated that world spending on defence reached a peak of $1,000 billion (£681.523 billion) in 1986–87, about $200 (£136) per head of world population. Between 1993 and 1994 expenditure fell from $823 billion (£548 billion) to $795 billion (£529 billion) – a trend that has continued.

GUINNESS WORLD RECORDS™

disasters

DANGER IN THE SKIES

The world's worst mid-air collision involving balloons occurred on 13 Aug 1989, when two balloons (above) collided at a height of 610 m (2,000 ft), resulting in 13 fatalities. The two passenger balloons were launched a few minutes apart for a sightseeing flight over Alice Springs, Northern Territory, Australia. The basket of one of the balloons tore a hole in the fabric of the other, which then collapsed. The pilot and 12 passengers died.

The worst airship disaster involved the US Navy Airship Akron, which killed 73 people when it was ripped apart in a storm off the New Jersey coast on 3 April 1933.

The worst mid-air collision involving an aeroplane happened when a Saudi Boeing 747 scheduled flight crashed with a Kazakh Ilushin 76 charter flight, killing 351 people. The crash occurred 80 km (50 miles) southwest of New Delhi, India, on 12 Nov 1996.

 www.guinnessworldrecords.com/ballooncollision
← ACCESS CODE: ‹52449›

WORST TUNNELLING DISASTER
Between 1931 and 1935 at the Hawk's Nest hydroelectric tunnel, West Virginia, USA, around 2,500 people were killed – the majority through exposure to rock dust that contained silica. Many contracted silicosis, a condition that decreases lung capacity and can lead to diseases like pneumonia and TB. This was the worst occupational-health disaster in American history.

WORST FAMINE DEATH TOLL
In the years between 1959 and 1961 approximately 40,000,000 people died from malnutrition in the Great Famine of China. In part, the famine was a direct result of unsuccessful new farming methods that were introduced by Chairman Mao after the formation of the People's Republic of China in 1949.

WORST ROAD ACCIDENT
On 3 Nov 1982 a petrol tanker exploded inside the Salang Tunnel, Afghanistan. Local estimates suggest that 176 people died (Western estimates quote over 1,100). Either way, it is the worst road accident ever. The Salang Pass, which is 108 km (67 miles) long, is one of the most expensive stretches of road in the world, having cost £24 million ($42 million) to build.

WORST NUCLEAR REACTOR DISASTER
At 1:23 am local time on 26 April 1986, a nuclear reactor disaster at Chernobyl's No. 4 reactor in the former USSR (now the Ukraine), resulted in an official Soviet death toll of 31 people. No systematic records were kept of subsequent deaths, but over 1.7 million people were exposed to varying amounts of radiation. A total of 135,000 people were evacuated, while another 850,000 people are still living in the contaminated regions. The contamination covers a total area of 28,200 km² (10,900 miles²) in Russia and Belarus. An estimated 200,000 people were involved in the clean-up operation.

WORST YEAR FOR AIR CRASHES
In 1988 the average fatality rate for scheduled flights was 175 per million departures, making it the worst year for air crashes. The African continent had an average of 190 fatalities per million departures for scheduled flights; Latin America, including Mexico, had 70 to 80 fatalities per million departures; North America and Canada had 25 fatalities per million departures, followed by Europe, which had an average of six to seven fatalities per million departures. The risk of air fatalities has fallen by a third since then.

WORST SINGLE AIRCRAFT DISASTER
The crash of JAL's Boeing 747 flight 123, near Tokyo on 12 Aug 1985, in which 520 passengers and crew perished, was the worst single-plane crash in aviation history.

WORST UNDERGROUND TRAIN DISASTER
On 28 Oct 1995 about 300 people were killed (and at least 250 people injured), when their underground train caught fire in a tunnel at Baku, Azerbaijan. Official reports blamed the fire on an electrical malfunction. Some reports suggested a bomb. Many of the passengers were killed by carbon-monoxide poisoning, when toxic materials in the train carriages caught fire. Other victims were crushed in the ensuing panic.

WORST TRAIN DISASTER
On 6 June 1981 more than 800 passengers died when seven coaches of their passenger train plunged off a bridge into the Bagmati River at Samastipur, Bihar, India. Confusion exists over the exact cause – some reports claim that the train struck a buffalo, while others say that its brakes failed catastrophically. Some reports put the death toll at 900, although it could have been twice that number.

WORST PEACETIME SINGLE-SHIP DISASTER
The paddle steamer Sultana sank on the Mississippi River, Memphis, Tennessee, USA, on 21 April 1865, when her boilers exploded, with the loss of more than 1,650 lives. Poor recordkeeping at the time of boarding has meant that the actual number of passengers aboard the Sultana will always be unclear. Some historians believe that between 2,200 and 2,300 people were probably aboard. By law, she was allowed to carry only 376 people.

WORST SUBMARINE DISASTER
The French submarine Surcouf sank with 159 crewmen on board after it was rammed in the Caribbean by the US merchantman Thompson Lykes on 18 Feb 1942. At the time of her sinking, Surcouf was the world's largest submarine – 110 m (361 ft) long. Today the largest are the Russian Typhoon class nuclear submarines, which are 170 m (558 ft) in length.

WORST YEAR FOR FOREST FIRES
Deliberately lit forest fires made 1997 the worst year in recorded history for the destruction of the natural environment. The largest and most numerous forest fires were in Brazil, where they raged along a 1,600 km (1,000 mile) front near the Amazon rainforest. The Brazilian Government and the international community were put on the alert due to the severity of the situation.

The second most destructive forest fires in 1997 were in Indonesia. As a result, large areas of South-east Asia were covered with smog and over 40,000 people were hospitalized with breathing problems.

WORST DISASTER CAUSED BY MASS PANIC

Around 4,000 people were killed on 6 June 1941 at an air-raid shelter in Chongqing, China. The crowd was leaving the shelter after an air-raid when the warning siren sounded again. The 4,000 deaths were due to suffocation and trampling as the crowd tried to return to the shelter.

WORST MOUNTAINEERING DISASTER

On Peak Lenin (7,134 m or 23,406 ft) on the border between Tajikistan and Kyrgyzstan (then USSR), 43 people were killed in a massive ice and snow avalanche triggered by a small earthquake on 13 July 1990. Only two of the expedition's climbers survived the mountaineering accident.

WORST DEATH TOLL FROM AN OFFSHORE OIL DISASTER

The largest offshore oil disaster occurred on 6 July 1988 when a fire started on the Piper Alpha oil platform in the North Sea, killing 167 people.

WORST AVALANCHE DISASTERS

An estimated 40,000 to 80,000 men lost their lives during World War I in the Tyrolean Alps, after avalanches were triggered by gunfire. A total of 18,000 Austrian and Italian troops were lost in the Dolomite valleys of northern Italy on 13 Dec 1916 after more than 100 avalanches ripped through the region.

WORST SPACE-RELATED DISASTER

In the greatest space-related disaster that took place on the ground, 91 people were killed when an R-16 rocket exploded during fuelling at the Baikonur Space Centre, Kazakhstan, on 24 Oct 1960.

WORST MANNED SPACEFLIGHT DISASTERS

On 28 Jan 1986 the worst manned spaceflight disaster occurred when *Challenger 51L* exploded 73 seconds after lift-off from the Kennedy Space Center, Florida, USA, at a height of 14,020 m (46,000 ft). The crew of five men and two women died on board. NASA's other space shuttles were grounded for nearly three years while investigations took place to ensure that such a disaster never happened again.

Four people, all Soviet, have been killed during actual spaceflight – Vladimir Komarov of *Soyuz 1*, which crashed on landing on 24 April 1967; and Georgi Dobrovolsky, Viktor Patsayev and Vladislav Volkov died when their *Soyuz 11* spacecraft depressurized during re-entry to the Earth's atmosphere on 29 June 1971.

WORST INDUSTRIAL CHEMICAL DISASTER

Up to 4,000 people were killed and thousands more were left with permanent disabilities after a toxic cloud of methyl isocyanate (MIC) gas enveloped a settlement around the Union Carbide Corporation's pesticide plant in Bhopal, India, on 3 Dec 1984. Reports claimed that the gas leak occurred after a disgruntled employee added water to a storage tank, causing heat and pressure to build up inside until the lethal gas escaped. After legal wranglings, the Indian Supreme Court made Union Carbide Corporation pay £310 million ($470 million) in compensation to the victims and their families.

www.guinnessworldrecords.com/concordecrash

CONCORDE TRAGEDY

On 25 July 2000 an Air France Concorde (above) crashed, killing 113 people (all 100 passengers, nine crew members and four people on the ground). Concorde took off from Charles de Gaulle Airport, Paris, France, bound for New York City, USA. It was brought down soon after taking off by an explosion in one of its fuel tanks, which was pierced by rubber thrown up at high speed by a burst tyre. The tyre was punctured by a piece of metal on the runway. The aircraft nosedived and crashed into a three-storey hotel near Gonesse. This is the third supersonic passenger jet accident and the one with the highest death toll.

ACCESS CODE: ‹55378›

GUINNESS WORLD RECORDS

explosions

MOST POWERFUL NUCLEAR EXPLOSION

The most powerful thermonuclear device so far tested is one dubbed 'Tsar Bomba' with a power equivalent to that of approximately 57 megatons of TNT, which was detonated by the former USSR above the remote Arctic island of Novaya Zemlya. The 28-tonne (56,000-lb) bomb was air-dropped at 8.33 am GMT on 30 Oct 1961. The shockwave circled the world three times, with the first circuit taking 36 hr 27 min. Some estimates put the power of this device at between 62 and 90 megatons.

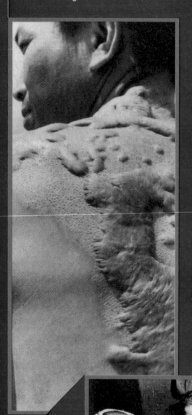

GREATEST EXPLOSION EVER

Most astronomers now believe that the universe began about 12 billion years ago in a cataclysmic explosion that we now call 'Big Bang'. All the matter and energy in the universe had its origins in this event, along with time itself. One second after Big Bang, the temperature was around 10,000 million degrees – around 600 times hotter than the interior of the Sun.

LARGEST IMPACT ON EARTH

Most astronomers now believe that, 4.5 billion years ago, a planet the size of Mars collided with the young Earth. Some of the debris from this cataclysm went into orbit around the Earth and collected under its own gravity to form the Moon. The effect of this impact would have been devastating to the Earth. The entire crust of the planet would probably have been blasted off leaving Earth with a surface made solely of molten magma.

MOST POWERFUL SPACE-BASED NUCLEAR EXPLOSION

On 9 July 1962 a 1.45-megaton nuclear explosion occurred in space 399 km (248 miles) above Johnston Island (Christmas Island) in the Pacific Ocean. The 7,550-kg (16,655-lb) warhead, codenamed 'starfish', was launched by the US Air Force. The explosion was 100 times more powerful than the 1945 Hiroshima blast and formed its own artificial aurora as radioactive particles interacted with the Earth's magnetic field. The height of this detonation equals the orbital altitude of the Space Shuttle.

LARGEST NUCLEAR EXPLOSION CRATER

A 104-kiloton nuclear device was detonated at the Semipalatinsk Test Site, Kazakhstan 178 m (583 ft) beneath the dry bed of the Chagan river on 15 Jan 1965. It left a crater that was 408 m (1,338 ft) wide with a maximum depth of 100 m (328 ft). A major lake later formed behind the 20–35-m (65–114-ft) upraised lip of the crater, which was then cut through with earth-moving equipment to allow it to be used as a reservoir.

HEAVIEST NUCLEAR BOMB

The heaviest known nuclear bomb in operational service was the MK 17 carried by US B-36 bombers in the mid-1950s. It weighed 19.05 tonnes (42,000 lb) and was 7.47 m (24 ft 6 in) long. It had a maximum yield of 20 megatons, equivalent to a thousand Hiroshima bombs. The MK 17 design was tested in the 1954 Castle Romeo nuclear test at Bikini Atoll in the South Pacific, producing an 11-megaton blast.

DEEPEST UNDERGROUND NUCLEAR EXPLOSION

A 2.5 kiloton nuclear device was detonated at the bottom of a 2,850-m-deep (9,350-ft) shaft at a location 60 km (37 miles) south of Nefte-yugamsk, Siberia, Russia, on 18 June 1985. This is roughly one eighth the size of the Hiroshima atomic explosion (the Hiroshima bomb had a yield of 20 kilotons). The detonation was carried out in an attempt to stimulate oil and gas production in the area.

GONE BALLISTIC!

The most destructive ICBM (intercontinental ballistic missile) is the former USSR's SS-18 Model 5 (above), which is accurate to within 250 m (820 ft), and is armed with 10 MIRVs (multiple independently targetable re-entry vehicles), each with a yield equivalent to 750 kilotonnes of TNT. During the Cold War the SS-18 was the most feared weapon in the Warsaw Pact armoury. START 2 (Strategic Arms Reduction Talks) requires that all SS-18s, and other ICBMs with more than one warhead, are eliminated.

www.guinnessworldrecords.com/ballisticmissile

ACCESS CODE: ‹46277›

MOST NUCLEAR WEAPONS DETONATED SIMULTANEOUSLY

A minimum of eight nuclear weapons were detonated simultaneously in an underground tunnel at the Russian test site at Novaya Zemyla on 24 Oct 1990. The simultaneous explosions were carried out for maximum power and to beat the deadline for the Soviet moratorium on nuclear testing.

LARGEST SINGLE CONVENTIONAL EXPLOSION

The demolition of the German fortifications at Heligoland, a North Sea island, on 18 April 1947 used a charge of 4,061 tonnes (8,952,970 lb). During both World Wars the island served as a major German naval base. The charge was detonated by a demolition team from *HMS Lasso*, which lay 14.5 km (9 miles) offshore.

HIROSHIMA HORROR

On 6 Aug 1945, 155,200 people were killed when an atomic bomb was dropped on Hiroshima, Japan – the largest death toll from an atomic bomb. This figure includes radiation deaths within a year. This first atomic bomb – dropped on Japan by the USA with the intention of bringing World War II to an end – had an explosive power equivalent to that of 12.5 kilotonnes (27,560 lb) of trinitrotoluene ($C_7H_5O_6N_3$), called TNT. Code named 'Little Boy' the bomb was 3.04 m (10 ft) long, weighed 4,080 kg (9,000 lb) and exploded 509 m (1,670 ft) above Hiroshima. The bomb completely devastated 10 km² (4 miles²) of the city as soon as it exploded. Over 65% of the city's structures were destroyed or damaged.

www.guinnessworldrecords.com/atombomb

ACCESS CODE: ‹49193›

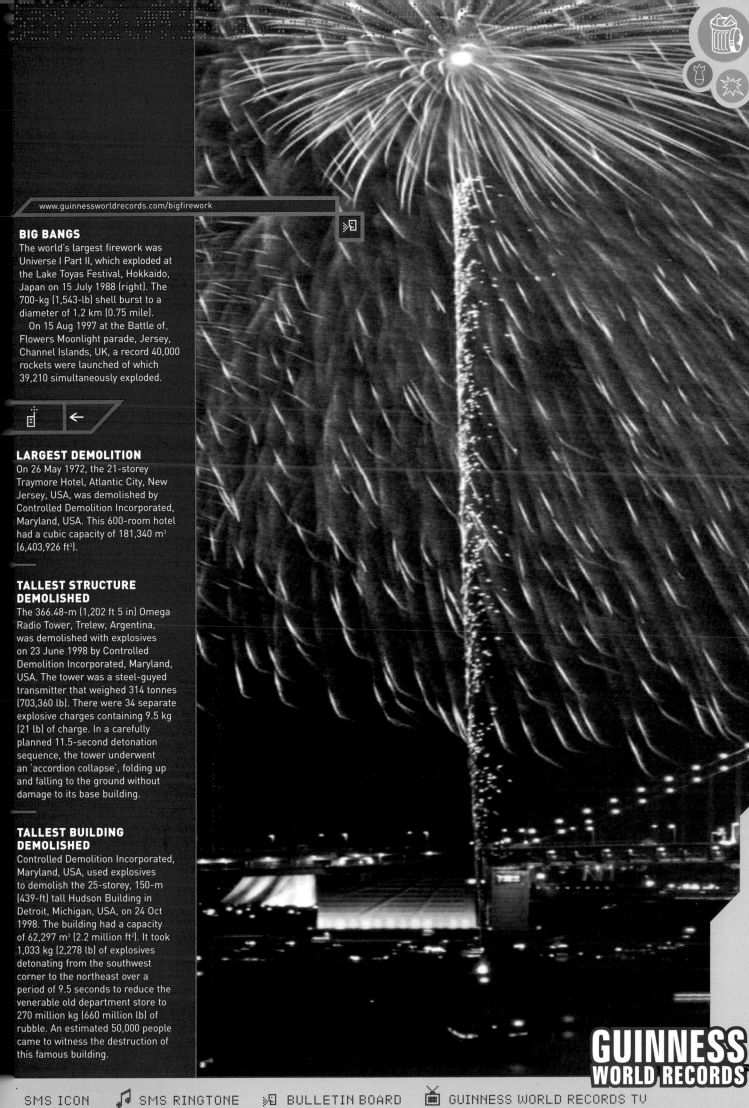

BIG BANGS

The world's largest firework was Universe I Part II, which exploded at the Lake Toyas Festival, Hokkaido, Japan on 15 July 1988 (right). The 700-kg (1,543-lb) shell burst to a diameter of 1.2 km (0.75 mile).

On 15 Aug 1997 at the Battle of, Flowers Moonlight parade, Jersey, Channel Islands, UK, a record 40,000 rockets were launched of which 39,210 simultaneously exploded.

LARGEST DEMOLITION

On 26 May 1972, the 21-storey Traymore Hotel, Atlantic City, New Jersey, USA, was demolished by Controlled Demolition Incorporated, Maryland, USA. This 600-room hotel had a cubic capacity of 181,340 m³ (6,403,926 ft³).

TALLEST STRUCTURE DEMOLISHED

The 366.48-m (1,202 ft 5 in) Omega Radio Tower, Trelew, Argentina, was demolished with explosives on 23 June 1998 by Controlled Demolition Incorporated, Maryland, USA. The tower was a steel-guyed transmitter that weighed 314 tonnes (703,360 lb). There were 34 separate explosive charges containing 9.5 kg (21 lb) of charge. In a carefully planned 11.5-second detonation sequence, the tower underwent an 'accordion collapse', folding up and falling to the ground without damage to its base building.

TALLEST BUILDING DEMOLISHED

Controlled Demolition Incorporated, Maryland, USA, used explosives to demolish the 25-storey, 150-m (439-ft) tall Hudson Building in Detroit, Michigan, USA, on 24 Oct 1998. The building had a capacity of 62,297 m³ (2.2 million ft³). It took 1,033 kg (2,278 lb) of explosives detonating from the southwest corner to the northeast over a period of 9.5 seconds to reduce the venerable old department store to 270 million kg (660 million lb) of rubble. An estimated 50,000 people came to witness the destruction of this famous building.

GUINNESS WORLD RECORDS

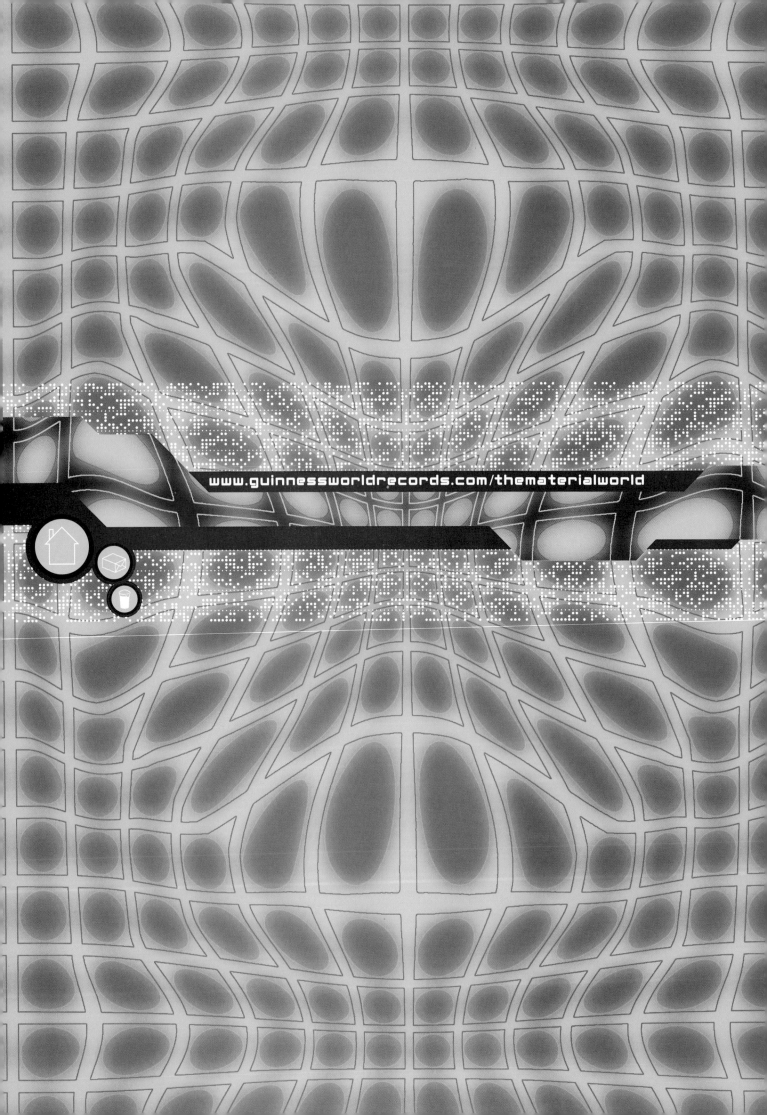

www.guinnessworldrecords.com/thematerialworld

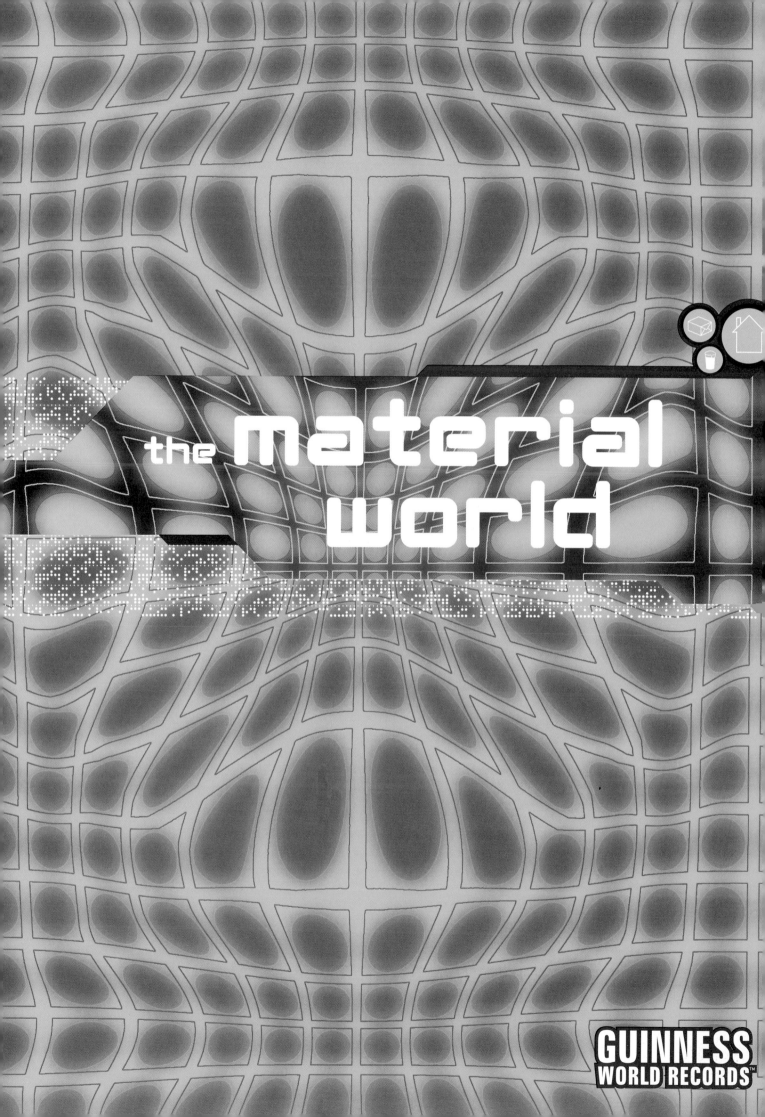

the material world

food and drink

LARGEST WINE TASTING
On 22 Nov 1986 a record 4,000 wine tasters consumed 9,360 bottles of wine. The event was sponsored by local San Francisco television station KQED in California, USA.

LARGEST MILKSHAKE
The Comfort Diners, Parmalat, USA, and the American Dairy Association made the world's largest milkshake of 22,712 litres (6,000 gal) in New York, USA, on 1 Aug 2000. This was the equivalent of 50,000 standard-sized milkshakes.

MOST VALUABLE FISH
The eggs of the Russian sturgeon (*Huso huso*) make it the most valuable fish in the world. A 1,227-kg (2,706-lb) female caught in the Tikhaya Sosna river in 1924 yielded 245 kg (540 lb) of best-quality caviar, worth $289,000 (£200,800) today.

MOST HOT DOGS EATEN IN 12 MINUTES
Kazutoyo 'The Rabbit' Arai of Saitama, Japan, ate 25 entire hot dogs and buns in 12 minutes to win the annual Nathan's Famous International Fourth of July Hot Dog Eating Contest on 4 July 2000.

LARGEST BEER FESTIVAL
Munich's Oktoberfest 99, which took place from 18 Sept to 5 Oct, was visited by seven million people, who consumed a record 5.8 million litres (1,532,197 gal) of beer in 11 beer tents, that stood on a site as large as 50 football pitches.

LARGEST BURGER
Loran Green and Friends of Hi Line Promotions made a burger of pure Montana beef weighing 2,740 kg (6,040 lb) and measuring 7.32 m (24 ft) in diameter at the Sleeping Buffalo Resort, Saco, Montana, USA, on 5 Sept 1999. More than 3,500 people gathered to watch the burger cook for about two hours on a gigantic specially made grill.

LARGEST BISCUIT
The largest biscuit ever made was a chocolate chip cookie with a diameter of 24.9 m (81 ft 9 in) and a circumference of 78.2 m (256 ft), made by Cookie Time, Christchurch, New Zealand, on 2 April 1996.

LARGEST BOWL OF SOUP
Wyler's, a division of Borden Foods Corporation (USA, prepared the world's largest bowl of beef and vegetable flavoured soup with a volume of 2,505.94 litres (661.99 gal) on 5 Oct 2000 to mark the company's 70th birthday.

MOST DIFFERENT DISHES ON DISPLAY
On 27 Oct 2000 Bochasanwasi Akshar Purushottam Swaminarayan Sanstha (BAPS – a social spiritual organisation) displayed 1,247

GIMME S'MORE!
S'more – short for "Some more!" is a classic American campfire treat made of roasted marshmallows, Hershey bars, and Graham crackers. The largest s'more (above), weighing 357 kg (789 lb) was created at the Cape Hatteras KOA Kampground in Rodanthe, North Carolina, on 19 June 1999. It contained 128 kg (284 lb) of Graham crackers, 170 kg (374 lb) of chocolate and 59 kg (131 lb) of marshmallows (10,000 marshmallows in all were roasted). It measured a lip-smacking 12 x 3 m x 5 cm (40 x 10 ft x 2 in).

www.guinnessworldrecords.com/smore
← ACCESS CODE: ‹53349›

different dishes of vegetarian food as an *Annakut* (offering) to mark the Hindu New Year. The record was set at the Shree Swaminarayan Mandir, Neasden, London, UK.

LARGEST COOKED BREAKFAST
The Chinook Centre, Calgary, Alberta, Canada, organized a cooked breakfast for 8,337 people in the Chinook Centre parking lot on 8 July 2000 between 8.11 am and 9.11 am. Food consumed comprised 1,500 kg (3,300 lb) pancake mix; 900 kg (1,980 lb) ham; 3,181.69 ml (107,586 fl.oz) orange juice; 400 litres (105.6 gal) maple syrup; 3,171 kg (6,372 lb) baked beans; and 20.43 kg (45 lb) ground coffee.

MOST OYSTERS EATEN IN THREE MINUTES
James Arney (UK) ate 64 oysters in three minutes at Bentley's Restaurant, London, UK, on 1 Sept 2000. Arney ran out of oysters after 2.5 min so he could probably have eaten more, given the chance.

LARGEST PIZZA COMMERCIALLY AVAILABLE
Since June 1999, Original Brooks Pizza 2 for 1 Ltd, Alberta, Canada, has sold 200 pizzas measuring 1 x 1.25 m (3 x 4 ft) and weighing between 11 and 16 kg (25–35 lb). 'The Colossal' takes two people to make, 5.89 kg (13 lb) of bread dough for the crust and 3.63 kg (8 lb) of cheese for the topping.

LARGEST CURRY COOKED
Abdul Salam, owner and chef of the Eastern Eye restaurant, Lichfield, Staffs, UK, cooked a vegetable curry weighing 3,106.5 kg (6,849.8 lb) on 17 July 2000. The curry fed about 7,500 people and the event raised £4,500 ($6,689) for charity.

FASTEST RICE EATER
Using chopsticks, Tae Wah Gooding (South Korea) ate 64 grains of rice, one by one, in three minutes. The

A SHIPLOAD OF CHOCOLATE
A chocolate model, in the shape of a traditional Spanish sailing ship (left), measuring 8.5 m (27 ft 10.5 in) tall, 13 m (42 ft 8 in) long and 2.5 m (8 ft 2.5 in) wide, was made by Gremi Provincial de Patisseria, Confiteria i Bolleria School, Barcelona, Spain, in Feb 1991. It was the tallest chocolate model ever made and weighed 4 tonnes (8,818 lb). It was displayed at the Palacio de Alfonso XIII at the international fair *Tecnoalimentaria* in Feb 1991.

www.guinnessworldrecords.com/chocship
← ACCESS CODE: ‹49162›

record was set at Peterborough Regional College, Cambs, UK, on 7 Nov 2000 (National Curry Day).

LARGEST JAR OF JELLYBEANS
Goelitz Confectionery, makers of Jelly Belly jellybeans, made a jar containing 2,160,000 jellybeans at the Empress Casino Hammond, Indiana, USA, on 15 Oct 1999. It weighed a massive 2,744.23 kg (6,050 lb) and measured a record 1.37 x 1.37 x 3 m (4 ft 6 in x 4 ft 6 in x 10 ft).

LARGEST TEQUILA SLAM
The world's largest tequila slam involving 154 people at Bar Madrid, London, UK, took place on 10 Feb 2001 to raise money for the Alejandro Magno Boys' Home, Bolivia.

FASTEST CREAM CRACKER EATER
Damian Howarth (UK) ate three cream crackers, in a record-

www.guinnessworldrecords.com/fastfood

ACCESS CODE: ‹56570›

AMAZING GRAZING
In 2000 Americans spent a record $110 billion (£76 billion) on fast food, more than on higher education, personal computers or new cars. On any one day approximately 25% of adults in the USA visit a fast-food outlet. The typical American eats about three burgers per week from one of the country's 300,000 fast-food outlets.

breaking time of 1 min 22.36 sec. He performed this feat on the set of Channel 4's *The Big Breakfast*, London, UK, on 6 March 2001.

HIGHEST-ALTITUDE FORMAL MEAL
The highest altitude at which a formal meal has been eaten is 6,768 m (22,205 ft), a record set when nine members of the Ansett Social

Donald A Gorske (USA) ate his 17,500th McDonalds Big Mac on 19 Feb 2001 – the most Big Macs ever consumed. On 17 May 2001 he completed his 29th year of eating Big Macs on a daily basis, sometimes at a rate of nine a day. His wife and he celebrated their 25th wedding anniversary in 2000 after he proposed to her in 1975 at his favourite McDonalds.

Climbers from Sydney, NSW, Australia, scaled Mt Huascarán, Peru, on 28 June 1989. They took a three-course meal with them, as well as wine, a Louis XIV dining table, chairs and candelabra.

MOST CHILLIS EATEN IN THREE MINUTES
Armando Martillana ate a record 550 chillis in three minutes at the annual Magayon Festival, Philippines, on 28 May 2000. He won PHP50,000 (£711.06; $1,042.75) in prize money. The chillis used for the competition were *capsicum frutescens* – one of the world's hottest chillis.

LONGEST CURRY DELIVERY
On 23 Feb 2001 fast food website, MadAboutCurry.co.uk arranged for a vegetable curry and a peshwari naan to be sent to Rachel Kerr (UK) from Newcastle-Upon-Tyne, Tyneside, UK, to Sydney, Australia, a distance of 17,398 km (10,811 miles) as the crow flies. It arrived three days later on 26 Feb 2001.

GUINNESS WORLD RECORDS

big stuff 1

LARGEST GUACAMOLE DIP

The world's largest guacamole dip weighing 1,288 kg (2,840 lb) was created at The Town Theater, Michoacan, Mexico, on 26 Nov 2000. The ingredients used were 1,000 kg (2,205 lb) avocado, 110 kg (242.50 lb) onions, 110 kg (242.50 lb) tomatoes, 15 kg (33 lb) chillis, 5 kg (11 lb) coriander, 12 kg (26 lb) salt, and 36 kg (79.36 lb) of limes.

LONGEST SUSHI

The world's longest futomaki (sushi roll) was created on 23 Sept 2000 by 315 staff of the Toyota Motor Corporation, Japan, and 3,050 members of the local community at the Toyota Gijyutu Fureai Fesuta 2000 in Aichi, Japan. It measured 1.11 km (0.69 miles) long, weighed about 2,200 kg (4,851 lb), was 5 cm (1.96 in) in diameter, and took about an hour to make.

LARGEST DOG BISCUIT

The world's largest dog biscuit measured 2.35 m (7 ft 9.4 in) long, 57 cm (1 ft 11.3 in) wide and 2.54 cm (1 in) thick. Produced by the People's Company Bakery in Minneapolis, Minnesota, USA, on 11 Aug 1999, the biscuit, weighing 4,014 kg (8,849 lb), was unveiled at the Phalen Pork Pavillion, St Paul, Minnesota, for the annual Walk and Talk for Homeless Animals. It was broken up and eaten by about 100 dogs who had been in the walkathon.

LARGEST BOX OF CHOCOLATES

A calorie-laden 8,000 Disaronno Amaretto-filled chocolates, weighing 81.2 kg (179 lb) went into the world's largest box of chocolates, which was created in the shape of a heart and measured 4.6 x 4.6 x 0.76 m (15 x 15 x 2.5 ft) in New York City, New York, USA, on 14 Feb 2000 to mark St Valentine's Day. 454.3 m² (4,890 ft²) of cardboard was used for the box. The full box of chocolates weighed 590 kg (1,300 lb).

LARGEST WOK

The world's largest wok, made by Tony Hancock (UK) measures 2.93 m (9 ft 7 in) in diameter and is 0.60 m (2 ft) deep. On 16 March 2000 at Wing Yip Chinese restaurant and supermarket, Croydon, Surrey, UK, Tony Hancock demonstrated the use of the giant double-handed wok by stir-frying 400 kg (882 lb) of vegetables and noodles. The large wok rested on a 0.68-m-high (2 ft 2.4 in) wok stand incorporating a propane burner carrier.

ARK DE TRIOMPHE!

Between Jan and Aug 1999, GP Reichelt (Germany), assisted by Ida Bagus Jiwartem (Bali), carved a 'Noah's Ark' measuring 1.5 m (4 ft 11 in) long, 0.64 m (2 ft 1 in) wide and 0.18 m (7 in) high from a single piece of wood (left). Mr. Reichelt initially intended to carve an ark that would hold just 42 pairs of animals but then decided to aim to carve one that would house 100 pairs. The result of his efforts was an ark that holds a record-breaking 71 pairs of animals – all individually carved. Reichelt cut the original shapes of the animals and formed them roughly with a grinder, then he and Jiwartem did the finer carving, with Reichelt performing the final finishes.

www.guinnessworldrecords.com/ark
← ACCESS CODE: ‹53394›

LONGEST PENCIL

On 15 Feb 1998 the Sri Chinmoy Marathon team (USA) made a pencil 6.24 m (20 ft 6 in) long and weighing 254 kg (560 lb). Six angled sections of pine were fitted together with a core of 8.25 cm (3.25 in) synthetic graphite running through it, forming a 33-cm (13-in) diameter. For the eraser, 15.87 kg (35 lb) of rubber was fixed on to one end with a sheet of aluminium. An electric plane sharpened the pencil so it could be used to write.

LARGEST DRINK CAN

On 16 March 1999 the world's largest aluminium drink can was first displayed in Sydney, Australia. Made by O'Brien Aluminium and launched on behalf of Guinness Australasia, the replica of a can of Draught Guinness had a capacity of 3,608 litres (6,349 pints), holding 8,200 times more beer than the 440-ml (15.48-fl oz) original. It was 4.5 m (14 ft 9 in) tall, 1.8 m (5 ft 10 in) wide and weighed 300 kg (661.39 lb).

LARGEST BRUSSELS SPROUT

In Oct 1992 Dr Bernard Lavery of Llanharry, South Wales, UK, grew a huge Brussels sprout that weighed an astounding 8.3 kg (18 lb 3 oz).

TALLEST CELERY PLANT

In 1998 Joan Priednieks of Bridgwater, Somerset, UK, grew a massive celery plant that measured 2.74 m (9 ft) tall. Normally these plants only grow to about 91 cm (3 ft).

LONGEST DRINK CAN CHAIN

Bexley Make A Difference Day (MADD) group created the longest chain of aluminium cans using 12,756 cans at Queen Mary's Hospital, Sidcup, Kent, UK, on 28 Oct 2000. The final length of the chain was 1.47 km (0.91 miles).

LONGEST GUM WRAPPER CHAIN

On 11 March 1965, Gary Duschl of Ontario, Canada, began making a gum-wrapper chain. By 31 March 2000 it measured 10,387 m (34,078 ft), was made up of 1,585,382 links from 792,691 wrappers, and weighed around 211 kg (465 lb).

ENOR-MOUSE

In May 1998 students from Columbiana Career Centre, Lisbon, Ohio, USA, constructed a fully operational mousetrap measuring 2.99 m (9 ft 10 in) long and 1.33 m (4 ft 5 in) wide (left). The new record holder is over a third larger than the previous 193-cm (6-ft 4-in) record-breaking model built by physics lecturers Mel McDaniel and Joseph Melancon of the University of Texas, USA. The Columbiana students built a full-scale replica of a Victor mousetrap, the world's most popular model. First patented a century ago, the steel-spring Victor, made in Litiz, Pennsylvania, USA, has sold millions of units. A mouse in proportion to this massive mousetrap would be around 3 m (9.84 ft) long – the size of a small car.

LARGEST BAR OF CHOCOLATE

Between 16 and 19 March 2000, at the Eurochocolate 2000 confectionery exhibition in Turin, Italy, Elah-Dufour United Food Companies Ltd made a scaled-up version of a chocolate bar, weighing an amazing 2,280 kg (5,026 lb). It measured 315 x 150 x 45 cm (124 x 59 x 17.7 in), equivalent to 22,800 100-g (4-oz) chocolate bars.

www.guinnessworldrecords.com/mousetrap
← ACCESS CODE: ‹48095›

ACCESS CODE: ‹48789›

SNOW BUSINESS

Residents of Bethel, Maine, USA, and surrounding towns, built an enormous snowman measuring 34.63 m (113 ft 7.5 in) high (right), over a period of 14 days, completing him on 17 Feb 1999. The 10-storey snowman named Angus (after Maine governor Angus King) was constructed using 5,600 m³ (197,762 ft³) of snow. He finally melted 15 weeks later on 10 June 1999 – the date had been the subject of a sweepstake.

LARGEST STICK OF ROCK

The Coronation Rock Company of Blackpool, Lancashire, UK, created the largest stick of rock weighing 424.5 kg (936 lb) and measuring 4.49 m (14 ft 9 in) long, with a circumference of 1.14 m (45 in) at their factory on 6 Dec 2000. The rock was broken up and sold for charity.

JIGSAW PUZZLE WITH MOST PIECES

A puzzle consisting of 209,250 pieces, each measuring 1.5 x 1.5 cm (0.59 x 0.59 in), was completed at the Mulan Jigsaw Puzzle contest at the Grand Formosa Regent Hotel, Taipei, Taiwan. The overall measurement was 6.75 m x 6.97 m (22 ft 1 in x 22 ft 10 in).

GUINNESS
WORLD RECORDS™

big stuff 2

BIGGEST NIGHTCLUB

The nightclub Privilege in Ibiza Spain, can hold 10,000 clubbers on its 6,500 m² (69,965 ft²) of dance space spread over three floors – altogether the size of a soccer pitch. Sheet glass at one end allows the morning sun to shine through. A swimming pool, fountains, gardens, trees and plants add to the ambience in the club.

LARGEST PARAFOIL

The largest parafoil parachute ever flown has a span of 43.6 m (143 ft) giving it a surface area of 700 m² (7,500 ft²), nearly one-and-a-half times the size of the wings of a Boeing 747. Essentially a parachute that is 'inflated' by air pressure as it descends, the parafoil was developed by NASA to bring its X-38 spacecraft down to the surface after re-entering the atmosphere. Most paragliders, which are also parafoils, have a surface area of 25–30 m² (270–323 ft²).

LARGEST CARDBOARD BOX

The world's largest corrugated cardboard box was constructed by Kappa Van Dam, a manufacturer of custom shipping cartons. It measured 7 m (22.9 ft) long, 2.6 m (8.5 ft) wide and 2.4 m (7.87 ft) high, and was unveiled on 20 Nov 1999 at Eindhoven market, Netherlands. The mammoth box was manufactured on mass-production equipment at the Kappa Van Dam production site, Helmond, Netherlands.

CALCULATED TO IMPRESS

The largest recognized abacus (left) measures 4.7 m (15.41 ft) long and 2.2 m (7.21 ft) high, contains 91 beads and weighs 380 kg (838 lb). It was made by Spectrum for Maths Year 2000 and unveiled at the Science Museum, London, UK, on 23 Jan 2001. The abacus is regarded as a universal mathematical icon. The frame was built from aluminium, the poles from stainless steel and the 91 shiny blue beads from plastic. According to Keith Greaves, head of the construction team, one problem was simply getting the huge abacus inside the Science Museum – it barely fitted through the doors. The abacus originated between 600 and 500 BC in either Egypt or China. They were, in effect, the first-ever hand-held calculators.

www.guinnessworldrecords.com/abacus
← ACCESS CODE: ‹56104›

LARGEST FOUNTAIN

The world's largest fountain is the Suntec City Fountain of Wealth in Singapore. Its cast-bronze superstructure weighs 85 tonnes (187,400 lb) and stands 14 m (46 ft) high, while the base of the fountain has a total area of 1,683 m² (18,116 ft²). It cost around £3.5 million ($6 million) to build in 1997.

LARGEST CATHERINE WHEEL

The world's largest self-propelled vertical Catherine wheel firework measured 25.95 m (85 ft) in diameter, and was designed by the Newick Bonfire Society Ltd (UK). It fired for 12 revolutions on 30 Oct 1999 at Newick, East Sussex, UK.

BIGGEST BRAZIER

A brazier that was 8 m (26 ft) tall, 9 m (30 ft) wide and weighed 25 tonnes (55,115 lb) was used to house the Millennium Beacon, lit on the river Thames, London, UK, on 31 Dec 1999. The beacon (the biggest in a national chain of about 2,000 beacons and bonfires) took 2,000 man-hours and eight weeks to construct. Although there is no official figure, reports state that the flame from this brazier, which was lit by Queen Elizabeth II, shot over 100 m (328 ft) into the air.

LARGEST PIGGY BANK

In Nov 1995 a giant pink piggy bank was constructed by the Canadian Imperial Bank of Commerce, Canada. It measured 4.70 m (15 ft 5 in) in length, 2.64 m (8 ft 8 in) in height and 6.52 m (21 ft 4 in) in circumference, and was named Maximillion.

LARGEST ACOUSTIC GUITAR

A fully-functional acoustic guitar, measuring 8.66 m (28 ft 5 in) long and 97.2 cm (3 ft 2 in) deep, is exhibited at the Stradivarium exhibition in The Exploratory, Bristol, UK. The dimensions are in proportion with those of the 18th-century classical guitar made by Antonius Stradivari in the Ashmolean Museum, Oxford, UK.

LARGEST CHANDELIER

The world's largest set of chandeliers was created by the Kookje Lighting Co Ltd of Seoul, South Korea. The set is 12 m (39 ft) high, weighs 10.67 tonnes (23,500 lb) and has 700 bulbs. Completed in Nov 1988, it occupies three floors of the Lotte Chamshil department store in Seoul.

LARGEST AXE

A steel axe measuring 18.3 m (60 ft) long, 7 m (23 ft) wide and weighing 7 tonnes (15,400 lb) was designed and built by BID Ltd of Woodstock, New Brunswick, Canada. It would take a 140-tonne (308,500-lb) lumberjack to swing the axe, and a crane was used to lift it into its concrete 'stump'.

LARGEST CLOCK

The world's largest clock is the astronomical clock in the Cathedral of St Pierre, Beauvais, France, constructed between 1865 and 1868. It consists of 90,000 parts and is 12.1 m (40 ft) high, 6.1 m (20 ft) wide and 2.7 m (9 ft) deep.

LARGEST FOOTBALL

A football made from 52.03 m² (560 ft²) of PU leather and sewn by hand had a diameter of 3.53 m (11 ft 7 in) when measured on 1 July 1999. Made by Tianjin Nanhua of Lisheng Sports Products Co, Beijing, China, the ball had 12,870 stitches, a circumference of 11.075 m (36 ft 4 in) and weighed 142 kg (313 lb). To be in proportion with this ball, a player would have to be around 28 m (92 ft) tall – as high as a six-storey building.

ANGELIC PROPORTIONS

An angel (left) constructed from 2,946 glass bottles (still containing beer) and punctured metal sheets from which bottle caps had been made, was designed and built by artist Sergio Rodriguez Villarreal (Mexico). It measured 5.57 m (18 ft 3 in) high, 3.6 m (11 ft 9 in) wide, with a base diameter of 2.5 m (8 ft 2 in) and was displayed at Alfonso Reyes Avenue, Nuevo León, Mexico, in Jan 2000. This work of art holds the record for the largest Christmas angel sculpture. The artist was inspired by the creative spirit of Christmas to become a multiple Guinness record holder.
Villarreal also designed and built the largest ever Christmas bauble, which measured 2.75 m (9 ft) tall and 2.2 m (7 ft 2 in) in diameter. It was displayed at Alfonso Reyes Avenue, Neuvo Len, Mexico, in 2000.

www.guinnessworldrecords.com/angelsculpture
← ACCESS CODE: ‹48146›

LARGEST GREETINGS CARD

A giant free-standing Christmas card, as big as 4,500 regular-sized greeting cards put together, was made from one piece of card measuring a total of 251 m² (2,700 ft²) or 30 x 8.3 m (98 ft 0.6 in x 27 ft 2 in) on 3 Dec 1990 at University College, Dublin, Republic of Ireland. Once folded, the card front measured 15 x 8.3 m (49 ft 2 in x 27 ft 2 in).

LARGEST BEDFRAME

A total of 223 students, aged 14 to 18, lay side by side in three rows upon a mattress on a giant wooden bedframe measuring 8 x 10 m (26 ft 2 in x 32 ft 10 in). Starlight Ltd exhibited it at the Furniture World exhibition from 14 to 18 Nov 2000 in Budapest, Hungary.

BIGGEST BRA

In Sept 1990 Triumph International Japan Ltd made a bra with an underbust measurement of 24 m (78 ft 8 in) and a bust measurement of 28 m (91 ft 10 in). It was made from 70 m (229 ft 7 in) of fabric, enough to make 1,000 regular-sized bras.

LONGEST SCARF

Karen Dengate (UK) began knitting a scarf on 1 Oct 1997 and has spent three hours a day working on it since. It was 174.21 m (571 ft 6 in) long and 19 cm (7.5 in) wide when measured in March 2000. She intends to carry on knitting.

TALLEST PAPER CUP

The tallest paper cup, 2.53 m (8 ft 3 in) high, was created by Bunzl Disposables Europe with the help of Polarcup on 1 Feb 2000 in Epsom, Surrey, UK. The paper cup was filled to hold 4,930 litres (1,302.37 gal) of water by the local fire brigade. To ensure that the cup was a scaled-up version of a normal paper cup, it was made with 13 layers of paper and had a watertight seam.

www.guinnessworldrecords.com/cowboyboots

IF THE BOOT FITS . . .

Texas, known for big ranches and big hats, is also home to the world's biggest pair of authentic cowboy boots. The boots (right) are 1.38 m (4 ft 6.75 in) tall and 1.19 m (3 ft 11 in) long. They were made by the co-owner of Rocketbuster Boots, El Paso, Texas, USA, Marty Snortum. A team of 15, headed by designer Nevena Christi, used $5,000 (£3,463) of materials and took three months to make the brightly coloured pair of boots, finishing them on 13 Jan 1999. They weigh 45 kg (100 lb) and have soles stitched with nylon clothesline.

The world's largest shoe measures 3.12 m (10 ft 3 in) in length, 1.05 m (3 ft 5.5 in) in width and 1.23 m (4 ft 0.8 in) in height. Zahit Okurlar (Turkey) used three-cows' worth of leather just for the sole. The right shoe was exhibited in Feb 2000 at the Konya International Shoe Fair.

Edmund Kryza (Poland) made a giant ladies' shoe 1.84 m (6 ft) long and 1.12 m (3 ft 8 in) high from 6 m² (64 ft²) of artificial leather on 8 May 1996.

GUINNESS WORLD RECORDS

small stuff

SMALLEST NIGHTCLUB

The world's smallest nightclub is The Miniscule of Sound, London, UK, which is a box only 2.4 m (8 ft) long, 1.2 m (4 ft) wide and 2.4 m (8 ft) high. Constructed in Aug 1998 from Dexion shelving and hardboard walls, and decorated with fake fur, strobe lighting and a mirror ball, it contains a full DJ and sound system and a dance floor measuring only 2 m² (21.5 ft²). The maximum capacity is 14 people including the DJ.

SMALLEST WINE GLASS

The smallest wine glass was unveiled on 7 Dec 2000 by NEC (Japan). This tiny vessel measures just 2,750 nanometres across (one nanometre is one billionth of a metre). This is approximately 20,000 times smaller than a conventional wine glass.

SMALLEST ABACUS

In Nov 1996 scientists at the IBM Research Division's Zurich laboratory in Switzerland built an abacus with individual molecules as beads with a diameter of less than one nanometre (one billionth of a metre). They formed rows of 10 molecules along steps one atom high, which acted as the rails for each molecule.

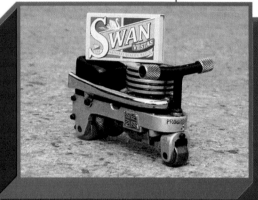

MICRO MOTOR

Simon Timperley and Clive Williams of Progressive Engineering Ltd, Manchester, UK, designed and constructed the world's smallest motorcycle (left) with a wheelbase of 108 mm (4.25 in), a seat height of 95 mm (3.74 in) and with a wheel diameter of 19 mm (0.74 in) for the front and 24 mm (0.94 in) for the back. The bike was ridden a distance of 1 m (3.28 ft). All parts of the motorcycle were hand made, except for the engine, which had to be modified to fit on to the chassis. The 10 cc model aircraft engine buzzes at 13,000 rpm, pushing the cycle along at a sedate 3.2 km/h (2 mph).

www.guinnessworldrecords.com/micromotorcycle
← ACCESS CODE: ‹43595›

SMALLEST PENKNIFE

The world's smallest fully-operational handmade penknife measures 8 mm (0.3 in) long and 3 mm (0.1 in) wide when closed. With the sharp blade snapped open, the knife extends to 14.5 mm (0.5 in) long and 2.5 mm (0.09 in) wide.

SMALLEST SCISSORS

In 1998 Ramesh Chand Dhiman (India) constructed, by hand, a pair of working scissors measuring just 3.12 mm (0.12 in) long and 2.17 mm (0.08 in) wide. Although they work, the scissors would be completely impractical for any kind of application. Ramesh Chand Dhiman also made the smallest razor blade in the world.

SMALLEST MICROPHONE

A silicon microphone only 40 microns (one micron is one millionth of a metre) wide was produced by the Electrical Engineering and Physics departments of the University of Bilkent, Turkey. It is hoped it will be used in the medical technique for ultra-sound scans.

SMALLEST PAPER MONEY

The smallest national note issued was the 10-bani note of the Ministry of Finance of Romania in 1917. Its printed area measured 27.5 x 38 mm (1.08 x 1.49 in). This is about one tenth the size of a $1 banknote.

SMALLEST RULER

A ruler used for measuring very small lengths in an electron microscope was developed in 1994 by John McCaffrey and Jean-Marc Baribeau of the Institute for Microstructural Sciences at the National Research Council, Canada. The smallest division on the ruler is 18 atoms wide and individual atoms are visible. It is so small that 10 of the rulers stacked end to end would equal the diameter of a human hair.

SMALLEST TEST TUBE

The world's smallest test tube – a nanotube – was made at the École Polytechnique Fédérale de Lausanne in Switzerland in 1996. Each tube is one micron long and has an internal diameter of less than 10 nanometres (10 billionths of a metre). End to end you could fit 15,000 of these nanotubes across your thumb.

SMALLEST HOLDING

Because of a legal technicality, the Electricity Trust of South Australia is the proprietor of a registered and separately delineated piece of land in Adelaide, South Australia, measuring just 25.4 mm (1 in) on all four sides, i.e. the same size as the average postage stamp.

THE BEE'S KNEES!

Rutherford Appleton Laboratory, Oxfordshire, UK, created the world's smallest advertisement for Guinness World Records, measuring just 100 microns x 100 microns. It featured on a knee-band worn by a bee on 25 Oct 2000 (left). Made from Kapton (a flexible and light plastic film), the letters, which were between 5-20 microns high read, 'Guinness World Records.com' and were made from deposited gold. As a comparison, a human hair on average measures between 40 and 100 microns in diameter. The whole process of making the advert took just half a day. The bee chosen had been selected from a colony of bees and was found dead at the bottom of the hive – so no harm was actually inflicted on a live bee.

www.guinnessworldrecords.com/microadvert
← ACCESS CODE: ‹55977›

MINUTE SURVEILLANCE

The PC-53XP pinhole micro-video camera (below), manufactured by US-based video security firm Supercircuits, is the smallest colour video camera commercially available in the world. It measures just 4.25 cm³ (0.26 in³) and provides full-colour video pictures. Weighing just 7 g (0.25 oz), this camera outputs standard NTSC format images that are digitally controlled to give a high-quality picture despite being smaller than a sugar cube.

The camera provides a horizontal resolution of 380 lines and consumes just 50 milliamps at 12 volts DC. When combined with the AVX-900T3 (also manufactured by Supercircuits), the result is the world's smallest wireless video camera. Ideal for covert operations and surveillance, the combined camera and transmitter (the AVX-900S5) can transmit colour video over a distance of 230 m (750 ft).

ACCESS CODE: ‹48050›

SMALLEST BICYCLE

The world's smallest-wheeled rideable bicycle has a front wheel with a diameter of 11 mm (0.43 in) and a rear wheel of 13 mm (0.51 in). On 11 Aug 1999 its constructor, Zbigniew Rózanek (Poland), rode it a distance of 5 m (16 ft).

SMALLEST CRYSTAL BOWL

A crystal bowl made by Jim Irish of Rathculliheen, Waterford, Ireland, measured 8.55 mm (0.336 in) wide, 4.6 mm (0.18 in) tall, 2.1 mm (0.08 in) thick and was made with 208 cuts. It took eight hours to complete the bowl over a two-week period, working in 45 tiny segments. The bowl can fit six times on to one Irish penny.

SMALLEST GUITAR

The world's smallest guitar carved from a block of silicon and based on a Fender Stratocaster, measures just 10 micrometres long – 1/20 of the thickness of a human hair. Made in 1997 in just 20 minutes by scientists at the Cornell University, New York, USA, each of its six strings were 0.05 mm (0.002 in) thick and, when plucked, they vibrated at frequencies 1,000 times higher than the human ear can hear. The guitar is the same size as a human blood cell.

SMALLEST RETURNING BOOMERANG

A boomerang measuring 48 mm (1.8 in) long and 45 mm (1.77 in) wide, was successfully thrown by Sadir Kattan at the Australian National Boomerang Championships, Melbourne, Vic, on 22 March 1997. The boomerang travelled past the qualifying 20 m (65.6 ft) and returned into the accuracy circles from where it had been thrown.

SMALLEST STEAM ENGINE

In 1993 a team of physicists at Sandia National Laboratories in Albuquerque, New Mexico, USA, invented a microscopic steam engine that was 6 microns long and 2 microns wide. Despite the engine's tiny size, its makers say that it is powerful enough to work in all manner of microtools such as the tweezers and scalpels used in eye or brain surgery.

SMALLEST SHIP-IN-A-BOTTLE

Arthur V. Pedlar (UK) constructed the smallest ship-in-a-bottle in a medical phial 24 mm (0.94 in) long and 9 mm (0.35 in) wide, with a neck of 2 mm (0.08 in) in 1956. The galleon has three masts, five sails and three flags and was inserted into the bottle in 28 pieces, each placed in position with a piece of fuse wire glued to a matchstick. The sea is sealing wax pulled into thin strands, the rigging is horsehair and the hull of the galleon is made of cork. A lighthouse was also placed inside the bottle.

GUINNESS WORLD RECORDS

collections 1

LARGEST PRIVATE ROLLS-ROYCE FLEET

Sultan Hassanal Bolkiah of Brunei is believed to have the biggest private collection of Rolls-Royce cars, consisting of an estimated 150 vehicles. Together with his brother, Prince Jefri, the Sultan is reported to own a further 1,998 luxury cars.

LARGEST COLLECTION OF MODEL COACHES AND BUSES

Ben Bradshaw (UK) has collected a total of 153 individual model buses and coaches – both single and double-decker – since he was three years old. The model and manufacturer most represented is Mercedes Benz and Corgi, with 45 and 59 models respectively.

LARGEST COLLECTION OF MODEL RAILWAY VEHICLES

The largest collection of model railway vehicles made by one person is the JP Richards Collection owned by the National Railway Museum in York, UK. There are 610 models in the collection handmade to scale by James Peel Richards (UK).

LARGEST JET-FIGHTER COLLECTION

The world's biggest private jet fighter collection numbers 110, and belongs to French winemaker Michel Pont. His hobby started in 1985, and includes Russian MiGs, British Jaguars and French Mirages. He buys them from governments, although they are not allowed to be flown over French airspace.

LARGEST COLLECTION OF TELEVISIONS AND RADIOS

By 22 Sept 1998 Göran Ågårdh (Sweden) had collected a record total of 10,060 televisions and radios.

LARGEST COLLECTION OF PENCILS

Emilio Arenas (Uruguay) has a collection of 5,500 different pencils, each printed with a distinct design, logo or brand. Emilio also owns impressive collections of key rings, ashtrays, soft drink and beer cans, perfume bottles, pencil sharpeners, pins, matchboxes and phone cards, all of which are on public display in four huge rooms in Emilio's house.

LARGEST BALL-POINT PEN COLLECTION

Angelika Unverhau (Germany) has a collection of ball-point pens that in Oct 2000 numbered 205,050 units (excluding duplicates) and represents 146 countries. She has been collecting unusual pens since childhood, but decided to take her

SUPERMODELS

The record for the largest collection of model cars is held by Mr Suhail Mohd. Al Zarooni of Dubai (UAE) who owns more than 1,500 miniature model cars. This huge collection – his passion since 1990 – is worth nearly $3 million (£2,100,000). Many of his models are rare cars such as Queen Elizabeth II's Rolls Royces and some are painted in 24-carat gold. A large portion of the cars are models from the 1960s – classic cars, police cars, and limousines – most of which he purchased in the UK and Europe. He often buys a real car to match a favourite model.

www.guinnessworldrecords.com/modelcars
ACCESS CODE: ‹55947›

hobby more seriously in 1990. She founded a club with 90 members from all over Germany who meet twice a year to trade pens and share pen-related experiences.

MOST BANK NOTES FROM DIFFERENT COUNTRIES

Shail Kumar and Larry and Dallys Arias Beebe (USA) share the record for the largest collection of bank notes – both with collections representing a grand total of 217 different countries.

LARGEST WINE AND CHAMPAGNE LABEL COLLECTION

Since 1984, Sophia Vaharis-Tsouvelekakis (Greece) has collected 15,403 labels from champagne and wine bottles, representing 50 different countries. She catalogues the labels using a special computer program that will not accept duplicate entries. She also has a unique, thermostat-controlled wine cellar where she stores thousands of bottles of wine and champagne.

LARGEST BOTTLE OPENER COLLECTION

Dale Deckert (USA) started his collection of 20,884 individual bottle openers representing 136 countries, after being discharged from the US Army in 1945. Including duplicates, the entire collection numbers 28,146.

LARGEST BAR TOWEL COLLECTION

Alan Alcott (UK) has collected 504 individual bar towels since 1977. When displayed end to end, these towels stretch 159.77 m (524 ft 2 in). Alan's longest bar towel is an Australian 'bar runner' from Castlemaine, which measures 3 m (9 ft 10 in) long.

PLANE CRAZY

The largest collection of handmade model airplanes is owned by Robert Humphrey of West Jordan, Utah, USA (left). Robert's collection consists of 1,642 plastic airplane models all of which he has assembled himself. He has an emergency back-up kit on hand for every single plane in case something should happen to it. Robert, born in 1952, built his first plane with his father's help in 1958. He subsequently received a model plane each year on his birthday. Robert now searches for rare models and his collection grows by about 100 airplanes every year. The plastic airplane models represent army forces, marine air forces and air forces of 61 different nations.

www.guinnessworldrecords.com/modelplanes
ACCESS CODE: ‹55815›

LARGEST BEER BOTTLE COLLECTION

Ron Werner (USA) has collected 11,644 different beer bottles since 1982. Of these, 7,128 are unopened. He has sampled almost every one of his 1,704 brands of beer.

LARGEST GASOLINE-PUMP COLLECTION

The Fisogni Museum, Palazzolo Milanse, Italy, currently houses 164 gasoline pumps. They range in age from a 1910 Tokheim self-measuring pump to a 1981 FIMAC Benaglia 'Lux 60 Puma' volumetric pump. There are 7,500 pieces of gasoline pumps, oil tanks, gadgets and toys in the museum. Guido Fisogni has been building his collection for more than 30 years and is dedicated to documenting the history of technological improvements.

LARGEST STAR WARS MEMORABILIA COLLECTION

Jason Joiner (UK) started collecting *Star Wars* memorabilia as a 12 year-old, and has never stopped. A special effects expert who has worked on the *Star Wars* films made in the UK, he has a collection of over 20,000 *Star Wars* toys. In addition, Joiner has one of the original C3PO robots, an original R2D2 and an original Darth Vader costume. Only *Star Wars* creator George Lucas has a larger collection of props and costumes. Joiner hopes to open a museum to house some of his collection.

www.guinnessworldrecords.com/gnomes

WHEREFORE ART THOU GNOMEO?

Since 1978, Ann Atkin (UK, above) has collected a record total of 2,010 gnomes and pixies, all of which live in a massive 1.6-ha (4-acre) Gnome Reserve in North Devon, UK. Some are fishing, others pushing wheelbarrows, some are musically inclined, mining or gambling. Every year, for the last 18 years, over 25,000 visitors have donned hats to turn temporarily into gnomes to journey through the woodland. The largest gnome in the reserve is 115 cm (45 in) tall and the smallest is only 2 cm (0.75 in) tall. They are all brought out once a year for an annual bath and a new outfit.

LARGEST SWATCH WATCH COLLECTION

Fiorenzo Barindelli (Italy) has a collection of 3,677 Swatch watches, which includes an example of every Swatch watch produced since 1983. His collection is on display at the World Museum 2000, Cesano, Italy.

GUINNESS WORLD RECORDS

collections 2

LARGEST LIBRARY

The United States Library of Congress (founded on 24 April 1800) in Washington, DC, USA, contains 125,198,175 items, including over 18 million books, 2.5 million recordings, 12 million photographs, 4.5 million maps and 54 million manuscripts. The library occupies about 265,000 m² (2.85 million ft²) in the Capitol Hill buildings alone, with 856.5 km (532.2 miles) of shelving.

LARGEST FOUR-LEAF CLOVER COLLECTION

George J Kaminski (USA) has single-handedly collected 72,928 four-leaf clovers since 1995. A total of 13,383 were collected from within the 2-ha (5-acre) prison yard, during his recreation time at the State Correctional Institution, Somerset, Pennsylvania, USA, and a further 59,545 were collected from the prison yard at the State Prison in Houtzdale, Pennsylvania, USA.

LARGEST COLLECTION OF BADGES

Daniel Hedges (UK) has collected 8,662 different badges. He began collecting when he was 14 years old. Danny's badges range from cheeky

www.guinnessworldrecords.com/celebhair
← ACCESS CODE: ‹56181›

GENTLEMEN PREFER BLONDES

John Rezinkoff of Connecticut, USA, has collected hair from 115 different historical celebrities. This collection of famous locks is insured for $1 million (£698,470) and includes tresses from the heads of Abraham Lincoln, John F Kennedy, Marilyn Monroe (left), Albert Einstein, Napoleon, Elvis Presley, King Charles I, and Charles Dickens. He aspires to finding locks from Mark Twain and Shakespeare. Despite offers of up to $100,000 (£69,847) for individual items, the collection is not for sale. All hair specimens in Mr Reznikoff's collection have documentation and/or DNA tests to back them up.

messages like 'no farting zone' to a rather more elegant example from the Royal Enclosure at Ascot.

LARGEST AIRLINE SICKNESS BAG COLLECTION

Marketing and investment consultant Niek Vermeulen (Netherlands) has 2,112 airline sickness bags from 470 different airlines, topping a list of over 50 serious airline sickness bag collectors. He currently resides in Vietnam. His favourite is an airline sickness bag from a NASA space shuttle. Be it barf bag, vomit bag,

motion sickness bag, hurl bag, spew bag, Sac Vomitoire, Sac pour mal de l'air, Bolsa de mareo, prullenzakje, Spucktüte, Spuckbeutel, Beg Mabuk Udara, Torba chorobowa, Etiquette bukuro, Oksennuspussi, Sacchetto Per Il Mal D'aria, Kräkpåse, Spypåse, Gero-Bukuro, Sanitarinis Maiselis ... whatever you call it, Vermeulen collects them all.

LARGEST FILM STILLS COLLECTION

The National Film Archive Stills Collection in London, UK, houses 6.5 million black-and-white stills and over 1 million colour transparencies from over 80,000 films from all over the world.

LARGEST MOVIE CAMERA COLLECTION

The largest unique collection of movie cameras, with no duplicates, belongs to retired postman Dimitrios Pistiola (Greece). He has accumulated 440 movie cameras dating from 1901 and has created a small museum for them.

MOST VALUABLE CAMERA COLLECTION

The record total for any camera auction is £296,043 ($424,090) for a collection of 'spy', subminiature and detective cameras sold at Christie's, London, UK, on 9 Dec 1991.

LARGEST COLOURED VINYL RECORD COLLECTION

Alessandro Benedetti (Italy) has collected 934 music records made of coloured vinyl. His massive collection is made up of 647 LPs (601 coloured, 46 with pictures) and 287 singles (255 coloured, 13 with pictures, and 19 in unusual shapes).

LARGEST MENU COLLECTION

Daniel Barlow (USA) has been collecting restaurant menus for 52 years, and has accumulated 3,908 different menus. His favourites are a papyrus menu from Egypt, scroll-style menus from China, a menu from a floating restaurant in Hong Kong and one from a nudist resort in Florida. Daniel believes they depict change and progression in world cuisine.

HIT ME WITH YOUR RHYTHM STICK

The record for the largest autographed drumstick collection in the world is held by Peter Lavinger (USA), who has collected over 1,300 drumsticks since 1980 when he caught his first drumstick from the front row of a Good Rats concert. Although Peter is not a drummer himself, the origins of his drumsticks vary from rock to blues, country to folk, soul to ska, and reggae to jazz. He boasts drumsticks once used by Pink Floyd, The Beatles, R.E.M., Nirvana, The Doors, Fleetwood Mac, Pearl Jam, The Rolling Stones, and U2, plus hundreds more. In 1989, the collection was displayed in the New York Hard Rock Café and is currently on show at the Rock and Roll Hall of Fame and Museum in Cleveland, Ohio, USA. His collection is worth over $1 million (£695,601).

NAVEL VICTORY

The largest collection of navel fluff belongs to plucky Australian Graham Barker, who has collected 15.41 g (0.54 oz) of his own navel fluff since 1984. "Some people gaze into their navel for inspiration: I look into mine and see navel fluff," says Graham Barker, who has collected the fluffy substance that forms in his bellybutton consistently for the last 16 years. When asked "why?" Graham simply replies, "why not?" Though he now owns two-and-a-half jars of this bizarre bodily by-product (one jar shown, right) Graham's ultimate goal is to collect enough fluff to stuff a cushion. He began his collection one day when he found himself cooped up in a youth hostel in Brisbane, Australia, extremely bored. Now Graham says collecting his navel fluff has become an ingrained, daily habit. He claims his navel fluff is in mint condition since he makes a point of immediately storing it in a jar to ensure that it remains uncontaminated.

LARGEST BANANA COLLECTION

Kevin Bannister's International Banana Club Museum in Altadena, California, USA, houses 17,000 banana-related articles. The museum was opened in 1972 and has 9,000 members from 27 countries. The collection includes banana slippers, suits, games, pots, pipes and puppets.

LARGEST BUNNY COLLECTION

Husband and wife Steve Lubanski and Candace Frazee (USA) have acquired 8,437 bunny-themed collectibles since they began collecting on 14 Feb 1993.

LARGEST FROG COLLECTION

Wendy Scower (Canada) has accumulated a collection of 1,202 different frog items since she was 10 years old in 1967.

LARGEST PIG COLLECTION

Carl Kinney's collection of pig memorabilia contains 2,250 different items, including banks, books, toys, napkin rings, cookie jars, figurines and comic books. Carl (USA) began collecting in 1978 to build upon his grandmother's collection, which was made up of 200 pig items.

LARGEST FRIDGE MAGNET COLLECTION

Louise J Greenfarb (USA) has collected 29,000 refrigerator magnets. Her collection is displayed at the Guinness World Records Museum in Las Vegas, Nevada, USA. Louise's magnets portray everything from food to US presidents, and such is her love of her collection that she even wants to be buried in her fridge.

LARGEST HANDCUFF COLLECTION

Locksmith Chris Gower (UK) has 530 pairs of antique and modern handcuffs that he has been collecting since 1968. They range from ancient slave shackles to the most up-to-date high-security cuffs. His favourite item in the collection is a famous pair of Plug Lock Figure '8' leg-irons from which Houdini, his big hero, failed to escape in 1903.

LARGEST VALID CREDIT CARD COLLECTION

Walter Cavanagh (USA) has collected 1,397 individual valid credit cards. The cost of acquisition to 'Mr Plastic Fantastic' was nil, but the cards are worth more than £1.15 million ($1.65 million) in credit. Walter Cavanagh keeps them in the world's longest wallet – 76.2 m (250 ft) in length and weighing 17.49 kg (38 lb 8 oz). If laid end-to-end, Cavanagh's credit cards would reach to the top of a four-storey building.

LARGEST COLLECTION OF PAPER AND PLASTIC BAGS

Heinz Schmidt-Bachem (Germany) has collected 150,000 plastic and paper bags since 1975. They range from simple plastic bags from a corner grocers to bags from designer boutiques. His oldest bag dates from 1853 and is the first industrially manufactured paper bag ever made.

Navel Fluff
1994-97

GUINNESS WORLD RECORDS

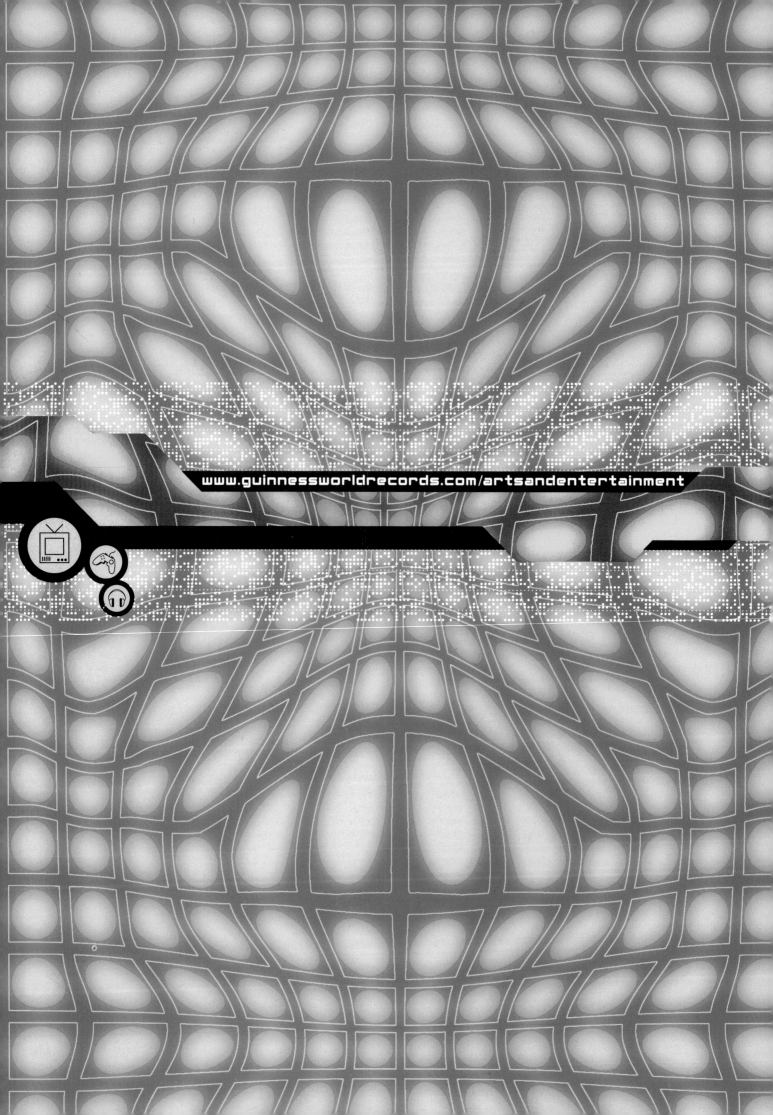
www.guinnessworldrecords.com/artsandentertainment

arts and entertainment

movies 1

LONGEST FILM TAKE

The longest take in a movie comprises the whole of Kevin du Toit's non-commercial *BugNight* (USA, 1998). It consists of 84 minutes of a flashback at a diner where nine hostages are being held.

LONGEST TAKE IN A COMMERCIAL FILM

In *A Free Soul* (USA, 1931), there is a 14-minute uninterrupted monologue by Lionel Barrymore. Since a reel of camera film only lasts 10 minutes, it was achieved by using more than one camera.

LONGEST FILM EVER MADE

The longest film ever made was the 85-hour *The Cure for Insomnia* (USA, 1987), directed by John Henry Timmis IV. It premiered at The School of the Art Institute of Chicago, USA, between 31 Jan and 3 Feb 1987.

MOST COSTUME CHANGES FOR A FILM CHARACTER

Madonna changed costume 85 times in *Evita* (USA, 1996) and wore 39 hats, 45 pairs of shoes, 56 pairs of earrings and 42 hair designs to transform her into Eva Perón, First Lady of Argentina. The costumes were designed by Penny Rose. After making thousands of samples, an army of costume-makers went to work, taking 14 weeks to stitch, sew, bead and recreate Eva's wardrobe.

www.guinnessworldrecords.com/lostworld

← ACCESS CODE: ‹50750›

JURASSIC ADVENTURES

Universal's *Jurassic Park: The Lost World* was given the widest release of any film in history when it opened on America's Memorial holiday weekend (23 May 1997) on more than 5,000 screens across the country, with some multiplexes showing the film simultaneously on six screens. This film was the sequel to *Jurassic Park* (USA, 1993), reuniting actors Jeff Goldblum and Richard Attenborough.

From 26 May 1997 *Jurassic Park: The Lost World* (USA, 1997) took a four-day gross of $90.1 million (£54.9 million) from 3,281 screens. This is the all-time record for highest box-office gross on an opening weekend. (This figure excludes the preview night of $2.6 million (£1.5 million) from 1,755 theatres.)

LARGEST MAKE-UP BUDGET

A total of $1 million (then £345,542) was budgeted for make-up in *Planet of the Apes* (USA, 1968). This would equal $4.95 million (£2.92 million) today. This amount represents nearly 17% of the film's total production cost of $5.8 million (£2,004,146). Today's equivalent value would be $28.71 million or £16.92 million.

MOST FILM EXTRAS

Over 300,000 extras appeared in the funeral scene of *Gandhi* (UK, 1982), the epic directed by Richard Attenborough. For this scene, 11 camera crews shot 6,096 m (20,000 ft) of film, more than the total footage of the final 188-minute released film. The edited funeral sequence ran for only 125 seconds of screen time.

MOST EXPENSIVE FILM MADE

Paramount's *Titanic* (USA, 1997) cost just over $200 million (£118,934,350) to make. The retelling of the UK's worst single ship disaster

in peace time became one of Hollywood's greatest triumphs. It was originally given a $125 million (£74,333,969) budget, and was due to have been released in July 1997, but post-production problems set the date back to Dec 1997, which, in turn, added to the cost.

In terms of real costs (adjusted for inflation) the most expensive film ever made was *Cleopatra* (USA, 1963). Its $44 million (then £15,712,602) budget would be equivalent to $306,867,120 (£175,352,640) today.

ONLY FILM MADE WITHOUT A CAMERA

Artist Jose Antonio Sistiagas (Spain) is credited with the only full-length film made without a camera. He completed his 75-minute animated one-man production *Scope, Colour, Muda* (Spain, 1970) in 17 months between 1968 and 1970. Sistiaga single-handedly painted directly on to the film stock, frame by frame.

AGAIN AND AGAIN AND AGAIN . . .

Director Stanley Kubrick demanded the record number of retakes for one scene in a film with dialogue. The scene with Shelley Duvall in *The Shining* (USA, 1980), also starring Jack Nicholson (left), had an unbelievable 127 takes.

Marilyn Monroe did 59 takes of a scene in *Some Like it Hot* (USA, 1959) in which her only line of dialogue was "Where's the Bourbon?"

The scene in Charlie Chaplin's *City Lights* (USA, 1931) in which a blind girl sells him a flower thinking that he is a wealthy tycoon, took 342 takes, and is the overall record for the film with the most retakes for one scene. This silent movie, generally considered to be Chaplin's best, was released three years after the start of the talkies.

www.guinnessworldrecords.com/retakes

← ACCESS CODE: ‹54546›

MOST EDITED SCENE

Editor Lloyd Nosler (USA) had to compress 60,960 m (200,000 ft) of film into 228.6 m (750 ft) for the chariot race scene in *Ben Hur* (USA, 1925), starring Ramon Navarro – the most edited scene in cinema history with a ratio of 267:1 (film shot to film shown).

LARGEST PRODUCTION CREW FOR A FEATURE FILM

The largest number of craftsmen and technicians employed on a dramatic feature was 532 for the World War I flying story *Gunbus* (USA title *Sky Bandits*; UK, 1986). The crew built enormous sets for war scenes, constructed buildings that were to be exploded, and built aeroplanes that matched those used in 1917.

LONGEST PRE-CREDIT SEQUENCE

Before the opening title of Dennis Hopper's *The Last Movie* (USA, 1971), the pre-credits ran for 30 minutes.

LONGEST CREDIT SEQUENCE

The credits for Sergio Leone's *Once Upon a Time in the West* (Italy/USA, 1968) lasted for 12 minutes.

LONGEST FILM TITLE

The official title of Lina Wertmüller's film was *Un Fatto di sangue nel comune di Sculiana fra due uomini per causa di una vedova si sospetano moventi politici. Amore-Morte-Shimmy. Lugano belle. Tarantelle. Tarallucci é vino.* (Italy, 1979). It has 179 characters, including punctuation. The English title was *Revenge!*

HIGHEST BOX-OFFICE GROSS

Rising cinema ticket prices mean the all-time top-grossing movies are nearly all recent films. Although *Gone with the Wind* (USA, 1939) took just $393.4 million (then £88 million) at the international box office, in an inflation-adjusted list it comes top with a total gross of $3,785,107,801 (£2,365,692,376). In the USA alone, *Gone with the Wind* had 283,100,000 admissions compared to 130,900,000 for *Titanic* (USA, 1997).

LARGEST BOX-OFFICE LOSS

MGM's *Cutthroat Island* (USA, 1995), starring Geena Davis and directed by Renny Harlin, cost over $100 million (£63 million) to produce, promote and distribute and reportedly earned back just $11 million (£7 million).

LARGEST FILM BUDGET

The largest production budget given to a movie before filming started is $145 million (£93,428,437) for the war epic *Pearl Harbor*. Shooting began on 3 April 2000 and the film, starring Ben Affleck, was released in May 2001.

HIGHEST-GROSSING SCIENCE FICTION FILM

Star Wars (USA, 1977) originally took $513.7 million (£294.29 million) worldwide. In an inflation-adjusted list, the film comes second only after *Gone with the Wind* (USA, 1939), with an international gross of $1,561,189,344 (£975,743,340).

www.guinnessworldrecords.com/hannibal

ACCESS CODE: ‹56244›

MONEY SPINNERS

In its opening weekend (starting on 9 Feb 2001) *Hannibal* (USA, 2001), directed by Ridley Scott and starring Anthony Hopkins and Julianne Moore (below), took $58 million (£40.1 million) from 3,230 screens. This is the highest box-office gross for a film with an over-18 rating on an opening weekend.

Opening in 2,970 cinemas, *Star Wars; Episode 1 – The Phantom Menace* (USA, 1999), reached the $100-million (£60.33-million) mark in a record five days from 23 to 28 May 1999, breaking the previous record set by *Jurassic Park:The Lost World* for the fastest time to reach $100 million. When the trailer was first released, cinemas reported that some people bought tickets, only to walk out once they had seen the *Star Wars: Episode I* trailer.

HIGHEST-GROSSING AUSTRALIAN FILM

Crocodile Dundee (Australia, 1986), starring Paul Hogan and Linda Kozlowski, has grossed $328 million (£218 million) since its release.

HIGHEST-GROSSING UK FILM

The Full Monty (UK, 1997), released in Aug 1997, grossed a record total of £160.5 million ($256.9 million).

HIGHEST-GROSSING WESTERN

The Western *Dances with Wolves* (USA, 1990), directed by and starring Kevin Costner, has grossed $424.2 million (£297.6 million) at the international box office since being first released in the USA in Nov 1990.

HIGHEST-GROSSING HORROR FILM

The Exorcist (USA, 1973), which was directed by William Friedkin with a $12 million (then £4.89 million) budget, has taken a record $292.7 million (£205.3 million) at the international box office.

LARGEST ANNUAL FILM OUTPUT

India produces more feature-length films than any other country. In 1990 a record 948 films were produced and, in 1994, a total of 754 films were produced in a record 16 languages at the three major centres of production, Mumbai (Bombay), Calcutta and Madras. Since the 1980s, traditional Hindi musical love stories have dominated the screen in India.

GUINNESS WORLD RECORDS™

movies 2

LARGEST ASSEMBLAGE OF ANIMALS IN A FILM

Around the World in Eighty Days (USA, 1956) directed by Daniel Anderson and starring David Niven as Phileas Fogg, involved a total of 8,552 animals – 3,800 sheep, 2,448 buffalo, 950 donkeys, 800 horses, 512 monkeys, 17 bulls, 15 elephants, six skunks and four ostriches.

MOST EXTENSIVE SCREEN TEST

To find the actress to play the role of Scarlett O'Hara in *Gone with the Wind* (USA, 1939), MGM shot 45,415 m (149,000 ft) of black-and-white test film and another 3,962 m (13,000 ft) of colour with 60 actresses, none of whom got the part. After discarding 27 hours of test film, producer David O'Selznick narrowed the choice to four. Vivien Leigh eventually landed the part after shooting had already commenced. The total cost of the 49,377 m (162,000 ft) of tests was $105,000 (£23,452) – approximately the budget then of an average second feature film. Today this would be equivalent to $1.63 million (£1.16 million).

MOST FILM SEQUELS

The American film series 'Blondie', starring Penny Singleton (b.15 Sept 1908) in the title role of Blondie Bumstead, first hit the screen in 1939 with *Blondie Meets the Boss*, followed by 26 sequels, the last being

Beware of Blondie (US 1950). Naturally a brunette, Singleton bleached her hair especially for the role. Starring in an average two to three 'Blondie' films a year, the most made in a year were four in 1947.

SMALLEST FILM SET

The smallest film set was built for *Bill and Coo* (USA, 1947). It was filmed entirely in a model village mounted on a table measuring 9.14 m x 4.57 m (30 ft x 15 ft). The performers were

love birds. The success of the film was rewarded with an Honorary Academy Award in 1948.

LARGEST INDOOR FILM SET

The UFO landing site built for Steven Spielberg's *Close Encounters of the Third Kind* (USA, 1977) was 27 m (90 ft) high, 137 m (450 ft) long and 76 m (250 ft) wide. The structure included 6.4 km (4 miles) of scaffolding, 1,570 m² (16,900 ft³) of fibreglass and 2,740 m² (29,500 ft²) of nylon canopy.

LONG TIME NO SEE

Walt Disney Production's sequel *Return To Oz* (USA, 1985) was made 46 years after the original, *The Wizard of Oz* (USA, 1939), which starred Judy Garland and Jack Haley (left). This is the longest interval between an original and its sequel. The sequel was based on the second and third of Frank Baum's 14 Oz books, *The Land of Oz* and *Ozma of Oz*.

The record for the longest interval between an original film and a remake stands at 74 years 267 days in the case of *Seven Chances* (USA, 1925) directed by and starring Buster Keaton and *The Bachelor* (USA, 1999) directed by Gary Sinyor. Both films tell the story of Jimmie Shannon who has 24 hours in which to find a woman to marry in order to claim his recently deceased grandfather's fortune.

 www.guinnessworldrecords.com/wizardofoz
← ACCESS CODE: ‹50608›

LONGEST FILM SERIES

The longest film series are the 103 features made in Hong Kong about the 19th-century martial arts hero Huang Fei-Hong, starting with *The True Story of Huang Fei-Hong* (HK, 1949). The latest production, after 46 years, was *Once Upon a Time in China 5* (HK, 1995).

LONGEST OSCAR SPEECH

The longest speech at the Oscars lasted 5 min 30 sec, and was made by Greer Garson at the 1942 Academy

HORROR UPON HORROR

The character most often portrayed in horror films is Count Dracula, created by Irish writer Bram Stoker. One such portrayal of Dracula (left) is *Bram Stoker's Dracula* (USA, 1992). Representations of the Count or his immediate descendants outnumber those of his closest rival, Frankenstein, by 162 to 117.

The year 1972 was the most prolific year for horror films – it saw a record total of 189 horror films released. Of these, 83 came from the USA. The boom rapidly abated within three years, when only 58 screamers were produced in 1975. This was, however, the year that horror pictures took the largest share of film rentals, largely due to the overwhelming success of *Jaws* (USA, 1975).

www.guinnessworldrecords.com/dracula
← ACCESS CODE: ‹50723›

Awards on 4 March 1943, after receiving Best Actress award for her title role in *Mrs Miniver* (USA, 1942). Speeches have been restricted to 45 seconds since the 1990 Awards.

MOST PEOPLE THANKED BY AN OSCAR WINNER

When Olivia de Havilland won Best Actress for Josephine Norris in *To Each His Own* (USA, 1946) at the 1946 Academy Awards on 13 March 1947, she thanked a record 27 people.

MOST OSCAR NOMINATIONS FOR FOREIGN LANGUAGE FILM

The martial arts film *Wo hu zang long* or *Crouching Tiger, Hidden Dragon* (Taiwan, 2000), directed by Ang Lee and starring Yun-Fat Chow and Michelle Yeoh, was nominated for a record 10 Oscars on 23 Feb 2001. Also nominated for Best Picture, Best Director, Music (Song), Writing (Adapted Screenplay), Film Editing and Costume Design, it won Oscars for Best Foreign Language Film, Art Direction, Music (Score) and Cinematography.

MOST OSCAR NOMINATIONS FOR FOREIGN FILMS

France holds the record for having a film nominated in the Foreign Language Film category 31 times between 1956 and 2001. France has won the category on nine occasions, in 1958, 1959, 1962, 1966, 1972, 1973, 1977, 1978 and 1992.

MOST OSCAR NOMINATIONS WITHOUT WINNING

Art director Roland Anderson received 15 Oscar nominations for Art Direction but never won. Composer Alex North also had 15 nominations without winning, but was awarded an Honorary Oscar in 1986.

MOST OSCAR NOMINATIONS FOR A FILM

The most Oscar nominations a film has received is 14, given to *All About Eve* (USA, 1950) in 1951 and *Titanic* (USA, 1997) in 1998. *All About Eve* eventually won six Oscars, while *Titanic* came away with 11 – a record it shares with *Ben Hur* (USA, 1959).

ACCESS CODE: ‹54705›

PRETTY WOMAN

Julia Roberts (right) commanded a fee of $20,000,000 (£12,500,000) for her lead role in *Erin Brokovich* (USA, 2000). This makes her the highest-paid actress for a single film. Her previous highest fee was $17,000,000 (£10,625,000) for *Runaway Bride* (USA, 1999). On 25 March 2001 she received an Oscar for Best Actress for portraying Erin Brokovich. Other big film hits include *Notting Hill* (UK, 1999) as well as *Pretty Woman* (USA, 1990).

WESTERN HERO MOST OFTEN PORTRAYED ON SCREEN

William Frederick Cody (1846–1917), otherwise known as 'Buffalo Bill', has appeared in 48 films, since first appearing in *Buffalo Bill* (Australia, 1909) and last being portrayed by Keith Carradine in *Wild Bill* (USA, 1995).

MOST COSTUMES USED IN A FILM

The largest number of costumes used for any one film was 32,000 for *Quo Vadis?* (USA, 1951), starring Robert Taylor and Deborah Kerr.

MOST OSCAR NOMINATIONS FOR A LIVING PERSON

The composer John Williams has had 38 Academy Awards nominations, making him the most-nominated living person. His first nomination was for Best Music, Scoring of Music, Adaptation or Treatment for *Valley of the Dolls* (USA, 1967). His 38th nomination for Best Original Score was for *The Patriot* (USA, 2000) in 2001.

MOST OSCAR-WINNING GENERATIONS

The only family with three generations of Oscar winners are the Hustons. Walter Huston (1884–1950) won Best Supporting Actor for *The Treasure of the Sierra Madre* (USA, 1948). His son John (1906–1987) won Best Director for the same film and John's daughter Angelica (b. 1951) won best Supporting Actress for *Prizzi's Honour* (USA, 1985).

MOST OSCAR WINS FOR ACTING AND WRITING

Emma Thompson won best actress in 1993 for her role in *Howard's End* (UK, 1991) and was awarded Best Screenplay Written Directly for the Screen for *Sense and Sensibility* (USA/UK, 1995) in 1996, making her the first person ever to win Oscars for both acting and writing.

MOST OSCARS WON FOR BEST FOREIGN LANGUAGE FILM

Italy has won 12 Oscars for Best Foreign Language Film, the most recent being *Life Is Beautiful* (1997) at the 71st Academy Awards in 1999. The Italian Academy-Award winners have been as follows: *Mediterraneo* (1991), *Cinema Paradiso* (1989), *Amarcord* (1974), *The Garden of the Finzi Continis* (1971), *Investigation of a Citizen Above Suspicion* (1970), *Yesterday, Today and Tomorrow* (1964), *Federico Fellini's 8½* (1963), *The Nights of Cabira* (1957), *La Strada* (1956), *The Walls of Malapaga* (1950) and *The Bicycle Thief* (1949).

GUINNESS WORLD RECORDS

tv ads and production

THE BIG APPLE
The most expensive TV ad ever made was a commercial for computer manufacturer Apple Macintosh (above), based on the novel *1984* by George Orwell. It cost $600,000 (£360,000) to produce and $1,000,000 (£600,000) to show during the NFL Super Bowl in Jan 1984. Its impact was so great and the recall so high that it is considered to be one of the most cost-effective commercials ever made. It was shown only twice – the other occasion was on a small station in the US in Dec 1983. It depicted an IBM world being overrun by a new machine – the Mac.

The highest rate for an ad broadcast during a TV series was a half-minute network spot during the advert breaks for the last ever episode of NBC's *Seinfeld*, starring Jerry Seinfeld. It cost $575,000 (£359,375) on 14 May 1998. That is $15,000 (£9,225.09) more than the second-highest rate commanded by the medical drama *ER*.

 www.guinnessworldrecords.com/apple

← ACCESS CODE: ‹48001›

LARGEST REVENUE BY A TV NETWORK ON A SINGLE DAY
Fox TV (USA) is reputed to have earned $150 million (£90.5 million) on Super Bowl Sunday (31 Jan 1999) – the most advertising revenue earned by a network in one day.

SHORTEST TV AD
A subliminal ad for Bon Marche's Frango sweets lasted four frames (there are 30 frames in a second) when it was aired on KING-TV's *Evening Magazine* (USA) on 29 Nov 1993.

EARLIEST AD IN SPACE
On 22 Aug 1997 an advertising campaign for Tnuva Milk showed cosmonaut Vasily Tsibliyev drinking milk aboard the Russian space station, Mir, making it the first ad to be filmed in space.

MOST TV ADS FOR ONE PRODUCT IN ONE NIGHT
On 1 Oct 1996 Granada Sky Broadcasting (UK) aired all 17 versions of the Castlemaine XXXX ad.

LARGEST CAST OF BABIES FOR AN AD
A British television commercial made for the Vauxhall Astra car by Tony Kaye in 1996 featured 2,000 babies.

LARGEST SIMULTANEOUS TV AD PREMIER
The Ford Motor Company (USA) aired their two-minute *Global Anthem* advertisement on more than 140 pan-regional or local market networks in a record 190 countries on 1 Nov 1999 at 9 pm local time.

BIGGEST TV AUDIENCE RATING SHARE
The final episode of *M*A*S*H*, *Goodbye, Farewell and Amen*, was transmitted by CBS on 28 Feb 1983 to 60.3% of all households in the USA. About 125 million people tuned in – 77% of the viewing public.

EARLIEST PROGRAMME BUDGET
In 1936, Cecil Madden, programme organizer and senior producer at Alexandra Palace, London, UK, was allotted a budget of £1,000 (then $4,971) for a week's entire television output for the BBC – equivalent today to £28,850 ($40,390). This, in part, accounted for the audience viewing pattern – one hour in the afternoons, one hour in the evenings and no television on Sundays.

FASTEST VIDEO PRODUCTION
Live filming of the Royal Wedding of HRH Prince Andrew and Sarah Ferguson (UK) on 23 July 1986 ended with the departure of the honeymoon couple from Chelsea Hospital by helicopter at 4:42 pm. The first fully edited and packaged VHS tapes produced by Thames Video Collection were purchased from the Virgin Megastore in Oxford Street, London, UK, at 10:23 pm – 5 hr 41 min later.

HIGHEST EARNINGS FOR A TV PRODUCER
In 1999 David E. Kelley (USA), the creator of *Ally McBeal* and *The Practice*, became the world's highest-earning TV producer according to the 2000 *Forbes* Celebrity 100 list, after his earnings topped $118 million (£73.1 million).

HIGHEST EARNINGS FOR A TV WRITER
Larry David, co-writer and co-creator of the hit US comedy *Seinfeld*, earned an estimated $242 million (£146 million) in 1998. David left the show in 1996, returning to pen the final episode in 1998.

SHORTEST-LIVED TV MONOPOLY
The shortest-lived monopoly in the history of broadcasting was the BBC's *Breakfast Time*, launched on 17 Jan 1983 on BBC1. It operated for 15 days before ITV introduced TV-AM on 1 Feb 1983 as a rival.

LONGEST-SERVING PURPOSE-BUILT TRANSMITTING TOWER
A steel TV transmitting mast was erected in 1935 on top of the south-east tower of Alexandra Palace, London, UK, to the specifications of John Logie Baird, the BBC and EMI-Marconi. It transmitted the world's first high-definition TV service from Nov 1936, and is still being used for BBC and ITV television and digital radio signals.

LONGEST TIME SPENT SUBTITLING A LIVE SHOW
The BBC's subtitling team employed eight stenographers, working shifts throughout the night, to bring verbatim subtitles of the BBC's *1997 Election Special* programme to a deaf and hard-of-hearing audience. They worked for 17 hr 55 min from 9:55 pm on 1 May until 4 pm on 2 May. The only break in the coverage was between 1:30 pm and 2 pm, when local news programmes were broadcast.

LARGEST TV AUDIENCE FOR A SPACE EVENT
The most televised event in space was the first moonwalk by the Apollo 11 astronauts in July 1969. It was watched on TV by an estimated 600 million people – a fifth of the world's population at the time.

LARGEST MUSIC TV NETWORK
MTV is beamed into 281.7 million households in 79 countries around the globe, which means it can be seen by one in four of the world's total TV audience.

LARGEST TV NETWORK
CNN International can be seen in 212 countries and territories through a network of 23 satellites. About

A COSTLY OPERATION

The most expensive TV programme currently made is *ER*, America's No.1 prime-time show. It had a weekly audience of 33 million when, in Jan 1998, Warner Bros agreed to a three-year deal with NBC of a record $857.6 million (£536 million) for 22 episodes at $13.1 million (£8.2 million) per one-hour episode. Before the deal, NBC paid $1.6 million (£1 million) per episode, earning $16 million (£10 million) in advertising revenue. In April 2000, NBC paid a record $640 million (£400 million) for three more series until 2004, which works out at $9.6 million (£6 million) an episode. Pictured below are Goran Visnjic (left), as Dr Luka Kovac, James Cromwell (centre), as Bishop Stewart and Erik Palladino (right), as Dr Dave Malucci.

149 million households across the planet can tune in, making it the world's largest TV network.

MOST WATCHED TV NETWORK

The state-owned station China Central Television (CCTV) is transmitted to 84% of all Chinese viewers in China. It is estimated that over 900 million people in the country have access to television, making CCTV the world's most watched network. Its nine channels broadcast in Mandarin, Cantonese, English and French.

MOST EXPENSIVE TV DOCUMENTARY SERIES PER MINUTE

It cost over £37,654 ($61,112) per minute to produce the BBC's documentary series *Walking with Dinosaurs* (Oct 1999), which depicts how dinosaurs lived, reproduced and became extinct. The six-part series took more than two years to produce and cost £6.1 million ($9.9 million). It features computer graphics and animatronics with background footage filmed in locations around the world.

MOST EXPENSIVE TV RIGHTS

In June 1997, the Fox network paid a record $81 million (£50 million) for the TV rights to Steven Spielberg's film *Jurassic Park: The Lost World* (USA,1997) before it was even released on the international market. *Jurassic Park: The Lost World* was the sequel to *Jurassic Park* (1993).

GUINNESS WORLD RECORDS

tu shows

MOST MONEY DONATED TO A TELETHON

On 16 March 2001, UK supermarket chain Sainsbury's presented Comic Relief with a cheque for £4.5 million ($6.4 million) during *The Night of Comic Relief* on BBC1. Money was raised through the sales of Comic Relief products and staff fundraising.

MOST TV EPISODES SOLD

On 31 May 1971 Granada Television sold 1,144 episodes of *Coronation Street* (UK) to CBKST Saskatoon,

MONEY MONEY MONEY

The largest cash prize ever won on television is £1 million, and has been given on three occasions. On 24 Dec 1999, Ian Woodley (UK) won his million (then equivalent to $1,618,000) on Channel 4's *TFI Friday* quiz thanks to knowing that in the film *American Pie*, the pie was made from apples.

On 19 Nov 2000 Judith Keppel (above) won £1 million (then worth $1,423,000) on ITV's *Who Wants To Be A Millionaire?* She answered 15 questions correctly, the last being, "Which King was married to Eleanor of Aquitaine?" Her correct answer was "Henry II".

The show gave away another £1 million (then $1,439,500) on 9 April 2001 to science teacher David Edwards (UK). He won the grand total on the question, "If you planted the seeds of *Quercus Robur*, what would you grow?" He answered correctly – "trees".

www.guinnessworldrecords.com/ millionaire

ACCESS CODE: ← ‹47849›

Saskatchewan, Canada. This number of episodes equalled 20 days 15 hr 44 min continuous viewing.

LONGEST FILM SHOWN ON TV

The longest film shown on television in a single day was the 8-hr-27-min epic *War and Peace* (USSR, 1967). It was transmitted by Mexico's Channel II on 28 Feb 1981.

LONGEST-RUNNING CHILDREN'S MAGAZINE PROGRAMME

The BBC's *Blue Peter* was transmitted for the first time from London's Lime Grove Studios on 16 Oct 1958. So far there have been 29 presenters and 3,456 shows broadcast up to 18 April 2001.

LONGEST-RUNNING CHILDREN'S PROGRAMME

Since 1949, over 150,000 individual episodes of the TV show *Bozo the Clown* (USA) by Larry Harmon Pictures have been aired daily on 150 stations in the USA.

LONGEST-RUNNING POP SHOW

The first edition of the UK's *Top of the Pops* was presented by Jimmy Savile on 1 Jan 1964 on BBC1 and is still running. Dusty Springfield, the Rolling Stones, the Dave Clark Five, the Swinging Blue Jeans and the Hollies all appeared in the first programme. The Beatles and Cliff Richard and the Shadows were shown on film. The programme had reached its 1,939th edition on 18 May 2001 and celebrated its 2000th edition in summer 2001.

LONGEST-RUNNING PRIME-TIME ANIMATED SERIES

The Simpsons (USA), created by Matt Groening, is the longest-running prime-time animated television show. Up to 4 March 2001, 263 episodes had been shown on the Fox television network in the USA.

LONGEST-RUNNING TV DRAMA

Granada's *Coronation Street* (UK) is the longest-running domestic drama

DON'T TRY THIS AT HOME! USA

The world's most extreme game show is Japan's *Za Gaman* (above), or in English, *Endurance*. Contestants have to endure different types of mental and physical torture, such as standing on their heads with hot coals on their feet, or hanging between swinging cactii above a tank of snakes – the winners endure the challenge for the longest. *Za Gaman* is a prime-time series on the Fuji Network and is the No.1 show. In the test of endurance shown here, which took place on 15 Jan 1998, the contestants braved the cold and doused themselves in freezing water during a heavy snowfall.

 www.guinnessworldrecords.com/endurance
← ACCESS CODE: ‹53821›

serial with the first episode shown on 9 Dec 1960. The programme is shown four times a week and up to 16 April 2001 there had been a total of 5,021 episodes broadcast.

LONGEST-RUNNING TV SHOW

NBC's *Meet the Press*, which first transmitted in the USA on 6 Nov 1947 and was subsequently shown weekly from 12 Sept 1948, has had 2,649 shows aired up to 4 Feb 2001.

LONGEST TV DOCUMENTARY ON A SINGLE SUBJECT

Every seven years since 1963, the '7 Up' documentary film series, shown on the UK's ITV, has followed the lives of the same 14 children selected from different social groups in the UK at the age of seven. The first in the series, *7 Up*, was followed by *7 times 7* (1970), which filmed the children when aged 14. A further four instalments have been added.

LONGEST TV TALK SHOW MARATHON

The record for the longest continuous talk show hosted by an individual is 24 hours. It is held by

Peter Imhof, who started at 1:30 pm on 23 June 2000 and chatted to more than 450 people in front of a studio audience in Potsdam-Babelsberg on Germany's station SAT.1.

LONGEST UNINTERRUPTED LIVE TV BROADCAST

The Swiss television station Suisse 4 broadcast the 1996 Olympic Games held in Atlanta, Georgia, USA, around the clock for 16 days 22 hr 45 min.

MOST DAYTIME SERIES EMMY NOMINATIONS IN A SEASON

A grand total of 21 nominations for Daytime Emmy Awards were given to the US soap opera *The Young and the Restless* (ABC) on 11 March 1999. It won three awards at the ceremony on 21 May 1999 for Supporting Actress in a Drama Series (Sharon Case); Younger Actress in a Drama Series (Heather Tom); and Drama Series Writing Team.

SHORTEST TV PROGRAMME

Election Thoughts, a series of 15 programmes just 30 seconds long, complete with titles, programme content, credits and original music score, were broadcast by Channel 4 during the three weeks leading up to the UK General Election of 1997.

LARGEST TV AUDIENCE FOR A WEDDING
On 29 July 1981 the marriage of HRH Prince Charles to Lady Diana Spencer was seen by an estimated 750 million people in 74 countries. At the time the largest outside broadcast in British history, it had an audience in Britain of 39 million.

LARGEST TV AUDIENCE FOR A COMEDY
The final episode of the US television comedy *Seinfeld*, starring Jerry Seinfeld, was screened on 14 May 1998, attracting 108 million viewers.

MOST POPULAR CHILDREN'S EDUCATIONAL PROGRAMME
Sesame Street (USA) produced since 10 Nov 1969 by the Children's Television Workshop, New York, is sold to 180 countries. This figure includes co-productions (such as *Open Sesame*) and dubbed versions.

CONTESTANT WITH MOST TV QUIZ APPEARANCES
Since March 1986, Marc Vanacker (Belgium) has appeared on 29 TV quiz shows that have been broadcast in Belgium, Germany, the Netherlands and the UK. The shows include *Going for Gold* (Grundy Television) and *Einstein* (NCRV), and he has won a total of BFr 1,520,326, ($34,577; £23,721), trips to the USA, Paris and Vienna, and a car.

MOST SUCCESSFUL TV SOAP
The American TV series, *Dallas*, began quietly in 1978 with just five episodes. By 1980, it was watched by an estimated 83 million people in the US, giving it a then record 76% share of the television audience. It has been seen in more than 90 countries, often in dubbed versions. A sister series, *Knots Landing*, was made, but it did not achieve the same level of success.

MOST POPULAR TV GAME
The game show *Wheel of Fortune* is currently seen in 204 US markets as well as in 54 overseas markets with an estimated 100 million viewers a week. Since its 1983 syndication launch, the US show has awarded over $112 million (£70 million) in cash and prizes, averaging in excess of $7 million (£4.3 million) per year.

ACCESS CODE: <51843>

www.guinnessworldrecords.com/westwing

LANDSLIDE VICTORY
NBC's drama series *The West Wing* (below), which is set behind-the-scenes at the White House, won a record nine awards for a single season at the 52nd Annual Prime Time Emmy Awards held from 9 to 10 Sept 2000.

The series shared the record for the most nominated show with HBO's *The Sopranos* with 18. *The Sopranos* went home in 2000 with one win. Premiered on US television on 22 Sept 1999, *The West Wing* was created by Aaron Sorkin, and stars Rob Lowe as the White House deputy communications director and speechwriter and Moira Kelly, Bradley Whitford, John Spencer, Richard Schiff, Allison Janney and Martin Sheen, playing President Josiah Bartlet, a New Hampshire Democrat.

GUINNESS WORLD RECORDS

stunts and special fx

BALLOONATIC! 📺 USA

On 20 May 1998 Mike Howard (UK, above), walked, with no parachute, between two hot air balloons at the frightening height of 5,486.4 m (18,800 ft) – the highest altitude at which anyone has completed a balloon skywalk. The two balloons flew over Marshall, Michigan, USA, with Howard balancing on a tiny beam 5.79 m (19 ft) long and only 7.62 cm (3 in) wide. By the time Howard finished his return journey across the beam, the hot air balloons had risen to 5,791.2 m (19,000 ft). and travelled over 104 km (65 miles) at a speed of more than 74.4 km/h (46.2 mph). The balloons were connected by two safety ropes and were piloted by Mike's wife Renée and his fellow balloonists Scott Lorenz, Steve Davis and Doug Davis, who also filmed Mike's breathtaking steps through the sky, as did additional film crews in a helicopter above the action, and below on the ground.

 www.guinnessworldrecords.com/balloonwalk
← ACCESS CODE: ‹48863›

MOST CLAY PIGEONS 📺 USA
SHOT UPSIDE DOWN

Kimberly Rhode (USA) managed to shoot 21 out of 24 clay targets while she was hanging upside down in a 12.19-m (40-ft) clear tunnel on 20 Dec 2000.

LARGEST
TIGHTROPE PYRAMID

On 27 and 30 June 1998 the children's high-wire act of the Peru Amateur Circus, Peru, Indiana, USA, achieved an eight-person pyramid on a high wire 6.09 m (20 ft) above the floor of the circus arena.

MOST 📺 USA
INVERTED FLAT SPINS

The most inverted flat spins made in one attempt is 78 at 4,500 m (14,764 ft) by Wayne Handley (USA). The record was set in a super light stunt plane G202, on 2 April 1999.

LONGEST HUMAN 📺 USA
SUCTION SUSPENSION

By pressing a rice bowl on his abdomen, Cuong Chu-Tan of Saale, Germany, was able to create enough suction to suspend himself from a helicopter on a 5-m (16-ft 5-in) rope for 3 min 37 sec. He travelled for 0.8 km (0.5 miles) at a height of 60.96 m (200 ft) on 27 Feb 2001.

LONGEST STRETCHED
BUNGEE-JUMP CORD

Gregory Riffi made a bungee jump from a helicopter above the Loire Valley, France, in Feb 1992. His 249.9-m (820-ft) cord stretched to 610 m (2,001 ft) during the jump. This record refers to the length of the elasticated bungee cord at maximum elongation, so after freefall the cord stretched a further 360.1 m (1,181 ft) – greater than any cord used before.

LONGEST UNSTRETCHED
BUNGEE-JUMP CORD

On 19 Sept 1997 Jochen Schweizer (Germany) used a cord, that when unstretched, measured 284 m (931 ft 9 in). When he jumped from an SA 365 Dauphine helicopter at a height of 2,500 m (8,202 ft) over Reichelsheim, Germany, the cord stretched to 380 m (1,246 ft 8 in). As this is the longest bungee cord ever used, the freefall distance and duration were longer than on any other bungee jump.

MOST SWORDS SWALLOWED

Martin Henshaw (USA) swallowed 14 swords simultaneously on 6 April 2000 at Fremantle, Perth, Western Australia. The swords were 4 cm (1.57 in) wide, 58.9 cm (23.19 in) long and weighed a total of 4.5 kg (9.92 lb). Martin can also cook a sausage between his pectoral muscles by passing 240 volts of electricity through his body jewellery.

MOST 📺 SE
CHAINSAWS JUGGLED

Karoly Donnert (Hungary) juggled three chainsaws, managing 12 rotations (36 throws) on 30 Jan 2001.

HIGHEST JUMP WITHOUT A
PARACHUTE BY A STUNTMAN

AJ Bakunas (USA) jumped from 70.7 m (232 ft) on to an air mattress while doubling for Burt Reynolds in *Hooper* (USA, 1978). On 9 Sept 1980, during the filming of *Steel* (USA, 1980), Bakunas was fatally injured when he fell from the top of a construction site in Lexington, VA, USA.

HIGHEST FREEFALL
BY A STUNTMAN

For the film *Highpoint* (Canada, 1979), stuntman Dar Robinson freefell from the record height of 335 m (1,100 ft), from a ledge at the summit of the CN Tower, Toronto, Canada. The freefall lasted six seconds before his parachute opened 91.4 m (300 ft) from the ground.

MOST EXPENSIVE
AERIAL STUNT

Simon Crane (UK) performed one of the most dangerous aerial stunts ever when he moved between two

DOUBLE JEOPARDY

Vic Armstrong (UK) is the world's most prolific movie stuntman. He has been the stunt double for many top actors including Sean Connery, Donald Sutherland, Timothy Dalton, Roger Moore, Pierce Brosnan and Harrison Ford (left). In a career spanning 30 years, he has performed stunts in over 200 films, including *Raiders Of The Lost Ark* (USA, 1981) and the Indiana Jones series. He has also co-ordinated stunts for movies such as *Tomorrow Never Dies* (UK/USA, 1997) and is married to stuntwoman Wendy Leech, whom he met when they doubled for the stars of *Superman* (USA, 1978).

www.guinnessworldrecords.com/stuntman

← ACCESS CODE: ‹53683›

film which has 50. The movie, about two 1990s teenagers (always shown in colour) who are transported into the black-and-white world of a 1950s television show, was shot on colour film. All colour then had to be painstakingly removed from each frame where the characters and backgrounds were monochrome. The 82-minute film spent over a year in post-production as every shot in the movie had to be adjusted.

MOST EXPENSIVE SPECIAL EFFECTS IN A MUSIC VIDEO

The video for 'What's It Gonna Be?' (1999) by Busta Rhymes and Janet Jackson, directed by Hype Williams, cost $2.4 million (£1.44 million) to produce. Inspired by the *Terminator* movies, computer-morphing effects, such as liquid being moulded into different objects – including Busta – accounted for much of the expenditure. The track was taken from Rhymes' millennium-themed album *E.L.E. – The Final World Front.*

jets at an altitude of 4.75 km (2.95 miles) for the movie *Cliffhanger* (USA, 1993). The stunt, performed only once because it was so risky, cost a record $1 million (£568,000). Sylvester Stallone, the film's star, is said to have offered to reduce his fee by the same amount to ensure that the stunt was made.

LARGEST CO-ORDINATOR OF FILM AERIAL STUNTS

Flying Pictures (UK) has planned and co-ordinated air stunts for more than 200 feature films, including *Cliffhanger* (USA, 1993), *GoldenEye* (UK/USA, 1995) and *Mission Impossible* (USA, 1996).

LARGEST SPECIAL EFFECTS BUDGET

The special effects budget for Stanley Kubrick's movie *2001: A Space Odyssey* (USA, 1968) came to $6.5 million (£2.25 million), the equivalent of around $27 million (£19 million) today. This represents over 60% of the total $10.5 million (£3.63 million) production cost. Compared to *Star Wars – The*

Phantom Menace (USA, 1999), this would be the equivalent of spending $69 million (£48 million) of its $115 million (£81 million) budget on special effects.

LARGEST FILM STUNT BUDGET

More than $3 million (£1.87 million) of the $200-million (£125-million) budget for *Titanic* (USA, 1997) went towards film stunts. In the most complex scene, 100 stuntpeople leapt, fell and slid 229 m (751 ft) as the ship broke in half and rose out of the water to a 90º angle. The exterior set was a 236.22-m (775-ft) long copy of *Titanic* – only 10% smaller than the actual ship.

MOST STILL CAMERAS USED IN A FILM SEQUENCE

When shooting the 'bullet time' sequence during the filming of *The Matrix* (USA, 1999), 120 specially modified film cameras were used by directors Larry and Andy Wachowski to achieve a panning shot of Neo (Keanu Reeves) as he dodged bullets from a pursuer.

Slow-motion filming that used 12,000 frames a second was added to the still shots and normal filming, which were all computer-manipulated later.

MOST COMPUTER-GENERATED FILM EFFECTS

Pleasantville (USA, 1998) had 1,700 separate digital visual effect shots, compared to the average Hollywood

www.guinnessworldrecords.com/firewall

GREAT WALLS OF FIRE

On 14 Oct 2000 the Marine Corps Air Station (MCAS) Miramar Explosive Ordnance Disposal Team created a wall of fire measuring a record 762 m (2,500 ft) in San Diego, California, USA, during the MCAS Miramar Twilight Air Show. The firewall (below) consisted of 334 23-litre (5-gal) bags of unleaded fuel connected by a detonation cord. Once this cord was lit the firewall

ACCESS CODE: ‹56058›

lasted for a few seconds as the fuel consumed itself almost immediately. The flames rose 60-90 m (200-300 ft) into the air and the heat of the blast could be felt from 380 m (1,250 ft) away. The length of the firewall was equivalent to approximately 80 London Transport double-decker buses placed end-to-end in a straight line.

GUINNESS WORLD RECORDS™

music best sellers

GREATEST ADVANCE SALES FOR A SINGLE
'Can't Buy Me Love' by The Beatles (UK) sold 2.7 million copies before its release on 21 March 1964.

BEST-SELLING CANTONESE POP FEMALE
Faye Wong (Hong Kong) had sold an estimated 9.7 million copies of her 20 albums by March 2000. Her most recent album, *Lovers & Strangers*,

was released in Sept 1999 and has so far sold over 800,000 copies, reaching No.1 in Hong Kong, China, Taiwan, Singapore and Malaysia.

BEST-SELLING GROUP EVER
The Beatles have amassed the greatest sales of any group, with all-time sales estimated by EMI at over one billion discs and tapes to date.

BEST-SELLING DRUM 'N' BASS ALBUM
New Forms by British act Reprazent has sold a total of 763,910 copies worldwide since its release in 1997. The Mercury Music Prize-winning debut album achieved sales of 250,000 in the UK alone.

BEST-SELLING COUNTRY SINGLE
'How Do I Live' by LeAnn Rimes (USA) is the best-selling single by a country artist in the USA, with sales of over 3 million. The single spent a record 33 weeks in the Top 10 and was still on the Country Sales chart in June 2001, a massive 208 weeks after it was released.

BEST-SELLING ALBUM BY A BRITISH GROUP
The best-selling album in the world by a British group is *The Wall* by the highly influential Pink Floyd, with global sales estimated at the 23 million mark. Released in 1979, the LP spent 15 weeks at the top of the US charts and was made into a movie starring Bob Geldof in 1982.

BEST-SELLING FILM SOUNDTRACK ALBUM
The best-selling movie soundtrack is *Saturday Night Fever* (USA, 1977), with sales of over 30 million. Taken from the film starring John Travolta (USA), this disco classic included an incredible six No.1 US hit singles.

BEST-SELLING SINGLE BY A GROUP
The best-selling single by a group is 'Rock Around the Clock' by Bill Haley and his Comets (USA), which sold an estimated 25 million copies. This track was recorded in 1954 and used as the title track to the hit movie *The Blackboard Jungle* (USA, 1955).

BEST-SELLING ALBUM EVER
The best-selling album of all time is the Quincey Jones-produced *Thriller* by Michael Jackson (USA), with global sales of over 47 million copies since its release in 1982.

BEST-SELLING CLASSICAL ALBUM
Recorded by José Carreras, Plácido Domingo (both Spain) and Luciano Pavarotti (Italy) in Rome on 7 July 1990 during the 1990 World Cup Finals, the world's best-selling classical album is *In Concert*, with global sales of 10.5 million copies sold to date.

BEST-SELLING REGGAE ALBUM
Legend by Bob Marley is the best-selling reggae album ever. The album topped the UK chart, selling

1.8 million copies, and sold more than 10 million in the USA despite never reaching the US Top 40. Marley was awarded the Jamaican Order of Merit after he died in 1981 and is officially known as The Honourable Bob Marley.

BEST-SELLING ALBUM IN AUSTRALIA
Best of ABBA, a compilation of hits by the Swedish pop group ABBA, has sold over 1.2 million copies in Australia since 1976.

BEST-SELLING ALBUM IN THE USA BY A GROUP
The best-selling album in the USA by a group is *Their Greatest Hits 1971-75* by the Eagles, with total sales of over 27 million copies beating the previous holder *Thriller*.

BEST-SELLING ALBUM ON UK CHART
The UK's best-selling album of all time is *Sgt Pepper's Lonely Hearts Club Band* by The Beatles, with a reported 4.5 million sales since its release in June 1967.

BEST-SELLING AUSTRALIAN ALBUM
The best-selling album by an Australian act is AC/DC's *Back in Black* with estimated global sales of 19 million copies since 1980. Formed in 1973, in Sydney, NSW, Australia, this heavy metal act reportedly found their name after a band member's sister read the label on a vacuum cleaner.

BEST-SELLING COUNTRY ALBUM BY A GROUP
The best-selling album by a country group is *Wide Open Spaces* (1998) by the Dixie Chicks (USA), which has sold 10 million copies. Within 12 months of release, the album was certified as quadruple platinum.

BEST-SELLING LIVE ALBUM
Double Live by country star Garth Brooks (USA) is the best-selling live album in the USA with certified sales of 14 million (seven million double LPs) since being released on 17 Nov 1998. Brooks won Entertainer Of The Year at the 1997 Country Music Awards.

COUNTRY COMES ON OVER
The best-selling album in the USA by a female solo artist is Shania Twain's record-breaking album *Come On Over* (1997), which has sold a total of 18 million copies in the USA and 30 million worldwide. The album was produced and co-written by Twain's husband Robert 'Mutt' Lange and also holds the record for the best-selling country album in the USA by a solo artist. Born Eileen Regina Edwards in Canda in 1965, Shania (above left) is one of the few country artists to make the successful crossover into pop. Her husband also produced *The Woman In Me* (1995), which was an enormous success, selling over 10 million copies by 1998 and including four Top 10 US country chart hits. She released *Come On Over* and won most of the country music awards, including the Entertainer Of The Year trophy, in 1997 – a phenomenal year for her. *Come On Over* remained in the Top 40 of the Billboard 200 chart 127 weeks after its release.

 www.guinnessworldrecords.com/shania
← ACCESS CODE: ‹56273›

A P-LATIN-UM ARTIST

The best-selling album by a Latin artist is Carlos Santana's (above) *Supernatural* album, which has sold 14 million copies in the USA since its release in June 1999. Hailing from Mexico, Santana's musical career has now spanned five decades. His influential group, also known as Santana, has experimented with diverse cultural elements and sounds including blues, acid rock, Latin, African and pop.

www.guinnessworldrecords.com/santana

 ACCESS CODE: ← ‹54238›

MOST PLATINUM CERTIFICATES

Elvis Presley (USA) holds the record for the most platinum certificates, with 54 since the RIAA (Recording Industry Association of America) introduced its sales-based awards on 14 March 1958. The Beatles hold the record for the group with the most platinum certificates (awarded for sales of one million units) with 33.

BEST-SELLING SINGLE SINCE THE CHARTS BEGAN

The best-selling single since the UK chart records began (14 Nov 1952) is Elton John's 'Candle In The Wind 1997/Something About The Way You Look Tonight', with worldwide sales of 33 million. As of 20 Oct 1997 it had reached the top of the charts in 22 countries. 'Candle In The Wind 1997' was recorded as a tribute to Diana, Princess of Wales and all Elton John's artist and PolyGram profits were donated to the Diana, Princess of Wales Memorial Fund.

BEST-SELLING SINGLE OF ALL TIME

'White Christmas', written by Irving Berlin (USA) and recorded by Bing Crosby (USA) on 29 May 1942, is the best-selling single of all time. It is estimated to have sold in excess of 50 million copies, although there are no exact figures available. If all formats such as 78s and albums are included, this figure rises to more than 100 million.

BEST-SELLING MUSIC VIDEO

The Making of Michael Jackson's Thriller, released in Dec 1983, is the world's best-selling music home video, with more than 900,000 units sold. The extravagant 14-minute-long *Thriller* was directed by John Landis (USA), and famously mocked the style of big-budget horror movies.

www.guinnessworldrecords.com/tlc

ALL SOULED OUT

The best-selling rap/hip hop album in the USA is *CrazySexyCool* (1994) by TLC, which achieved worldwide sales of 11 million copies, surpassing MC Hammer's *Please Hammer Don't Hurt 'Em* (1990), which sold 10 million copies. TLC is made up of Rozonda 'Chilli' Thomas, Tionne 'T-Boz' Watkins and Lisa 'Left Eye' Lopes (right), all from Atlanta, Georgia, USA. *CrazySexyCool*, which featured guest performances by Busta Rhymes and Phife of A Tribe

Called Quest won two Grammy Awards for Best R&B Performance by a Duo/Group for 'Creep' and Best R&B Album. Other awards included two Billboard Music Awards, three Soul Train Music Awards and a Blockbuster Entertainment Award. Chilli is quoted on their website as saying that she wishes "to be the biggest female group of all time, to sell so many albums that it will be a few years before any other group can catch up"

 ←

GUINNESS WORLD RECORDS

chart toppers

YOUNGEST NO.1 SOLO ARTIST ON US ALBUM CHART
Stevie Wonder (USA) was 13 years 3 months old when his album *Little Stevie Wonder – The Twelve Year Old Genius* (1963) topped the US charts.

YOUNGEST SINGER IN UK ALBUM CHART TOP 10
Lena Zavaroni (UK) was just 10 years 146 days old when she hit the album charts in March 1974 with *Ma*, which reached No.8.

ALL YOU NEED IS POP
The record for the most consecutive No.1 hits in the UK is held by The Beatles (above), who had 11 in a row between 1963 and 1966 (from 'From Me to You' through to 'Yellow Submarine'). They also share the record for most consecutive UK Christmas No.1 singles with the Spice Girls, both of whom have had three festive chart-toppers in a row. Formed in the late 1950s as The Quarry Men, The Beatles went through various line-ups and name changes, with John Lennon, Paul McCartney and George Harrison at the core before adding Ringo Starr on drums in 1962. Guided by manager Brian Epstein and the production skills of George Martin they became a worldwide sensation, causing hysteria amongst their fans and amassed the greatest record sales for any group with over one billion units sold.

www.guinnessworldrecords.com/beatles

ACCESS CODE: ‹50847›

FASTEST-SELLING DEBUT SINGLE ON UK CHART
Released on 12 March 2001, 'Pure And Simple' by Hear'Say (UK), the group comprised of the five winners of ITV's *Popstars* series, became the best selling debut single on the UK chart, with 549,823 sales in the first week, taking them straight to No.1. The group, consisting of Noel, Danny, Suzanne, Kym and Myleene, are also the first-ever act to top the UK single and album charts simultaneously with their debut releases.

LONGEST SPAN OF UK NO.1 SINGLES
Cliff Richard (UK) has had a span of 40 years between his first and most recent No.1 singles on the UK chart – 'Living Doll' in 1959 and 'The Millennium Prayer' in 1999.

LONGEST WAIT FOR A US NO.1 SINGLE
Santana (Mexico) hold the record for the longest gap between their first chart entry – 'Jingle' in October 1969 – and their first No.1 – 'Smooth', which became the US No.1 in Oct 1999.

MOST UK CHRISTMAS NO.1 SINGLES
The Beatles (UK) have had four singles in the coveted Christmas top spot – 'I Wanna Hold Your Hand' (12 Dec 1963), 'I Feel Fine' (10 Dec 1964), 'Day Tripper/We Can Work it Out' (16 Dec 1965) and, last but not least, 'Hello Goodbye' (6 Dec 1967).

MOST CONSECUTIVE WEEKS AT NO.1 ON US SINGLES CHART
The record that has spent most consecutive weeks at No.1 on the US singles charts is 'One Sweet Day', a collaboration between Mariah Carey and Boyz II Men, (both USA), which topped the chart for 16 weeks in 1995.

MOST CONSECUTIVE SINGLES TO ENTER THE UK CHART AT NO.1 SINCE DEBUT
In 1999/2000, Irish boy-band Westlife became the only group to have their first seven singles enter the UK

HOUSTON, WE HAVE A RECORD BREAKER!
The record for the most consecutive No.1 singles on the US charts is seven, a total achieved by R&B vocalist/actress Whitney Houston (USA, above) between 1985 and 1988. The songs were 'Saving All My Love For You' (1985), 'How Will I Know' (1985), 'Greatest Love Of All' (1986), 'I Want To Dance With Somebody (Who Loves Me)' (1987), 'Didn't We Almost Have It All' (1987), 'So Emotional' (1987), and 'Where Do Broken Hearts Go' (1988). Born on 27 March 1970, in Long Island, New York, USA, Whitney's record sales total over 100 million copies worldwide to date.

www.guinnessworldrecords.com/whitney

 ACCESS CODE: ‹54592›

charts at No.1 when their single 'My Love' entered at the top spot on 11 Nov 2000.

MOST UK NO.1 SINGLES BY A FEMALE GROUP
The most No.1 singles on the UK charts by a female group is nine by the Spice Girls, and was achieved on 4 Nov 2000 when their double-A side single 'Holler/Let Love Lead The Way' reached the top spot.

MOST US NO.1 ALBUMS
The record for the most US No.1 albums is 19, held by The Beatles – more than doubling the number held by closest rivals The Rolling Stones (UK) with nine. 'The Fab Four' have now reached the top of the US album chart in five different decades.

MOST NO.1 SINGLES BY A SOLO ARTIST
Elvis Presley holds the record for the most No.1 hit singles by a solo artist. Since the beginning of the rock era in 1955, 'the King' has scored 17 UK No.1 hit singles and

18 in the USA, which stayed at No.1 for a grand total of 80 weeks – more than any other artist in the USA.

MOST UK NO.1 SINGLES
The Beatles and Elvis Presley both share the record for the most No.1 hit singles on the UK charts, with 17 chart toppers each.

MOST US NO.1 SINGLES
The Beatles have the most No.1 hits on the US singles chart with 20, the first of which was 'I Want To Hold Your Hand' on 1 Feb 1964.

MOST WEEKS AT NO.1 ON AUSTRALIAN SINGLES CHART
The Beatles' 'Hey Jude' (1968) and ABBA's 'Fernando' (Sweden,1976) both spent 15 weeks at No.1 in Australia.

MOST WEEKS AT NO.1 ON UK ALBUM CHART
The soundtrack to *South Pacific* (USA 1958) was the first No.1 album and stayed at the top for 70 consecutive weeks from 8 Nov 1958. It eventually spent a record 115 weeks at No.1.

ACCESS CODE: •56344•

DESTINATION NO.1

The most weeks spent at No.1 on the US singles chart by a girl band is 'Independent Woman' by Grammy Award-winning R&B trio Destiny's Child (USA, right). It was released on 20 Nov 2000, and spent a record 11 weeks at the top of the US chart. The song was the title track from the hit movie *Charlie's Angels*, and the first single by a US female trio to top the UK chart for over 26 years.

YOUNGEST MALE SOLO ARTIST TO ENTER AT NO.1 ON UK SINGLES CHART

The youngest male solo artist to enter the UK singles chart at No.1 is R&B singer Craig David (UK), who was 18 years 339 days old when his single 'Fill Me In' reached the top of the charts on 9 April 2000, selling over 165,000 copies.

YOUNGEST SINGER AT NO.1 ON UK ALBUM CHART

Neil Reid (UK) was 12 years 9 months old when his self-titled debut album topped the chart on 19 Feb 1972.

MOST SUCCESSFUL POP FAMILY

The Jackson family have scored 26 US No.1 singles – 13 by Michael, nine by Janet and four by the Jackson 5, who achieved the first Jackson No.1 with 'I Want You Back' on 6 Dec 1969.

MOST INTERNATIONAL CHARTS TOPPED BY AN ALBUM

Since being released on 13 Nov 2000, the album *1* by The Beatles – a compilation of all of their UK and US No.1 singles – has topped the charts in 35 countries from Australia to Venezuela. Furthermore, it was the biggest album of the year in Australia, Germany, Ireland, Italy, Portugal and the UK.

MOST UK NO.1 SINGLES BY A TEENAGE FEMALE ARTIST

Two artists share this record with three UK No.1 hits. Britney Spears (USA) was 18 years 158 days old when 'Oops! I Did It Again' became her third single to reach No.1 on 7 May 2000; and Billie Piper (UK) was 17 years 242 days old when 'Day & Night' became her third No.1 debuting at the top of the charts on 21 May 2000.

GUINNESS WORLD RECORDS

chart hits

MOST NO.1 SINGLES PRODUCED BY AN ADVERTISING CAMPAIGN

Seven songs have reached No.1 in the UK pop charts after having appeared on Levi Strauss and Co TV advertisements. The chart successes include 'Stand By Me' by Ben E King (USA), 'Inside' by Stiltskin (UK) and 'The Joker' by The Steve Miller Band (USA). The seventh No.1 hit to be associated with Levi's TV adverts, 'Flat Beat' by French artist Mr Oizo, debuted at No.1 in Britain on 3 April 1999 after selling nearly 284,000 copies.

LONGEST STAY ON UK ALBUM CHART

The longest stay on the UK album chart is a record 477 weeks by Fleetwood Mac's *Rumours*, released on 26 Feb 1977. The album hit No.1 and included four singles chart entries, though none hit the Top 20.

LONGEST TIME SPENT AT US RAP NO.1 SPOT

'Hot Boyz' by Missy 'Misdemeanor' Elliott (USA) featuring guest rappers Nas, Eve and Q-Tip, spent a record 18 weeks at the top of the US Rap singles chart in 1999/2000.

LONGEST TIME SPENT ON UK SINGLES CHART

'My Way' by Frank Sinatra (USA) has spent 124 weeks on the UK chart since its original release on 2 April

SINGING LA VIDA LOCA

The fastest-selling album of all time in Spain was *El Alma Al Aire* (The Bared Soul) by Alejandro Sanz, released in Oct 2000. A record 500,000 advance orders were taken and over one million copies were sold in its first week of release (equivalent to 20 million in the USA). A total of 800,000 were shipped to North and South America.

'Macarena' by Spanish duo Los Del Rio (Spanish for 'People of the river') is the most successful Latin single of all time, selling over 10 million copies worldwide. It topped the US chart for 14 weeks in 1996 and spent 60 weeks in the Top 100. Despite its huge success, an internet poll recently voted it, 'Most irritating summer single of all time', and some US schools banned it owing to its suggestive lyrics.

www.guinnessworldrecords.com/sanz
← ACCESS CODE: ‹56330›

1969 when it reached its peak position of No.5. It has since re-entered the chart no fewer than 10 times.

LONGEST US CHART SPAN

The jazz trumpeter Louis Armstrong (USA) first appeared on a chart in 1926 with 'Muskrat Ramble'. His most recent entry came in 1988, with 'What A Wonderful World' after it was included in the film soundtrack to *Good Morning Vietnam* (USA, 1987), thus taking his span of hits to more than 61 years. He also holds the record for the longest gap between US album chart entries. His album *Satch Plays Fats* entered on 1 Oct 1955 and *Ken Burns Jazz – The Definitive Louis Armstrong* entered in Jan 2001, 45 years 3 months later.

MOST US HIT ALBUMS BY A FEMALE ARTIST

Barbra Streisand (USA) holds the female record for the most albums to enter the US chart with 48, since her first *The Barbra Streisand Album* hit

the charts on 25 Feb 1962, reaching No.8. Her most recent, *Timeless – Live in Concert* was released on 19 Sept 2000 and reached No.21.

MOST US HIT SINGLES BY A MALE ARTIST

Elvis Presley (USA) had a record 149 hit singles on the Billboard Hot 100 between 1956 and 1996. He took his first step towards a musical career at the age of 10, when he won $5 (then £1.24) in a local singing contest in Tupelo, Mississippi, performing the Red Foley ballad, 'Old Shep'.

MOST UK HIT ALBUMS BY A MALE ARTIST

The record for the most UK album chart entries is held by Elvis Presley with 100 by Feb 2001.

MOST CONSECUTIVE WEEKS ON UK SINGLES CHART

Elvis Presley stayed on the UK chart with 13 hit singles, from 'A Mess of

Blues' in 1960 to 'One More Broken Heart for Sale' in 1963 for an unbroken 144 weeks on the chart.

MOST NEW UK HIT SINGLES IN ONE YEAR

British group The Wedding Present and Elvis Presley share this record with 12 new hits in the UK singles chart in one year, Elvis in 1957 and The Wedding Present in 1992. In both cases all 12 hit the Top 30.

MOST UK HIT SINGLES BY A MALE ARTIST

Cliff Richard (UK) has had 123 UK hit singles to March 2001. His first hit was 'Move It', which reached No.2 on 12 Sept 1958 and his latest was 1999's No.1 'The Millennium Prayer'.

THE BEATLES, THE MONKEES, PEARL JAM, AND THE BEST BAND IN THE WORLD

The Beatles (UK), The Monkees (USA), Pearl Jam (USA) and U2 (Ireland, left), hold the record, with seven albums each, for having the most albums on the US chart (Top 200) at the same time. The Beatles achieved this on 31 Jan 1981 in the aftermath of John Lennon's death with *Beatles 1967-1970*, *Beatles 1962-1966*, *White Album*, *Sgt Pepper's Lonely Hearts Club Band*, *Rubber Soul*, *Abbey Road* and *Love Songs*. The Monkees', whose success was based largely on their TV show, achieved their record in 1987. U2, Bono's self proclaimed 'Best Band in the World' joined the Beatles and the Monkees as record-holders in the same year. Pearl Jam were the last to hit the spot on 17 March 2001.

www.guinnessworldrecords.com/mostalbums
← ACCESS CODE: ‹56340›

MOST SIMULTANEOUS US ALBUM CHART ENTRIES IN A WEEK

Rock group Pearl Jam (USA) had seven different albums enter the US Top 200 chart on 17 March 2001. They were part of a series of 23 albums recorded live at different venues around the USA during the group's world tour, and broke their own record of five entries, held five months before, from a series of 25 simultaneously-released live albums from concerts across the world.

MOST WEEKS ON US COUNTRY CHART BY A FEMALE ARTIST

Patsy Cline's *12 Greatest Hits* (USA) was still on the US country catalogue album chart in Feb 2001, 722 weeks after it first entered. The album spent 251 weeks (almost five years) at No.1 and sold over seven million copies. Cline died alongside US Country stars Hawkshaw Hawkins and Cowboy Copas in a light aircraft crash in March 1963, and her funeral was attended by 25,000 grieving fans.

MOST WEEKS SPENT ON UK SINGLES CHART

Elvis Presley's 111 hits have spent a total of 1,168 weeks on the UK singles chart since 'Heartbreak Hotel' debuted on 11 May 1956. In the weeks after his death on 16 Aug 1977, his record sales predictably rocketed and 'Way Down' proved a fittingly final UK No.1.

MOST WEEKS SPENT ON US ADULT CONTEMPORARY ALBUM CHART

Australian duo Savage Garden's single 'Truly Madly Deeply' spent a record 123 weeks on the US adult contemporary chart before it dropped out of the chart in May 2000. Their debut album sold 11 million copies.

MOST US SOLO NO.1 ALBUMS

Elvis Presley has had a record nine No.1 albums – *Elvis Presley* (1956), *Elvis* (1956), *Loving You* (1957), *Elvis Christmas Album* (1957), *GI Blues* (1960), *Something For Everybody* (1961), *Blue Hawaii* (1961), *Roustabout* (1964) and *Elvis – Aloha From Hawaii* (1973).

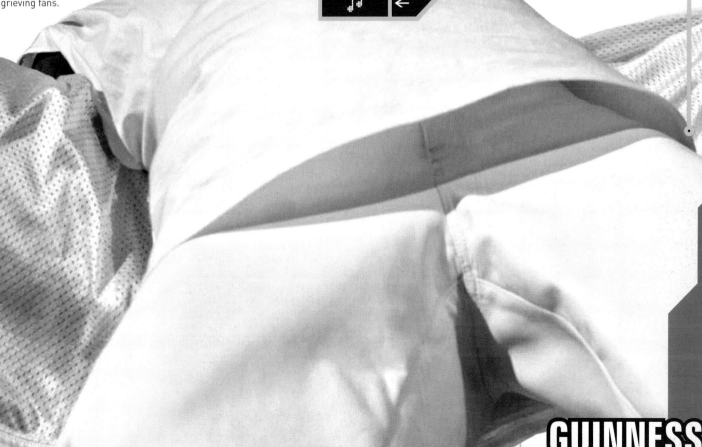

www.guinnessworldrecords.com/puffdaddy

ACCESS CODE: ‹55719›

THE MACK DADDY

Sean 'Puffy' Combs, a.k.a. Puff Daddy (USA, left), is the world's most successful rap producer, having been responsible for four singles that consecutively headed the US rap chart for a record 36 weeks in 1997. Stars he has worked with include Lil' Kim, Mariah Carey and Usher. He took part in the record-breaking run himself with a tribute record to his friend Christopher Wallace (US), a.k.a. rapper Notorious B.I.G. who recorded for Puffy's record label Bad Boy. When B.I.G. was tragically shot, Puffy recorded a tribute single with B.I.G.'s wife, Faith Evans. 'I'll Be Missing You' was a massive international chart success and all proceeds were donated to his children.

GUINNESS WORLD RECORDS

music facts and feats

MOST GRAMMY AWARDS WON BY AN INDIVIDUAL

The late Hungarian-born British conductor Sir Georg Solti won an all-time record of 31 Grammy awards (including a special Trustees award presented in 1967) between 1958 and 1997.

BEST-SELLING JAZZ ARTIST

The best-selling jazz artist is Kenny G (USA), who has sold an estimated 55 million albums worldwide to date.

THE CAT IN THE HAT

The best-selling funk album of all time is *Travelling Without Moving* by Jamiroquai (UK), which has sold more than seven million albums globally since its release in 1996. In total, Jamiroquai, led by vocalist Jay Kay (above), have sold 11 million albums and have become one of the most sought-after live jazz funk acts in the world. The album spawned hit after hit in the UK, including 'Cosmic Girl', 'Alright' and 'Virtual Insanity', and it saw them break the American market, collecting four US MTV awards and a Grammy in 1997. In 1998 Jamiroquai wrote 'Deeper Underground' for the Hollywood movie *Godzilla* and most recently released the 1999 album *Synkronized*. Their career started way back in 1992 when they released 'When You Gonna Learn' on a small independent London label, Acid Jazz, before they signed to Sony.

www.guinnessworldrecords.com/
bestfunk

ACCESS CODE:
← ‹54242›

This includes 12 million copies of *Breathless*, the best-selling jazz album of all time, released in 1992. Born Kenneth Gorelick, Kenny has won many awards, including Grammy, American Music Awards, Soul Train Awards and World Music Awards.

MOST VALUABLE JAZZ INSTRUMENT

The most valuable jazz instrument is a saxophone, once owned by Charlie 'Bird' Parker (USA), which sold for £93,500 ($144,500), at Christie's, South Kensington, London, UK, on 7 Sept 1994.

MOST VALUABLE VIOLIN

A violin made by Guarneri del Gesu (Italy) in 1742, and owned by the late Yehudi Menuhin (UK), was sold to an anonymous collector in Zurich, Switzerland, on 29 Oct 1999. Swiss dealer Musik Hug said it sold for "approximately $1.25 million (£781,250) above what had ever been paid for a violin" – which was £947,500 ($1,585,452) in 1998.

HIGHEST ALTITUDE CONCERT

A concert commemorating the 150th anniversary of the death of composer Gaetano Donizetti (Italy) took place at a record height of 5,050 m (16,568 ft) above sea level, on 24 Oct 1998 at the Laboratory-Observatory, a three-storey glass and aluminium pyramid, in Mt Everest's Khumba Valley, Nepal. The concert was performed by flautist Ombretta Maffeis and pianist Gianni Bergamelli.

GREATEST VOCAL RANGE

Marta Maria Kupeczik (Hungary), has a vocal range extending from great B Flat to D4 – from the male bass to the highest coloratura – an incredible range of more than four octaves.

LARGEST CD MUSIC EDITION

Great Pianists of the 20th Century, compiled by Philips is the largest single edition ever recorded. It consists of 200 CDs and was released over a period of 12 months from Sept 1998. The edition features 74 pianists, the youngest of whom is Evgeny Kissin

THERE WERE 470 GLASS BOTTLES, SITTING ON THE WALL, 470 GLASS BOTTLES ...

On 12 Oct 2000 in Toledo, Ohio, USA, local flautists Patricia Rentner and Roselyn Smith broke the record for the largest bottle orchestra by blowing into a line of 470 strategically arranged glass bottles (above). Patricia conducts Ottawa Hills Flute Choir, while Roselyn is a flautist with the 555th Air National Guard of Toledo, Ohio, USA. Both strayed from their normal repertoires to play a nursery-rhyme medley on the bottles including 'This Old Man', 'Hickory Dickory Dock' and 'Mary had a Little Lamb'.

www.guinnessworldrecords.com/glassbottles
← ACCESS CODE: ‹50521›

(b. 10 Oct 1971, Russia), and the oldest, deceased musician Ignaz Paderewski (1860–1941, Poland).

LARGEST ELECTRONIC KEYBOARD ENSEMBLE

The largest electronic keyboard ensemble consisted of 100 students and teachers from the Music School, Gorsium, Hungary, performing on keyboards programmed to sound like traditional orchestral instruments. They played Strauss's *Blue Danube* and Monti's *Monti Czardas* during the first Roland Keyboard Festival on 2 June 2000, in the Pesti Vigado Concert Hall, Budapest, Hungary.

MOST GUITAR PARTS PLAYED SIMULTANEOUSLY BY AN INDIVIDUAL

On 12 Jan 2000 Jack 'Hoss' Linneman (USA) played the four guitar parts – two types of rhythm, melody and fill notes – of the tune 'Greenback Dollar' simultaneously on the *Jimmy Smart Show*. He played on a standard six-string Epiphone guitar and maintained a speed of 240 beats per minute, which works out at 36 notes per second.

LONGEST APPLAUSE

Spanish tenor Plàcido Domingo was applauded for a grand total of 1 hr 20 min through 101 curtain calls after a performance of *Otello* by Verdi at the Vienna Staatsoper on 30 July 1991.

LARGEST SIMULTANEOUS PERCUSSION PERFORMANCE

The largest simultaneous percussion performance was *Beat This!*, an event organized as part of the BBC Music Live festival on 29 May 2000. Across the UK, from 12–12.30 pm, 2,140 people played a common percussive rhythm especially devised for the event. Groups were linked by radio or television to the TV centre, and a live broadcast was shown on TV.

YOUNGEST WINNER OF THE BIGGEST MUSIC PRIZE

British composer Thomas Adès won the Grawemeyer Award for Music Composition in 2000 at the age of 28, to become the youngest and only the third British winner of the award. It is the world's largest single music writing award worth $200,000 (£125,000).

A SAW POINT FOR EMINEM

The record for the fastest-selling rap artist of all time is held by Detroit rapper Eminem. *The Marshall Mathers LP* sold a record 1.76 million copies in its first week in the US in May 2000. He is seen by some people as a genius lyricist reflecting social problems in American society, and by others as a bad influence on adolescents worldwide, who are influenced by his aggressive lyrics. Eminem's 'Stan', an ode to an obsessive fan, was an international smash hit. He is currently so popular that a search on the internet will offer at least 215,000 links. Tongue-in-cheek references to members of his own family in his songs have led to multi-million dollar lawsuits, dwarfed only by the even larger profits from his album and video sales, which show no sign of slowing down.

HIGHEST-PAID PIANIST

Wladziu Valentino Liberace (USA) earned more than $2 million (£716,845) for each 26-week season at Madison Square Garden, New York City, New York, USA, with a peak of $138,000 (then £49,285) for a single night's performance in 1954, equivalent to $1,085,252 (£775,180) today.

LARGEST ONE-MAN BAND

Rory Blackwell (UK), aided by his double left-footed perpendicular percussion-pounder, plus his three-tier, right-footed, horizontal, 22-pronged differential beater as well as his 12-outlet, bellow-powered horn-blower, played 108 different instruments (19 melody and 89 percussion), simultaneously in Dawlish, Devon, UK, on 29 May 1989. The entire collection of instruments measured 4.57 x 3.65 m (15 ft x 12 ft).

LARGEST PIANO REPERTOIRE

Richard Järnefelt of Helsinki, Finland, has a repertoire of 3,000 songs that he can play from memory. The list consists mainly of pop songs but also includes classical pieces.

OLDEST PLAYABLE INSTRUMENT

Archaeologists uncovered a 9,000-year old Chinese bone flute and managed to play a tune on it. The flute, which is 22 cm (8.6 in) long, has seven holes and is made from the leg bone of a red crowned crane. It was found at Jiahu, the site of an ancient farming village on the Yellow River flood plain, China.

LONGEST SYMPHONY

The symphony *Victory at Sea*, written by Richard Rodgers (USA) for the film of the same name, and arranged by Robert Russell Bennett (USA) in 1952, lasted 13 hours.

GUINNESS WORLD RECORDS

theatrical performance

HIGHEST THEATRE BOX-OFFICE GROSS

Since first opening at Her Majesty's Theatre, London, UK, on 9 Oct 1986, Andrew Lloyd Webber's (UK) musical *The Phantom of the Opera* has played in 18 countries and has taken £2 billion ($3.2 billion) at the box office. The second-highest grossing theatre show ever is *Cats*, another Lloyd Webber musical, with a box-office take of £1.25 billion ($2 billion).

HIGHEST INSURANCE FOR A SHOW

When the musical *Barnum* opened at the London Palladium on 11 June 1981, it became the most highly insured show in theatre history. Producers put the total cover at £5 million (then $9,867,000) – £3 million (then $5,920,200) of which was the cost of insuring Michael Crawford (UK), who walked the high-wire and slid down a rope to the stage from the topmost box during the show.

MOST EXPENSIVE STAGE PRODUCTION

The stage adaptation of Disney's 1994 film *The Lion King* is the most expensive theatrical production ever. The Broadway production, which opened in Nov 1997, cost an estimated $15 million (£9.3 million).

GREATEST THEATRICAL LOSS

The Royal Shakespeare Company's musical *Carrie* closed after five performances on Broadway, New York City, New York, USA, on 17 May 1988 at the huge cost of $7 million (£3,745,000). *King*, the musical about Martin Luther King, lost £3 million ($5,128,200) in a six-week run ending on 2 June 1990, equalling the record London losses of *Ziegfeld* in 1988.

LONGEST THEATRICAL RUN

The longest continuous run of any show is Agatha Christie's (UK) *The Mousetrap*, which opened on 25 Nov 1952. It had its 20,126th performance on 23 April 2001 at St Martin's Theatre, London, UK, and has grossed more than £20 million ($33.3 million) from more than 10 million theatre-goers in its 49 years.

LONGEST-RUNNING MUSICAL

The off-Broadway musical *The Fantasticks*, by Tom Jones and Harvey Schmidt (both USA) opened on 3 May 1960. By 2000, it had been performed a record 16,562 times at the Sullivan Street Playhouse, New York City, New York, USA.

SHORTEST PLAY

Nobel prize-winner Samuel Beckett (Ireland), author of one of the most influential plays in post-war drama, *Waiting For Godot* (1953), also wrote the shortest play in world drama, the 30-second *Breath* (1969).

LONGEST PLAY

The longest recorded theatrical production was *The Warp* by Neil Oram (UK), a 10-part play cycle that was performed at the Institute of Contemporary Art, London, UK, between 18 and 20 Jan 1979. Actor Russell Denton was on stage for all but five minutes of the 18-hr 5-min production.

FASTEST THEATRICAL PRODUCTION

Velvet Jacket Ltd's production of the musical *Oklahoma!* performed by Act 24 at The Playhouse, Edinburgh, UK, was put on stage 23 hr 55 min after the cast and crew first received the script at 8 pm on 6 May 2000.

MOST TONY AWARDS

Harold Prince (USA) has won a total of 20 Tony Awards in 40 years. The Tony Awards, named in honour of stage actress Antoinette Perry (USA), are one of theatre's most coveted accolades. Harold Prince's record is made up of eight Tonys each for directing and producing, two as producer of the year's Best Musical and two special Tony Awards.

MOST TONY AWARDS FOR AN ACTRESS

With five Tony awards to her credit – her first win was in 1952 – Julie Harris (USA) has won more than any other actress. Julie Harris also holds the record for the most Tony Award nominations, with 10 over a period of 45 years. She made her Broadway debut in 1945.

MOST TONY AWARDS FOR A PLAY

Five plays have each won five Tony Awards – *A Man for all Seasons* by Robert Bolt (1962); *Who's Afraid of Virginia Woolf?* by Edward Albee (1963); *Child's Play* by Robert Marasco (1971); *Amadeus* by Peter Shaffer (1981); and *The Real Thing* by Tom Stoppard (1984).

MOST FREQUENTLY ADAPTED PLAY

A Day Well Spent, a one-act farce written by John Oxenford (UK) in 1835, has been adapted five times as follows – *Einen Jux will er sich machen* (1842) by Johann Nestroy; *The Merchant of Yonkers* (1938) by Thornton Wilder; *The Matchmaker* (1954) by Thornton Wilder; *Hello Dolly* (1963) by Jerry Herman and Michael Stewart; and *On The Razzle* (1981) by Tom Stoppard.

LARGEST SIMULTANEOUS PERFORMANCE OF ONE SHOW

At 7 pm on 20 Nov 1999 the children's musical *The Rainbow Juggler* was performed in 56 theatres across the UK, Ireland, Germany, USA and Australia by 4,568 Stagecoach Theatre Arts students. The shows were staged to mark the 10th anniversary of the Convention on the Rights of the Child, and raised £50,000 ($78,947) for the United Nations Children's Fund (UNICEF).

LARGEST TAP DANCE

The greatest-ever number of tap dancers in a single routine was 6,776 outside Macy's department store in New York City, New York, USA, on 17 Aug 1997. The event was staged on 34th Street, with a two-minute routine to the tune of 'Puttin' on the Ritz'. The dancers' ages ranged from one year old to an impressive 91 years old.

MOST ROLES IN A SINGLE PLAY

For the play *For Love or Money*, put on at the Grand Theatre, Lancaster, UK, in Sept 2000 by the Lancaster Red Rose Amateur Operatic and Dramatic Society, Phil Gibson (UK) was credited for six production roles – original idea; composer; librettist; orchestration; chorus master; and the lead role of 'Sam'.

FLY BY NIGHT ACTOR?

Performing a stunt known in Japanese as *chunori*, kabuki actor Ichikawa Ennosuke (Japan, left) has flown across the stage and audience for 5,000 performances since April 1968. His record-breaking 5,000th stage flight was achieved on 19 April 2000 at 3.08 pm at the Shimbashi Ebujo Theatre in Tokyo, performing in *Shin Sankokushi*. Ennosuke plays a hero who dies and flies to heaven with his lover in his arms. *Chunori*, performed using pulleys and a safety belt, was developed in Edo (today's Tokyo) in the 17th century and remained a popular stage trick for nearly three centuries. Ennosuke revived the stunt at the National Theatre in Tokyo for the play *Yoshitsune and the Thousand Cherry Trees* and continued the *chunori* in numerous guises and drama throughout the following 32 years.

www.guinnessworldrecords.com/chunori
← ACCESS CODE: ‹54812›

www.guinnessworldrecords.com/chairstack

HIGH CHAIRS
 USA

On 16 Oct 1999 the Peking Acrobats (China, right) created the tallest human chair-stack, measuring 6.4 m (21 ft) high, with six people stacked onto seven chairs. Once in place, they held a handstand for five seconds. The Peking Acrobats have performed together since 1952, mastering disciplines dating back to the Ch'in Dynasty (225–207BC).

MOST THEATRE PERFORMANCES IN THE SAME ROLE
From Nov 1966 to June 1983, Kanbi Fujiyama (Japan) played the lead role in 10,288 performances as part of the comedy company Sochiku Shikigek.

MOST ACTING ROLES
Jan Leighton (USA) holds the record for playing the greatest recorded number of theatrical, film and TV parts with 3,395 different roles to his credit since 1951. He owns over 200 wigs and hats, over 70 pairs of glasses, five Santa suits and 36 pipes.

VIETNAMESE VICTORY
Miss Saigon, the musical written by Alain Boubil and Claude-Michel Schonberg (both France) and produced by Cameron Mackintosh (UK), opened on Broadway, in April 1991, having set a record of $36 million (£20.5 million) as the highest advance sales for a musical. The show includes a life-size helicopter, a 1959 Cadillac and a cast of 44. *Miss Saigon*'s world première took place in London's Theatre Royal (above) on 20 Sept 1989. The show opened in Tokyo in May 1992 and broke all box-office records there to become the longest consecutive-running musical in Japan.

www.guinnessworldrecords.com/
misssaigon

MOST PLAYS RUNNING SIMULTANEOUSLY BY ONE WRITER
Somerset Maugham (UK) set the record in 1908 when he had four plays running simultaneously in the West End, London, UK – *Lady Frederick* at the Court, *Mrs Dot* at the Comedy, *Jack Straw* at the Vaudeville and *The Explorer* at the Lyric.

MOST ACTORS SUSPENDED IN THE AIR SIMULTANEOUSLY
Período Doma, a show by the Argentinian dance-theatre group De La Guarda, featured 33 actors suspended together in the air simultaneously. Five performances of *Período Doma* were watched by an audience of 14,000 at the Velódromo, Buenos Aires, Argentina, in April 1998.

MOST MEMBERS OF A FAMILY TO PERFORM ON STAGE TOGETHER
On 12 June 1906 at Ellen Terry's (UK) Jubilee Matinée at the Drury Lane Theatre, London, UK, 22 members of the Terry family appeared in the ball scene from *Much Ado About Nothing*.

THICKEST MAKE-UP
Chutti, the make-up unique to the Indian Kathakali dance-theatre tradition is built up using rice paste and paper and can extend 15 cm (6 in) from the face.

GUINNESS WORLD RECORDS

books and magazines

BEST-SELLING AUTHOR

The world's best-selling fiction writer is Agatha Christie (UK), whose 78 crime novels have sold an estimated two billion copies in 44 languages. Agatha Christie also wrote 19 plays and, under the pseudonym Mary Westmacott, six romantic novels. Annual royalty earnings are worth around £2.5 million ($4 million).

BEST-SELLING NON-FICTION

The world's best-selling and most widely distributed book is the Bible, with an estimated 2.5 billion copies sold since 1815. Parts of the Bible are available in 2,123 languages.

The King James Bible holds the record for the largest CD edition of a talking book. It was recorded over seven years, creating a collection of 78 CDs with 88 hours of playtime. 147 actors from the Royal Shakespeare Company (UK) and the BBC Repertory Company (UK) read onto 1,600 km (1,000 miles) of tape.

BIGGEST ADVANCE FOR A BOOK

In 1992 Berkeley Putnam paid $14 million (then £7.3 million) for the North American rights to *Without Remorse*, a spy-thriller by Tom Clancy (USA), the author of *Patriot Games* and *The Hunt for Red October*. This is the greatest-ever advance for a single book.

FULLY BOOKED

Kazuko Hosoki (Japan, left) is the best-selling author of fortune-telling books. She has written a series of 81 books and has sold 34 million copies. She published her first book in May 1982.

There are three contenders for the record for the best-selling work of fiction. However, due to a lack of audited figures, it is impossible to state which single work of fiction has the highest sales. Three novels have been credited with sales of around 30 million – *To Kill a Mockingbird* (1960) by Harper Lee, *Gone with the Wind* (1936) by Margaret Mitchell and *Valley of the Dolls* (1966) by Jacqueline Susann (all USA). The latter sold 6.8 million copies in its first six months, although it is now out of print.

www.guinnessworldrecords.com/fortunebooks
← ACCESS CODE: ‹55598 ›

LONGEST NOVEL

A la recherche du temps perdu (or, in English, *Remembrance of Things Past*) by Marcel Proust (France) consists of 13 volumes, containing about 9,609,000 characters (letters and spaces). The first volume of this masterpiece was published in 1913. The last six unrevised volumes were finished before his death in 1922.

MOST PROLIFIC NOVELIST

Brazilian author José Carlos Ryoki de Alpoim Inoue had 1,058 novels published between June 1986 and Aug 1996. He writes westerns, science fiction and thrillers.

YOUNGEST SERIES WRITER

Randy Nahle's (Lebanon) first book, *Revenge*, was published in July 1998 when he was 12 years old. He wrote the second book in his *Hawk Archives* detective series, *Mirror Image*, aged 13, and it was published in Feb 2000 when he was aged 14.

LONGEST BIOGRAPHY

The longest biography in publishing history is the ongoing biography of Sir Winston Churchill, co-authored by his son Randolph and the historian Martin Gilbert (both UK). It currently comprises eight volumes plus 16 companion volumes, together containing around 10 million words.

BIGGEST LITERARY AWARD

The International IMPAC Dublin Literary Award (Eire) for novels has a prize of IR£100,000 ($130,900). Contenders for the prize are nominated by public libraries in major cities around the world. Nicola Barker (UK) won the 2000 award for her novel *Wide Open*.

OLDEST NOVEL

Chaireas and Callirhoe, written by the Greek author Chariton around 100 AD, is the oldest known novel. It describes the adventures of a beautiful bride named Callirhoe. The only Latin novel that still survives in its entirety is Apuleius's *The Golden Ass* (also known as *Metamorphoses*) written in 123 AD.

SLOWEST-SELLING BOOK

The world's slowest-selling book was David Wilkins' translation of the New Testament from Coptic into Latin. 500 copies were published by Oxford University Press in 1716. It had an average sales rate of one copy sold every 20 weeks and took 191 years to sell out.

LARGEST BOOK

The *Super Book* measures 2.74 x 3.07 m (9 x 10 ft 1in), weighs 252.6 kg (557 lb) and has 300 pages. It was published in Denver, Colorado, USA, in 1976. The cover of the *Super Book* is 122 times the size of the book you are reading now.

SMALLEST BOOK

The smallest bound book ever marketed is printed on 22 gsm paper and measures 1 mm^2 (0.04 in^2). It comprises the children's story *Ole King Cole!*, and 85 copies of it were published in March 1985 by The Gleniffer Press (UK). The pages can only be turned using a needle.

LARGEST READING BY AN AUTHOR

JK Rowling (UK) was one of three authors who read from their works to an audience of 20,264 at Toronto's SkyDome stadium (Canada) on 24 Oct 2000, as part of Harborfront Center's International Festival of

READ ALL ABOUT IT

The most massive single issue of a newspaper was the 14 Sept 1987 edition of the *Sunday New York Times* (left), which weighed more than 5.4 kg (12 lb) and contained a staggering 1,612 pages. This newspaper has an average circulation of 1,650,000.

The longest newspaper published was the 19 Dec 1997 edition of the Brazilian daily newspaper *Diàrio Oficial da União*, which ran to 2,112 pages and weighed 5.27 kg (11 lb 8oz).

The world's oldest existing weekly newspaper is the Swedish official journal *Post och Inrikes Tidningar*, founded in 1645 and published by the Royal Swedish Academy of Letters. In 1766, Sweden became the first country to introduce a law guaranteeing freedom of the press.

www.guinnessworldrecords.com/massivenewspaper
← ACCESS CODE: ‹47978›

www.guinnessworldrecords.com/harrypotter

POTTY ABOUT POTTER!

The first three books in JK Rowling's (UK) Harry Potter (right) series hold the record for the highest one-year sales for a book series. In 1999 the series sold over 18.5 million copies in the USA and over 4.5 million in the UK and Commonwealth. Rowling is also the first novelist to have three titles in the top four slots of the *New York Times* bestsellers list for 16 weeks. Book four, *Harry Potter and the Goblet of Fire*, received record advance orders of 5.3 million copies.

Authors. She read from *Harry Potter and the Goblet of Fire*. Canadian author Kenneth Oppel read from his novel *Silverwing*, while his compatriot Tim Wynne-Jones read from *The Boy in the Burning House*.

LARGEST BOOK-SIGNING EVENT

On 3 Dec 1999, 60 Citron Press authors signed their books for the public at an event held at the Business Design Centre, London, UK. A total of 1,200 books were signed in two hours.

MOST OVERDUE LIBRARY BOOK

A German biography of the Archbishop of Bremen, published in 1609, was borrowed from Sidney Sussex College, Cambridge, UK, by Colonel Robert Walpole in 1668. Prof Sir John Plumb found the book 288 years later in the library of the then Marquess of Cholmondeley at Houghton Hall, Norfolk, UK. He returned it, but was not fined.

BIGGEST INITIAL PRINT RUN FOR A NOVEL

JK Rowling's (UK) *Harry Potter and the Goblet of Fire*, the fourth in the record-breaking series, had an initial print run of 4.8 million copies, of which 3.8 million were printed in the USA (40 times as many as an average bestseller) and one million in the UK.

LARGEST PUBLICATION

The *Yongle Dadian* is a thesaurus compiled under the instructions of the Ming emperor Yongle in the 15th century. The 11,095 volumes containing 22,937 manuscript chapters (of which 370 still survive), were written by 147 Chinese scholars and subsequently revised by another 3,000 scholars between 1403 and 1408.

LARGEST ENCYCLOPEDIA

The largest encyclopedia in use is the *Arabic Legislations Encyclopaedia*, written by Mohamed Abu Baker Ben Younis (Greece). Its 200 volumes have a total of 164,000 pages and weighed of 420 kg (925 lb). It contains every piece of legislation from all the Arab countries. The general index is contained in a further six volumes and there are also additional annexes.

LARGEST ENGLISH DICTIONARY

The second edition of the *Oxford English Dictionary* (1989) contains 21,543 pages in 20 volumes, comprising over 231,000 main entries. The longest entry is for the verb 'set', with over 60,000 words of text. In 1993 an annual series of *Additions Volumes* began, in which approximately 4,000 new vocabulary entries are listed. The dictionary is now also available on CD-ROM.

LARGEST DICTIONARY

Deutsches Wörterbuch (or *German Dictionary*), started in 1854 by Jacob and Wilhelm Grimm, best known for their collection of fairy tales, was completed in 1971 and consists of 34,519 pages in 33 volumes. It is available as a special order over the internet for around £1,200 ($1,695).

OLDEST PERIODICAL MAGAZINE

The oldest continuing periodical in the world is the Royal Society's *Philosophical Transactions*, first published in London, UK, on 6 March 1665. Isaac Newton's rise to scientific prominence owes much to *Transactions* – he had 17 papers published in it. It also published work by Charles Darwin.

HEAVIEST MAGAZINE

The Feb/March 1999 issue of *Brides* magazine (UK) weighed 1.952 kg (4 lb 5 oz). It had 1,242 pages, including 1,065 pages of advertisements. This monster edition kept its usual cover price.

MOST EXPENSIVE MAGAZINE

Visionaire magazine (USA), established by Stephan Gan, Cecilia Dean and James Kalian, is sold at $100 (£70) per issue, but can fetch $5,000 (£3,450) on the black market. The magazine format and theme varies with each edition but it generally combines fashion, photography and art, and has no advertisements. The magazine always has a striking cover or case design, which in the past, has featured fabric, Plexiglas™ and even a jewellery box.

GUINNESS WORLD RECORDS

art and sculpture

MOST PROLIFIC PAINTER

Pablo Diego José Francisco de Paula Juan Nepomuceno de los Remedios Crispín Cipriano de la Santísima Trinidad Ruíz y Picasso (Spain, 1881–1973) was the most prolific of all painters in a career that lasted 75 years. Picasso produced about 13,500 paintings or designs, 100,000 prints or engravings, 34,000 book illustrations and 300 sculptures or ceramics. His *oeuvre* has been valued at £500 million ($709,600,000).

MOST VALUABLE 20TH-CENTURY PAINTING

Picasso's (Spain) *Woman With Crossed Arms* (1901-02) sold for a record $55 million (£38.47 million) on 8 Nov 2000 at a Christie's auction in New York City, New York, USA.

By 9 May 1997 works of art by Pablo Picasso had been sold at auctions no fewer than 3,579 times. This makes him the artist with the most auction sales. The total value of these sales is £668, 817,963 ($954,710,889).

MOST STOLEN PAINTING

Jacob III de Cheyn (1632) by the Dutch artist Rembrandt van Rijn (1609–69), has been stolen from museums no fewer than four times. It was once found on the back of a bicycle, and once underneath a graveyard bench. It has been returned anonymously each time and, as a result, no one has ever been charged with theft.

Rembrandt's portrait of a tranquil young man is so well known that thieves would find it nearly impossible to sell.

MOST VALUABLE SCULPTURE

The Three Graces (1814) by Antonio Canova (Italy, 1752–1822) was jointly purchased by the Victoria and Albert Museum, London, UK, and the National Gallery of Scotland, Edinburgh, UK, for a record £7.5 million ($11.5 million) in 1994.

LARGEST COW ART EXHIBITION

CowPARADE began in Zurich, Switzerland, in 1998, to promote retail and the arts downtown. This event had 812 artistically painted life-size fibreglass cows, with names such as PiCOWso and Lady Cowdiva, exhibited along streets, on buildings, in parks, airport terminals, railway stations, etc – bringing in more than 1.5 million additional visitors to the city to experience the exhibit.

LARGEST ABSTRACT DRAWING BY TYRE MARKS

At an event called Burnout 2001, the world's largest abstract tyre drawing was produced in the Melbourne Docklands (Australia) by eight drivers who burned tyre marks on to an area of concrete measuring 70 x 30 m (229.6 x 98.4 ft). Thousands of excited spectators (art lovers and car lovers alike) watched as the drivers spun their wheels, where and as they pleased, in order to leave indelible rubber traces on the cement surface.

KIDS' STUFF

More than 200 children from Gaithersburg, Maryland, USA, created the biggest-ever finger painting on 19 July 1999. They used just their bare hands and feet to make the painting entitled *Ten Fingers, Ten Toes* (left), which measured 8.53 x 10.66 m (28 x 35 ft) in celebration of Sigma-Tau Pharmaceutical's first decade of commercial operations.

The largest-ever jellybean mosaic, made from 210,000 STARBURST® jellybeans, was created by 60 children from Public School 166, New York City, New York, USA. The 29.7-m² (320-ft²) mosaic was designed by Stephanie Logsdon and made at the Children's Museum of Manhattan on 18 and 19 April 2000. It was displayed on 22 April 2000 at the 'Easter Eggstravaganza' in Central Park.

www.guinnessworldrecords.com/fingerpainting
← ACCESS CODE: ‹54735›

LARGEST FLORAL SCULPTURE

A sculpture created to resemble an Aspirin package measured 76 x 26.48 m (249 ft 4 in x 86 ft 10 in) and was prepared and constructed in a week by 1,914 people, using 75,000 white chrysanthemums, 1,200,000 edelweiss and 71,500 polybags of Pangus kuning leaves. The event was organized by advertising agency Ammirati Puris Lintas for PT Bayer on 17 Oct 1999 in Jakarta, Indonesia.

LARGEST STONE SCULPTURE

The mounted figures of American confederate giants Jefferson Davis, Robert Edward Lee and Thomas Jonathan (Stonewall) Jackson are 27.4 m (90 ft) high and cover 0.5 ha (1.33 acres) on the face of Stone Mountain, near Atlanta, Georgia, USA. Sculptor Roy Faulkner (USA) worked on the mountain face for eight years and 174 days, between 12 Sept 1963 and 3 March 1972, with a thermo-jet torch, working with Walker Kirtland Hancock (USA).

LARGEST COTTON-WOOL SCULPTURE

In April 1999, after 11 months' work, Anant Narayan Khairnar (India) completed a sculpture of Mahatma Gandhi that was 2.28 m (7.5 ft) tall and weighed 20 kg (44 lb). Although it looks like marble, it is made entirely from white surgical cotton wool soaked in chemicals to make it harden.

LONGEST SAND SCULPTURE

The longest sand sculpture ever made was the GTE Directories Ultimate Sand Castle, at 26,375.9 m (86,535 ft) long, built by more than 10,000 volunteers at Myrtle Beach, South Carolina, USA, on 31 May 1991.

LARGEST HORNET NEST SCULPTURE

Yoshikuni Shiozawa (Japan) created a model of Mount Fuji by joining together 160 hornet nests, containing around 160,000 live yellow hornets. It was 3.766 m (12 ft 4 in) high and 4.8 m (15 ft 7.4 in) wide at the base.

THE SKY'S THE LIMIT

The Statue of Liberty (left), the world's heaviest statue, weighs 24,635 tonnes (54.31 million lb); 28 tonnes (61,729 lb) of copper, 113 tonnes (249,122 lb) of steel and 24,493 tonnes (53.99 million lb) of concrete foundation. She stands 92.99 m (305 ft 1 in) from the ground to the tip of her torch; 354 steps inside lead up to the crown; her nose is 1.48 m (4ft 9 in) long; and her index finger 2.44 m (8 ft). It was made by Frederic-Auguste Bartholdi, Richard Morris Hunt and Alexandre Gustave Eiffel, and France gave it to the USA in 1885 to commemorate liberty and friendship.

The world's tallest statue is a bronze Buddha that is 120 m (394 ft) high, 35 m (115 ft) wide and weighs 1,000 tonnes (2.2 million lb). It took seven years to build and was completed in Jan 1993 in Tokyo, Japan.

www.guinnessworldrecords.com/statueliberty
← ACCESS CODE: ‹54191›

MOST PAINT IN A PAINTING

In June 1998 the US duo The Art Guys (Michael Galbreth and Jack Massing) were commissioned to design a billboard entitled *ABSOLUTly A Thousand Coats of Paint*, to advertise the *Absolut* brand of vodka. The billboard, in Houston, Texas, USA, features a 4.3-m (14-ft) tall picture of an *Absolut* bottle and was covered with 1,000 coats, or 900 kg (1,984 lb) of paint, in various colours. Artist Bernard Brunon did the painting over a nine-month period.

LARGEST PAINTING

ID Cultur completed a huge painting of the sea, the size of four American football fields (8,586 m² or 92,419 ft²) at The Arena, Amsterdam, Netherlands, on 14 Aug 1996.

LARGEST 3-D BALLOON SCULPTURE

A display of 52,000 balloons in the shape of a football was shown at the Northampton Balloon Festival, Northampton, UK, between 14 and 16 Aug 1998.

MOST BEADS IN A WORK OF ART ◻USA

Liza Lou (USA) used 40 million glass beads to create a life-size kitchen and garden, first displayed at the Kemper Museum of Contemporary Art in Kansas City, Kansas, USA. If strung out, the beads would stretch about 703.7 km (380 miles), or the distance between Los Angeles and San Francisco.

LARGEST ART GALLERY

One has to walk 24 km (15 miles) to visit each of the 322 galleries in the Winter Palace at the State Hermitage Museum in St Petersburg, Russia, to see the nearly three million works of art and objects of archaeological interest.

MOST BATTERIES IN A WORK OF ART

Gilberto Macías Enríquez (Mexico) has made a European medieval castle using 11,380 button-shaped batteries. He has been collecting batteries since 1988 and by recycling them in this way, he aims to make people aware of the high toxicity of the nitric acid used in them. He has already collected over 33,000 batteries.

www.guinnessworldrecords.com/carsculpture

LONG-TERM PARKING

The art sculpture containing the most whole cars (right) is entitled *Long-term Parking* and was commissioned by the Cartier Foundation in Jouy-en-Josas, France. The towering structure contains 60 cars embedded in 1,600 tonnes (3.53 million lb) of concrete, rising over 20 m (65.6 ft) into the air. The automotive sculpture was created by artist Armand Fernandez, better known as Arman, who is celebrated for his 'accumulation' artwork.

GUINNESS WORLD RECORDS

cartoons and animation

MOST VALUABLE COLOUR ANIMATION CELL

One of the 150,000 colour animation cells from Walt Disney's *Snow White and the Seven Dwarfs* (USA), which premiered on Christmas Eve 1937, was sold in 1991 for the record price of £115,000 ($222,525).

LARGEST CARICATURE

Paul Slattery (UK) drew a caricature of footballer Alan Shearer (UK) that measured 18.89 x 9.24 m (62 x 30 ft 4 in) on a giant canvas. The drawing began with the subject's eye and was completed in three days by 22 April 1999. The caricature was hung off the Tyne Bridge, Newcastle, UK, and then auctioned off to raise funds for the NSPCC (National Society for the Prevention of Cruelty to Children).

MOST EXPENSIVE CARTOON

DreamWorks' *Prince of Egypt* (USA, 1998) cost $60 million (£37.5 million) to make. With 350 artists and animators working on the project, it took four years to create. With a running time of 90 minutes, the film has 1,192 special effects. The four-minute 'Red Sea' sequence alone took 350,000 man-hours to complete.

LONGEST-RUNNING CARTOON SERIES

Between 1933 and 1957, Max Fleisher's (USA) *Popeye the Sailor Man* had 233 one-reelers and a single two-reeler, *Popeye the Sailor Meets Sinbad the Sailor* (USA, 1936). A further 220 *Popeye* cartoons were produced for TV by King Features from 1960 to 1962, followed by 192 *All New Popeye* cartoons made for the CBS Network from 1978 to 1983. The series was first aired on TV in Sept 1956, making it the longest-running syndicated cartoon series.

HIGHEST-GROSSING ANIMATION

Walt Disney's *The Lion King* (USA, 1994) is the animation with the highest box-office gross, taking in $777.9 million (£486.1 million). The film featured the voices of celebrities Rowan Atkinson (UK), Jeremy Irons (UK) and Whoopi Goldberg (USA). Walt Disney's first full-length feature film, *Snow White and the Seven Dwarfs* (USA, 1937), which took four years to make, took $184.9 million (then £37.38 million) at the box office worldwide. If inflation is taken into account, this would be the equivalent of $1.63 billion (£1.02 billion) today.

www.guinnessworldrecords.com/smallestcomic
ACCESS CODE: ‹53243›

SIZE ISN'T EVERYTHING

The smallest comic of all time is *Agent 327* (left), drawn and written by Martin Lodewijk (Netherlands). It was published by Comicshop Sjors in June 1999, measuring just 2.58 x 3.7 cm (1 x 1.4 in). Printed in full colour, 2,000 copies of the 16-page comic were produced, and it was sold with a free magnifying glass. The record holder edition of the comic was called *Minimum Bug*.

MOST CARTOON SERIES EPISODES

Harry Bud Fisher's (USA) cartoon *Mutt and Jeff*, which began as supplement to *Pathé's Weekly* with the issue of 10 Feb 1913, continued as separate weekly reels from 1 April 1916 to 1 Dec 1926. Allowing for a gap between 1923 and 1924, for which no titles have been traced, there were at least 323 *Mutt and Jeff* episodes shown at the cinema. Several have been colourized and synchronized for video release, making them also the oldest cartoons in distribution.

MOST FAN MAIL IN HOLLYWOOD

Mickey Mouse was reported to have received 800,000 fan letters in 1933 – an average of 66,000 a month.

MOST CONSECUTIVE OSCAR NOMINATIONS

Walt Disney (USA) received nine consecutive Oscar nominations in the category Best Short Subject, Cartoons between 1942 and 1950, beginning the run with *Truant Officer Donald* (USA, 1941) and ending with *Toy Tinkers* (1949). From 1933 to 1940, Walt Disney was nominated for eight years in a row, including two films in 1933 and 1934, and three in 1939. During this period, he won a record eight consecutive times.

MOST EDITIONS OF A COMIC

The Mexican comic *Pepín*, which printed its first edition on 4 March 1936 as a weekly anthology of comics, eventually became a daily and ran until 23 Oct 1956 with a total of 7,561 issues. At the height of its popularity, sales were estimated at 320,000 copies a day, a number that doubled on Sundays.

LONGEST-RUNNING COMIC STRIP STILL SYNDICATED

The Katzenjammer Kids, Hans and Fritz, created by Rudolph Dirks (USA), was first published in the *New York Journal* on 12 Dec 1897 and was inspired by 'Max Und Moritz', an 1860s' German children's story. This comic strip is the oldest still in syndication and is now drawn by cartoonist Hy Eisman (USA) and syndicated to 50 newspapers.

MOST PROLIFIC CARTOONIST

Joe Martin (USA), creator of *Mr Boffo*, *Willy 'N Ethel*, *Cats with Hands* and *Porterfield*, produces 25 cartoon series, including single-panel cartoons and cartoon strips, totalling 1,300 cartoons a year. He has published 20,865 cartoons since 1978. Among hundreds of others, Martin's cartoons appear in newspapers such as the *Chicago Tribune*, the *San Francisco Chronicle* and the *Boston Globe*.

LARGEST CARTOON MUSEUM

The International Museum of Cartoon Art in Boca Raton, Florida, USA, has a collection of over 160,000 original animated drawings from 50 countries. The collection includes 10,000 books on animation and 1,000 hours of cartoons, interviews and documentaries on film and tape. The museum covers 25,000 ft² (2,322.5 m²) and there is also a 250-seat theatre.

ZORRO MAKES HIS MARK

Zorro, the world's most-filmed cartoon character, was originated by Johnston McCulley (USA), and has been portrayed in 69 films. Wise, brave, charming and romantic, Zorro was the first comic strip character to be the subject of a major feature film, *The Mark of Zorro* (USA, 1920) starring Douglas Fairbanks (USA). It appeared a year after the comic strip was printed, making Zorro the comic-strip character to make it fastest from strip to screen. The most recent Zorro movie, *The Mask of Zorro* (USA, 1998) starring Antonio Banderas (Spain, left), Anthony Hopkins and Catherine Zeta-Jones (both UK) opened in the US on 19 July 1998. It made $22.54 million (£13.69 million) in sales from 2,515 screens in its opening weekend.

www.guinnessworldrecords.com/zorro
ACCESS CODE: ‹50724›

LONGEST CARTOON STRIP

The longest cartoon strip measured 53.5 m x 1.5 m (175 ft 6 in x 4 ft 11 in) and was made up of 20 panels. Drawn by 26 cartoonists on 17 Oct 1999 in homage to the 16th-century Spanish humourist Quevedo, the strip was drawn during the *VI Muestra Iberoamericana de Humor Gráfico*, a cartoon festival held by the University of Alcalá, Spain.

MOST SWEARING IN AN ANIMATED MOVIE

The record for the most swearing ever featured in an animated movie

MOST COMIC READERS

In Japan, 40% of all printed material sold belongs to *manga* (the Japanese word for comic) sales. Throughout the 1990s, yearly sales of *manga* reached an average of 600 billion yen (£3.83 billion; $5.5 billion). Initially the *manga* storylines were primarily written for children (one of the characters with worldwide success is *Pokémon*), but about 50% of the material is now aimed at adults. *Manga* culture is so entrenched in Japanese society that it pervades every aspect of their lifestyle, from entertainment to design and education.

www.guinnessworldrecords.com/chickenrun

CHICK FLICK

The most plasticine ever used in a movie was squeezed and shaped during the filming of Aardman Animation's *Chicken Run* (UK, 2000) in which animators used 2,380 kg (5,247 lb) of plasticine. The 82-minute *Chicken Run* also holds the record for the longest stop-motion film, made up of 118,080 separate stop-motion special effects shots. In comparison, a live-action feature would use 500–1000 shots. Each plasticine character on the miniature film set had to be adjusted 24 times for every second of film.

Pictured right is DreamWorks Pictures co-founder Jeffrey Katzenberg (USA) with stars of the movie, Rocky (left) and Ginger (right).

is held by *South Park: Bigger, Longer and Uncut* (USA, 1999), which included 399 swear words during its running time. Despite its 'uncut' label, it ran between 75 and 82 minutes depending on which country it was released in. It also included 128 offensive gestures and 221 acts of violence.

LONGEST-RUNNING COMIC

The children's comic weekly *Comic Cuts*, published from 17 May 1890 to 12 Sept 1953 in London, UK, ran for 63 years 128 days. Its 3,006 editions offered 'A hundred laughs for half a penny'.

GUINNESS WORLD RECORDS™

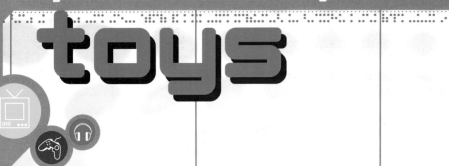

toys

LARGEST WATER PISTOL
The Monster XL water pistol of the Supersoaker range measures 99 cm (39 in) in length and can hold 4.6 litres (162 fl oz) of water. A pump-action stock pressurizes the water, which is fired from two nozzles that shoot to a range of around 10 m (33 ft).

FASTEST TIME TO SOLVE A RUBIK CUBE
Minh Thai, a 16-year-old Vietnamese refugee, won the World Rubik Cube Championship in Budapest, Hungary, on 5 June 1982. His winning time was 22.95 seconds. Before the timer started, each contestant was allowed to lift the cube and look at it for 15 seconds. The best time out of three attempts determined the winner.

FASTEST TIME TO SOLVE A RUBIK CUBE BLINDFOLDED
Ralf Laue (Germany), solved a Rubik Cube while blindfolded in a record-breaking time of 5 min 42 sec on 11 March 2001 in Los Angeles, USA.

LARGEST RUBBER-BAND BALL
EdVenture Children's Museum, Columbia, South Carolina, USA, made the world's largest rubber band ball, weighing 1,111 kg (2,450 lb), out of about 500,000 rubber bands. The ball is 1.32 m (4 ft 4 in) high, 1.37 m (4 ft 6 in)

TOY STOREY
A LEGO® tower built in Tallinn, Estonia, between 18 and 21 Aug 1998 (left), reached a height of 24.91 m (81 ft 12 in) and contained 391,478 plastic, eight-stud LEGO® bricks with no adhesive to help them stick together. More than 6,000 children participated in the event, organized by AS Rekato Ltd to beat the previous record, set in Moscow, Russia, in July 1998, by 25 cm (9 in).

The longest LEGO® structure is a millipede, measuring 610.8 m (2,003.93 ft) and comprising a total of 1,679,100 bricks. It was assembled by thousands of children at LEGOland® California, USA, between 8 and 13 July 2000. It has a total of 474 links and 948 legs. It was built in connection with the first LEGO® Maniac Kidvention.

www.guinnessworldrecords.com/lego
← ACCESS CODE: ‹48833›

wide and has a circumference of 4.34 m (14 ft 3 in). The project lasted from 1 Dec 2000 to 3 Feb 2001.

MOST CONSECUTIVE SWITCHES WITH ASTROJAX®
Maximilian Leidolf (Germany) performed a record 3,208 consecutive mid-air end ball switches with a set of AstroJax®, (three spherical balls on a rope with the central ball acting as a yoyo) in 24 min 52 sec on 12 Feb 2000.

FASTEST YO-YO
The fastest time to complete 100 m while throwing and catching a yo-yo is 13.9 seconds by Taro Yamashita (Japan) at the Yolympics, New Hampshire, USA, on 25 May 1996.

MOST YO-YO TRICKS
Eddie McDonald – alias 'Fast Eddie' (USA) managed to complete a record-breaking 35 yo-yo tricks in one minute on 22 July 1999.

GREATEST DISTANCE TRAVELLED BY A MODEL CAR
The greatest distance travelled by a 1:64-scale car is 342.9 km (213.07 miles) in 24 hours. This was set by Team USA at Derby HO Racing Club, UK, under BSCRA (British Slot Car Racing Association) rules between 15 and 16 Nov 1997.

Between 5 and 6 July 1986, the North London Society of Model Engineers team achieved a 24-hour distance record of 492.36 km (305.94 miles) for a 1:32-scale car, a Rondeau M482C Group C sports car.

FASTEST RADIO-CONTROLLED MODEL CAR
The highest speed achieved by a radio-controlled model car is 95.1 km/h (59.09 mph) by an Audi TT Coupe (scale 1:10) controlled by Petri Kivikoski, Leo Hongisto and Petri Väätäinen of the Audi Sport Team in Finland, on 7 June 2000. It was 20 cm (7.87 in) wide, 40 cm (15.74 in) long and weighed 2 kg (4.41 lb).

HIGHEST ALTITUDE BY A SINGLE KITE
Henry H Clayton and AE Sweetland (both USA) flew a single kite at a height of 3,801 m (12,471 ft) at the Blue Hill Weather Station, Milton, Massachusetts on 28 Feb 1898.

HIGHEST ALTITUDE BY A TRAIN OF EIGHT KITES
A record-breaking height of 9,740 m (31,955 ft) was reached by a train of eight kites over Lindenberg, Germany, on 1 Aug 1919.

FASTEST KITE
The fastest speed attained by a kite was 193 km/h (120 mph) flown by Pete DiGiacomo (USA) at Ocean City, Maryland, USA, on 22 Sept 1989. The kite was a modified Super 10 Flexifoil. Readings were taken by a local police officer with a radar gun.

MOST FIGURE-OF-EIGHTS WITH A KITE
On 25 Sept 1988 Stu Cohen (USA) achieved a record number of 2,911 figure-of-eights with a kite in one hour at Ocean City, Maryland, USA.

FASTEST POGO-STICK JUMPING
Ashrita Furman (USA) travelled one mile (1.6 km) on a pogo stick in 17 min 45 sec on the frozen runway of the Marambio Argentinian Research Base in Antarctica on 15 Jan 2000. He set this record in Antarctica as he wishes to have a record for setting a record on each of the seven continents.

READY TEDDY GO
Tornado Ted (UK, left) a teddy-bear mascot for the Northdale Horticulture Centre charity appeal (UK), flew a total distance of 251,925 km (156,539 miles) between 6 Jan and 7 Sept 1998, making him the world's most well-travelled teddy bear. Travelling with the RAF, the USAAF, the Red Arrows, the Slovak, Hungarian and Austrian Air Forces, British Airways, Cathay Pacific and British Midland, he flew in over 15 different types of aircraft, including Concorde, Tornado F3s, and VC10s, to raise money and awareness of the charity.

Ted has now gained celebrity status, including being made an honorary member of the Dutch Air Force 9G Club after flying in an F16. His latest flight was in a Hawk jet.

www.guinnessworldrecords.com/tornadoted
← ACCESS CODE: ‹48817›

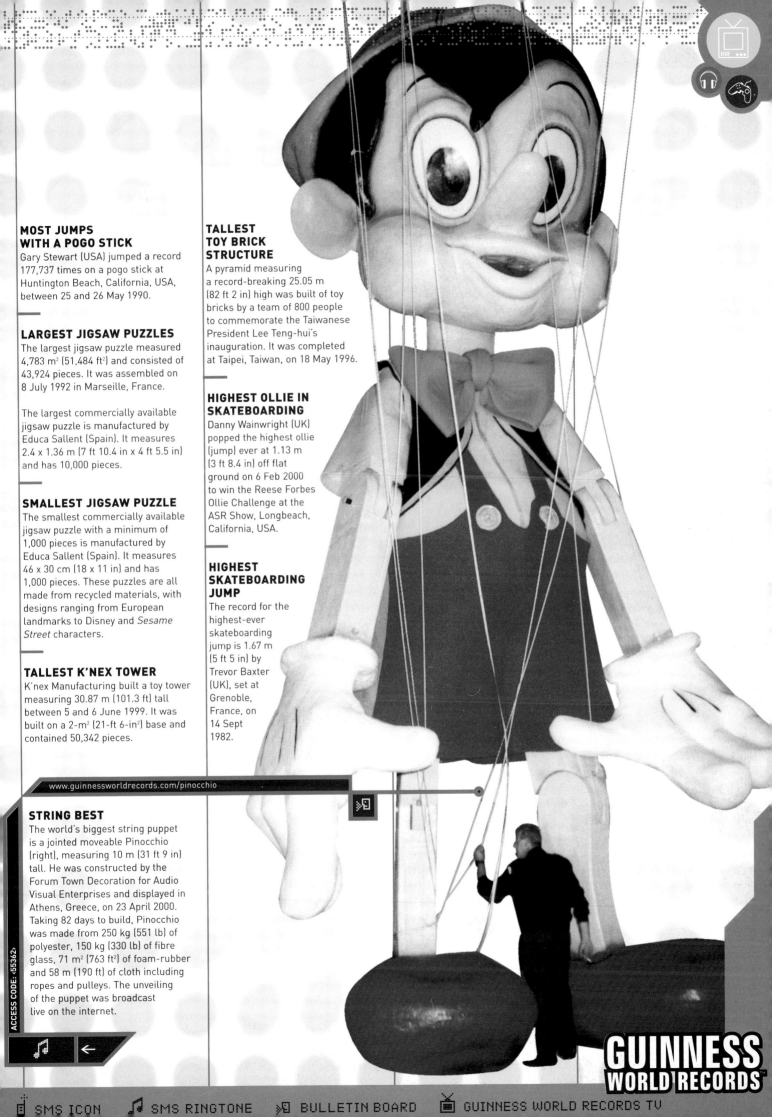

MOST JUMPS WITH A POGO STICK

Gary Stewart (USA) jumped a record 177,737 times on a pogo stick at Huntington Beach, California, USA, between 25 and 26 May 1990.

LARGEST JIGSAW PUZZLES

The largest jigsaw puzzle measured 4,783 m² (51,484 ft²) and consisted of 43,924 pieces. It was assembled on 8 July 1992 in Marseille, France.

The largest commercially available jigsaw puzzle is manufactured by Educa Sallent (Spain). It measures 2.4 x 1.36 m (7 ft 10.4 in x 4 ft 5.5 in) and has 10,000 pieces.

SMALLEST JIGSAW PUZZLE

The smallest commercially available jigsaw puzzle with a minimum of 1,000 pieces is manufactured by Educa Sallent (Spain). It measures 46 x 30 cm (18 x 11 in) and has 1,000 pieces. These puzzles are all made from recycled materials, with designs ranging from European landmarks to Disney and *Sesame Street* characters.

TALLEST K'NEX TOWER

K'nex Manufacturing built a toy tower measuring 30.87 m (101.3 ft) tall between 5 and 6 June 1999. It was built on a 2-m² (21-ft 6-in²) base and contained 50,342 pieces.

TALLEST TOY BRICK STRUCTURE

A pyramid measuring a record-breaking 25.05 m (82 ft 2 in) high was built of toy bricks by a team of 800 people to commemorate the Taiwanese President Lee Teng-hui's inauguration. It was completed at Taipei, Taiwan, on 18 May 1996.

HIGHEST OLLIE IN SKATEBOARDING

Danny Wainwright (UK) popped the highest ollie (jump) ever at 1.13 m (3 ft 8.4 in) off flat ground on 6 Feb 2000 to win the Reese Forbes Ollie Challenge at the ASR Show, Longbeach, California, USA.

HIGHEST SKATEBOARDING JUMP

The record for the highest-ever skateboarding jump is 1.67 m (5 ft 5 in) by Trevor Baxter (UK), set at Grenoble, France, on 14 Sept 1982.

www.guinnessworldrecords.com/pinocchio

STRING BEST

The world's biggest string puppet is a jointed moveable Pinocchio (right), measuring 10 m (31 ft 9 in) tall. He was constructed by the Forum Town Decoration for Audio Visual Enterprises and displayed in Athens, Greece, on 23 April 2000. Taking 82 days to build, Pinocchio was made from 250 kg (551 lb) of polyester, 150 kg (330 lb) of fibre glass, 71 m² (763 ft²) of foam-rubber and 58 m (190 ft) of cloth including ropes and pulleys. The unveiling of the puppet was broadcast live on the internet.

ACCESS CODE: ‹55362›

♪   ←

GUINNESS WORLD RECORDS

games and gambling

MOST FOOTBAG KICKS

Footbag, also known as hacky-sack, involves keeping a beanbag in the air using only your foot. Andy Linder (USA) managed 1,019 kicks of a footbag in five minutes on 7 June 1996.

The world record for keeping a footbag airborne is 63,326 consecutive kicks in 8 hr 50 min 42 sec by Ted Martin (USA) at Lions Park, Mount Prospect, Illinois, USA, on 14 June 1997.

The doubles record is 132,011 consecutive kicks by Gary Lautt and Tricia George (both USA), at Chico, California, USA, on 21 March 1998.

FASTEST TIDDLYWINKS MILE

The fastest time for a tiddlywink to be propelled over a measured mile (1.6 km) is 2 hr 25 min 24 sec by a relay team of 23 people from AGS Home Improvements Ltd of Newton Abbot, Devon, UK, on 20 Nov 1999.

FASTEST TIDDLYWINKS POTTING

Allen Astles from the University of Wales (UK) potted 10,000 winks in 3 hr 51 min 46 sec at Aberystwyth, Dyfed, Wales, in Feb 1966.

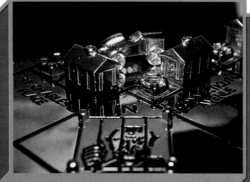

PASS 'GO' AND COLLECT $2 MILLION!
USA

An exclusive $2-million (£1.15-million) *Monopoly* set (left) was created by the jeweller Sidney Mobell, San Francisco, USA, in 1988 – the most expensive *Monopoly* game ever. The board is made from 23-carat gold. Rubies and sapphires top the chimneys of the solid gold houses and hotels, and the dice has 42 full-cut diamonds for spots!

By 1999, *Monopoly* had been played by 500 million people worldwide. *Monopoly* is the most played and best-selling board game in the world, sold in 80 countries and produced in 26 different languages.

www.guinnessworldrecords.com/monopoly
← ACCESS CODE: ‹43436›

YOUNGEST CHESS GRAND MASTER

Aged 14 yr 59 days, Etienne Bacrot (France) became the youngest person to qualify as an International Grand Master on 22 March 1997.

MOST SIMULTANEOUS CHESS OPPONENTS

The most games played simultaneously is 310 by Ulf Andersson (Sweden) at Alvsjö, Sweden, between 6 and 7 Jan 1996. Of the 310 games played Ulf Andersson was defeated in only two.

SLOWEST CHESS MOVE

Francisco Torres Trois took 2 hr 20 min to play his seventh move against Luis Santos at Vigo, Spain, in 1980 – the slowest move since time clocks were introduced in the 19th century.

LEAPFROG OVER THE MOST STANDING PEOPLE

Andy Wiltz (USA) leapfrogged over 10 standing people during a local variety show at Seaman High School, Topeka, Kansas, USA. All 10 people were over age 16 and over 1.53 m (5 ft) tall. Without using a trampoline, Wiltz had a running start before he pushed off the shoulders of the first person in line and flew through the air over all 10 heads.

MOST EXPENSIVE BOARD GAME

The most expensive commercially available board game is the deluxe version of *Outrage!* (by Imperial Games of Southport, Merseyside, UK). The game, which is based on stealing the Crown Jewels from the Tower of London, retails at £3,995 ($6,290).

LARGEST BOARD GAME

The world's biggest commercially available board game is *Galaxion*, created by Cerebe Design Int (Hong Kong). The board measures 83.8 x 83.8 cm (33 x 33 in).

LARGEST PRIZE IN A POKER TOURNAMENT

John Duthie (UK) won £1 million ($1,423,000) in the Ladbroke's Casinos Poker Million tournament held at the Hilton Casino, Douglas, Isle of Man, on 19 Nov 2000.

Chris 'Jesus' Ferguson (USA) won $1.5 million (£995,000) in the 31st World Series of Poker tournament, held at the Binion's Horseshoe Casino, Las Vegas, Nevada, USA, on 15 May 2000.

LARGEST POKER POT

The largest pot accrued in a poker tournament is $4.5 million (£3.1 million) for the final hand of the 31st World Series of Poker between TJ Cloutier (Canada) and eventual winner Chris 'Jesus' Ferguson (USA).

TWIST 'N' SHOUT!

The world's biggest *Twister* board (left), measuring 18.28 x 6 m (60 x 19 ft 8.5 in) was created by the digital printing company Vision International of Salt Lake City, Utah, USA, in Feb 1998. The classic American party game was originally created by Milton Bradley in 1967, but on 6 Feb 1998 it was simultaneously enjoyed by hundreds of Vision International employees. They intertwined their limbs with their co-workers' and twisted themselves into all sorts of contorted shapes before collapsing into heaps of laughter on the massive coloured board.

The record number of participants in a game of *Twister* is 4,160 people at the University of Massachusetts, Amherst, USA, on 2 May 1987. The game was won by Allison Culler.

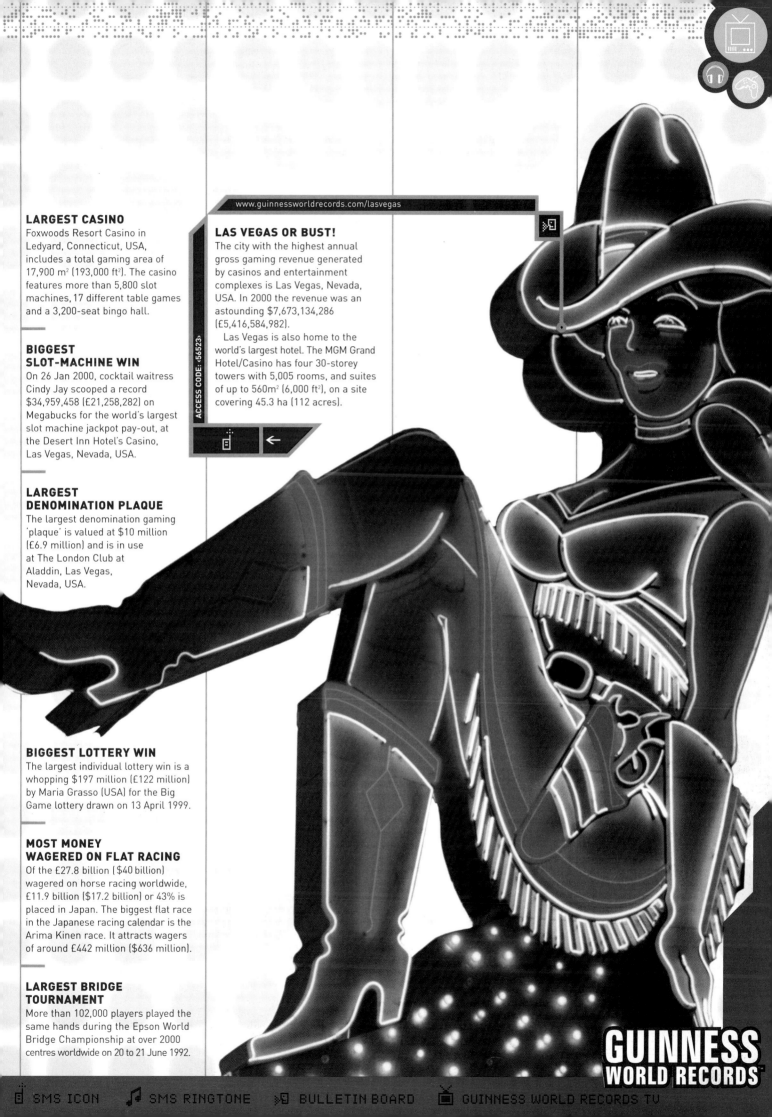

LARGEST CASINO

Foxwoods Resort Casino in Ledyard, Connecticut, USA, includes a total gaming area of 17,900 m² (193,000 ft²). The casino features more than 5,800 slot machines, 17 different table games and a 3,200-seat bingo hall.

BIGGEST SLOT-MACHINE WIN

On 26 Jan 2000, cocktail waitress Cindy Jay scooped a record $34,959,458 (£21,258,282) on Megabucks for the world's largest slot machine jackpot pay-out, at the Desert Inn Hotel's Casino, Las Vegas, Nevada, USA.

LARGEST DENOMINATION PLAQUE

The largest denomination gaming 'plaque' is valued at $10 million (£6.9 million) and is in use at The London Club at Aladdin, Las Vegas, Nevada, USA.

BIGGEST LOTTERY WIN

The largest individual lottery win is a whopping $197 million (£122 million) by Maria Grasso (USA) for the Big Game lottery drawn on 13 April 1999.

MOST MONEY WAGERED ON FLAT RACING

Of the £27.8 billion ($40 billion) wagered on horse racing worldwide, £11.9 billion ($17.2 billion) or 43% is placed in Japan. The biggest flat race in the Japanese racing calendar is the Arima Kinen race. It attracts wagers of around £442 million ($636 million).

LARGEST BRIDGE TOURNAMENT

More than 102,000 players played the same hands during the Epson World Bridge Championship at over 2000 centres worldwide on 20 to 21 June 1992.

www.guinnessworldrecords.com/lasvegas

ACCESS CODE: ‹56523›

LAS VEGAS OR BUST!

The city with the highest annual gross gaming revenue generated by casinos and entertainment complexes is Las Vegas, Nevada, USA. In 2000 the revenue was an astounding $7,673,134,286 (£5,416,584,982).

Las Vegas is also home to the world's largest hotel. The MGM Grand Hotel/Casino has four 30-storey towers with 5,005 rooms, and suites of up to 560m² (6,000 ft²), on a site covering 45.3 ha (112 acres).

GUINNESS WORLD RECORDS

theme parks and rides

OLDEST AMUSEMENT PARK

Bakken, located in Klampenborg, Denmark, opened in 1583 and is currently the oldest operating amusement park in the world. In medieval Europe, most major cities featured what is the origin of the amusement park – a pleasure garden. These gardens were usually on the edges of the city, featuring live entertainment, fireworks, dancing, games and some primitive amusement rides. Most closed down during the 1700s, and Bakken, located in woodland beside a lake, is the only one to survive.

MOST VISITED THEME PARK

Disneyland Tokyo is the most visited theme park in the world. An estimated 16.5 million people passed through its gates in 2000 (17.4 million in 1999). During the 1990s, the park had an estimated 179.11 million visitors, the most visited park of the decade. This is well above the total population of Japan (which is about 126 million).

LARGEST TEMPORARY AMUSEMENT PARK

The world's largest temporary amusement park springs up around the Oktoberfest Beer Festival in Munich, Germany, each year, and attracts up to 50 portable mechanical rides. The centrepieces of the amusement park are several world-class steel roller coasters, such as the five-inversion 'Olympia Looping Bahn'. This transportable roller coaster was designed by the world famous Bavarian roller-coaster designer, Anton Schwarzkopf.

OLDEST ROLLER COASTERS

'Leap-The-Dips', a traditional side-friction roller coaster at Lakemont Park, Altoona, Pennsylvania, USA, was built by the Edward Joy Morris Company in 1902. It was closed to the public in 1985, seemingly at the end of its life, but was fully restored and re-opened in 1999.

The oldest continually operating roller coaster is 'The Scenic Railway' at Luna Park, St Kilda, Vic, Australia. It originally opened to the public on 13 Dec 1912 and has

remained in operation ever since. This traditional wooden roller coaster was designed by La Marcus Adna Thompson (USA), who is regarded as the father of the modern roller coaster.

TALLEST ROLLER COASTER

'Superman The Escape' at Six Flags Magic Mountain, Valencia, California, USA, a dual-track, vertical reverse-point, free-fall roller coaster, designed by Intamin AG of Switzerland, features 15-seater gondolas which, when launched along the track by means of a linear induction motor, reach a height of 126.5 m (415 ft) before falling vertically back along the same track at a speed of 160 km/h (100 mph).

TALLEST LOOPING ROLLER COASTER

'Viper' at the Six Flags Magic Mountain in Valencia, USA, is 57.30 m (188 ft) high. It turns upside down seven times at a speed of 112.65 km/h (70 mph).

LONGEST WOODEN ROLLER COASTER

'The Beast', built in 1979 at Paramount's Kings Island, near Cincinnati, Ohio, USA, is the longest traditional wooden laminated-track roller coaster at 2,286 m (7,400 ft). A new roller coaster called 'Son of Beast' is being built and will hold the following records – tallest wooden roller coaster (66.5 m or 218 ft), tallest wooden roller coaster drop (65.2 m or 214 ft), fastest wooden

COMING FULL CIRCLE

The 'British Airways London Eye' (above), designed by London architects David Marks and Julia Barfield, is the world's biggest observation wheel with a diameter and height of 135 m (443 ft). It had its first 'flight' on 1 Feb 2000. The wheel turns continuously during normal operation. Each of the 32 fully enclosed high-tech capsules carries up to 25 passengers and completes a full 360° rotation every 30 minutes. At the highest point this giant wheel offers views across a 48-km (30-mile) radius of London.

www.guinnessworldrecords.com/londoneye

ACCESS CODE: ← ‹51872›

roller coaster (125.5 km/h or 78 mph), most loops in a wooden roller coaster (although it will have only one). The loop is contained in a steel section incorporated into the laminated wooden tracks – standard wooden structures would not be able to withstand the forces of a loop.

ROLLER COASTER WITH STEEPEST DROP

The steepest drop of any steel roller coaster in the world is at the 'Oblivion' in Alton Towers, UK, at 87.5°. The drop is 60 m (197 ft) long and the two-row cars reach a speed of up to 113 km/h (70 mph). Oblivion can accommodate up to 1,900 riders per hour.

The record for the steepest drop in a wooden roller coaster is 58.5° and belongs to the 'Cyclone' in Astroland, New York City, New York, USA.

RIDING HIGH

Cedar Point Amusement Park, Sandusky, Ohio, USA, (left, above), which dates back to 1870, has 68 rides – more than any other single amusement or theme park. This park also has the most roller coasters with 14 – two traditional wooden-track and 12 steel-track roller coasters featuring, among others, the 'Millennium Force', which opened in 2000 and is taller than the Statue of Liberty.

A team of seven (left) holds the record for most roller coaster rides in 24 hours. Patricia Byron, Denise Lau Cortopassi, David Escalante, John Sutherland, David Curley, John Green and Steven Wilson (all USA) rode on 40 different roller coasters at eight different parks from 14 to 15 Oct 2000.

www.guinnessworldrecords.com/cedarpoint

ACCESS CODE: ← ‹51868›

EARLIEST FERRIS WHEEL

The original Ferris wheel, designed by engineer George Washington Gale Ferris Jr (USA), was erected in 1893 in Chicago, Illinois, USA. It had a maximum height of 80 m (264 ft) above the ground, with a diameter of 76 m (250 ft) and a circumference of 240.8 m (790 ft). Each of the 36 fully enclosed gondolas could carry up to 40 passengers in revolving chairs and the wheel weighed 1,300 tonnes (2.87 million lb) unladen.

OBSERVATON WHEEL WITH BIGGEST CAPACITY

British naval officer Walter Bassett constructed his first and largest observation wheel for the Oriental Exhibition, Earl's Court, London, UK, in 1895. It had 10 first-class and 30 second-class cars, each carrying 30 people. It could carry up to a total of 1,200 passengers to a maximum height of 84 m (276 ft), but was scrapped in 1906.

FERRIS WHEEL WITH THE WIDEST DIAMETER

On 18 March 1999 'The Cosmoclock 21' opened at Yokohama City, Japan. It is 100 m (328 ft) in diameter and 112.5 m (369 ft) high, equivalent to a 30-storey building. It has 60 gondolas with eight seats in each. It is illuminated by laser beams and features acoustic effects by sound synthesizers. Fireworks are presented at 15-minute intervals to light up the wheel.

LONGEST MECHANICAL RODEO RIDE

Pauline Farrington (UK) was able to ride a mechanical bull set at level seven for a duration of 58.1 sec in Paris, France, on 30 Sept 2000.

LONGEST VERTICAL DROP RIDE

At 'Drop Zone' at Kings Island theme park in Cincinnati, Ohio, USA, the 40 riders are seated in a circle around a central pole. They fall for 80 m (262 ft 6 in) from a 91.4-m (300-ft) tower, reaching speeds of up to 105 km/h (65 mph). Only 43 m (141 ft) of the 80 m (262 ft) are free-falling. While braking, riders experience 4 G of force (four times the force of gravity) meaning that they effectively weigh four times their usual weight.

OLDEST CAROUSEL IN OPERATION

The world's oldest operating carousel is the Vermolen Boden-Karussel at Efteling Theme Park in Kaatsheuvel, Netherlands, and was built in 1865. It was originally powered by horses, but was later restored and is now electrically driven.

TALLEST SPEED WATER SLIDE

The tallest water slide in the world is 'Insane' at Beach Park, Fortaleza, Brazil, which is 41 m (135 ft) high. Riders reach speeds of up to 104 km/h (64.6 mph) in only 4 seconds – quite uncomfortable as the riders wear only their bathing costumes. This slide is as tall as an 11-storey building.

TALLEST ENCLOSED WATER FLUMES

The 'Turbo Twisters' at Myrtle Waves, Myrtle Beach, South Carolina, USA, which opened in 1994, are 22.8 m (75 ft) high and 61 m (200 ft) long – the world's tallest tubular water flumes. Riders reach speeds of up to 55 km/h (34 mph) in complete darkness.

HIGHEST WAVE-POOL WAVE

The highest artificial waves are 2.8 m (9.18 ft) high, and are in the Valley of the Waves at Sun City, South Africa.

MOST WATERSLIDE FLUMES

The Splash Garden, Rokko Island, Kobe, Japan, has a record 50 waterslide flumes on a single tower.

LARGEST WAVE POOL

According to the World Waterpark Association, the largest wave pool, often called an artificial sea, covers 16,000 m^2 (172,000 ft^2 or four acres) and can be found at Siam Park, Bangkok, Thailand.

www.guinnessworldrecords.com/steeldragon

ACCESS CODE: '55358'

BIG DIPPER 📺 JP

The 'Steel Dragon' (left), which opened on 1 Aug 2000 at Nagashima Spaland, Mie, Japan, is a non-inversion steel-track giga-coaster, designed by Steve Okamoto. It is the fastest full-circuit roller coaster on earth and also holds the world records for the longest drop and the longest track. It lifts riders 95 m (311 ft 8 in) before dropping them 93.5 m (306 ft 9 in), while accelerating to 149 km/h (92.5 mph). Before completing the amazing 2,479 m (8,133 ft) of track, riders have additional 74-m (243-ft) and 64-m (210-ft) hills ahead of them. In total, riders are dropped 365 m (1,200 ft).

GUINNESS WORLD RECORDS

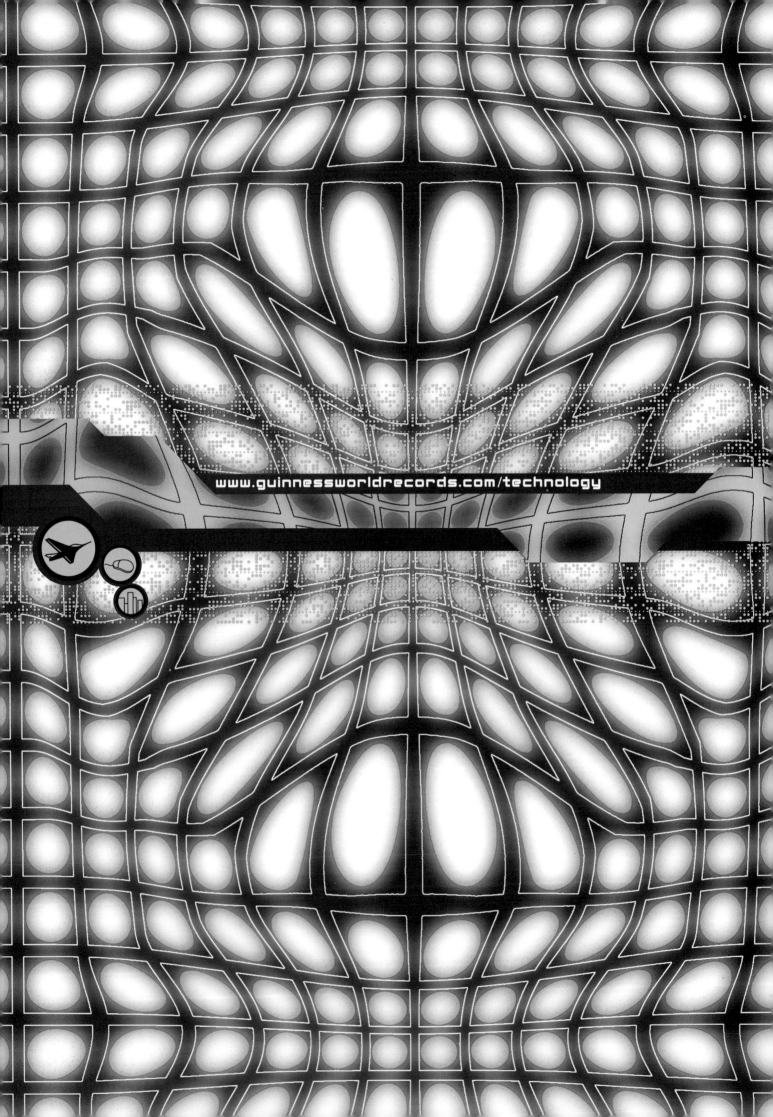

www.guinnessworldrecords.com/technology

technology

computers 1

FASTEST-SELLING PC GAME

The role-playing PC game *Diablo II* by Blizzard Entertainment sold more than one million copies within the first two weeks of being released in June 2000. By Jan 2001 it had sold 2.75 million copies worldwide. The original *Diablo* role-playing computer game has sold more than 2.3 million copies since its release in 1997.

OLDEST GIGA PET

The world's oldest-known Giga Pet is Elvis, owned by Jessica Troiano (USA). According to its manufacturer, Tiger Electronics, Elvis' 'life' began on 3 July 1997. It claimed the record on 13 Jan 1998, at the age of 194 days, when its batteries ran out.

BEST-SELLING COMPUTER

About 30 million Commodore 64 computers were sold between the model's launch in 1982 and its commercial decline in 1993. The computer contained 64K RAM, 16K graphics and 16K sound.

LENGTHIEST COMPUTATION FOR A YES/NO ANSWER

In 1986, the 20th Fermat number, $2^{220}+1$ (named after mathematician Pierre de Fermat 1601–65) was tested on a CRAY-2 supercomputer to see if it was a prime number. After 10 days, the answer 'no' came back, making this the longest-ever computer computation to give a yes/no answer.

WOULD YOU CREDIT IT?

Just 60% the size of a credit card, the smallest computer keyboard with a full complement of alphanumeric, symbol and command keys was patented on 18 March 1997 by David Levy (USA). The keyboard (left) has 64 keys, which are big enough to be operated with a thumb, yet the whole device measures just 7.62 x 3 cm (3 x 1.2 in).

www.guinnessworldrecords.com/tinykeyboard
◄— ACCESS CODE: ‹47158›

BEST-SELLING SOCCER GAME

The FIFA series of games, developed by EA Sports (USA), have sold more than 16 million units. Launched in PC format on 27 Nov 1998, the game features a full pop soundtrack, including recording artists such as Fatboy Slim (UK).

SHORTEST COMPUTER INSTRUCTION MANUAL

The Apple iMac personal computer comes with an instruction manual that consists of just six pictures and 36 words, allowing the computer to live up to the sales pitch that a user can just take it out of the box and plug it in.

LARGEST COMPUTERISED ROBOT DOG

The RS-01 RoboDog, manufactured by RoboScience (UK), measures 82 x 67 x 37 cm (32 x 26 x 14 in). RoboDog has an internal computer and connects remotely to the internet via a radio transmitter. It can monitor and read out emails sent to its owner, and responds to voice commands.

BEST-SELLING FLIGHT SIMULATOR

MS Flight Simulator was released by Microsoft in April 1992 and had sold a total of 21 million units by June 1999. *Flight Simulator 2000* allows players to 'fly' Concorde, the Boeing 737-400 and Boeing 777-300, the Learjet 45, the Bell 206B JetRanger helicopter and the Sopwith Camel.

BEST-SELLING DRIVING SIMULATOR

Gran Turismo Real Driving Simulator, a Sony PlayStation game, had sold a record seven million units worldwide by Feb 2000. The game was developed by Polyphony Digital, a satellite company of Sony Computer Entertainment. A sequel, *Gran Turismo 2*, was launched in 1999, and *Gran Turismo 2000* is one of the headline titles showcasing the

'Emotion Engine' processor of the PlayStation2, which was released in Japan on 4 March 2000.

LARGEST COMPUTATION

SETI@home, which was launched by the University of California at Berkeley, California, USA, on 17 May 1999, had made a total of 7.7×10^{20}, or 300 billion billion, computer calculations as of July 2000. SETI@home is a scientific experiment that harnesses the power of hundreds of thousands of internet-linked computers in the search for extraterrestrial intelligence. Participants download and run a free program that analyses data from radio telescopes.

FASTEST COMPUTER

The fastest supercomputer is the RS/6000 *ASCI White*, which was completed by IBM in June 2000. The size of two basketball courts, this supercomputer is capable of 12 trillion calculations per second. It has more than six trillion bytes (terabytes) of memory along with 160 terabytes of storage memory – enough to hold six times the whole book collection of the US Library of Congress – the largest library in the world. In one second it could solve a problem that would take one person with a calculator 10 million years to complete. The purpose of *ASCI White* is to allow the testing of nuclear weapons using computer simulations instead of detonating actual bombs.

MOST 'HUMAN' COMPUTER PROGRAM

A computer running the program *Albert* was awarded the 1999 Loebner Prize for the 'most human' computer system after convincing 11% of judges that it was a real person. *Albert* won $2,000 (£1,250) for its author, Robby Garner (USA). *Albert* is a program that a user can communicate with using human speech and is capable of holding a quirky, spontaneous conversation full of sarcastic and witty one-liners.

BIGGEST SCANNER

The SLC972C colour scanner, produced by Widecom Group Inc of Brampton, Ontario, Canada, has a 1.82-m (6-ft) scan width. Unveiled at

YU'RE IN THE MONEY

The most expensive computer game to be developed is the Dreamcast game *Shenmue*, which cost over £12 million ($20 million). The project (left) took seven years to complete and was the brainchild of Yu Suzuki (Japan), the head of Sega's game-development AM2 division. Suzuki built his reputation on arcade titles – credits include *Virtual Fighter* (1993), *Virtual Racing* (1992) and *Out Run* (1986).

Shenmue is about a Japanese high-school student who begins a quest to avenge the death of his father. The game is polished with ultra-realistic scenery, in-depth plot and martial arts fighting. There are also over 200 characters to interact with, all of whom lead their own lives within the game.

www.guinnessworldrecords.com/dreamcast
ACCESS CODE: ‹53483›

PERSONAL BEST

The Compaq H3360 iPaq Pocket PC (above), a PDA (personal digital assistant) launched in 2001, has a 206-MHz processor and a 240 x 320-pixel touch-sensitive colour LCD screen, making it the most powerful PDA in the world. It has 64 MB of RAM and 16 MB of ROM, and weighs 170 g (6 oz), including its battery.

The Palm range of Personal Digital Assistants from 3Com are the best-selling PDAs, having sold over five million units since their launch in 1996. 3Com dominates the US market for PDAs, with a 73.6% market share as of Jan 2000.

www.guinnessworldrecords.com/pda

ACCESS CODE:
← ‹53693›

a Californian trade show in May 1999, it is targeted at people who work in industries such as automotive and aircraft manufacturing and shipbuilding, who deal with huge drawings that require a scanning capacity of this size.

FASTEST-SELLING VIDEO GAME

The Nintendo Game Boy title *Pokémon Yellow* was released in the USA on 18 Oct 1999 and had sold one million copies within 10 days. If you played each one of the 100 million Game Boys that exist in the world for just 60 seconds without stopping, it would take 190 years.

BEST-SELLING HAND-HELD GAME SYSTEM

The world's most popular video game system is the Nintendo Game Boy, which sold more than 100 million units between 1989 and 2000 – an average of more than 1,000 units per hour. Nintendo currently occupies more than 99% of the US market through its *Game Boy*, *Game Boy Pocket* and *Game Boy Colour* units. More than 1,000 Game Boy titles are now available worldwide.

www.guinnessworldrecords.com/playstation

CRASH BANDICOOT WALLOP

The fastest-selling video game console is Sony's PlayStation2 (PS2) with a record 980,000 units of the game, which features the character Crash Bandicoot (right), being sold in the 48 hours following its release on 4 March 2000. That is more than 10 times the sales scored by the original PlayStation console over the same period when it was launched in 1996. The console currently costs JPY39,800 (£233.50; $369.62). The character Crash Bandicoot was developed by Naughty Dog (USA), a company of 10 people.

←

GUINNESS WORLD RECORDS

computers 2

LARGEST NUMBER CRUNCHED

The largest number ever 'crunched' is $(10^{211}-1)/9$: ie multiply 10 by itself 211 times, subtract 1 from the total and then divide the result by 9. The number consists of 211 digits, all of which are ones. A group called 'The Cabal', led by Herman teRiele, found two factors (whole numbers by which a larger number can be divided) to this massive figure. The factors themselves were 93 and 118-digits long. Number crunching, or 'factorisation' as it is known, is very useful in writing complex codes and in coded military communications.

LARGEST PERSONAL COMPUTER MANUFACTURER

In 1998 US firm Compaq sold a total of 13,275,204 PCs – the equivalent of one every 2.38 seconds. Compaq provides the systems for 75% of the world's cashpoint transactions and 60% of all lotteries.

FIRST PROGRAMMABLE ELECTRONIC COMPUTER

The 1500-valve Colossus, formulated by Prof Max Newman and built by TH Flowers, was run in Dec 1943 at Bletchley Park, Bucks, UK, to break codes created by the German-made Lorenz-Schlussel-zusatz 40 machine, or 'Tunny' as the British called it. Colossus was not declassified until 25 Oct 1975.

MOST DAMAGING VIRUS

The CIH virus or 'Chernobyl' virus has affected one million PCs since it was first triggered on 26 April 1998, the 12th anniversary of the nuclear reactor disaster in Chernobyl, USSR. According to the Taipei authorities, the virus was written by Chen Ing-hau, whose initials make up the name of the virus. CIH irreversibly alters a computer's BIOS chip, which is soldered on to the motherboard. The damage can make a computer totally useless.

BEST CHESS COMPUTER

IBM's Deep Blue was the first computer to beat a chess grandmaster when it defeated Gary Kasparov (Azerbaijan) in Feb 1996. The victory was part of a six-match series that Kasparov ultimately won 4-2. In 1997 a new and improved Deep Blue returned to beat Kasparov in a second series. The computer, which could consider a mind-boggling 200 million positions a second, won the series by 3.5 points to Kasparov's 2.5.

MOST ADVANCE ORDERS FOR A VIDEO GAME

More than 325,000 US consumers put down advance orders and deposits for the Nintendo 64 game, *The Legend of Zelda: Ocarina of Time*. The game hit the stores on 23 Nov 1998.

BEST-SELLING GAME

The Nintendo game *Super Mario Brothers* has sold a total of 40.23 million copies worldwide since its launch in 1983.

CORE VALUE

Steve Jobs (USA, left), the co-founder of Apple Computer Inc, is the world's lowest paid Chief Executive Officer – he receives a salary of just $1 (62 pence) a year. But the Apple chief gets a lot more than his annual wage – in Jan 2000, Jobs received a Gulfstream luxury airliner and 10 million stock options for agreeing to stay with Apple as its permanent chief executive. From 31 Jan 2000, he was able to exercise the options to buy and sell half of these 10 million shares. Jobs co-designed the Apple II computer, which ignited the personal computer revolution in the 1970s. He then led the development and marketing of the Macintosh computer in the 1980s, presiding over the growth of Apple into a $2-billion (£1.4-billion) company.

www.guinnessworldrecords.com/applemacchief
ACCESS CODE: ‹54029›

MOST CHARACTERS HANDLED BY SOFTWARE

Japan's Personal Media Corporation has developed a computer operating system called B-right/V2, which is capable of handling 128,175 different characters as part of its TRON code system. This includes most of the characters in all the world's alphabets, and special characters such as braille. The program was launched in 1999 and runs on all IBM PC-compatible computers.

BEST-SELLING GAMES CONSOLE

The Sony PlayStation console had sold around 79.61 million units worldwide by Jan 2001, making it the world's best-selling games console. Sony Computer Entertainment Inc spent more than £181 million ($300 million) developing the console, which runs hit games such as *Tomb Raider* and *Final Fantasy VII*. Around 430 million PlayStation software units have been produced.

LONGEST-RUNNING COMPUTER GAME CHARACTER

Nintendo's 'Mario' character, a plumber by trade, first appeared in the arcade version of *Donkey Kong* in 1981. Mario has since made an appearance in over 70 games, although he is a 'playable' character in only around 30 of these. In the original *Donkey Kong* game, Mario was a carpenter initially called 'Jumpman', but he was renamed after the president of Nintendo noticed the character resembled his landlord, Mario. The character's look owes a lot to the limitations of early computer technology. On the low-resolution hardware of the early 1980s, it was easier to animate a moustache than a mouth, and a cap was easier to draw than hair.

LOVESICK COMPUTERS

The virulent 'I Love You' computer virus (left) was the most widespread the world has ever known. It was first detected in Hong Kong on 1 May 2000. Within four days it had mutated into three different generations. The Love Bug combined sophisticated programming with a cunning appeal to the human psyche. When users opened the 'I Love You' attachment, the virus was instantly forwarded to all the addresses in the victim's e-mail directory. Governments, multinational corporations and small businesses were all affected. At its height, the virus forced the closure of the White House and US State Department e-mail networks. Figures published on 8 May 2000 by Trend Micro Inc. showed that 'I Love You' had infected 3.1 million computers worldwide.

MOST PARTICIPANTS IN A VIDEO-GAME TOURNAMENT

On 24 March 1996 a record 9,066 people participated in Compile Corporation's second annual 'Puyo Puyo' tournament, held at Makuhari Messe, Hiroshima, Japan.

www.guinnessworldrecords.com/lovebug
ACCESS CODE: ‹52411›

MOST ADVANCED GAMES CONSOLE

Microsoft's Xbox, which launched in the US in Autumn 2001, is powered by a 733 MHz Intel chip, the fastest of any games console. The Xbox's graphics processor, which runs at 250 MHz, is also the field leader. The Xbox's rivals, the Sony PlayStation 2 and the Nintendo Gamecube, have clock speeds of 300 and 405 MHz respectively. The PlayStation 2 has a graphics chip that runs at 150 MHz. The Gamecube's graphics chip runs at 202.5 MHz. The PlayStation 2, however, also supports DVD and audio CD formats.

MOST TREES WITH MICROCHIPS

During 1999, 90,000 trees in Paris, France, were implanted with tiny 3-cm (1.4 in) glass and carbon-fibre electronic microchips. The chips were programmed with information about each individual tree's health. The microchip-tagging system allowed the city's tree surgeons to identify trees in need of treatment more precisely. About 1,200 trees die every year in Paris due to the effects of human and car pollution, winter salting and dehydration.

FASTEST E-COMMERCE SET-UP

In 1999 Computer Experts of Brighton, UK, set up the website http://www. jcamping.instant-net.co.uk and received its first order in a record-breaking 20 min 6.83 sec.

OLDEST COMPUTER

The first fully-automated, software-driven computer was designed and run by Tom Kilburn and Freddie Williams (both UK) on 21 June 1948. They used a 17-instruction program on a machine called 'Baby', which calculated the highest factor of 2^{18}. 'Baby' is 4.87 m (16 ft) long, 2.13 m (7 ft) high and 0.6 m (2 ft) deep and its wires and vacuum tubes occupied an entire room. The computer had 1,024 bytes of memory and could work out seven instruction types. 'Baby' could perform a maximum of 700 operations per second – modern machines can carry out tens of millions.

www.guinnessworldrecords.com/minimouse

ACCESS CODE: ‹56137›

MINI MOUSE

The smallest computer mouse is the Cat Eye FinRing (right). Made by Luckytech Technology (Taiwan), it is worn on the index finger like a ring. The wireless device is powered by two small batteries and it has three thumb-operated buttons. The user's finger movement is tracked by internal sensors, and information is transmitted to a receiver plugged into the computer's mouse port. Users can roam up to 8 m (26 ft 3 in) away from the receiver and still control the cursor accurately.

BIGGEST STORAGE CAPACITY

Ted Williams (UK) has invented a new type of double-sided solid-state memory that can hold as much as 270 gigabytes/cm^2 (1,742 gigabytes/in^2) of random access memory (RAM). This means that it could hold 10.8 terabytes on a chip the size of a credit card. Solid-state memory involves no moving parts.

THINNEST DIGITAL DISC

The *ThinDisc*, introduced on 1 Dec 2000, is five times thinner than normal CDs or DVD discs. Designed to be played in virtually any CD or DVD drive, the *ThinDisc* is also very flexible and can be wrapped around a drink can without breaking.

EARLIEST COMPUTER GAME

Spacewar was the earliest computer game, first implemented between 1961 and 1962 at the Massachusetts Institute of Technology, USA, on a PDP-1 computer. It was a space combat game in which two ships, revolving around a central star, had to shoot each other down. Written for fun by students at MIT, this game was an important precursor to all modern computer games. The PDP-1 computer first became available in 1960 and cost $120,000 (£56,900) – the equivalent today of $930,000 (£654,000). Fifty units were sold in total. The PDP-1 was the ancestor of the microcomputer and was designed for use in scientific institutions. It had a memory of 4K and operators used a keyboard and paper tape to input data.

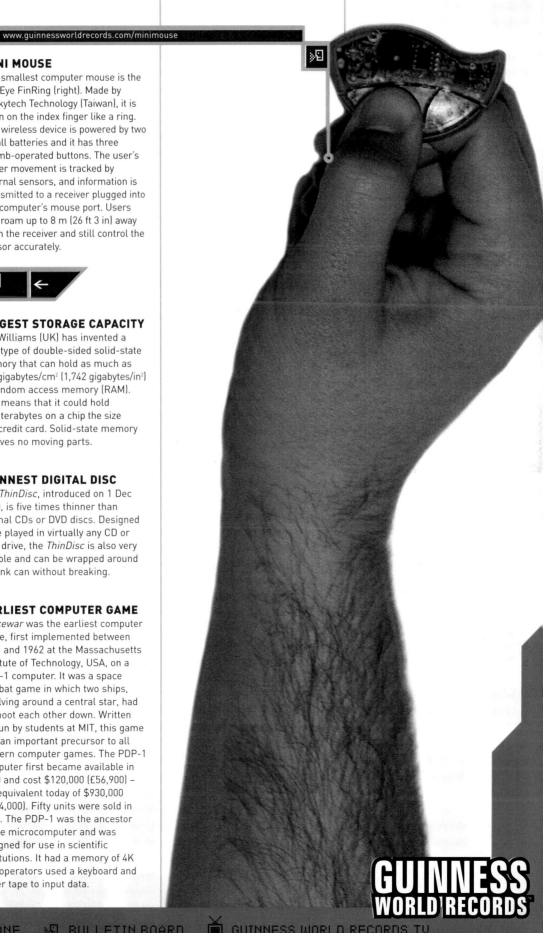

GUINNESS WORLD RECORDS

LONGEST-RUNNING WEBCAM
Computer scientists at Cambridge University (UK) were so frustrated with trekking down the corridor to find that the coffee pot was empty, that they rigged up a camera and a computer so that they could see instantly if there was any coffee left. In Nov 1993 Daniel Gordon hooked the camera up to the World Wide Web, where live images of the now-famous coffee pot have been available ever since at web address: www.cl.cam.ac.uk/coffee/qsf/coffee.html. It will be turned off in late 2001.

HIGHEST ANNUAL ADVERTISING REVENUE
The year 2000 saw a rise in internet advertising revenues to a record $2.9 billion (£1.94 billion), a 52.6% increase on 1999 figures.

LARGEST INTERNET ADVERTISER
The largest internet advertiser in 2000 was General Motors, who spent £32.09 million ($47.9 million), a 96.5% increase on their advertising expenditure in 1999.

LARGEST BRAND ADVERTISER
The bookstore Barnes & Noble (USA) spent $15,903,892 (£10,654,446) on brand advertising in 2000, a 55.8% increase on their advertising expenditure in 1999.

WRIST BANDS
The smallest MP3 player and watch is the SV-SD75 by Panasonic (left), which measures 50.8 x 49.2 x 15.0 mm (2 x 1.9 x 0.59 in). It comes with 64MB memory on an SD memory card and is designed to be worn as a watch or around the neck. It connects to a home PC using a USB cable and, as it has no moving parts, it will never 'jump' or 'skip' while playing music.

www.guinnessworldrecords.com/mp3player
← ACCESS CODE: ‹56559›

INDUSTRY SECTOR WITH MOST INTERNET ADS
The industry sector that spent the most on internet advertising in the year 2000 with a combined expenditure of £363,204,731 ($542,155,702) was Media and advertising. Retail came second, spending a grand total of £342,234,362 ($510,853,232).

WEBSITE WITH HIGHEST ADVERTISING REVENUE
Yahoo! Inc, based in Sunnydale, California, USA, generated an advertising revenue of $442,336,726 (£296,333,306) from their website Yahoo.com in 2000, according to Competitive Media Reporting (CMR).

COSTLIEST E-MAIL
In 1997 a subsidiary of US-based petroleum company Chevron Corporation paid $2.2 million (£1.3 million) to settle a sexual-harassment lawsuit filed by four female employees. Evidence presented by the women's lawyers included e-mail records listing 25 reasons why beer is supposedly better than women. In settling, Chevron Corporation denied the women's allegations.

EARLIEST LIVE DEBUT PERFORMANCE OF A CLASSICAL WORK ONLINE
On 19 Nov 1997 Sir Paul McCartney (UK) performed his new classical work, the 75-minute symphonic poem *Standing Stone*. It was broadcast live from Carnegie Hall, New York City, New York, USA, in a multi-faceted presentation of radio, TV, interactive online interview and internet audio and video broadcast across the World Wide Web.

BIGGEST FINE FOR AN INTERNET CRIME
US anti-abortion activists who operated a site called The Nuremberg Files, containing 'Wanted' posters with the names and addresses of doctors who perform abortions, had to pay more than $107.7 million (£65 million) in damages on 3 Feb 1999.

SMALLEST WEB SERVER
The web page of the Wearables Laboratory at Stanford University, California, USA, is supported by Jumptec's DIMM-PC, a 'matchbox' server measuring a tiny 6.86 x 4.32 x 0.64 cm (2.7 x 1.7 x 0.25 in), making it only slightly higher and wider than a box of matches but just one third of the thickness. The server weighs a mere 20 g (0.71 oz).

BIGGEST MULTILINGUAL WEB BROADCAST
In Dec 1997 the opening and closing ceremonies of the Third Conference of the Parties of the United Nations Framework Convention on Climate Change, which took place in Kyoto, Japan, were broadcast at the same time via the internet in seven languages — Arabic, Chinese, English, French, Japanese, Russian and Spanish.

BIGGEST INTERNET GOLF TOURNAMENT
More than 11,000 players signed up for the 1999 Jack Nicklaus Online Golf Championship. The final round was held on 10 Dec 1999. Chet Stone (USA) won the title and $5,000 (£3,492) after 36 holes of matchplay on a digitally-rendered version of the golf course at the Pelican Hill Golf Club, California, USA.

BIGGEST SCHOOLS INTERNET PROJECT
The world's biggest schools internet project is Tesco SchoolNet 2000 (UK), launched in Sept 1998. The aim of the project is to create an electronic 'Domesday Book' for the 21st century, made up of children's investigations into their local communities. By March 2001 up to 133,986 pupils and 17,312 schools had registered. The project was meant to finish at the end of 2000, but is so popular that it is continuing.

LARGEST URL
The largest internet URL ever to be displayed is www.rawmart.com. A global commodities trading site, its

ACCESS ALL AREAS
A record 11 million people watched Madonna (left) perform a concert at the Brixton Academy, London, UK, on 28 Nov 2000. It was broadcast live on the internet by Microsoft Network online. MSN e-mailed their 75 million Hotmail users to let them know of the event and also had homepage promotions in 17 different languages on more than 30 internet sites across the world.

The largest concert that took place exclusively via the internet was on 24 Sept 1998. Roger Taylor and five band members performed a 45-minute gig at the Cyberbarn, Thursley, Surrey, UK. The audience consisted of a record 9,804 people who logged on via the internet – which was the only way to see the concert.

www.guinnessworldrecords.com/madonna
← ACCESS CODE: ‹54431›

TRADING PLACES

If you can't find what you want in a shop, the Internet Mall (above) has a record 27,000 on-screen virtual shops and more than one million subscribers in the UK alone. It is available in more than 150 countries, with products ranging from popcorn to car insurance.

The most expensive internet domain name – business.com – was sold by entrepreneur Marc Ostrofsky (USA) on 1 Dec 1999 for $7.5 million (£4.6 million). This tops the $3.3 million (£2,340,000) paid by Compaq for altavista.com and the $3 million (£2,130,000) paid for wine.com.

www.guinnessworldrecords.com/
internetmall

ACCESS CODE:
← ‹54144›

name was painted on the side of the carrier ship *E-Trader* in letters 4.1 m (13.45 ft) high in July 2000. The full address was 118.59 m (389 ft) long.

LONGEST URL

The longest URL belongs to http://llanfairpwllgwyngyllgogerychwyrndrobwlllllantysiliogogogoch.co.uk/, a site about an ancient rural village in North Wales, UK called Llanfairpwllgwyngyllgogerychwyrn-drobwlllllantysiliogogogoch. The name means 'Saint Mary's Church in the hollow of the white hazel, near a rapid whirlpool and the church of Saint Tysilio of the red cave'.

MOST ATTACKS IN A HACKING COMPETITION

A total of 5.23 million attacks were recorded during eWeek's 17-day-long Openhack III competition, in which

the latest security software, Pitbull, from Argus Systems Group Inc was probed for weaknesses by the hacking community. Despite the offered prize of $50,000 (£35,000), not one hacker was able to penetrate Pitbull. During Openhack I and II, the software that was being tested was successfully accessed.

MOST SEARCHED-FOR SPORTSWOMAN

The Russian tennis player Anna Kournikova is reported to be the most searched-for sportswoman on the internet.

MOST SEARCHED-FOR SPORTSMAN

The American golfer Tiger Woods is reported to be the most searched-for sportsman on the internet.

MOST REMOTE CONCIERGE

Anna Morris (USA) works 130 km (80 miles) from the hotel where she is employed as a concierge. Guests at the Westin Hotel, Santa Clara, California, USA, speak to Anna via an interactive webcam and she can see guests via a camera in the hotel. So instead of driving through heavy traffic each day, she can work from home.

www.guinnessworldrecords.com/napster

NAPPY DAYS

Shawn Fanning (USA, right) was a 19-year-old computer science student at Northeastern University, Boston, Massachusetts, USA, when he wrote the source code for the music file-sharing program Napster in mid-1999. Napster has since become the world's fastest-growing internet company, with more than 32 million users worldwide. The program got its name from Shawn's high-school nickname – the Napster – a reference to his perpetually 'nappy' (messy) hair.

ACCESS CODE: ‹90746›

GUINNESS WORLD RECORDS

internet 2

MOST DOWNLOADED CYBERPET

More than 14 million people worldwide have downloaded *MOPy*, a lifelike pet fish screensaver, since it was first released in Oct 1997.

MOST CYBERSTAR VARIATIONS

There are an estimated 2,000 variations of *Dancing Baby*, a cyberstar originally created as an animated 3-D graphics model in Oct 1996 by Kinetix, a subsidiary of Autodesk Inc. (USA). *Dancing Baby* is the only character originated on the internet that has achieved a popular following prior to its appearance in mainstream media. The internet spurred the creation of new variations of *Dancing Baby* by amateur animation artists on hundreds of websites. The official *Dancing Baby* page has an average monthly view rate of 55,000.

HIGHEST CYBERSTAR MERCHANDISE SALES

During 1998 *Dancing Baby* T-shirt sales in the USA totalled more than $2.8 million (£1.7 million) wholesale. Music CD sales exceeded $425,000 (£256,000) wholesale, while international and US wholesale figures of the electronic *Dancing Baby* doll topped $550,000 (£331,845). Other merchandise across the USA, Australia and Europe grossed over $900,000 (£543,019).

ONE FOR THE BOOKS

Amazon.com (left), founded in 1994 by Jeff Bezos (USA), opened its virtual doors in July 1995 and has now sold products to more than 13 million customers in over 160 countries, making it the largest online bookshop. It has a catalogue of 4.7 million books, CDs and videos, including titles presently out of print. Although there are over three million books actively in print, no one could build a bookstore large enough to hold them. The largest known conventional bookstores carry 170,000 titles. When Bezos started this business, he worked out of an office from his garage in Seattle, Washington, USA – wrapping book orders himself and delivering them to the post office in the family car.

MOST QUESTIONS ASKED ONLINE

On 17 May 1997 Sir Paul McCartney was asked over three million online questions in 30 minutes. Fans questioned him during a web event to promote his album *Flaming Pie*.

MOST STOCK TRADING ONLINE

During Jan 2000, 44.6% of all stock trading in South Korea was executed online, according to the Korea Securities Dealers Association. A total of 51,000 billion won ($45.5 billion or £28.1 billion) worth of stocks listed on the Korea Stock Exchange and the Kosdaq were traded online.

LARGEST SINGLE E-COMMERCE TRANSACTION

Internet tycoon Mark Cuban (USA) bought a Gulfstream V business jet over the internet in Oct 1999. The jet changed hands for $40 million (£25 million).

LARGEST FREE E-MAIL PROVIDER

Hotmail is the world's largest free web-based e-mail service provider and had more than 70 million subscribers in April 2001. Every day Hotmail adds 100,000 new users. It is available in 230 countries and has 12 million unique logins per month.

EARLIEST REGISTERED DOMAIN NAME

Symbolics.com was the first domain name ever registered, according to NetNames Ltd. It was registered on 15 March 1985.

MOST POPULAR TOP-LEVEL DOMAIN

'.com' is the most popular top-level domain. It is used by 22.3 million hosts, out of a possible 35.3 million in existence worldwide in April 2001. There are no general restrictions relating to who can register because '.com' is a top-level domain (TLD) and is considered to be global.

LARGEST CONCENTRATION OF DOMAIN NAMES

The greatest concentration of domain names is in the New York Metropolitan area, USA. These domain names account for 4.8% of the world's total.

LARGEST HOLDER OF DOMAIN NAMES

US company Namezero holds a record 1,307,300 domain names – more than any other company in the world.

YOUNGEST INTERNET COUNTRY CODE

Palestine, still battling for international recognition as an independent state, acquired autonomy in cyberspace on 22 March 2000. The Internet Corporation for Assigned Names and Numbers (ICANN), which regulates net addresses, granted the Palestinian National Authority its own two-letter suffix for online real estate. As with other so-called country codes, such as '.fr' for France and '.it' for Italy, the Palestinian group will be able to register addresses under its own domain, '.ps'.

MOST POPULAR COUNTRY-LEVEL DOMAIN

As of March 2001 the most popular country-level domain is '.uk' (United Kingdom) with over two million domain registrations, according to NetNames Ltd. The UK is closely followed by Germany ('.de'). Although America has the most internet sites, few of them use '.us' in their URL.

EASY DOES IT

easyEverything (left) in Times Square, New York City, New York, USA, is the world's biggest internet café. It opened on 28 Nov 2000 and has 760 computer terminals. The 5,221-m² (17,130-ft²) cybercafé has two floors of PCs offering internet access to the web 24 hours a day, seven days a week. The New York café was the first easyEverything to open in the USA. Previously, branches had been confined to Europe. By April 2001 there were 21 easyEverything internet cafés around the world – five in London, two in Amsterdam, two in Barcelona and one each in New York, Edinburgh, Glasgow, Manchester, Brussels, Antwerp, Rotterdam, Berlin, Munich, Rome, Paris and Madrid. The creator of easyEverything is Greek-born, UK-based businessman, Stelios Haji-Ioannou.

MOST VOTES RECEIVED BY A WEBPAGE

Between 2 pm on 4 Oct and midday on 11 Nov 1999, the MTV Europe Music Awards website (www.mtv-vote.com), powered by Compaq, registered 1,643,863 votes. The site featured a built-in spam-trap to prevent hackers setting up an automated voting system to register thousands of bogus votes.

MOST ELECTRONIC BIRTHDAY GREETINGS

To mark the birthday of 'Posh Spice' (Victoria Beckham), a website on www.dotmusic.com was reserved for birthday greetings from 2 pm on 9 April until 2 pm on 10 April 2000. In the 24-hour period 2,600 messages were received from all over the globe.

MOST DAY-TO-DAY WEBSITE VISITS

The Microsoft Corporation website www.msn.com received 10.5 billion page views in March 2000, according to web statisticians, alexa.com. Of this total figure, 62% of page views came from Microsoft's free e-mail provider, www.hotmail.msn.com.

MOST VISITED ROYAL WEBSITE

The memorial page of the official website of the British monarchy was visited by 14 million people in Sept 1997, following the death of Diana, Princess of Wales. A record 580,000 messages of condolence were also left on the site.

MOST VISITED WEBSITE FOR AN EVENT

During the Fédération Internationale de Football Association (FIFA) World Cup held in France between 10 June and 12 July 1998, the official website, www.france98.com, received a record total of 1,137,218,296 hits.

On 29 June 1998 this website received a record 235,356 hits in one minute alone. On 30 June 1998, this site received 10,290,429 hits in just 60 minutes. On the same date it also had a record 73,030,828 hits in 24 hours.

HIGHEST PERCENTAGE OF AIRLINE TICKETS SOLD OVER THE INTERNET

The airline company easyJet sells 86.6% of all of its tickets via its website www.easyjet.com (as of March 2001). The airline specializes in flights in Europe and keeps the prices of tickets to a minimum by selling directly to its customers, by using less congested airports and by only using one type of aircraft, the Boeing 737-300.

www.guinnessworldrecords.com/battledotnet

BATTLE IT OUT

Battle.net, owned by Blizzard Entertainment, provides players of games such as *Diablo 2* (featuring characters such as The Sorceress, right) and *Starcraft*, with an internet arena where they can play multiplayer games on the web. Since its launch in 1997, its popularity has risen to over 8.2 million active accounts that log more than six million games daily. Peak concurrent usage tops more than 210,000 players per day. This is the largest free online game service.

ACCESS CODE: ‹56574›

gadgets

SMALLEST PERSONAL DIGITAL ASSISTANT

The REX PC Companion, built in 1998 by Franklin Electronic Publishers, Burlington, USA, is the size and weight of a credit card – 8.6 x 5.3 x 0.63 cm (3.4 x 2.1 x 0.25 in) and 39.7 g (1.4 oz). The user can slide it into any compatible laptop computer and then download. REX can also store up to 2,500 personal items, such as names, addresses and appointments.

MOST VERSATILE PEN

The Space Pen range made by Fisher Space Pen Co (USA) uses special nitrogen-pressurised cartridges to dispense visco-elastic ink. This allows these pens to work perfectly upside down, and under a wide range of environmental conditions including extreme heat and cold, underwater and even the zero gravity of space. They were first used in space on the *Apollo 7* mission in 1968 and have become the standard pen for astronauts, including those currently working on the International Space Station. Before the Space Pen was invented, astronauts used pencils when they wanted to write anything in space. The ink is pressurised at nearly 50 psi and is fed to a tungsten

carbide ball point. Inside the cartridge, the ink has a consistency similar to that of thick rubber cement. The shearing action of the ball point rolling in its socket liquifies the ink, allowing it to flow out like any normal ball point pen.

MOST 'INTELLIGENT' PEN AND PAPER

The Swedish company Anoto has created a digital pen that allows the user to digitally store up to 50 fully written pages in its memory. This can be transferred directly to a

www.guinnessworldrecords.com/gpswatch
ACCESS CODE: ‹56399›

WATCH OUT!

The smallest-ever GPS watch is the Casio PAT2GP-1V (left), measuring 58.5 x 51.5 x 21.0 mm (2.3 x 2.0 x 0.8 in). It receives data from the constellation of Global Positioning System (GPS) satellites in order to pinpoint the location of the wearer within an accuracy of 10 m (33 ft), anywhere on Earth. It can be connected to a home computer to plan map routes, which can be stored in the watch itself.

The Casio WQV1D-8CR is the most advanced digital watch camera and weighs only 32 g (1.12 oz). Its 1 MB of memory allows up to 100 pictures, 28,000 pixels each, to be taken and stored. Images can also be uploaded to a PC.

nearby computer or (via bluetooth technology) straight to any computer in the world over the internet. The pen writes on special digital paper that enables the pen to locate its exact position on the paper. The paper is divided into a grid system with squares of 2 x 2 mm (0.08 x 0.08 in). Inside each square is a pattern of dots that is different depending upon where one looks on the paper. The huge number of possible dot combinations means that, theoretically, a single sheet of paper larger than Asia and Europe combined could be created, and the pen would still know exactly where it was.

PUBLICATION WITH THE MOST USELESS INVENTIONS

Chindogu, (Japanese for 'weird tool') is the art of inventions that appear to be useful but, on closer inspection, reveal their utter uselessness. Kenji Kawakami (Japan) has written *101 Unuseless Japanese Inventions*, containing *chindogu* inventions such as tiny dusters that slip on to a cat's paws, enabling it to clean dusty surfaces as it walks around.

MOST ENERGY-EFFICIENT SHOE

The Electric Shoe Company (founded by Trevor Baylis (UK) and Texon Int) aims to develop a shoe that generates electricity through the act of walking. In Aug 2000 prototypes were tested by Trevor Baylis and John Grantham (UK) during a 120-km (75-mile) trek into the Namibian desert. At the end of the walk, Baylis made a phone call to Richard Branson in the UK, using a mobile phone that had been charged by the shoes.

MOST SUCCESSFUL CLOCKWORK RADIO

In 1993 inventor Trevor Baylis (UK) created a spring system that, when wound for several seconds, would give several minutes airplay. Freeplay Energy refined his idea and have to date produced 2.5 million units of these self-sufficient wind-up radios.

LIGHTEST BINOCULARS

The Minolta UCIII binoculars weigh just 120 g (4.23 oz) and are available

WALKING AWAY WITH THE GLORY

The Walkman was developed by The Sony Corporation in 1979 and has proved to be the most successful portable music system ever. The first model on the market was the TPS-L2. Cassette Walkman sales to April 2001 total between 200 and 250 million units. Up to April 1999 the CD Discman had sold 54 million units and the MiniDisc Walkman 6.9 million units. As the Sony Walkman has evolved through the years, it has become more and more compact. The Sony NW-E3 (left) is the latest version and has no moving parts. This MP-3 player measures 8.1 x 3.2 x 1.46 cm (3.18 x 1.26 x 0.57 in) and weighs 33 g (1.16 oz). It has 64 MB of Flash memory embedded, can be connected to a PC via a USB connection and can store up to two hours of music.

www.guinnessworldrecords.com/walkman

with magnifications of six and eight. The 6 x 16 version can focus on objects just 1 m (3.3 ft) away.

MOST ADVANCED HOLOGRAPHIC UNDERWATER CAMERA

The HOLOMAR underwater holographic camera was developed by a team led by Aberdeen University, Scotland (UK). It can record 3-D images of objects as small as 100 microns across in up to 100 litres (26 gal) of water.

LARGEST MOBILE-PHONE PENETRATION

Finland is the country with the greatest mobile-phone penetration. There are 651 cellular telephone subscribers for every 1,000 people.

www.guinnessworldrecords.com/thincamera

ACCESS CODE: ‹56541›

THROUGH THICK AND THIN

The Ultra-Pocket digital camera (below), designed and developed by SMaL Camera Technologies in Massachusetts, USA, is only 6 mm (0.2 in) thick and weighs a mere 63.3 g (0.14 lb) – including the lithium-ion rechargeable battery. This, the thinnest camera ever, is the size of a credit card and can store approximately 40 colour images on the included 8 MB MultiMediaCard. This card can also be upgraded to a larger memory capacity. Images can be uploaded to a PC via a USB cable. The camera's full dimensions are 85.6 x 6 x 54 mm (3.4 x 0.2 x 2.1 in). The Ultra-Pocket was introduced at the International Consumer Electronics Show 2001 in Las Vegas, Nevada, USA, on 8 Jan 2001.

PENKNIFE WITH MOST BLADES

The Year Knife was made in 1822 by Joseph Rodgers & Sons (UK). Initially, it had 1,822 blades – one for every year. The tradition of adding a new blade for every year was continued. Stanley Works (UK) Ltd of Sheffield, S Yorks, UK, restored the knife in 1999 and added a final silver blade to mark the coming of the year 2000.

SMALLEST VIDEO TRANSMITTER

The AVX900T3 measures 0.9 x 1.9 x 0.5 cm (0.36 x 0.75 x 0.20 in) and is manufactured by Supercircuits of Texas, USA. Designed to be used in covert operations and micro-robotics, it can transmit video images over a distance of more than 230 m (750 ft), despite being smaller than the average thumb and weighing less than 7.1 g (0.35 oz).

S M a L
ULTRA-POCKET *DIGITAL*

Autobrite™ Exposure

SMaL Lens 6.3mm

GUINNESS WORLD RECORDS

robots

MOST EXPENSIVE DOMESTIC ROBOT

The most expensive commercially available domestic robot is the TMSUK IV robot, developed by the Japanese Thames company. It was first exhibited in Tokyo, Japan, on 23 Jan 2000. The 99.8-kg (220-lb) humanoid robot stands 1.22 m (4 ft) high and costs £30,000 ($43,037) to buy. It is totally obedient, can be controlled remotely by mobile phone, runs errands and even gives massages.

FASTEST INDUSTRIAL ROBOT

The LR Mate 100I high-speed conveyance robot can carry objects for up to 3 km (1.86 miles), can move up and down 2.5 cm (1 in) and can move back and forth over 30 cm (12 in) in just 0.58 seconds. Its speed and movement capabilities enable fast and precise loading and unloading in factory and assembly situations. The robot was developed by Japanese company Fanuc in 1997 and is estimated to be 79% faster than previous models.

LARGEST ROBOTIC ARM IN SPACE

The Canadarm 2, built by the Canadian Space Agency measures 17.5 m (57.7 ft) in length and weighs 1,641 kg (3,618 lb). It was attached to the International Space Station on 22 April 2001 during a spacewalk by US astronaut Scott Parazynski and Canadian astronaut Chris Hadfield.

HANDLE WITH CARE

The most advanced robotic hand available is the BH8-262 BarrettHand (left), launched by Barrett Technology Inc (USA), in April 2001, which has three articulated fingers. Unlike more conventional robotic grippers, which work with a simple pincer movement, the BH8-262 can move its three fingers independently over their full range in either direction in less than one second. Weighing just 1.18 kg (2.6 lb), the hand can apply a force of up to 2 kg (4.4 lb) at each fingertip, allowing it to pick up and handle a variety of objects. The BarrettHand does not need to be physically customized for each specific job. Instead, all changes to its function can be accomplished using software.

www.guinnessworldrecords.com/robothand
← ACCESS CODE: ‹56227›

MOST HUMANOID ROBOT

The 1.6-m (5-ft 3-in) P3 robot was launched by the Japanese company Honda in 1997. P3 resembles a normal human, with arms and legs. It can walk sideways and backwards, as well as walk up and down stairs and on sloped floors. The robot, with its 3-D sight, can also turn its head, step over obstacles, change direction and correct its balance if pushed. It took 11 years, 150 engineers and £49 million ($80 million) to produce and was designed to be used in nursing or in tasks too dangerous or strenuous for humans to do – such as bomb disposal.

MOST WIDELY USED INDUSTRIAL ROBOT

PUMA (Programmable Universal Machine for Assembly), designed by Vic Schienman (Switzerland) in the 1970s and manufactured by Swiss company Staubli Unimation, is the most commonly used robot in university laboratories and automated assembly lines.

MOST EMOTIONALLY RESPONSIVE ROBOT

Kismet, created by Cynthia Breazeal (USA) at the Massachusetts Institute of Technology, is a robotic head powered by 15 networked computers and 21 motors. It is designed to recognize different emotions while interacting with humans and to respond to them. Nine of the 15 computers are used to control Kismet's vision alone.

MOST SUCCESSFUL BIONIC EAR

In 1978, 48-year-old Rod Saunders (Australia) was the first person to be fitted with a bionic ear (or cochlear implant). Saunders had become profoundly deaf after a head injury. Designed by the Department of Otolaryngology at the University of Melbourne, Vic, Australia, the prototype became available commercially in 1982. By 2000, more than 20,000 people worldwide had bionic ears, including more than 10,000 children. The bionic ear, made by Australian firm Cochlear Limited, has been implanted in 10 times more patients than its nearest rival.

MOST ADVANCED ROBOTIC ARM

In 1997 the US company Barrett Technology Inc developed a $250,000 (£153,000) robotic arm, complete with cables that act like human tendons, which can hold weights of up to 5 kg (11 lb) in any position. The arm has a total of seven gearless joints, driven by brushless motors. Potential uses include cleaning, assisting people in and out of the bath, opening doors and preparing meals.

MOST ADVANCED CYBERNETIC LIMB IMPLANT

On 24 Aug 1998 Kevin Warwick of the University of Reading, Berkshire, UK, had a cybernetic silicon chip implanted in his forearm. This enabled a computer to monitor him, using signals transmitted from the chip. Kevin was able to operate computers and other electronic items such as lights and heaters without actually touching them.

BEST-SELLING ROBOT LAWNMOWER

The RL500 Robomower, developed and manufactured in Israel by Friendly Robotics, has sold over 5,000 units worldwide. It retails for under £1,000 ($1,450). This battery-powered 'cutting edge' gardener can cut an area equivalent to a tennis court on a single charge.

ROBOHOP!

Sandia National Laboratories, USA, have developed experimental 'hopper' robots (left) that use combustion-driven pistons to jump to heights of 9 m (29.5 ft). These small robots have potential applications in planetary exploration, where several hoppers could be released by a lander to survey the surrounding landscape. The idea for these robots came from Rush Robinett (USA) of Sandia's Intelligent Systems and Robotics Center while he was catching grasshoppers to use in trout fishing. The high-jumping hoppers could theoretically travel 100 hops on a single tank of fuel. On planetary bodies like the Moon and Mars, where the force of gravity is lower, these hoppers would be able to jump higher and travel further.

www.guinnessworldrecords.com/jumpingrobot
← ACCESS CODE: ‹56526›

MOST LIFELIKE ROBOT FISH

The world's most lifelike robot fish has been developed by Mitsubishi Heavy Industries in Japan in a four-year project. A whole series of robot fish have been constructed, and only the closest inspection can distinguish them from the real thing. Future applications include the development of super-fast submarines and robot fish that could scour the oceans detecting sources of pollution. Mitsubishi is also developing robotic replicas of extinct fish for use in virtual aquariums.

FASTEST-SELLING ENTERTAINMENT ROBOT

When Sony Corporation's pet robot dog (AIBO Entertainment Robot ERS-110) made its debut on Sony's Japanese website on 31 May 1999, 3,000 – retailing at £1,439 ($2,066) each – were sold within 20 minutes. AIBO ('partner' in Japanese) is 27.9 cm (11 in) tall and can recognize its surroundings with a built-in sensor. It can be programmed to perform tricks or 'play' on its own. On 1 June 1999, 2,000 AIBOs became available over the internet in America, and the initial rush to buy the robot caused webservers to crash.

CHEAPEST ROBOT

The world's cheapest robot cost just $1.75 (£1.15) as it was made from the remains of a Sony Walkman at the Los Alamos National Laboratory, New Mexico, USA, in 1996. Walkman was just 12.7 cm (5 in) tall and was highly unpredictable. In tests it was reported that the robot struggled to get free when its legs were held without being programmed to do so, and without making the same movement twice.

LARGEST ROBOT EXHIBITION

The International Robot Exhibition held every two years in Tokyo, Japan, demonstrates new and important feats of technology. The Oct 1999 event saw over 700 human exhibitors, both private and corporate, take part in displaying their latest robots.

LARGEST PERMANENT DISPLAY OF COLLECTIVE ROBOTS

A unique set of three small collective robots (ie. they are programmed to act as a team) are permanently housed in the Wellcome Wing of the Science Museum in London, UK. Visitors can control the movements of one of them using a joystick, and the other two can be instructed either to mimic, line up with, follow or run away from the lead robot.

www.guinnessworldrecords.com/robonaut

MEET THE REAL C3PO

The most advanced robot astronaut is NASA's Robonaut (right). This prototype mechanical astronaut is designed to assist space travellers with vital and dangerous tasks, particularly during spacewalks. Anticipated to fly in space for the first time within the next few years, it has dexterous human-like hands, stereo vision and a single leg to allow it to move easily around the exterior of the International Space Station, where it will be deployed on a permanent basis. The design of Robonaut's crude nervous system – a web of sensors, software and circuits – was borrowed from human anatomy. As there is no 'brain' required in the small head, engineers concentrated most of the controls and command structures in a mechanical backbone. Cameras in Robonaut's head beam visual information to eyeglasses worn by a NASA technician, who can then direct the robot's arms and fingers by moving his own hands inside gloves wired with sensors linked directly to the robot. This gives the robot the full range of manoeuvres.

GUINNESS WORLD RECORDS

space exploration

MOST PEOPLE IN SPACE AT ONE TIME

On 14 March 1995 a record 13 people were in space at the same time – seven Americans aboard the US *STS 67 Endeavour*; three CIS cosmonauts aboard the Russian *Mir* space station; and two CIS cosmonauts and a US astronaut aboard the CIS *Soyuz TM21*.

SMALLEST PLANETARY BODY EVER LANDED UPON

The *NEAR-Shoemaker* spacecraft landed on asteroid Eros on 12 Feb 2001. The spacecraft transmitted 69 images of the surface of Eros during its descent, showing details of rocks that were just centimetres across.

LARGEST TELESCOPE

The twin Keck Telescopes, on the summit of Hawaii's Mauna Kea volcano, are the world's largest optical and infra-red telescopes. Each one is eight storeys high and weighs 2,998 tonnes (661,000 lb). Both have a mirror 9.8 m (32 ft) wide, made up of 36 hexagonal segments that together create a single reflective surface. With this telescope, you would be able to see a golf ball 150 km (93.2 miles) away.

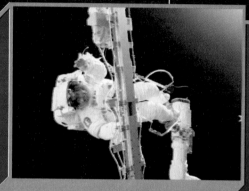

SPACED OUT

The longest spacewalk was made by astronauts Jim Voss (left) and Susan Helms (both USA), who spent 8 hr 56 min outside in space on 11 March 2001. Their job was to make room on the International Space Station for the Italian cargo module *Leonardo*, launched into space by the space shuttle *Discovery*. Around five tonnes (11,000 lb) of equipment was included in *Leonardo*'s payload. When construction is completed, the station will measure 96.3 m (316 ft) from end to end. Sixteen nations are involved in the station's construction – one of the largest international non-military collaborations in history.

www.guinnessworldrecords.com/spacewalk
← ACCESS CODE: ‹46910›

LARGEST SOLAR PANEL ARRAY IN SPACE

On 5 Dec 2000 astronauts on the space shuttle *Endeavour* deployed the first of four sets of solar panels to provide electrical power to the International Space Station. The remaining sets will be added over the next few years, making the station one of the brightest objects in the night sky – outshone only by the Moon, the brightest planets and the star Sirius. Unfurled, the panels span 73 m (240 ft) and generate 64 kW of electricity between them (enough to power 30 households).

HEAVIEST ROCK RETURNED FROM SPACE

The only rock samples returned to Earth from space are Moon rocks brought back during the Apollo programme. Of these, the largest was sample number 61016 nicknamed 'Big Muley', returned by *Apollo 16*. It has a mass of 11.7 kg (25.79 lb).

LONGEST MANNED SPACEFLIGHT

The longest manned spaceflight was made by Valeriy Poliyakov (Russia). Launched to the *Mir* space station aboard *Soyuz TM18* on 8 Jan 1994, he returned to Earth in *Soyuz TM20* on 22 March 1995, after a spaceflight lasting 437 days 17 hr 58 min 16 sec.

SHORTEST MANNED SPACEFLIGHT

Alan Bartlett Shepard (USA) boarded *Mercury-Redstone 3* on 5 May 1961. His sub-orbital mission lasted only 15 min 28 sec because the *Redstone* booster rocket upon which his *Freedom 7* capsule was launched was not powerful enough to reach orbit. Instead, *Freedom 7* went up and down in an arc trajectory. Shepard reached an altitude of 187.49 km (116.5 miles) and during the flight he was subjected to acceleration forces 11 times stronger than the force of gravity.

MOST DISTANT IMAGE OF EARTH

On 4 Feb 1990, after 12 years 6 months in space, NASA's *Voyager 1* spacecraft turned its camera back towards the Sun and the planets of the Solar System to take photographs of our home planet from a distance of 6.5 billion km (4 billion miles). The photos were transmitted back to NASA and showed the Sun as a bright star and the Earth as a pale blue dot.

MOST POWERFUL GAMMA RAY TELESCOPE

Launched in 1991, the Compton Gamma Ray Observatory is the most powerful gamma ray telescope to date. It weighed 15.4 tonnes

MOON'S-TRUCK

The lunar speed record was set by the manned *Apollo 16* Rover, driven by John Young (USA, left), who achieved 18 km/h (11.2 mph) downhill. He also set the manned distance record with 33.8 km (21 miles). John Young is one of NASA's most experienced astronauts and has been called the 'Godfather of Space'.

The furthest distance travelled on another planet is 37 km (23 miles). The record was set on the surface of the Moon by the unmanned Soviet *Lunokhod 2* Rover between 16 and 23 June 1973. *Lunokhod 2* moved during the lunar day, using its solar panels to charge its batteries, and hibernated during the long lunar night. Over four months, the Rover transmitted over 80,000 TV pictures and 86 panoramic images back to Earth.

www.guinnessworldrecords.com/lunarspeed

www.guinnessworldrecords.com/mir

A MIR TRIFLE!

The heaviest man-made object to re-enter the Earth's atmosphere is the Russian space station *Mir* (right). It was taken out of orbit during a successful controlled re-entry of the Earth's atmosphere on 23 March 2001. After an amazing 15 years in space, the 130-tonne (286,600-lb) outpost broke into thousands of incandescent pieces that splashed down in the Pacific Ocean, east of New Zealand.

(37,475 lb) and was placed in a low orbit around the Earth on 5 April 1991 by the space shuttle *Atlantis*. After nine years of observation it was guided to a controlled re-entry into the Earth's atmosphere and burned up on 4 June 2000.

FURTHEST RESTING PLACE

On 31 July 1999 the American *Lunar Prospector* spacecraft crashed on to the surface of the Moon, carrying a polycarbonate container holding 28 g (1 oz) of the remains of Dr Eugene Shoemaker (USA). Brass foil inscribed with some of the images of Shoemaker's pioneering work in planetary science was wrapped around the container. This first lunar 'funeral' was a fitting tribute to the man who trained Apollo astronauts to become lunar field geologists.

LARGEST SPACE LABORATORY

The largest single research laboratory ever launched was the US *Skylab* in 1973, which was 24.9 m (82 ft) long and weighed 26,762 kg (59,000 lb). It was the largest manmade object to re-enter the Earth's atmosphere until *Mir* re-entered in 2001.

LONGEST SPACE FLIGHT BY A DOG

The two dogs Veterok (Little Wind) and Ugolek (Little Piece of Coal) spent 22 days orbiting the Earth during the Soviet *Kosmos 110* mission (launched 22 Feb 1966). This record was not surpassed by humans until the *Skylab 4* mission in 1974.

GUINNESS WORLD RECORDS

aircraft

LARGEST HELICOPTER EVER

The Russian Mil Mi-12 weighed 103.3 tonnes (227,737 lb) and was 37 m (121 ft 48 in) long. It was powered by four 4,847-kW (6,500-hp) turboshaft engines and had a rotor diameter of 67 m (219 ft 10 in). A prototype was demonstrated in 1971 but it never entered service.

LARGEST HELICOPTER IN PRODUCTION

The largest helicopter in service is the Russian Mil Mi-26, with a maximum take-off weight of 56 tonnes (123,458 lb). Its overall length is 40 m (131 ft) and the eight-bladed rotor has a diameter of 32 m (105 ft). It can be converted into an assault-troop carrier or can carry up to 80 stretchers.

FASTEST HELICOPTER CIRCUMNAVIGATIONS

John Williams and Ron Bower (both USA) flew round the world in a Bell 430 helicopter in 17 days 6 hrs 14 min 25 sec at an average speed of 91.76 km/h (57.02 mph). They left Fair Oaks, London, UK, on 17 Aug 1996 and flew westabout, against prevailing winds, arriving back on 3 Sept 1996.

Jennifer Murray (UK) circumnavigated the globe solo in a Robinson R44 helicopter in 99 days, from 31 May to 6 Sept 2000, at an average speed of 16.99 km/h (10.55 mph). Her journey began and ended at Brooklands airfield, Weybridge, Surrey, UK, and covered 30 countries.

LONGEST HELICOPTER HOVER

Doug Daigle, Brian Watts and Dave Meyer of Tridair Helicopters, and Rod Anderson of Helistream, Inc. (all USA), maintained a continuous hover in a 1947 Bell 47B model for 50 hr 50 sec between 13 and 15 Dec 1989.

LARGEST OBJECT TRANSPORTED BY AIR

The largest single objects to be transported by air are the 37.23-m (122.17-ft) NASA space shuttles, which are 'piggy-backed' on top of modified Boeing 747s from alternative landing strips back to Cape Canaveral. The shuttles – Columbia, Discovery, Atlantis and Endeavour – weigh 100 tonnes (220,500 lb) each.

LARGEST CARGO AIRCRAFT

The aircraft with the largest cargo hold is the Airbus A300-600ST Super Transporter ('Beluga'). The cargo deck has a volume of 1,400 m^3 (49,440 ft^3), and is 37.7 m (123 ft 8 in) long, with a maximum height and width of 7.1 m (23 ft 3 in). Its maximum payload weight is 47 tonnes (103,607 lb). The main section of the cargo bay is two storeys high, and longer than a basketball court.

HEAVIEST AIRCRAFT

The aircraft with the heaviest take-off weight is the Antonov An-225 ('Mriya', meaning Dream) at 600 tonnes (1.323 million lb). The aircraft lifted a payload of 156,300 kg (344,582 lb) to an altitude of 12,410 m (40,715 ft) and covered a distance of 2,100 km (1,305 miles) on 22 March 1989. In comparison, the maximum take-off weight of a Boeing 747-400 ('Jumbo') is 396.89 tonnes (874,990 lb).

LARGEST WING SPANS

The eight-engined 193-tonne (425,490-lb) Hughes H4 Hercules flying boat, more commonly known as the 'Spruce Goose', had the largest wing span of any aircraft ever constructed. Its wing span was 97.51 m (319 ft 11 in) and its length 66.65 m (218 ft 8 in). It was raised 21.3 m (70 ft) into the air in a test run of 914 m (2999 ft) by Howard Hughes, off Long Beach Harbor, California, USA, on 2 Nov 1947, but never flew again. At 73.3 m (240 ft 6 in), the Ukranian Anotov An-124 has the largest wing span of any modern aircraft. In comparison, the Boeing 747-400 has a wing span of 64.4 m (211 ft 5 in).

FASTEST COMBAT JET

The fastest combat jet is the Russian Mikoyan MiG-25 fighter (NATO code name 'Foxbat'). The reconnaissance 'Foxbat-B' has been tracked by radar at Mach 3.2 (3,395 km/h or 2,110 mph). It has a wing span of 13.95 m (45 ft 9 in), is 23.82 m (78 ft 2 in) long and has an estimated maximum take-off weight of 37.4 tonnes (82,450 lb).

LARGEST WATER BOMBER

The largest firefighting aircraft is the Russian-made Ilyushin 76TD air tanker, which can carry 42,000 litres (11,000 gal) of water or fire retardants. Owned by the Russian ministry for Civil Defence, Emergencies and Elimination of Consequences of Natural Disasters (EMERCOM), five such aircraft are available at short notice for humanitarian missions and leasing to governments and organisations around the world. In one 8-10 second pass it is capable of soaking an area 1,200 m (0.75 miles) long and 90 m (295 ft) wide with water.

BOMBER WITH GREATEST WING SPAN

The 10-engined Convair B-36J ('Peacemaker'), had a wing span of 70.1 m (230 ft), the longest ever for a bomber, and a maximum take-off weight of 185 tonnes (410,000 lb). The B-36J has been out of service since the late 1950s, when it was replaced by the Boeing B-52.

HEAVIEST BOMBER

The former Soviet four-jet Tupolev Tu-160 ('Blackjack') bomber has a take-off weight when fully loaded with bombs of 275 tonnes (606,250 lb). Its empty weight is 110 tonnes (242,500 lb). The 'Blackjack' has a maximum speed of Mach 2.05 (2,200 km/h or 1,350 mph) and is 54.1 m (177.5 ft) long, with a wing span of 55.7 m (182.7 ft).

LARGEST PROPELLER

The largest aeroplane propeller ever to fly was the 6.9-m (22.6-ft) diameter Garuda propeller, fitted to the Linke-Hofmann R II, which flew in 1919. It was driven by four 195-kW (260-hp) Mercedes engines and turned at only 545 rpm. Today's small aircraft propellers are roughly 2 m (6.56 ft) in diameter, and turn at approximately 2,500 rpm.

BLACKBIRD JOINS THE JETSET

The USAF Lockheed SR-71 ('Blackbird'), a reconnaissance aircraft (left), is the world's fastest aeroplane, with a top speed in excess of Mach 3 (3,185 km/h or 1,979 mph) although the exact figure is classified. The two-seater aircraft flew top-secret missions for nearly 25 years, making its first flight on 22 Dec 1964. The fastest transatlantic flight record is 1 hr 54 mins 56.4 secs, by Major James V Sullivan and Major Noel F Widdifield (both USA), flying a 'Blackbird' eastwards on 1 Sept 1974. The average speed for the New York–London stage of 5,570.8 km (3,461.53 miles) was 2,908.02 km/h (1,806.96 mph).

The Lockheed SR-71 'Blackbird' was decommissioned by the USAF in 1990, but several re-entered service for NASA in 1995 for research purposes.

www.guinnessworldrecords.com/fastjet

ACCESS CODE: ‹43994›

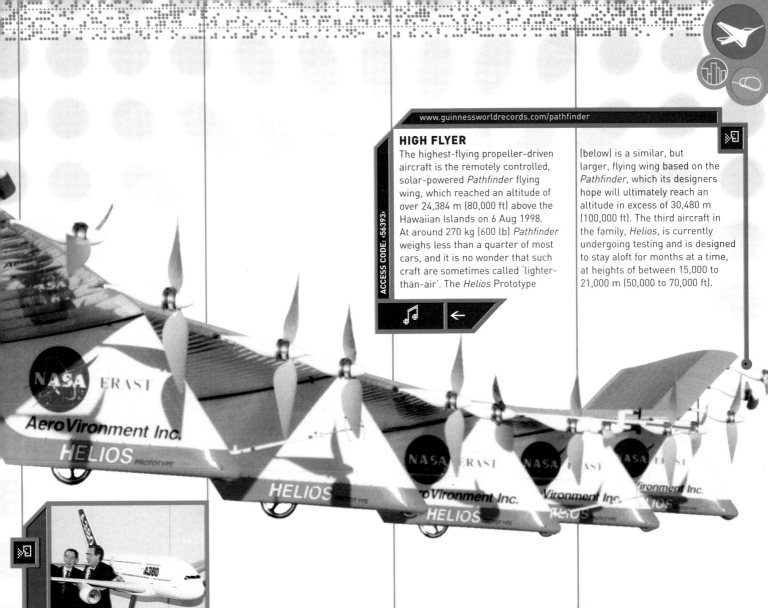

www.guinnessworldrecords.com/pathfinder

HIGH FLYER

The highest-flying propeller-driven aircraft is the remotely controlled, solar-powered *Pathfinder* flying wing, which reached an altitude of over 24,384 m (80,000 ft) above the Hawaiian Islands on 6 Aug 1998. At around 270 kg (600 lb) *Pathfinder* weighs less than a quarter of most cars, and it is no wonder that such craft are sometimes called 'lighter-than-air'. The *Helios* Prototype (below) is a similar, but larger, flying wing based on the *Pathfinder*, which its designers hope will ultimately reach an altitude in excess of 30,480 m (100,000 ft). The third aircraft in the family, *Helios*, is currently undergoing testing and is designed to stay aloft for months at a time, at heights of between 15,000 to 21,000 m (50,000 to 70,000 ft).

ACCESS CODE: ‹56393›

SPACE TRAVEL

The largest passenger aircraft in development is the Airbus A380 (above), launched in Dec 2000 and expected to enter service by 2007. It has a wing span of 79.8 m (261 ft 10 in) and is 73 m (239 ft 6 in) long. It will have a maximum take-off weight of 560 tonnes (1.23 million lb) and will carry 555 passengers in considerable comfort, as its size allows for facilities such as casinos, bars and gyms.

The Boeing 747-400 holds the record for the greatest capacity, holding a maximum of 566 people, but it is a smaller plane, with a wingspan of 64.9 m (212 ft 11 in), and a length of 70.6 m (231 ft 7 in).

www.guinnessworldrecords.com/airbus

ACCESS CODE: ‹56382›

FASTEST BOMBER

The US variable-geometry, or 'swing-wing' General Dynamics FB-111A has a maximum speed of Mach 2.5, which is two-and-a-half times the speed of sound (2,655 km/h or 1,650 mph).

The Russian swing-wing Tupolev Tu-22M, which is known to NATO as 'Backfire', has an estimated speed of Mach 2, but may reach Mach 2.5.

LARGEST AIRSHIPS

The world's largest airships were the 213.9-tonne (471,568 lb) German *Hindenburg* (LZ 129) and *Graf Zeppelin II* (LZ 130), both of which were 245 m (803 ft 10 in) long with a hydrogen gas capacity of 200,000 m³ (7,062,100 ft³). The *Hindenburg* first flew in 1936, exploding and crashing on 6 May 1937 at Lakehurst, New Jersey, USA, and the *Graf Zeppelin II* first flew in 1938.

FASTEST FLYING BOAT

The Martin XP6M-1 *SeaMaster*, the US Navy four-jet-engined minelayer flown in 1955-59, was the fastest flying boat ever built, with a top speed of 1,040 km/h (646 mph).

EARLIEST AEROPLANE HOP

On 9 Oct 1890, the first hop by a manned aeroplane entirely under its own power was made when Clément Ader (France) flew in his *Éole* for about 50 m (164 ft) at Armainvilliers, France. It was powered by a light-weight steam engine of his own design, which developed about 15 kW (20 hp), but the flight was neither sustained nor controlled.

EARLIEST JET FLIGHT

The first flight by an aeroplane powered by a turbojet engine was made in the Heinkel He 178, piloted by Flugkapitän Erich Warsitz, at Marienehe, Germany, on 27 Aug 1939. Despite its success, it was not until towards the end of World War II, in 1944, that the jet-propelled Messerschmidt Me 262 entered service as Germany's first active jet fighter.

LARGEST PAPER AIRCRAFT

The largest flying paper aircraft, was constructed by a team of students from the Faculty of Aerospace Engineering at Delft University of Technology, Netherlands. It had a wing span of 13.97 m (45 ft 10 in), and was flown on 16 May 1995. It was launched indoors and flew a distance of 34.8 m (114 ft 2 in). Founded in 1940, the 1,300-student faculty is equipped with a wind tunnel test centre and a supercomputer centre and works closely with aerospace giants Airbus and Boeing.

MOST AIRCRAFT BUILT

The Cessna Aircraft Company of Wichita, Kansas, USA, has been the world's most productive aerospace company, with total production of 182,804 aircraft by the end of 2000. Company founder Clyde Cessna built and flew his first aeroplane in 1911.

GUINNESS WORLD RECORDS

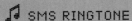

ships and submarines

FASTEST SAILING VESSEL

On 26 Oct 1993 the trifoiler *Yellow Pages Endeavour* reached a record speed of 46.52 knots (86.21 km/h or 53.57 mph) on a timed run of 500 m (1,640 ft) at Sandy Point near Melbourne, Vic, Australia.

FASTEST REGULAR ATLANTIC CROSSING

The fastest regular commercial Atlantic crossings were by the liner *United States*. On her maiden voyage between 3 and 7 July 1952 from New York, USA, to Le Havre, France, and Southampton, UK, she averaged 35.39 knots (65.95 km/h or 40 mph) over 3 days 10 hr 40 min. The *United States* was decommissioned in 1969 and today is anchored in Philadelphia, Pennsylvania, USA.

LARGEST BATTLESHIPS IN ACTIVE SERVICE

The largest battleships ever used in active service were the *USS Missouri* and *USS Wisconsin.* They were 270 m (887 ft) long and had a full-load displacement (the amount of water they displace when fully loaded) of 58,930 tonnes (130 million lb). Weapons included nine 40.6-cm (16-in) guns which were used in the

SAIL OF THE CENTURY

Taller above the waterline than a 15-storey building, the *Royal Clipper* (left) is 133.8 m (439 ft) in length and has five masts and 42 sails, which use 5,202 m² (56,000 ft²) of canvas. This makes her the largest square rigger in service. Weighing 5,000 tonnes (11 million lb), she has a crew of 106 and can carry up to 228 passengers in luxury accommodation. Facilities include three swimming pools, a piano lounge, deluxe shops, a spa and gym, a large dining room and a forward observation lounge for up to 90 people. The *Royal Clipper* cruises in the Caribbean and the western Mediterranean.

www.guinnessworldrecords.com/clipper

← ACCESS CODE: ‹43704›

Gulf War in 1991 and were capable of firing 1,225-kg (2,700-lb) projectiles a distance of 39 km (23 miles).

OLDEST COMMISSIONED WARSHIP IN USE

Ordered in 1758, the *HMS Victory* took six years to build and is the oldest serving warship still in commission, retaining her own captain, officers and crew. Docked at the Portsmouth Historic Dockyard, Hampshire, UK, *HMS Victory* looks the same today as she did at the Battle of Trafalgar in 1805.

LARGEST CRUISE LINER 📺 FI

The *Voyager of the Seas* is the world's largest cruise liner, measuring 310 m (1,020 ft) long and 48 m (157.5 ft) wide. She weighs 144,000 tonnes (317.4 million lb), has a crew of 1,181 and a total capacity of 3,114 passengers. The ship has its own five-storey theatre with 1,350 seats, plus a golf course, an ice skating rink and a wedding chapel.

MOST MASTED SAILING SHIP

The only seven-masted sailing schooner ever built was the *Thomas W Lawson*, measuring 114.4 m (375 ft) long. It was built at Quincy, Massachusetts, USA, in 1902, and was wrecked off the Isles of Scilly, Cornwall, UK, in 1907.

TALLEST MAST

The 47.9-m (157-ft) sloop *Hyperion*, built by Wolter Huisman (Netherlands), has a mast 59 m (193 ft) high. *Hyperion* was commissioned in 1995 by Jim Clark (USA), the founder of internet browser company Netscape.

MOST POWERFUL ICEBREAKERS

The most powerful icebreakers are the *Rossiya*, *Sovetskiy Soyuz* and *Oktyabryskaya Revolutsiya*. Built in Leningrad (USSR), now St Petersburg, Russia, in 1985, the *Rossiya* weighs 23,460 tonnes (51.7 million lb) and is powered by 55.930-kW (75,000-hp) nuclear engines.

LARGEST WING-IN-GROUND VEHICLE

Built by the Soviet Central Design Bureau of Hydrofoil Vehicles in the 1960s, the 540-tonne (1.9 million-lb) *Caspian Sea Monster* was the largest wing-in-ground (WIG) effect vehicle ever built. A cross between an aircraft and a hovercraft, it skimmed just above the waves at speeds of up to 500 km/h (311 mph). It was powered by 10 turbofan jet engines, but was destroyed in a crash in 1980.

LARGEST SHIPWRECK

The 321,186-tonne (708 million-lb) VLCC (very large crude carrier) *Energy Determination* blew up and

DHOW AMAZING!

Al Hashemi II, a wooden Arabic dhow (left) built and owned by Radisson SAS Hotels Resorts, Kuwait, is a record 80.4 m (263 ft 7 in) long and 18.7 m (61 ft 3 in) wide. This richly decorated traditional Arabic cargo ship is held together by approximately 80 tonnes (78,737 lb) of hand-made nails and bolts, and is used as a conference and reception venue. It was completed in Jan 2000. Dhows are traditional wooden ships with distinctive triangular sails, common in the Persian Gulf and Indian Ocean ports. *Al Hashemi II* was the brainchild of Husain Marafie, one of the owners of the Radisson SAS hotel. It is modelled on a cargo-carrying dhow of the Baghlah type, built by his great-grandfather and named *Al Hashemi* in the late 19th century.

PLANE SAILING

The warships with the largest full-load displacement are the Nimitz-class US Navy aircraft carriers *USS Nimitz, Dwight D Eisenhower, Carl Vinson, Theodore Roosevelt, Abraham Lincoln, George Washington, John C Stennis, Harry S Truman* and *Ronald Reagan* (below), the last five of which displace approximately 98,550 tonnes (217.2 million lb). They are 332.9 m (1,092 ft) long, have 1.82 ha (4.49 acres) of flight deck, can reach speeds over 30 knots (56 km/h or 35 mph) and are driven by four nuclear-powered 194,000-kW (260,000-shp) geared steam turbines.

Tasked with a multi-mission attack/anti-submarine warfare role, the *Nimitz* has four C-13 Mod 1 catapults, or 'cats', that propel aircraft off the flight deck. These can accelerate even the heaviest carrier-based aircraft to speeds of 273 km/h (170 mph) from a standing start and launch one aircraft every 20 seconds.

broke in two in the Strait of Hormuz, Persian Gulf, on 12 Dec 1979. The ship was not carrying cargo at the time, but the hull value alone was $58 million (£26 million).

EARLIEST SURVIVING VESSEL

The earliest surviving vessel is a pine logboat or dugout found in Pesse, Netherlands, which has been dated to around 6315 BC. It is now in the Provincial Museum, Assen, Netherlands. The second oldest surviving vessels are a fleet of 12 funeral river boats discovered in 1991 at Abydos, Egypt, which have been tentatively dated to around 3000 BC.

FASTEST SUBMARINE

The Russian Alpha class nuclear-powered submarines had a top speed of over 40 knots (74 km/h or 50 mph), and were believed to be capable of diving to 760 m (2,500 ft). Only one now remains in service.

MOST SUBMARINES

The largest navy in the world in terms of submarines is the Russian navy, with 128 (92 nuclear) in 1997.

LARGEST SUBMERGED NUCLEAR CARGO

On 6 Oct 1986 Russian nuclear submarine K-219 (Project 667-A Yankee Class) sank in the Atlantic Ocean 965 km (600 miles) north of Bermuda. The submarine carried two nuclear reactors and 16 nuclear missiles, making it the largest cargo of this type resting in the sea, at a depth of 5,800 m (19,000 ft).

GUINNESS WORLD RECORDS

trucks, trains and buses

www.guinnessworldrecords.com/trams

← ACCESS CODE: ‹43477›

STAR TRACK:
TO BOLDLY GO WHERE NO TRAM HAS GONE BEFORE

The world's oldest trams in revenue service are cars 1 and 2 of the Manx Electric Railway (above), running regularly on the 28.5-km (17.7-mile) line between Douglas and Ramsey, Isle of Man, UK. The trams date back to the opening of the railway in 1893. Today the MER is a popular tourist attraction on the island, as the journey provides views of the coastline.

The city of St Petersburg, Russia, has the most extensive tramway system, with 2,402 cars on 64 routes covering 690.6 km (429.1 miles) of track. St Petersburg is Russia's second-largest city and former capital. It is also known as the 'Tram Capital of the World'. The first horse-drawn tram began moving freight in the outskirts of the city in 1854. The system continued to grow in the 19th and 20th centuries, but in recent years sections of the track have been dug up to make way for roads.

FASTEST TRUCK WHEELIE

FR

Patrick Bourny (France) drove his modified truck cab in a wheelie at a speed of 90 km/h (55.92 mph) at Lure, France, on 21 Oct 2000.

FASTEST MONSTER TRUCK

The highest recorded speed ever reached by a monster truck is 111.5 km/h (69.3 mph), achieved by Dan Runte (USA) in his vehicle 'Bigfoot 14' on 11 Sept 1999 at Symrna Airport, Nashville, Tennessee, USA. The record was set in the run-up to the longest-ever monster truck ramp jump of 61.6 m (202 ft). The same truck and driver also hold the record for the highest monster truck jump, reaching 7.3 m (24 ft) on 14 Dec 1999.

LARGEST DUMPER TRUCK

The world's largest two-axle dumper truck is the T-282, manufactured by the Liebherr Mining Equipment Co (USA). It has a payload capacity of 327 tonnes (720,910 lb), or more than one-and-a-half times its own weight.

LONGEST ROAD TRAIN

The longest line of trailers pulled by a single truck stretched 610.7 m (2,003 ft 7 in). The 45 trailers were pulled by a Kenworth Tri-Drive Cab model K100G, driven by

Greg Marley (Australia) along the Great Eastern Highway at Merredin, Western Australia, on 3 April 1999.

FASTEST LONDON UNDERGROUND CIRCUIT

The record time for doing a tour of all 272 stations on the London Underground is 19 hr 57 min 47 sec. Robert Robinson, Chris Loxton, Chris Stubley, Chris Whiteoak, Olly Rich and Adam Waller Berks (all UK) made the journey on 16 March 2000.

FASTEST TRAIN JOURNEY

The West Japan Railway Company runs its 500-Series-Nozomi bullet trains (*Shinkansen*) at an average speed of 261.8 km/h (162.7 mph) on the line between Hiroshima and Kokura on the island of Honshu. The Nozomi, meaning 'dream', entered service in 1997 and each train can carry up to 1,324 people.

FASTEST RAIL SYSTEM

The highest speed recorded on a national rail system is 515.3 km/h (320.2 mph), by the French SNCF high-speed train TGV *Atlantique*, travelling from Courtalain to Tours on 18 May 1990.

FASTEST MAGLEV VEHICLE

The highest recorded speed of a Maglev (magnetically levitated) train is

552 km/h (343 mph), by the MLX01 on the Yamanashi Maglev Test Line between Otsuki and Tsuru, Japan, on 14 April 1999. Operated by the Central Japan Railway Company and Railway Technical Research Institute, the record-breaking Maglev harnesses the power of magnetism to lift itself off the ground and move forwards, with electromagnets made from superconductive metals.

LONGEST JOURNEY BY A RUNAWAY TRAIN

On 26 March 1884 eight coal cars were set in motion by high winds in Akron, Colorado, USA, and ran a distance of 160 km (100 miles) on the Chicago, Burlington & Quincy Railroad, east of Denver, Colorado. The cars are thought to have reached a maximum speed of 106 km/h (66 mph) on a downhill stretch. A freight engine gave chase and brought them under control.

FURTHEST DISTANCE TRAVELLED BY TRAIN

Mona Tippins (USA) travelled a record 128,492 km (79,024 miles) by rail, without duplicating any part of her journey, between 7 Oct 1994 and 11 Feb 1997. She visited 33 countries in North America and Europe.

THE LONG AND WINDING UNDERGROUND RAILROAD

The most extensive underground rail system is the New York City subway (USA, left), covering a total track distance of 1,355 km (842 miles). This includes 299 km (186 miles) of track in yards, workshops and storage, as well as 370 km (230 miles) of actual transport routes. The network serves about 1.3 billion passengers per year and, with 468 stations, has more stations than any other system. Trains operate 24 hours a day, seven days a week, throughout the city, and on an average weekday cover around 1.6 million km (1 million miles).

 www.guinnessworldrecords.com/newyorksubway

← ACCESS CODE: ‹43824›

German state of North Rhine Westphalia, it is 220 m (722 ft) long, 94.5 m (310 ft) tall at its highest point, and can shift 240,000 m³ (8.475 million ft³) of earth a day. It has 18 buckets fitted to a massive wheel. As the wheel revolves the buckets scoop up and dump earth.

LARGEST BUS FLEET

Andhra Pradesh State Road Transport Corporation (India) has the largest bus fleet. As of 31 Oct 1999, the company owned 18,397 buses.

FURTHEST DISTANCE TRAVELLED BY TRAIN IN SEVEN DAYS

Andrew Kingsmell, Sean Andrews and Graham Bardouleau (all UK) travelled 21,090 km (13,105 miles) on French national railways from 28 Nov to 5 Dec 1992, with a total journey time of 6 days 22 hr 38 min.

LONGEST FREIGHT TRAIN

The world's longest freight train, measuring 7.3 km (4.8 miles) long and made up of 660 wagons, a tank car and a guard's van, made a run on the Sishen-Saldanha railway in South Africa from 26 to 27 Aug 1989. Moved by a total of nine 50-kV-electric and seven diesel-electric locomotives, it travelled 861 km (535 miles) in 22 hr 40 min. It took 7 km (4.3 miles) to come to a complete standstill after the brakes were first applied.

LARGEST LAND VEHICLE

The largest land vehicle is the 14,196-tonne (31.3 million-lb) RB293 bucket wheel excavator, an earthmoving machine made by MAN TAKRAF of Germany. Used in an open-cast coal mine in the

www.guinnessworldrecords.com/fireengine

THE BACKDRAFT BUSTERS

 USA

The world's fastest fire engine is the rocket-powered Hawaiian Eagle (below), owned by Tom Seydel (USA). It reached a speed of 655 km/h (407 mph) in Brainerd, Florida, on 11 July 1998. The vehicle is a 1941 truck, powered by two Rolls Royce Bristol Viper engines, each boasting 4,500 kW (6,000 hp) and generating 5,450 kg (12,000 lb) of thrust.

ACCESS CODE: ‹53934›

The fire engine with the greatest pumping capacity is the 640-kW (860-hp), eight-wheel Oshkosh firetruck manufactured by Oshkosh Truck Corporation, Wisconsin, USA. It can discharge a record 189,000 litres (49,900 gal) of foam through two turrets in just 150 seconds. This powerful pumping vehicle weighs 60 tonnes (132,277 lb) and is used for aircraft and runway fires.

KEEP BACK 300 FEET OR ELSE!

GUINNESS WORLD RECORDS

cars

BEST-SELLING SPORTS CAR

Mazda has manufactured a record 531,890 MX-5 Miata sports cars since production began in April 1989.

FASTEST PRODUCTION CAR

The highest speed achieved by a standard production car is 386.7 km/h (240.25 mph), by a McLaren F1, driven by Andy Wallace (UK) at the Volkswagen Proving Ground, Wolfsburg, Germany, on 31 March 1998. Only 100 of these supercars have been manufactured.

The McLaren F1 is also the most powerful standard production car ever produced, accelerating to 96 km/h (60 mph) in 3.2 seconds.

FASTEST DIESEL-POWERED CAR

The Mercedes C111–III, powered by a five-cylinder three-litre diesel engine reached a top speed of 327.3 km/h (203.3 mph) in tests on the Nardo Circuit, Italy, from 5 to 15 Oct 1978.

FASTEST STEAM CAR

On 19 Aug 1985 Robert E Barber (USA) broke the 79-year-old record for a steam car when *Steamin' Demon*,

FIRST-CLASS TRAVEL

The greatest confirmed price paid for a car is $15 million (£8.41 million) for the 1931 Bugatti Type 41 Royale Sports Coupé (left), sold by Nicholas Harley to the Meitec Corporation of Japan on 12 April 1990.

A Bugatti also holds the record for the largest car ever produced – the Bugatti Royale Type 41, built by the Italian Ettore Bugatti. First made in 1927, it has an eight-cylinder engine with a capacity of 12.7 litres and is over 6.7 m (22 ft) in length. Perhaps the only thing more remarkable than the massive bulk of this car is its rarity – only six were ever produced.

www.guinnessworldrecords.com/priceycar
← ACCESS CODE: ‹43465›

built by Barber-Nichols Engineering Co, reached a speed of 234.33 km/h (145.58 mph) at Bonneville Salt Flats, Utah, USA.

FASTEST SOLAR-POWERED CAR

The highest recorded speed for a solar/battery-powered vehicle is 135 km/h (83.88 mph) achieved by the Star Micronics solar car, *Solar Star*. The car was driven by Manfred Hermann (Australia) on 5 Jan 1991 at Richmond RAAF Base, NSW, Australia.

FASTEST ROCKET-ENGINED CAR

The Blue Flame, a rocket-powered four-wheeled vehicle driven by Gary Gabelich (USA) reached a speed of 1,016.086 km/h (631.366 mph) on the Bonneville Salt Flats, Utah, USA, on 23 Oct 1970. The car was powered by a liquid natural gas/hydrogen peroxide engine, which could develop thrust of up to 9,979 kg (22,000 lb).

FASTEST ELECTRIC CAR

On 22 Oct 1999 *White Lightning Electric Streamliner*, an electric car driven by Patrick Rummerfield (USA), achieved a speed of 395.821 km/h (245.951 mph) at the Bonneville Salt Flats, Utah, USA. With its slender, aerodynamic carbon-fibre body, the 7.62-m (25-ft) *White Lightning* looks more like a rocket than a car and can reach a speed of 161 km/h (100 mph) in eight seconds.

FASTEST LAND SPEED

The *Thrust SSC*, driven by Andy Green (UK), broke the sound barrier and achieved the one-mile

(1.6 km) land-speed record on 15 Oct 1997. It reached a top speed of 1,227.99 km/h (763.03 mph) in the Black Rock Desert, Nevada, USA.

HIGHEST REVERSE-DRIVING SPEED

Alistair Weaver (UK) reached a speed of 138.4 km/h (86 mph) in reverse, driving a Caterham Seven Blackbird at Bruntingthorpe Proving Ground, Leicestershire, UK, on 7 March 2001. Weaver reached his record speed in 16.63 seconds, accelerating to 96 km/h (60 mph) in 9.32 seconds, a respectable rate even for cars travelling forwards.

LONGEST CAR

The world's longest car is the 26-wheeled limo designed by Jay Ohrberg (USA). It is 30.5 m (100 ft) long and features include a king-sized water bed and a swimming pool with diving board. It is designed to be driven as a rigid vehicle but it can be changed to 'bend' in the middle. Its main purpose is for use in films and exhibitions.

MINI DRIVER

The longest journey in a Mini was achieved by Duncan Mortimer (UK, left), who drove 36,460.3 km (22,655.4 miles) around the world in his bright yellow 1978 Mini Clubman 1275 GT between 25 May 1999 and 13 Feb 2000. Starting in New York, USA, and finishing back home in England, Duncan's journey took him through parts of the USA, Australia, India, Pakistan, Iran, Turkey, Greece, Italy, France and England.

The greatest number of people to fit in a Mini was achieved on 3 July 2000, when a total of 18 women crammed into a Mini Cooper outside the National Indoor Arena in Birmingham, West Midlands, UK, beating the previous record, set by the Reading Ladies' Rugby Club (UK), by one person.

LIGHTEST CAR

Louis Borsi (UK) has built and driven a 9.5-kg (21-lb) car with a 2.5-cc engine. It is capable of 25 km/h (15 mph).

OLDEST MANUFACTURED CAR

The Morgan 4/4 celebrated its 65th birthday in Dec 2000. Produced by the Morgan Motor Car Company of Malvern, Worcester, UK, (founded 1910), all Morgans are hand-built and production time is an average of 23 days. The company's total production for all four of its models is around 540 per year. There is still a six-to-eight-year waiting list for delivery.

www.guinnessworldrecords.com/caracceleration

FAST AND FURIOUS

The fastest road-tested acceleration recorded is 0–96 km/h (0–60 mph) in 3.07 seconds by a Ford RS200 *Evolution* (below), driven by Graham Hathaway (UK) at the Millbrook Proving Ground, Bedfordshire, UK, on 25 May 1994. They were developed in the 1980s to compete in the high-performance Group B Rally competition. Although most RS200s were fitted with turbo-charged 1.8-litre engines, the *Evolution* models had a 2.1-litre powerplant, capable of an incredible 485 kW (650 hp).

The record for the highest speed achieved by a wheel-driven car where the engine is connected to a transmission that drives the wheels, is 659.808 km/h (409.986 mph), the average over two runs, with a peak speed of 696.331 km/h (432.692 mph), by Al Teague (USA) in *Spirit of '76* on Bonneville Salt Flats, Utah, USA on 21 Aug 1991.

MOST EXPENSIVE PRODUCTION CAR

The world's most expensive car is the Mercedes Benz CLK/LM, which costs $1,547,620 (£957,093). It has a top speed of 320 km/h (200 mph) and can travel from 0–100 km/h (62 mph) in 3.8 seconds.

HEAVIEST CAR

The world's heaviest car is the Soviet-built Zil-41047 limousine, which has a 3.88-m (12.73-ft) wheel-base and weighs 3,335 kg (7,353 lb). A 'stretched' Zil was used by former USSR President Mikhail Gorbachev until Dec 1991. It weighed 6 tonnes (13,227 lb), including 75 mm (3 in) of steel armoured-plating. The first Zil was produced in 1936 for Russian dictator Stalin. The side mirrors were removed as they were redundant – no one dared overtake him. Russian President Vladimir Putin imported two Zils to the UK for his visit in 2000.

HIGHEST CAR MILEAGE

The highest recorded mileage for a car is 3,029,685 km (1,882,559 miles) for a 1966 Volvo P-1800S owned by Irvin Gordon (USA) up to April 2001. He bought the car in 1966 and used to make a daily 201-km (124-mile) round trip to work. In 1998 he said that "it still handles like a new car."

AMPHIBIOUS CIRCUMNAVIGATION BY CAR

On 8 May 1958 Ben Carlin (Australia) arrived in Montreal, Quebec, Canada, in his amphibious jeep *Half-Safe*, having completed a circumnavigation of 62,765 km (39,000 miles) over land and 15,450 km (9,600 miles) by sea or river – the only amphibious vehicle ever to achieve this.

LONGEST RAMP JUMP LANDING ON WATER

Philippe Leveque (Belgium) jumped a distance of 57 m (187 ft) in his car from a ramp into a river at Tournai, Belgium, on 10 Oct 2000. When the car was fully submerged, Leveque got out of the vehicle unharmed.

LONGEST RAMP JUMP 📺USA

The longest ramp jump in a car, with the car landing on its wheels and continuing to drive, is 72.23 m (237 ft), by Ray Baumann (Australia) in a VH Valiant at Ravenswood International Raceway, Perth, Western Australia, on 23 Aug 1998.

Ray Baumann also achieved the furthest ramp jump ever with a standard caravan attached to the back of his car. For this record he launched from a ramp and landed on a collection of burned-out cars that acted as a cushion. The event took place at the Ravenswood International Raceway, Ravenswood, Australia, on 4 Oct 1999.

GUINNESS WORLD RECORDS

bikes and motorbikes

THREEWHEELING

The world's largest tricycle (above) was designed and constructed by 16 students at Bay de Noc Community College, Michigan, USA, in July 1998. The front wheel had a diameter of 4.67 m (15 ft 3 in), the back wheels measured 2.23 m (7 ft 3 in) and the trike had an overall height of 7.13 m (23 ft 4 in). It cost about $6,000 (£4,200) to build, with cash donated by local businesses and residents, and was ridden 76 m (250 ft) during testing. Chuck Gold, the Dean of Technology at the college, needed the help of a fire-truck ladder and crane to help him reach the trike's seat, which is 6 m (20 ft) off the ground. In reality, the seat is for show, with the two riders sitting nearer the ground between the trike's back wheels.

The greatest number of penny-farthing bicycles freestanding in a line with the riders holding hands, is 69 by members of the Velocipede Society at Evandale, Tasmania, Australia, on 26 Feb 2000.

www.guinnessworldrecords.com/3wheelers

ACCESS CODE: ‹43650›

HIGHEST MOTORCYCLE JUMP

The highest motorcycle jump of all time was achieved by Tommy Clowers (USA) on 21 Jan 2001. Clowers achieved a height of 7.62 m (25 ft) from the top of a 3.04-m (10-ft) ramp after a run-up of 12.19 m (40 ft) at Van Nuys Airport, California, USA.

LARGEST MOTORCYCLE WEDDING PROCESSION

Peter Schmidl and Anna Turcekova (Slovakia) had a wedding procession of a record-breaking 597 motorcycles when they got married in Bratislava, Slovakia, on 6 May 2000.

LONGEST REVERSE MOTORCYCLE JUMP

Roger 'Mr Backward' Riddell (USA) jumped seven cars – a record distance of 18 m (60 ft) – riding backwards on a 650-cc Honda motorcycle in May 1987.

LONGEST RAMP-TO-TRUCK MOTORCYCLE JUMP

The longest ramp-to-truck jump on a motorcycle is 41.1 m (135 ft) into a 2.13 x 6.09-m (7 x 20-ft) van travelling at 96 km/h (60 mph). The jump was made by Roger Wells (USA), on a Honda CR500 on 17 Sept 1999.

LONGEST MOTORCYCLE JUMP WITH PASSENGER

On 12 Nov 2000 Jason Rennie (UK) jumped his Yamaha YZ250 motorcycle a record distance of 29.26 m (96 ft), with his girlfriend Sian Phillips on the back at the Rednall airfield, Shropshire, UK.

LONGEST MOTORCYCLE RIDE BY A COUPLE

Jim Rogers and Tabitha Estabrook (both USA) drove 91,766 km (57,022 miles), covering six continents between March 1990 and Nov 1991.

LONGEST MOTORCYCLE RAMP JUMP

On 9 July 2000 Jason Rennie (UK) jumped 77.1 m (253 ft) on a Yamaha YZ250 at Donington Park Grand Prix Circuit, Leicestershire, UK, beating the record by Doug Danger (USA) that had stood for nine years.

BIGGEST PARADE OF TRIUMPH MOTORCYCLES

The greatest number of Triumph motorcycles in a single parade is 313 for the Rally of the Tigers at Chislehurst, Kent, UK, on 12 July 1998. The title refers to one of Triumph's famous models, the Tiger.

EARLIEST MOTORCYCLE

The earliest internal combustion-engined motorized bicycle was a wooden-framed machine built at Bad Cannstatt, Germany, between Oct and Nov 1885. It had a top speed of 19 km/h (12 mph). Known as the *Einspur*, it was lost in a fire in 1903.

GREATEST ENGINE EFFICIENCY

The best fuel-economic performance achieved with a road-legal vehicle is 0.28 litres per 100 km (1,015 mpg) by a motorized tricycle, invented and driven by James Ouchterlony (UK), in the Shell Mileage Marathon at Silverstone, Northants, UK, in 1998.

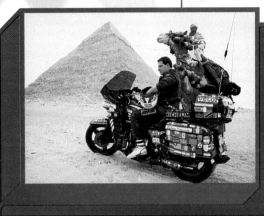

KING OF THE ROAD

Emilio Scotto (Argentina, left) completed the longest-ever journey on a motorcycle, covering over 735,000 km (457,000 miles) between 17 Jan 1985 and 2 April 1995. Riding a Honda Gold Wing motorcycle, he circumnavigated the planet both clockwise and anticlockwise, visiting 214 countries and travelling a distance equivalent to a round-trip to the moon.

The first woman to circumnavigate the world solo on a motorcycle was Monika Vega (Brazil) on a Honda 125-cc. She covered 83,500 km (51,885 miles) and visited 53 countries between 7 March 1990 and 24 May 1991.

www.guinnessworldrecords.com/motorbikes

← ACCESS CODE: ‹43612›

www.guinnessworldrecords.com/roadski

ACCESS CODE: ‹53432›

IRON IN THE SOLE UK

On 18 April 1999 Gary Rothwell (UK, below) road-skied at a record speed of 251.54 km/h (156.3 mph). This daredevil stunt involved climbing from the seat to the rear of a speeding motorcycle and hanging off the back, using 2 mm (0.07 in) titanium-soled boots as 'skis'. In addition to 'skiing' behind the motorcycle with metal shoes, Gary's full repertoire consists of a series of courageous motorcycle tricks and stunts that often seem to defy the laws of physics. He can ride backwards while lying down and steering only with his feet. He also does wheelies while sitting on the handlebars and multi-person wheelies with as many as 12 people on board.

MOST EXPENSIVE MOTORCYCLE

The most expensive production motorcycle in the world is the Morbidelli 850 V8, retailing at 180,000,000 Italian Lira (£56,665 or $79,425) in 2000. The motorbike was styled by Pininfarina, a company best known for its work for Ferrari.

LONGEST STANDING BIKE JUMP FR

Marc Caisso (France) achieved a standing bike jump distance of 2.9 m (9.51 ft) on 26 Oct 2000.

MOST BMX 360° FRONT-WHEEL SPINS IN A MINUTE SE

Using a standard freestyle BMX bike and balancing on just the front wheel, Andreas Lundqvist (Sweden) completed 34 continuous rotations in a minute on 2 Feb 2001.

MOST EXPENSIVE SCOOTER

The world's most expensive production scooter is the Yamaha XP500 Tmax, currently available at an on-the-road price of £6,199 ($8,958). The scooter boasts the largest disc brakes and most powerful engine ever for a production scooter, with a top speed of 168 km/h (105 mph).

LONGEST PEDAL-POWERED VEHICLE

Roger Dumas (USA) built a 55-seater 'bicycle', 42.875 m (140.67 ft) long, made of several bicycle frames welded together and supported by wheels at regular intervals along its length. It was pedalled a distance of 986 m (3,235 ft) by 52 members of Dumas' family in Augusta, Maine, USA, on 29 July 2000.

FASTEST BICYCLE

The highest speed ever achieved on a bicycle is 268.831 km/h (166.944 mph) by Fred Rompelberg (Netherlands) at Bonneville Salt Flats, Utah, USA, on 3 Oct 1995. He was towed until he reached 80 km/h (50 mph) and then continued under his own power, protected by the slip-streaming effect of the lead vehicle.

FASTEST 50 KM CYCLING BACKWARDS

On 28 Aug 1999 Matthew Poynter (Canada) covered 50 km (31 miles) on a bicycle in 2 hr 52 min 11 sec, while facing backwards. For the attempt, he sat on the handlebars and pedalled backwards.

GUINNESS WORLD RECORDS™

 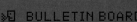

travel and transport

LONGEST ESCALATORS

The world's longest escalator system is Hong Kong's Central Hillside Escalator Link. The 800-m-long (2,624-ft) system of covered moving walkways carries commuters from the Mid-Levels district to the Central Market, which is near the waterfront on Hong Kong Island. After the morning rush, the escalator direction is reversed for the rest of the day.

SHORTEST ESCALATOR

The world's shortest escalator is the 83.4-cm (32-in) moving walkway at Okadaya More's Shopping Mall at Kawasaki-shi, Japan. It was installed by Hitachi Ltd and is 20 times smaller than the average escalator.

BUSIEST AIRPORT

The world's busiest airport for both international and domestic passengers is Hartsfield International Airport in Atlanta, Georgia, USA. In 1999, 78,092,940 passengers passed through its doors. The highest-ranked non-US airport was London Heathrow, with 62,263,365 annual passengers.

LONGEST AIR TICKET

The longest-ever single air ticket measured 12 m (39.37 ft) and was issued to Bruno Leunen (Belgium) in Dec 1984 for a 85,623-km (53,206-mile) round trip, using 80 airlines with a total of 109 stopovers.

GO THE DISTANCE

The world's most travelled couple are Dr Robert Becker and his wife Carmen (USA, left), both of whom have visited all of the sovereign countries and all but six of the non-sovereign or other territories, making a grand total of 234. The Emperor of Japan once gave Bob a shirt while on his travels, and the careful couple have only lost their luggage once, while in Korea.

Frederick W Finn (UK) had flown more air-miles than anyone else, with a record distance of 19,247,750 km (11,960,000 miles) by 2000. Mr Finn commutes regularly from London to New Jersey, USA, and also holds the record for the most flights as a supersonic passenger, having made 714 Atlantic crossings on Concorde.

www.guinnessworldrecords.com/traveltwo
← ACCESS CODE: ‹48606›

FASTEST TRIP FROM LONDON TO NEW YORK

The speed record from central London, UK, to New York City, USA, by helicopter and Concorde, is 3 hr 59 min 44 sec, set by David J Springbett and David Boyce (both UK). The return journey took them 3 hr 40 min 40 sec. Both journeys were taken between 8 and 9 Feb 1982.

FASTEST TRIP AROUND THE WORLD

Michael Bartlett and David J Springbett (both UK) successfully circumnavigated the globe on scheduled flights in a record-breaking 62 hr 15 min between 18 and 21 March 2000. In total they covered 41,010 km (25,484 miles) on their journey between London, Ti Tree Point, Auckland, Los Angeles, Chicago, Madrid and London. The rules of this 'antipodal' record mean that the record holders have to pass through two points on the globe that are exactly opposite one another, and Springbett and Bartlett used Ti Tree Point (New Zealand) and Madrid (Spain) as their two antipodal points of reference.

HIGHEST AIRPORT

Situated in a mountainous region known as 'the roof of the world', Bangda Airport in eastern Tibet lies at 4,739 m (15,548 ft) above sea level. Bangda also holds the record for the longest runway, at 5,500 m (18,045 ft).

LOWEST INTERNATIONAL AIRPORT

The lowest international airport is Schiphol, Amsterdam, Netherlands, at 4.5 m (15 ft) below sea level.

BUSIEST AIRLINE

The busiest scheduled domestic and international airline in the world is Delta Air Lines (USA). In 1999 Delta carried 105,534,000 passengers, the majority of whom (98,298,000) went to destinations within the USA. United Airlines and American Airlines were second and third, with 87,049,000 and 81,452,000 passengers respectively.

BUSIEST INTERNATIONAL AIRLINE

According to the International Air Transport Association (IATA), British Airways (UK) is the world's largest carrier of international passengers, with 36.609 million annual passengers. German airline Lufthansa is in second place, with 27.287 million passengers.

BUSIEST INTERCONTINENTAL AIR ROUTE

The world's busiest intercontinental route is London–New York, with over 3.82 million passengers flying the 5,539 km (3,442 miles) between these two cities annually.

BUSIEST INTERNATIONAL ROUTE

The world's busiest international scheduled air route runs between Hong Kong and Taipei, Taiwan, with 3.96 million passengers recorded in 1999 by the International Civil Aviation Organization. In 1997 the world's 25 top airports handled a total of 968 million passengers.

WIDEST ROAD

The world's widest road is the Monumental Axis, running for 2.4 km (1.8 miles) from the Municipal Plaza to the Plaza of the Three Powers in Brasilia, Brazil. The six-lane boulevard was opened in April 1960 and is 250 m (820.2 ft) wide.

TOWERING OVER THE COMPETITION

France (left) attracts more tourists than any other country. According to the World Tourism Organization, France received 73 million foreign tourists in 1999, representing 11.2% of the global market and easily outnumbering its own population of 59 million.

As a whole, Europe is the world's most popular destination for international tourists, with 379.8 million arrivals in 1999, accounting for 58.4% of the world total.

The USA spends more on foreign tourism than any other nation, with $54 billion (£32.56 billion) spent while travelling in 1999, down from $56.1 billion (£33.82 billion) in 1998. Germany and the UK hold second and third place in the spending stakes respectively.

www.guinnessworldrecords.com/mosttourists
← ACCESS CODE: ‹46014›

MOST LANES IN ONE ROAD

The San Francisco–Oakland Bay Bridge Toll Plaza has 23 lanes (17 westbound) serving the bridge in Oakland, California, USA.

STEEPEST STREET

The world's steepest public road is Baldwin Street in Dunedin, New Zealand, which has a maximum gradient of 1:1.266 (38° or 42.2%). Baldwin Street is so steep that there are warning signs discouraging motorists from attempting to drive up it. In comparison, San Francisco's steepest streets, Filbert Street and 22nd Street, both have a maximum gradient of 1:1.853 (28.35° or 31%).

NARROWEST STREET

The world's narrowest street is in the village of Ripatransone in Italy. It is called Vicolo della Virilita (Virility Alley) and is 43 cm (16.9 in) wide.

GREATEST TRAFFIC DENSITY

International Road Federation statistics show that Monaco is the country with the highest number of vehicles in relation to its road network. In 1996, the most recent year for which statistics are available, there were 480 vehicles for each kilometre of road in the principality. If all the vehicles were parked behind one another on Monaco's streets, nearly half would have nowhere to park.

BIGGEST 'SPAGHETTI' JUNCTION

The most complex road interchange in the world is the 2/22/57 Interchange (known unofficially as the Orange Crush Interchange) in Orange County, California, USA. It consists of 34 routes on just two levels and has an average daily traffic flow of 629,000 vehicles. The most complex interchange on the British road system is that at Gravelly Hill, north of Birmingham on the Midland Link Motorway section of the M6, opened on 24 May 1972. Popularly known as 'Spaghetti Junction', it includes 18 routes on six levels (together with a diverted canal and river).

GREATEST ROAD MILEAGE

According to the International Road Federation, the country with the greatest length of road is the United States (all 50 states), which had 6,348,227 km (3,944,788 miles) of graded roads in 1999. India had 3,319,664 km (2,062,839 miles) and Brazil 1,724,924 km (1,071,867 miles) of graded roads.

www.guinnessworldrecords.com/spacetourist

OUT OF THIS WORLD!

US businessman Dennis Tito (right, centre) paid the Russians a reported $20 million (£14 million) to visit the International Space Station (ISS) as it orbited above the Earth. He took off on 28 April and returned on 6 May 2001. Tito's 'holiday' can officially be called the most expensive tourist trip ever because he paid for it entirely out of his own pocket. Previous civilians who have made the trip into space have either been active crew members such as Helen Sharman (UK) and Salman al-Saud (Saudi Arabia), or have been paid for by an employer, as was the case with Japanese broadcaster Yoyohiro Akiyama.

The largest space-launch vehicle was the Saturn V, used to send astronauts to the Moon between 1968 and 1972. It was 110.6 m (363 ft) long.

The smallest satellite launch vehicle was Pegasus, a three-stage booster, which was 15.5 m (50.85 ft) long. Pegasus has now been succeeded by an operational Pegasus XL version. The original Pegasus, first launched in 1990, was air-launched from an aircraft.

ACCESS CODE: ‹56604›

GUINNESS
WORLD RECORDS™

buildings and structures 1

LARGEST CINEMA

The largest cinema in the world is the Radio City Music Hall, New York City, New York, USA, which opened on 27 Dec 1932 with 5,945 (now 5,910) seats. Designated a New York City landmark in 1979 and a National Historic Landmark in 1987, over 300 million people have passed through its doors.

OLDEST ICE THEATRE

The oldest purpose-built ice theatre is the Ice Drome at Blackpool Pleasure Beach, Lancashire, UK, which opened in Oct 1937. The theatre has been in continuous use ever since.

LARGEST AMPHITHEATRE

The Flavian amphitheatre or Colosseum of Rome, Italy, completed in 80 AD, covers 20,000 m² (5 acres) and has a capacity of 87,000. It has a maximum length of 187 m (613 ft) and a maximum width of 175 m (574 ft). At the height of Rome's power, the Colosseum was the site of countless battles between gladiators, slaves and wild beasts. The arena was even flooded to recreate naval battles.

SOUTHERNMOST LIGHTHOUSE

In 1884 the Argentine navy built a lighthouse on the Isla de los Estados, 100 nautical miles from Cape Horn

TEMPLE-TASTIC

The largest Buddhist temple in the world is Borobudur, central Java, Indonesia (left), built between 750 and 842 AD. The 6-ha (14.83-acre) stone structure is 34.5 m (113 ft) tall. The temple is built in three layers – a pyramidal base with five concentric square terraces, a cone with three circular platforms and at the top, a monumental bell-shaped stupa.

www.guinnessworldrecords.com/borobudur
← ACCESS CODE: ‹49868›

in Patagonia. The light guided ships and boats as they sailed through the Magellan Strait. Abandoned in 1902, the lighthouse has now been rebuilt and continues to operate.

SMALLEST CHURCH

The world's smallest church is Santa Isabel de Hungría, in Colomares, at Benalmádena, Málaga, Spain. Built out of polychromed stone, it was consecrated on 7 April 1990 and has a total floor area of 1.96 m² (21.1 ft²). Mass is held on special occasions and only one person can fit in to pray at a time.

FURTHEST BUILDING RELOCATION

The linked five-storey Gem Theater and Century Club building in Detroit, Texas, USA, was moved five blocks away – a distance of 563 m (1,850 ft) – on 72 dollies, each with eight rubber tyres. It took 25 days to move the 2,750-tonne (6.061 million-lb) building, beginning on 16 Oct 1997.

HEAVIEST BUILDING RELOCATED

On 1 March 1998 the 3,700-tonne (8.157 million-lb) Empire Theater, New York City, New York, USA, was moved on rails 51.81 m (170 ft) west, as part of the 42nd Street Development Project. Moving at less than 1 ft (30 cm) a minute, it was transferred in less than five hours on to temporary foundations by hydraulic cylinders along eight rails.

TALLEST STRUCTURES

The tallest structure ever was the guyed Warszawa Radio mast at Konstantynow, Poland, which was 646.38 m (2,120 ft 8 in) tall before it collapsed during renovation work on 10 Aug 1991. It was designed by Jan Polak (Poland) and weighed 550 tonnes (1.102 million lb).

The tallest structure that is still standing, is a stayed television transmitting tower, between Fargo and Blanchard, North Dakota, USA, which is 629 m (2,063 ft) tall.

TALLEST BUILDING

The free-standing CN Tower in Toronto, Ontario, Canada, which rises to 553.34 m (1,815 ft 5 in), is the tallest building. At 351 m (1,150 ft) it has a revolving restaurant from which you can see 120 km (75 miles).

TALLEST OFFICE BUILDING

The Petronas Towers in Kuala Lumpur, Malaysia, became the world's tallest office building in March 1996, when stainless steel pinnacles measuring 73.5 m (241 ft) long were placed on top of the 88-storey towers, bringing their height to 451.9 m (1,482 ft 8 in). As these spires are non-functional, the Sears Tower, Chicago, Illinois, USA, can still boast the highest occupied storey.

TALLEST HOTEL

The Grand Hyatt Shanghai in Pudong, China, is the tallest hotel in the world. It occupies the top 35 floors of the 88-storey Jin Mao Tower and contains the world's highest health club on the 57th floor.

HIGHEST-ALTITUDE HOTEL

The Hotel Everest View above Namche, Nepal – the town closest to Everest base camp – is located at a record height of 3,962 m (13,000 ft) above sea level. The hotel commands an excellent view of the Himalayas, including Mt Everest, the world's highest mountain.

HIGHEST-ALTITUDE RESTAURANT

The highest restaurant in the world is on the mountain summit at the Chacaltaya ski resort, Bolivia, 5,340 m (17,520 ft) above sea level. Lake Titicaca, the world's highest navigable lake, can be glimpsed through the restaurant windows.

LARGEST ADMINISTRATIVE BUILDING

The Pentagon, in Arlington, Virginia, USA, covers the largest ground area of any office building. Built to house the US Defense Department's offices, the exterior side of each wall is 281 m (921 ft) long, and the perimeter measures 1,405 m (4,610 ft) long. Its five storeys enclose a floor area of

THE BIGLOO
FI

The largest igloo ever built is the Ice Hotel in Jukkasjärvi, Sweden (left), 200 km (124 miles) north of the Arctic Circle. It has a total floor area of 4,000 m² (43,055 ft²), with the capacity to sleep up to 150 guests per night. It was first built in 1989 as the 'Art-ic' exhibition, with a 60 m² (645 ft²) gallery. It has been rebuilt every Nov, since 1990, increasing in size each year. It opens in Dec and usually stays open until the end of April or the beginning of May, depending on the weather. The temperature inside the hotel hovers between -4° and -9°C (25° and 16°F) depending on the weather outside. It currently features ice sculptures, a cinema, saunas, an ice chapel and an ice bar. The guests even have to sleep on ice beds, but thankfully they are covered with thick reindeer pelts.

www.guinnessworldrecords.com/igloo
← ACCESS CODE: ‹52782›

SMALL IS BEAUTIFUL

The smallest house in the world is a 19th-century fisherman's cottage (above) at The Quay, Conwy, Wales, UK, which consists of two tiny rooms, a staircase and a tiny bedroom – everything in fact but a bathroom. It has only 1.82 m (72 in) of frontage, is 3.09 m (122 in) high and measures 2.54 m (100 in) deep. An average-height man could just manage to lie across its width. At the beginning of the century the owner, Robert Jones, travelled across Britain measuring all small houses to prove that his was really the smallest.

www.guinnessworldrecords.com/tinyhouse

ACCESS CODE: ← ‹50055›

604,000 m² (149.2 acres), and the corridors total 28 km (17.5 miles) in length. 23,000 military and civilian employees work in the building. It was completed on 15 Jan 1943 and cost an estimated $83 million (£57.89 million) to build.

LARGEST INDUSTRIAL BUILDING

The largest multi-level industrial building that is a single structure, is the container freight station of Asia Terminals Ltd at Hong Kong's Kwai Chung container port. The 15-level building has a total area of 865,937 m² (9,320,868 ft²).

LARGEST ANCIENT CASTLE

The largest ancient castle in the world is Prague Castle in the Czech Republic, which dates back to the 9th century. It is an irregular oblong polygon with an axis of 570 m (1,870 ft) and an average diameter of 128 m (420 ft), giving a surface area of 72,800 m² (18 acres).

SMALLEST DETACHED HOUSE

Thimble Hall, located in the Peak District village of Youlgreave, Derbyshire, UK, holds the record for the smallest detached house, externally measuring 3.63 m (11 ft 10 in) by 3.14 m (10 ft 3 in) and 3.7 m (12 ft 2 in) high. It was reputedly occupied by a family of eight in the 19th century.

LARGEST MOSQUE

The world's largest mosque is Shah Faisal Mosque, near Islamabad, Pakistan. The total area of the complex is 189,700 m² (46.87 acres), with the covered area of the prayer hall being 4,800 m² (1.19 acres). It can accommodate 100,000 worshippers in the prayer hall and courtyard and a further 200,000 people in the adjacent grounds.

www.guinnessworldrecords.com/largestwindows

EXTREME PANE

The largest windows in the world are those in the Palace of Industry and Technology at Rondpoint de la Défense, Paris, France (below). The three matching windows, made up of a large number of panes of glass, have an extreme width of 218 m (715 ft) and a maximum height of 50 m (164 ft). The Palace of Industry and Technology was built by General de Gaulle's government in the late 1950s as a national exhibition centre. It spearheaded

ACCESS CODE: ‹49682›

LARGEST TRADITIONAL HINDU TEMPLE OUTSIDE INDIA

The largest traditionally built Hindu temple outside India is the Shree Swaminarayan Mandir, Neasden, London, UK, which covers an area of 6,071 m² (65,344 ft²) and is built with 26,300 pieces of stone. Opened on 20 Aug 1995, it was carved by 1,526 craftsmen in India and then reassembled in London a year later.

the redevelopment of the La Défense area of the city, and was soon surrounded by offices, shops and apartment buildings. Its three windows are 15 mm (0.6 in) thick, and were manufactured by the Chantereine-Thourotte factory outside Paris.

The largest sheets of glass ever manufactured were two identical panes 21.64 m (71 ft) long and 2.9 m (9 ft 6 in) wide, made by the Saint Gobain Co in France and installed in their Chantereine factory at Thourotte, France, in Aug 1996.

GUINNESS WORLD RECORDS

buildings and structures 2

SMALLEST COMMERCIAL THEATRE

The Theatre of Small Convenience, Malvern, Worcestershire, UK, a former Victorian gentleman's toilet, seats 12 people and covers an area of 10.14 m² (109.1 ft²). It opened on 6 Nov 1999 and is used by amateur and professional performers.

LARGEST OPERA HOUSE

The Metropolitan Opera House at the Lincoln Center, New York City, New York, USA, is the biggest opera house in the world, with a people capacity of 4,065. The auditorium is 137 m (451 ft) deep and the stage measures 70 m (230 ft) wide and 45 m (148 ft) deep.

LARGEST OBELISK

The obelisk of Pharaoh Tuthmosis III was brought from Aswan, Egypt, by Emperor Constantinus in 357 AD and repositioned in the Piazza San Giovanni in Laterano, Rome, Italy, on 3 Aug 1588. The obelisk stands up to 32.81 m (107 ft 7 in) high and weighs 455 tonnes (1,003,102 lb).

DEEPEST UNDERWATER POSTBOX

The world's deepest underwater postbox is located 10 m (32.8 ft) beneath the waters of Susami Bay, Japan. Sports divers can post special waterproof plastic postcards in the box, which is officially part of the Susami post office and opened daily.

www.guinnessworldrecords.com/djoser
ACCESS CODE: ‹49728›

ETERNAL TRIANGLE

The Djoser Step Pyramid (left) at Saqqâra, Egypt, is the world's oldest pyramid. It was constructed by Imhotep (Djoser's royal architect) during the Third Dynasty (around 2,630 BC) to a height of 62 m (204 ft) and is thought to be the first tomb in Egypt to have been built entirely of stone.

The world's largest pyramid, and the largest monument ever constructed, is the Quetzalcóatl Pyramid at Cholula de Rivadavia, 101 km (63 miles) south-east of Mexico City, Mexico. It is 54 m (177 ft) tall, and its base covers an area of nearly 18.2 ha (45 acres). Its total volume has been estimated at 3.3 million m³ (4.3 million yd³), compared with the volume of 2.4 million m³ (3.1 million yd³) for the Pyramid of Khufu or Cheops, at Giza, Egypt.

More than 4,273 undersea letters were collected in the postbox's first year of operation in 1999.

MOST ROOMS IN HOUSE

The house with the most rooms is Knole House, near Sevenoaks, Kent, UK, which is believed to have had 365 rooms, one for each day of the year. Built around seven courtyards, its total depth from front to back is about 120 m (400 ft). Building began in 1456 by Thomas Bourchier, Archbishop of Canterbury, and the house was extended by Thomas Sackville, first Earl of Dorset, around 1603. Knole is now administered by the National Trust.

LARGEST DOOR

The four doors in the Vehicle Assembly Building near Cape Canaveral, Florida, USA, reach a record-breaking height of 140 m (460 ft). The building is used by NASA to assemble and prepare space vehicles.

LARGEST MARQUEE

An enormous marquee covering an area of 17,500 m² (188,350 ft²) was erected by the firm of Deuter from Augsburg, Germany, for the Welcome Expo in Brussels, Belgium, in 1958.

HIGHEST-ALTITUDE PRE-FABRICATED ROAD BRIDGE

The highest-altitude road bridge is a 5,602-m-high (18,380-ft) Bailey bridge invented by Sir Donald Bailey which was made up of pre-fabricated sections. Erected in Aug 1982 near Khardung-La, in Ladakh, India, it is 30 m (98 ft) across. Such bridges played a major role in the Allied invasion of Nazi-occupied Europe, enabling speedy river crossings even after the retreating Germans dynamited fixed bridges.

LONGEST BRIDGE

At 38.42 km (23 miles), the longest bridge in the world is the Second Lake Pontchartrain Causeway, which joins Mandeville and Metairie,

Louisiana, USA. Completed in 1969, the causeway is so long that it is possible to stand in the middle of it and be unable to see land in either direction.

LONGEST CABLE SUSPENSION BRIDGE

The Tsing Ma Bridge in Hong Kong, opened to the public in May 1997, has a span of 1,377 m (4,518 ft), making it the longest suspension-bridge span for combined road and railway traffic.

TALLEST BRIDGE

The towers of the Akashi-Kaikyo Bridge, between Honshu and Awaji islands, Japan, rise to a height of 299 m (984 ft) and their foundations extend 70 m (230 ft) beneath the seabed. The suspension cables are 1 m (3 ft) thick. The bridge has been built to withstand winds of 80 km/h (50 mph), as well as earthquakes of 8.5 on the Richter scale.

LARGEST WALL OF BOOKS

On 30 Nov 2000 a wall made of 649,000 books designed by Luz Darriba (Spain), was unveiled in Lugo, Spain. It has an area of 11,800 m² (127,014 ft²), took 6,000 people 100 days to build, and was built on a structure 6 m (19.7 ft) long.

LARGEST TEEPEE

The world's largest teepee is 12.8 m (42 ft) high, 76.8 m (252 ft) in circumference and has a diameter of 15.2 m (50 ft). It was built by Dr Michael Doss (USA) of the Crow

UP THE GARDEN PATH

The largest beach-front garden in the world (left) stretches from Emissario Submarino, next to Urubuquecaba Island, to the entrance of the port channel between Sao Vicente and Santo Amaro Islands in Santos, Brazil. It covers an area of 218,800 m² (2,355,143 ft²) and has 719 flowerbeds, 1,746 trees and the path running through it is 5,247 m (17,214 ft) long.

The world's largest garden is arguably the one created by Andre Le Notre at Versailles, France, in the late 17th century for Louis XIV. The magnificent formal gardens and parkland were created in what had been a muddy swamp. They cover over 6,070 ha (15,000 acres) of which the famous formal garden covers 100 ha (247 acres).

 www.guinnessworldrecords.com/beachgarden
ACCESS CODE: ‹52135›

ACCESS CODE: ‹50947›

STATE OF THE ART

The Getty Center in Los Angeles, California, USA (below), is the world's most expensive museum, and is funded by a $4.3-billion (£2.4-billion) trust established after the death of oil tycoon J Paul Getty in 1976. It cost an unprecedented $1 billion (£600 million) to build and took 13 years to construct on its 10-acre hilltop site, offering views to the city and the sea. It covers 93,000 m² (1 million ft²) and was designed by Richard Meier (USA).

Getty first opened a museum to the public in 1954 in the grounds of his Malibu home. The first art to be displayed consisted of antiquities and French decorative art and paintings. In 1974 he constructed a new villa for the display of his collections.

The new building, which opened in 1997, also holds the record for the largest museum acquisitions budget. It was first established with an initial budget of $700 million (£300 million) in Jan 1974. Today the museum has an annual budget of over $100 million (£70.4 million), which is used for acquisitions for its 38 galleries.

Indian Reservation, Montana, USA, and is a Crow Nation teepee modelled directly on one owned by Chief Medicine Crow.

LARGEST SHOWER

The largest shower in the world was built at Jones Beach State Park, New York, USA, on 27 May 2000. It measures 24.47 m (80 ft 3.5 in) long, 2.43 m (8 ft) wide and 3.65 m (12 ft) tall, big enough for up to 200 people to shower simultaneously.

LARGEST SHOPPING CENTRE

West Edmonton Mall in Edmonton, Alberta, Canada, covers an area of 492,387 m² (5.3 million ft²). The mall contains over 800 stores and services, as well as 11 major department stores. Parking is provided in the world's largest car park for over 20,000 vehicles. The mall also has the world's largest indoor amusement park, indoor waterpark and man-made lake.

TALLEST CHIMNEY

The coal power-plant No. 2 stack at Ekibastuz, Kazakhstan, is 420 m (1,378 ft) tall. The diameter tapers from 44 m (144 ft) at the base to 14.2 m (46 ft 7 in) at the top.

LARGEST HANGING BASKET

Jos de Troyer (Belgium) created a hanging basket measuring 10.5 m (34.4 ft) in diameter and weighing 45 tonnes (99,207 lb) in Ghent, Belgium. It went on display on 20 April 2000 and is hanging above the Emile Braunplein square in Ghent's historic centre. A special flower beer was brewed to celebrate the occasion.

GUINNESS WORLD RECORDS™

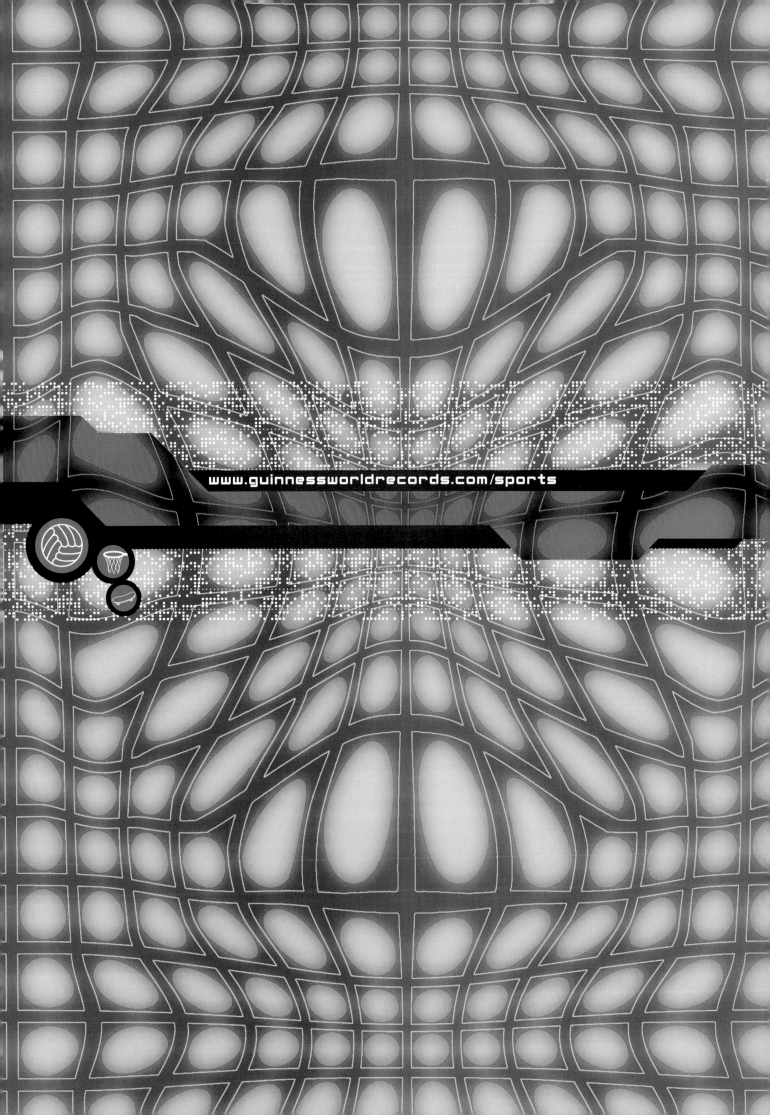

www.guinnessworldrecords.com/sports

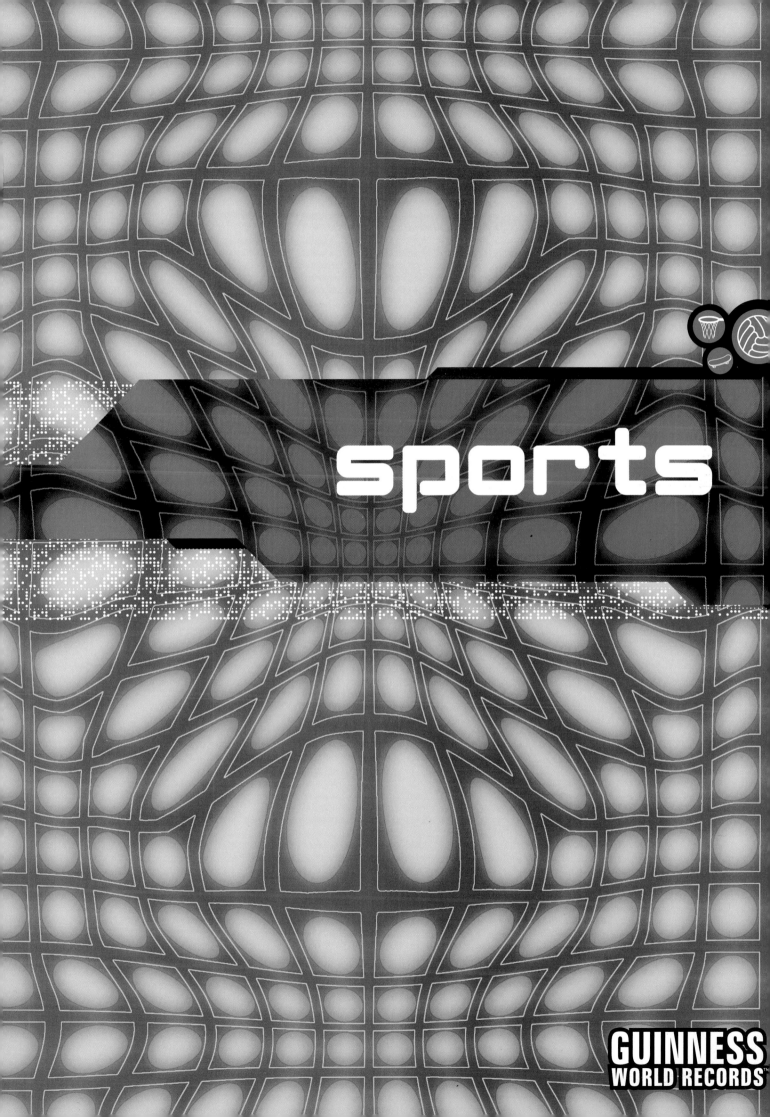

sports

baseball

HIGHEST OLYMPIC BATTING AVERAGE

Luigi Carrozza (Italy) hit .571 at the 1996 Olympic Games, Atlanta, Georgia, making this the highest batting average achieved by a player during an Olympic tournament.

MOST GAMES WON BY A PITCHER AT AN OLYMPICS

The greatest number of games won by a pitcher at an Olympic Games tournament is three by Chieh-Fu Kuo Lee (Chinese Taipei) in 1992, Seth Greisinger (USA) and Omar Luis (Cuba) in 1996 and Ryan Franklin (USA) in 2000. A pitcher is credited with winning the game when he pitches for the majority of the inning in which his team scores the winning run.

MOST STRIKEOUTS AT THE OLYMPICS

The most strikeouts thrown by a pitcher in an Olympic Games is 27 by Tomohito Ito (Japan) at Barcelona, Spain, in 1992.

MOST HITS BY A PLAYER IN OLYMPICS

The most hits at an Olympic Games tournament by a player is 20 by Omar Linares (Cuba) at Barcelona, Spain, in 1992, and again at Atlanta, Georgia, USA, in 1996.

BORN TO RUN

The most home runs in a career was achieved by Henry Louis 'Hank' Aaron (USA, left) with 755 home runs; 733 for the Milwaukee Braves (1954–65) and Atlanta Braves (1966–74) in the National League and 22 for the Milwaukee Brewers (AL) from 1975 to 1976. Born in 1943, Aaron grew up in a segregated neighbourhood in Mobile, Indiana, USA. From a young age he was determined to play professional baseball, and taught himself the game at the local playground. With no team at his high school, Aaron played in local amateur leagues until he was eventually recruited by the Milwaukee Braves. There he became one of the first black players to cross the colour divide that was then in force.

www.guinnessworldrecords.com/aaron
ACCESS CODE: ‹45657›

MOST HOME RUNS AT THE OLYMPICS

The record for the most home runs hit by an individual at an Olympic Games tournament is nine (in nine games) by Orestes Kindelan (Cuba) at Atlanta, Georgia, USA, in 1996.

MOST MAJOR LEAGUE TEAM TITLES

There are two leagues in US baseball, the National League (NL) formed in 1876 and the American League (AL) formed in 1901. The champions of each league meet in the World Series and the best players meet in an All Star Game: NL v. AL.

The greatest number of title wins of the American League is 37 by the New York Yankees between 1921 and 2000.

The record for the most National League titles is 18, held by the LA Dodgers (formerly the Brooklyn Robins and the Brooklyn Dodgers).

MOST WORLD SERIES WINS

The World Series was first staged unofficially in 1903, and officially from 1905. The most wins is 26 by the New York Yankees (AL) between 1923 and 2000, from a record-breaking 37 Series appearances.

MOST WORLD SERIES PLAYED

The most series played is 14 by Lawrence Peter 'Yogi' Berra (USA) playing for the New York Yankees (AL) between 1947 and 1963.

MOST HOME RUNS IN A WORLD SERIES GAME

The most home runs in a World Series game is three by George Herman 'Babe' Ruth (USA) playing for the New York Yankees (AL) on 6 Oct 1926 and again on 9 Oct 1928, and by Reggie Jackson (USA) also playing for the New York Yankees (AL) on 18 Oct 1977. Babe Ruth's impact on baseball remains unsurpassed, and he has been called 'the greatest player of all time'.

MOST HOME RUNS IN A SINGLE GAME

The most home runs hit in a major league game is four, first achieved by Robert Lincoln Lowe (USA) for Boston (NL) v. Cincinnati (NL) on 30 May 1894. The feat has been achieved a further 11 times since then, most recently on 7 Sept 1993 by Mark Whiten (USA), for St Louis (NL) playing against Cincinnati (NL).

LONGEST HOME RUN HIT

The longest measured home run for a major league game is 193 m (634 ft) by Mickey Mantle (USA) for the New York Yankees (AL), against the Detroit Tigers (AL) at Briggs Stadium, Detroit, Michigan, USA, on 10 Sept 1960.

MOST BASE HITS IN CAREER

Pete Rose (USA), nicknamed 'Charlie Hustle', has the most base hits in a career, with 4,256 achieved for Cincinnati (NL), followed by Philadelphia (NL), Montreal (NL) and Cincinnati (NL) from 1963 to 1986.

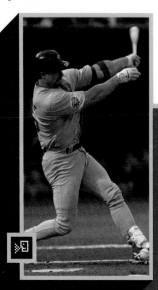

HIT AND RUN

The USA major league record for home runs in a season is 70 by Mark McGwire (USA, left) of the St Louis Cardinals (NL) in 162 games in 1998. Born in Pomona, California, USA, in 1963, Mark McGwire attended Damien High School where he played basketball and golf as well as baseball. He graduated in 1981 and went to the University of Southern California before turning professional. Initially he played pitcher but when his hitting power became apparent, he switched to third base. He was a member of the US Olympic team that won silver in 1984, when baseball was a demonstration sport, and he has reached the World Series three times with the Oakland Athletics (AL). McGwire is active in charity work, frequently appearing at charity golf tournaments.

MOST STOLEN BASES IN CAREER

'Man of Steal' Rickey Henley Henderson (USA) has stolen the greatest number of bases (when the batter gets to the next base without needing to hit the ball) in a baseball career. He notched up a record 1,376 stolen bases between 1979 and 2001 for, in sequence, Oakland (AL), New York (AL), Oakland (AL), Toronto (AL), Oakland (AL), San Diego (NL), Anaheim (AL), San Diego (NL), Oakland (AL), New York (NL), Seattle (AL) and San Diego (NL).

www.guinnessworldrecords.com/mcgwire
ACCESS CODE: ‹45653›

MOST STRIKEOUTS IN A CAREER

Nicknamed 'The Ryan Express', Nolan Ryan (USA) playing for New York (NL), California (AL), Houston (NL), Texas (AL), pitched a record 5,714 strikeouts during his career, from 1966 to 1993.

Nolan Ryan also achieved the most strikeouts in a season when he fanned 383 batters in one season in 1973, playing for California (AL).

MOST STRIKEOUTS IN ONE GAME

A record-breaking 20 strikeouts were pitched in one major league game of nine innings by Roger 'The Rocket' Clemens, playing for Boston (AL) v. Seattle (AL) on 29 April 1986 and v. Detroit (AL) on 18 Sept 1996; by Kerry Wood for Chicago (NL) v. Houston (NL) on 6 May 1988; and most recently by Randy Johnson for Arizona (NL) against Cincinnati (NL) on 8 May 2001.

MOST GAMES WON BY A PITCHER

The pitcher with the most games won in a career is baseball legend Denton True 'Cy' Young (USA), with 511 games won between 1890 and 1911 for Cleveland (NL), St Louis (NL), Boston (AL), Cleveland (AL) and Boston (NL). He pitched a record total of 7,356 innings in the 749 games of his career.

MOST SHUTOUTS IN A PITCHER'S CAREER

The pitcher with the most shutouts (when the opposition fails to score a single run) in a career is Walter Perry Johnson (USA) playing for Washington (AL) with 110 shutouts achieved from 1907 to 1927. Nicknamed 'Big Train', Johnson has been ranked as one of the fastest-ever pitchers.

MOST CONSECUTIVE GAMES

One of the most respected players in the game, Cal Ripken Jr (USA), played 2,632 consecutive games for the Baltimore Orioles (AL) between 30 May 1982 and 19 Sept 1998.

MOST GAMES PLAYED

Pete Rose (USA) played in 3,562 games and was at-bat 14,053 times for the Cincinnati Reds (NL), the Philadelphia Phillies (NL) and the Montreal Expos (NL). After retiring from playing, Rose served as Reds' manager, steering the team to four consecutive second place finishes.

MOST WORLD CUP TEAM WINS

Instituted in 1938, the World Cup has been won a record 21 times by Cuba in 1939–40, 1942–43, 1950, 1952–53, 1961, 1969–73, 1976, 1978, 1980, 1984, 1986, 1990, 1994 and 1998. Baseball was introduced into Cuba in 1866 and it continues to flourish there.

www.guinnessworldrecords.com/rodriguez

BALL PARK FIGURE

The richest contract, based on the average annual salary for the duration of the contract, is the $25.2 million (£16.8 million) earned by Alex Rodriguez (USA, right) of the Texas Rangers (AL). This earned him $252 million (£168 million) over 10 years and was signed in Dec 2000. He made his major league debut in 1994, aged 18, at shortstop for the Seattle Mariners, one of the youngest-ever players to start a game in this position. He was also the youngest-ever shortstop for an All Star Game, playing in 1996 aged 20.

ACCESS CODE: ‹45664›

GUINNESS WORLD RECORDS

SMS ICON   SMS RINGTONE   BULLETIN BOARD   GUINNESS WORLD RECORDS TV

american football

HIGHEST NFL SCORE

The highest score ever in a regular season National Football League (NFL) game occurred when the Washington Redskins beat the New York Giants by 73 points to 41 in Washington, DC, on 27 Nov 1966. The aggregate score of 114 points is also a world record.

LONGEST FIELD GOAL

The longest field goal kicked in an NFL game is 63 yd by two players – Tom Dempsey for the New Orleans Saints on 8 Nov 1970, and Jason Elam for the Denver Broncos on 25 Oct 1998.

LONGEST PASS

A 99-yd-long pass has been achieved on eight occasions in NFL history and has always resulted in a touchdown. The most recent was a pass from Brett Favre to Robert Brooks, for the Green Bay Packers when they played the Chicago Bears on 11 Sept 1995.

MOST TOUCHDOWNS IN AN NFL GAME

The most touchdowns scored in an NFL game is six by Ernie Nevers for the Chicago Cardinals against

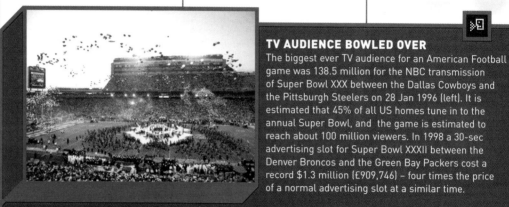

www.guinnessworldrecords.com/superbowl

← ACCESS CODE: ‹47871›

TV AUDIENCE BOWLED OVER

The biggest ever TV audience for an American Football game was 138.5 million for the NBC transmission of Super Bowl XXX between the Dallas Cowboys and the Pittsburgh Steelers on 28 Jan 1996 (left). It is estimated that 45% of all US homes tune in to the annual Super Bowl, and the game is estimated to reach about 100 million viewers. In 1998 a 30-sec advertising slot for Super Bowl XXXII between the Denver Broncos and the Green Bay Packers cost a record $1.3 million (£909,746) – four times the price of a normal advertising slot at a similar time.

the Chicago Bears on 28 Nov 1929; by William Jones for the Cleveland Browns against the Chicago Bears on 25 Nov 1951; and by Gale Sayers for the Chicago Bears against the San Francisco 49ers on 12 Dec 1965.

MOST FIELD GOALS

The most field goals scored by an individual in an NFL game is seven, by Jim Bakken for the St Louis Cardinals against the Pittsburgh Steelers on 24 Sept 1967; and Rick Karlis for Minnesota Vikings against the LA Rams on 5 Nov 1989.

MOST YARDS GAINED

Glyn Milburn gained a record 404 combined net yards for the Denver Broncos against the Seattle Seahawks on 10 Dec 1996. Milburn received Pro Bowl honours in 1995 when he led the NFL with a 27-yd average on kickoff returns and has not missed one game, playing in 96 consecutive games.

MOST TOUCHDOWN PASSES

The greatest number of touchdown passes thrown in the same NFL game by the same player is seven; by Sid Luckman for the Chicago Bears on 14 Nov 1943; Adrian Burk for the Philadelphia Eagles on 17 Oct 1954; George Blanda for the Houston Oilers on 19 Nov 1961; YA Tittle for the New York Giants on 28 Oct 1962; and Joe Kapp for the Minnesota Vikings on 28 Sept 1969.

MOST YARDS GAINED RUSHING IN AN NFL GAME

Corey Dillon rushed for a record 278 yd for the Cincinnati Bengals against the Denver Broncos on 22 Oct 2000.

MOST PASSES CAUGHT IN AN NFL GAME

Tom Fears of the LA Rams caught 18 passes in an NFL game against the Green Bay Packers on 3 Dec 1950. Frears was inducted to the American Football Hall of Fame in 1970.

MOST YARDS PASSING IN AN NFL GAME

Norm Van Brocklin of the LA Rams passed for 554 yd against the New York Yanks on 28 Sept 1951. Van Brocklin, a quarterback, was inducted to the American Football Hall of Fame in 1971.

MOST YARDS RECEIVING IN AN NFL GAME

Willie Lee Anderson of the Los Angeles Rams had a record 336 receiving yards in an NFL game against the New Orleans Saints on 26 Nov 1989. He caught a total of 15 passes and helped the Los Angeles Rams to a 20–17 victory after 6 min 38 sec of overtime, when his 26-yd pass reception laid the ground for the game-winning field goal.

THE GOLDEN BOYS

Jerry Rice of the San Francisco 49ers (left) holds the record for the most touchdowns in a professional career, with 187 between 1985 and 2000. He also holds the Super Bowl career records for touchdowns (seven), yards gained receiving (512) and pass receptions (28). Born in Starkville, Mississippi, in 1962, Jerry Rice first came to prominence at Mississippi Valley State University, setting a college career record of 4,693 yards gained as receiver. He joined the San Francisco 49ers in 1985 forming one of the NFL's best passing partnerships with Joe Montana. Rice was voted Most Valuable Player (MVP) in the 1989 Super Bowl and has recently joined the Oakland Raiders. The 49ers also share the record for the highest attendance for a regular season game with a crowd of 102,368 when they played the LA Rams at the LA Coliseum, California, on 10 Nov 1957

www.guinnessworldrecords.com/dallascowboys

ACCESS CODE: ‹45813›

DALLAS DYNASTY

The greatest number of Super Bowl wins is five; by the Dallas Cowboys (1972, 1978, 1993, 1994 and 1996) and by the San Francisco 49ers (1982, 1985, 1989, 1990 and 1995). The Super Bowl was first held in 1967 between the winners of the NFL and the AFL. The Dallas Cowboys (right), nicknamed 'America's Team', is the most successful team in the history of the NFL, and has appeared in eight Super Bowls in total.

MOST HOME GAMES OF DIFFERENT TEAMS SEEN BY AN INDIVIDUAL

Paul Sansone (USA) attended a home game for each of the 30 NFL teams in the 1998 season. Paul embarked on his tour of the teams in aid of the American Cancer Society.

HIGHEST ATTENDANCE

The greatest number of spectators at any game is 103,985, for Super Bowl XIV between the Pittsburgh Steelers and the LA Rams at the Rose Bowl, Pasadena, California, on 20 Jan 1980.

MOST YARDS RUSHING IN A CFL CAREER

George Reed rushed for a Canadian Football League (CFL) career-record 16,116 yd, for the Saskatchewan Roughriders, 1963–75.

MOST CFL TOUCHDOWNS

The most touchdowns scored in a career is 137, by George Reed for the Saskatchewan Roughriders between 1963 and 1975.

MOST CFL POINTS SCORED

Lui Passaglia scored 3,984 points for the BC Lions between 1976 and 2000. During this time Passaglia played in a record-breaking 408 games.

GUINNESS WORLD RECORDS

basketball

MOST POINTS IN AN NBA GAME

The most points ever scored by an individual in an NBA (National Basketball Association) game is 100. Wilt Chamberlain (USA) set the record while playing for the Philadelphia Warriors against the New York Knicks on 2 March 1962. In NBA games, a successful shot is worth three points, except for shots taken within an area near to the basket. Throws from this area, which is marked with a semicircle drawn from the end of the court to a radius of 6.25 m (20.5 ft), are worth two points. Violations can be penalised with free throws, which are worth one point.

HIGHEST SCORE IN AN NBA MATCH

The highest points total in an NBA match is 370. This occurred when the Detroit Pistons (186) beat the Denver Nuggets (184) at Denver on 13 Dec 1983. Overtime was played after regulation time ended in a 145–145 tie.

HIGHEST POINT AVERAGE IN AN NBA CAREER

The highest point-scoring average per game for players exceeding 10,000 points is 31.5 by Michael Jordan (USA). Jordan scored 29,277 points in 930 games for the Chicago Bulls between 1984 and 1998.

MOST GAMES PLAYED IN AN NBA CAREER

Between 1976 and 1997 Robert Parish (USA) played 1,611 regular-season games. He achieved this over 21 seasons and with four different teams – the Golden State Warriors (1976–80), Boston Celtics (1980–94), Charlotte Hornets (1994–96) and Chicago Bulls (1996–97).

MOST POINTS IN AN NBA CAREER

The most points scored in an NBA career is 38,387 (at an average of 24.6 points per game) by Kareem Abdul-Jabbar (USA) from 1969 to 1989. This includes 15,837 field goals scored in regular-season games, and 5,762 points scored in play-off games.

MOST POINTS IN AN NBA SEASON

The most points ever scored in an NBA season is 4,029 by Wilt Chamberlain (USA) for the Philadelphia Warriors in the 1961/62 season. (His career average was 30.1 points per game.)

MOST GAMES PLAYED IN AN NBA SEASON

The most complete games played in an NBA season is 79 by Wilt Chamberlain (USA) for the Philadelphia Warriors in the 1961/62 season. Chamberlain was on court for a record total time of 3,882 minutes.

MOST CONSECUTIVE NBA GAMES

From 19 Nov 1986 to 20 March 2001, AC Green (USA) played a total of 1,177 consecutive games. During this time Green played for four teams – the Los Angeles Lakers, Phoenix Suns, Dallas Mavericks and Miami Heat.

MOST WINS IN AN NBA SEASON

The most wins in an NBA season is 72 by the Chicago Bulls in the 1995/96 season.

MOST CONSECUTIVE WINS

The record for the most consecutive NBA wins is held by the Los Angeles Lakers. The Lakers won a record-breaking total of 33 NBA games in succession from 5 Nov 1971 to 7 Jan 1972.

MOST NBA TITLES

The Boston Celtics have won more NBA Championship titles than any other team. They have taken the title a total of 16 times, winning in 1957, 1959–66, 1968–69, 1974, 1976, 1981, 1984 and 1986.

OLDEST NBA PLAYER

The oldest player to participate in an NBA game is Robert Parish (USA, b. 30 Aug 1953). Parish played his last game with the Chicago Bulls aged 43 years 231 days on 19 April 1997.

TALLEST NBA PLAYER

The tallest player in NBA history is Gheorghe Muresan (Romania) of the Washington Bullets. Muresan measures up at 2.31 m (7 ft 7 in). He made his professional debut in 1994.

TALLEST BASKETBALL PLAYER

Suleiman 'Ali Nashnush was reputed to be 2.45 m (8 ft 0.25 in) tall when he played for the Libyan national team in 1962.

MOST PARALYMPIC WOMEN'S BASKETBALL GOLD MEDALS

The most Paralympic titles won is three, by Canada. The Canadians took the title in 1992, 1996 and 2000.

MOST MEN'S WHEELCHAIR BASKETBALL WORLD CHAMPIONSHIP TITLES

The most World Championship wins is five, by the USA, who won in 1979, 1983, 1986, 1994 and 1998. The first Championships were held in 1973, and the most recent were played in 2000. Twelve men's teams and eight women's teams competed at the 2000 Championships.

MOST WOMEN'S WHEELCHAIR BASKETBALL WORLD CHAMPIONSHIPS

Canada has won the women's wheelchair basketball title twice, in 1994 and 1998. The first Championships were held in 1990.

WOMEN ON TOP!

The US women's basketball team has won the Olympic gold medal a record-breaking four times. They took the title in 1984, 1988, 1996 and 2000. Teresa Edwards (USA, left) has been a member of every American Olympic gold medal winning team.

Women's basketball was introduced as an Olympic sport in 1976 at the Montreal Olympics. The USSR entered the inaugural competition with an unbeaten international winning streak stretching back to 1958. The Soviets extended this unbeaten run by taking gold in both the 1976 Games and at the 1980 Moscow Olympics. Their dominance of the competition was confirmed in 1980 by a record-breaking 66-point margin of victory over the Italian team, whom they beat 119–53. The American team, however, has won the women's basketball gold at every Olympics since 1980, excluding 1992, when the Commonwealth of Independent States (CIS) took the title.

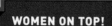
www.guinnessworldrecords.com/womensbasketball

← ACCESS CODE: ‹45627›

CHECK THE RARE CHAIR-FLAIR!

The US men's wheelchair basketball squad (above) have taken a record five Paralympic titles. They won in 1960, 1964, 1972, 1976 and 1988. Wheelchair basketball is largely identical to the standing game. The basket is set at the same height and the court is the same size. Wheelchair basketball demands high levels of skill and physical fitness.

www.guinnessworldrecords.com/chairflair

 ACCESS CODE: ← ‹56470›

MOST WOMEN'S BASKETBALL WORLD CHAMPIONSHIPS

The USSR and the USA have both won the women's Basketball World Championships a record-breaking six times. The Soviet Union took the title in 1959, 1964, 1967, 1971, 1975 and 1983. The USA won in 1953, 1957, 1979, 1986, 1990 and 1998. The first women's World Championship was staged in 1953.

MOST MEN'S BASKETBALL WORLD CHAMPIONSHIPS

Yugoslavia has won the most men's Basketball World Championships, taking the title a total of four times – in 1970, 1978, 1990 and 1998. The first men's Basketball World Championships were held in 1950.

MOST MEN'S BASKETBALL OLYMPIC GOLD MEDALS

The USA has won a record-breaking 12 men's Olympic basketball titles. The sport was first played at the Games in 1936, and the Americans won 63 consecutive matches after its introduction.

The USA's 36-year-long winning streak ended in Munich (West Germany) in 1972, when they lost 50–51 to the USSR in a hotly disputed final.

MOST CONSECUTIVE FREE THROWS

On 28 April 1996 Ted St Martin (USA) scored a record-breaking 5,221 consecutive free throws. The record was set at Jacksonville, Florida, USA.

LONGEST THROW

On 8 April 1996 Iain McKinney (UK) scored with a record-breaking long-distance throw of 27.6 m (90 ft 6 in). The shot was thrown for the Sheffield Sharks during an exhibition match at Ponds Forge, Sheffield, UK.

FURTHEST BASKETBALL SLAM-DUNK FROM A TRAMPOLINE

Joseph Gibby (USA) successfully slam-dunked a basketball by leaping from a trampoline placed 5.79 m (19 ft) from the net's backboard. The slam-dunk was sunk on 21 Jan 2001 at Van Nuys Airport, California, USA.

HIGHEST SLAM-DUNK

On 1 April 2000 Michael 'Wild Thing' Wilson (USA) of the Harlem Globetrotters successfully slam-dunked a

www.guinnessworldrecords.com/bryant

LAKERS RECRUIT YOUNG HOOP-FUL

The youngest player ever to start an NBA game is Kobe Bryant (USA, above), the son of former NBA player Joe 'Jellybean' Bryant. The record-breaker started for the Los Angeles Lakers on 28 Jan 1997, aged just 18 years 158 days. His first match was against the Dallas Mavericks. Bryant is also the youngest player ever to have appeared in an NBA All Star game. He played in the 1998 match aged 19 years 169 days.

ACCESS CODE: ‹56524›

regulation-sized basketball through a basket set at a record height of 3.65 m (12 ft).

FURTHEST DISTANCE DRIBBLED

Jamie Borges (USA) dribbled a regulation basketball for a distance of 155.9 km (96.89 miles) in 24 hours at Barrington High School, Rhode Island, USA, between 3 and 4 May 1998.

MOST BASKETBALLS DRIBBLED

The most basketballs dribbled simultaneously is five, by Joseph Odhiambo (USA). He dribbled two on each hand and one between his feet.

LARGEST ATTENDANCE FOR A BASKETBALL MATCH

A total of 80,000 people attended the European Cup Winners Cup final between AEK Athens and Slavia Prague on 4 April 1968. AEK Athens beat Slavia Prague 89 to 82.

MOST FREETHROWS SCORED IN 10 MINUTES

On 12 Oct 1998 Jim Connolly (USA) scored 280 free throws from 326 attempts, in 10 minutes at St Peter's School, Pacifica, California, USA.

GUINNESS WORLD RECORDS

ice hockey

MOST INDIVIDUAL WINS IN CONSECUTIVE NHL GAMES
Gerry Cheevers (Canada) holds the record for the most consecutive individual NHL (National Hockey League) wins, with 32 for the Boston Bruins in the 1971/72 season.

MOST GOALS SCORED IN AN NHL SEASON
Wayne Gretzky (Canada) scored a record-breaking 92 goals for the Edmonton Oilers in the 1981/82 NHL season.

MOST GOALS SCORED BY AN INDIVIDUAL IN AN NHL GAME
The most goals scored by any individual in an NHL game is seven by Joe Malone for the Quebec Bulldogs v. Toronto St Patricks in Quebec City, Quebec, Canada, on 31 Jan 1920.

MOST POINTS SCORED IN AN NHL CAREER
The most points scored in an NHL career is 2,857 by Wayne Gretzky (Canada) for the Edmonton Oilers, Los Angeles Kings, St Louis Blues and New York Rangers between 1979 and 1999. This massive points total is from 894 goals and 1,963 assists, achieved in 1,487 games.

MOST POINTS SCORED IN A FULL NHL SEASON, INCLUDING PLAYOFFS
The most points scored in a full NHL season, including the playoffs, is 255 points by Wayne Gretzky (Canada) for the Edmonton Oilers in the 1984/85 season. The points total comprises 90 goals and 165 assists.

MOST POINTS SCORED IN AN NHL SEASON
Ice hockey legend Wayne Gretzky (Canada) scored 215 points for the Edmonton Oilers in the 1985/86 season. The points total includes 163 assists.

HIGHEST PERCENTAGE OF WINS IN AN NHL SEASON
The highest percentage of wins to games in an NHL season was 87.5%, achieved by the Boston Bruins with 38 wins in 44 games in 1929/30.

MOST GOALTENDING SHUTOUTS IN AN NHL CAREER
The most goaltending shutouts in an NHL career were by Terry Sawchuk, while playing for Detroit, Boston, Toronto, Los Angeles and the New York Rangers from 1949 to his death in 1970. He did not concede a single goal in 103 of his games.

WINGING IT
The most wins in an NHL season is 62 by the Detroit Red Wings (team member Sergei Fedorov above, left) in the 1995/96 season. Between 1935 and 1955, the team won seven Stanley Cups and boasted some of the all-time best players. Following the team's 1955 win, it hit a 42-year barren patch, the team's famed stability disappeared and they changed coaches and players frequently. 1993 saw a new era of stability when coach Scotty Bowman joined and reversed the fortunes of a team that had become known as the 'Detroit Dead Things' because of their inability to win.

www.guinnessworldrecords.com/redwingwin
← ACCESS CODE: ‹44947›

HIGHEST SCORE IN AN ICE HOCKEY GAME
The highest score in a World Championship game was Australia's 58–0 victory over New Zealand at Perth, Australia, on 15 March 1987.

FEWEST DEFEATS IN A SEASON
In the 1976/77 season, the Montreal Canadiens lost just eight games, the fewest in a season of 70 or more games, from 80 played (60 wins and 12 ties) earning a record 132 points.

LONGEST GAME
The longest ice hockey game was 19 hr 8 min 44 sec, played by a team of 34 in the Labatt Blue NHL Pick-up Marathon at Red Deer, Alberta, Canada, beween 23 and 24 Feb 2001.

MOST STANLEY CUP WINS
The Montreal Canadiens have won the Stanley Cup a record 24 times. They won in 1916, 1924, 1930–31, 1944, 1946, 1953, 1956–60, 1965–66, 1968–69, 1971, 1973, 1976–79, 1986, 1993, from a record 32 finals.

MOST INDIVIDUAL STANLEY CUP WINS
Henri Richard (Canada) has a record 11 Stanley Cup wins to his credit between 1956 and 1973, playing for the Montreal Canadiens. He was on the winning side in 1956–60, 1965, 1966, 1968–69, 1971 and 1973.

MOST GOALS SCORED IN A STANLEY CUP GAME
Five players (all Canadian) share the record for the most goals scored in a Stanley Cup game. Five goals each were scored by Newsy Lalonde for Montreal v. Ottawa on 1 March 1919; by Maurice Richard for Montreal v. Toronto on 23 March 1944; by Darryl

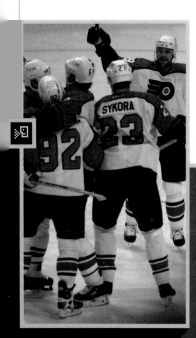

BROTHERLY LOVE
The longest undefeated run for a team in an NHL season is 35 games – 25 wins and 10 ties – established by the Philadelphia Flyers (left) between 14 Oct 1979 and 6 Jan 1980. The Philadelphia Flyers came into existence on 5 June 1967 as part of the NHL's expansion. Fittingly, the team that comes from the 'City of Brotherly Love' is known to treat its players as part of a 'family'. The team was an instant success, topping the division in their first season. In the 1970s they became known as the 'Broad Street Bullies' for their aggressive on-ice presence. The Flyers had consecutive Stanley Cup wins in 1974 and 1975 – their only successes in this particular competition.

www.guinnessworldrecords.com/phillyflyers
← ACCESS CODE: ‹44948›

Glen Sittler for Toronto v. Philadelphia on 22 April 1976; by Reggie Leach for Philadelphia v. Boston on 6 May 1976; and by Mario Lemieux for Pittsburgh v. Philadelphia on 25 April 1989.

QUICKEST GOAL SCORED

The quickest goal scored in an NHL game occurred after five seconds. This record is shared by three players – Doug Smail (Canada) for the Winnipeg Jets v. St Louis Blues at Winnipeg on 20 Dec 1981; Bryan Trottier (Canada) for the New York Islanders v. Boston Bruins at Boston on 22 March 1984; and Alexander Mogilny (USSR, now Russia) for the Buffalo Sabres v. Toronto Maple Leafs at Toronto on 21 Dec 1991.

MOST OLYMPIC TEAM GOLD MEDALS

Ice hockey was first contested at the 1920 Olympics, and the USSR have a record eight wins: in 1956, 1964, 1968, 1972, 1976, 1984, 1988 and 1992 (as the CIS).

Women's ice hockey was first contested at the 1998 Winter Olympics. The USA defeated Canada to win gold.

MOST INDIVIDUAL OLYMPIC GOLDS

The most individual Olympic ice-hockey golds won is three, achieved by Soviet players Vitaliy Davydov, Anatoliy Firsov, Viktor Kuzkin and Aleksandr Ragulin, who each won gold in 1964, 1968 and 1972; Vladislav Tretyak, who won gold in 1972, 1976 and 1984; and by Andrey Khomutov, who won gold in 1984, 1988 and 1992.

MOST WORLD CHAMPIONSHIP WINS

The Ice Hockey World Championships were first held for amateurs in 1920, in conjunction with the Olympic Games. From 1976, the World Championships have been separate and open to professionals. The USSR won 22 world titles between 1954 and 1990 (and Russia won in 1993), including the Olympic titles of 1956, 1964 and 1968.

World Championships for women have been held since 1990, and have been won on each occasion by Canada, in 1990, 1992, 1994, 1997, 1999, 2000 and 2001. In winning the seven titles, the team has not lost a single game.

www.guinnessworldrecords.com/roygoaltend

PUCKER UP

The most NHL career wins by a goaltender is 481 by Patrick Roy (Canada, right) of the Colorado Avalanche, up to 22 March 2001. This record was set on 17 Oct 2000 in a game against the Washington Capitals, and Roy continues to play. The previous record holder was Terry Sawchuk. Throughout Roy's 16-year career he has only missed one season's playoffs, in 1994/95, and has been on the Stanley Cup winning side twice with the Canadiens in 1986 and 1993, and once with the Avalanche in 1996. A sporty child, he decided on becoming a goaltender at the age of eight after watching the sport on television and liking the look of the goaltender's uniform.

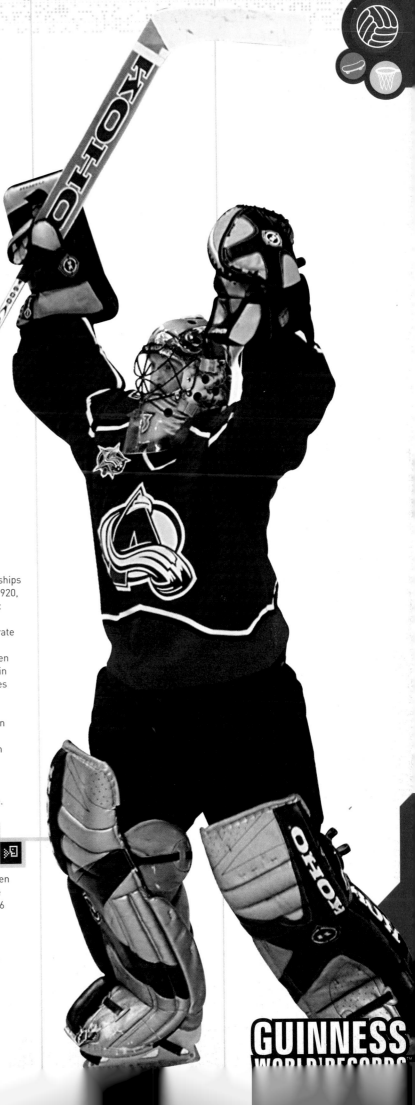

GUINNESS WORLD RECORDS

golf

BIGGEST PRIZE MONEY FOR A TOURNAMENT
The Players Championship, contested from 23 to 27 March 2000 at Sawgrass, Florida, USA, had a total prize pool of $6,113,400 (£3,835,250), with $1.08 million (£677,500) going to the winner, who was Hal Sutton (USA).

HIGHEST CAREER EARNINGS ON THE US LPGA TOUR
The record career earnings for a woman on the US Ladies Professional Golf Association (LPGA) tour belong to Annika Sorenstam (Sweden), with $6,957,044 (£4,874,371) earned between 1993 and April 2001.

MOST BRITISH OPEN TITLES
Harry Vardon (UK) won six British Open titles in 1896, 1898, 1899, 1903, 1911 and 1914. He started out as caddy, rose progressively to the top and became one of golf's first international celebrities. Amazingly, he won two of the Opens after contracting tuberculosis.

MOST US OPEN TITLES
Willie Anderson, Bobby Jones Jr, Ben Hogan and Jack Nicklaus have all won the US Open four times – Willie Anderson (USA) in 1901 and 1903–05; Bobby Jones (USA) in 1923, 1926, 1929 and 1930; Ben Hogan (USA) in 1948, 1950, 1951 and 1953; and Jack Nicklaus (USA) in 1962, 1967, 1972 and 1980.

HITTING THE JACKPOT
Jack Nicklaus (USA, left) won a total of six US Masters titles – more than any other golfer – in 1963, 1965, 1966, 1972, 1975 and 1986. He is considered by many to be the greatest golfer in the history of the sport. After turning professional in 1962, he dominated the golfing world during the 1960s and 1970s. Nicklaus became the first player to take his career earnings to the $2-million (then £816,000) mark in 1973, and in 1986 became the oldest player to win the Masters, at the age of 46.

Jack Nicklaus and Walter Hagan (USA) jointly hold the record for most US PGA titles won with five titles each. Walter Hagan won in 1921 and 1924–27, and Jack Nicklaus in 1963, 1971, 1973, 1975 and 1980.

www.guinnessworldrecords.com/jacknicklaus
ACCESS CODE: ‹55734›

MOST RYDER CUP WINS BY A TEAM
The biennial Ryder Cup professional match between the USA and Europe (British Isles or Great Britain prior to 1979) was instituted in 1927. The USA has won 24 to 7 (with two draws) up until 1999.

MOST RYDER CUP WINS BY AN INDIVIDUAL
Nick Faldo (UK) has won 23 out of 46 matches and also holds a record 25 points scored, having halved four other matches.

Arnold Palmer (USA) holds the US record for most matches won, with 22 out of 32 played. Billy Casper scored a US record 23.5 points from 37 matches.

MOST SOLHEIM CUP WINS
The female equivalent of the Ryder Cup is contested biennially between the top professional players of Europe and the USA, and was first held in 1990. The USA has won four times, in 1990, 1994, 1996 and 1998, with Europe winning in 1992 and 2000.

MOST SOLHEIM CUP WINS BY AN INDIVIDUAL
Dottie Pepper (USA) has won 13 out of 20 matches between 1990 and 2000. Laura Davies (UK) has won 13 out of 23 matches in the same period. The most points scored is 14, by both Davies and Pepper.

LOWEST SCORE OVER 18 HOLES BY A MAN
At least five players have played a long course (over 5,950 m or 6,500 yd) in a score of 58. Shigeki Maruyama (Japan) shot a round of 58 (29 + 29), which included 11 birdies and one eagle, in a qualifying event for the 2000 US Open, at Woodmont Country Club, Rockville, Maryland, (par 71, 5,979 m or 6,539 yd) on 5 June 2000. (A birdie is one under par for the hole; an eagle is two under par and an albatross three.)

The US Professional Golf Association (PGA) tournament record for 18 holes is 59. This is jointly held by Al Geiberger, Chip Beck and David Duval (all USA). Al Geiberger scored 30 + 29 in the second round of the Danny Thomas Classic, on the 72-par (6,628-m or 7,249-yd) Colonial GC course, Memphis, Tennessee, on 10 June 1977. Chip Beck played in a score of 59 in the third round of the Las Vegas Invitational, on the 72-par (6,381-m or 6,979-yd) Sunrise GC course, Las Vegas, Nevada, on 11 Oct 1991. David Duval scored 31 + 28 in the final round of the Bob Hope Chrysler Classic, La Quinta, California, on 24 Jan 1999.

LOWEST SCORE OVER 18 HOLES BY A WOMAN
The lowest recorded score on an 18-hole course (over 5,120 m or 5,600 yd) for a woman is 59 by Annika Sorenstam (Sweden) in the 2001 Standard Register PING at Moon Valley Country Club, Phoenix, Arizona, USA, on 16 March 2001.

LOWEST TOTAL SCORE OVER 72 HOLES BY A WOMAN
The lowest four-round total in a US LPGA Championship event is 261. It is held by two people – Se Ri Pak (South Korea) with 71, 61, 63, 66 at the Jamie Farr Kroger Classic, Sylvania, Ohio, USA, held from 9 to 12 July 1998; and Annika Sorenstam (Sweden) with 65, 59, 65, 68 in the 2001 Standard Register PING at Moon Valley Country Club, Phoenix, Arizona, USA, held from 15 to 18 March 2001.

KARRIE'D AWAY
In 1999 Karrie Webb (Australia, left) had the highest season's earnings on the US LPGA tour. She won a record total of $1,591,959 (£1,115,387). Karrie began playing golf at the age of eight. By the time she had turned professional in 1994, she had already represented Australia six times in international competition. Webb qualified for the LPGA tour despite playing with a broken bone in her wrist. During her rookie season in 1996, she won four tournaments, making her the second most successful rookie ever. She was the first woman to reach the $1-million mark in a single season, winning this sum in only 10 months and 3 days.

www.guinnessworldrecords.com/karriewebb
ACCESS CODE: ‹53361›

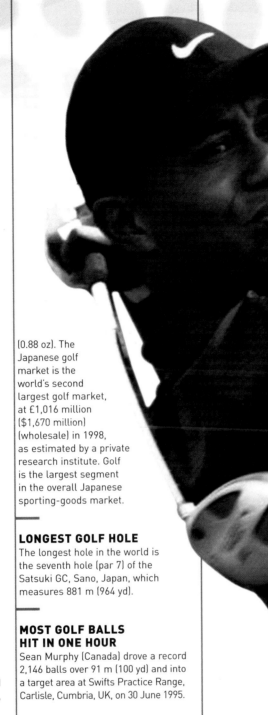

FASTEST ROUND OF GOLF BY AN INDIVIDUAL
The fastest round played when the golf ball comes to rest before each new stroke is 27 min 9 sec by James Carvill (UK) at Warrenpoint Golf Course, Co. Down, Ireland (18 holes; 5,628 m or 6,154 yd) on 18 June 1987.

FASTEST ROUND OF GOLF BY A TEAM
The Fore Worcester's Children team of golfers completed 18 holes in 9 min 28 sec at the Tatnuck Country Club, Worcester, Massachusetts, USA, on 9 Sept 1996. They scored 70.

BEST GOLF BALL CONTROL
Jonas Belander (Sweden) managed to keep a regulation golf ball aloft, alternating touches between two sandwedge golf clubs, for 13 min 47 sec on 3 Feb 2001.

GREATEST DISTANCE BETWEEN TWO ROUNDS OF GOLF IN ONE DAY
Nobby Orens (USA) played at Stockley Park, Uxbridge, Greater London, UK, as well as Braemar Country Club, Tarzana, California, USA – 9,582 km (5,954 miles) apart – on 20 July 1999.

HIGHEST-ALTITUDE SHOT
Vladímir Mysík (Czech Republic) played a shot from the peak of Gasherbrum I, 8,068 m (26,470 ft), Karakoram Range, Kashmir (on the border of India and Pakistan), on 9 July 1997.

LARGEST BUNKER
The world's biggest bunker (called a 'trap' in the USA) is Hell's Half Acre on the 535-m (585-yd) seventh hole of the Pine Valley course, Clementon, New Jersey, USA, built in 1912. It is generally regarded as the world's most difficult course.

LIGHTEST GOLF CLUB
The lightest full-size golf club is the driver JBeam Win.1, manufactured by Japan Golf Equipment Co Ltd of Tokyo, Japan, which weighs just 220 g (7.75 oz). The titanium head weighs 160 g (5.64 oz), the carbon fibre shaft 35 g (1.23 oz) and grip 25 g

(0.88 oz). The Japanese golf market is the world's second largest golf market, at £1,016 million ($1,670 million) (wholesale) in 1998, as estimated by a private research institute. Golf is the largest segment in the overall Japanese sporting-goods market.

LONGEST GOLF HOLE
The longest hole in the world is the seventh hole (par 7) of the Satsuki GC, Sano, Japan, which measures 881 m (964 yd).

MOST GOLF BALLS HIT IN ONE HOUR
Sean Murphy (Canada) drove a record 2,146 balls over 91 m (100 yd) and into a target area at Swifts Practice Range, Carlisle, Cumbria, UK, on 30 June 1995.

www.guinnessworldrecords.com/tigerwoods

WHAT A TIGER!
The all-time career earnings record on the US PGA circuit is held by Tiger Woods (USA, right) with $23,767,307 (£16,652,285), between Aug 1996 and March 2001. Eldrick 'Tiger' Woods was born on 30 Dec 1975. His interest in golf started at an early age – at six months, he would imitate his father's swing as he hit balls into a net, and at the age of two he putted with Bob Hope on *The Mike Douglas Show*. Since turning professional in 1996, Woods has emerged as one of the most gifted players in the history of golf, becoming the only player to achieve a grand slam as well as being the game's highest-ever earner.

The record for the highest season's earnings for the US PGA tour is also held by Tiger Woods. In 2000 he won a total of $9,188,321 (£6,437,698).

In June 2000 Tiger Woods won the US Open by 15 strokes. This is a record for a major tournament. He finished the tournament with a total of 272, an amazing 12 under par.

ACCESS CODE: ‹53362›

GUINNESS WORLD RECORDS

soccer 1

LARGEST FOOTBALL TOURNAMENT

The second Bangkok League Seven-a-side Competition, which was held from 9 Jan to 25 April 1999, was contested by a record-breaking 5,098 teams (35,686 players).

MOST SUCCESSIVE NATIONAL LEAGUE CHAMPIONSHIPS

The greatest number of successive National League Championships is 11 by Al-Ansar Sporting Club, Lebanon, from 1988 to 1999. For all 11 championships, the team was coached by Adnan Mekdashi and presided over by the same club president, Salim Diab.

MOST FOOTBALL MATCHES PLAYED

Peter Shilton (UK) made a record 1,390 senior appearances, including a record 1,005 league appearances – 286 for Leicester City (1966–74); 110 for Stoke City (1974–77); 202 for Nottingham Forest (1977–82); 188 for Southampton (1982–87); 175 for Derby County (1987–92); 34 for Plymouth Argyle (1992–94); one for Bolton Wanderers (1995) and nine for Leyton Orient (1996–97); one league play-off; 86 FA Cup; 102 League Cup; 125 internationals; 13 under-23; four Football League XI and 53 various European and other club competitions.

MOST CAREER GOALS

The most goals ever scored in a career is a record 1,279 by Edson Arantes do Nascimento (Brazil), who is better known as Pelé. He set his record between 7 Sept 1956 and 1 Oct 1977 in 1,363 games. His best year was 1959 when he scored 126 goals, and the Milésimo (1,000th) came from a penalty for his club Santos at the Maracanã Stadium, Rio de Janeiro, Brazil, on 19 Nov 1969 when playing his 909th first-class match.

MOST GOALS BY A TEAM IN ONE GAME

The highest score recorded in a first-class match is 36. This occurred in a Scottish Cup tie between Arbroath v. Bon Accord on 12 Sept 1885, when Arbroath won 36–0 at home.

HIGHEST SCORE IN A NATIONAL CUP FINAL

In 1935 Lausanne-Sports recorded the highest-ever score in a national

cup final when they beat Nordstern Basel 10–0 in the Swiss Cup final, but later lost by the same scoreline at the hands of Grasshopper-Club (Zurich) in the 1937 Swiss Cup final.

FASTEST GOAL

Goals scored in three seconds or less after the kick-off have been claimed by a number of players. From video evidence, Ricardo Olivera (Uruguay) scored in 2.8 seconds for Río Negro against Soriano at the José Enrique Rodó stadium, Soriano, Uruguay, on 26 Dec 1998. When the referee blew his whistle, Olivera blasted the ball towards goal when he saw the goalkeeper was off his line.

FASTEST TIME TO SCORE A HAT TRICK

The fastest time taken to score three goals is 2 min 13 sec by Jimmy O'Connor (Ireland) for Shelbourne against Bohemians at Dallymount Park, Dublin, Ireland, on 19 Nov 1967.

THE REAL DEAL

The most European Champions Cup (instituted in 1957) wins is eight by Real Madrid (Spain, left), in 1955/56, 1956/57, 1957/58, 1958/59, 1959/60, 1965/66, 1997/98 and 1999/2000. Named by FIFA as Team of the Century in 1998, Real Madrid's remarkable success can be traced back to the arrival of its 10th president, Santiago Bernabéu, in 1943, as it was his dream of turning them into the best team in the world that led him to pursue the best players and coaches to share his vision.

Real Madrid also own the world's most expensive player, winger Luis Figo (Portugal), who was transferred from Barcelona in July 2000 for a record 9.90 billion pesetas (£37 million or $52.89 million).

 www.guinnessworldrecords.com/realmadrid

← ACCESS CODE: ‹45617›

MOST CONSECUTIVE HAT TRICKS

The most consecutive league games in which a player has scored hat tricks in a national top division side is four by Masashi Nakayama for Jubilo Iwata in the Japanese League – First Stage. He scored five goals against Cerezo Osaka at Nagai Stadium on 15 April 1998, four goals against Sanfrecce Hiroshima at Jubilo Iwata Stadium on 18 April 1998, four goals against Avispa Fukuoka at Kumamoto City Stadium on 25 April 1998 and three goals against Consadole Sapporo at Jubilo Iwata Stadium on 29 April 1998.

YOUNGEST PLAYER TO SCORE A HAT TRICK

The youngest scorer of a hat trick in UK football was Tommy Lawton, aged 17 years 5 days, on his debut for Burnley v. Spurs at Turf Moor on 10 Oct 1936. The person to score a hat trick in the Premiership is Michael Owen, (UK), aged 18 years 62 days for Liverpool v. Sheffield Wednesday on 14 Feb 1998.

MOST GOALS SCORED BY A GOALKEEPER IN ONE GAME

Paraguayan goalie José Luis Chilavert scored a hat trick of penalties for Vélez Sarsfield in their 6-1 defeat of Ferro Carril Oeste in the Argentine professional league.

MOST GOALS SCORED FROM A CORNER

The greatest number of goals anyone has scored in a match direct from a corner is two by Luis 'Gita' Barroso

RIO GRANDE

Rio Ferdinand (UK, left) became the world's most expensive defender in Nov 2000 when he joined Leeds United from West Ham United in a deal worth £18 million ($25.6 million). Born on 8 Nov 1978, in London, UK, Rio Ferdinand joined West Ham United as a schoolboy in 1994. He made his senior debut in 1996 and has since established himself as a regular in the senior England squad.

The most expensive goalkeeper of all time is Angelo Peruzzi (Italy), who was transferred from Juventus to Inter Milan (both Italian clubs) in June 1999 for a record fee of £10.5 million ($17.4 million), a full £3 million ($4.3 million) more than his nearest rival Fabien Barthez (France) who was bought by Manchester United (UK) from Monaco for £7.5 million ($11.66 million).

www.guinnessworldrecords.com/riogrande

← ACCESS CODE: ‹54326›

(Portugal) for FC de Famalicão against SC Olhanese in a Portuguese Cup match on 2 July 1946.

LONGEST TIME WITHOUT A GOALKEEPER CONCEDING A GOAL

Thomas McKenna (UK), of Folkestone Invicta Under-13s, played 1,417 minutes without conceding a goal, from 24 Sept 1995 to 5 May 1996.

LONGEST THROW-IN

The longest throw-in is 48.17 m (158 ft 0.4 in) achieved by Michael Lochner (USA) at Bexley High School, Ohio, USA, on 4 June 1998.

FASTEST INDOOR FOOTBALL KICK

The fastest indoor football kick is 109.43 km/h (68 mph), by Moroccan international footballer Hassan Kachloul of Southampton FC, UK, on 27 April 2000.

LONGEST PENALTY SHOOTOUT

In the Freight Rover Trophy Southern Section quarter-final between Aldershot Town and Fulham at Aldershot, Surrey, UK, on 10 Feb 1987, a total of 28 penalty kicks were taken after the match had finished 1–1 after normal and extra-time. Seven penalties were missed, with Aldershot winning 11–10.

LONGEST CONTROL OF A FOOTBALL

Ricardinho Neves (Brazil) juggled a regulation soccer ball for 19 hr 5 min 31 sec non-stop with his feet, legs and head and without the ball ever touching the ground at the Los Angeles Convention Centre, California, USA, on 15 and 16 July 1994. The longest duration by a woman is 7 hr 5 min 25 sec by Cláudia Martini (Brazil) at Caxias do Sul, Brazil, on 12 July 1996.

MOST FOOTBALL TOUCHES IN 30 SECONDS

The greatest number of touches of a football in 30 seconds, while keeping the ball in the air, is 136 by Ferdie Adoboe (USA), at Fort Lowell Park, Tucson, Arizona, USA, on

22 Jan 1999. On the same occasion, Adoboe completed 262 touches in just one minute.

MOST UNDISCIPLINED FOOTBALL MATCH

On 3 Nov 1969, in the local cup match between Tongham Youth Club, Surrey v. Hawley, Hants (both UK), the referee booked all 22 players, including one who went to hospital, and a linesman.

FURTHEST DISTANCE TRAVELLED BY TEAMS

The furthest distance travelled between two clubs in the top division of a professional national league is 4,766 km (2,961 miles) between the home grounds of LA Galaxy, Los Angeles, California, and New England Revolution, Foxboro, Massachusetts, in the US Major League.

MOST VALUABLE FOOTBALL SHIRT

The red football shirt worn by striker Geoff Hurst (UK) during the 1966 World Cup final between England and Germany was sold for £91,750 ($134,393) at Christie's, London, UK, on 28 Sept 2000.

www.guinnessworldrecords.com/manunited

ACCESS CODE: ‹54710›

UNITED THEY STAND

Manchester United Football Club (below), in the English Premier League, is the world's most valuable football club. They had a market capitalization of over £1 billion ($1.59 billion) on 8 March 2000 – the first football club ever to reach that milestone. Their finest hour came in 1999 when their victory over Bayern Munich in the European Champion's League final completed the treble (they also won the FA Cup and the Premier League) – a unique achievement in English football.

KEANE
16

soccer 2

MOST WORLD CUP WINS

FIFA (Fédération Internationale de Football Association), founded on 21 May 1904, instituted the first World Cup on 13 July 1930, in Montevideo, Uruguay. It is held quadrennially and Brazil has won a record-breaking four times, in 1958, 1962, 1970 and 1994.

MOST WOMEN'S WORLD CUP WINS

Initiated in 1991, the women's World Cup also takes place quadrennially. The USA won in 1991 and 1999. The winner in 1995 was Norway.

YOUNGEST PLAYER IN A WORLD CUP TOURNAMENT

The youngest person ever to play in a World Cup finals match is Norman Whiteside (UK), who played for Northern Ireland v. Yugoslavia, aged 17 years 41 days, on 17 June 1982.

MOST WORLD CUP APPEARANCES

Antonio Carbajal (Mexico) appeared in a record five World Cup final tournaments, keeping goal for Mexico in 1950, 1954, 1958, 1962 and 1966, and playing 11 games in all.

WOMAN'S WORLD

The most international football appearances by a woman for a national side is officially 225 by No.13 player Kristine Lilly (USA, left) between 1987 and 2000.

In the women's international game, the highest score ever recorded is 21–0. This incredible score has occurred on four occasions – Japan v. Guam at Guangzhou, China, on 5 Dec 1997; Canada v. Puerto Rico at Centennial Park, Toronto, Canada, on 28 Aug 1998; and Australia v. American Samoa and New Zealand against Samoa, both at Mt Smart Stadium, Auckland, New Zealand, on 9 Oct 1998.

www.guinnessworldrecords.com/kristinelilly
← ACCESS CODE: ‹56488›

This record was equalled by Lothar Matthäus (Germany), who played in 1982, 1986, 1990, 1994 and 1998, playing a record 25 games in total.

FASTEST GOAL IN A WORLD CUP MATCH

The quickest goal in a World Cup finals match was after 15 seconds by Vaclav Masek (Czechoslovakia) v. Mexico at Viña del Mar, Chile, on 7 June 1962. In a preliminary match, Davide Gualtieri scored after seven seconds for San Marino v. England at Bologna, Italy, on 17 Nov 1993.

YOUNGEST SCORER IN A WORLD CUP FINAL

The youngest scorer in a World Cup final match is Edson Arantes do Nascimento (Brazil), known as Pelé, who scored for Brazil against Wales, at Gothenburg, Sweden, on 19 June 1958, aged 17 years 239 days. A Brazilian hero, he is also known as 'Perola Negra' (Black Pearl).

MOST FEDERATIONS IN FIFA WORLD CUP QUALIFIERS

A record 198 federations registered to play the FIFA qualifiers for the 2002 Football World Cup to be played jointly in South Korea and Japan. The exceptions were the football federations of North Korea, Niger, Afghanistan, Burundi and New Guinea. In terms of revenue and viewing figures, the World Cup is the world's largest single-sport competition.

MOST FUTSAL WORLD CUP TITLES

Since it was first held in 1989, Brazil holds the record for the most wins at the Futsal (indoor football) World

Cup, which is held every four years, with three in 1989, 1992 and 1996.

MOST EUROPEAN CHAMPIONSHIPS

Germany has won the European Championships a record three times, in 1972, 1980 and 1996 (the first two as West Germany).

A women's Championship was held for the first time in 1984. Germany holds the record for the most wins, winning four times in 1989, 1991, 1995 and 1997.

MOST EUROPEAN CUP-WINNERS CUPS

The European Cup-Winners Cup, contested until 1999 by the winners of European National Cups, has been won a record four times by Barcelona in 1979, 1982, 1989 and 1997. One of the top football clubs in the world, Barcelona has won every major European competition and is the only club in Europe to have taken part annually since 1955 when European competitions were first introduced.

KEEP THE BALL ROLLING

The oldest player to take part in a World Cup match was Albert Roger Milla (left, centre) for Cameroon v. Russia on 28 June 1994, aged 42 years 39 days. He also scored in the match, making him the oldest scorer in the finals. Africa's Footballer of the Year in 1976, Milla moved to France in 1977 and won the French Cup with Monaco in 1980 and with Bastia in 1981. He retired from international football having won 81 full caps, but was persuaded to rejoin the Cameroon squad for the 1994 tournament.

The oldest player to take part in an international game was William Henry 'Billy' Meredith (UK), who played outside right for Wales v. England at Highbury, London, UK, on 15 March 1920, aged 45 years 229 days. He played internationally for a record span of 26 years.

DOUBLE WHAMMY

Two records were broken at the same time when the highest score ever in an international match was achieved by Australia v. American Samoa during the Oceania Group One World Cup qualifying match at Coffs Harbour, NSW, Australia, on 11 April 2001. Australia won 31–0 with Archie Thompson (Australia, right) scoring 13 goals in the match – the most goals ever scored by an individual in a World Cup match.

MOST AFRICA CUP OF NATIONS WINS

The record for the most wins at the Africa Cup of Nations, which is held every two years, is four. It is held jointly by Ghana (1963, 1965, 1978, 1982) and Egypt (1957, 1959, 1986, 1998). The Africa Cup began in 1957 and had just three entrants. Now there are 49 participants.

MOST ASIAN CUP WINS

The most wins in the Asian Cup is three – by Iran – in 1968, 1972 and 1976; and Saudi Arabia in 1984, 1988 and 1996.

MOST CONCACAF CHAMPIONSHIPS

Costa Rica has won the CONCACAF Championships (Confederation of North, Central American and Caribbean Association Football) 10 times between 1941 and 1989.

A women's version, held for the first time in 2000, was won by the USA.

MOST COPA AMERICA CHAMPIONSHIPS

Argentina has won the South American Championship (Copa America since 1975) a record 15 times between 1910 and 1993.

MOST GOALS IN A MATCH BY ONE PLAYER

On 13 Dec 1942 Stephan Stanis (France), playing for Racing Club de Lens v. Aubry-Asturies, in Lens, France, scored 16 goals – the most goals scored by one player in a match. The most goals scored by one player in a match at the Olympics is 10, a record shared by Sofus Nielsen playing for Denmark v. France (final score 17–1) in the 1908 London Olympic Games and Gottfried Fuchs of Germany, who beat Russia 16–0 in the 1912 Stockholm Olympic Games.

MOST INTERNATIONAL CAPS

Hossam Hassan (Egypt) has made the most international appearances, representing his national team 156 times between 1985 and 2001.

FASTEST INTERNATIONAL HAT TRICK

Japanese international Masashi 'Gon' Nakayama scored a hat trick in 3 min 15 sec against Brunei during an Asian Cup qualifying match played on 16 Feb 2000. Nakayama netted the ball after 1 min, 2 min and 3 min 15 sec.

LARGEST MATCH ATTENDANCE

The greatest crowd attendance at a football match numbered 199,854 people at the Brazil v. Uruguay World Cup match in the Maracanã Municipal Stadium, Rio de Janeiro, Brazil, on 16 July 1950.

LONGEST CLEAN SHEET IN SOCCER

The longest that any goalkeeper has succeeded in keeping goals out of his net in top-class competition is 1,275 minutes (just over 14 matches) by Abel Resino (Spain) of Atlético Madrid from 10 Dec 1990 to 1 April 1991.

The record in international matches is 1,142 minutes (nearly 13 matches) for Dino Zoff (Italy) from Sept 1972 to June 1974.

The British club match record is 1,196 minutes by Chris Woods (UK) for Glasgow Rangers from 26 Nov 1986 to 31 Jan 1987.

GUINNESS WORLD RECORDS

 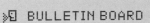

tennis

MOST GRAND SLAM SINGLES TITLES

Between 1960 and 1973 Margaret Court (*née* Smith, Australia) won 24 grand slam tournament singles tennis titles. She won 11 Australian Open titles, five US Open titles, five French Open titles and three Wimbledon titles.

MOST GRAND SLAM MEN'S SINGLES TITLES

Pete Sampras (USA) won 13 grand slam tournament singles tennis titles between 1990 and 2000. These include seven Wimbledon titles, four US Open titles and two Australian Open titles. When he won his first US Open in 1990, he became the youngest man to have done so, at 19.

BEST MALE GRAND SLAM PLAYERS

The only man to hold all four Championships (Wimbledon, US, Australian, and French Open Championships) simultaneously was Don Budge (USA) in 1938. He also won Wimbledon and the US Open in 1937, giving him six successive grand slam tournaments. The first man to

have won all four of the world's major Championship singles was Fred Perry (UK) when he won the French title in 1935. The only man to achieve the grand slam twice was Rod Laver (Australia) as an amateur in 1962 and again in 1969 when the titles were open to professionals.

BEST FEMALE GRAND SLAM PLAYERS

Four women have achieved the grand slam – Maureen Connolly (USA) in 1953; Margaret Court (Australia) in 1970; and Martina Navrátilová (USA) in 1983 and 1984. (These three also won six successive grand slam tournaments.) The fourth was Steffi Graf (Germany) in 1988, when she also won the women's singles Olympic gold medal. Pam Shriver (USA) won a record eight successive grand slam tournament women's doubles titles with Navrátilová, and 109 successive matches in all events from April 1983 to July 1985.

MOST WIMBLEDON WINS

Pete Sampras (USA) won seven Wimbledon men's singles tennis titles in 1993–95 and 1997–2000. This record was set after the Challenge Round was abolished in 1922. Before this, William Charles Renshaw (UK) won seven men's singles titles in 1881–86 and 1889.

Martina Navrátilová (USA) won a record nine Wimbledon women's singles tennis titles in 1978, 1979, 1982, 1983, 1984, 1985, 1986, 1987 and 1990.

FOR PETE'S SAKE

Pete Sampras (USA, above) has earned a record £28,664,619 ($41,314,315) over the course of his career up to March 2001, and also holds the records for the highest earnings in a single season (£3,944,825 or $6,498,311) in 1997, and the greatest prize money ever won (£1.2 million or $2 million) at the Grand Slam Cup in Munich, Germany, in 1990. Steffi Graf (Germany) is the woman with the highest career earnings – £13,481,398 ($21,807,509) between 1982 and 1999, while the highest earnings by a woman in a single season is £2,064,102 ($3,400,196) by Martina Hingis (Switzerland) in 1997.

www.guinnessworldrecords.com/sampras
← ACCESS CODE: ‹44300›

The most Wimbledon doubles tennis titles is 19, held by Elizabeth Montague Ryan (USA) who won them between 1914 and 1934. The 19 titles comprise 12 women's doubles titles and seven mixed doubles titles. The seven mixed doubles titles is a record in itself.

Billie-Jean King (*née* Moffitt, USA) won a record 20 Wimbledon titles between 1961 and 1979, comprising six singles, 10 women's doubles and four mixed doubles titles. This is the most Wimbledon titles won

by a woman. King helped form the Women's Tennis Association (WTA) in 1974, becoming its first president.

The most Wimbledon tennis titles won by a man is 13 by Laurie Doherty (UK), comprising five singles titles (1902–06) and eight men's doubles titles (1897–1906). For his men's doubles titles he was partnered by his brother Reginald Frank Doherty (UK).

MOST FRENCH OPEN WINS

Margaret Court (Australia) holds the women's record with 13 French Open titles between 1962 and 1973, consisting of five singles titles, four doubles titles and four mixed doubles titles.

Henri Cochet (France) holds the men's record with nine titles at the French Open. He won four singles titles, three doubles titles and two mixed doubles titles between 1926 and 1930.

Björn Borg (Sweden) won the French Open men's singles title a record six times, in 1974–75 and 1978–81.

Chris Evert (USA) won the French Open women's singles title seven times – in 1974, 1975, 1979, 1980, 1983, 1985 and 1986. She was voted

CAN'T COMPLAIN ABOUT THE SERVICE . . .

The fastest tennis service by a man is 239.8 km/h (149 mph) by Greg Rusedski (UK, left) during the ATP Champions' Cup at Indian Wells, California, USA, on 14 March 1998. Rusedski's best year came in 1997 when he was voted BBC TV's Sports Personality of the Year and was ranked fourth in the world.
   The fastest tennis service by a woman is 205 km/h (127.4 mph) by Venus Williams (USA) during the European Indoor Championships, Zurich, Switzerland, on 16 Oct 1998. In 1997 she became the first unseeded woman ever to reach the final of the US Open, and has since won seven grand slam titles.

www.guinnessworldrecords.com/rusedski
← ACCESS CODE: ‹44299›

the Women's Sports Foundation's greatest athlete of the past 25 years in 1985 and won the WTA Award in 1992.

MOST US OPEN WINS
The most US Open singles tennis titles won by a man is seven and is shared by Bill Tilden (USA) in 1920–25 and 1929, Richard Sears (USA) in 1881–87 and William Larned (USA) in 1901, 1902 and 1907–11.

The most US Open singles titles won by a woman is eight by Molla Mallory (*née* Bjurstedt, USA) in 1915–18, 1920–22 and 1926.

The most US Open titles won by a man is 16 by Bill Tilden (USA).

The most US Open titles won by a woman is 25 by Margaret Du Pont (USA), who won 13 women's doubles, nine mixed doubles and three singles titles between 1941 and 1960. The women's doubles titles were won with Louise Brough (USA) as her partner.

MOST AUSTRALIAN OPEN WINS
The most Australian Open singles tennis titles won by a man is six. This was won by Roy Emerson (Australia) in 1961 and 1963–67. In total he won 12 grand slam singles titles and 16 grand slam doubles titles.

The most Australian Open tennis titles won by a woman is 21 by Margaret Court (Australia) who won the women's singles 11 times

(1960–66, 1969–71 and 1973), the women's doubles eight times (1961–63, 1965, 1969–71 and 1973) and the mixed doubles twice (1963 and 1964).

The most Australian Open women's doubles titles won is 16 by Thelma Long (*née* Coyne, Australia), who won 12 women's doubles and four mixed doubles titles.

MOST DAVIS CUP WINS
The most wins in the Davis Cup, the men's international team championship, is 31 by the USA between 1900 and 1995. The most appearances for Cup winners is eight by Roy Emerson (Australia), 1959–62 and 1964–67. Bill Tilden (USA) played in a record 28 matches in the final, winning a record 21 (17 out of 22 singles and four out of six doubles). He was in seven winning sides in 1920–26 and then four losing sides in 1927–30.

LONGEST MATCH
The longest match in a grand slam tournament is 5 hr 31 min between Alex Corretja (Spain) and Hernán Gumy (Argentina), in the third round of the French Open on 31 May 1998. Corretja eventually won 6–1, 5–7, 6–7, 7–5, 9–7.

MOST CONSECUTIVE SERVES
The most consecutive 'good' serves (without a double fault) is 8,017 by Rob Peterson (USA) at Port Aransas, Texas, USA, on 5 Dec 1998. The attempt lasted 10 hrs 7 min.

www.guinnessworldrecords.com/kournikova

GAME, SET AND MATCH
The youngest-ever winner of a Federation Cup match is Anna Kournikova (Russia, right). On 25 April 1996, when she was only 14 years old, she beat Anna-Karin Svensson (Sweden) 6–0, 6–3, helping Russia to defeat Sweden 3–0. Anna began playing tennis at the age of five and turned professional in 1995.

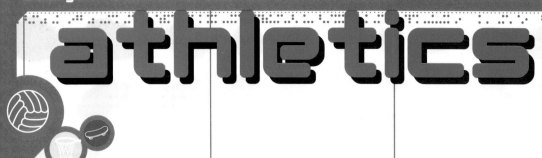

athletics

MOST WORLD RECORDS IN ONE DAY

Jesse Owens (USA) set six world records in 45 minutes at Ann Arbor, Michigan, USA, on 25 May 1935 with a 9.4-sec 100-yd race at 3:15 pm; a 8.13-m (26-ft 8.25-in) long jump at 3:25 pm; a 20.3-sec 220-yd race at 3:45 pm (which included a separate record for the 200 m); and a 22.6-sec 220-yd low hurdles race at 4 pm (which also included a separate record for the 200-m hurdles).

LONGEST TRACK EVENT WINNING SEQUENCE

For over a decade Ed Moses (USA) dominated the men's 400-m hurdling event. His remarkable record of 122 consecutive wins began on 2 Sept 1977 and ended when he was beaten by Danny Harris (USA) in Madrid, Spain, on 4 June 1987. Moses's domination of the sport was such that at one time he held the 13 fastest times ever recorded.

LONGEST FIELD EVENTS WINNING SEQUENCE

Iolanda Balas (Romania) won a record 150 consecutive competitions at the high jump between 1956 and 1967 in National, European, World and Olympic Championships.

MOST SUCCESSFUL IAAF GOLDEN LEAGUE INDIVIDUAL

The only athlete to have twice won a share of the jackpot in the IAAF (International Amateur Athletics Federation) Golden League is runner Hicham El Guerrouj (Morocco). For the jackpot, an athlete must win five of the seven IAAF Grand Prix meetings in a season and remain undefeated. Originally the jackpot was $1 million (£670,000) but it is currently 50 kg (110 lb) of gold.

OLDEST OLYMPIC ATHLETICS GOLD MEDALLIST

The oldest athlete to win an Olympic title was Irish-born Patrick Joseph 'Babe' McDonald (USA) who was aged 42 years 26 days when he won the 56-lb (25.4-kg) weight throw at Antwerp, Belgium, on 21 Aug 1920.

The oldest female champion was Lia Manoliu (Romania) who was aged 36 years 176 days when she won the discus event at the Mexico City Olympics on 18 Oct 1968, with a throw of 58.28 m (191 ft 6 in).

YOUNGEST OLYMPIC ATHLETICS GOLD MEDALLIST

The youngest Olympic athletics gold medallist was Barbara Pearl Jones (USA) who, at 15 years 123 days, was part of the 4 x 100-m relay team that won the gold at Helsinki, Finland, on 27 July 1952.

The youngest male champion was Robert Bruce Mathias (USA) who was aged 17 years 263 days when he won the decathlon at the Olympic Games held in London between 5 and 6 Aug 1948.

OLDEST SPORTING WORLD-RECORD BREAKER

The oldest person to set an official world record in sport was Gerhard Weidner (Germany), who set a 20-mile walk record of 2 hr 30 min 38.6 sec on 25 May 1974, aged 41 years 71 days.

YOUNGEST ATHLETICS WORLD-RECORD HOLDER

The youngest male to set an official world record is Thomas Ray (UK), who was 17 years 198 days when he set a pole-vault record of 3.42 m (11 ft 2.75 in) on 19 Sept 1879.

The youngest female athletics record breaker is Wang Yan (China) who set a women's 5,000-m walk record of 21 min 33.8 sec when aged 14 years 334 days on 9 March 1986.

MOST INDOOR ATHLETICS WORLD CHAMPIONSHIP GOLD MEDALS

Iván Pedroso (Cuba) holds the record for the most individual titles with five, won in the long jump in 1993, 1995, 1997, 1999 and 2001.

The most individual golds by a woman is four by Stefka Kostadinova (Bulgaria) in the high jump in 1985, 1987, 1989, 1993; and Gabriela Szabo (Romania) for the 3,000 m in 1995, 1997, 1999 and the 1,500 m in 1999.

MOST ATHLETICS WORLD CHAMPIONSHIP GOLD MEDALS

The World Championships were inaugurated in 1983 in Helsinki, Finland. The most golds won to date is nine by Michael Johnson (USA), who won the 200 m in 1991 and 1995, the 400 m in 1993, 1995, 1997 and 1999, and the 4 x 400-m relay in 1993, 1995 and 1999.

The most World Championship gold medals won by a woman is five, by Gail Devers (USA). She won the 100 m in 1993, the 100-m hurdles in 1993, 1995 and 1999; and the 4 x 100-m relay in 1997.

MOST CROSS-COUNTRY RUNNING WORLD CHAMPIONSHIPS

The individual women's World Championship Cross-country race has been won five times by Grete Waitz (Norway), in 1978–81 and 1983.

The greatest number of men's individual victories is five by John Ngugi (Kenya) in 1986–89 and 1992; and Paul Tergat (Kenya) in 1995–99.

The greatest number of team victories in the World Cross-country Championships (first held in 1973) is 15 by Kenya, between 1986 and 2000.

The record for team victories in the World Cross-country Championships is held by the USSR, who won a record eight women's team victories in 1976–77, 1980–82, and 1988–90.

LONGEST-EVER RUNNING RACE

The longest race ever staged was the 1929 5,850-km (3,635-mile) trans-continental race from New York City to Los Angeles, California, USA. Johnny Salo (Finland) won in 79 days, running from 31 March to 17 June 1929. His time of 525 hr 57 min 20 sec (averaging 11.12 km/h or 6.91 mph) left him only 2 min 47 sec ahead of Pietro Gavuzzi (UK).

LONGEST ANNUAL RUNNING RACE

The longest race staged annually is the Sri Chinmoy 3,100-mile (4,989-km) race, held on a 400-m track in Jamaica, New York, USA. The fastest time to complete the race

IN THE LONG RUN

The fastest time for a men's half-marathon (21.097 km or 13 miles 192.5 yd) is 59 min 5 sec by Paul Tergat (Kenya, left). This record was set in Lisbon, Portugal, on 26 March 2000.

The women's official half marathon record is 66 min 43 sec by Masako Chika (Japan) in Tokyo, Japan, set on 19 April 1997.

Paul Tergat also holds the record for the most individual wins in the men's IAAF Half Marathon World Championships. He won in 1999 and 2000.

Tegla Loroupe (Kenya), holds the record for wins in the same event for women. She won in 1997, 1998 and 1999.

The most wins by a team at the same event is six by the Kenyan men's team in 1992–95, 1997 and 2000, and the Romanian women's team 1993–97 and 2000.

www.guinnessworldrecords.com/halfmarathons
ACCESS CODE: ‹45718›

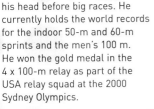

GREENE FLASH

Sprinter Maurice 'The Phenomenon' Greene (USA, right) always shaves his head before big races. He currently holds the world records for the indoor 50-m and 60-m sprints and the men's 100 m. He won the gold medal in the 4 x 100-m relay as part of the USA relay squad at the 2000 Sydney Olympics.

is 46 days 17 hr 2 min 6 sec by Istvan Sipos (Hungary) who ran from 13 June to 28 July 1998, taking breaks at his own discretion.

OLDEST MARATHON

With a continuous 104-year history, the Boston Marathon is officially the oldest. The first Boston Marathon took place on 19 April 1897, inspired by the Olympic Marathon the previous year.

GOING FOR GOLD

The most medals won in the biennial World Championships by a woman is 14 by Merlene Ottey (Jamaica, above) who won three gold (4 x 100-m 1991; 200 m 1993 and 1995); three silver (100 m 1993 and 1995, 4 x 100-m 1995) and eight bronze (100 m 1987–1991; 200 m 1987,1991, 1997; 4 x 100-m 1983, 1993).

The most World Championship medals won by a man is 10 by Carl Lewis (USA). He won eight gold (100 m, long jump and 4 x 100-m 1983; 100 m, long jump and 4 x 100-m 1987; 100 m and 4 x 100-m 1991); one silver (long jump in 1991) and one bronze (200 m in 1993).

MOST MARATHON FINISHERS

The record number of confirmed finishers in a marathon is 38,706 at the centennial Boston Marathon on 15 April 1996.

FASTEST 100 X ONE-MILE RELAY RACE

The men's record for 100 miles by 100 runners is 7 hr 35 min 55.4 sec by the Canadian Milers Athletic Club at York University, Toronto, Canada, on 20 Dec 1998.

The women's record is 9 hr 38 min 39.14 sec by the Anderson College Athletics Club of San Francisco at Foothill College, Los Altos Hills, California, USA, on 15 June 1997.

MOST PARTICIPANTS IN A RELAY RACE

The most participants in a relay race is 7,175, (287 teams of 25), for the 175-km *Batavierenrace* run from Nijmegen to Enschede, Netherlands, which was run on 24 April 1999. This annual race starts at midnight and takes about 18 hours to complete with each runner carrying a micro-chip to register each completed section.

FASTEST TRANS-AMERICA RUN

The fastest time recorded for the trans-America (San Francisco to New York) run is 46 days 8 hr 36 min by Frank Giannino Jr (USA) who ran the 4,989 km (3,100 miles) from 1 Sept to 17 Oct 1980.

The women's trans-America record is 69 days 2 hr 40 min by Mavis Hutchinson (South Africa) who ran from 12 March to 21 May 1978.

GUINNESS WORLD RECORDS

olympics

LONGEST SPAN AS MALE OLYMPIC COMPETITOR

The longest span of an Olympic competitor is 40 years. Ivan Joseph Martin Osiier (Denmark) competed in fencing (1908–32 and 1948); Magnus Andreas Thulstrup Clasen Konow (Norway) in yachting (1908–20, 1928 and 1936–48); Paul Elvstrom (Denmark) in yachting (1948–60, 1968–72 and 1984–88); and Durward Randolph Knowles (UK 1948, then Bahamas) in yachting (1948–72 and 1988).

LONGEST SPAN AS FEMALE OLYMPIC COMPETITOR

The longest span as an Olympic competitor for women is 28 years and both record holders competed in dressage. Anne Jessica Ransehousen (née Newberry, USA) competed in 1960, 1964 and 1988 and Christilot Hanson-Boylen (Canada) in 1964–76, 1984 and 1992.

MOST CONSECUTIVE OLYMPIC TEAM GOLD MEDALS WON

The most successive gold medal wins in Olympic history is six by Aladár Gerevich (Hungary), who was a member of the winning sabre team from 1932–60.

BIGGER AND BETTER DOWN UNDER

The very successful Summer Olympic Games held from 15 Sept to 1 Oct 2000 in Sydney, NSW, Australia, had a record number of participants. The Games (opening ceremony, left) were attended by 11,084 athletes, of which 4,245 were women.

The 2000 Sydney Games also holds the record for the most countries participating in the Summer Olympics. A total of 199 countries took part. The Sydney Games also saw the most medal-winning countries at an Olympic Games, with 80 countries winning at least one medal.

www.guinnessworldrecords.com/sydney2000
← ACCESS CODE: ‹44741›

MOST CONSECUTIVE OLYMPIC INDIVIDUAL GOLD MEDALS WON

The only Olympians to win four consecutive individual titles in the same event are Al Oerter (USA) for discus 1956–68, and Carl Lewis (USA) for long jump 1984–96. However, Raymond Clarence Ewry (USA) won both the standing long jump and the standing high jump at four games in succession in 1900, 1904, 1906 and 1908. (This is if the Intercalated Games of 1906, which were staged officially by the International Olympic Committee, are included).

Paul Elvstrom (Denmark) also won four successive gold medals at monotype yachting events between 1948 and 1960, although there was a class change (1948 Firefly class, 1952–60 Finn class).

MOST CONSECUTIVE GOLD MEDALS WON BY A WOMAN

The most consecutive Olympic gold medals won by a woman is four by Birgit Fischer (née Schmidt, Germany) for canoeing. She first competed at the Olympic Games held in South Korea in 1988, and also participated at the Sydney Olympics in 2000.

MOST MEDALS WON AT THE SUMMER GAMES

The USA has won more medals than any other country in the history of the Summer Olympic Games, 1896–2000. A total of 2,112 medals have been won during this time. Of these, a record 872 were gold.

The USA is the country that has won the most gold medals at a single Games. They won 83 gold medals at the XXIIIrd Olympic Games held in Los Angeles, California, USA, in 1984.

The USA also holds the record for the most medals won at a single Games. They were awarded 242 medals at the IIIrd Olympic Games, held at St Louis, Missouri, USA, in 1904.

MOST MEDALS WON AT THE WINTER GAMES

Norway has won a record total of 239 medals in the history of the Winter Olympic Games, 1924–98.

The most medals won by a country at a single Winter Olympic Games is 29 by the Soviet Union (USSR) at the XVth Winter Games at Calgary, Alberta, Canada, in 1988. This total was equalled by Germany at the XVIIIth Winter Games held at Nagano, Japan, in 1998.

The Soviet Union (USSR) has won the most gold medals at the Winter Olympic Games, with 87. They also won a record 13 gold medals at a

ERIC THE EEL

Eric Moussambani (Equatorial Guinea, left) clocked the slowest-ever recorded time in Olympic history for the 100-m freestyle, with a time of 1 min 52.72 sec at the Sydney Games on 19 Sept 2000. Remarkably he won his heat, the two other participants in the heat having been disqualified for false starts. Eric, who acquired the nickname 'Eric the Eel' for his unique swimming style, had never seen an Olympic-size (50-m) pool before and had only learned to swim nine months previously. Training for the Games had been done in Equatorial Guinea's unique 20-m pool and in local rivers. Sadly his time was outside the qualifying time and he was eliminated from the competition. His time was over seven seconds slower than the gold-winning time for the men's 200-m freestyle.

single Winter Games, the XIIth Winter Olympiad held at Innsbruck, Austria, in 1976.

MOST MEDALS WON AT THE PARALYMPICS

Since the first Summer Paralympics, held in 1960 in Rome, Italy, the most medals won by a country is 1,938 by the USA. This includes a record 693 gold medals.

Since the first Winter Paralympics, held in 1976 at Örnsköldsvik, Sweden, Austria has won the most medals with a total of 250. The country that has won the most gold medals at the Winter Paralympic Games is Norway, with a total of 97.

MOST PARTICIPANTS AT A PARALYMPIC GAMES

The Paralympic Games held in 2000 in Sydney, NSW, Australia, saw more athletes than any other Paralympics, with a total of 3,824. The participants came from a record 125 countries.

www.guinnessworldrecords.com/redgrave

ACCESS CODE: ‹55805›

ROW, ROW, ROW YOUR BOAT

The most consecutive Olympic gold medals ever won in an endurance event is five by Steve Redgrave (UK). Redgrave (below, centre) won a gold medal in rowing at five consecutive Olympic Games, from 1984 to 2000. He has also won a record nine World Championships. These were for coxed pair in 1986, coxless pair in 1987, 1991, 1993–95, and coxless four in 1997–99.

Redgrave took up rowing at school in Marlow, Bucks, UK, after having proved himself talented at all other sports. He left school aged 16 and devoted himself to training, but liked to unwind with a game of golf at his local club. In 1989 he took up bobsledding and was a member of the crew that won the British four-man Championship that year. Steve Redgrave was knighted for services to rowing on 1 May 2001.

MOST OLYMPIC MEDALS WON BY A MAN

The most Olympic medals won by a man is 15 by the gymnast Nikolay Andrianov (USSR). In 1972–1980, between the ages of 19 and 27, he won seven gold, five silver and three bronze medals.

MOST OLYMPIC MEDALS WON BY A WOMAN

The most Olympic medals won by a woman is 18 by gymnast Larisa Semyonovna Latynina (USSR). In 1956–64, between the ages of 21 and 29, she won nine gold, five silver and four bronze medals.

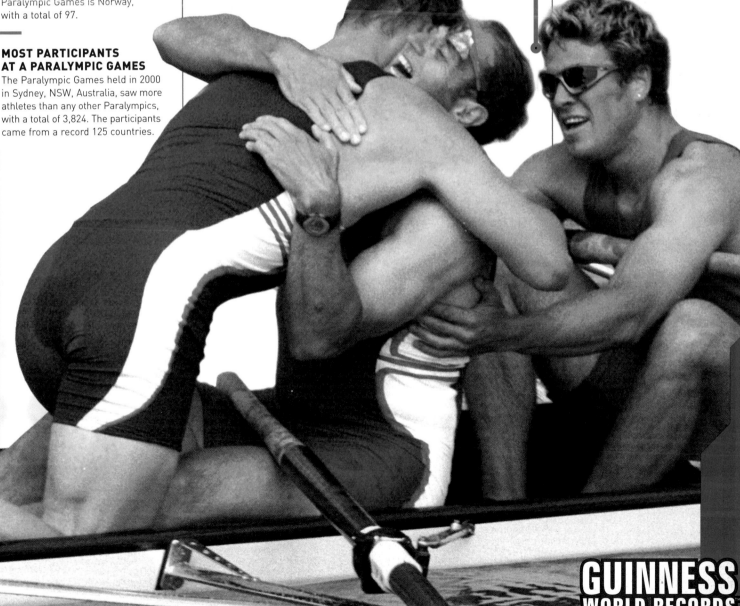

GUINNESS WORLD RECORDS™

auto sports

MOST MAJOR NASCAR RACE WINS

Of the four major races in the NASCAR (National Association for Stock Car Auto Racing) series – the Daytona 500, Winston 500, Southern 500 and Coca Cola 600 – three US drivers share the record for winning three races in one season – Dave Pearson (1976), Bill Elliott (1985) and Jeff Gordon (1997). In 1969, Lee Roy Yarbrough (USA) won all three of the races contested that year – the Winston 500 was run for the first time in 1970.

FAST MOVER

Alain Prost (France, above) holds the record for the most Grand Prix points in a Formula 1 driving career, with 798.5 points from 199 races, between 1980 and 1993.

He also holds the record for the most Grand Prix victories by a driver. He won 51 out of a total of 199 races, between 1980 and 1993. He has appeared a record number of times on the podium, stepping up 106 times to collect a first, second or third place. Not surprisingly, as the world's greatest Formula 1 driver, his nickname is 'Professor of the Track'.

He retired from competitive racing in 1992 and since then has continued working in Formula 1, first as PR for Renault and then as an advisor for McLaren. In 1997 he bought the Ligier team, renaming it Prost in 1998.

www.guinnessworldrecords.com/prost

ACCESS CODE: ‹44854›

MOST NASCAR RACE VICTORIES

Richard Petty (USA) has achieved the most victories in a NASCAR career, winning 200 out of a possible 1,184 races, between 1958 and 1992.

MOST NASCAR TITLES

The most titles won in the annual NASCAR Championship is seven; by Richard Petty (USA), in 1964, 1967, 1971–72, 1974–75 and 1979 and Dale Earnhardt (USA), in 1980, 1986–87, 1990–91 and 1993–94.

MOST NASCAR POLE POSITIONS IN CAREER

The greatest number of pole positions (starting the race from the front after qualifying as the fastest driver) achieved in a NASCAR career is 126 by Richard Petty (USA), from 1958 to 1992.

MOST COCA COLA 600 RACE VICTORIES

Darrell Waltrip (USA) has achieved the greatest number of wins of the Coca Cola 600 – the longest race in the NASCAR series – winning five in 1979–80, 1985 and 1988–89.

MOST DAYTONA 500 RACE VICTORIES

The most wins of the Daytona 500 – the richest race in the NASCAR series with a prize of $10 million (£6.9 million) – is seven by Richard Petty (USA) in 1964, 1966, 1971, 1973–74, 1979 and 1981.

MOST SOUTHERN 500 RACE VICTORIES

The greatest number of wins of the Southern 500 – the oldest race in the NASCAR series, first run in 1950 – is five by Cale Yarborough (USA), in 1968, 1973–74, 1978 and 1982.

MOST WINSTON 500 RACE VICTORIES

Dale Earnhardt (USA) has achieved the greatest number of wins at the Winston 500 – the fastest race in the NASCAR series – with four victories in 1990, 1994, 1999 and 2000.

GET RICH QUICK

The highest earnings in a NASCAR career is $41,445,551 (£29,011,885) by Dale Earnhardt (USA, above), between 1975 and 2001. Tragically, Dale was killed during the 2001 Daytona 500 race on 18 Feb 2001. His son, Dale Jr is following in his father's tyre tracks, as Dale followed in his father Ralph's, so the Earnhardt name continues in NASCAR racing.

Al Unser Jr (USA) holds the record for the highest earnings purely from winning races in the CART (Championship Auto Racing Teams) Championship. He had won $18,828,406 (£13,179,884) to the end of the 2000 season.

www.guinnessworldrecords.com/earnhardt

ACCESS CODE: ‹56448›

MOST CART CHAMPIONSHIP TITLES

The greatest number of wins in the CART (Championship Auto Racing Teams) National Championship is seven by AJ Foyt (USA), in 1960–61, 1963–64, 1967, 1975 and 1979.

MOST POLE POSITIONS IN CART RACES

The greatest number of pole positions achieved in a CART racing career is 67 by Mario Andretti (USA) between 1965 and 1994.

MOST WORLD RALLY CHAMPIONSHIP RACE WINS IN A SEASON

The most World Rally Championship race wins in a season is six by Didier Auriol (France), in 1992. He took up rallying in 1979, following in the footsteps of his elder brother.

MOST WORLD RALLYING CHAMPIONSHIP TITLES

The most World rallying title wins is four, shared by Juha Kankkunen 1986–87, 1991 and 1993, and Tommi Makinen (both Finland) 1996–99.

YOUNGEST WORLD RALLY CHAMPION

The youngest World Rally champion is Colin McRae (UK), who was aged 27 years 89 days when he won the title in 1995.

YOUNGEST FORMULA 1 GRAND PRIX WINNER

The youngest Formula 1 champion is Bruce McLaren (New Zealand), who won the US Grand Prix at Sebring, Florida, on 12 Dec 1959, aged just 22 years 104 days.

OLDEST FORMULA 1 WORLD CHAMPION

Juan Manuel Fangio (Argentina) won his last World Championship for the Mercedes-Benz team on 4 Aug 1957, aged 46 years 41 days, the oldest-ever Formula 1 champion.

YOUNGEST FORMULA 1 WORLD CHAMPION

The youngest-ever Formula 1 world champion was Emerson Fittipaldi (Brazil), who won his first World Championship on 10 Sept 1972, aged 25 years 273 days.

MOST GRAND PRIX FORMULA 1 WINS BY A MANUFACTURER

The greatest number of Grand Prix race wins by a manufacturer is 139 by Ferrari (Italy), out of a total number of 656 races. Ferrari won all seven races in 1952 and the first eight (of nine) in 1953 – an unbroken record for a manufacturer.

MOST WINS BY A MANUFACTURER IN A FORMULA 1 SEASON

In 1998 McLaren (UK) achieved the most wins by a manufacturer in a season, with 15 out of a possible 16 Grand Prix victories. Ayrton Senna (Brazil) took eight wins and Alain Prost (France) seven. The McLarens, powered by Honda engines, amassed over three times the points of their nearest rival, Ferrari.

FASTEST SPEED FOR A FUNNY CAR DRAG RACER

All drag races are run over 440 yd (402 m). John Force (USA) reached a top speed of 521.50 km/h (324 mph) from a 440-yd standing start in a '99 Ford Mustang at Gainesville, Florida, USA, on 21 March 1999.

FASTEST TIME FOR A FUNNY CAR DRAG RACER

The fastest time to cover 440 yd in a funny car is 4.788 sec by John Force (USA), driving a '99 Ford Mustang, at Houston, Texas, USA, on 11 April 1999.

FASTEST SPEED FOR A PRO STOCK MOTORBIKE

The top speed for a petrol-driven piston-engined (Pro Stock) motorcycle is 308.15 km/h (191.45 mph) by Matt Hines (USA) on a '95 Suzuki GSX-R on 31 Oct 1999.

FASTEST TIME FOR PRO STOCK MOTORBIKE

On 19 May 2000 Matt Hines (USA) covered 440 yd on a Pro Stock motorbike in a record time of 7.138 seconds on a '95 Suzuki GSX-R, at Englishtown, New Jersey, USA.

TOP SPEED FOR A NHRA DRAG RACER

The highest speed reached by a NHRA (National Hot Rod Association) drag racer over 440 yd is a cracking 526.11 km/h (326.92 mph) by Tony Schumacher (USA) on 22 Oct 1999.

FASTEST TIME FOR A TOP-FUEL DRAGSTER

The fastest time to cover 440 yd in a top-fuel dragster is 4.48 seconds by Gary Scelzi (USA), at Houston, Texas, USA, on 31 Oct 1999.

www.guinnessworldrecords.com/formula1

WINNING FORMULA

The most Grand Prix victories in a year is nine by Michael Schumacher (Germany, right) in 1995 and 2000 and Nigel Mansell (UK) in 1992.

Mansell quit Formula 1 to race Indy cars in 1993, becoming the first rookie to win the IndyCar title.

Schumacher's career began at the age of four when he discovered go-karting. He was runner-up in the Junior World Championships at the age of 16, and two years later he became European champion. After 15 years of go-kart racing, he switched to racing cars, and in 1990 became the Mercedes-Benz team driver in the sports car World Championship and the German Formula 3 champion. In 1991, at the Belgian Grand Prix, he made his debut as a driver for the Formula 1 Jordan team and his F1 career was born.

GUINNESS WORLD RECORDS

bike sports

MOST TOUR OF ITALY WINS

The greatest number of *Giro d'Italia* (Tour of Italy) wins is five and is shared by Alfredo Binda (Italy) in 1925, 1927–29 and 1933; Fausto Coppi (Italy) in 1940, 1947, 1949, 1952–53; and Eddy Merckx (Belgium) in 1968, 1970, 1972–74.

MOST TOUR OF SPAIN WINS

The most wins in the *Vuelta a España* (Tour of Spain) cycling race is three, by Tony Rominger (Switzerland), from 1992 to 1994.

GREATEST DISTANCE CYCLED IN 24 HOURS

The 24-hr record behind pace is 1,958.2 km (1,216.8 miles) by Michael Secrest (USA) at Phoenix International Raceway, Arizona, USA, on 26 and 27 April 1990.

MOST WORLD CHAMPIONSHIP TITLES WON BY A WOMAN

Jeannie Longo (France) won 12 World Championship titles from her first in 1985 to her last in 1997. During this time, she won five road race titles, the only woman ever to do so, with four coming in consecutive years from 1985 to 1989. The remainder of her titles came in the time trial, points and pursuit events.

LARGEST CYCLING EVENT

The most participants in a cycling event is 48,615 for Udine Pedala 2000, organized by Rolo Banca 1473 at Udine, near the Slovenian border, Italy, on 11 June 2000. The cyclists completed a circuit measuring 29.3 km (18.2 miles) around Udine.

FASTEST TRANS-AMERICA CROSSING BY A TWO-MAN CYCLE TEAM

The fastest trans-America crossing by a two-man cycle team was 7 days, 9 hr and 56 min by Ricardo S Arap and Alexandre Ribeiro (both Brazil) from 22 to 30 July 1998. They travelled 4,828 km (3,000 miles) at an average speed of 28.6 km/h (17.8 mph).

GREATEST DISTANCE CYCLED IN ONE HOUR

The official UCI (Union Cycliste Internationale) one-hour record from an unassisted standing start is 49.441 km (30.722 miles) held by Chris Boardman (UK), in Manchester, England, on 27 Oct 2000.

The official UCI one-hour record by a woman from an unassisted standing start is 45.094 km (28.02 miles) by Jeanie Longo (France) in Mexico City, Mexico, on 7 Dec 2000. She also won a 1996 Olympic road-race gold medal.

I LIKE TO RIDE MY SUPERBIKE

The record for the most World Superbike Championship titles won is four by Carl Fogarty (UK, above). Known as the Lion King, he made his racing debut in 1983, but did not gain his first win until 1985, when he won the Manx 250GP. Racing for Ducati, he won his first World Superbike Championship in 1994, and repeated the feat the following year. He moved from Ducati to Honda in 1996 but only managed a fourth place in the Championship. Fogarty returned to Ducati in 1997, finishing runner-up in that season, before taking the title for two consecutive years again in 1998 and 1999.

www.guinnessworldrecords.com/superbike

← ACCESS CODE: ‹52800›

MOST PROFESSIONAL WORLD CHAMPIONSHIP TITLES

The most professional World Championship cycling titles won by a man is 10 by Koichi Nakano (Japan), in the professional sprint event between 1977 and 1986.

MOST WORLD CHAMPIONSHIP SPEEDWAY TITLES

Hans Hollen Nielsen (Denmark) has been the most successful rider in World Championship competitions, with eight Team (formerly Pairs), nine team and four individual World titles, for a record 21 Championship titles in total.

MOST SPEEDWAY WINS

The most individual World Speedway Championship wins is six by Ivan Mauger (New Zealand), in 1968–70, 1972, 1977 and 1979.

MOST APPEARANCES IN SPEEDWAY FINALS

Barry Briggs (New Zealand) appeared a record 18 times in the World Speedway Championship finals between 1954 and 1972. Briggs won four times in 1957, 1958, 1964 and 1966.

MOST WORLD CHAMPIONSHIP POINTS

Barry Briggs (New Zealand) scored a record 201 points in 87 World Championship appearances between 1954 and 1972.

MOST WORLD TRIALS CHAMPIONSHIP TITLES

The record for the most World Trials Championships won is seven, held by Jordi Tarrés (Spain), in 1987, 1989–91 and 1993–95.

LANCE IN FRANCE

The fastest average speed in the Tour de France is 40.276 km/h (25.026 mph) by Lance Armstrong (USA, left) in 1999.

The greatest number of wins in the Tour de France is five, shared by Jacques Anquetil of France (1957 and 1961–64), Eddy Merckx of Belgium (1969–72 and 1974), Bernard Hinault of France (1978–79, 1981–82 and 1985) and Miguel Induráin of Spain (1991–95).

The closest Tour de France race ever was in 1989. After 3,267 km (2,030 miles) and 23 days (1–23 July) of racing, Greg LeMond (USA) completed the Tour in 87 hr 38 min 35 sec, beating Laurent Fignon (France) in Paris by only eight seconds.

www.guinnessworldrecords.com/tourdefrance

← ACCESS CODE: ‹45315›

MOST SUPERBIKE WINS BY A MANUFACTURER

The record for the most superbike races won by a manufacturer is 161 by Ducati, between 1989 and 1999. Ducati also holds the record for the most World Superbike Championship titles, with eight from 1991 to 1996 and 1998 to 2000.

MOST WORLD PAIRS CHAMPIONSHIP TITLES

The World Pairs Championships have been held unofficially since 1968, and officially since 1970. They were renamed the World Team

Championships in 1994, and have been won a record nine times by Denmark, 1979, 1985–91 and 1995.

MOST WORLD MOTORCYCLE CHAMPIONSHIP 125CC TITLES

The most World Motorcycle Championship 125cc titles won is seven by Angel Roldán Nieto (Spain), in 1971, 1972, 1979 and 1981–84.

MOST WORLD CHAMPIONSHIP SIDE-CAR TITLES

The most World Motorcycle Championship side-car titles won is

seven by Rolf Biland (Switzerland), in 1978, 1979, 1981, 1983 and 1992–94. Biland was runner-up in the 1980 and 1982 Championships.

MOST MOTORCYCLE CAREER RACE WINS IN A SINGLE CLASS

The record for the most World Motorcycle Championship career wins in a single class is 79, set by Rolf Biland (Switzerland) in the side-car class.

MOST WORLD MOTORCYCLE CHAMPIONSHIP TITLES

The record for the most World Motorcycle Championship titles is 15, held by Giacomo Agostini (Italy), with seven 350cc titles between 1968 and 1974, and eight 500cc titles from 1966 to 1972 and in 1975.

MOST NATIONAL SIDE-CAR TITLES

Milcho Georgiev Mladenov (Bulgaria) is the holder of a record-breaking 16 consecutive Bulgarian national titles in motorcycle side-car class 500cc, between 1981 and 1999.

MOST MOTORCYCLE CAREER RACE WINS

The most World Motorcycle Championship career race wins is 122 (68 at 500cc class and 54 at 350cc class), held by Giacomo Agostini between 24 April 1965 and 25 Sept 1977.

MOST WORLD MOTORCYCLE CHAMPIONSHIP 250CC TITLES

The most World Motorcycle Championship 250cc titles won is four by Phil Read (UK), in 1964, 1965, 1968 and 1971.

www.guinnessworldrecords.com/poleposition

MAGNIFICENT MEN ON THEIR FLYING MACHINES

The world record for the most pole positions achieved in the World Superbike Championship is 25 by Troy Corser (Australia, right), between 1996 and March 2001. In 1996 he won the World Superbike Championship, aged 24, the youngest-ever winner of the title. Corser has consistently taken 3rd place ever since.

GUINNESS WORLD RECORDS™

extreme sports 1

LONGEST ABSEIL

On 2 Nov 1993 a team of four Royal Marines (all UK) set an abseiling distance record by abseiling 1,105.5 m (3,627 ft) down the Boulby Potash Mine, Cleveland, UK. They started their descent 7.6 m (25 ft) below ground level, and abseiled deeper to finish at the bottom of the shaft.

GREATEST DISTANCE ABSEILED DOWN A BUILDING

The record for abseiling down a building is 446.5 m (1,465 ft), by two teams of 12 representing the UK Royal Marines and the Canadian School of Rescue Training. All 24 abseiled to the ground from the Space Deck of the CN Tower, Toronto, Ontario, Canada, on 1 July 1992.

LONGEST ROPE SLIDE

The greatest distance covered in a rope slide is 1,746.5 m (5,730 ft), by Lance-Corporal Peter Baldwin (UK) of the Royal Marines and Stu Leggett (Canada) of the Canadian School of Rescue Training. They slid from the summit of Mt Gibraltar, Alberta, Canada, down to ground level on 31 Aug 1994. For some of the descent, they both reached speeds in excess of 160 km/h (100 mph).

ON THE ROPES?

The world's longest Tyrolean traverse (a static rope running over an obstacle such as a canyon or a river) measured 953.63 m (3,128 ft 3 in) and spanned the Elbe River between Belveder and Dolni Zleb, Czech Republic. The traverse was erected by the Czech Speleological Emergency Service, and was crossed by Zdenek Kadlec (Czech Republic, left), who pulled himself along the rope upside down, while attached to a harness, in 59 min 6 sec on 3 July 1998. This distance beat the previous record set the year before by their Slovak counterparts.

www.guinnessworldrecords.com/tyrolrope
← ACCESS CODE: ‹44786›

FASTEST FREE CLIMBER

🖳 USA

Dan Osman (USA) climbed the 120-m (400-ft) 'Lover's Leap' rock face at Lake Tahoe, California, USA, in 5 min 52 sec. He achieved this amazing feat without using ropes or harnesses on 29 May 1997.

LONGEST ROPE JUMP 🖳 USA

Dan Osman (USA) made a 305-m (1,000-ft) rope jump at the 'Leaning Tower' rock formation in Yosemite National Park, California, USA, on 12 Oct 1998. Dan's jump involved him freefalling for hundreds of metres until a rope tied to his full-body harness stopped his fall. Tragically, he died less than three weeks after setting this record, while attempting another jump at the same location.

LONGEST CLIMB BY A HUMAN FLY

The record for the longest climb by a 'human fly' was set on 25 May 1981, when Daniel Goodwin (USA) climbed 443.2 m (1,454 ft) up the outside of the Sears Tower, Chicago, Illinois, USA. For this death-defying feat, he used only a system of suction cups and metal clips for support.

FASTEST GRASS-SKIER

The grass-skiing speed record is 92.07 km/h (57.21 mph), by Klaus Spinka (Austria) at Waldsassen, Germany, on 24 Sept 1989.

HIGHEST LAND YACHT SPEED

The highest land yacht speed recorded is 187.8 km/h (116.7 mph), by Bob Schumacher (USA) on *Iron Duck* at Ivanpah Dry Lake, Prim, Nevada, USA, on 20 March 1999. The yacht was designed and built by Bob Dill in Burlington, Vermont, USA.

HIGHEST INDOOR HALFPIPE JUMP ON IN-LINE SKATES

🖳 FR

Taïg Khris (France) made an in-line skate jump of 3.1 m (10 ft 2 in) from a halfpipe on 6 Dec 2000.

MOST IN-LINE SKATE BACK FLIPS

🖳 USA

Jason Stinsmen (USA) achieved an in-line skate double back flip using a ramp at Van Nuys Airport, California, USA, on 20 Jan 2001.

HIGHEST 'AIR' ON A SKATEBOARD

Danny Way (USA) pulled off a 5 m-high (16-ft 6-in) 'method air' jump from a halfpipe at Brown Field, San Diego, California, USA, on 3 Aug 1998. A method air is one of the most straightforward of the aerial tricks: the front hand grabs the heel edge,

SPIN DOCTOR

Tony Hawk (USA, left) completed the world's first-ever 900-degree spin on a skateboard from a halfpipe during the 1999 X Games, held in San Francisco, California, USA, on 27 June 1999. The so-called '900' entails two-and-a-half airborne rotations and Hawk remains the only person to have achieved it in competition. As a youth, he seemed an unlikely athlete, but his love of skateboarding inspired him to overcome his weak build and he had turned pro by the age of 14. Hawk is one of the few skateboarders to have achieved superstar status and has merchandise and computer games bearing his name. His autobiography, *Hawk: Occupation Skateboarder*,

www.guinnessworldrecords.com/flipboard

FLIPPIN' GOOD

Skateboarder Josh Tenge (USA, right), performed an amazing record-breaking back flip while on a sandboard on 20 May 2000. The flip measured 13.6 m (44 ft 10 in). The record was set at the X-West Huck Fest, Sand Mountain, Nevada, USA. Sandboarding is related to surfing and dates back as far as the 1940s. Sandboards run on laminated thermoplastics (Formica™) and, when waxed, can reach speeds in excess of 80 km/h (50 mph).

both knees are bent, and the board is pulled up behind the rider. In the halfpipe, the rider's body can become parallel with the ground.

HIGHEST SKATEBOARD DROP ON TO A QUARTER PIPE 📺 USA

Jason Ellis (Australia) achieved the highest skateboard drop on to a quarter pipe from a height of 8.53 m (28 ft) at Van Nuys Airport, California, USA, on 21 Jan 2001.

LONGEST SKATEBOARD JUMP 📺 USA

Brian Patch (USA) jumped a record distance of 17.06 m (56 ft) on his skateboard at Van Nuys Airport, California, USA, on 21 Jan 2001.

FASTEST SKATEBOARDER

The highest speed ever recorded by a skateboarder is 126.12 km/h (78.37 mph) by Roger Hickey (USA) on a course near Los Angeles, California, USA, on 15 March 1990. He was riding in a prone position.

With an amazing speed of 100.66 km/h (62.55 mph), Gary Hardwick (USA) holds the record for the fastest speed reached in the standing position, which he achieved at Fountain Hills, Arizona, USA, on 26 Sept 1998.

FASTEST SANDBOARDERS

Erik Johnson (USA) achieved a record sandboarding speed of 82 km/h (51 mph) during the Sand Master Jam at Dumont Dunes, California, USA, on 12 April 1999.

The fastest female sandboarder is Nancy Sutton (USA), who achieved a speed of 71.94 km/h (44.7 mph) at Sand Mountain, Nevada, USA, on 19 Sept 1998.

MOST DOWNHILL MOUNTAIN BIKING WORLD CHAMPIONSHIPS

Nicolas Vouilloz (France) holds the record for the most Downhill World Championship wins with seven – three in the Junior Championships from 1992 to 1994 and four in the senior class from 1995 to 1998.

Anne-Caroline Chausson (France) holds the record in the women's event, also with five wins – two in the Junior Championships (1994 and 1995) and three in the senior class (from 1996 to 1998).

HIGHEST MOTOCROSS STEP-UP JUMP

On 18 Aug 2000 Tommy Clowers (USA) achieved a record-breaking height of 10.67 m (35 ft) in the X Games Motocross Step-Up event. Essentially a 'high-jump' on motorbikes, the sport involves riders trying to clear a bar placed at the top of a steep take-off ramp. Clowers's feat is the equivalent of jumping onto the roof of a two-storey building.

LONGEST POWER ASSISTED BMX RAMP JUMP 📺 USA

Professional stunt rider Colin Winkelmann (USA) achieved a ramp jump of 35.63 m (116 ft 11 in) on his BMX bicycle at the Agoura Hills, California, USA, on 20 Dec 2000. His BMX was towed behind a motorcycle at a speed approaching 100 km/h (60 mph) – to give him the necessary velocity – before being released just before he hit the ramp.

MOST 📺 USA BACKFLIPS FROM A SINGLE SCOOTER JUMP

Jarret Reid (USA) managed a scooter back flip, landing with both feet on the scooter, when travelling from a ramp at a height of 5.48 m (18 ft). The record was achieved at Van Nuys Airport, California USA, on 21 Jan 2001.

GUINNESS WORLD RECORDS™

extreme sports 2

MOST HELICOPTER SKYSURFING SPINS
🖥 UK

The most helicopter spins in the skysurfing position (spinning upside down with a board attached to the feet) is 64 in 20 seconds by Chris Gauge of St Agnes, Cornwall, UK, in the skies above the Aerodrome Sierra Morena, Spain, on 31 March 1999.

LONGEST DISTANCE BY KITE SURFER

Three surfers from kite manufacturer Flexifoil International crossed the English Channel using kite surfers – custom-made boards with 4.9-m² (52.7-ft²) two-blade traction kites. Chris Calthrop and Andy Preston (both UK) crossed the 42.9 km (23.2 nautical miles) from Hythe, Kent, UK, to Wissant, France, on 17 Sept 1999, in 2 hr 30 min, while Jason Furness (UK) completed the record-breaking journey in three hours.

LONGEST PARACHUTE DROP

The longest time spent in a parachute drop is 40 min by Lt Col Wm H Rankin (USA), of the US Marine Corps, due to thermal updraughts on 26 July 1956.

FURTHEST FREEFALL DROP
🖥 USA

The longest-ever freefall was by Capt Joseph W Kittinger, who dropped 25,820 m (84,715 ft) from a balloon at 31,330 m (102,800 ft), at Tularosa, New Mexico, USA, on 16 Aug 1960. The maximum speed reached in rarified air was 1,006 km/h (625 mph) at 27,400 m (90,000 ft), which is slightly faster than the speed of sound. He fell for 4 min 37 sec before his parachute was deployed automatically.

MOST PARACHUTE JUMPS IN 24 HOURS

The most descents made in 24 hours (in accordance with United States Parachute Association rules) is 476, by Jay Stokes (USA), at Yuma, Arizona, USA, from 12 to 13 Nov 1999. There were medics on hand who quizzed Jay to ensure that he was alert enough to keep jumping.

HIGHEST BASE JUMP

On 26 Aug 1992 Nicholas Feteris and Glenn Singleman (both Australia) jumped from a ledge known as the 'Great Trango Tower', Pakistan, which stands at 5,880 m (19,300 ft).

LONGEST BUNGEE JUMP

On 19 Sept 1997 the renowned stuntman and bungee jumper Jochen Schweizer (Germany), jumped from an SA 365 Dauphine helicopter for a total distance of 1,012 m (3,320 ft) above Reichelsheim, Germany. Schweizer leapt from the helicopter

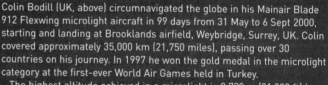

A MIGHTY FLIGHT IN A MICROLIGHT

Colin Bodill (UK, above) circumnavigated the globe in his Mainair Blade 912 Flexwing microlight aircraft in 99 days from 31 May to 6 Sept 2000, starting and landing at Brooklands airfield, Weybridge, Surrey, UK. Colin covered approximately 35,000 km (21,750 miles), passing over 30 countries on his journey. In 1997 he won the gold medal in the microlight category at the first-ever World Air Games held in Turkey.

The highest altitude achieved in a microlight is 9,720 m (31,890 ft) by Serge Zin (France), at Saint Auban, France, on 18 Sept 1994.

🎵 www.guinnessworldrecords.com/microlight
← ACCESS CODE: ‹52011›

at 2,500 m (8,200 ft), then cut the rope and went into a freefall, finally parachuting to safety near Frankfurt.

HIGHEST COMMERCIALLY OPERATED BUNGEE JUMP

The highest commercial bungee jump in the world is from the 216-m-high (708-ft) Bloukrans River Bridge, South Africa. Jumpers typically freefall for five seconds before the bungee cord begins to slow their fall. However, the jump usually lasts a further four

seconds, taking the total length jumped to between 160 and 180 m (525 to 590 ft).

LONGEST WATERFALL DESCENT IN A CANOE
🖥 USA

The longest descent over a waterfall by canoe is 30 m (98.4 ft) by Tao Berman (USA) at the Upper Johnstone Canyon Falls in Banff National Park, Alberta, Canada, on 23 Aug 1999.

LONGEST WATER-SKI JUMP

The International Water Ski Federation record for the longest ski jump is 70.9 m (232.6 ft) by Jimmy Siemers (USA) at the Tri-Lakes Late Bloomer event at Zachary, Louisiana, USA, on 22 Oct 2000.

The record for the longest jump by a woman is 52.7 m (172.9 ft) by Toni Neville (Australia) at the US Open event at Sacramento, California, USA, on 25 June 2000.

LONGEST BAREFOOT WATER-SKI JUMP

The world record for the longest barefoot water-ski jump is 25.8 m (84.6 ft) by Jon Kretchman (USA) in the USA in Aug 1998.

IN AT THE DEEP END

The highest regularly performed head-first dives are those of professional divers, aged between 12 and 50 years old, from La Quebrada, Acapulco, Mexico. They have been diving head-first from a record height of 35 m (115 ft) into a mere 3.6 m (12 ft) of crashing water since 1934. La Quebrada (left) is a rock formation with a large crevice between the two cliffs. It was formed when a cliff top was dynamited and split in two and its name means 'the break in the rocks'. This feat is equivalent to jumping off a 10-storey building in a vertical freefall, although the divers must also clear the edge of the cliffs by 8.2 m (27 ft) to avoid jutting base rocks and wait for a wave to fill the channel to deepen the water.

🎵 www.guinnessworldrecords.com/divers
← ACCESS CODE: ‹48667›

SURFER DUDES

The women's professional surfing title (instituted 1979) has been won a record four times by Frieda Zamba (USA) in 1984–86 and 1988; Wendy Botha (Australia, formerly South Africa) in 1987, 1989 and 1991–92; and Lisa Andersen (Australia, below) in 1994–97. Andersen pulled out of the 1998 season, citing chronic back troubles, but returned to the professional fray late in 1999,

finishing fourth in the 2000 season. Combining prodigious talent with glamour, she is often credited with helping to popularize the sport among women.

The World Professional men's title has been won six times by Kelly Slater (USA), in 1992 and 1994–98, making him the man with the most World titles for surfing.

LONGEST DISTANCE SKI FLYING

The International Water Ski Federation record for ski flying (a more extreme form of water-ski jumping) is 91.1 m (298.9 ft), by Jaret Llewellyn (Canada) at the Big Air Challenge event at Orlando, Florida, USA, on 14 May 2000.

The record for ski flying by a woman is 66.6 m (218.5 ft), a distance achieved by both Toni Neville and Emma Sheer (both Australia) at the America's Cup event at West Palm Beach, Florida, USA, in Sept 2000.

MOST WAKEBOARDING INVERTS IN ONE MINUTE

On 30 Aug 1999 Julz Heany achieved 15 inverts (somersaults) in one minute on a wakeboard measuring 125 cm (49 in) long, and 39.8 cm (15.5 in) wide. Wakeboarding involves being pulled

behind a speed boat, but with both feet attached to a small board, which gives great freedom for performing tricks.

FASTEST WATER-SKIERS

The fastest water-skiing speed recorded is 230.26 km/h (143.06 mph) by Christopher Massey (Australia) on the Hawkesbury River, Windsor, NSW, Australia, on 6 March 1983.

Donna Patterson Brice set a women's record of 178.8 km/h (111.11 mph) at Long Beach, California, USA, on 21 Aug 1977.

MOST BODYBOARDING CHAMPIONSHIPS

Mike Stewart (USA) has won nine World Championships, eight National tour titles and 21 Pipeline Bodyboarding Championships.

GUINNESS WORLD RECORDS

winter sports 1

FASTEST SNOWBOARD ON A BOBSLEIGH RUN
Reto Lamm (Switzerland) surfed down a bobsleigh run on his snowboard at a record speed of 80 km/h (49.7 mph) in Nov 1998.

MOST SNOWBOARDING CHAMPIONSHIP TITLES
Karine Ruby (France) has won a record three Championship titles (including Olympic titles). She won the giant slalom in 1996, the Olympic title in 1998 and the snowboard cross (a race between four riders over a downhill course) in 1997.

LONGEST SNOWBOARDING VERTICAL DESCENT
On 20 April 1998 Tammy McMinn (USA) snowboarded down a slope at Atlin, British Columbia, Canada, 101 times, making a total vertical descent of 93,124 m (305,539 ft).

MOST US OPEN SNOWBOARDING WINS
The greatest number of halfpipe victories at the US Open has been achieved by Terje Haakonsen (Norway) with three wins in 1992, 1993 and 1995.

ONE JUMP AHEAD
The longest competitive ski jump by a man is 225 m (738 ft) by Andreas Goldberger (Austria, left) at Planica, Slovenia, on 18 March 2000. The day before, his previous world record of a 223-m (731-ft) jump had been broken by 18-year-old Austrian Thomas Hoerl. Goldberger is reported as to have admitted that the wind played in his favour when he regained the title the next day. He has also won the World Cup three times in 1993, 1995 and 1996.

The women's record is 112 m (367 ft) by Eva Ganster (Austria) at Bischofshofen, Austria, on 7 Jan 1994. She began skiing competitively when she was 10 years old.

www.guinnessworldrecords.com/goldberger
← ACCESS CODE: ‹44485›

FASTEST SNOWBOARDING SPEED
The fastest recorded speed reached by a snowboarder is 201.907 km/h (125.44 mph) by Darren Powell (Australia) at Les Arcs, France, on 2 May 1999.

MOST OLYMPIC BIATHLON GOLDS
In the biathlon – shooting and Nordic (cross-country) skiing – the most Olympic individual titles won is two by Magnar Solberg (Norway) in 1968 and 1972; and Frank-Peter Rötsch (GDR) in 1988 at 10 km and 20 km. Aleksandr Tikhonov (USSR) won four relay golds at 7.5 km in the biathlon in 1968 and 1980, and a silver for the 20 km in 1968.

Anfissa Restzova (Russia) and Myriam Bédard (Canada) hold the most Olympic titles in the women's biathlon competition. Restzova won gold for the 7.5 km in 1992, and another in the 4 x 7.5 km in 1994; Bédard won gold in the 7.5 km and the 15 km in 1994.

MOST BIATHLON CHAMPIONSHIP TITLES
Frank Ullrich (GDR) has won a record six individual Biathlon World titles, with four victories at 10 km, from 1978 to 1981, including the 1980 Olympics, and two wins at 20 km, between 1982 and 1983.

GREATEST DISTANCE COVERED IN NORDIC SKIING IN 24 HOURS
A Nordic ski is only attached to the point of the toe of a boot, which resembles a running shoe. The furthest distance achieved by a Nordic skier in 24 hours is 415.5 km (258.2 miles), by Seppo-Juhani Savolainen (Finland) between 8 and 9 April 1988 at Saariselkä, Finland.

The women's distance record for Nordic skiing in 24 hours is 333 km (206.92 miles), held by Kamila Horakova (Czech Republic) between 12 and 13 April 2000 at the Canmore Nordic Centre, Alberta, Canada.

MOST NORDIC SKIING TITLES
Bjørn Dæhlie (Norway) has won the most Nordic skiing titles (including the Olympics) with a total of 17, consisting of 12 individual and five relay wins between 1991 and 1998. Dæhlie won a record 29 medals in total (gold, silver and bronze) between 1991 and 1999.

The most Nordic skiing titles won by a woman is 17, achieved by Yelena Välbe (Russia). She won 10 individual and seven relay titles between 1989 and 1998. With an additional seven silver and bronze medals, her total of 24 is a record.

X-TREME MEASURES
The Winter X (extreme) Games were launched by ESPN in 1977 and feature ice-climbing, snow mountain biking, free-skiing, skiboarding, snowboarding and snowcross. Shaun Palmer (USA, left) has won a record three gold medals in the Boarder X (a race between four riders over a downhill course) discipline at the Winter ESPN X Games in 1997, 1998 and 1999. Shaun took up snowboarding aged 14 and turned professional three years later.

The women's record for the most X Games snowboarding medals is six, by Barrett Christy (USA). Christy took the gold medal in the Big Air (jump tricks off a ramp) event and the silver medal in the Slopestyle (performing tricks on a slope that has rails and other props)

MOST WORLD CUP RACE WINS

The most World Cup wins for Alpine individual events is 86 (46 giant slalom and 40 slalom, from a total of 287 races) by Ingemar Stenmark (Sweden) between 1974 and 1989, including a men's record of 13 in one season between 1978 and 1979. Ten of these were part of a record 14 successive giant slalom wins from 18 March 1978, his 22nd birthday, to 21 Jan 1980.

Annemarie Moser (Austria) achieved a women's record for 62 individual event wins from 1970 to 1979. She had a record 11 consecutive downhill wins from Dec 1972 to Jan 1974.

MOST WORLD CUP DOWNHILL WINS

Franz Klammer (Austria) won a record-breaking 25 downhill races between 1974 and 1984.

MOST WORLD CUP FREESTYLE WINS

The most overall titles won by a woman in the World Cup is 10 by Connie Kissling (Switzerland) between 1983 and 1992.

The most men's overall titles in the World Cup is five by Eric Laboureix (France) between 1986 and 1988 and between 1990 and 1991.

MOST FREESTYLE SKIING TITLES

The first Freestyle World Championships were held at Tignes, France, in 1986, with titles being awarded in ballet, moguls, aerials and combined (a combination of results from the other disciplines). Edgar Grospiron (France) has won a record three titles – moguls in 1989 and 1991, and aerials in 1995. He also won the Olympic freestyle title in 1992.

The most World titles for a woman is also three, achieved by Candice Gilg (France), who won the moguls in 1993, 1995 and 1997.

FASTEST OLYMPIC SKIING SPEED

The fastest average speed in the Olympic downhill race was 107.24 km/h (66.62 mph) by Jean-Luc Cretier (France) at Nagano, Japan, on 13 Feb 1998.

FASTEST SKIING SPEED

The fastest speed for a skier is 248.105 km/h (154.147 mph) by Harry Egger (Austria) at Les Arcs, France, on 2 May 1999.

The fastest speed by a female skier is 234.528 km/h (145.71 mph) by Karine Dubouchet (France) at Les Arcs, France, on 2 May 1999.

MOST NATIONS CUPS WON

The Nations Cup, awarded for the best combined results of men and women taking part in the World Cup, has been won a record-breaking 22 times by Austria in 1969, from 1973 to 1980, in 1982 and from 1990 to 2001.

MOST SKI FLIPS (SOMERSAULTS) IN 10 MINUTES

Tommy Waltner (USA) completed 23 front inverted aerial jumps within 10 minutes on 25 April 2000. The event took place on Aspen Mountain, Colorado, USA, in order to raise money for Tommy's 'Loops for Lupus' (a disease of the immune system) campaign, which aims to heighten awareness of the condition. He achieved his record at the age of 50.

www.guinnessworldrecords.com/ruby

ACCESS CODE: ‹55454›

JEWEL IN THE CROWN

Snowboarding became an Olympic sport in 1998 and is part of the Fédération Internationale du Ski. A World Cup series began in 1995, with World Championships inaugurated the following year. Karine Ruby (France, below) has won the greatest number of World Cup snowboarding titles, with 14 victories consisting of the overall from 1996 to 1998 and 2001, the slalom between 1996 and 1998, the giant slalom from 1995 to 1998 and 2001, and snowboard cross between 1997 and 2001.

The most men's titles won in the World Cup is five by Mathieu Bozzetto (France), made up of the overall from 1999 to 2000 and the slalom/parallel slalom from 1999 to 2001.

GUINNESS WORLD RECORDS

 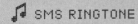

winter sports 2

FASTEST LUGEING SPEED

The fastest-ever recorded, photo-timed lugeing speed is 137.4 km/h (85.36 mph) by Asle Strand (Norway) on 1 May 1982 at Tandådalens Linbana, Sälen, Sweden.

MOST FOUR-MAN BOBSLEIGH WINS

The World Four-man Bobsleigh title has been won a record-breaking 20 times by Switzerland, in 1924, 1936, 1939, 1947, 1954–57, 1971–73, 1975, 1982–83, 1986–90 and 1993. These include five Olympic victories, in 1924, 1936, 1956, 1972 and 1988.

MOST TWO-MAN BOBSLEIGH WINS

Switzerland has won the two-man bobsleigh title a record 17 times – in 1935, 1947–50, 1953, 1955, 1977–80, 1982–83, 1987, 1990, 1992 and 1994. These include four Olympic wins in 1948, 1980, 1992 and 1994.

MOST MEDALS WON IN INDIVIDUAL BOBSLEIGH EVENTS

The greatest number of individual World Bobsleigh titles won is 11, achieved by Eugenio Monti (Italy) between 1957 and 1968. He did this by winning eight two-man titles as well as three four-man titles, becoming the most successful bobsleigher in the history of these two events.

THE FAST LANE

The most victories in the women's Short-track Speed Skating Championships have been achieved by Sylvie Daigle (Canada), in 1983 and between 1988 and 1990; and Yang Yang (China, left), between 1998 and 2001.

In the men's Championships, the holder of the most titles is Marc Gagnon (Canada), from 1993 to 1994, 1996 and 1998.

MOST INDIVIDUAL OLYMPIC BOBSLEIGH MEDALS

Bogdan Musiol (GDR) has won the most individual bobsleigh medals, with seven accumulated between 1980 and 1992 – one gold, five silver and one bronze. During his bobsleigh career, Musiol took part in four Olympic Games and never came home without a medal.

MOST BOBSLEIGH OLYMPIC GOLD MEDALS

The most Olympic gold bobsleigh medals won by an individual is three and is shared by Meinhard Nehmer (GDR) and Bernhard Germeshausen (GDR) in the 1976 two-man, 1976 and 1980 four-man events. Following his retirement in 1991, Nehmer became the coach of the US bobsleigh team.

FASTEST CRESTA RUN FROM JUNCTION

The Cresta Run course, at St Moritz, Switzerland, is a 1,212-m-long (3,977-ft) ice run with a drop of 157 m (514 ft). It has two start points – at Junction (when the full length cannot be run owing to snowfall) and at Top (the whole run). Johannes Badrutt (Switzerland) set a record from Junction (890 m or 2,921 ft) of 41.02 seconds on 17 Jan 1999.

FASTEST CRESTA RUN COMPLETION TIME

The fastest-ever recorded time to complete the Cresta Run is 50.09 seconds at an average speed of 87.11 km/h (54.13 mph), achieved by James Sunley (UK) on 13 Feb 1999.

JM Baguley (UK) was the last woman to ride the Cresta in a race on 13 Jan 1925. Women were banned from riding on 6 Jan 1929 as it was considered too dangerous.

FASTEST 16-ENDER

Curling is played between two teams of four players each. The object is to push a 20-kg (44-lb) stone down a sheet of ice towards a ring of concentric circles. A team scores a point for each stone that is closest to the centre of the rings. A match consists of eight ends, with each player throwing two stones for a total of 16 – hence a 16-ender. Curling teams led by Hammy McMillan (UK) completed the fastest end in 6 min 49.90 sec at the 16-ender National Finals in Stirling, Scotland, UK, on 22 Dec 1999.

MOST WORLD CURLING CHAMPIONSHIP TITLES

The most World Curling titles have been won by Canada with a record 26 titles – in 1959–64, 1966, 1968–72, 1980, 1982–83, 1985–87, 1989–90, 1993–96, 1998 and 2000.

The Canadian women's team has won 12 titles – in 1980, 1984–87, 1989, 1993–94, 1996–97 and 2000–01.

MOST OLYMPIC GOLD SPEED-SKATING MEDALS

Lidiya Pavlovna Skoblikova (USSR) has won the greatest number of Olympic speed-skating gold medals with six victories – two in 1960 and four in 1964.

The greatest number of Olympic gold speed-skating medals won by a man is five. The record is shared between Clas Thunberg (Finland) who won his medals in the 1924 and 1928 Games; and Eric Arthur Heiden (USA), who won all his gold medals at Lake Placid, New York, USA, in 1980.

MOST OLYMPIC SPEED-SKATING MEDALS

The most Olympic speed-skating medals won by a man is seven. This record is shared by Clas Thunberg (Finland) and Ivar Ballangrud (Norway). Thunberg, in addition to winning a record five golds, won one silver and one tied bronze between 1924 and 1928; Ballangrud won four golds, two silvers and a bronze medal between 1928 and 1936.

MOST WORLD CHAMPIONSHIPS SINGLE DISTANCE SPEED-SKATING

Gunda Niemann-Stirnemann (Germany) has won the most women's titles at the World Single Distance Championships with

BACK-SEAT DRIVER

The most World Championship Lugeing titles won (including the Olympics) is six by Georg Hackl (GDR/Germany, left), in a single-seater, in 1989, 1990, 1992, 1994, 1997 and 1998. Stefan Krausse and Jan Behrendt (both GDR/Germany) have won a record six two-seater titles, in 1989, 1991–93, 1995 and 1998.

The most Olympic gold luge medals won by a woman is two by Steffi Walter (GDR), with victories at the women's single-seater luge event in 1984 and 1988.

The most World Championships in lugeing won by a woman is four, by Margit Schumann (GDR), in 1973–1975 and in 1977. She also won the Olympic gold medal in 1976.

SPEED DEMON

The most World Championship titles won in women's speed-skating is eight by Gunda Niemann-Stirnemann (Germany, above), between 1991 and 1993 and from 1995 to 1999. Very popular in her homeland, she is nicknamed the 'Ice Queen' and has won several major sporting awards in Germany, including the German Athlete of the Year in 1995.

The greatest number of men's World Speed-skating titles is five, and is shared by Oscar Mathisen (Norway) from 1908 to 1909 and from 1912 to 1914; and by Clas Thunberg (Finland) in 1923, 1925, 1928–29 and 1931.

www.guinnessworldrecords.com/niemann-stirnemann

ACCESS CODE:
← ‹44913›

11 victories – the 1,500 m (1997), 3,000 m (1996–1999, 2001) and the 5,000 m (1997–2001).

The most titles won by a man is seven, achieved by Gianni Romme (Netherlands) in the 5,000 m (1998–2000) and 10,000 m (1996–98 and 2000). He was helped to success by an innovative new skate design.

MOST OLYMPIC FIGURE-SKATING MEDALS

The greatest number of Olympic gold figure-skating medals won is three, a record that is shared by Gillis Grafstrom (Sweden) who won in 1920, 1924 and 1928; by Sonja Henie (Norway) – whom Grafstrom trained – at the Winter Olympics of 1928, 1932 and 1936; and by Irina Rodnina (USSR) – who won three pairs figure-skating gold medals with two different partners. In 1972 she won the gold medal skating with Alexei Ulanov

(USSR), and in 1976 and 1980 she won gold skating with Alexandr Zaitsev (USSR). Following retirement from the sport in 1980, Rodnina now coaches in California, USA, and has trained the 1995 World Figure Skating champions.

GREATEST DISTANCE SKATED IN 24 HOURS

Martinus Kuiper (Netherlands) skated a record-breaking distance of 546.65 km (339.68 miles) in 24 hours at Alkmaar, Netherlands, between 12 and 13 Dec 1988.

MOST CONTINUOUS SPINS ON ICE

The greatest number of continuous spins made on one foot on ice is 60 rotations achieved by Neil Wilson (UK) at the Spectrum Centre, Guildford, Surrey, UK, on 1 July 1997.

MOST X GAMES ICE-CLIMBING MEDALS

Kim Csizmazia (USA) has won a record three X Games gold medals for ice-climbing – the difficulty medal in 1998 and 1999, and the speed medal in 1998.

www.guinnessworldrecords.com/coomber

NO BONES ABOUT IT

Alex Coomber (UK, right) holds the most skeleton sled titles with two World Cups and one World Championship. The skeleton sled will be contested at the Winter Olympic Games, at Salt Lake City, Utah, USA, in Feb 2002 after an absence of 54 years. For the first time there will be a women's competition with current women's World Cup champion Alex Coomber a favourite for success.

Coomber successfully defended her World Cup title during the 2000/01 season. She could not,

however, retain her World Championship title success of 2000, losing to Maya Pedersen (Switzerland) by just 7/100 second at the 2001 Championships.

The sport of skeleton sledging originated at the Swiss resort of St Moritz in the 1800s and is noted for its head-first style of riding. The sport got its name from the early metal toboggans that were used. People commented that they looked like skeletons.

ACCESS CODE: ‹56666›

←

GUINNESS WORLD RECORDS™

water sports

BOLD GOLD

Krisztina Egerszegi (Hungary, above) has won more Olympic gold medals for individual swimming than any other person. She won a record five gold medals, for 100-m backstroke (1992), 200-m backstroke (1988, 1992 and 1996) and 400-m medley (1992). In 1988, when she was only 14 years old, she won silver and gold medals at the Seoul Olympic Games.

The most individual Olympic gold medals awarded to a man for swimming are four. This record is jointly held by Charles Meldrum Daniels (USA) for 220-yd freestyle (1904), 440-yd freestyle (1904), 100-m freestyle (1906, 1908); Roland Matthes (GDR) for 100-m backstroke (1968, 1972) and 200-m backstroke (1968, 1972); Mark Spitz (USA) for 100-m and 200-m freestyle, and 100-m and 200-m butterfly (all 1972); Tamás Daryni (Hungary) for 200-m medley (1988, 1992) and 400-m medley (1988, 1992); and Aleksandr Popov (Russia) for 50-m freestyle (1992, 1996) and 100-m freestyle (1992, 1996).

 www.guinnessworldrecords.com/egerszegi

← ACCESS CODE: ‹44333›

MOST CONSECUTIVE OLYMPIC GOLD MEDALS FOR SWIMMING

Only two swimmers have won the same event on three occasions. Dawn Fraser (Australia) won the 100-m freestyle in 1956, 1960 and 1964, and Krisztina Egerszegi (Hungary) won the 200-m backstroke in 1988, 1992 and 1996.

MOST GOLD MEDALS FOR SWIMMING AT ONE OLYMPIC GAMES BY A WOMAN

Kristin Otto (GDR) won six golds for swimming. They were for the 50-m freestyle, the 100-m freestyle, the 100-m backstroke, the 100-m butterfly, the 4 x 100-m freestyle and the 4 x 100-m medley in 1988.

MOST OLYMPIC GOLD MEDALS FOR SWIMMING BY A MAN

Mark Spitz (USA) won a total of nine Olympic gold medals. They were for 100-m and 200-m freestyle (1972), 100-m and 200-m butterfly (1972), 4 x 100-m freestyle (1968 and 1972), 4 x 200-m freestyle (1968 and 1972), 4 x 100-m medley (1972). All but one of these performances (the 4 x 200-m freestyle of 1968) were new world records. He also won a silver (100-m butterfly) and a bronze (100-m freestyle) in 1968, for a record of 11 medals in total.

Spitz's record seven medals at one Games in 1972 was equalled by Matt Biondi (USA) who took five gold, one silver and one bronze in 1988. Biondi has also won a record 11 medals in total, winning a gold in 1984 and two golds and a silver in 1992.

MOST OLYMPIC MEDALS FOR SWIMMING BY A WOMAN

The most medals won by a woman is eight. Dawn Fraser (Australia) won four golds and four silvers (1956–64); Kornelia Ender (GDR) won four golds and four silvers (1972–76); and Shirley Babashoff (USA) won two golds and six silvers (1972–76).

MOST OLYMPIC GOLD MEDALS FOR CANOEING BY A MAN

Gert Fredriksson (Sweden) won a record six Olympic gold medals from 1948 to 1960. He added a silver and a bronze for a record eight medals.

MOST OLYMPIC GOLD MEDALS FOR CANOEING BY A WOMAN

The most golds won by a woman is seven by Birgit Fischer (née Schmidt, GDR/Germany) between 1980 and 2000. She has also won three silvers for a record total of 10 medals.

MOST WORLD AND OLYMPIC TITLES FOR CANOEING BY A MAN

The record of 13 World and Olympic titles is jointly held by Gert Fredriksson (Sweden, 1948–60), Rüdiger Helm (GDR, 1976–83) and Ivan Patzaichin (Romania, 1968–84).

MOST WORLD AND OLYMPIC TITLES FOR CANOEING BY A WOMAN

In addition to her five Olympic titles, Birgit Fischer (née Schmidt) has won 29 World titles between 1979 and 1998, to make a record 34 titles overall.

LONGEST CANOE JOURNEY WITH PORTAGES

Verlen Kruger and Steven Landick (both USA) travelled a distance of 45,129 km (28,043 miles), starting from Red Rock, Montana, and finishing at Lansing, Michigan, USA, from 29 April 1980 to 15 Dec 1983. They travelled via the Missouri, Great Lakes, Atlantic Coast, Gulf of Mexico, Mississippi, through Canada and Alaska, down the Pacific Coast to the Gulf of California, up the Colorado River and back to Michigan. All portages (carrying the canoe) were human powered.

LONGEST CANOE JOURNEY WITHOUT PORTAGES

Without portages or aid of any kind, the longest canoe journey is 9,820 km (6,102 miles) by Richard H Grant (USA) and Ernest Moose Lassy (USA). They circumnavigated the eastern USA via Chicago, New Orleans, Miami, New York and the Great Lakes between 22 Sept 1930 and 15 Aug 1931.

HIGHEST CANOE SPEED OVER 200 M

At the 1998 World Championships held in Szeged, Hungary, the Hungarian four won the 200-m title in a time of 31.155 sec. This represents an average speed of 23.11 km/h (14.36 mph).

HIGHEST CANOE SPEED OVER 1,000 M

The German four-man kayak Olympic champions covered 1,000 m in 2:51.52 to win gold in Atlanta, Georgia, USA, on 3 Aug 1996. This represents an average speed of 20.98 km/h (13.04 mph).

MOST OLYMPIC GOLD MEDALS FOR YACHTING

The first sportsman ever to win individual gold medals for yachting in four successive Olympic Games was Paul B Elvstrom (Denmark) in the firefly class in 1948 and the finn class in 1952, 1956 and 1960. He also won eight other World titles in a total of six classes.

LONGEST SOLO NON-STOP YACHTING RACE

The world's longest non-stop solo sailing race is the Vendée Globe Challenge, which starts and finishes at Les Sables d'Olonne, France. The first one took place on 26 Nov 1989. The distance currently sailed without stopping is 22,500 nautical miles (41,652 km or 25,881 miles). The race is for single-handed yachts, between 50 and 60 ft long.

MAKING WAVES

The world record for the women's long-course 4 x 100-m freestyle relay is 3:36.61, by the US Olympic team, consisting of Amy van Dyken, Dara Torres, Courtney Shealy and Jenny Thompson (left; from left to right). The time was set at the Olympic Games in Sydney, NSW, Australia, on 16 Sept 2000. The US team broke the world record that had stood for six years. Jenny Thompson, who swam the fastest leg, has been a member of the winning relay team at the last three Olympic Games, equalling the record achievement of fellow American Matt Biondi.

www.guinnessworldrecords.com/usswimteam

ACCESS CODE: ‹52934›

www.guinnessworldrecords.com/ianthorpe

ACCESS CODE: ‹52321›

IAN THORPEDO

The fastest time set in the men's 400-m freestyle race is 3:40.59 by Ian Thorpe (Australia, below) at the Olympic Games in Sydney, NSW, Australia, on 16 Sept 2000. Since March 2001 he also holds the world records for 200-m freestyle (1:44:69) and 800-m freestyle (7:41:59). He is regarded as one of the greatest swimmers the world has ever seen.

FURTHEST WHITEWATER SWIM

On 5 June 1999 Thom Stanton (USA) swam up the James River in Virginia, USA, from Mayo Island to Bosher's Dam, a distance of 12.07 km (7.5 miles). Armed only with flippers and web-fingered gloves, Stanton swam, dragged and clawed his way up the Class II–IV+ rapids of the Falls of the James. Stanton took breaks totalling 29 min 24 sec. The event, without breaks, lasted 5 hr 50 min 30 sec.

BIGGEST SEA-WAVE RIDES

Four to six times each year rideable surfing waves break in Matanchen Bay near San Blas, Nayarit, Mexico, which makes surfing rides of around 1,700 m (5,700 ft) possible.

BIGGEST RIVER BORE RIDES

The longest recorded rides on a river bore have been set on the Severn bore, UK. The official British Surfing Association record for riding a surfboard is 9.1 km (5.7 miles) by David Lawson (UK), from Windmill Hill to Maisemore Weir, on 29 Aug 1996.

MOST WORLD TITLES FOR WINDSURFING

World Championships were first held in 1973 and windsurfing (also known as boardsailing) was added to the Olympic Games in 1984. The winner was Stephan van den Berg (Netherlands), who also won five World titles between 1979 and 1983.

MOST SOUTHERLY ESKIMO ROLL

On 3 Feb 1998 Christopher Patalano (UK) performed an eskimo roll (rotating through 360°) in icy waters at 77° 04.8'S. Sea temperatures in the area are normally little more than just above 0°C (32°F).

MOST CONTINUOUS ROTATIONS UNDER WATER

Virginie Dedieu (France), a bronze medallist in synchronized swimming at the Sydney Olympics, completed 22 rotations in one breath in Paris, France, on 26 Oct 2000.

rugby

FASTEST INTERNATIONAL RUGBY LEAGUE TRY

The record for the fastest try in an international match is 15 seconds, by Bobby Fulton for Australia v. France at Odsal Stadium, Bradford, UK, on 1 Nov 1970.

The fastest try in a rugby league match was by Lee Jackson (UK) who scored after nine seconds for Hull v. Sheffield Eagles in a Yorkshire Cup semi-final at Don Valley Stadium, Sheffield, UK, on 6 Oct 1992.

HIGHEST RUGBY LEAGUE SCORE

The record for the highest score in a rugby league match is held by Ngati Pikiao of Rotorua. The team beat Tokoroa United 148–0 in a Bay of Plenty Rugby League under-17s league match at Pikiao, New Zealand, on 10 July 1994.

MOST AMATEUR RUGBY LEAGUE TRIES SCORED IN A SEASON

Richard Lopag (UK) has scored the most tries in an amateur rugby league season, with 142 in the 1998/99 season for the Deighton Juniors under-9s side, West Yorkshire, UK. Richard started playing for the team at the age of five. His grandfather spotted the youngster's talent and, with the record books in mind, began compiling the statistics.

UP AND UNDER – DOWN UNDER

First held in 1954, the Rugby League World Cup has been won by Australia (left) a record eight times. They won the Cup in 1957, 1968, 1970, 1977, 1988, 1992, 1995 and 2000 as well as a win in the International Championship of 1975.

Australia also holds the record for the most wins of the Webb Ellis Trophy (the Rugby Union World Cup). Instituted in 1987, Australia won the 1991 and 1999 contests and is the only team to have won it more than once. An early form of rugby is believed to have been played in Australia since the 1820s, although the first rugby club at Sydney University was not established until 1864. The Australian Rugby Union was formed in 1949.

www.guinnessworldrecords.com/ausrugby
ACCESS CODE: ‹44564›

MOST POINTS IN AN INTERNATIONAL RUGBY LEAGUE MATCH

The greatest number of points scored in a professional game is 48 (16 goals, 4 tries) by Hazen El Masri of Lebanon v. Morocco in a World Cup qualifying match at Avignon, France, on 17 Nov 1999.

YOUNGEST INTERNATIONAL RUGBY LEAGUE PLAYER

The youngest international player in a rugby league match is Paul Newlove (UK) who played in the first Test for the UK against New Zealand on 21 Oct 1989 at Old Trafford, Manchester, UK, aged 18 years 72 days.

LONGEST RUGBY LEAGUE DROP GOAL

The longest drop goal in a rugby league match is 56 m (183 ft) by Joseph 'Joe' Lydon (UK) for Wigan, v. Warrington in a Challenge Cup semi-final at Maine Road, Manchester, UK, on 25 March 1989.

HIGHEST RUGBY UNION POSTS

The world's highest rugby union goal posts measure 33.54 m (110 ft) and are at the Roan Antelope Rugby Union Club, Luanshya, Zambia. This is equivalent to 12 buses on top of one another.

HIGHEST ATTENDANCE AT A RUGBY UNION MATCH

The largest paying attendance for an international rugby match is 109,874 for New Zealand's 39–35 victory over Australia at Stadium Australia, Sydney, NSW, Australia, on 15 July 2000.

MOST SUCCESSFUL RUGBY UNION TEAM

The Feilding Senior 4ths of New Zealand played 108 successive games without defeat from 1984 to 1989. At junior level, the Chiltern mini rugby side played 213 games without defeat, from their formation as an under-8s side on 29 Sept 1985 to 8 April 1990.

FASTEST RUGBY UNION TRY

The fastest try was scored in just eight seconds by Andrew Brown (UK) for Widden Old Boys v. Old Ashtonians at Gloucester, UK, on 22 Nov 1990.

INTERNATIONAL RUGBY UNION APPEARANCES

Frenchman Philippe Sella played in a record-breaking 111 internationals for France between 1982 and 1995. In the 13 years since his first appearance against Romania, Sella scored 30 tries and appeared in three World Cups, winning a runners-up medal in 1987.

MOST INTERNATIONAL RUGBY UNION PENALTIES

The greatest number of penalties successfully kicked in an international is nine by Keiji Hirose for Japan, v. Tonga (44–17) in Tokyo, Japan, on 9 May 1999; and by Andrew Mehrtens for New Zealand v. Australia (34–15) in Auckland, New Zealand, on 24 July 1999.

MOST INTERNATIONAL RUGBY UNION TRIES

The most tries in an international career is 64 by David Campese, in 101 internationals for Australia between 1982 and 1996. Campese is Australia's most capped player, and in 1996 he was awarded a UNESCO (United Nations Educational, Scientific and Cultural Organization) prize as one of the most outstanding sportsmen of the century.

I GET A KICK OUT OF VIEW

Neil Jenkins (UK, left) has scored the most rugby union international points in a career with a record 1,052 points in 86 matches for Wales (1,011 points in 83 matches) and British Lions (41 points in 3 matches), between 1991 and March 2001. Much of this tally comes from Jenkins's formidable kicking skills, to the extent that he has become the most prolific goal kicker in the history of international rugby.

The longest recorded successful drop goal in rugby union history is 82 m (269 ft) by Gerald 'Gerry' Hamilton Brand for South Africa v. England at Twickenham, London, UK, on 2 Jan 1932. This was taken 6 m (19.69 ft) inside the England 'half', 50 m (164 ft) from the posts, and it dropped over the dead ball line.

www.guinnessworldrecords.com/kickrugby
ACCESS CODE: ‹52110›

MOST WINS IN THE HONG KONG SEVENS

The record for the greatest number of wins in the Hong Kong Rugby Union Sevens is held by Fiji, with nine wins in 1977–78, 1980, 1984, 1990–92 and 1998–99. In 1997 the contest was replaced by the World Cup Sevens and was also won by Fiji. The world's most prestigious international competition for seven-a-side teams, the first Hong Kong tournament was held in 1976.

MOST WOMEN'S HONG KONG SEVENS TITLES

The women's version of the world's most famous seven-a-side rugby competition was first held in 1997, and New Zealand has won the title a record four times, in 1997, 1999, 2000 and 2001.

MOST INDIVIDUAL POINTS SCORED IN A RUGBY UNION WORLD CUP MATCH

The most points scored in a match by an individual is 45 by Simon Culhane for New Zealand v. Japan (145–17) at Bloemfontein, South Africa, on 4 June 1995. In the same match, Culhane scored a match-record 20 conversions. The final score earned New Zealand the record for most points scored by a team in a World Cup match. They also scored a record 21 tries during the match.

MOST INDIVIDUAL POINTS IN A RUGBY UNION INTERNATIONAL

On 27 Oct 1994 Ashley Billington (Hong Kong) scored a record-breaking 50 points from 10 tries in the Rugby Union World Cup qualifying match between Hong Kong and Singapore at Kuala Lumpur, Malaysia, on 27 Oct 1994.

MOST OUTRIGHT INTERNATIONAL CHAMPIONSHIP TITLES

England has won the Rugby International Championship more times than any other international side, with 23 outright wins between 1884 and 2000. This does not take into account any ties, as the title is then shared.

www.guinnessworldrecords.com/tryrugby

ACCESS CODE: ‹53873›

A GOOD TRY

Jonny Wilkinson (UK, above) holds the record for the most individual points scored in a Rugby Union International Championship match. His record-breaking 35 points in the England v. Italy (80–23) game at Twickenham, London, UK, on 17 Feb 2001, consisted of four penalties (three points each), nine conversions (two points each) and a try (five points).

The 13 goals he kicked in this match are a record for an International Championship match. England's 80 points in this game was also the highest team score in a Rugby Union International Championship match.

The highest score for a Rugby League International is Australia's defeat of Russia (110–4) during the Rugby League World Cup at Hull, Yorkshire, UK, on 4 Nov 2000.

GUINNESS WORLD RECORDS

cricket

MOST WORLD CUP CATCHES
The most catches by a fielder is 14, by Steve Waugh (Australia) in 32 matches between 1987 and 1999.

The most catches in a tournament is eight by Anil Kumble (India) in 1996.

The most catches in a match is four by Chris Cairns (New Zealand) v. United Arab Emirates at Faisalabad, Pakistan, on 27 Feb 1996.

MOST WORLD CUP RUNS
The most runs scored by an individual in World Cup matches is 1,083, by Javed Miandad (Pakistan) in 33 matches from 1975 and 1996.

The greatest number of runs scored in a World Cup tournament is 523 by Sachin Tendulkar (India) in 1996.

The highest individual score in a World Cup match is 188 not out by Gary Kirsten (South Africa) v. the United Arab Emirates at Rawlpindi, India, on 16 Feb 1996.

MOST WICKET-KEEPING DISMISSALS IN WORLD CUP
The most dismissals by a wicket-keeper in the World Cup is 29 by Moin Khan (Pakistan), in 20 matches between 1992 and 1999.

The most dismissals by a wicket-keeper in a tournament is 16 by Jeff Dujon (West Indies) in 1983.

The most dismissals in a match by a wicket-keeper is five by Syed Kirmani (India) v. Zimbabwe at Leicester, UK, on 11 June 1983; Jimmy Adams (West Indies) v. Kenya at Pune, India, on 29 Feb 1996; Rashid Latif (Pakistan) v. New Zealand, Lahore, Pakistan, on 6 March 1996; Nayan Mongia (India) v. Zimbabwe at Leicester, UK, on 19 May 1999; and Ridley Jacobs (West Indies) v. New Zealand at Southampton, UK, on 24 May 1999.

MOST WINS IN WORLD CUP
The greatest number of wins is two by the West Indies, in 1975 and 1979; and Australia in 1987 and 1999.

MOST EXTRAS IN A ONE DAY INTERNATIONAL
The most extras conceded in a One Day International is 59 by the West Indies (eight byes, 10 leg byes, four no balls and 37 wides) v. Pakistan at Brisbane, Australia, on 7 Jan 1989; and Scotland (five byes, six leg byes, 15 no balls and 33 wides) v. Pakistan at Chester-le-Street, Durham, UK, on 20 May 1999.

HIGHEST INDIVIDUAL SCORE IN A ONE DAY INTERNATIONAL
The highest individual score is 194 by Saeed Anwar for Pakistan v. India, at Madras, India, on 21 May 1997.

HIGHEST MARGIN OF VICTORY IN A ONE DAY INTERNATIONAL
The largest victory margin is 233 runs by Pakistan v. Bangladesh (320–3 to 87), at Dhaka, Bangladesh, on 2 June 2000.

MOST ONE DAY INTERNATIONAL MATCHES PLAYED
The most matches played is 334 by Mohammad Azharuddin (India), between 1985 and 2000.

HIGHEST AND LOWEST SCORES IN ONE DAY MATCHES
The highest team score achieved in a World Cup match is 398–5 by Sri Lanka v. Kenya at Kandy, Sri Lanka, on 6 March 1996.

The lowest team score is 45 by Canada v. England at Old Trafford from 13 to 14 June 1979.

LOWEST TEAM SCORE IN A ONE DAY INTERNATIONAL
The lowest innings total is 43 by Pakistan v. the West Indies at Newlands, Cape Town, South Africa, on 25 Feb 1993.

MOST ONE DAY INTERNATIONAL CATCHES IN A CAREER
The greatest number of catches by a fielder is 156 in 334 matches by Mohammad Azharuddin (India), between 1985 and 2000.

MOST ONE DAY INTERNATIONAL WICKETS TAKEN IN A CAREER
The most wickets taken is 440 (av. 23.81), by Wasim Akram (Pakistan) in 316 matches from 1985 to Feb 2001.

HIGHEST BATTING AVERAGE IN FIRST-CLASS CRICKET
Don Bradman (Australia) holds the record for the highest batting average of 95.14, playing for New South Wales, South Australia and Australia between 1927 and 1949 (28,067 runs in 338 innings, including 43 not outs).

MOST 150S SCORED AGAINST TEST-PLAYING NATIONS
On 26 March 2000, during the third day of the second Test between New Zealand and Australia, Australian captain Steve Waugh became the first man to score 150 runs in an innings against each of the eight Test-playing nations. Waugh went on to lead Australia to victory by six wickets, thereby setting a new Australian record for consecutive Test-match victories (nine).

HIGHEST BATTING AVERAGE IN TEST CRICKET
Don Bradman (Australia) has the highest average of 99.94, playing for Australia in 52 Tests (6,996 runs in 80 innings) between 1928 and 1948.

MOST RUNS IN FIRST-CLASS CRICKET
Jack Hobbs (UK) scored a record 61,237 (av. 50.65) runs playing for Surrey and England between 1905 and 1934.

MOST RUNS IN TEST CRICKET
Allan Border (Australia) scored 11,174 runs in 156 Tests (av. 50.56) between 1978 and 1994.

MOST RUNS OFF AN OVER
The first batsman to score 36 runs off a six-ball over was Garfield Sobers (West Indies) off Malcolm Andrew Nash for Nottinghamshire v. Glamorgan at Swansea, UK, on 31 Aug 1968. His feat was emulated by Ravishankar Jayadritha Shastri for

HE JUST GETS BATTER AND BATTER!
Sachin Tendulkar (India, left) has scored the most centuries in One Day Internationals during his career, with a record 28 centuries, having played 268 matches between 1989 and 2001.
  He has also scored the most runs in One Day Internationals, amassing a grand total of 10,179 (av. 42.58) in 268 matches, from 1982 to 2001.
  Sachin Ramesh Tendulkar, born on 24 April 1973 in Mumbai (Bombay), India, is regarded by many to be the world's greatest batsman currently playing and has been compared to legendary Australian Don Bradman for his finesse and impeccable technique. Among his greatest assets, Tendulkar shows great timing and power, with the addition of a mental strength that has been tested in a number of international games.

www.guinnessworldrecords.com/bats

← ACCESS CODE: ‹51995›

BOWLED OVER!

The best bowling analysis in a One Day International is 7–30 by Muttiah Muralitharan (Sri Lanka, right) v. India at Sharjah, on 27 Oct 2000.

Wasim Akram (Pakistan) has taken the most wickets in World Cup matches, with 43 in 32 matches from 1987 to 1999.

The most wickets in a single tournament is 20 by Geoff Allott (New Zealand) and Shane Warne (Australia), both in 1999.

The best bowling figures in a World Cup match is 7–51 by Winston Davis (West Indies) v. Australia at Headingley, W Yorks, UK, from 11 to 12 June 1983.

Courtney Walsh (Jamaica) has taken the greatest number of Test-match wickets with 519 (av. 24.44 runs per wicket) in 132 matches between Nov 1984 and April 2001.

Mumbai (Bombay) v. Baroda at Mumbai (Bombay), India, on 10 Jan 1985 off the bowling of Tilak Raj Sharma (India).

MOST CONSECUTIVE DUCKS

The greatest number of consecutive 'ducks' (when a batsman scores zero) in Test cricket is the five ducks achieved by Bob Holland (Australia), between Aug and Nov 1985 and Ajit Agarkar (India), between Dec 1999 and Jan 2000.

HIGHEST BATTING AVERAGE

The highest batting average in a league season is 330 by Colin Gill (UK) for Plymstock 2nd XI in 1998. Gill batted 10 times and was dismissed just once.

HIGHEST TEST SCORE

Sri Lanka scored a record 952 for six, v. India at Colombo, Sri Lanka between 4 and 6 Aug 1997.

England scored a record 903 runs for seven wickets declared in 15 hr 17 min, v. Australia at The Oval, London, between 20 and 23 Aug 1938.

LOWEST TEST INNINGS TOTAL

The lowest innings total in Test cricket is 26 by New Zealand v. England at Auckland on 28 March 1955.

PUSHING OUT THE BOUNDARIES

Seven women's Cricket World Cups have been staged since 1973. The greatest number of World Cup titles is four won by Australia, in 1978, 1982, 1988 and 1997. England won in 1973 and 1993 and New Zealand was victorious in 2000. The picture above shows Karen Rolton (Australia) in action while scoring 154 not out during the Australia v. Sri Lanka match in the 2000 World Cup, which was played at Hagley Oval, Christchurch, New Zealand. Australia beat Sri Lanka by 200 runs but were in turn beaten by New Zealand.

SINGER

GUINNESS WORLD RECORDS™

ball sports 1

MOST MEN'S OLYMPIC HANDBALL TITLES

The USSR (the Unified Team from the republics of the former USSR) has won the men's Olympic handball title three times in 1976, 1988 and 1992.

MOST WOMEN'S OLYMPIC HANDBALL TITLES

The USSR and South Korea have both won the women's Olympic handball title twice. The USSR triumphed in 1976 and 1980, and South Korea won in 1988 and 1992.

HIGHEST MEN'S OLYMPIC HANDBALL SCORE

The highest handball team score in an Olympic match is 44, reached by Yugoslavia v. Kuwait at the 1980 Games in Moscow, USSR (now Russia). Sweden shares the record with a 44 score against Australia at the 2000 Olympics in Sydney, NSW, Australia.

HIGHEST WOMEN'S OLYMPIC HANDBALL SCORE

The record for the highest score by a female handball team at the Olympics is 45, by Austria v. Brazil at the 2000 Games in Sydney, NSW, Australia.

HIGHEST HANDBALL SCORE

The USSR reached the highest-ever score in an international handball match when they beat Afghanistan 86–2 in Hungary in Aug 1981.

THE KNOCK-IT-IN-THE-NET KNOCK OUTS

The Australian netball team (left) is one of the most successful teams in the history of Australian sport. The wonder women have won the World Championships a record eight times – in 1963, 1971, 1975, 1979, 1983, 1991, 1995 and 1999. As well as being world champions, they are also Open winners and were the first team to win the official Commonwealth Games gold medal in 1998. Every year, 20 athletes are picked for the Australian netball squad after the Qantas Netball Nationals have ended. They train throughout the year and a team of 12 is selected to represent Australia. The current team is captained by Kathryn Harby who plays all three defensive positions and was 1995's Netballer of the Year.

www.guinnessworldrecords.com/netball
← ACCESS CODE: ‹44764›

MOST WOMEN'S HANDBALL WORLD CHAMPIONSHIPS

Romania, Germany and the USSR have all won three women's Handball World Championship titles. The Romanians were the outdoor victors in 1956 and 1960, and the indoor champs in 1962. Germany won indoors in 1971, 1975 and 1978. The USSR also tasted victory indoors in 1982, 1986 and 1990.

MOST WORLD CHAMPIONSHIP NETBALL GOALS SCORED

Irene van Dyk (South Africa) has scored the most goals at a Netball World Championship contest. Over the course of the 1995 tournament she put the ball in the net 543 times.

HIGHEST NETBALL WORLD CHAMPIONSHIP TEAM SCORE

The Cook Islands are the highest scoring Netball World Championship team. They beat Vanuatu 120–38 on 9 July 1991 in Sydney, NSW, Australia.

MOST AFL TITLES

Australia has three major football leagues – the AFL (Australian Football League), the South Australian National Football League and the Western Australian Football League. The AFL is the biggest and has been won by the Carlton Blues 16 times between 1906 and 1995. Port Adelaide has had 36 South Australian NFL wins from 1884 to 1991 and East Fremantle had 30 Western Australia FL wins between 1900 and 1998.

MOST AFL CAREER GOALS

The most goals scored in an AFL career is 1,357, by Tony Lockett between 1983 and 1999. He averaged five goals per match.

LARGEST AFL GRAND FINAL CROWD

The most people to attend an AFL Grand Final is 121,696. They watched Carlton beat Collingwood at the Melbourne Cricket Ground, Victoria, Australia, on 26 Sept 1970.

HIGHEST TEAM SCORE IN AN AFL MATCH

The highest team score in the Australian Football League is 239 (37–17) reached by Geelong v. Brisbane on 3 May 1992.

HIGHEST AGGREGATE SCORE IN AN AFL MATCH

The highest aggregate score (combined scores of both sides) in an Australian football match is 345 points, reached when St Kilda beat Melbourne 204–141 on 6 May 1978.

MOST MEN'S WORLD VOLLEYBALL CHAMPIONSHIP TITLES

The USSR has won six men's Volleyball World Championships. They were the victors in 1949, 1952, 1960, 1962, 1978 and 1982.

MOST WOMEN'S OLYMPIC VOLLEYBALL TITLES

The USSR has won four women's volleyball Olympic titles, in 1968, 1972, 1980 and 1988.

MOST MEN'S OLYMPIC VOLLEYBALL TITLES

The USSR has won a record three men's Olympic volleyball titles. The team won in 1964, 1968 and 1980. Introduced into the Olympics in 1964 for both men and women, volleyball has been dominated by the Russians. They have only come away from the Olympics without a medal twice – in 1992 in Barcelona and 1996 in Atlanta. In 1984 they boycotted the games.

YOU'VE REALLY GOT TO HAND IT TO THEM . . .

Sweden (left, playing Australia at the 2000 Sydney Olympics) has won the most men's indoor handball titles, with four wins in 1954, 1958, 1990 and 1999. Romania equals the record with victories in 1961, 1964, 1970 and 1974. Germany has won the outdoor title five times between 1938 and 1966. Handball originated in Germany in the 1920s and developed from the basics of association football, with 11-a-side teams using their hands instead of their feet. It was originally an outdoor sport, played on a football-sized pitch. An indoor seven-a-side version developed and is the game solely played today. The original sport was only ever once contested at the Olympics, in 1936, with the indoor version introduced to the games in 1972.

www.guinnessworldrecords.com/handball
← ACCESS CODE: ‹45019›

BRILLIANT BRAZILIAN BEACH BALL BABES!

Brazil is the holder of the most Beach Volleyball World Championship titles. The tournament was first staged for both men and women in 1997, and is held biennially. Brazil won both titles, for men and women (below), in 1997 and 1999.

Beach volleyball began in the 1920s. Its birthplace is generally recognized as Santa Monica, California, USA. Courts were set up on the beach and standard six-a-side games were played. The sport soon became widespread in the USA,

with interest spreading to Europe when American troops played on the beach during and after World War II. The format of the current game, two-a-side, was played during the 1930s, with the first official two-man competition at State Beach, California, USA, in 1947. Long before hitting the beach, volleyball had been invented as 'Mintonette' in 1895 by a YMCA physical training instructor as a non-contact alternative to basketball, which had begun four years earlier.

MOST INTERNATIONAL WATER POLO GOALS

The most goals scored by an individual in an international water polo match is 13, achieved by Australia's Debbie Handley, when her team beat Canada 16–10 at the World Championship tournament in Guayaquil, Ecuador, in 1982.

MOST OLYMPIC WATER POLO TITLES

Hungary has won the most men's Olympic water polo titles, with six victories in 1932, 1936, 1952, 1956, 1964 and 1976. The sport is thought to have originated in Hungary, and the national team dominated international competitions from the early 1930s until the 1980s.

MOST WATER POLO WORLD CHAMPIONSHIPS

Three countries have won the Water Polo World Championship tournament twice – the USSR in 1975 and 1982; Yugoslavia in 1986 and 1991; and Italy in 1978 and 1994.

MOST GOALS SCORED IN A KORFBALL WORLD CHAMPIONSHIP

The most goals scored in a Korfball World Championship tournament is 191 by the Netherlands in 1999. Korfball was invented in 1901 by an Amsterdam schoolmaster, Nico Broekhuysen, and is similar to netball and basketball. The big difference is that it is designed to be played by mixed teams. Broekhuysen wanted it to be a game in which boys and girls in his school could compete at the same level. It is the world's only real mixed sport and was first demonstrated in 1902 in Holland.

MOST KORFBALL WORLD CHAMPIONSHIP TEAM WINS

The Netherlands have won the most Korfball World Championships since the tournament began in 1978. They have taken home the title a record five times in 1978, 1984, 1987, 1995 and 1999.

NARROWEST MARGIN OF VICTORY IN A KORFBALL WORLD CHAMPIONSHIP

The narrowest margin of victory in the final of the Korfball World Championships is one. There have been two such slim wins – in 1978 when the Netherlands defeated Belgium 14–13, and in 1991 when Belgium defeated the Netherlands 11–10.

HIGHEST KORFBALL SCORE IN A WORLD CHAMPIONSHIP FINAL

The highest team score in the final of the Korfball World Championships is 23 when the Netherlands beat Belgium 34–11 in 1999.

MOST KORFBALL WORLD GAMES TITLES

The Netherlands has won a record four Korfball World Games titles, with victories at every tournament held so far, in 1985, 1989, 1993 and 1997.

ball sports 2

MOST MEN'S TABLE TENNIS OLYMPIC GOLDS

Liu Guoliang (China) won a record two gold medals at the 1996 Atlanta Olympics, one in the singles, and one in the doubles with Kong Linghui.

MOST WOMEN'S TABLE TENNIS OLYMPIC GOLDS

Deng Yaping (China) has clinched a record four Olympic titles. She won gold in the women's singles in 1992

and 1996, and two in the women's doubles, with Qiao Hang, in 1992 and 1996. She has won a total of 18 World titles during her 10-year career.

MOST MEN'S TEAM TABLE TENNIS WORLD CHAMPIONSHIP TITLES

The Chinese and Hungarian men's table tennis teams have won the most World Championship titles. They have taken home the coveted Swaythling Cup 12 times. China triumphed in 1961, 1963, 1965, 1971, 1975, 1977, 1981, 1983, 1985, 1987, 1995 and 1997. Hungary won in 1926, 1928–31, twice in 1933 (when two tournaments were held), and once in 1935, 1938, 1949, 1952 and 1979.

MOST WOMEN'S TEAM TABLE TENNIS WORLD CHAMPIONSHIP TITLES

China has won the most women's team Table Tennis World titles, with 13 Corbillon Cup victories. They first won in 1965, then followed with eight successive biennial wins from 1975 to 1989 and further victories in 1993, 1995, 1997 and 2000.

MOST TABLE TENNIS HITS IN ONE MINUTE

Between them, Jackie Bellinger and Lisa Lomas (both UK) broke the record for the most table tennis hits in one minute. They tapped the ball across the table to each other a total of 173 times at the Northgate Sports Centre, Ipswich, Suffolk, UK, on 7 Feb 1993.

MOST MEN'S TEAM SQUASH WORLD CHAMPIONSHIPS

The Australian men's squash team has clinched the World Championship title a record six times. They won in 1967, 1969, 1971, 1973, 1989 and 1991. They share the record with Pakistan, who triumphed in 1977, 1981, 1983, 1985, 1987 and 1993.

MOST WOMEN'S TEAM SQUASH WORLD CHAMPIONSHIPS

The Australian women's team has won a record six World Championships, in 1981, 1983, 1992, 1994, 1996 and 1998.

MOST WOMEN'S SQUASH WORLD CHAMPIONSHIPS

Susan Devoy (New Zealand) has won the most women's Squash World Championship titles. She has been the World Open champion four times – in 1985, 1987, 1990 and 1992.

FASTEST SHUTTLECOCK SMASH

In tests at Warwickshire Racquets and Health Club, Coventry, UK, on 5 Nov 1996, Simon Archer (UK) hit a shuttlecock at a record speed of 260 km/h (162 mph).

MOST BADMINTON SINGLES WORLD CHAMPIONSHIP TITLES

Four Chinese players have won a record two individual Badminton World titles. Yang Yang won the men's singles twice, in 1987 and 1989. The women's singles have

been won by Li Lingwei in 1983 and 1989; Han Aiping in 1985 and 1987; and Ye Zhaoying in 1995 and 1997.

MOST BADMINTON WORLD CHAMPIONSHIP TITLES

Park Joo-bong (South Korea) has won five World Championship Badminton titles. He triumphed in the men's doubles in 1985 and 1991, and in the mixed doubles in 1985, 1989 and 1991.

MOST WOMEN'S TEAM BADMINTON WORLD CHAMPIONSHIP TITLES

China has won the most women's team Badminton World Championships, taking home the Uber Cup seven times – in 1984, 1986, 1988, 1990, 1992, 1998 and 2000.

SHORTEST BADMINTON MATCH

Ra Kyung-min (South Korea) tasted badminton victory in the fastest time ever when she beat Julia Mann (UK) 11–2, 11–1, in six minutes, during the 1996 Uber Cup in Hong Kong, on 19 May 1996.

HIGHEST SCORE IN MEN'S INTERNATIONAL HOCKEY

The Indian men's hockey team beat the USA with the highest-ever score of 24–1, in California, USA, at the 1932 Olympic Games. The unstoppable Indian team won an unbroken string of six Olympic gold medals between 1928 and 1956. At the 1936 Games in Berlin, Adolf Hitler was so impressed by the skill of Indian captain Dhyan Chand that he tried to buy his stick.

MOST MEN'S INTERNATIONAL HOCKEY APPEARANCES

From his debut in 1985 to Jan 2001, Jacques Brinkman (Netherlands) played hockey for his country a record 337 times.

MOST WOMEN'S INTERNATIONAL HOCKEY APPEARANCES

Karen Brown (UK) played hockey for England and Great Britain 355 times between 1984 and 1999.

KNOCK ME DOWN WITH A FEATHER!

Indonesia has won the most men's team Badminton World Championships. The team has taken home the Thomas Cup a record 12 times – in 1958, 1961, 1964, 1970, 1973, 1976, 1979, 1984, 1994, 1996, 1998 and 2000, with Hendrawan (above) a key player in clinching the last two trophies. The Thomas Cup is named after Sir George Thomas, a winner of 21 All-England titles, who donated the trophy in 1940. However, the competition did not actually begin until after World War II, in 1949. It was held every three years until 1982, when it became a biennial event. The competition is contested by teams of six, who play five singles and four doubles matches in each contest. Badminton gets its name from Badminton House in the UK, where it was played by the Duke of Beaufort's family in the 19th century. Its origins come directly from the children's game of battledore and shuttlecock, and a similar game played in China over 2,000 years ago.

 www.guinnessworldrecords.com/badminton

← ACCESS CODE: ‹45671›

SQUASH THE OPPOSITION

Pakistan's Jahangir Khan (above) has won the most Squash World Open titles. He has triumphed a record six times between 1981 and 1985, and in 1988. He is considered the most successful player in the history of squash. The son of Roshan Khan, winner of the 1956 British Open, Jahangir started playing squash at the age of 10 and won his first World amateur title at 15.

www.guinnessworldrecords.com/squash

ACCESS CODE:
 ← ‹44362›

MOST ALL-IRELAND HURLING FINAL WINS

The greatest number of All-Ireland Championships won by one team is 28 by Cork, from 1890 to 1999.

LARGEST CROWD AT A HURLING MATCH

A record crowd of 84,865 spectators turned out for the All-Ireland Hurling final between Cork and Wexford at Croke Park, Dublin, in 1954.

LONGEST HIT IN HURLING

The greatest distance for a hurling 'lift and stroke' hit is a record 118 m (387.16 ft), credited to Tom Murphy of Three Castles, Kilkenny, Ireland, during a 'long puck' contest in 1906.

MOST SHINTY TEAM WINS

Similar to the Irish sport of hurling, the mainly Scottish sport of shinty has its own champion of champions. The Newtonmore team from Highland, UK, has won the Camanachd Association Challenge Cup a record 28 times between 1907 and 1986.

HIGHEST MEN'S LACROSSE SCORE

The highest score in a Lacrosse World Cup match is Scotland's 34–3 win over Germany on 25 July 1994 in Greater Manchester, UK. In the World Cup Premier division, the record score is the USA's 33–2 win over Japan at Greater Manchester on 21 July 1994.

HIGHEST WOMEN'S LACROSSE SCORE

The highest score by an international female lacrosse team was notched up by Great Britain and Ireland when they beat Long Island 40–0 during their 1967 tour of the USA.

MOST WOMEN'S LACROSSE WORLD CHAMPIONSHIPS

The US women's team has won a record five Lacrosse World titles. They won the World Championships in 1974, and went on to win the World Cup (which replaced the World Championships) in 1982, 1989, 1993 and 1997.

MOST MEN'S LACROSSE WORLD CHAMPIONSHIPS

The USA has won seven of the eight Lacrosse World Championships in 1967, 1974, 1982, 1986, 1990, 1994 and 1998. Canada won the other, in 1978, beating the USA 17–16.

www.guinnessworldrecords.com/hockey

JOLLY HOCKEY STICKS

The most women's Hockey Champions' Trophies have been won by Australia (right). The team has triumphed a record five times – in 1991, 1993, 1995, 1997 and 1999. First held in 1987, the tournament takes place every two years, with the world's top six teams competing against one another to take home the coveted cup.

ACCESS CODE: ‹45007›

  ←

GUINNESS WORLD RECORDS

animal sports

MOST THREE-DAY BADMINTON WINS

The Badminton Three-Day Event has been won six times by Lucinda Jane Green (née Prior-Palmer, UK) on Be Fair (1973), Wide Awake (1976), George (1977), Killaire (1979), Regal Realm (1983) and Beagle Bay (1984).

BIGGEST CAREER WINNINGS BY A RACE-HORSE TRAINER

Trainer Wayne Lukas (USA) began training horses full-time in 1967. He won $177 million (£118 million) in horse racing during his career. He was also awarded the Eclipse Award four times by the National Thoroughbred Racing Association for Trainer of the Year. His total winnings for 1988 was $17,842,358 (£11,947,234) – the biggest amount won in one year by a trainer.

HIGHEST-PRICED RACE HORSE

On 23 July 1985 Robert Sangster (UK) and partners paid $13.1 million (£9 million) for yearling Seattle Dancer at Keeneland, Kentucky, USA.

FASTEST RACE HORSE

The highest race speed recorded is 69.62 km/h (43.26 mph) or 20.8 sec for 0.5 miles (804 m), by Big Racket in Mexico City, Mexico, on 5 Feb 1945, and Onion Roll at Thistledown, Cleveland, Ohio, USA, on 27 Sept 1993. The record for 1.5 miles (2,414 m) is 60.86 km/h (37.82 mph) by 3-year-old Hawkster, carrying 54.9 kg (121 lb), at Santa Anita Park, Arcadia, California, USA, on 14 Oct 1989 with a time of 2 min 22.8 sec.

HIGHEST HORSE JUMP

The official Fédération Equestre Internationale record for high jump is 2.47 m (8 ft 10 in) by Huaso, ridden by Alberto Larraguibel Morales (Chile) at Viña del Mar, Santiago, Chile, on 5 Feb 1949.

HIGHEST INDOORS HORSE JUMP

On 9 June 1991 Optibeurs Leonardo, ridden by Franke Sloothaak (Germany), at Chaudefontaine, Switzerland, jumped a record 2.4 m (7 ft 9 in).

BEST RODEO ATTENDANCE

The largest rodeo in the world is the National Finals Rodeo (USA), organized by the Professional Rodeo Cowboys Association (PRCA) and the Women's Professional Rodeo Association (WPRA). The 1991 finals had a paid attendance of 171,414 for 10 performances – the highest ever.

GOOD FORTUNE

From 1974 to April 2000 jockey Christopher McCarron (USA, left) won a total of $236 million (£148 million) – the greatest amount won in a horse-racing career. McCarron regards his Kentucky Derby win on Alysheba as a career highlight. He was also a regular rider of John Henry. In 1994 he posted his 6,000th win at Hollywood Park, California, USA.

www.guinnessworldrecords.com/mccarron
← ACCESS CODE: ‹55548›

MOST SUCCESSFUL RODEO BULL

The top-bucking bull, Red Rock, dislodged 312 riders between 1980 and 1988, and was finally ridden to the eight-second bell by world champion Bull Rider 1987, Lane Frost (USA), on 20 May 1988. Red Rock, a red brindle Brahma-Hereford mix bull, had retired at the end of the 1987 season but still continued to make guest appearances.

BIGGEST FIRST PRIZE FOR A GREYHOUND RACE

The biggest first prize for a greyhound race is $125,000 (£87,000), won by Ben G Speedboat in the Great Greyhound Race of Champions at Seabrook, New Hampshire, USA, on 23 Aug 1986.

SPORT OF KINGS ... ... KINGS OF SPORT

Of the five Polo World Championships contested, three have been won by Argentina – the record for the most Polo World Championships won by one country. They won in 1987 in Argentina, in 1992 in Chile and in 1998 in the USA. World Championships are held every three years under the auspices of the Federation of International Polo (FIP). Mariano Uranga (left) was one of the Argentinian team members who competed in the World Cup Polo held in Australia in March 2001.
   The highest aggregate number of goals scored in an international match is 30, when Argentina beat the USA 21–9 at Meadowbrook, Long Island, New York, USA, in Sept 1936.

www.guinnessworldrecords.com/polochamps
← ACCESS CODE: ‹54456›

FASTEST GREYHOUND

The fastest speed at which a greyhound has been timed is 67.32 km/h (41.83 mph) or 366 m (400 yd) in 19.57 seconds by Star Title on the straightaway track at Wyong, NSW, Australia, on 5 March 1994.

HIGHEST JUMP BY A DOG

The canine high-jump record for a leap and scramble over a smooth wooden wall (without ribs or other aids) is 3.72 m (12 ft 2 in), achieved by an 18-month-old Lurcher dog named Stag, at the annual Cotswold Country Fair in Cirencester, Glos, UK, on 27 Sept 1993. The dog is owned by Mr and Mrs PR Matthews (UK).

LONGEST SLED-DOG RACING TRAIL

The longest sled-dog race is the 2,000-km (1,243-mile) Berengia Trail from Esso to Markovo, Russia, which started as a 250-km (155-mile) route in April 1990. Now established as an annual event, the fastest time to complete the trail was achieved in 1991 by Pavel Lazarev (Russia) in 10 days 18 hr 17 min 56 sec. Lazarev's time is equivalent to an average rate of 8 km/h (5 mph).

OLDEST SLED-DOG RACING TRAIL

The oldest established sled-dog trail is the 1,688-km (1,049-mile) Iditarod Trail from Anchorage to Nome, Alaska, USA, which has existed since 1910 and has been the route of an annual race since 1967. The fastest time, 9 days 58 min 6 sec, was set by Doug Swingley (USA) between 6 and 14 March 2000. This is equivalent to an estimated average rate of 8 km/h (5 mph).

GREATEST DISTANCE FLOWN BY A PIGEON

The greatest distance flown in a competitive career is 41,050 km (25,508 miles) between 1990 and 1997 by Brazilian Beauty, a blue-check hen, owned by Robert Koch (South Africa).

HIGHEST-PRICED PIGEON

A four-year-old cock bird, winner of the 1992 Barcelona International race and

FABULOUS FERRET

On 11 July 1999 at the North England Ferret Racing Championships held in Blythe, Northumberland, UK, an albino ferret named Warhol (above), owned by Jacqui Adams (UK), ran the 10-m (32-ft) tube race in a record 12.59 sec – beating 150 other ferret competitors. The fact that this was his very first race, makes this achievement even more remarkable. At the time of the race, Warhol weighed 2.7 kg (6 lb). Ferrets belong to the weasel family and have elongated bodies, short legs and a long, bushy tail.

www.guinnessworldrecords.com/ferret

ACCESS CODE: ← ‹53067›

subsequently named Invincible Spirit, was sold for £110,800 ($160,000) – the highest sum ever paid for a pigeon. Louella Pigeon World (UK) bought the bird from Martin Biemans (Netherlands) in July 1992.

FASTEST SNAIL RACE

The annual World Snail Racing Championships, held in July at Congham, Norfolk, UK, is conducted on a 33-cm (13-in) circular course outside St Andrew's Church. The runners race from the centre to the perimeter. Some race several times as they are divided into heats to cater for the 150 snail competitors who enter every year. The all-time record holder is Archie, trained by Carl Bramham, who sprinted to the winning post in 2 min 20 sec in 1995. Like all great racing champions, he was sent to stud in a cabbage patch.

www.guinnessworldrecords.com/camelfight

CAMEL COMBAT

At the 1994 Camel Wrestling Festival in Selçuk, Turkey, 20,000 people gathered to watch 120 dromedaries wrestle in a 2,000-year-old stadium in the city of Ephesus. This was the largest audience that has ever attended a camel-wrestling festival. Camel wrestling (below) is one of Turkey's oldest forms of entertainment. A male wrestling camel is brought before a female in the arena. As a courtship ritual the male immediately drops to the ground and writhes in front of the female.

ACCESS CODE: ‹56083›

She is then taken away and replaced by a male, provoking a jealous battle for the female. As camels are expensive, muzzles are used so they do not seriously harm one another. Two breeds of camel are crossed to obtain the *tulu*, the camel used in wrestling.

The owner of a winning camel collects a cash prize of £40 ($60) as well as a carpet. There are approximately 1,200 wrestling camels in Turkey and the sport extends over the Marmara, Aegean and Mediterranean coasts of western Turkey.

GUINNESS WORLD RECORDS™

combat and martial arts

HIGHEST ATTENDANCE AT A BOXING MATCH

The greatest paying attendance at any boxing match is 132,274 for four World title fights at the Aztec Stadium, Mexico City, Mexico, on 20 Feb 1993, headed by the successful WBC super lightweight defence of Julio César Chávez (Mexico) over Greg Haugen (USA).

The highest non-paying attendance is 135,132 at the fight between Tony Zale and Billy Pryor (both USA) at Juneau Park, Milwaukee, Wisconsin, USA, on 16 Aug 1941.

LOWEST ATTENDANCE AT A BOXING MATCH

The smallest attendance at a World Heavyweight title fight was 2,434, at the Cassius Clay (Muhammad Ali) v. Sonny Liston (both USA) fight at Lewiston, Maine, USA, on 25 May 1965.

MOST JUDO WORLD TITLES WON BY A MAN

David Douillet (France) has won six World and Olympic titles – Over 95 kg (1993, 1995 and 1997), Open (1995), the Olympic Over 95 kg (1996) and Over 100 kg (2000). Yasuhiro Yamashita (Japan), who won nine

AND THE WREST IS HISTORY

A student of literature, opera and ballet, Aleksandr Karelin (Russia, left) began wrestling at the age of 13. He quickly achieved success and was world junior champion in 1987. He has won 12 World titles in the Greco-Roman Under-130-kg class in 1988 to 1999 – more than any other wrestler. In addition to his World titles, Karelin has won Olympic gold medals at Seoul, Barcelona and Atlanta as he continued to dominate world Greco-Roman wrestling. He developed a manoeuvre known as the 'reverse body lift', with which he would slam his opponents to the mat. He is regarded as a national hero in Russia.

www.guinnessworldrecords.com/karelin

← ACCESS CODE: ‹44189›

consecutive Japanese titles between 1977 and 1985, has won five World and Olympic titles – Over 95 kg (1979, 1981 and 1983), Open (1981) and the Olympic Open category (1984). He retired undefeated in 1985 after 203 successive wins.

MOST OLYMPIC GOLD MEDALS FOR JUDO

The only men to have won two Olympic gold medals are Wilhelm Ruska (Netherlands) for Over 93 kg and Open (1972), Peter Seisenbacher (Austria) for 86 kg (1984 and 1988),

Hitoshi Saito (Japan) for Over 95 kg (1984) and Open (1988), Waldemar Legien (Poland) for 78 kg (1988) and 86 kg (1992), David Douillet (France) for Over 95 kg (1996) and Over 100 kg (2000), and Tadahiro Nomura (Japan) for 60 kg (1996 and 2000).

MOST JUDO WORLD TITLES WON BY A WOMAN

Ingrid Berghmans (Belgium) has won a record six women's World titles for Open (1980, 1982, 1984 and 1986) and Under 72 kg (1984 and 1989).

MOST JUDO THROWS IN 10 HOURS

Patrick Hurley and Tony Cox (both UK) of the Leeds Central Aikido Club completed 46,261 judo and aikido throwing techniques in a 10-hour period at the Aireborough Leisure Centre, Leeds, UK, on 30 May 1998.

RAREST SUMO LOSS

On 13 May 2000, during the May tournament at the Kokugikan, Sumida-ku, Tokyo, Japan, *sandanme*

rikishi Asanokiri (Japan) lost a bout against opponent Chiyohakuho (Japan) because his loin cloth fell off – the first time in the 83 years since the introduction of the rule that a bout has been settled in this fashion. The fight was stopped after a ringside Sumo elder saw Asanokiri's genitals exposed when his *mawashi* (belt) fell off. *Mawashi* are about 8 m (26 ft) long and are wrapped tightly several times around the wrestlers' expansive bodies.

HEAVIEST LIVING ATHLETE

The heaviest living athlete in the world is Sumo wrestler Emmanuel 'Manny' Yarborough (USA). He stands 2.03 m (6 ft 8 in) tall and weighs a colossal 319.3 kg (704 lb).

HIGHEST MARTIAL ARTS KICK

🔳 USA

The highest martial-arts kick measured is 2.94 m (9 ft 8 in) by Jessie Frankson (USA), who kicked a target with a pin attached, which in turn burst a balloon, on 21 Dec 2000.

QUITE A HEAVYWEIGHT!

Up to May 2001, Ricardo López (Mexico, left) has remained unbeaten throughout his professional career, with 48 wins and one draw out of 49 fights over a total of 16 years and 8 months. No other boxer has been able to remain unbeaten for such a long period of time.

Joe Louis (USA) holds the record for the longest reign of a boxing world champion. His heavyweight duration record of 11 years 252 days undefeated stands for all divisions. When he died in 1981, he was considered one of the greatest fighters of all time. Tony Canzoneri (USA) was world light-welterweight champion from 21 May to 23 June 1933. This period of 33 days is the shortest for a boxer to have won and lost the World title in the ring.

ACCESS CODE: ·56478›

CHAMP CHYNA

The highest earnings by a female wrestler in a year, as reported by the *Forbes* Celebrity 100 list, is $1 million (£700,000) by 'Chyna' (right) in 2000. Chyna's real name is Joanie Laurer (USA). She was born on 27 Dec 1971 and started lifting weights when she was 15. In 1995 she went on to train under Walter 'Killer' Kowalski. She is a full-time professional wrestler who has been a member of the World Wrestling Federation (WWF) since 1997. She was the first woman in the history of the sport to complete the Royal Rumble Match in 1999. In the same year she also became the first female intercontinental champion and was voted by her fans as WWF's Diva of the Year. Outside the ring she has appeared three times in NBC's *3rd Rock from the Sun* and in Sept 2000 released her video, *Chyna Fitness: More than Meets the Eye.* In 2001 she released her autobiography, *If Only They Knew.*

MOST KICKBOXING WORLD TITLES

Don 'The Dragon' Wilson (USA) has won 11 World titles in three weight divisions (light-heavyweight, super light-heavyweight and cruiserweight) and for six sanctioning organizations (WKA, STAR, KICK, ISKA, PKO and IKF).

MOST CONCRETE BLOCKS 📺 SE BROKEN IN ONE MINUTE

Mikael Bigersson (Sweden) smashed 21 concrete blocks by hand in one minute on 3 Feb 2001 in Stockholm, Sweden. The blocks, each measuring 60 x 20 x 7 cm (23.62 x 7.87 x 2.7 in), were stacked in piles of one, two, three, four, five and finally six high.

MOST CONCRETE BLOCKS SMASHED IN A GROIN BREAK 📺 USA

On 12 Aug 1998 a record two concrete blocks were placed over martial-arts expert Cliff Flenoy's (USA) groin and then smashed with a sledgehammer by another person, in Los Angeles, California, USA.

LARGEST KARATE AUDIENCE

The Sabaki Challenge is the standard for bare-knuckle full-contact karate in the USA. This tournament has a live audience of 7,500 as well as millions of television viewers all over the world.

MOST SHEETS OF GLASS BROKEN IN KARATE 📺 USA

With a single karate chop, Maurice Elmalem (USA) broke 50 glass sheets, each measuring 9.84 cm (3.875 in) wide, 38.1 cm (15 in) long and 0.4 cm (0.16 in) thick, in Los Angeles, USA, on 12 March 2001. The sheets were spaced using blocks measuring 8.9 cm (3.5 in) long,1.27 cm (0.5 in) wide and 0.32 cm (0.125 in) thick. To avoid being cut, Elmalem had to use twice the power he uses to break wood.

SLOWEST TAI-CHI WALK

The greatest time taken to travel 10 m (32 ft) using tai chi is 54 min 30 sec by Ken Poole (Canada) at the SlowDown ShowDown Race, Toronto, Canada, on 6 Feb 1999.

FASTEST 100-MAN KUMITE KARATE

On 22 March 1995 Francisco Alves Filho (Brazil) defeated 100 consecutive opponents in full-contact knockdown fighting in 3 hr 8 min. He won 26 fights by *Ippon* (full points), won 50 by decision, drew 24 and lost none. The One Hundred Man Kumite is the ultimate test in Kyokushin karate and is unique to this discipline. It involves fighting 100 opponents in full-contact knockdown fighting, with each bout lasting two minutes. If knocked down for more than five seconds, you would fail – even if it were your last fight.

GUINNESS WORLD RECORDS™

gymnastics and weights

MOST PUSH-UPS IN ONE MINUTE

Sgt Paul Dean (UK) of the Royal Marines achieved a record 116 push-ups in one minute at the Marine Training Base, Lympstone, Devon, UK, on 25 July 2000.

MOST PARALLEL BAR DIPS IN ONE HOUR

Simon Kent (UK) achieved 3,989 parallel bar dips at Farrahs Health Centre, Lincoln, UK, on 5 Sept 1998.

FASTEST MILE DOING FORWARD ROLLS

Ashrita Furman performed 1.6 km (one mile) of gymnastically correct forward rolls in 19 min 11 sec, around Victory Field Track in Forest Park, New York City, New York, USA, on 25 Nov 2000.

MOST CONSECUTIVE FORWARD ROLLS

Ashrita Furman performed 8,341 forward rolls in 10 hr 30 min over 19.67 km (12.22 miles) from Lexington to Charleston, Massachusetts, USA, on 30 April 1986.

MOST CARTWHEELS IN ONE MINUTE

The most complete cartwheels achieved in 60 sec is 48 by Brianna Schroeder (USA) at the GymCarolina Gymnastics Academy, Raleigh, North Carolina, USA, on 1 Nov 1997.

FASTEST 50-M REVERSE SOMERSAULTS

On 31 Aug 1995 Vitaliy Scherbo (Belarus) somersaulted backwards for a record 50 m (164 ft) in 10.22 sec at Makuhar Messe Event Hall, Chiba, Japan.

MOST ROTATIONS ON A POMMEL HORSE

Tyler Farstad (Canada) completed 97 consecutive double-leg circles on a pommel horse at Surrey Gymnastic Society, Surrey, British Columbia, Canada, on 27 Nov 1993.

MOST SQUAT THRUSTS IN ONE HOUR

The most squat thrusts in one hour is 3,743 by Paddy Doyle (UK) at the Stamina Boxing Kickboxing Gym, Erdington, Birmingham, W Midlands, UK, on 4 May 1998.

MOST VAULTS IN ONE HOUR

A team of 10 gymnasts from the Blue Falcons gymnastic display team of Chelmer Valley High School, Chelmsford, Essex, UK, completed a world–record 4,095 vaults in one hour (6.8 vaults each per minute) on 2 Dec 1999.

YOU'RE BARRED!

The heaviest weight lifted in the women's 53-kg snatch weightlifting competition is a record-breaking 100 kg by Yang Xia (China, above) at the Olympic Games in Sydney, Australia, on 18 Sept 2000. Yang also achieved an Olympic and world record-breaking 125 kg in the women's 53-kg clean and jerk weightlifting competition on the same day. These two weights are combined to calculate the total weight lifted. With a combined weight of 225 kg in the women's 53-kg category, Yang takes her record-breaking tally to three world records and three Olympic records.

 www.guinnessworldrecords.com/barred
← ACCESS CODE: ‹51810›

YOUNGEST INTERNATIONAL GYMNAST

Pasakevi Voula Kouna (b. 6 Dec 1971) was aged 9 years 299 days at the start of the Balkan Games at Serres, Greece, on 1 Oct 1981, when she represented Greece.

MOST OLYMPIC MEDALS WON BY A FEMALE GYMNAST

The most Olympic gymnastic medals won by a woman is 18 by Larisa Latynina (USSR) who won six individual gold medals, three team gold medals, five silver and four bronze medals at three Olympic Games, between 1956 and 1964.

MOST OLYMPIC MEDALS WON BY A MALE GYMNAST

The most Olympic gymnastic medals won by a male is 15 by Nikolay Andrianov (USSR) between 1972 and 1980. Andrianov won seven gold, five silver and three bronze medals.

MOST INDIVIDUAL OLYMPIC GOLD MEDALS WON

The most men's individual gold medals won is six. Boris Shakhlin (USSR) won one in 1956, four (two shared) in 1960 and one in 1964; and Nikolay Yefimovich Andrianov (USSR) won one in 1972, four in 1976 and one in 1980.

SHE'S GOT RHYTHM

The most individual World All-around Rhythmic Gymnastics titles is three, a record shared by Maria Petrova (Bulgaria, left), in 1993, 1994 and 1995 (shared), and Maria Gigova (Bulgaria) in 1969, 1971 and 1973 (shared). The all-around competition involves each competitor performing in four separate gymnastic disciplines chosen out of a possible five – rope, ball, ribbon, hoop and clubs – with each discipline being marked individually.
The most individual Olympic gold gymnastics medals won by a woman is seven by Vera Cáslavská (Czechoslovakia). She won three gold medals in Tokyo, Japan, in 1964 and four (one shared) in Mexico City, Mexico, in 1968.

24-HOUR DEADLIFT

A deadlifting record of 3,137,904 kg (6,917,886 lb) was set by a team of 10 at the Pontefract Sports and Leisure Centre, W Yorks, UK, between 3 and 4 May 1997.

The individual 24-hour deadlift record is 455,677.5 kg (1,004,595 lb) by Steph Smit at Warren's Health Club, Pietermaritzburg, South Africa,

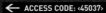 www.guinnessworldrecords.com/rhythmicgym
← ACCESS CODE: ‹45037›

between 13 and 14 Sept 1997. In a deadlift, the lifter has to lift the bar from the floor, lock the knees and stand erect with shoulders back. The bar is not lifted above the head or to the shoulders, and the arms are held straight down.

MOST TIMES OWN BODYWEIGHT LIFTED

Lamar Gant (USA) deadlifted a record-breaking five times his own bodyweight, lifting 299.5 kg (660 lb) while weighing 59.5 kg (131 lb) in 1985.

Cammie Lynn Lusko (USA) is the only woman to lift more than her bodyweight with one arm. She lifted 59.5 kg (131 lb) with a bodyweight of 58.3 kg (128.5 lb), at Milwaukee, Wisconsin, USA, on 21 May 1983.

HEAVIEST DEADLIFT WITH THE LITTLE FINGER

The heaviest deadlift with the little finger is 89.6 kg (197.5 lb) by Barry Anderson (UK) on 14 Oct 2000 at the Bass Museum, Burton-upon-Trent, Staffordshire, UK. Competing in the Masters division for contestants between the ages of 65 and 69 in the 100-kg (200.5-lb) weight class, Barry lifted the weight with the little finger of his right hand.

www.guinnessworldrecords.com/weights

HEAVY METTLE

The most Olympic weightlifting gold medals won is three by Pyrros Dimas (Greece, right), and Turkey's Naim Suleymanoglü. Dimas won his gold medals in Barcelona, Spain, in the 82.5-kg weight class (1992); in Atlanta, USA, in the 83-kg weight class (1996); and Sydney, Australia, in the 85-kg weight class (2000).

MOST BODY RAISES IN ONE HOUR

The greatest number of body raises on a gymnastic bar (from hanging vertically to lying horizontally on the bar) in one hour is 493 by Tomasz Szanca (Poland) at Szczecin, Poland, on 23 May 1999.

24-HOUR BENCH PRESS

A bench press record of 4,748,283 kg (10,469,964 lb) was set by a nine-man team at the Pontefract Sports and Leisure Centre, W Yorks, UK, between 11 and 12 April 1998.

MOST WORLD CHAMPIONSHIP POWERLIFTING TITLES

The winner of the most women's World Championship Powerlifting titles is Natalya Rumyantseva (Russia) with seven at 82.5 kg, from 1993 to 1999.

LONGEST STATIC WALL SIT

Rajkumar Chakraborty (India) stayed in an unsupported sitting position against a wall for 11 hr 5 min at Panposh Sports Hostel, Rourkela, India, on 22 April 1994.

GUINNESS
WORLD RECORDS

sports reference

BASEBALL

AL – American League
NL – National League

LONGEST BASEBALL THROW BY A WOMAN
90.2 m (296 ft), Mildred Ella Zaharias (USA), 25 July 1931

WORLD SERIES

MOST RUNS BATTED IN
6, Robert Richardson (New York AL), 8 Oct 1960

MOST SERIES PLAYED BY A PITCHER
Game: 11, Whitey Ford (New York AL), 1950–64

MOST STRIKEOUTS
Game: 17, Robert Gibson (St Louis NL), 2 Oct 1968

PERFECT GAME (9 INNINGS)
Donald James Larsen (New York AL) v. Brooklyn, 8 Oct 1956

MOST VALUABLE PLAYER AWARDS
2, Sandy Koufax (Los Angeles NL, 1963, 1965); Bob Gibson (St Louis NL, 1964, 1967); and Reggie Jackson (Oakland AL, 1973, New York AL, 1977)

MAJOR LEAGUE PITCHING RECORDS

MOST NO-HIT GAMES
Career: 7, Nolan Ryan, 1973–91

MOST PITCHED SHUTOUT GAMES
110, Walter Johnson (Washington AL), 1907–27

MOST GAMES WON
Consecutive: 24, Carl Owen Hubbell (New York Giants NL), 1936–37
Season: 60, Hoss Radbourn (Providence NL), 1884
Career: 511, Cy Young (Cleveland NL, St Louis NL, Boston AL, Cleveland AL, Boston NL), 1890–1911

TOTAL INNINGS
7,356, Cy Young (Cleveland NL, St Louis NL, Boston AL, Cleveland AL, Boston NL), 1890–1911

MAJOR LEAGUE BATTING RECORDS

MOST RUNS BATTED IN
Inning: 7, Edward Cartwright (St Louis AL), 23 Sept 1890
Season: 191, Lewis Robert Hack Wilson (Chicago NL), 1930
Career: 2,297, Henry Hank Aaron, 1954–76

MOST RUNS
Season: 196, William Robert Hamilton (Philadelphia NL), 1894
Career: 2,245, Tyrus Raymond Ty Cobb, 1905–28

MOST TOTAL BASES
Game: 12, James Bottomley (St Louis NL), 16 Sept 1924; and Mark Whiten (St Louis NL), 7 Sept 1993
Career: 6,856, Henry Hank Aaron, 1954–76

AMERICAN FOOTBALL

SUPER BOWL RECORDS

MOST FIELD GOALS
Game: 4, Don Chandler (Green Bay Packers), 1968; and Ray Wersching (San Francisco 49ers), 1982
Career: 5, Ray Wersching (San Francisco 49ers), 1982–85

MOST PASSES COMPLETED
Game: 31, Jim Kelly (Buffalo Bills), 1994
Career: 83, Joe Montana (San Francisco 49ers), 1982, 1985, 1989–90

MOST PASSES CAUGHT
Game: 11, Dan Ross (Cincinnati Bengals), 1982; and Jerry Rice (San Francisco 49ers), 1989
Career: 28, Jerry Rice (San Francisco 49ers), 1989–90, 1995

MOST POINTS
Game: 18, Roger Craig (San Francisco 49ers), 1985; Jerry Rice (San Francisco 49ers), 1990, 1995; Ricky Watters (San Francisco 49ers), 1995; and Terrell Davis (Denver Broncos), 1998
Career: 42, Jerry Rice (San Francisco 49ers), 1989–90, 1995

MOST VALUABLE PLAYER AWARDS
3, Joe Montana (San Francisco 49ers), 1982, 1985, 1990

MOST TOUCHDOWN PASSES
Game: 6, Steve Young (San Francisco 49ers), 1995
Career: 11, Joe Montana (San Francisco 49ers), 1982, 1985, 1989–90

MOST TOUCHDOWNS
Game: 3, Roger Craig (San Francisco 49ers), 1985; Jerry Rice (San Francisco 49ers), 1990, 1995; Ricky Watters (San Francisco 49ers), 1995; and Terrell Davis (Denver Broncos), 1998

MOST PASSING YARDS
Game: 414, Kurt Warner (St Louis Rams), 30 Jan 2000
Career: 1,142, Joe Montana (San Francisco 49ers), 1982, 1985, 1989–90

MOST RECEIVING YARDS
Game: 215, Jerry Rice (San Francisco 49ers), 1989

MOST RUSHING YARDS
Game: 204, Timmy Smith (Washington Redskins), 1988
Career: 354, Franco Harris (Pittsburgh Steelers), 1975–76, 1979–80

NFL RECORDS

MOST COMBINED NET YARDS
Season: 2,535, Lionel James (San Diego Chargers), 1985
Career: 21,803, Walter Payton (Chicago Bears), 1975–87

MOST FIELD GOALS
Season: 39, Olindo Mare (Miami Dolphins), 1999
Career: 461, Gary Anderson, Pittsburgh Steelers (1982–94), Philadelphia Eagles (1995–96), San Francisco 49ers (1997), Minnesota Vikings (1999–2000)

MOST PASSES COMPLETED
Season: 404, Warren Moon (Houston Oilers), 1991
Career: 4,967, Dan Marino (Miami Dolphins), 1983–2000

MOST PASSES RECEIVED
Season: 123, Herman Moore (Detroit Lions), 1995
Career: 1,281, Jerry Rice (San Francisco 49ers), 1985–2000

MOST POINTS

Season: 176, Paul Hornung
(Green Bay Packers), 1960
Career: 2,059, Gary Anderson,
Pittsburgh Steelers (1982–94),
Philadelphia Eagles (1995–96),
San Francisco 49ers (1997),
Minnesota Vikings (1999–2000)

MOST TOUCHDOWN PASSES

Season: 48, Dan Marino
(Miami Dolphins), 1984
Career: 420, Dan Marino
(Miami Dolphins), 1983–99

MOST TOUCHDOWNS

Career: 180, Jerry Rice (San
Francisco 49ers), 1985–99

MOST YARDS
GAINED PASSING

Season: 5,084, Dan Marino
(Miami Dolphins), 1984
Career: 61,631, Dan Marino
(Miami Dolphins), 1983–99

MOST YARDS
GAINED RECEIVING

Season: 1,848, Jerry Rice
(San Francisco 49ers), 1995
Career: 19,247, Jerry Rice
(San Francisco 49ers), 1985–2000

MOST YARDS
GAINED RUSHING

Season: 2,105, Eric Dickerson
(Los Angeles Rams), 1984
Career: 16,726, Walter Payton
(Chicago Bears), 1975–87

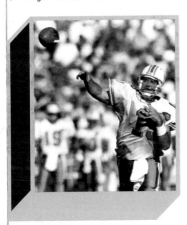

BASKETBALL
NBA – National Basketball Association

HIGHEST
SCORING AVERAGE

NBA play-off career: 33.4
(5,987 points in 179 games),

Michael Jordan, Chicago Bulls,
1984–98
NBA season: 50.4 points per
game, Wilt Chamberlain,
Philadelphia Warriors, 1961/62

MOST BASKETBALL
FIELD GOALS

NBA game: 36, Wilt Chamberlain,
Philadelphia Warriors, 2 March 1962
NBA season: 1,597, Wilt
Chamberlain, Philadelphia Warriors,
1961/62

MOST POINTS
SCORED BY A TEAM

NBA quarter: 58, Buffalo Braves,
20 Oct 1972
NBA half: 107, Phoenix Suns,
11 Nov 1990
NBA game: 186, Detroit Pistons,
13 Dec 1983

MOST FREE
THROWS SCORED

NBA game: 29, Wilt
Chamberlain, Philadelphia
Warriors, 2 March 1962; and
Adrian Dantley, Utah Jazz,
5 Jan 1984

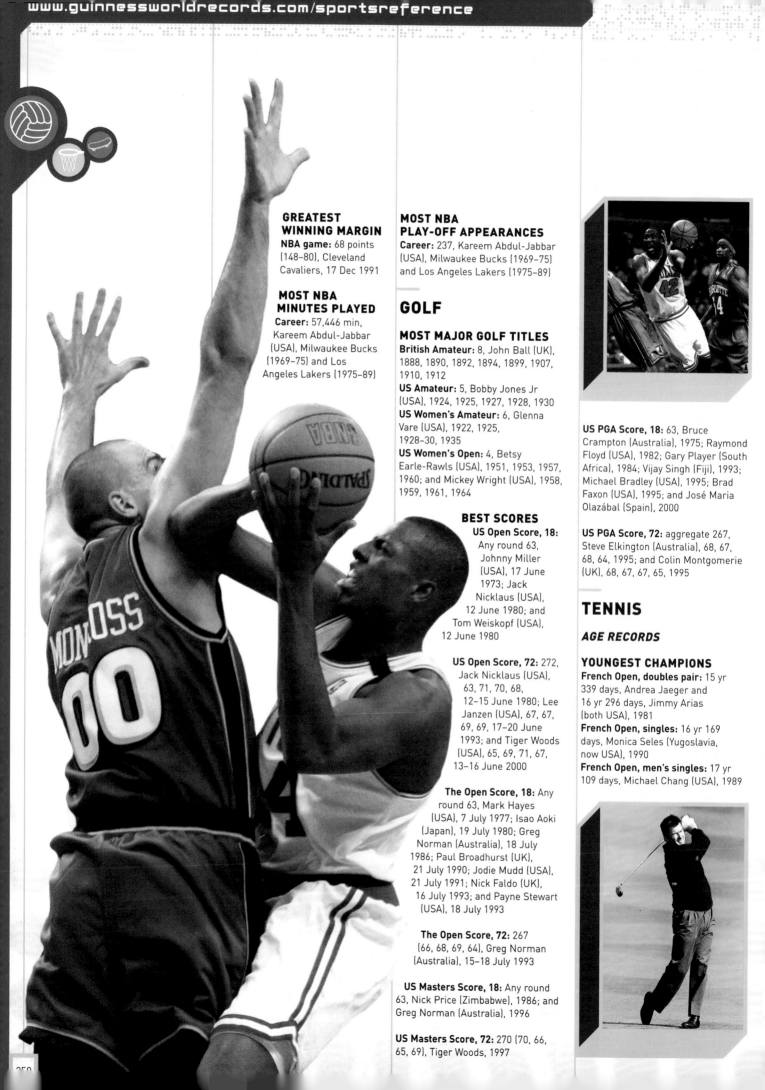

GREATEST WINNING MARGIN

NBA game: 68 points (148–80), Cleveland Cavaliers, 17 Dec 1991

MOST NBA MINUTES PLAYED

Career: 57,446 min, Kareem Abdul-Jabbar (USA), Milwaukee Bucks (1969–75) and Los Angeles Lakers (1975–89)

MOST NBA PLAY-OFF APPEARANCES

Career: 237, Kareem Abdul-Jabbar (USA), Milwaukee Bucks (1969–75) and Los Angeles Lakers (1975–89)

GOLF

MOST MAJOR GOLF TITLES

British Amateur: 8, John Ball (UK), 1888, 1890, 1892, 1894, 1899, 1907, 1910, 1912

US Amateur: 5, Bobby Jones Jr (USA), 1924, 1925, 1927, 1928, 1930

US Women's Amateur: 6, Glenna Vare (USA), 1922, 1925, 1928–30, 1935

US Women's Open: 4, Betsy Earle-Rawls (USA), 1951, 1953, 1957, 1960; and Mickey Wright (USA), 1958, 1959, 1961, 1964

BEST SCORES

US Open Score, 18: Any round 63, Johnny Miller (USA), 17 June 1973; Jack Nicklaus (USA), 12 June 1980; and Tom Weiskopf (USA), 12 June 1980

US Open Score, 72: 272, Jack Nicklaus (USA), 63, 71, 70, 68, 12–15 June 1980; Lee Janzen (USA), 67, 67, 69, 69, 17–20 June 1993; and Tiger Woods (USA), 65, 69, 71, 67, 13–16 June 2000

The Open Score, 18: Any round 63, Mark Hayes (USA), 7 July 1977; Isao Aoki (Japan), 19 July 1980; Greg Norman (Australia), 18 July 1986; Paul Broadhurst (UK), 21 July 1990; Jodie Mudd (USA), 21 July 1991; Nick Faldo (UK), 16 July 1993; and Payne Stewart (USA), 18 July 1993

The Open Score, 72: 267 (66, 68, 69, 64), Greg Norman (Australia), 15–18 July 1993

US Masters Score, 18: Any round 63, Nick Price (Zimbabwe), 1986; and Greg Norman (Australia), 1996

US Masters Score, 72: 270 (70, 66, 65, 69), Tiger Woods, 1997

US PGA Score, 18: 63, Bruce Crampton (Australia), 1975; Raymond Floyd (USA), 1982; Gary Player (South Africa), 1984; Vijay Singh (Fiji), 1993; Michael Bradley (USA), 1995; Brad Faxon (USA), 1995; and José Maria Olazábal (Spain), 2000

US PGA Score, 72: aggregate 267, Steve Elkington (Australia), 68, 67, 68, 64, 1995; and Colin Montgomerie (UK), 68, 67, 67, 65, 1995

TENNIS

AGE RECORDS

YOUNGEST CHAMPIONS

French Open, doubles pair: 15 yr 339 days, Andrea Jaeger and 16 yr 296 days, Jimmy Arias (both USA), 1981

French Open, singles: 16 yr 169 days, Monica Seles (Yugoslavia, now USA), 1990

French Open, men's singles: 17 yr 109 days, Michael Chang (USA), 1989

Australian Open, singles: 16 yr 117 days, Martina Hingis (Switzerland), 1997
Australian Open, men's singles: 17, Rodney Heath (Australia), 1905
Wimbledon: 15 yr 282 days, Martina Hingis (Switzerland), in women's doubles with Helena Sukova (Czech Republic), 1996
Wimbledon, women's singles: 15 yr 285 days, Charlotte Dod (UK), 1887

Wimbledon, men: 17 yr 227 days, Boris Becker (West Germany), 1985
US Open: 15 yr 139 days, Vincent Richards, (USA), 1918 (men's doubles)
US Open, women's singles: 16 yr 271 days, Tracey Austin (USA), 1979
US Open, men's singles: 19 yr 28 days, Pete Sampras (USA), 1990

YOUNGEST WORLD TENNIS NUMBER ONE
Women: 16 yr 182 days, Martina Hingis (Switzerland), 31 March 1997
Men: 20 yr 234 days, Marat Mikhailovich Safin (Russia), 17 Sept 2000

YOUNGEST WIMBLEDON PLAYER
Match winner: 14 yr 89 days, Jennifer Capriati (USA), 1990
Seeded competitor: 14 yr 89 days, Jennifer Capriati (USA), 1990

OLDEST CHAMPIONS
French Open: 42 yr 88 days, Elizabeth Ryan (USA), 1934 (women's doubles)
French Open, singles: 34 yr 301 days, Andrés Gimeno (Spain), 1972
Australian Open: 46 yr 60 days, Norman Everard Brookes (Australia), 1924 (men's doubles)

Australian Open, singles: 37 yr 62 days, Kenneth Robert Rosewall (Australia), 1972

GRAND SLAM RECORDS

MOST DOUBLES PARTNERSHIP TITLES
Women: 20 (12 US, 5 Wimbledon, 3 French), Althea Louise Brough (USA) and Margaret Evelyn du Pont (*née* Osborne, USA), 1942–57; and Martina Navratilova (USA) and Pam Shriver (USA), 7 Australian, 5 Wimbledon, 4 French, 4 USA, 1981–89

Men: 12, (5 Wimbledon, 4 Australian, 2 French, 1 US), John Newcombe (Australia) and Tony Roche (Australia), 1965, 1976

ATP TOUR RECORDS

MOST WINS
Doubles: 7, John McEnroe and Peter Fleming (both USA), 1978–84
Singles: 5, Ivan Lendl (Czech Republic), 1982, 1983, 1986, 1987

MOST QUALIFICATIONS
ATP tour: 16 (14 consecutive), Jimmy Connors (USA), 1972–85, 1987, 1988

ATHLETICS

WOMEN'S INDOOR RECORDS

50 M
5.96, Irina Privalova (Russia), Madrid, Spain, 9 Feb 1995

50-M HURDLES
6.58, Cornelia Oschkenat (GDR), Berlin, Germany, 20 Feb 1988

60 M
6.92, Irina Privalova (Russia), Madrid, Spain, 11 Feb 1993 and 9 Feb 1995

60-M HURDLES
7.69, Lyudmila Narozhilenko (Russia), Chelyabinsk, Russia, 4 Feb 1993

200 M
21.87, Merlene Ottey (Jamaica), Liévin, France, 13 Feb 1993

400 M
49.59, Jarmila Kratochvílovà (Czechoslovakia), Milan, Italy, 7 March 1982

800 M
1:56.40, Christine Wachtel (GDR), Vienna, Austria, 13 Feb 1988

1,000 M
2:30.94, Maria Mutola (Mozambique), Stockholm, Sweden, 25 Feb 1999

1,500 M
4:00.27, Doina Melinte (Romania),
East Rutherford, NJ, USA, 9 Feb 1990

1 MILE
4:17.14, Doina Melinte (Romania),
East Rutherford, NJ, USA, 9 Feb 1990

3,000 M
8:32.88, Gabriela Szabo (Romania),
Birmingham, UK, 18 Feb 2001

5,000 M
14:47.36, Gabriela Szabo (Romania),
Dortmund, Germany, 13 Feb 1999

4 X 200 M RELAY
1:32.55, SC Eintracht Hamm, West
Germany (Helga Arendt, Silke-Beate
Knoll, Mechthild Kluth, Gisela Kinzel),
Dortmund, Germany, 19 Feb 1988;
LG Olympia Dortmund, Germany
(Esther Moller, Gabi Rockmeier,
Birgit Rockmeier, Andrea Phillip),
Karlsruhe, Germany, 21 Feb 1999

4 X 400 M RELAY
3:24.25, Russia (Tatyana Chebykina,
Svetlana Goncharenko, Olga
Kotlyarova, Natalya Nazarova),
Maebashi, Japan, 7 March 1999

3,000-M WALK
11:40.33, Claudia Iovan (Romania),
Bucharest, Romania, 30 Jan 1999

PENTATHLON
4,991 points, Irina Belova (Russia),
Berlin, Germany, 14–15 Feb 1992,
60-m hurdles: 8.22; **High jump:**
1.93 m (6 ft 4 in); **Shot:** 13.25 m
(43 ft 5.5 in); **Long jump:** 6.67 m
(21 ft 10.5 in); **800 m:** 2:10.26

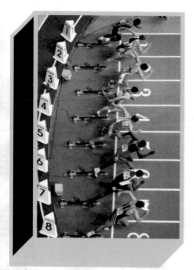

LONG JUMP
7.37 m (24 ft 2 in), Heike Drechsler
(GDR), Vienna, Austria, 13 Feb 1988

TRIPLE JUMP
15.16 m (49 ft 8.75 in), Ashia Hansen
(UK), Valencia, Spain, 28 Feb 1998

HIGH JUMP
2.07 m (6 ft 9.5 in), Heike Henkel
(Germany), Karlsruhe, Germany,
9 Feb 1992

POLE VAULT
4.70 m (15 ft 5 in), Stacy Dragila
(USA), Pocatello, Idaho, USA,
17 Feb 2001

SHOT PUT
22.50 m (73 ft 10 in), Helena
Fibingerová (Czechoslovakia),
Jablonec, Czechoslovakia,
19 Feb 1977

MEN'S INDOOR RECORDS

50 M
5.56, Donovan Bailey (Canada),
Reno, NV, USA, 9 Feb 1996; and
Maurice Greene (USA), Los Angeles,
USA, 13 Feb 1999

50-M HURDLES
6.25, Mark McCoy (Canada), Kobe,
Japan, 5 March 1986

60 M
6.39, Maurice Greene (USA),
Madrid, Spain, 3 Feb 1998 and
3 March 2001

60-M HURDLES
7.30, Colin Jackson (UK),
Sindelfingen, Germany, 6 March 1994

200 M
19.92, Frank Fredericks (Namibia),
Liévin, France, 18 Feb 1996

400 M
44.63, Michael Johnson (USA),
Atlanta, USA, 4 March 1995

800 M
1:42.67, Wilson Kipketer
(Denmark), Paris, France,
9 March 1997

1,000 M
2:14.96, Wilson Kipketer (Denmark),
Birmingham, UK, 20 Feb 2000

1,500 M
3:31.18, Hicham El Guerrouj
(Morocco), Stuttgart, Germany,
2 Feb 1997

1 MILE
3:48.46, Hicham El Guerrouj
(Morocco), Ghent, Belgium,
12 Feb 1997

3,000 M
7:24.90, Daniel Komen (Kenya),
Budapest, Hungary, 6 Feb 1998

5,000 M
12:50.38, Haile Gebrselassie
(Ethiopia), Birmingham, UK,
14 Feb 1999

4 X 200 M RELAY
1:22.11, Great Britain (Linford
Christie, Darren Braithwaite,
Ade Mafe, John Regis), Glasgow,
Scotland, UK, 3 March 1991

4 X 400 M RELAY
3:02.83, USA (Andre Morris,
Dameon Johnson, Deon Minor,
Milton Campbell), Maebashi,
Japan, 7 March 1999

5,000-M WALK
18:07.08, Mikhail Shchennikov
(Russia), Moscow, Russia,
14 Feb 1995

HEPTATHLON
6,476 points, Dan Dion O'Brien (USA),
Toronto, Canada, 13–14 March 1993.
60 m: 6.67; **Long jump:** 7.84 m (25 ft
8.5 in); **Shot:** 16.02 m (52 ft 6.5 in);
High jump: 2.13 m (6 ft 11.75 in);
60-m hurdles: 7.85; **Pole vault:**
5.20 m (17 ft 0.75 in); **1,000 m:** 2:57.96

LONG JUMP
8.79 m (28 ft 10 in), Carl Lewis (USA),
New York, USA, 27 Jan 1984

TRIPLE JUMP
17.83 m (58 ft 6 in), Aliecer Urrutia
(Cuba), Sindelfingen, Germany,
1 March 1997

HIGH JUMP
2.43 m (7 ft 11.5 in), Javier
Sotomayor (Cuba), Budapest,
Hungary, 4 March 1989

POLE VAULT
6.15 m (20 ft 2 in), Sergei Bubka
(Ukraine), Donetsk, Ukraine,
21 Feb 1993

SHOT PUT
22.66 m (74 ft 4 in) Randy Barnes
(USA), Los Angeles, USA,
20 Jan 1989

**WOMEN'S OUTDOOR
RECORDS**

100 M
10.49, Florence Griffith-Joyner (USA),
Indianapolis, USA, 16 July 1988

100-M HURDLES
12.21, Yordanka Donkova (Bulgaria),
Stara Zagora, Bulgaria, 20 Aug 1988

200 M
21.34, Florence Griffith-Joyner (USA),
Seoul, South Korea, 29 Sept 1988

400 M
47.60, Marita Koch (GDR), Canberra, Australia, 6 Oct 1985

400-M HURDLES
52.61, Kim Batten (USA), Gothenburg, Sweden, 11 Aug 1995

800 M
1:53.28, Jarmila Kratochvílova (Czechoslovakia), Munich, Germany, 26 July 1983

1,000 M
2:28.98, Svetlana Masterkova (Russia), Brussels, Belgium, 23 Aug 1996

1,500 M
3:50.46, Qu Yunxia (China), Beijing, China, 11 Sept 1993

1 MILE
4:12.56, Svetlana Masterkova (Russia), Zurich, Switzerland, 14 Aug 1996

2,000 M
5:25.36, Sonia O'Sullivan (Ireland), Edinburgh, Scotland, UK, 8 July 1994

3,000 M
8:06.11, Wang Junxia (China), Beijing, China, 13 Sept 1993

3,000-M STEEPLECHASE
9:40.20, Cristina Iloc-Casandra (Romania), Reims, France, 30 Aug 2000

5,000 M
14:28.09, Jiang Bo (China), Beijing, China, 23 Oct 1997

10,000 M
29:31.78, Wang Junxia (China), Beijing, China, 8 Sept 1993

1 HOUR
18,340 m, Tegla Loroupe (Kenya), Borgholzhausen, Germany, 7 Aug 1998

20,000 M
1:05:26.6, Tegla Loroupe (Kenya), Borgholzhausen, Germany, 3 Sept 2000

25,000 M
1:29:29.2, Karolina Szabó (Hungary), Budapest, Hungary, 23 April 1988

30,000 M
1:47:05.6, Karolina Szabó (Hungary), Budapest, Hungary, 23 April 1988

4 X 100 M RELAY
41.37, GDR (Silke Gladisch, Sabine Rieger, Ingrid Auerswald, Marlies Gohr), Canberra, Australia, 6 Oct 1985

4 X 200 M RELAY
1:27.46, United States 'Blue' (LaTasha Jenkins, Chryste Gaines, Nanceen Perry, Torri Edwards), Philadelphia, USA, 29 April 2000

4 X 400 M RELAY
3:15.17, USSR (Tatyana Ledovskaya, Olga Nazarova, Maria Pinigina, Olga Bryzgina), Seoul, South Korea, 1 Oct 1988

4 X 800 M RELAY
7:50.17, USSR (Nadezhda Olizarenko, Lyubov Gurina, Lyudmila Borisova, Irina Podyalovskaya), Moscow, Russia, 5 Aug 1984

HEPTATHLON
7,291 points, Jacqueline Joyner-Kersee (USA), Seoul, South Korea, 23–24 Sept 1988
100-m hurdles: 12.69;
High jump: 1.86 m (6 ft 1.25 in);
Shot: 15.80 m (51 ft 10 in);
200 m: 22.56; **Long jump:** 7.27 m (23 ft 10.25 in); **Javelin:** 45.66 m (149 ft 10 in); **800 m:** 2:08.51

LONG JUMP
7.52 m (24 ft 8 in), Galina Chistyakova (USSR), Leningrad, USSR, 11 June 1988

TRIPLE JUMP
15.50 m (50 ft 10.25 in), Inessa Kravets (Ukraine), Gothenburg, Sweden, 10 Aug 1995

HIGH JUMP
2.09 m (6 ft 10.25 in), Stefka Kostadinova (Bulgaria), Rome, Italy, 30 Aug 1987

POLE VAULT
4.70 m (15 ft 5 in), Stacy Dragila (USA), Pocatello, USA, 27 April 2001

SHOT PUT
22.63 m (74 ft 3 in), Natalya Lisovskaya (USSR), Moscow, Russia, 7 June 1987

DISCUS
76.80 m (252 ft), Gabriele Reinsch (GDR), Neubrandenburg, Germany, 9 July 1988

HAMMER
76.07 m (249 ft 6 in), Mihaela Melinte (Romania), Rüdlingen, Germany, 29 Aug 1999

JAVELIN
69.48 m (227 ft 11 in), Trine Solberg-Hattestad (Norway), Oslo, Norway, 28 July 2000

MEN'S OUTDOOR RECORDS

100 M
9.79, Maurice Greene (USA), Athens, Greece, 16 June 1999

110-M HURDLES
12.91, Colin Jackson (UK), Stuttgart, Germany, 20 Aug 1993

200 M
19.32, Michael Johnson (USA), Atlanta, Georgia, USA, 1 Aug 1996

400 M
43.18, Michael Johnson (USA), Seville, Spain, 26 Aug 1999

400-M HURDLES
46.78, Kevin Young (USA), Barcelona, Spain, 6 Aug 1992

800 M
1:41.11, Wilson Kipketer (Denmark), Cologne, Germany, 24 Aug 1997

1,000 M
2:11.96, Noah Ngeny (Kenya), Rieti, Italy, 5 Sept 1999

1,500 M
3:26.00, Hicham El Guerrouj (Morocco), Rome, Italy, 14 July 1998

1 MILE
3:43.13, Hicham El Guerrouj (Morroco), Rome, Italy, 7 July 1999

2,000 M
4:44.79, Hicham El Guerrouj (Morocco), Berlin, Germany, 7 Sept 1999

3,000 M
7:20.67, Daniel Komen (Kenya), Rieti, Italy, 1 Sept 1996

3,000-M STEEPLECHASE
7:55.72, Bernard Barmasai (Kenya), Cologne, Germany, 24 Aug 1997

5,000 M
12:39.36, Haile Gebrselassie (Ethiopia), Helsinki, Finland, 13 June 1998

10,000 M
26:22.75, Haile Gebrselassie (Ethiopia), Hengelo, Netherlands, 1 June 1998

20,000 M
56:55.6, Arturo Barrios (Mexico, now USA), La Flèche, France, 30 March 1991

1 HOUR
21,101 m, Arturo Barrios (Mexico, now USA), La Flèche, France, 30 March 1991

25,000 M
1:13:55.8, Toshihiko Seko (Japan), Christchurch, New Zealand, 22 March 1981

30,000 M
1:29:18.8, Toshihiko Seko (Japan), Christchurch, New Zealand, 22 March 1981

4 X 100 M RELAY
37.40, USA (Michael Marsh, Leroy Burrell, Dennis A Mitchell, Carl Lewis), Barcelona, Spain, 8 Aug 1992; USA (John Drummond Jr, Andre Cason, Dennis Mitchell, Leroy Burrell), Stuttgart, Germany, 21 Aug 1993

4 X 200 M RELAY
1:18.68, Santa Monica Track Club, USA (Michael Marsh, Leroy Burrell, Floyd Wayne Heard, Carl Lewis), Walnut, CA, USA, 17 April 1994

4 X 400 M RELAY
2:54.20, USA (Jerome Young, Antonio Pettigrew, Tyree Washington, Michael Duane Johnson), New York, USA, 23 July 1998

4 X 800 M RELAY
7:03.89, Great Britain (Peter Elliott, Garry Peter Cook, Stephen Cram, Sebastian Coe), London, UK, 30 Aug 1982

4 X 1,500 M RELAY
14:38.8, West Germany (Thomas Wessinghage, Harald Hudak, Michael Lederer, Karl Fleschen), Cologne, Germany, 17 Aug 1977

DECATHLON
9,026 points, Roman Sebrle (Czech Republic), Götzis, Austria, 26–27 May 2001
Day 1
100 m: 10.64; **Long jump:** 8.11 m (26 ft 7.25 in); **Shot:** 15.33 m (50 ft 3.5 in); **High jump:** 2.12 m (6 ft 11.25 in); **400 m:** 47.79
Day 2
110-m hurdles: 13.92; **Discus:** 47.92 m (157 ft 2.5 in); **Pole vault:** 4.80 m (15 ft 9 in); **Javelin:** 70.16 m (230 ft 2 in); **1,500 m:** 4:21.98

LONG JUMP
8.95 m (29 ft 4.5 in), Mike Powell (USA), Tokyo, Japan, 30 Aug 1991

TRIPLE JUMP
18.29 m (60 ft 0.25 in), Jonathan Edwards (UK), Gothenburg, Sweden, 7 Aug 1995

HIGH JUMP
2.45 m (8 ft 0.5 in), Javier Sotomayor (Cuba), Salamanca, Spain, 27 July 1993

POLE VAULT
6.14 m (20 ft 1.75 in), Sergei Bubka (Ukraine), Sestriere, Italy, 31 July 1994

SHOT PUT
23.12 m (75 ft 10.25 in), Randy Barnes (USA), Los Angeles, USA, 20 May 1990

DISCUS
74.08 m (243 ft), Jürgen Schult (GDR), Neubrandenburg, Germany, 6 June 1986

HAMMER
86.74 m (284 ft 7 in), Yuriy Sedykh (USSR, now Russia), Stuttgart, Germany, 30 Aug 1986

JAVELIN
98.48 m (323 ft 1 in), Jan Zelezný (Czech Republic), Jena, Germany, 25 May 1996

CYCLING

WOMEN'S WORLD RECORDS

UNPACED STANDING START
500 m: 34.017, Felicia Ballanger (France), Bogotá, Colombia, 29 Sept 1995
3 km: 3:30.816, Leontien Zijlaard-van Moorsel (Netherlands), Sydney, Australia, 17 Sept 2000

UNPACED FLYING START
200 m: 10.831, Olga Slyusareva (Russia), Moscow, Russia, 25 April 1993

MEN'S WORLD RECORDS

UNPACED STANDING START
1 km: 1:00.148, Arnaud Tournant (France), Mexico City, Mexico, 16 June 2000
4 km: 4:11.114, Chris Boardman (UK), Manchester, UK, 29 Aug 1996

UNPACED FLYING START
200 m: 9.865, Curtis Harnett (Canada), Bogotá, Colombia, 28 Sept 1995
500 m: 26.649, Aleksandr Kiritchenko (USSR), Moscow, Russia, 29 Oct 1988

TEAM PURSUIT
4 km: 3:59.710, Germany (Robert Bartko, Guido Fulst, Jens Lehmann, Daniel Becke), Sydney, Australia, 19 Sept 2000

SKIING

WOMEN'S RECORDS

MOST OLYMPIC TITLES
Alpine: 3, Vreni Schneider (Switzerland) giant slalom, slalom

1988; slalom 1994; Katja Seizinger (Germany), downhill 1994; combined, downhill 1998; and Deborah Campagnoni (Italy), super giant slalom 1992; giant slalom 1994; giant slalom 1998
Nordic: 6, Lyubov Yegorova (Russia), 10 km, 15 km, 4 x 5 km 1992; 5 km, 10 km, 4 x 5 km 1994

MOST WORLD CUP ALPINE TITLES
Overall: 6, Annemarie Moser-Pröll (Austria), 1971–75, 1979
Downhill: 7, Annemarie Moser-Pröll (Austria), 1971–75, 1978–79
Slalom: 6, Vreni Schneider (Switzerland), 1989–90, 1992–95
Giant slalom: 5, Vreni Schneider (Switzerland), 1986–87, 1989, 1991, 1995
Super giant slalom: 5, Katja Seizinger (Germany), 1993–96, 1998

MOST WORLD CUP NORDIC TITLES
Cross-country: 4, Yelena Välbe (USSR/Russia), 1989, 1991–92, 1995

MEN'S RECORDS

MOST OLYMPIC TITLES
Alpine: 3, Anton 'Toni' Sailer (Austria), downhill, slalom, giant slalom, 1956; Jean-Claude Killy (France), downhill, slalom, giant slalom, 1968; Alberto Tomba (Italy), slalom, giant slalom, 1988; giant slalom, 1992
Nordic: 8, Bjørn Dæhlie (Norway), 15 km, 50 km, 4 x 10 km, 1992; 10 km, 15 km, 1994; 10 km, 5 km, 4 x 10 km, 1998
Jumping: 4, Matti Nykänen (Finland), 70 m hill, 1988; 90 m hill, 1984, 1988; Team 1988

MOST WORLD CUP ALPINE TITLES
Overall: 5, Marc Girardelli (Luxembourg), 1985–86, 1989, 1991, 1993
Downhill: 5, Franz Klammer (Austria), 1975–78, 1983
Slalom: 8, Ingemar Stenmark (Sweden), 1975–81, 1983
Giant slalom: 7, Ingemar Stenmark (Sweden), 1975–76, 1978–81, 1984
Super giant slalom: 4, Pirmin Zurbriggen (Switzerland), 1987–90

MOST WORLD CUP NORDIC TITLES
Jumping: 4, Matti Nykänen (Finland), 1983, 1985–86, 1988
Cross-country: 5, Gunde Svan (Sweden), 1984–86, 1988–89; Bjørn Dæhlie (Norway), 1992–93, 1995–97

SPEED SKATING

WOMEN'S RECORDS

500 m: 37.29, Catriona LeMay Doan (Canada), Salt Lake City, USA, 9 March 2001
1,000 m: 1:14.13, Monique Garbrecht-Enfeldt (Germany), Salt Lake City, Utah, USA, 10 March 2001
1,500 m: 1:54.38, Anni Friesinger (Germany), Calgary, Canada, 4 March 2001
3,000 m: 3:59.26, Claudia Pechstein (Germany), Calgary, Canada, 2 March 2001
5,000 m: 6:52.44, Gunda Niemann-Stirnemann (Germany), Salt Lake City, USA, 10 March 2001

GUINNESS
WORLD RECORDS

**LOWEST WORLD
CHAMPIONSHIP SCORE**
161.479 points, Gunda Niemann-Stirnemann (Germany), Hamar, Norway, 6–7 Feb 1999

SHORT TRACK
500 m: 43.873, Evgenia Radanova (Bulgaria), Lake Placid, NY, USA, 18 Feb 2000
1,000 m: 1:31.991, Yang Yang (China), Nagano, Japan, 21 Feb 1998
1,500 m: 2:25.146, Evgenia Radanova (Bulgaria), Szekesfehervar, Hungary, 6 Nov 1998
3,000 m: 5:01.976, Eun-kyung Choi (South Korea), Calgary, Canada, 22 Oct 2000
3,000-m relay: 4:16.260, South Korea (An Sang-mi, Chun Lee-kyung, Kim Yun-mi, Won Hye-kyung), Nagano, Japan, 17 Feb 1998

MEN'S RECORDS
500 m: 34.32, Hiroyasu Shimizu (Japan), Salt Lake City, USA, 10 March 2001
1,000 m: 1:08.28, Jeremy Wotherspoon (Canada), Salt Lake City, USA, 11 March 2001
1,500 m: 1:45.20, Kyu-Hyuk Lee (South Korea), Calgary, Canada, 15 March 2001
3,000 m: 3:42.75, Gianni Romme (Netherlands), Calgary, Canada, 11 Aug 2000
5,000 m: 6:18.72, Gianni Romme (Netherlands), Nagano, Japan, 30 Jan 2000
10,000 m: 13:03.40, Gianni Romme (Netherlands), Heerenveen, Netherlands, 26 Nov 2000

**LOWEST WORLD
CHAMPIONSHIP SCORE**
152.651 points Rintje Ritsma (Netherlands), Hamar, Norway, 6–7 Feb 1999

SHORT TRACK
500 m: 41.938, Nicola Franceschina (Italy), Bormio, Italy, 29 March 1998
1,000 m: 1:28.23, Marc Gagnon (Canada), Seoul, South Korea, 4 April 1997
1,500 m: 2:15.50, Kai Feng (China), Groningen, Netherlands, 11 Nov 1997
3,000 m: 4:46.727, Kim Dong-sung (South Korea), Szekesfehervar, Hungary, 8 Nov 1998
5,000-m relay: 6:49.618, South Korea, Chang Chun, China, 5 Dec 1999

FIGURE SKATING

GRAND SLAM RECORDS
The figure-skating grand slams comprise the European, World and Olympic titles.

MOST FIGURE-SKATING GRAND SLAMS
Women: 2, Sonja Henie (Norway), 1932, 1936; and Katarina Witt (West Germany), 1984, 1988
Men: 2, Karl Schäfer (Austria), 1932, 1936

WORLD CHAMPIONSHIP RECORDS

MOST TITLES
Individual titles, women: 10, Sonja Henie (Norway), 1927–36
Individual titles, men: 10, Ulrich Salchow (Sweden), 1901–05, 1907–11

World titles, pairs: 10, Irina Rodnina (4 with Aleksey Nikolayevich Ulanov, 1969–72; 6 with Aleksandr Gennadyevich Zaitsev, 1973–78)
Dance titles, pairs: 6, Lyudmila Alekseyevna Pakhomova and husband Aleksandr Georgiyevich Gorshkov (USSR), 1970–74, 1976

YOUNGEST WORLD CHAMPION
Individual title: 14 yr 286 days, Tara Lipinski (USA), 22 March 1997

COMPETITION RECORDS

HIGHEST MARKS
Women: 7 perfect 6.0s, Midori Ito (Japan), World Figure Skating Championships, Paris, France, 1989
Men: 7 perfect 6.0s, Donald George Jackson (Canada), Prague, Czechoslovakia, 1962
Pairs (dancing): 29 perfect 6.0s, Jayne Torvill and Christopher Dean (both UK), Ottawa, Canada, 22–24 March 1984

SWIMMING

WOMEN'S SHORT-COURSE RECORDS

BACKSTROKE
50 m: 27.25, Haley Cope (USA), Indianapolis, USA, 7 March 2000
100 m: 58.45, Mia Nakamura (Japan), Sagamihara, Japan, 23 March 2001

200 m: 2:06.09, He Cihong (China), Palma de Mallorca, Spain, 5 Dec 1993

BREASTSTROKE
50 m: 30.60, Penny Heyns (South Africa), Durban, South Africa, 26 Sept 1999
100 m: 1:05.40, Penny Heyns (South Africa), Durban, South Africa, 26 Sept 1999
200 m: 2:19.25, Hiu Qi (China), Paris, France, 28 Jan 2001

BUTTERFLY
50 m: 25.36, Anne-Karin Kammerling, (Sweden), Stockholm, Sweden, 25 Jan 2001

100 m: 56.56, Jenny Thompson (USA), Athens, Greece, 18 March 2000
200 m: 2:04.16, Susan O'Neill (Australia), Sydney, Australia, 18 Jan 2000

FREESTYLE
50 m: 23.59, Therese Alshammar (Sweden), Athens, Greece, 18 March 2000
100 m: 52.17, Therese Alshammar (Sweden), Athens, Greece, 17 March 2000
200 m: 1:54.17 Claudia Poll (Costa Rica), Gothenburg, Sweden, 18 April 1997
400 m: 4:00.03, Claudia Poll (Costa Rica), Gothenburg, Sweden, 19 April 1997
800 m: 8:15.34, Astrid Strauss (GDR), Bonn, Germany, 6 Feb 1987
1,500 m: 15:43.31, Petra Schneider (GDR), Gainesville, FL, USA, 10 Jan 1982
4 x 50 m relay: 1:38.21, Sweden (Annika Lofstedt, Therese Alshammar, Johanna Sjöberg, Anna-Karin Kammerling), Valencia, Spain, 15 Dec 2000

4 x 100 m relay: 3:34.55, China (Le Jingyi, Na Chao, Shan Ying, Nian Yin), Gothenburg, Sweden, 19 April 1997

4 x 200 m relay: 7:49.11, Great Britain (Claire Huddart, Nicola Jackson, Karen Legg, Karen Pickering), Athens, Greece, 16 March 2000

MEDLEY

100 m: 59.30, Jenny Thompson (USA), Hong Kong, 2 April 1999

200 m: 2:07.79, Allison Wagner (USA), Palma de Mallorca, Spain, 5 Dec 1993

400 m: 4:29.00, Dai Gouhong (China), Palma de Mallorca, Spain, 2 Dec 1993

4 x 50 m relay: 1:48.31, Sweden (Therese Alshammar, Emma Igelström, Anna-Karin Kammerling, Johanna Sjöberg), Valencia, Spain, 16 Dec 2001

4 x 100 m relay: 3:57.46, University of Georgia, USA (Courtney Shealy, Kristy Kowal, Keegan Walkley, Maritza Correia), Indianapolis, USA, 16 March 2000

MEN'S SHORT-COURSE RECORDS

BACKSTROKE

50 m: 23.42, Neil Walker (USA), Athens, Greece, 16 March 2000

100 m: 50.75, Neil Walker (USA), Athens, Greece, 19 March 2000

200 m: 1:51.62, Matt Welsh (Australia), Melbourne, Australia, 13 Oct 2000; and Gordon Kozulj (Croatia), Berlin, Germany, 21 Jan 2001

BREASTSTROKE

50 m: 26.70, Mark Warnecke (Germany), Sheffield, UK, 11 Dec 1998

100 m: 57.66, Ed Moses (USA), Minneapolis, USA, 24 March 2000

200 m: 2:06.40, Ed Moses (USA), Minneapolis, USA, 25 March 2000

BUTTERFLY

50 m: 22.87, Mark Foster (UK), Sheffield, UK, 17 Jan 2001

100 m: 50.44, Lars Frolander (Sweden), Athens, Greece, 17 March 2000

200 m: 1:51.58, Franck Esposito (France), Antibes, France, 13 Jan 2001

GUINNESS
WORLD RECORDS™

FREESTYLE
50 m: 21.13, Mark Foster (UK), Paris, France, 28 Jan 2001
100 m: 46.74, Aleksandr Popov (Russia), Gelsenkirchen, Germany, 19 March 1994
200 m: 1:41.10, Ian Thorpe (Australia), Berlin, Germany, 5 Feb 2000
400 m: 3:35.01, Grant Hackett (Australia), Hong Kong, 2 April 1999
800 m: 7:34.90, Kieren Perkins (Australia), Sydney, Australia, 25 July 1993
1,500 m: 14:19.55, Grant Hackett (Australia), Sydney, Australia, 27 Sept 1998
4 x 50 m relay: 1:26.78, USA (Bryan Jones, Matt Ulricksson, Robert Bogart, Leffie Crawford), Minneapolis, USA, 23 March 2000
4 x 100 m relay: 3:09.57, Sweden (Johan Nystrom, Lars Frolander, Mattias Ohlin, Stefan Nystrand), Athens, Greece, 16 March 2000
4 x 200 m relay: 7:01.33, USA (Josh Davis, Neil Walker, Scott Tucker, Chad Carvin), Athens, Greece, 17 March 2000

MEDLEY
100 m: 52.79, Neil Walker (USA), Athens, Greece, 18 March 2000
200 m: 1:54.65, Jani Sievinen (Finland), Kuopio, Finland, 21 Jan 1994; and Atilla Czene (Hungary), Minneapolis, USA, 23 March 2000

400 m: 4:04.24, Matthew Dunn (Australia), Perth, Australia, 24 Sept 1998
4 x 50 m relay: 1:35.51, Germany (Thomas Rupprath, Mark Warnecke, Alexander Luderitz, Stephane Kunzelmann) and Sweden (Daniel Carlsson, Patrik Isaksson, Jonas Akesson, Lars Frolande), Sheffield, UK, 13 Dec 1998
4 x 100 m relay: 3:29.88, Australia (Matt Welsh, Phil Rogers, Michael Klim, Chris Fydler), Hong Kong, 4 April 1999

WOMEN'S LONG-COURSE RECORDS

BACKSTROKE
50 m: 28.25, Sandra Voelker (Germany), Berlin, Germany, 17 June 2000
100 m: 1:00.16, He Cihong (China), Rome, Italy, 10 Sept 1994
200 m: 2:06.62, Krisztina Egerszegi (Hungary), Athens, Greece, 25 Aug 1991

BREASTSTROKE
50 m: 30.83, Penny Heyns (South Africa), Sydney, Australia, 28 Aug 1999
100 m: 1:06.52, Penny Heyns (South Africa), Sydney, Australia, 23 Aug 1999
200 m: 2:22.99, Hiu Qi (China), Hangzhou, China, 3 April 2001

BUTTERFLY
50 m: 25.64, Inge de Bruijn (Netherlands), Sheffield, UK, 26 May 2000

100 m: 56.61, Inge de Bruijn (Netherlands), Sydney, Australia, 17 Sept 2000
200 m: 2:05.81, Susan O'Neill (Australia), Sydney, Australia, 17 May 2000

FREESTYLE
50 m: 24.32, Inge de Bruijn (Netherlands), Sydney, Australia, 23 Sept 2000
100 m: 53.77, Inge de Bruijn (Netherlands), Sydney, Australia, 20 Sept 2000
200 m: 1:56.78, Franziska van Almsick (Germany), Rome, Italy, 6 Sept 1994

400 m: 4:03.85, Janet Evans (USA), Seoul, South Korea, 22 Sept 1988
800 m: 8:16.22, Janet Evans (USA), Tokyo, Japan, 20 Aug 1989
1,500 m: 15:52.10, Janet Evans (USA), Orlando, USA, 26 March 1988
4 x 100 m relay: USA (Amy van Dyken, Dara Torres, Courtney Shealy, Jenny Thompson), Sydney, Australia, 16 Sept 2000

4 x 200 m relay: 7:55.47, East Germany (Manuela Stellmach, Astrid Strauss, Anke Möhring, Heike Friedrich), Strasbourg, France, 18 Aug 1987

MEDLEY
200 m: 2:09.72, Wu Yanyan (China), Shanghai, China, 17 Oct 1997
400 m: 4:33.59, Yana Klochkova (Ukraine), Sydney, Australia, 16 Sept 2000
4 x 100 m relay: 3:58.30, USA (Megan Quann, Jenny Thompson, BJ Bedford, Dara Torres), Sydney, Australia, 23 Sept 2000

MEN'S LONG-COURSE RECORDS

BACKSTROKE
50 m: 24.99, Lenny Krayzelburg (USA), Sydney, Australia, 28 Aug 1999
100 m: 53.60, Lenny Krayzelburg (USA), Sydney, Australia, 24 Aug 1999
200 m: 1:55.87, Lenny Krayzelburg (USA), Sydney, Australia, 27 Aug 1999

BREASTSTROKE
50 m: 27.39, Ed Moses (USA), Austin, USA, 31 March 2001
100 m: 1:00.29, Ed Moses (USA), Austin, USA, 28 March 2001

200 m: 2:10.16, Mike Barrowman (USA), Barcelona, Spain, 29 July 1992

BUTTERFLY
50 m: 23.60, Geoff Huegill (Australia), Sydney, Australia, 14 May 2000
100 m: 51.81, Michael Klim (Australia), Canberra, Australia, 12 Dec 1999
200 m: 1:54.92, Michael Phelps (USA), Austin, USA, 30 March 2001

FREESTYLE
50 m: 21.64, Alexander Popov
(Russia), Moscow, Russia,
16 June 2000
100 m: 47.84, Pieter van den
Hoogenband (Netherlands),
Sydney, Australia, 19 Sept 2000
200 m: 1:44.69, Ian Thorpe
(Australia), Hobart, Tasmania,
Australia, 27 March 2001
400 m: 3:40.59, Ian Thorpe
(Australia), Sydney, Australia,
16 Sept 2000
800 m: 7:41.59, Ian Thorpe
(Australia), Hobart, Tasmania,
Australia, 26 March 2001
1,500 m: 14:41.66, Kieren Perkins
(Australia), Victoria, Canada,
24 Aug 1994
4 x 100 m relay: 3:13.67, Australia
(Michael Klim, Chris Fydler, Ashley
Callus, Ian Thorpe), Sydney,
Australia, 16 Sept 2000
4 x 200 m relay: 7:07.05, Australia
(Ian Thorpe, Michael Klim, Todd
Pearson, Bill Kirby), Sydney,
Australia, 19 Sept 2000

MEDLEY
200 m: 1:58.16, Jani Sievinen
(Finland), Rome, Italy, 11 Sept 1994
400 m: 4:11.76, Tom Dolan (USA),
Sydney, Australia, 17 Sept 2000
4 x 100 m relay: 3:33.73, USA (Lenny
Krayzelburg, Ed Moses, Ian Crocker,
Gary Hall Jr), Sydney, Australia,
23 Sept 2000

ROWING

ROWING EIGHT (NON-TIDAL WATER)

FASTEST 2,000 M (2,187 YD)
Women: 5:58.50 (20.08 km/h;
12.48 mph), Romania,
Duisburg, Germany,
18 May 1996
Men: 5:20.92 (22.43 km/h;
13.94 mph), Poland, Plovdiv,
Bulgaria, 5 Aug 1999

ROWING SINGLE SCULLS

FASTEST 2,000 M
Women: 7:17.09 (16.47 km/h;
10.23 mph), Silken Laumann
(Canada), Lucerne, Switzerland,
17 July 1994
Men: 6:35.67 (18.19 km/h;
11.30 mph), Leonid Gulov
(Estonia), Plovdiv, Bulgaria,
5 Aug 1999

RIVER THAMES SCULL
**Roundhouse, Lechlade
to Gravesend Pier, UK
(234 km; 146 miles):**
60 hr 23 min, Peter Goodchild
(UK), 15–17 Dec 1996

GUINNESS
WORLD RECORDS

CONCEPT II INDOOR ROWER

FASTEST 1,000,000 M
Men's team (of 12): 66 hr 44 min 54 sec, HMP Downview team, Sutton, Greater London, UK, 3–6 Aug 1999

FASTEST 2,000 M
Women: 6:33.4, Kathrin Boron (Germany), 1998
Men: 5:38.3, Rob Waddell (New Zealand), 1998

CRICKET

INNINGS RECORDS

LONGEST INDIVIDUAL CRICKET INNINGS
16 hr 55 min, Rajiv Nayyar (India), scoring 271 for Himachal Pradesh, India, 1–3 Nov 1999

LONGEST INNINGS WITHOUT SCORING
First class: 101 min, Geoff Allott, New Zealand v. South Africa, Auckland, New Zealand, 2 March 1999. Allott faced a total of 77 deliveries

HIGHEST CRICKET INNINGS
Score: Brian Lara, 501 not out in 7 hr 5 min for Warwickshire v. Durham at Edgbaston, UK, 3 and 6 June 1994. Innings included: most runs in a day (390 on 6 June), most runs from strokes worth four or more (308, 62 fours and 10 sixes)
Test: Brian Lara, 375 in 12 hr 48 min for West Indies v. England, St John's, Antigua, 16–18 April 1994

WICKET-KEEPING RECORDS

MOST CAREER CATCHES
First class: 1,473, Bob Taylor, Derbyshire/England, 1960–88.
Test: 353, Ian Healy, Australia, 1988–99 (111 Tests)

MOST CAREER STUMPINGS
First class: 418, Leslie Ames, Kent/England, 1926–51
Test: 52, William Oldfield, Australia, 1920–37 (54 tests)

MOST CAREER DISMISSALS
First class: 1,649, Bob Taylor, Derbyshire/England, 1960–88
Test: 381, Ian Healy, Australia, 1988–99 (111 Tests)

One Day International: 234 (195 ct, 39 st), Ian Andrew Healy, in 168 matches, 1988–97

BOWLING RECORDS

MOST WICKETS
Innings (test): 10–53, Jim Laker (UK), England v. Australia, 31 July 1956; and 10–74, Anil Kumble, India v. Pakistan, New Delhi, India, 7 Feb 1999
Match (first class): 19 for 90 (9–37 and 10–53), Jim Laker, England v. Australia, 27–31 July 1956
Career (first class): 4,187, Wilfred Rhodes (av 16.71) Yorkshire/England, 1898–1930

FASTEST BOWLING
160.45 km/h (99.7 mph), Jeffrey Robert Thomson, Australia v. West Indies, Dec 1975

BATTING RECORDS

MOST CENTURIES
First class: 197, Jack Hobbs (in 1,315 innings), Surrey/England, 1905–34
Test: 34, Sunil Gavaskar (in 214 innings), India, 1971–87

FIELDING RECORDS

MOST CATCHES
Test: 157, Mark Taylor (in 104 tests), Australia, 1989–99

BLIND CRICKET RECORDS
The first Cricket World Cup for the blind was held in New Delhi, India, in November 1998.

HIGHEST INDIVIDUAL SCORE
262 not out, Mansood Jan, Pakistan v. South Africa, 19 Nov 1998

BEST BOWLING ANALYSIS
3–12, Bhalaji Damor, India v. Sri Lanka, 18 Nov 1998

PLAYERS

YOUNGEST CAPTAIN
Test: 21 yr 77 days, the Nawab of Pataudi (later Mansur Ali Khan), India v. West Indies, Barbados, 23 March 1962

YOUNGEST PLAYERS
First class: 11 yr 261 days, Esmail Ahmed Baporia (India), Gujarat v. Baroda, Ahmedabad, India, 10 Jan 1951
Test: 15 yr 124 days, Mushtaq Mohammad, Pakistan v. West Indies, 26 March 1959

OLDEST CAPPED CRICKETER
International Cricket Council member country: 65 yr 269 days, Wally Glynn, Malta v. Greece, 21 Aug 1997

ARCHERY
Archery featured in the Olympic Games of 1900, 1904, 1908 and 1920, with participating countries using their own rules. Owing to the confusion, archery was removed from the Olympics. In 1972 it returned to the Games, with the Fédération Internationale de Tir à l'Arc (FITA) as the international governing body for the sport, and with standardized international rules.

WOMEN'S RECORDS

HIGHEST SCORES IN SINGLE FITA ROUNDS
FITA: 1,384 of 1,440 points, Chung Chang-sook (South Korea), Wonju, South Korea, Nov 2000
Team: 4,094 of 4,320 points (3 x 144), South Korea (Cho Youn-jeong, Kim Soo-nyung and Lee Eun-kyung), South Korea, 1992

30 m: 360 of 360 points, Ha Na-young (South Korea), Wonju, South Korea, Aug 1998
50 m: 345 of 360 points, Kim Moon-sun (South Korea), Ch'ungjo, South Korea, Nov 1996
60 m: 350 of 360 points, Kim Jo-soon (South Korea), Ye-chun, South Korea, Sept 1998
70 m: 345 of 360 points, Choi Nam-nak (South Korea), Wonju, South Korea, Aug 2000

MEN'S RECORDS

HIGHEST SCORES IN SINGLE FITA ROUNDS

FITA: 1,379 of 1,440 points, Oh Kyo-moon (South Korea), Wonju, South Korea, Nov 2000
Team: 4,053 of 4,320 points (3 x 144), South Korea (Oh Kyo-moon, Lee Kyung-chul and Kim Jae-pak), Jakarta, Indonesia, Aug 1995
30 m: 360 of 360 points, Han Seuong-hoon (South Korea), Seoul, South Korea, June 1994; and Oh Kyo-moon (South Korea), Wonju, South Korea, Nov 2000
50 m: 351 of 360 points, Kim Kyung-ho (South Korea), Wonju, South Korea, in Sept 1997
70 m: 345 of 360 points, Jackson Fear (Australia), Kyongju, South Korea, June 1997
90 m: 332 of 360 points, Oh Kyo-moon (South Korea), Wonju, South Korea, Nov 2000

HORSE SPORTS

OLYMPIC RECORDS

MOST OLYMPIC GOLDS
Dressage: 6, Reiner Klimke (Germany), team: 1964–88, individual: 1984
Show jumping: 5, Hans Günter Winkler (Germany), team: 1956, 1960, 1964, 1972, individual: 1956

MOST INDIVIDUAL GOLDS
Dressage: 2, Henri St Cyr (Sweden), 1952, 1956; and Nicole Uphoff (Germany), 1988, 1992

MOST TEAM GOLDS
Dressage: 10, Germany (West Germany 1968–90), 1928, 1936, 1964, 1968, 1976, 1984, 1988, 1992, 1996, 2000

MOST TEAM MEDALS
Show jumping (Prix des Nations): 7, Germany, 1936, 1956, 1960, 1964, 1996 (as Germany), and 1972, 1988 (as West Germany)

LOWEST SCORE (NO FAULTS)

Show jumping: Frantisek Ventura (Czechoslovakia), 1928; Alwin Schockemöhle (West Germany), 1976; and Ludger Beerbaum (Germany), 1992

WORLD RECORDS

MOST WORLD SHOW JUMPING CHAMPIONSHIP TITLES

Women: 2, Janou Tissot (*née* Lefebvre, France), 1970, 1974
Men: 2, Hans Günter Winkler (Germany), 1954, 1955; and Raimondo d'Inzeo (Italy), 1956, 1960
Team: 2, France, 1982, 1990; and Germany, 1994, 1998

SHOOTING

WOMEN'S RECORDS

RIFLE

50 m (3 x 20 shots): 689.7 (592 + 97.7), Vessela Letcheva (Bulgaria), Munich, Germany, 15 June 1995; and 689.7 (591 + 98.7), Wang Xian (China), Milan, Italy, 29 May 1998

AIR RIFLE

10 m (40 shots): 503.5 (398 + 105.5), Gaby Buehlmann (Switzerland), Munich, Germany, 24 May 1998

PISTOL

25 m (60 shots): 696.2 (594 + 102.2), Diana Jorgova (Bulgaria), Milan, Italy, 31 May 1994

AIR PISTOL

10 m (40 shots): 493.5 (390 + 103.5), Jie Ren (China), Munich, Germany, 22 May 1998

TRAP

100 targets: 95 (71 + 24), Satu Pusila (Finland), Nicosia, Cyprus, 13 June 1998; and Delphine Racinet (France), Sydney, Australia, 26 March 2000

DOUBLE TRAP

120 targets: 150 (115 + 35), Yafei Zhang (China), Nicosia, Cyprus, 20 Oct 2000

SKEET

100 targets: 99 (75 + 24), Svetlana Demina (Russia), Kumamoto City, Japan, 1 June 1999

MEN'S RECORDS

RIFLE

50 m (3 x 40 shots): 1,287.9 (1,186 + 101.9), Rajmond Debevec (Slovenia), Munich, Germany, 29 Aug 1992
50 m prone: 704.8 (600 + 104.8), Christian Klees, (Germany), Atlanta, USA, 25 July 1996

AIR RIFLE

10 m: 700.7 (597 + 103.7), Artem Khadjibekov (Russia), Munich, Germany, 18 Nov 2000

RAPID FIRE PISTOL

25 m: 699.7 (596 + 103.7), Ralf Schumann (Germany), Barcelona, Spain, 8 June 1994

AIR PISTOL

10 m: 695.1 (593 + 102.1), Sergey Pyzhyanov (former USSR), Munich, Germany, 13 Oct 1989
50 m: 676.2 (577 + 99.2), William Demarest (USA), Milan, Italy, 4 June 2000

RUNNING TARGET

10 m: 687.9 (586 + 101.9), Ling Yang (China), Milan, Italy, 6 June 1996

TRAP

125 targets: 150 (125 + 25), Marcello Tittarelli (Italy), Suhl, Germany, 11 June 1996

DOUBLE TRAP

150 targets: 194 (prelim 146 + 48), Daniele di Spigno (Italy), Tampere, Finland, 7 July 1999

SKEET

125 targets: 150 (125 + 25), Jan Henrik Heinrich (Germany), Lonato, Italy, 5 June 1996; Andrea Benelli (Italy), Suhl, Germany, 11 June 1996; Ennio Falco (Italy), Lonato, Italy, 19 April 1997; Harald Jensen (Norway), Kumamoto City, Japan, 1 June 1999; Franck Durbesson (France), Sydney, Australia, 31 March 2000; and Mikola Milchev (Ukraine), Sydney, Australia, 23 Sept 2000

BENCH REST (CLOSEST GROUP)

10 shots at 1,000 yd (914 m): 8.003 cm (3.151 in), John Voneida (USA), Williamsport, PA, USA, 8 July 1995
5 shots at 500 m (546 yd): 26.6 mm (1.048 in), Dave Goodridge (Australia), Canberra, Australia, 29 Aug 1998

SPORTING CLAY TARGETS

500 shot and broken: 30 min 31 sec, Scott Hutchinson (USA), Lake Placid, NY, USA, 18 Sept 1999
Broken in one minute: 27, Scott Hutchinson (USA), Lake Placid, NY, USA, 18 Sept 1999

OLYMPIC RECORDS

MOST INDIVIDUAL GOLD MEDALS

3, Gudbrand Gudbrandsönn Skatteboe (Norway), 1906

MOST MEDALS

Women: 5 (2 gold, 1 silver, 2 bronze), Marina Logvinenko (*née* Dobrancheva, Russia), 1988–96
Men: 11 (5 gold, 4 silver, 2 bronze), Carl Townsend Osburn (USA), 1912, 1920 and 1924

WEIGHTLIFTING

From 1 Jan 1998, the International Weightlifting Federation (IWF) introduced modified bodyweight categories, thereby making the then world records redundant. This is the new listing with the world standards for the new bodyweight categories. Results achieved at IWF-approved competitions exceeding the world standards by 0.5 kg for snatch or clean & jerk, or by 2.5 kg for the total, are recognized as world records.

WOMEN'S IWF RECORDS

48 KG BODYWEIGHT

Clean & jerk: 113.5 kg, Donka Mincheva (Bulgaria), Athens, Greece, 21 Nov 1999
Snatch: 87.5 kg, Liu Xiuhua (China), Montreal, Canada, 6 June 2000
Total: 197.5 kg, Liu Xiuhua (China), Montreal, Canada, 6 Sept 1999

53 KG BODYWEIGHT

Clean & jerk: 125 kg, Yang Xia (China), Sydney, Australia, 18 Sept 2000
Snatch: 100 kg, Yang Xia (China), Sydney, Australia, 18 Sept 2000
Total: 225 kg, Yang Xia (China), Sydney, Australia, 18 Sept 2000

58 KG BODYWEIGHT

Clean & jerk: 131.5 kg, Ri Song Hui (North Korea), Osaka, Japan, 3 May 2000
Snatch: 105 kg, Chen Yanqing (China), Athens, Greece, 22 Nov 1999
Total: 235 kg, Chen Yanqing (China), Athens, Greece, 22 Nov 1999

63 KG BODYWEIGHT

Clean & jerk: 132.5 kg, Xiong Meiyin (China), Athens, Greece, 23 Nov 1999
Snatch: 112.5 kg, Chen Xiaomin (China), Sydney, Australia, 19 Sept 2000

Total: 242.5 kg, Chen Xiaomin (China) Sydney, Australia, 19 Sept 2000

69 KG BODYWEIGHT
Clean & jerk: 143 kg, Sun Tianni (China) , Athens, Greece, 24 Nov 1999
Snatch: 112.5 kg, Erzsebet Markus (Hungary), Sydney, Australia, 19 Sept 2000
Total: 252.5 kg, Lin Weining (China), Wuhan, China, 3 Sept 1999

75 KG BODYWEIGHT
Clean & jerk: 142.5 kg, Sun Tianni (China), Osaka, Japan, 6 May 2000
Snatch: 116 kg, Tang Weifang (China), Wuhan, China, 4 Sept 1999
Total: 257.5 kg, Sun Tianni (China), Osaka, Japan, 6 May 2000

+75 KG BODYWEIGHT
Clean & jerk: 160.5 kg, Ding Meiyuan (China), Osaka, Japan, 6 May 2000
Snatch: 135 kg, Ding Meiyuan (China), Sydney, Australia, 22 Sept 2000
Total: 285 kg, Ding Meiyuan (China), Athens, Greece, 27 Nov 1999

MEN'S IWF RECORDS

56 KG BODYWEIGHT
Clean & jerk: 168 kg, Halil Mutlu (Turkey), Trenčín, Slovakia, 24 April 2001
Snatch: 138.0 kg, Halil Mutlu (Turkey), Sydney, Australia, 16 Sept 2000
Total: 305.0 kg, Halil Mutlu (Turkey), Sydney, Australia, 16 Sept 2000

62 KG BODYWEIGHT
Clean & jerk: 180.5 kg, Le Maosheng (China), Athens, Greece, 23 Nov 1999
Snatch: 152.5 kg, Shi Zhiyong (China), Osaka, Japan, 3 May 2000
Total: 325 kg (world standard)

69 KG BODYWEIGHT
Clean & jerk: 196.5 kg, Galabin Boevski (Bulgaria), Sydney, Australia, 20 Sept 2000
Snatch: 165 kg, Georgi Markov (Bulgaria), Sydney, Australia, 20 Sept 2000
Total: 357.5 kg, Galabin Boevski (Bulgaria), Athens, Greece, 24 Nov 1999

77 KG BODYWEIGHT
Clean & jerk: 210 kg, Oleg Perepetchenov (Russia), Trenčín, Slovakia, 27 April 2001
Snatch: 170.5 kg, Khach Kyapanaktsyan (Armenia), Athens, Greece, 25 Nov 1999
Total: 375 kg, Oleg Perepetchenov (Russia), Trenčín, Slovakia, 27 April 2001

85 KG BODYWEIGHT
Clean & jerk: 218 kg, Zhang Yong (China), Tel Aviv, Israel, 25 April 1998
Snatch: 181 kg, Georgi Asanidze (Georgia), Sofia, Bulgaria, 29 April 2000
Total: 395 kg (world standard)

94 KG BODYWEIGHT
Clean & jerk: 232.5 kg, Szymon Kolecki (Poland), Sofia, Bulgaria, 29 April 2000
Snatch: 188 kg, Akakios Kakiashvilis (Greece), Athens, Greece, 27 Nov 1999
Total: 417.5 kg (world standard)

105 KG BODYWEIGHT
Clean & jerk: 242.5 kg (world standard)
Snatch: 197.5 kg (world standard)
Total: 440 kg (world standard)

+105 KG BODYWEIGHT
Clean & jerk: 262.5 kg (world standard)
Snatch: 212.5 kg, Hossein Rezazadeh (Iran), Sydney, Australia, 26 Sept 2000
Total: 472.5 kg, Hossein Rezazadeh (Iran), Sydney, Australia, 26 Sept 2000

be a record breaker!

We are always on the look out for interesting new records and categories, so if you think you could break or make a record, get in touch and we will tell you whether your idea is suitable and what you have to do. Make sure you contact us early so that we can consult our experts and draw up new guidelines if necessary.

Getting in touch has never been easier – contact us via the web, or by letter, fax or phone and we will consider your claim and send you all the relevant rules, guidelines and a list of all the documentation you will need as valid proof for your record claim.

Remember that you must follow these, otherwise your record attempt will not be accepted by our rigorous judges!

Once you know what you have to do to make or break a world record, get in touch with us just before you make your attempt to ensure that no one else has broken the record in the meantime.

CONTACT US!

• Visit our website at:
http://www.guinnessworldrecords.com

Our online service is a fast-track way of submitting your record application. Just fill in the form and we'll give you a personal ID number so that you can track your claim's progress on the website.

• Write to:
Records Research Services
Guinness World Records
338 Euston Road
London NW1 3BD

• Phone/fax:
To contact us from the UK, ring 0870 241 6632

Calls will be charged at the national rate.

To fax us from the UK, ring 020 7891 4501

Please note that if you contact us by letter, fax or phone, it will take us longer to acknowledge your claim.

The World's Largest Ice Cream Cake (left)

GUINNESS
WORLD RECORDS™

stop press!

Records are being broken all the time, and our meticulous verification process means that we cannot always include all the latest details in the main body of the book. Here are some of the records that had just been confirmed as we went to press.

CITY WITH THE MOST NO.1 HIT SINGLES PER CAPITA

According to Guinness World Records *British Hit Singles*, the city with the most No.1 hit singles on the UK chart per head of population is Liverpool (pop. 461,481), UK, with local bands achieving a record 53 hits – one for every 8,707 Liverpudlians. The most recent No.1 was Atomic Kitten's 'Whole Again'. The City of Liverpool was presented with a *British Hit Singles* No.1 Award on 28 June 2001.

MOST NO.1 BILLBOARD CHART ACTS PERFORMING ON SAME STAGE IN ONE DAY

A total of 53 artists with Billboard chart No.1 hits performed at 'Beatstock 2000' on Staten Island, New York, USA, on 19 Aug 2000. Acts at the record-breaking event included Pink, the Outhere Brothers, C+C Music Factory, Thelma Houston and Deborah Gibson (all USA).

FASTEST TIME TO MAKE ONE LITRE OF ICE CREAM

On 10 June 2001 Peter Barham (UK) made one litre (1.75 pint) of ice cream in a record 54.5 seconds, as part of the 'Ice Cream Sunday' event, organized by the Royal Institution and the Royal Society of Chemistry. The ingredients – single cream, double cream, icing sugar and vanilla essence – were mixed with liquid nitrogen at approximately –196°C (–320°F) until they reached the right temperature and consistency.

LARGEST CROQUEMBOUCHE

Chefs from the Dubai World Trade Centre prepared a 5-m (16-ft) tall croquembouche (tower of profiteroles), containing 137,000 choux buns, on 23 March 2001. It weighed approximately 9 tonnes (20,000 lb) and was created during the Dubai Shopping Festival, UAE.

MOST DOUGHNUTS EATEN IN THREE MINUTES

Ben Munday-Chanin (UK) ate two sugar jam doughnuts in three minutes, without licking his lips, on the set of Channel 4's *The Big Breakfast*, London, UK, on 7 March 2001.

LARGEST SERVING OF FISH AND CHIPS

Tadeusz Hupa (Poland), chef of the Wroclaw Hotel, prepared the world's largest serving of fish and chips at the Third Cookbook Fair held at the Wroclaw Hotel, Poland, on 1 Dec 2000. The fish, once battered and fried, weighed 5.505 kg (12.13 lb) and the chips weighed 5.435 kg (11.98 lb).

LARGEST SNOW CONE

Mammoth Mountain Ski Area created the world's largest snow cone, weighing 2,104.66 kg (4,640 lb) with 322.77 litres (71 gal) of syrup (cherry, grape and lemon flavours) at Mammoth Lakes, California, USA, on 11 Nov 2000. It took almost five hours to fill the 3.43-m (11-ft 2-in) cone with ice and syrup. The contents of the cone were served to 1,000 guest skiers.

MOST EXPENSIVE WATERMELON

In June 2001 approximately 400 square watermelons were put on sale for £60 ($85) each, by growers from a farmers' association in Zentsuji on the western Japanese island of Shikoku. The unusual shape, chosen to make storing the fruit easier, was achieved by placing a segment of vine bearing a bud inside a flexible square glass container. As the fruit grew it was forced into a square shape by the glass, which also acted as a hothouse and protected and encouraged the fruits to grow.

LARGEST KING CAKE

SAV-A-CENTER Food Market New Orleans Division, in partnership with Pillsbury Bakeries Food Service, made the world's largest king cake at the Lakeside Mall, Metairie, Louisiana, USA, between 3 and 4 March 2000. It was 56.76 m (186 ft 3 in) long, 22.86 cm (9 in) wide and weighed 464.79 kg (1,024.69 lb). King cakes are special sponge cakes cooked to celebrate Mardi Gras in New Orleans, Louisiana, USA.

MOST CANDLES ON A CAKE

On 23 March 2001, chefs at the Al Bustan Rotana Hotel, Dubai, UAE, made a cake with a record 2,100 candles to celebrate the same number of rooms at the hotel.

LARGEST SILVER-SERVICE DINNER

The world's largest silver-service dinner party took place on 28 April 2001, when 11,483 people were guests at a dinner party hosted by Vodafone Group plc at Earls Court, London, UK. The event was organized by Skybridge Group plc and the caterers were Beeton Rumford Ltd.

LARGEST SHOT SLAM

A total of 190 people took part in the world's largest shot slam at the Delta King Hotel, Sacramento, California, USA, on 9 April 2001. JB Scotch was used for the attempt.

TALLEST SUGAR-CUBE TOWER

Dean O'Loughlin (UK), a contestant on Channel 4's *Big Brother*, London, UK, built a sugar-cube tower (one cube at a time) to a height of 1.20 m (47.24 in) on 27 June 2001, breaking the existing record by 18.1 cm (7.12 in).

MOST SWEETCORN EATEN IN THREE MINUTES

On 5 July 2001 Paul Ferguson, alias 'Bubble' (UK), a contestant on the UK *Big Brother* television show ate a total of 185 sweetcorn kernels in three minutes (using an ordinary wooden toothpick to individually stab each kernel). The record was broken at the studios of E4's *Little Brother*, Bromley-on-Bow, London, UK. He broke his own UK record by 20 kernels and the world record by 16.

LARGEST SHOPPING BAG

The world's largest shopping bag measures 1.80 m (6 ft) high, 1.20 m (4 ft) wide and 20 cm (7.8 in) deep. It was made by the luxury goods store Paris Gallery and presented on 23 March 2001, during the Dubai Shopping Festival, UAE.

LARGEST LABEL

On 1 May 2001 Germark SA, a label company based in Cornellà de Llobregat, Barcelona, Spain, produced the world's largest label, measuring 100 m x 29 cm (328 ft x 11.4 in). Once it had been printed, it took approximately 100 people standing side-by-side to hold it up.

LARGEST KIMONO

The largest kimono in the world was created as part of the National Kimono Festival in Cho Kagoshima City, Japan, on 23 March 2001. The giant kimono was 11.72 m (38 ft 3 in) wide, 12.80 m (41 ft 11 in) high and weighed 100 kg (220.5 lb).

LONGEST KEYBOARD PLAYING MARATHON

Between 30 March and 1 April 2001, Ginés Borges Belza (Spain) played a Yamaha MC-600 electric organ for a record 49 hr 15 min (including six breaks of 15 min) at the Royal Nautical Club of Santa Cruz de Tenerife, Canary Islands, Spain. He played a total of 800 individual arrangements.

LARGEST NUDE PHOTO SHOOT

On 5 May 2001 over 2,500 people bared their all in the name of art, lying naked on the streets of Montreal, Quebec, Canada, for US photographer Spencer Tunick. The volunteers lay outside the city's Place des Arts, shivering in temperatures as low as 13°C (55°F). Tunick's project was to illustrate the vulnerability of humanity.

LARGEST OUTDOOR PHOTOGRAPHIC EXHIBITION
A total of 10,610 photographs based on the theme 'One Family' were displayed on the 'Kodak DSF Wall of Fame' on 23 March 2001, during the Dubai Shopping Festival, UAE.

LARGEST INCENSE BURNER
A hand-crafted ash wood and brass incense burner (*mabkhara*) measuring a record 3 m (10 ft) tall and weighing 1,000 kg (2,200 lb) was made by fragrance company AJMAL on 23 March 2001, during the Dubai Shopping Festival, UAE.

TALLEST TOWER OF WALKING FRAMES
Staff and residents of The Royal Palm Retirement Center, Port Charlotte, Florida, USA, built a tower 30 ft (9.1 m) high with 103 walking frames on 21 Oct 2000.

FASTEST TIME TO CLEAR TWO POOL TABLES
USA

The fastest time to clear two pool tables is 1 min 36 sec, which was achieved by Dave Pearson (USA) on 12 March 2001. Dave is a full-time professional pool player and world champion based in Las Vegas.

MOST PUSH-UPS USING BACK OF HANDS IN ONE HOUR
Mario Sirotiæ (Bosnia-Herzegovina) completed a record 671 push-ups, using the back of his hands, in one hour, at the Hotel Sol Park, Rovinj, Croatia, on 8 March 2001.

FASTEST TIME TO PUNCH TEN TV SETS
SE

Mike Yikealo (Japan) punched ten 53-cm (21-in) television sets placed on tables in a time of 7.66 seconds, in Stockholm, Sweden, on 3 Feb 2001. He wore boxing gloves for the attempt.

MOST HAIR WASHED AND BLOW-DRIED IN EIGHT HOURS BY 60 PEOPLE
On 15 Jan 2000, 948 people had their hair washed and blow-dried by 60 hair stylists in eight hours during the Rejoice Shampoo-a-thon organized by Procter & Gamble in Singapore. The event attracted large crowds of people who lined up to have a free shampoo and blow-dry in one of the four salons taking part.

MOST SYSTEMATIC SCIENTIFIC STUDY INTO 'HAUNTED' LOCATIONS
Between 4 and 17 April 2001 psychologist Richard Wiseman (UK) led an in-depth scientific experiment to test the reactions of more than 250 volunteers who were exposed to supposed 'haunted' locations in Edinburgh, Scotland, UK. Equipment used included a magnetometer, thermal imager, movements sensors and a light meter as well as photographic and video cameras.

MOST ENDANGERED WILDCAT
In 2000 it was estimated that the number of Iberian lynx (*Lynx pardinus*) – once widespread in Spain – had dwindled to just 600. A major cause of the decline has been the introduction of the disease *myxomatosis* to reduce the rabbit population. As rabbits are the Iberian lynx's main food source, this had a devastating impact on the population. The wild cat is now legally protected and efforts are being made to increase numbers.

MOST ENDANGERED CANID
In 2000 there were less than 400 Ethiopian Wolves (*Canis simensis*) left in Ethiopia – their main habitat – making this the most endangered genus of the canid (dog) family. Their numbers have been greatly reduced because of agricultural activities and they exist only in a few mountain ranges. Their scarcity is such that they are in danger of extinction.

TALLEST FLOWER ARRANGEMENT
On 3 June 2000 the Campaign for the Promotion of Flowers and Plants created a flower arrangement in Cadiz, Spain, measuring a record 13 m (42 ft 5 in) tall and weighing 170,000 kg (374,000 lb). The arrangement took 40 florists 3,000 hours in total to make and consisted of 31,500 blooms.

TALLEST TREE TRANSPLANTED
David Fountain and former pop star Kim Wilde (both UK) transplanted a 60-year-old London plane tree (*Platanus acerifolia*) measuring 17.65 m (57 ft 11 in) high from The Big Tree Company Ltd in Houtvenne, Belgium to Warrington, Lancashire, UK, in Jan 2001.

MOST HEADS ON ONE SUNFLOWER
Rose Marie Roberts, Waterford, Michigan, USA, grew a 2.4-m (8-ft) sunflower that bloomed a record 129 heads in Oct 2000.

MOST GLASSES BALANCED ON CHIN
Ashrita Furman (USA) balanced 75 pint (568-ml) beer glasses on his chin for 10.6 sec in his backyard, Jamaica, New York, USA, on 26 April 2001.

LARGEST ROCKING CHAIR
A giant wooden rocking chair measuring a record 3.9 m (13 ft) tall, 2.4 m (8 ft) wide and weighing 771 kg (1,700 lb) was constructed by The Solid Wood Bed and Table Company, Ontario, Canada, in Feb 2001.

LARGEST LEGO® FLAG
On 29 July 2000 a Saudi Arabian flag measuring a record 4.62 m x 7.57 m (15 ft 1 in x 24 ft 10 in) was made by 12,000 children using 470,000 LEGO® bricks. The record took place at the Jeddah Science and Technology Museum, Saudi Arabia.

LONGEST FLIGHT OVER WATER BY A POWERED PARAGLIDER
The longest flight over water in a powered paraglider (PPG) is 264 km (164 miles), achieved by Haim Raveh (Israel) on 12 May 2001, between Haifa, Israel, and Larnaca, Cyprus. A powered paraglider is a standard paraglider with a light, three-wheeled frame slung below it. A small engine is attached to the frame and the aircraft has a maximum airspeed of around 50 km/h (31 mph). Haim's PPG carried emergency equipment and enough fuel for a 12-hour flight.

OLDEST COMPETING AEROBATIC PILOT
Ian Metcher (Australia) was 85 years old when he won the basic aerobatics section of the Western Australia Light Aircraft Championships at Jandakot Airport near Fremantle, WA, Australia, on 24 Feb 2001.

FURTHEST DISTANCE WALKED ON HANDS IN EIGHT HOURS
Roger Rank (USA) walked on his hands a record-breaking distance of 640.08 m (2,100 ft) between 9.30 am and 5 pm at the Wal-Mart Super Center, Pittsburg, Kansas, USA, on 17 March 2001.

LARGEST FULLY MOVEABLE MOTOR-DRIVEN STRUCTURE ON LAND
The Robert C Byrd Green Bank Telescope is a radio telescope at the National Radio Astronomy Observatory in West Virginia, USA. It is fully moveable and its highest point stands 146 m (480 ft) tall. The dish measures 100 m x 110 m (328 ft x 360 ft) and can move to observe the whole sky from five degrees above the horizon.

YOUNGEST PERSON TO TRAVEL TO EACH CONTINENT
By Dec 2000, at age 12, Mario Casuga II (USA), had visited all seven continents in the world, becoming the youngest person ever to have done so. Travelling with his parents Mario and Rebecca, Mario Jr had visited nearly 40 countries before completing his quest in Antarctica.

index

A

GUINNESS
WORLD RECORDS

GUINNESS
WORLD RECORDS

GUINNESS
WORLD RECORDS

GUINNESS
WORLD RECORDS

picture credits

acknowledgements

inness World Records would like to thank
e following for their contributions to
inness World Records 2002:

ports Council International (ACI)
Turner, World Waterparks Association
dy Milroy
hrita Furman
ilio Costaguta, ICAO
rry Norman, WKVL Amusement
esearch Library
l Palantonio, Marty Tenney and Eric
hotz for LMNO Productions
itish Antarctic Survey
ristie's
ve Everton
aig Hilton Taylor, Coordinator of Red List
ogram, UK
rrell Kirk Nordstrom and Charles Alpers,
Geological Survey
ve McAleer
ve Roberts
vid Wallechinsky
mma Dixon
ic Schlosser
tève Font Canadell
van Vinnicombe
rbes
rtune
x Television
les Marion
uinness - Die Show Der Rekorde, ARD
uinness Rekord TV, TV3
uinness World Records, Channel 4
uinness World Records, ITV
uinness World Records, NTV
uinness World Records: Primetime, Fox
elevision
oover's
mi
ternational Road Federation (World Road
atistics 2000)
ternational Union for the Conservation of
ature
mes Carlyle, Casella CEL Inc.
eff Sniegowski
l Paski, North Coast Redwood
terpretive Association, USA
Steel
arl Shuker
arola Gadja
ate Stuart-Cox
evin Warwick
Émission des Records, TF1
M.J.F. Cunningham
alcolm Smith
ark Carwardine
ark Hertsgaard
aureen Kane
ike Cowley
ike Foster, Jane's Information Group
unich Re
ASA
ational Science Foundation
etNames
igel Richards
ik Bambrick
ne Bad Monkey Limited
eter Matthews
PARC

Rebecca Adcock
RIAA
Roger Hawkins
Roger Launius
Salvador Pujol
Simon Gold
Sir Peter Johnson
Sotheby's
Stan Greenberg
Suzanne Collins
The Economist
Tim Footman
World Tourism Organisation
World Wildlife Fund
W.B.J. Rees
Yamaha